The Fall of the
British Monarchies
1637–1642

The Fall of the
British Monarchies
1637–1642

Oxford University Press, Walton Street, Oxford OX2 6DP

Oxford New York
Athens Auckland Bangkok Bombay
Calcutta Cape Town Dar es Salaam Delhi
Florence Hong Kong Istanbul Karachi
Kuala Lumpur Madras Madrid Melbourne
Mexico City Nairobi Paris Singapore
Taipei Tokyo Toronto
and associated companies in
Berlin Ibadan

Oxford is a trade mark of Oxford University Press

Published in the United States by
Oxford University Press Inc., New York

First published 1991
Reprinted 1992
First published as Clarendon Paperback 1995

British Library Cataloguing in Publication Data
Russell, Conrad, 1937-
The fall of the British monarchies 1637-1642.
1. Great Britain. Political events, 1625-1649
I. Title
941.062
ISBN 0-19-822754-X

Library of Congress Cataloging in Publication Data
Russell, Conrad.
The fall of the British monarchies, 1637-1642/Conrad Russell.
p. cm.
Includes index.
1. Great Britain—Politics and government—1625-1649. 2. Ireland—
Politics and government—17th century. 3. Scotland—Politics and
government—1625-1649. 4. Monarchy—Great Britain—History—17th
century. 5. Charles I, King of England, 1600-1649. I. Title.
DA395.R87 1991 941.06'2—dc20 90-41302
ISBN 0-19-822754-X
ISBN 0-19-820588-0 pbk

Printed and bound in Great Britain by
Biddles Ltd, Guildford and King's Lynn

To the Members, Past, Present, and Future,
of the Tudor and Stuart Seminar
at the Institute of Historical Research

Preface

THIS is the work to which my Ford Lectures, on *The Causes of the English Civil War*, are an extended conclusion. Readers may be glad to know that although, in deference to the wishes of Oxford University Press, whom I would like to thank for many kindnesses, I have published my conclusion first, I did not write it first. This work was substantially complete by the summer of 1987. Because the University of Oxford's invitation to give the Ford Lectures, like time and tide, waits for no man, it then had to be set aside. However, this is the foundation on which that work rests.

Ever since I was an undergraduate, it has worried me that so much work on the causes of the English Civil War was accompanied by so little investigation into the effects for which causes had to be found. With some honourable exceptions, notably Professors Pearl, Hibbard, and Fletcher, the political events leading up to the English Civil War have been remarkably little studied since the days of S. R. Gardiner. This is the more unfortunate since the range of material available for their study has more than doubled in that time. Gardiner, no doubt, nodded as rarely as Homer, but a doubling of the amount of material available must change the story in some important points. *L'histoire événementielle* has been out of fashion recently, partly for good reasons, but there are some cases, of which the English Civil War is one, in which we cannot let the *événements* alone. In those cases, it is essential, if we are to match cause with effect, to know what those *événements* were. Future work on the causes of the English Civil War will, I hope, either explain the story here told, or else take up the challenge of revising the story itself.

Scottish and Irish colleagues will no doubt have already perceived the cloven hoof of anglocentricity. I confess freely that this work began, in 1977, as an attempt to study the events leading up to the English Civil War. No other focus would justify the decision to stop in 1642. As the work has progressed, I have become convinced that it is impossible to tell the English story by itself, and this book has been slowly transformed into an attempt at genuinely British history. The transformation is still incomplete, and there is much more to be done in this direction. This book makes no pretence to be definitive in the linking of the stories of the three kingdoms, but I hope at least it has provided a story detailed enough to be capable of being revised by future work.

I have also found, as the work progressed, that the King was a more active participant in the story than I had supposed; even at his lowest, he was still doing things, and not just having things done to him. The public records have been more helpful than I had expected in piecing together the sequence of events. Here too, there is much more to do, and I hope this book will point the way towards future work. Like others, I have found a linguistic problem in looking for a collective noun to describe the group of people for whom Pym acted as spokesman. On this, I have decided to follow Edward Nicholas, and describe the group as 'Pym's junto'. The phrase is no doubt a question-begging one, but the question it begs is precisely the one which ought to remain open.

Research in depth is an expensive pastime, and the more so in this case, since half the research for this book was done during five happy years in the History Department at Yale. The experience has given me a more lively sympathy for the budgetary difficulties of my American colleagues. It has also given me cause for gratitude to the many bodies which have provided financial help, and in particular to the American Council of Learned Societies, the American Philosophical Society, The Yale University Concilium on International and Area Studies, the A. Whitney Griswold Fund of Yale University, the Central Research Fund of the University of London, The Small Grants Fund of the British Academy, and the Dean's Fund of University College, London. Without their help bankruptcy would have brought this work to a halt long ago. I would like to thank Miss Kitty Stubbs and Dr Janina Giejgo for undertaking the laborious task of typing this book.

In the course of this work, I have incurred many debts to archivists who have helped with the production of material. Space forbids me to offer individual thanks to the staff of all thirty-seven repositories from which I have drawn material, but I would like to offer special thanks to the staff of the Public Record Office for their patience and helpfulness in dealing with immense orders while I was checking footnotes, and also to Mr H. C. Cobb of the House of Lords Record Office, Dr T. I. Rae of the National Library of Scotland, Mr Colin Shrimpton of Alnwick Castle, Dr David Jones of the House of Lords Library, and Mr Stephen Parkes of the Osborn Collection, Beinecke Library, Yale. I also owe special thank to the owners who have allowed me to consult their family papers, the Marquess of Anglesey, the Trustees of the Bedford Settled Estates, the Earl of Crawford and Balcarres, the Earl of Dartmouth, Viscount De L'Isle and Dudley, and His Grace the Duke of Northumberland. I am also particularly grateful to Dr Judith Maltby for allowing me to see her edition of Aston's diary before publication, and to Anne Steele Young for allowing me to see the texts of vols. ii and iii of *PJ* before publication.

Among my fellow scholars, I owe debts to more people than I can list.

In addition to directing me to innumerable sources, they have for many years allowed me to share my enthusiasms and helped to put them in many different perspectives. Historical research may be a cottage industry, but its cottagers could not flourish without their manorial court. Among those to whom I owe special thanks, pride of place must go to John Adamson. That he drew my attention to the Nicholas MSS at Guildford, the Nicholas MSS at Christ Church, the Crawford MSS, the Tollemache MSS, the Book of Petitions in the PRO, and the letter-book of the Elector Palatine, improbably lodged in the papers of the Treasury Solicitor, would alone be enough to put me permanently in his debt. That he has also brought a critical and open-minded scrutiny to all this material piles Pelion on Ossa, and I do not know how to thank him. That he has also read the whole of this work and made many helpful constructive comments is a work of supererogation. I also owe special thanks to Dr Peter Donald, for welcoming me to Scottish history and for guiding me through many of its intricacies. Without his help, Chapters 2 and 4, in particular, could not have been written. He has also read several chapters, and made many helpful comments, as well as saving me from a number of errors. I also owe special thanks to Maija Jansson, Bill Bidwell, and the Yale Center for Parliamentary History. I have had the benefit of their unrivalled knowledge of Parliamentary diaries. I also am grateful for the opportunity to use the facilities of the Center, which is the only place where it is possible to compare diaries from different repositories without transcribing them in full. That it was Maija Jansson who discovered, and has now edited, a vital new Parliamentary diary in the library of University College, London merely symbolizes the point.

I owe thanks to my Yale pupils, who first helped to point me in a British direction, especially to Jake Levich, Martin Flaherty, David Venderbush, and Jim Wilson. I also owe thanks, in no particular order, to Caroline Hibbard, Anthony Fletcher, Michael Mendle, Jenny Wormald, Michael Perceval Maxwell, Jane Ohlmeyer, Jonathan Israel, Bob Stacey, Andrew Thrush, Richard Cust, Tom Cogswell, John Elliott, Gerald Aylmer, Ed Morgan, John Morrill, David D'Avray, Michael Clanchy, Mark Kishlansky, Elizabeth Read Foster, Ken Fincham, Tom Barnes, David Underdown, Blair Worden, David Hebb, Jacqueline Levy, Anthony Milton, and David Smith. Between them, as well as giving me many ideas and much material, they have saved me from innumerable errors. For those which remain, I alone am responsible. Above all, I owe a special debt to the members of the Tudor and Stuart seminar at the Institute of Historical Research. In addition to their helpful comments on parts of Chapters 6 and 9, which were delivered to them as papers, they have supplied some forty pairs of spectacles to peruse almost every problem which has emerged. Usually, one of them has had the right focus. Since individual acknowledgement is insufficient, I would like to ask them to accept the dedication.

Finally, as always, I owe special thanks to my wife. She has been living with this material ever since she first wrote me essays on some of it in 1961. Since her focus is vitally different from mine, we have often managed to get that double observation which provides a fix on events, when neither of us could have done it singly. Many parts of this book, in particular the last part of Chapter 11 and the first part of Chapter 12, I could never have written if I had not enjoyed the advantage of seeing the participants from her point of view as well as my own. It is to be hoped that readers will think that two heads have in the event been wiser than one: I certainly believe so myself. Since the spring of 1988, when this book was going through what I have come to think of as its Report Stage, she has suffered the further trial of having to share her house with two Parliaments at once, those of 1640 and of 1987. Both have turned out to be addicted to long sittings and to heated debate. She has not yet complained that nothing is heard at their meetings but cries, shouts, and confusion, but if she should wish to greet the departure of this book for press with the same relief as the Long Parliament greeted the recess of September 1641, the fact should cause no surprise. Though we no longer own a pear tree, I understand very well what Roger Hill felt.

Conrad Russell

University College, London
September 1989

Contents

Notes

THE English pound was made up of 20 shillings and of 240 pennies. One shilling was made up of 12 pennies.

Place of publication for all references is London unless otherwise stated.

Dates remain in Old Style unless otherwise stated, save that the year has been taken to begin on 1 January. The Scottish year already did so. The possibility of confusion sometimes exists in dates given by Anglo-Scots (of both countries), who sometimes date the New Year from 1 January or 25 March indiscriminately. I do not guarantee that all such confusions are eliminated.

Many of the manuscripts cited (notably the diary of Sir Symonds D'Ewes) have a double foliation, in ink and pencil. In most cases, the archivist prefers the use of the pencil foliation. However, I have learnt by painful experience while in the United States that pencil foliations are often invisible in photographic reproductions. I have therefore in many cases continued to use the ink foliation.

The editions of Rushworth and Clarendon used are unusual ones, but I happen to possess them, and hope I may be forgiven for continuing to use them.

Abbreviations

Aldis	H. G. Aldis, *List of Books printed in Scotland before 1700* (Edinburgh Bibliographic Society, Edinburgh, 1904)
APC	*Acts of the Privy Council*
APS	*Acts of the Parliaments of Scotland*, ed. T. Thomson and C. Innes (Edinburgh, 1814–75)
Baillie	Robert Baillie, *Letters and Journals*, 2 vols., ed. David Laing (Bannatyne Club, Edinburgh, 1841–2)
BIHR	*Bulletin of the Institute of Historical Research*
BL	British Library
BL Add. MSS	British Library, Additional Manuscripts
BL E.	British Library, Thomason Tracts
BL Harl. MSS	British Library, Harleian Manuscripts
Bodl.	Bodleian Library, Oxford
CJ	*Commons' Journals*
CJ Ire.	*Commons' Journals of Ireland*
Clarendon, *History*	Edward, Earl of Clarendon, *The History of the Rebellion* (Oxford, 1732)
Clarendon, *Life*	Edward, Earl of Clarendon, *Life* (Oxford, 1857)
Clarendon SP	*State Papers collected by Edward, Earl of Clarendon* (Oxford, 1767)
Cope	*Proceedings of the Short Parliament of 1640*, ed. Esther S. Cope and Willson H. Coates (Camden Society⁴, 19, 1977)
Crawford MSS	Manuscripts of the Earl of Crawford and Balcarres, formerly in the John Rylands Library, now transferred to the National Library of Scotland
CSPD	*Calendar of State Papers, Domestic*
CSP Ire.	*Calendar of State Papers, Ireland*
CSP Ven.	*Calendar of State Papers, Venetian*
CUL	*Cambridge University Library*
d.	an old penny
D'Ewes (N)	*The Journal of Sir Symonds D'Ewes*, ed. Wallace Notestein (New Haven, Conn., 1923). Nov. 1640–Mar. 1641
D'Ewes (C)	*The Journal of Sir Symonds D'Ewes*, ed. Willson H. Coates (New Haven, Conn., 1942, repr. Hamden, Conn., 1970). Oct. 1641–Jan. 1642:
DO	Diurnal Occurrences: vol. i, PRO 30/53/9/11 vol. ii, PRO 30/53/12

Donald	Peter Harry Donald, 'The King and the Scottish Troubles, 1637–1641', Ph.D. thesis (Cambridge, 1987)
Dover	House of Lords diary of the Earl of Dover, Bodl. MS Clarendon, vol. 21, no. 1603
ECR	*An Exact Collection of Remonstrances* (Edward Husbands, 1643)
EHR	*English Historical Review*
EUL	*Edinburgh University Library*
Evelyn	*Diary and Correspondence of John Evelyn*, 4 vols., ed. H. B. Wheatley (1906)
Fletcher	Anthony Fletcher, *The Outbreak of the English Civil War* (1981)
Galloway	Bruce Galloway, *The Union of England and Scotland, 1603–1608* (Edinburgh, 1986)
Gardiner, *History*	S. R. Gardiner, *History of England 1603–1642*, 10 vols. (1893)
Gardiner, *Documents*	S. R. Gardiner, *The Constitutional Documents of the Puritan Revolution 1625–1660* (Oxford, 1889, repr. 1979)
Gawdy	Rushworth, Parliamentary diary of Sir Framlingham Gawdy: vol. i, BL Add. MS 56103 vol. ii, BL Add. MS 14827 vol. iii, BL Add. MS 14828
Gilbert	*History of the Irish Confederation*, ed. J. T. Gilbert (Dublin, 1882)
Groen Van Prinsterer	G. Groen Van Prinsterer, *Archives ou correspondence inédité de la maison d'Orange–Nassau*, iii (Utrecht, 1859)
Guildford MSS.	Surrey Record Office (Guildford), Bray MSS. NB: I have used the description 'Guildford MSS' in order to avoid any risk of confusion with the Braye MSS in the House of Lords Record Office
Hamilton MSS	Scottish Record Office GD 406/1, Hamilton MSS
Hardwicke SP	*Hardwicke State Papers* (London, 1778)
Hibbard	Caroline M. Hibbard, *Charles I and Popish Plot* (Chapel Hill, 1983)
Hill	Parliamentary diary of Roger Hill, Bucks. Record Office, no catalogue reference: transcript in the possession of Yale Center for Parliamentary History
HJ	*Historical Journal*
HMC	*Historical Manuscripts Commission*
Holland	Parliamentary diary of Sir John Holland: vol. i, Bodl. MS Rawlinson C 956

	vol. ii, Bodl. MS Rawlinson D 1099
	vol. iii, Bodl. MS Rawlinson D 932
JBS	*Journal of British Studies*
JEH	*Journal of Ecclesiastical History*
JRL	John Rylands Library, Manchester
KAO	Kent Archive Office
Keeler	Mary Frear Keeler, *The Long Parliament, 1640–1641: A Biographical Study of its Members* (American Philosophical Society, 36, Phil. 1954)
Kenelm Digby	Corporation of London Record Office, Historical Papers I no. 14, newsletter from Sir Kenelm Digby, 25 Sept. 1640
Knowler	*Strafforde Letters*, ed. W. Knowler (1739)
Knyvett Letters	*The Knyvett Letters*, ed. B. Schofield (Norfolk Record Society, 20, Norwich, 1949)
Lake, 'Calvinism'	Peter Lake, 'Calvinism and the English Church 1570–1635', *Past and Present*, 114 (1987), 32–76
Lake, 'Puritans'	Peter Lake, *Moderate Puritans and the Elizabethan Church* (Cambridge, 1982)
Larkin	*Stuart Royal Proclamations*, ii. *1625–1646*, ed. James F. Larkin (Oxford, 1983)
Laud, *Works*	W. Laud, *Works*, 7 vols., ed. W. Scott and J. Bliss (Oxford, 1847–60)
Letters of Queen Henrietta Maria	*Letters of Queen Henrietta Maria*, ed. Mary Ann Everett Green (1857)
LJ	*Lords' Journals*
LJ Ire.	*Lords' Journals of Ireland*
Maltby	*The Short Parliament (1640) Diary of Sir Thomas Aston*, ed. Judith D. Maltby (Camden Society[4], 35, 1988)
MM	House of Lords Record Office, Manuscript Minutes
MP	House of Lords Record Office, Main Papers
Napier	M. Napier, *Memorials of Montrose and his Times*, 2 vols. (Maitland Club, Edinburgh, 1848)
NHI	*New History of Ireland*, ed. T. W. Moody, F. X. Martin, and F. J. Byrne
NLS	National Library of Scotland
NLS Adv. MSS	National Library of Scotland, Advocates' Manuscripts
NLS Wodrow MSS	National Library of Scotland, Wodrow Manuscripts
NLW	National Library of Wales
Northcote	Northcote, *The Notebook of Sir John Northcote*, ed. A. H. A. Hamilton (1877)
NP	*Nicholas Papers*, i. *1641–1652*, ed. George F. Warner (Camden Society, NS 40, 1886)

Palmer	Parliamentary diary of Geoffrey Palmer, Cambridge University Library MS Kk vi 38
PC Reg.	Privy Council Register, Facsimile (1967–8)
Pearl	Valerie Pearl, *London and the Puritan Revolution* (Oxford, 1961)
Peyton	Parliamentary diary of Sir Thomas Peyton, University of Minnesota Library Z 942.062 qG79: Bodl. Library Microfilm 39
PJ	*The Private Journals of the Long Parliament*, ed. Willson H. Coates, Anne Steele Young, and Vernon F. Snow (New Haven, Conn., 1982–) vol. i, 3 Jan. to 5 Mar. 1642 (1982) vol. ii, 7 Mar. to 1 June 1642 (1987)
PRO	Public Record Office
PRO A	Public Record Office, Alienations Office
PRO C	Public Record Office, Chancery
PRO E	Public Record Office, Exchequer
PRO LC	Public Record Office, Lord Chamberlain
PRO LS	Public Record Office, Lord Steward
PRO Prob.	Public Record Office, Probate
PRO 30	Public Record Office, Gifts and Deposits
PRO 31	Public Record Office, Foreign Transcripts
PRO SO	Public Record Office, Signet Office
PRO SP	Public Record Office, State Papers
PRO TS	Public Record Office, Treasury Solicitor
PRO Wards	Public Record Office, Court of Wards
PRO WO	Public Record Office, War Office (shelved at Kew)
RO	Record Office
Rothes	John Leslie, Earl of Rothes, *A Relation of Proceedings concerning the Affairs of the Kirk of Scotland*, ed. D. Laing (Bannatyne Club, 37, Edinburgh, 1830)
RPCS	*Register of the Privy Council of Scotland*
Rushworth, *Collections*	J. Rushworth, *Historical Collections*, 7 vols. vol. i (1659) vol. ii (1680) vol. iii (1692) NB in some editions vol. iii, pt. 1 is listed as vol. iv.
Rushworth, *Trial*	J. Rushworth, *The Tryall of Thomas Earl of Strafford* (1680)
Russell, *1621–9*	Conrad Russell, *Parliaments and English Politics 1621–1629* (Oxford, 1979)
Russell (ed.), *Origins*	Conrad Russell (ed.), *The Origins of the English Civil War* (1973)
Russell, 'Pym'	Conrad Russell, 'The Parliamentary Career of

John Pym 1621–1629', in Peter Clarke, Alan G.
R. Smith, and Nicholas Tyacke (eds.), *The
English Commonwealth 1547–1660: Essays in
Politics and Society presented to Joel Hurstfield*
(Leicester, 1979)

Russell, 'Strafford'   Conrad Russell, 'The Theory of Treason in the
Trial of Strafford', *EHR* 80/314 (1965), 30–50

s.   shilling or shillings

1628 Debates   Parliamentary Debates in 1628, ed. Robert C.
Johnson, Mary Frear Keeler, Maija Jansson
Cole, and William B. Bidwell (New Haven,
Conn., 1977)

1629 Debates   *Commons Debates for 1629*, ed. Wallace
Notestein and Frances Helen Relf (Minn.,
1921)

ST   *State Trials*, ed. W. Cobbett and T. B. Howell, 33
vols. (1809–26)

STC   *Short Title Catalogue of Books ... 1475–1640*, ed.
A. W. Pollard and G. R. Redgrave (1926)

Stevenson   David Stevenson, *The Scottish Revolution
1637–1644* (Newton Abbot, 1973)

TRHS   *Transactions of the Royal Historical Society*

Tollemache MSS   Tollemache Manuscripts. Buckminster Park, nr.
Grantham, Lincs.

Two Diaries   *Two Diaries of the Long Parliament*, ed. Maija
Jansson (Gloucester, 1984)

Tyacke   Nicholas Tyacke, *Anti-Calvinists: The Rise of
English Arminianism c.1590–1640* (Oxford,
1987)

Verney's Notes   *Verney's Notes of the Long Parliament*, ed. J.
Bruce (Camden Series, 31, 1845)

Wing   *Donald Wing, Short Title Catalogue of Books
printed in England, Scotland, Ireland, Wales,
and British America*, 3 vols. (New York,
1945–51)

Winthrop Papers   *Winthrop Papers*, ed. R. Winthrop (Massachusetts
Historical Society, Boston, Mass., 1931)

I

England in 1637

'None could expect a Parliament, but on some great necessity not now imaginable'.[1] These words are Sir Roger Twysden's summary of the views of some Kentish gentry on the likely consequences of a victory for the King in the Ship Money trial. They are, among other things, a clear example of the indifference to matters British which left the English gentry to be so often caught by surprise in the long crisis in British relations which ran from 1637 to 1707. Yet they are also an accurate assessment of the situation in England in the summer of 1637: England in 1637 was a country in working order, and was not on the edge of revolution.

Twysden's judgement is one which seems in 1637 to have been generally shared. The massive collection of *State Papers, Domestic* is not the record of a regime which believed it was sitting on a powder-keg: there are frequent irritations at foot-dragging over Ship Money, or at the tedious behaviour of the godly, but there seems to be little sense that this represented more than the trials of a busy man's existence. The Earl of Salisbury was taking advantage of a period between wars, when his duties as Lord-Lieutenant were less onerous, to sort and catalogue his pictures.[2] Judgements from the other side of the fence, by their gloom, mirror the general guarded optimism perceptible in *State Papers*. In 1629 Robert Ryece, the Suffolk antiquary, seems to have been one of those who opposed Winthrop's plan to go to New England on the ground that the godly had a duty to stay and help the church at home. To judge by the despondent letters he was sending Winthrop (under disguised hands and names) by 1637, he seems to have concluded that he had been wrong.[3] Saye and Brooke, the King's most fundamental critics among the peerage, had seriously considered emigration, and Brooke had gone so far as to send his steward on a long trip to New England and Virginia, at a cost of £32 4s.9d.[4]

In local government, the Crown was still receiving the necessary

---

[1] Kenneth Fincham, 'The Judges' Decision on Ship Money in February 1637: The Reaction of Kent', *BIHR* 57 (1984), 236.

[2] *HMC Salis.* XXII, 250–2.

[3] *Winthrop Papers*, iii. 371–5, 355–63.

[4] E. S. Morgan, *Puritan Political Ideas* (Indianapolis, 1965), 160–73, Warwicks. RO, Warwick Castle MSS, CR 1886 (John Halford's accounts), 1640–1, foreign payments, in settlement of a bill of 20 Nov. 1635.

minimum of co-operation even from some of the most alienated of the gentry. The appointment of Oliver Cromwell as a JP for the Isle of Ely on 20 July 1638, coming as it did in the middle of the purge of the Bench over the issue of Ship Money, seems to be sufficient evidence that he paid his Ship Money.[5] In continuing to co-operate, Cromwell was only taking the same line as most of those who were the King's leading opponents five years later. The names of Pym, Hampden, Warwick, Earle, Harley, Barrington, and Masham are enough to sustain the point. In the absence of a Parliament, a pretender, or a foreign army, there was very little even the most alienated gentleman could do about his discontent. He could tear up his roots and emigrate, yet it is noteworthy that Winthrop seems to have been almost the only man of JP status who did so. He could retire to his country house and withdraw into his library or the hunting field, but in so doing, he would forfeit any influence he might exert, and also any chance he might have of securing a favourable deal next time he was bothered by a Ship Money assessment or a metropolitical visitation. This was a sensible course only for those who had very little to lose, and few gentlemen believed themselves to come into that category. Rebellion, apart from the fact that it was well known to be a sin, was not a practical option. To have any chance of success, it needed more co-ordination before the undertaking than it was safe to risk. Moreover, in the absence of any pretender to the throne, it was a major problem, and one never solved, what any rebellion would do in the event of success. More alarmingly, rebellion without a proper legal title would create a general threat to property of a sort no gentleman was likely to welcome. Popular riots, if they occurred without gentry support, were likely to be limited and local and easily put down. Even a Parliament, as was shown in May 1640, had a limited power to challenge the King while it could exist for no longer than he found it useful. From the failure of the Pilgrimage of Grace onwards, the Crown was never successfully challenged without one of two things: a pretender to the throne, or a foreign army. Charles I put a great deal of skill into avoiding the first of these, but was less successful with the second.

This discussion is in the strictest degree hypothetical, and designed only to argue that a zealous resort to 'revolution' was not practical politics. There is very little evidence in 1637 that any significant body of the King's subjects would have wanted to resort to revolution if it had been a practical possibility. Many were offended, often deeply offended, by a number of things the King was doing, but the history of the past century had shown that rebellion was not the cleverest way to tackle these things. Wyatt's rebels had done far less for the survival of Protestantism than William Cecil had, and the Gunpowder Plotters had

[5] Birmingham Reference Library, Coventry MSS, Commissions of the Peace, no. 457.

done far less for the survival of Catholicism than the Earl of Nor-thampton or Secretary Calvert. It was a lesson well learnt that a voice at the centre of power was a more effective way to support any cause than futile demonstrations of armed resistance. If such a man as the Earl of Essex ever doubted this, he only needed to remember the fate of his father in 1601.

For those who wished to approach the centre of power in order to influence the King in a different direction, the road was still open. Charles I's court and Council, for all the rude things which have been said about them, were no mere mirrors to the King's ideas. Men who disagreed with the King's approach, both to questions of politics and to questions of religion, were still able to obtain positions which brought them very near to the centre of influence. The court in 1637 was no more united in subservience to Charles than the country was united in opposition to him. As Professor Zagorin pointed out, the politics of 1640 to 1642 were not a confrontation between a monolithic court and a monolithic country.[6] Anyone who tries to treat them as one is likely to find them entirely unintelligible.

No one better symbolizes this point than the Earl of Holland. As Groom of the Stool he held the key office in the Bedchamber, giving him more constant and confidential access to the King's person than was enjoyed by any other courtier. Yet, at the same time, Holland as Governor of the Providence Company was acting as leader and patron for a group including such people as his brother Warwick, Saye, Brooke, and Pym, many of whom were willing to contemplate emigra-tion rather than come to terms with the King's ecclesiastical policy. For Holland, who was a believer in reconciliation, consensus, and freedom of information, there was no apparent inconsistency in these positions. When he was ultimately forced to choose, it was not the King's service which he chose. His case alone should go a long way to show that Charles was not gathering a one-party court.

The case of Holland is not unique. Among the great courtiers who attended the King on state occasions, Pembroke Lord Chamberlain and Hamilton Master of the Horse rank close behind Holland. Neither consistently backed the royal line, and both influenced the King regularly in the direction of reconciliation. The picture is similar in other ceremonial functions. The Chancellor of the Order of the Garter Sir Thomas Roe gave so many perceptive warnings of impending trouble that he deserves to be known as the Stuarts' Greek chorus. Those who held the ceremonial offices at the Garter feasts of 1638 and 1640, though they included hard-liners, also included the Earls of Bed-ford, Essex, and Hertford, or, in other words, 25 per cent of the

[6] Perez Zagorin, *The Court and the Country* (1969), 305.

signatories of the Petition of the Twelve Peers which called for a Parliament in August 1640. The Gentlemen of the Privy Chamber included, in addition to hard-liners like Kynaston and Killigrew, Bedford's son Francis Russell. They also included such unexpected figures as William Coryton, a prominent participant in the tumult in the House of Commons in 1629, and John Crew, later chairman of the Long Parliament's committee on religion.[7] Even the court masques, which used to be presented as the epitome of courtly isolationism, brought together people who would be on different sides in the great divisions of 1640 and 1642. The performance of *Britannia Triumphans* on Sunday after Twelfth Night in 1637 included two of Bedford's sons among the performers as well as the future Parliamentarian peer Lord Wharton. In 1640, at the performance of *Salmacida Spolia*, the performers again included two of Bedford's sons, and their father entered part of the text in his commonplace book.[8] It was the future Royalist Sir Thomas Knyvett, not Bedford, who was moved to ambivalence when offered a ticket to the Queen's masque.[9]

It was not only in ceremonial positions that Charles was capable of selecting people from all round the political spectrum. In 1637, as much as in 1627, Charles still had moderate Councillors, and was capable of engaging in dialogue with them. Among those who had been conspicuous in the moderate faction on the legal issues raised by the Forced Loan, Lord Keeper Coventry, Secretary Coke, and the Earl of Manchester were still there in 1637.[10] Sympathy both for Calvinism and for Parliaments could be found among newly elevated Councillors too. The Earl of Salisbury in 1636 insisted that his sons spend a season in Geneva 'for the exercise of their religion', and what they learnt there can hardly have been pleasing to Charles.[11] Northumberland, who became Lord Admiral in 1638, consistently expressed hostility to what he called the 'Spanish' influence on the Council, under which title he comprehended both those he thought hostile to Parliaments and those whose Protestantism seemed to him insufficiently zealous.[12] In 1640, when appointed General for the Second Bishops' War, he wrote to his friend Mandeville (later one of the Five Members) expressing the fear that his generalship might make him be thought 'almost as great a reprobate as

[7] PRO LC 5/134, pp. 256, 439, 245, 218, 265, PRO E 403/2813, fo. 3a.

[8] William Davenant, *Dramatic Works* (Edinburgh, 1872), ii. 290, 327; Bedford Estate Office, vol. 25, unfol.

[9] *Knyvett Letters*, p. 88.

[10] R. P. Cust, 'Charles I, the Privy Council and the Forced Loan', *JBS* 24 (1985), 208–35.

[11] J. S. A. Adamson, 'The Peerage in Politics 1645–1649', Ph.D. thesis (Cambridge, 1986), 93 n. I am grateful to Dr Adamson for permission to quote from his thesis.

[12] Alnwick Castle MSS, vol. 14 (BL Microfilm 285), fo. 237[r].

any bish'. (sic).[13] Sir Henry Vane, though capable of appearing a hard-
liner either when the King was instructing him in detail, or when he
thought his favour in danger, was a friend of the Earl of Bedford and of
John Hampden, and had been warned as early as 1632 that some
thought him 'too much German and Puritan'.[14]

There was, of course, another group on the Council which was giving
Charles a different sort of advice. The names of Windebank, Cottington, Laud, Wentworth (whenever he was not in Ireland), and the
Duke of Richmond and Lennox are not usually associated with leading
Charles in directions likely to please a future Parliament, though even in
these cases, there could be unexpected exceptions. Northumberland
once accused Windebank of being 'so mean and fearful' that he would
do nothing displeasing to the King, and said the King should be served
by abler men as Secretaries.[15] The key to these remarks is that they are
made by one Councillor about another: they are not the outsider protesting at the insider, but two insiders in competition with each other.
This is the way politics worked, and it merely underlines the point that
Northumberland's complaints about the Secretaries were part of a
campaign to replace one of them by his brother-in-law the Earl of
Leicester, to whom he was writing.

Whatever may have been wrong about Charles's ability to take counsel (and something clearly was wrong), it was not that he was unable to
take advice from those who disagreed with him. He knew that this was
one of the things a good king was supposed to do, and he knew, too,
that a good king was sometimes supposed to concede to the advice of
his councillors. Charles did in fact make major decisions against his own
inclination and as a result of the persuasion of his Councillors. The
decision to call a Parliament in 1628, the Pacification of Berwick in
1639, and the decision to call the Short Parliament in 1640 are all cases
in point. Yet what seems to have happened when Charles took the
advice of his moderate Councillors is a policy less successful than either
he or they would have followed in isolation. This seems to be, in each of
these three cases, because Charles did not see (or chose not to see) that
the policy being urged on him was not a policy viable in isolation, but
part of a wider reversal of policy which he was not prepared to adopt.
The assemblies of Parliament in 1628 and 1640 were only sensible
proposals if the King would let them at least discuss grievances before
insisting on supply, and the Pacification of Berwick was only a viable

---

[13] HMC Eighth Report, II. 56. (The term 'Five Members' is used throughout because of its
familiarity, though in fact, with the inclusion of Mandeville, they were six.)
[14] CSPD 1629–31, vol. cliii, no. 55; CSPD 1634–5, vol. cclxxiii, no. 71; CSPD 1631–3, vol. ccxxi,
no. 25. The warning about being 'too much German and Puritan' came from Will Murray of the
Bedchamber, who could have been acting on higher authority.
[15] Alnwick MSS, vol. 14 (BL Microfilm 235), fos. 237ʳ, 247ʳ.

policy if Charles would let the Scots abolish episcopacy. In none of these cases was Charles willing to make the concession of substance implied by his concession of form, and the result was a policy unsuccessful because inconsistent. Much of the tortuousness which makes Charles's policies so difficult to follow is the result of this sort of unsuccessful dialogue between him and his moderate Councillors. Meanwhile, however, the fact that such reversals happened encouraged those who believed that the insider's route to political change was the right one.

There is very little sign in 1637 that those who were to be on opposite sides in 1642 were divided by any social issues. The two biggest causes of social discontent in the 1630s, forest clearance and fen drainage, were ones which pitted rural protesters against those who were to be the leaders of both sides in the Civil War.[16] One of the Crown's most active agents in forest clearance was John Pym, and one of its leading partners in fen drainage was the Earl of Bedford. The Book of Orders, the main social policy of the Caroline government, seems to have done more to unite the Crown and the godly gentry than to divide them. Its leading draftsman, the Earl of Manchester, was a future Parliamentarian.[17] It makes a number of important points about English history that the reason why the Long Parliament's plague orders of 1641 so closely followed the Privy Council's Book of Orders is that both were drafted by the same man: the Earl of Manchester.[18] Sir William Masham, it is true, seemed to be more enthusiastic for the suppression of alehouses than for other items in the Book of Orders, but he is unlikely to have been the only man who picked and chose within a very large programme.[19] Sir Thomas Jervoise, a Hampshire JP and future Rumper, seems to have put his best efforts, which were considerable, into the programme for the relief of dearth.[20] Charles Fitzgeffrey, Pym's undergraduate and family friend, committed himself to it equally enthusiastically in three assize sermons at Exeter Bodmin and Fowey in 1631.[21] These things are much more typical than Oliver Cromwell's somewhat lonely championship of the fenmen against drainage schemes. Neither the history of the 1630s nor the history of the Long Parliament gives us any good reason to suppose that social issues were any significant part of the causes that divided the gentry. They were, it seems, a rare example of something the Civil War was clearly not about.

[16] R. Buchanan Sharp, *In Contempt of All Authority* (Berkeley, Calif., 1980), 8, 223, and *passim*.
[17] Paul Slack, 'Books of Orders: The Making of English Social Policy 1577–1631', *TRHS*⁵ 30 (1980), 1–22. Brian Quintrell, 'The Making of Charles I's Book of Orders', *EHR* 95/376 (1980), 558.
[18] Paul Slack, *The Impact of Plague in Tudor and Stuart England* (1985), 221; *LJ* iv. 391.
[19] *Barrington Family Letters 1628–1632*, ed. Arthur Searle (Camden Society⁴, 28, 1983), 91.
[20] Hants. RO Jervoise MSS o 13 and o 12.
[21] Charles Fitzgeffrey, *Curse of Corne-Hoarders* (Exeter, 1631).

Superficially, then, England in 1637 was still in the age before party politics. Divisions of opinion, however profound, separated people and not institutions, and most criticism, however heated, was still being absorbed within the political system. Yet, though England was not on the edge of revolution, it was a body politic subject to many visible signs of strain. Whenever the King was forced to make a major and unexpected demand on his subjects' goodwill, these strains were capable of becoming very serious indeed. Kings had always had to bargain with their subjects when they wanted exceptional political favours from them, and it was perfectly possible in 1637 for an informed observer to predict that the next bargain was likely to be a very hard one.

In any such bargain, Ship Money was almost certain to become one of the items of negotiation. If for no other reason, this would have been true because of the sheer financial weight of Ship Money, which came to something in the region of three subsidies every year except 1638. As Sir Roger Twysden wrote, 'the common sort of people are sencible of no losse of liberty so much as that which hath joined with it a parting from mony'.

Ship Money highlighted two serious and related issues. One was the breakdown of the principle of government by consent, 'the crossing of knowne maxims of law, of which they held this the chiefe, that a king of England could lay no taxe but by Parliament'.[22] The other was a growing gap between the maximum weight of taxation the King's subjects were likely to consent to and the minimum sum on which a King could preserve solvency and national security. The case for arguing that the King needed to be able to put out a fleet capable of matching the French or the Dutch was one which those who had reproved him for unpreparedness in 1626 could not easily answer. Such a fleet was unlikely to be financed for much less than £200,000 a year, if something was allowed for rigging, victualling, repairs, and other incidental expenses.[23] Yet the maximum amount of subsidies the King could expect on a regular basis in peacetime, assuming compliant and well-satisfied Parliaments, may perhaps have been a third of this, and on this sum, there would be many other calls as well. The critics of Ship Money were as likely as anyone else to reproach Charles for neglecting the defence of the kingdom, and Charles was entitled to ask them, as he did after the Short Parliament, in what form they were likely to give their consent. The answer seems to have been none, and it was an answer from which Charles was entitled to draw his own conclusions.[24]

[22] Fincham, 'Judges' Decision on Ship Money', pp. 234, 237.
[23] I am grateful to Andrew Thrush for numerous discussions of the complex issues involved in navy finance. The amount of money the navy needed depended on the strategic objectives allotted to it.
[24] *His Majesties Declaration* (1640), BL E. 203(1), pp. 13–14.

Meanwhile Ship Money was causing a series of administrative difficulties which fill the pages of the *State Papers, Domestic* for 1637–8. It
has been pointed out that the vast majority of the protests about Ship
Money concentrate on technical issues of rating and assessment.[25] Even
if these issues were no more than what they appear to be, they were
serious enough. Rating was the Achilles heel of the English taxation
system, and was already full of ambiguities and inconsistencies. Some
counties, like Devon, had an ancient rate which apportioned any new
levy in fixed proportions between the hundreds and parishes of the
county. Such rates of course became out of date through the increasing
prosperity of some parishes and the decreasing prosperity of others,[26]
though, as with modern rating revaluations, we hear much more from
those suffering increasing poverty than from those suffering increasing
prosperity. It was a regular county convention that rating reassessments,
like taxes, were decided by consent, and that the JPs in quarter sessions
were the proper body to give consent. The procedure for Ship Money
contained a further assault on government by consent, beyond that
implied in its very existence, in the fact that the rates were to be fixed,
not by the justices in quarter sessions, or by sworn local jurors, but by
the sheriff, acting arbitrarily and alone.[27]

There were other points of strain and ambiguity in the rating system.
There was a great deal of doubt, inadequately resolved by the 1633
resolutions of the judges, about whether rates should be assessed in
proportion to the area of land held or to its value.[28] Where a county-
wide rate was being imposed for a new levy, there was dispute which of
the county rates should be used as the basis for calculation. The subsidy
rate, the poor rate, and the purveyance rate were all used, at different
times and places, as a basis of calculation.[29] Since the sums were large
and a change in the basis of assessment could mean a considerable
alteration in the amount paid, the temptation to argue about rating and
assessment was considerable. The inhabitants of Tiverton also
attempted to bargain, arguing that they would pay their Ship Money
when they were repaid the money due to them for billeting rates for

[25] J. S. Morrill, *Revolt of the Provinces* (1976), 24–6.

[26] *CSPD 1635*, vol. ccci, no. 76.

[27] *ST* iii. 1208. Chief Baron Davenport said the procedure 'is as it were to make a rape'. He was
not using the word in its Sussex sense.

[28] *CSPD 1635*, vol. ccci, no. 39; Alnwick MSS, vol. 13 (BL Microfilm 285), fo. 302; KAO,
Sackville MSS U 269/0 273/13 (Cranfield's notes on a similar problem over a parish powder rate in
1627). On some of the underlying difficulties, see A. Hassell Smith, 'Militia Rates and Militia
Statutes', in Peter Clarke, Alan G. R. Smith, and Nicholas Tyacke (eds.), *English Commonwealth
1547–1640: Essays in Politics and Society presented to Joel Hurstfield* (Leicester, 1979), 93–111.

[29] *CSPD 1638–9*, vol. cccxcviii, no. 51; *CSPD 1634–5*, vol. cclxxviii, no. 100. For similar
problems in assessing the plague rate, see Paul Slack, *Impact of Plague in Tudor and Stuart England*
(1985), 279.

1627–8.[30] In Middlesex, Chelsea protested at being rated equally with Acton, though it paid less for the subsidy. The sheriffs replied saying Chelsea ought to pay more than it did for the subsidy because it had so many peeresses, who were assessed separately for the subsidy.[31] In Cambridge, the town complained that it found it hard to meet its assessment because so many people were getting exemption as privileged persons of the University. The Council, ever willing to oblige, then tried to assess privileged persons of the University, only to receive an outraged defence of the liberties of the University from the Laudian Vice-Chancellor.[32] The scope for such arguments was almost infinite: such questions as whether the Hundred of Bath Forum should be assessed with Bath or with Somerset provided scope for endless ingenuity. The game was one which any Stuart could play: anyone who sees Ship Money refusal as a 'country' cause should remember the instruction to distrain on Ship Money refusers living in Windsor Castle.[33] Other assessments which were unquestionably legal created lengthy rating disputes: the plague rate, though imposed by the legally impeccable method of a Parliamentary statute, led to many protests and disputes, while the attempts to raise rates for the repair of Fisherton Anger bridge may have made the assize judges feel that the place was sadly appropriately named.[34] It is possible, if no legal issue had arisen, that these rating disputes could have crippled the service.

As Dr Morrill and Dr Sharpe have pointed out, the vast majority of known protests about Ship Money concentrate on these issues of rating and assessment.[35] It cannot be presumed that rating disputes cloak legal objections to the payment of Ship Money, since some were patently made by people who fully accepted the legal principles of the levy. Yet, granted the silence, we are left with the central question of the 1630s: what weight can be placed on the *argumentum ex silentio*? Dr Lake has argued that our sources are the wrong place to look if we want to find objections of constitutional principle: the vast majority of them, coming as they do from the *State Papers, Domestic*, are documents addressed to the Privy Council and its associates.[36] These are not the places to look for what the Council would have taken for seditious words: it was far

[30] *CSPD 1634–5*, vol. cclxxxi, no. 14.

[31] *CSPD 1635–6*, vol. cccxvii, no. 94.

[32] *CSPD 1635*, vol. ccxcvii, no. 23, vol. cccxcviii, no. 29.

[33] *CSPD 1638–9*, vol. cccxcviii, no. 4.

[34] Paul Slack, *Impact of Plague*, pp. 267–8, 301; *Western Circuit Assize Orders 1629–1648*, ed. J. S. Cockburn (Camden Society⁴, 17, 1976), 23, 31, 68, 80–1, 165, 203.

[35] Morrill, *Revolt of the Provinces*, pp. 24–6; Kevin Sharpe, 'Personal Rule of Charles I', in Howard Tomlinson (ed.), *Before the English Civil War* (1983), 72.

[36] Peter Lake, 'Collection of Ship Money in Cheshire during the 1630s', *Northern History* 17 (1981), 71.

better to play according to rules the Council itself accepted, under which petitioners might actually win some relief from their burdens.

It is also very doubtful how far people felt free to express their feelings even in the most private of letters. The number of letters in which the writer says he will not express himself freely for fear the letter might fall into the wrong hands is beyond count.[37] This is not necessarily a fear of deliberate interception, though the list of letters now surviving in *State Papers, Domestic* is sufficient proof that such interception might take place. It is much more a fear of accidents to an undeveloped postal system. Even where there was no fear of interception, good manners often dictated a restraint in letters which was not needed in more impersonal public pronouncements. Viscount Saye and Sele, for example, was not one of the most mealy-mouthed seventeenth-century Englishmen, yet the letters he wrote to the Marquess of Hamilton during 1641–2 are much less freely expressed than his Parliamentary speeches during the same period.[38] The convention of free speech in Parliament did matter, and if we want to know what a man really thought, his Parliamentary speeches may be a better guide than even the most private of his letters.

When we find those objectors to their Ship Money assessments including such stalwarts of the 1628 Parliament as Sir Robert Phelips and Walter Long, we should not assume that they had forgotten all the things they said in Parliament because it was not at that time expedient to repeat them.[39] It is the balance of probability that these people, at least, objected to Ship Money because they saw it as an arbitrary and illegal tax imposed without consent in Parliament. When we find the comparatively short list of outright refusers including other Parliamentary stalwarts such as Sir Francis Seymour,[40] their actions are so clearly consistent with the views they expressed in public both before and after that it would be a perverse use of the *argumentum ex silentio* to argue that their convictions went into an eleven-year abeyance.

The depth of English attachment to the principle of taxation by consent is clear in the views of the only twelve people in England able to discuss Ship Money freely and in public: the judges. These were, from the King's point of view, a hand-picked sample: he or his father had appointed all of them, and some influence was brought to bear on them during the trial. Yet even in this sample, five out of twelve did not

---

[37] *HMC Eighth Report*, II. 58; *Winthrop Papers*, iii. 139; *CSPD 1635*, vol. ccxcvii, no. 39. It would be easy, but I hope unnecessary, to extend this list into double or even treble figures.

[38] Hamilton MSS 1505, 1506, and other refs.

[39] T. G. Barnes, *Somerset 1625–1640* (1961), 214 and many other refs.; *CSPD 1639*, vol. cccxxii, no. 45.

[40] Keeler, p. 337.

uphold his case. Even in the judgements of those who judged for the King, there are a number of ideas which show the depth of attachment to the notion of taxation by consent and to Parliamentary statute as the ultimate source of law. There are, it is true, numerous high-flown and provocative utterances as well, especially Finch's claim that the right to levy Ship Money was something which no Act of Parliament could take away.[41] Yet their principal argument, that in cases of necessity law could be overridden was one which, in its proper context, their opponents accepted. In cases such as the outbreak of fire, they admitted the principle to be valid. Berkeley and the others also devoted great effort to arguing that Ship Money was legal *because* it was not a tax: the effort put into trying to prove that Ship Money was a form of conscription and not of taxation shows the need to offer at least a powerful lip-service to the principle of taxation by consent.[42] When Berkeley discussed the claim by Hampden's lawyers that the Danegeld had been imposed by Parliament, he said it was a 'conjecture', but he did not dismiss it out of hand. He was prepared to entertain as possibilities, both that there had been Parliaments under the Saxons, and that one of them had imposed the Danegeld.[43] He even conceded the key constitutionalist case, that the kingdom of England was, as classified by Sir John Fortescue, *dominium politicum et regale*, in which the king could not do what he liked, but had to govern by rules of law. Berkeley's comment is: 'this needs no answer, it is agreed'.[44] The Ship Money judgements suggest, among much else, that the notion of Parliaments as the ultimate source of law was so deeply settled in legal thinking that it was going to take a very long time without Parliaments to get it out. All this argument was conducted before a packed courtroom, in which Oliver St John's arguments against Ship Money were applauded by the crowd.[45] It is not to be imagined that such discussion did not continue outside the walls of the courtroom. The Earl of Holland, reporting the judgement to Hamilton, thought it had done the king no good: '[it] occasions a great remisse in the businesse, our people being more enclined to beleeve that

[41] J. P. Kenyon, *The Stuart Constitution* (1966), 116. But note the admission of Justice Croke, on the other side, that 'if a statute were, that the king should not defend the kingdom, it were void, being against law and reason'. Croke was disputing, not Finch's constitutional principle, but his assessment of the facts; *ST* iii. 1160.

[42] *ST* iii. 1090, 1095–6: 'the ships and arms to be provided are to continue the subjects' own in property'. For Croke's concession of the principle, that the King could demand the persons and ships of his subjects, ibid. 1152. Again, Croke conceded the constitutional principle, but disputed its relevance to the facts of the case.

[43] Ibid. 1091.

[44] Ibid. 1124. For Berkeley's concession that the Petition of Right was a statute, ibid. 1109.

[45] *HMC Ninth Report*, II. 496–7; also Northcote, pp. 85–6. Sir Thomas Knyvett, although he was up 'by peepe of the day', could not get into the courtroom: *Knyvett Letters*, p. 91.

those that were against the king were lesse against their owen consciences'.[46]

We get occasional tantalizing hints of such debate. At Kilsby, North-amptonshire, the vicar took instructions to preach obedience seriously, only to find that he had turned the church into a debating society. On one occasion, 'when I exhorted the people to pay his Majesty's dues', the vicar said they owed both suit and service, only to be told from the congregation that Ship Money was neither 'which did not a little harm in the country'. He was left to face the parish constable saying that the King's taxes were more intolerable than Pharoah's on the Israelites.[47] It would be interesting to know whether many followed the King's Vice-Admiral Sir John Pennington in maintaining that the Ship Money fleets were achieving so little that the money should be 'as soon saved as spent'.[48] Dr Fincham has made the most valuable contribution to the debate on public reactions to Ship Money: he has saved us from discus-sions of the *argumentum ex silentio* by penetrating the wall of silence. The extract he has published from the commonplace book of Sir Roger Twysden shows us the debate on Ship Money as conducted by the Kentish gentry. As a sample, the Kentish gentry, and particularly Twysden's friends among them, may be unusual in their scholarship, but there is no reason to think them unusual in the depth of their convictions.

The Kentish gentry seem to have agreed that 'this was the greatest cause according to the general opinion of the world was ever heard out of parlyament in England'. Perhaps the most significant conclusion from Twysden's report was that what took place was not a universal protest, but a *debate*. Some, he reported, said that 'the king had full right to impose it, and all concluded that if a kingdom were in jeopardy it ought not to be lost for want of money if it were within it, which these men sayd wee were to beleeve the king affirming'. As his words suggest, Twysden was not one of 'these men'. Others, of whom he seems to have been one, fell back on the legal views of Sir John Fortescue, whose effect 'was to shew the king had not an absolute power, they considered in especiall the 9, 14, 34, 35, 37, 53 chapters'. This detailed analysis of chapter and verse did not come from people unaware of the issues involved. They also argued, even while holding the 'last parliaments' much to blame, 'that in a judgment that not may, but doth, touch every man in so hygh a poynt every man ought to be herd and the reasons of every one weyghed, which could not bee but in parlyament'.[49]

[46] Hamilton MS 374. Holland added his own opinion that Ship Money was necessary for the King's 'foreign businesses'.

[47] PRO SP 16/438/92.

[48] *CSPD 1635*, vol. ccxcv, no. 18.

[49] Fincham, 'Judges' Decision on Ship Money', pp. 230–7.

That Twysden became a Ship Money refuser will cause little surprise to readers of his commonplace book. What may cause more surprise is that by March 1642, he had also become one of the key figures in the group which became the Kentish Royalist party. In following this course, Twysden was by no means alone. The Ship Money refusers included Sir Francis Seymour; the Earl of Peterborough, an ex-Catholic; and Sir Marmaduke Langdale, a Catholic who was to command a wing of the King's cavalry at Naseby.[50] Opposition to Ship Money seems to have been a cause which united most of the English gentry, rather than dividing them, and belief in the rule of law, taxation by consent, and future meetings of Parliament, however passionately held, are not necessarily marks of a future Parliamentarian. It is, after all, hard to see how a principled attachment to legality can explain a decision to undertake the ultimate illegality of fighting a war against the king.

Probably most Englishmen looked forward to a time when there might be another Parliament. Garrard, Lord Deputy Wentworth's newsletter-writer, took the chance, when sending him good wishes for his Irish Parliament in 1634, to add: 'I wish as heartily to see an happy one in England'. The King, on the other hand, was much less encouraging when he wrote to Wentworth about his Irish Parliament: he said: 'as for that hidra, take good heed; for you know, that here I have found it as well cunning, as malitious'.[51] This passage seems to express a settled hostility, but one based on political, rather than constitutional, objections. The same hostility appeared the previous year when a benevolence was being raised for the relief of Charles's sister Elizabeth of Bohemia. The draft instructions, probably based on those for the Forced Loan, included the statement that co-operation in paying the benevolence would not make the King less willing, when the time was right, to meet his people in Parliament. Charles crossed these words out, and wrote a note that 'I have scored out thease eight lynes as nott judging them fitt to pass'.[52]

These were serious tensions, but ones whose resolution was not beyond all conjecture. They are not necessarily marks of impending catastrophe, though they did mean that the next Parliament, whenever it might come, was likely to be an unusually difficult one. For Charles, any restoration of trust would have had to include a new-found willingness to supply him with adequate finance, and before that could happen, the English gentry would need to go through a financial education. Had Charles seen Sir Roger Twysden's commonplace book, the passage

[50] Above, p. 10; *CSPD 1638–9*, vol. cccc, no. 27; J. S. Morrill, *Revolt of Provinces*, p. 25.
[51] Knowler, i. 267, 233.
[52] Bodl. MS Clarendon, vol. 5, no. 315 (fo. 117).

which would, perhaps, have made the deepest impression on him was the assertion that it was possible to defray the charges of a navy for £30,000 a year.[53] This statement is a mark of either strategic or financial illiteracy. £30,000 a year, it is true, was the amount of the ordinary estimate for the navy, but this would suffice only to keep the navy in port and to send out a few ships for a guard. To those who believed, as most of the gentry probably did, that the English navy should be capable of matching the continental navies, such a sum was laughably small.

Yet financial education, difficult though it may be, is easier than theological conversion. Charles had more chance of making his peace with gentlemen who believed Ship Money merely represented the insolence of office than he had of making his peace with those who believed, like the author of an anonymous squib of 1639, that Ship Money was wanted for the setting up of idolatry.[54] This was a crudely parodied form of the thesis which had been developed by Pym, Rous, and Rudyerd at the end of the 1620s. The key to this thesis was that the King, or some of those about him, wished to dispense with Parliaments because they were an obstacle to a plan to alter the country's religion. As Rous had put it in 1629, the object of these people was 'to set a distaste between prince and people, or to find out some other way of supply to avoid or break Parliaments, that so they may break in upon our religion, and bring in their own errors'.[55] The statement that Ship Money was wanted for the setting up of idolatry is a good caricature of this position. For those who thought this way, something more than a mere reaffirmation of the law was needed. For them, there would be no security for property, any more than for religion, until the theological tendencies associated with the name of Laud had been removed from the King's counsels. By the middle 1630s, this way of thought was widely disseminated. In 1636 one Raphael Britten of Olney, lace–buyer, was repeating a rumour that the King had fallen out with Laud, and there would be a Parliament. He added that Laud was a papist, and there was no need to read the Book of Sports in favour of Sunday recreations. In his mind, at least, the indissoluble association between religious and constitutional change was firmly established.[56]

The chief justification for this view was the fact that Charles had changed the church of England in a way many in his Parliaments found profoundly uncongenial. If Arminian clergy feared the prospect of a future Parliament, they had every excuse for doing so, since they were often threatened with one. That Charles's church was profoundly dif-

---

[53] Fincham, 'Judges' Decision on Ship Money', p. 234.
[54] PRO SP 16/438/93.
[55] Russell, 1621–9, pp. 404–8; id., Pym, pp. 161–4.
[56] CSPD 1636–7, vol. cccxxvii, no. 140.

ferent from James's is a case which it is fortunately unnecessary to argue here, since Dr Tyacke and Dr Lake have argued the case fully and convincingly.[57] In transferring dominance in the church from Calvinists to Arminians, Charles operated under a Declaration of December 1628, forbidding controversy, confirming the 'literal and grammatical sense' of the Thirty-Nine Articles, and, 'out of our princely care that the churchmen may do the work which is proper unto them', putting into the hands of the bishops and clergy in convocation the power to 'do all such things, as being made plain by them, and assented unto by us, shall concern the settled continuance of the doctrine and discipline of the church of England'. Meanwhile, these 'curious and unhappy differences' were to be 'shut up in God's promises', and not openly discussed.[58] This Declaration is sometimes ignorantly discussed as if it were an exercise in impartiality. The assertion that it was not does not merely depend on the way it was administered, though a case may easily be based on that.

As Bishop Davenant discovered in 1629, when he preached before the King what he believed to be 'the received doctrine of our church established in the 17th article' on predestination, the most controversial thing about this Declaration was its assessment of what was controversial.[59] To a Calvinist, speaking from a position of established dominance, predestination did not appear controversial. It was the Arminians, coming from behind, who benefited from a ruling regarding these questions as controversial. Moreover, the questions which were not to be discussed were ones an Arminian could safely regard as peripheral: it was no great hardship to most of them to do what they were in any case inclined to do, and move other questions into the centre of debate. To one of the firmer Calvinists, on the other hand, this Declaration was tantamount to a command not to preach the gospel of salvation, and that was a command no Christian preacher could obey without sin. For some of them, a command not to preach Christ crucified would hardly have been a more severe restriction.[60]

Charles's Declaration also conferred the power to interpret the Thirty-Nine Articles on the bishops and clergy in Convocation, that is to say, on a body whose upper ranks were hand-picked by himself. This was, in effect, to confer the power to interpret the Thirty-Nine Articles on the Arminians. In conferring a power to take enforceable religious decisions on the clergy alone, the Declaration also offended many of the deepest prejudices of English lawyers and gentry, including many, such

[57] Tyacke, *passim*; Lake, 'Calvinism', pp. 32–76. These two works are complementary and, it is to be hoped, definitive.
[58] Gardiner, *History*, vii. 21–3.
[59] Lake, 'Calvinism', p. 65. Davenant was immediately told that the King was much displeased.
[60] Tyacke, pp. 188, 182.

as John Selden, who could not by any stretch of the imagination be classified as Calvinists. The century after the Reformation was an anxious one for gentry, facing constant changes in the list of things they could not do or say without offence. One of the reactions to this anxiety was a growing stress on a creed which went back to Christopher St German, that the clergy had no legislative power, and nothing could be enforced on the laity but what had received general assent in Parliament. Edward Littleton, later Charles's Lord Keeper, said in the Parliament of 1629 that 'the convocation house hath noe power to make any cannon of the church or to put it upon the state but by the assent of the state, what the convocation house hath made for a cannon hath beene rejected by the Parliament'.[61] This Erastian, Parliamentary version of the Royal Supremacy seems to have grown in popularity during the 1630s. Edward Bagshawe in November 1640 claimed that 'the ornamts. off the church off England are settled by Act of parliament'. It perhaps helps to understand why Sir Edward Dering, no Puritan by any likely definition, began his Long Parliament assault on the bishops by taking up the case of the cleric Thomas Wilson, who had objected to reading the prayer against the Scots because 'noe man should read an arbitrary prayer in ye churche but what is enacted by Parliament to be read etc'.[62] To Charles, who thought the laity should not govern the church, the notion of an 'arbitrary prayer' would have made no sort of sense. This dislike of clerical attempts to impose new things on the laity deprived Charles and Laud of the support of many who were no friends to Calvinism, and also meant that any future Parliamentary battle to abolish Arminianism was likely to become merged in a struggle to impose Parliamentary limitations on the Convocation and the Royal Supremacy. It was thus likely to come into the area where Charles was least flexible: the area where his religious convictions and his sense of his 'authority' merged.

Much of the story of the 1630s seems to revolve round the failure of Charles and Laud to mobilize support from many people who were no friends either to predestinarian theology or to godly iconoclasm. Viscount Falkland, for example, was prepared in 1641 to accuse the Laudian bishops of having been 'the destruction of unity, under pretence of uniformity: to have brought in superstition and scandal, under the titles of reverence and decency; to have defiled our church by adorning our churches'. He said the King's Declaration had been used 'to tye up one side, and to let the other loose'. Yet this passionate enemy

---

[61] *1629 Debates*, pp. 117, 120.

[62] Bodl. MS Rawlinson C 956, fo. 16ᵃ; Peyton, fo. 31. Peyton, as a fellow Kentishman, probably had some previous knowledge of the case. He has marked the passage with a marginal hand. For the context, see S. P. Salt, 'Origins of Sir Edward Dering's Attack on the Ecclesiastical Hierarchy 1625–1640', *HJ* 30/1 (1987), 21–52. I am grateful to Dr Salt for lending me a proof of this article.

of the Laudian bishops was no friend to Calvinism: he wrote, probably in about 1636, that on the issue of free will, he would rather be a Pelagian than a Calvinist. He said the Calvinist view wholly overthrew God's justice, was directly contrary to Scripture, and that it said the kingdom of Heaven was to take us by violence. The key to Falkland's published writing is a sceptical doubt, both how far religious truths could be certainly known, and how far, if they could be known, they should be enforced. It is perhaps this dislike of enforcing doubtful matters which is at the bottom of his hostility to the Laudian bishops, and his key charge is that they had 'laboured to bring in an English, though not a Roman, popery: I mean not only the outside, and dress, of it, but equally absolute, a blind dependence of the people upon the clergy'.[63]

Sir Henry Slingsby, one of the Deputy-Lieutenants of Yorkshire, was one of the leaders of the local Arminians. His diary, the source of our information, was kept in imitation of Montaigne. For him, it was the clericalism of the Laudians which annoyed him. Archbishop Neile of York refused Slingsby's request to consecrate his chapel, 'having, as he saith, express command not to consecrate any, least it may be occasion of conventicles'. This attempt to restrict Slingsby's use of his own chapel moved him to fury. He wrote: 'it is not amiss to have a place consecrated for devotion, as our churches are, thereby to separate them for that use: but we cannot stay our self here, but must attribute a sanctity to the very walls and stones of the church; and herein we do of late draw near to the superstition of the church of Rome, who do suffer such external devotion to efface and wear out the inward devotion of the heart'. Behind this passage is an intense anticlericalism: 'but if in a place clergymen are, and enter into their acquaintance, for the most part we shall receive no benefit, but rather harm whose example shall teach us rather to embrace the world than to forsake the world; being covetous, contentious, proud, boasters, ambitious'.[64] In the Long Parliament, Falkland and Slingsby both followed the same course; they supported the exclusion of the bishops from the House of Lords, drew back from their abolition, and rallied to the King only when faced by Parliamentarians with a clericalism they found even more uncongenial than Laud's.

Among Calvinists, there was a considerable difference in their reactions to the changes of the 1630s. It may safely be assumed that none of them liked these changes, but there seems to have been a considerable difference between those who regarded them as antichristian and those

---

[63] Rushworth, *Collections*, III. i. 184–5: Falkland, *A Reply* with *A Discourse of Infallibility*, ed. Thomas Triplet (1651), 126, 54–5.
[64] *Diary of Sir Henry Slingsby*, ed. Daniel Parsons (Oxford, 1836), 19–21. On the Arminianism of Thurscross, see G. E. Aylmer and R. Cant (eds.), *History of York Minster* (Oxford, 1977), 212.

who merely regarded them as undesirable. Those in the second category seem to have been able to remain in attendance on Charles, and to accept a situation almost comically like that of the Arminians under James. They could still hold positions in the church, they could still attend on the King, and they could still preach before him, but at the price of not preaching on the convictions closest to their hearts. No new Calvinist bishops were appointed after Hall's appointment to Exeter in 1627, but those who were left over from the previous reign seem to have kept their places in the lists of Lent preachers and in other lists of those attendant on the King. Davenant Bishop of Salisbury, though his conduct was very carefully watched, seems to have almost succeeded to the court status of Lancelot Andrewes: as Andrewes had been James's tame Arminian, Davenant was becoming Charles's tame Calvinist. The part was undertaken under protest, but it was not until the Convocation of 1640, when Davenant moved for a canon for the suppression of Arminianism, that he firmly stepped out of line.[65]

Behind Davenant, there were others of the same ecclesiastical stamp. In February 1639 Daniel Featly, Abbot's old chaplain, was made a Chaplain Extraordinary to the King. Ralph Brownrigg, the Cambridge Calvinist, was preferred to the same office in May 1638.[66] Joseph Hall Bishop of Exeter had a sometimes uneasy relationship with the Laudians, but finally rallied to the defence of his order when moved to fellow-feeling by the sufferings of the Scottish bishops in 1639 simply for their membership of the episcopal order.[67] Thomas Morton Bishop of Durham, who of all the Calvinist bishops was perhaps most uncomfortable with the new dispensation, nevertheless preached against the Scots in 1639, and allowed the King to cut out of his text any passages which showed an excessive approval of Calvin.[68] For these Calvinist episcopalians of the Jacobean vintage, the Civil War was to ask them to choose between their Calvinist convictions and their episcopalian convictions. Not all of them found the choice an easy one.

Dr Lake has tentatively suggested that the distinction between Calvinists who could live with Laud and Calvinists who could not may

---

[65] Tyacke, pp. 210–12, 236. For an example of the care with which Davenant was watched, see *CSPD 1631–3*, vol. ccxxxiii, no. 88. He was, however, included in the list of Lent preachers for 1635, 1636, 1637, and 1638. In 1639 he was 'excused for his age and infirmity': PRO LC 5/134, flyleaves. On the 1640 Convocation, see Cope, p. 111.

[66] PRO LC 5/134, pp. 307, 233.

[67] PRO SP 16/429/40. Hall was writing to Laud, and saying what the recipient wanted to hear, but his complaint that Holy Island was again a receptacle for persecuted prelacy has the ring of sincerity. Both men retained the suspicion that when they defended episcopacy, they were not necessarily defending the same thing. This letter still shows reservations. It warns against any attempt by the King to 'reconquer his owne' in Scotland, and recommends instead a general synod of the three kingdoms: PRO 16/431/2 and 65; ibid. 16/432/38.

[68] Ibid. 16/437/56.

have something to do with the distinction made by Dr Kendall between credal and experimental predestinarians.[69] For the experimental predestinarians, of whom William Perkins had been the most distinguished, it was possible to know experimentally that one was saved. The less cautious among them believed or were tempted to believe, that it might be possible to have such knowledge about others also, and therefore to identify a visible community of 'the godly', as the most extreme among them would say, 'the saints' or, as Stephen Marshall put it to the Long Parliament, Gods 'owne separated people'.[70] Such a belief tended to weaken a commitment to a 'visible church', in which all professing Christians, elect or reprobate, were gathered together under one roof, and instead tempted them to apply references to 'the church', to the invisible church, the company of the Elect. Such a belief of course weakened the desire to make the compromises necessary to go on worshipping in the same visible church as others less likely to be regenerate. Such a suggestion must of course be made with caution. Even in Massachusetts, where visible evidence of conversion became essential for full church membership, clergy never asserted that the church were the Elect.[71] Only the Fifth Monarchists, much later, seem to have gone all the way to this point. Nevertheless, it does seem to be true that those who were experimental predestinarians often had a less intense belief in the importance of an institutional church.

Credal predestinarians, by contrast, followed Calvin against Perkins, and believed it was not possible to know who was elect or who was reprobate. Archbishop Ussher, for example, told his hearers in 1641 that 'tis not for us to search into the decree of election and reprobation'. A man might not say 'there's a reprobate (as if they had stood at God's elbow)': this was a 'desperate presumption'.[72] It is at least possible that those who believed this were more reluctant than other Calvinists to classify Laud as 'Antichrist' or 'the pander and broker to the Whore of Babylon'. The vicar of Brigstock (Northants), who said God had created the greatest part of mankind in order to damn them, had less need than others to make sacrifices for the unity of the visible church.[73]

For such people, there was nothing necessarily new about a gulf between them and the ecclesiastical authorities. On the other hand, the gulf which separated them from Charles and Laud was a great deal wider than any previous gulf. It was also a gulf of a different order. This fact follows from the doctrine of the marks of the true church. The

---

[69] Lake, 'Calvinism', p. 39; R. T. Kendall, *Calvin and English Calvinism* (Oxford, 1979).

[70] Lake, *Puritans*, pp. 104–5; Stephen Marshall, *A Sermon* (1641), 11.

[71] E. S. Morgan, *Visible Saints* (Ithaca, 1963), 93, 100–1, 109–10, 114–15, and *passim*.

[72] CUL MS Mm vi 55, fo. 6ʳ. I am grateful to Dr J. S. A. Adamson for drawing my attention to this MS.

[73] *CSPD 1634–5*, vol. cclxxx, no. 54.

Thirty-Nine Articles, which on this point follow Calvin exactly, set out that 'the visible church of Christ is a congregation of faithful men, in the which the pure word of God is preached, and the sacraments be duly ministered according to Christ's ordinance in all those things that of necessity are requisite to the same'.[74] For those who followed Calvin, so long as they could find these two things in their church, it was their duty to remain within it without separation. No matter what else they might find wrong in the church, it was theirs, and they had a duty to belong to it. Even if they could only find these things in some part of their church, it was their duty to attend and worship in that part of it. Failure to do so was schism, which was only a slightly lesser sin than heresy.

On the other hand, if they could not find these two things, the church to which they belonged was no true church, and it was their duty not to worship in it. Until the 1630s most had been able to find them without too much difficulty. In and after the 1630s it was rapidly becoming a very different matter. For many Calvinists, the preaching of the pure word of God was very nearly a synonym for predestination. For Henry Burton, for example, the fundamentals of true Protestantism were 'predestination, election, freewill [sic] justification, faith, perseverance in saving grace, certainty of salvation, and the like'.[75] None of these could he find anywhere where Charles's Declaration was duly observed, so he was reduced to finding the church of England in those unobserved corners where it was not. The sacraments duly administered, for many, could not be found anywhere where there was an altar, since an altar by definition implied a sacrifice, and therefore some change in the consecrated elements. For many, of whom Pym was the most prominent, bowing to the altar compounded this particular felony by introducing an element of worship of the altar. Worship of any created thing was idolatry. In the debate on the Grand Remonstrance, Pym said that 'altar-worship is idolatry, and that was injoyned by the bishopps in all there cathedrals'. This belief separated Pym very sharply indeed from Sir Edward Dering, who believed that the Laudian altar policy did not involve idolatry, but only superstition.[76] For Dering, the existence of altars, however undesirable, was possible inside a true church. For Pym, wherever there was an altar was neither a church nor Christian: idolatry was one of the sins with which no compromise was possible, and certainly incompatible with the sacraments duly administered.

There seems to be no evidence of godly gentry actually refusing to attend services on state occasions on the ground that the churches

---

[74] Article XIX; John Calvin, *Institutes*, IV. i. 8–12.
[75] Tyacke, pp. 187–8.
[76] *Verney's Notes*, p. 123; Rushworth, III. i. 426.

concerned were no part of the true church: the combination of ambition, social adaptability, and a principled horror of schism seems to have been too strong for them. Yet there are some who, on their own principles, should have done, and it is possible that later, when the boot was on the other foot, a sense of guilt at their own compliance contributed to their severity. Certainly, many of them were opposed to the regime in as fundamental a sense as the northern rebels of 1569, who restored the old order and held Mass in Durham cathedral.

It is hard to know from evidence before 1640 how many gentry were thinking this way. It was not the sort of conviction that could safely be avowed in public. Occasional chance documentary survivals show that views like this were held by gentlemen who, as far as the public record goes, were still loyal and hard-working local servants of the Crown. Sir Thomas Wroth, for example, is known in the public record as Deputy-Lieutenant during the Bishops' Wars, and as an apparently co-operative, even if not effective, ship-sheriff. Yet Wroth, in a letter we know because it was intercepted, said that

it will argue some patience if we quietly suffer *usquam* [*sic*] *ad rerum amissionem*, but it will be a great evidence of true Christian resolution if we suffer *usque ad sanguinis effusionem*, for preservation of faith and a good conscience. Good Doctor, I know you are so affected with the sad condition of these times, that you spare no prayers for yourself and others. Continue, I beseech you, and the Lord pour the spirit of prayer into my heart, that I may assault God incessantly with supplications and tears for myself, for you, and for his church in general.[77]

He was evidently looking forward to martyrdom. It tells us something about the 1630s, not only that this letter was intercepted, but that no action was then taken on it.

Lucy Jervoise, wife of a Hampshire JP, was another of the same stamp. Her husband Sir Thomas was a hard-working JP and Deputy-Lieutenant, whose efforts did a great deal to make a success of both the Forced Loan and the Book of Orders. He was a regular member of Parliament, though a silent one, and very little in his record prepares us for the fact that he became a Parliamentarian Deputy-Lieutenant in 1642, and ultimately a member of the Rump. In 1633, when Henry Sherfield smashed a picture of God the Father in a church window because it was idolatrous, he was facing a Star Chamber trial, and in such bad trouble that only his true friends wanted to know him. Lucy Jervoise wrote to him that 'it is your honor to suffer for Godes cause; it will be your Glory if you continewe to ye end'. She said that when he

---

[77] *CSPD 1635*, vol. ccxcvii, no. 35. Wroth was writing to Dr Stoughton, who sometimes acted as a postbox for New England.

went to London for his trial, Sir Thomas would go with him if his cold was not so bad as to prevent it. Sir Thomas's cold seems not to have been diplomatic, since he later undertook responsibility for Sherfield's debts.[78] Sir Robert Harley, whose household prayed for the conversion of the Queen and against Arminianism, seems to have been another of the same stamp.[79] Such people were opposed to the Crown in a sense in which almost no Jacobean gentleman had been. They enjoyed national, as well as county-wide, contact with each other, and came regularly to each other's support. In fact, by 1640 they had come to constitute something very close to a party. As such, in a society most of which still hoped to restore consensus, they could enjoy an advantage out of all proportion to their numbers. This was not only because, both in England and in Scotland, their congregations could help to get them ready and organized first. It was also because the political fixers, the Vanes, Hamiltons, and Hollands, would make big sacrifices in the hope of reuniting them with the political community and eradicating their party, and therefore potentially disloyal, character. In 1640 it was not necessarily too late for this technique to be practical, but it was a great deal harder to use than it would have been eleven years earlier.

This unwillingness to compromise was fuelled, for many of the godly, by the sense that they, and not their opponents, were the truly orthodox and conformable part of the church of England. When they used words like 'orthodox' and 'conformable', they, as well as the Laudians, were using words and ideas selectively. As Laudians more eagerly invoked conformity to the discipline than to the doctrine of the church of England, so Calvinists more readily claimed to be conformable to its doctrine than to its discipline. When a group of petitioners to the House of Lords in 1641 accused an Arminian vicar of disapproving of a lecture by clergy conformable to the *doctrine* of the church of England, they told a Laudian ear that the lecture was delivered by nonconforming Calvinists.[80] It is part of the price of the ambiguity of the 1559 settlement that the claim to be conformable, and therefore entitled to all the moral rightness of orthodoxy, was made equally by both sides. In November 1629 two petitions were delivered to Laud by groups of Essex clergy. One was from clergy 'obedient to his majesty's ecclesiastical laws', the other from clergy 'of the conformable part'. One of these petitions was for Thomas Hooker, lecturer at Chelmsford, and the other

---

[78] Hants. RO Jervoise MSS E 77: I would like to thank Dr Kevin Sharpe for this reference; *CSPD 1635–6*, p. 258 (docket).

[79] Jacqueline Levy, 'Perceptions and Beliefs: The Harleys of Brampton Bryan', Ph.D. thesis (London, 1983), 62, 164, and *passim*. I am grateful to Dr Levy for permission to quote from her thesis.

[80] MP 16. Jan 1641.

was against him.[81] In 1639 one of the Oxford proctors replied to an instruction to bow to the altar, professing his conformity, and asking, if anything 'besides what is established' were to be required of him, for an explicit order from Laud.[82] He was in the right of it: the argument for conformity to established practice worked neither for Laud nor for his opponents.[83] Much of what Laud was requiring was genuinely novel. A correspondent of John Winthrop's, reporting deprivations in East Anglia, distinguished perceptively (and honestly) between deprivations according to the 'new conformity' and deprivations according to the 'old conformity'.[84]

This fact increased sympathy for those who complained of the Laudian regime and, in the trial of William Prynne in 1637, produced such demonstrations of support that Wentworth commented perceptively: 'a prince that loseth the force and example of his punishments, loseth withal the greatest part of his dominion'.[85] If these had just been demonstrations of the godly, they would have been easier to ignore, but at least one report suggests that discontent at the bishops ranged a good deal wider than that. Henry Jacie, writing to John Winthrop, said that 'by these devices, the prelates hoped to have more prevailed; but its feared they have lost greatly by it. The poor credit they had with the vulgar is almost quite lost. Every wrech, and swearing and drunken beast almost, is ready on the least speech to cry out on them'.[86] The Laudians, it seems, had failed to communicate their sense of the dangerousness of Burton, Bastwick, and Prynne to the public at large, and so only alienated the public by measures taken against them.

There is a small but persistent undercurrent in the seditious words of the 1630s charging Laud, and sometimes Charles also, with popery. It is so patently clear that Charles and Laud were not papists that modern readers have been unable to take this charge seriously. Yet it is possible that this failure is because we have not quite understood what was being said: 'popery', as much as 'Puritanism', may be in the eye of the beholder. Both were terms of abuse, and both might vary in meaning according to the prejudices of the abuser. In the mouth of a man like Sir

---

[81] Tyacke, pp. 189–90. See *CSPD 1628–9*, vol. cxlii, no. 51, where Thomas Edwards, perhaps the future author of *Gangraena*, was described as 'every way conformable to the church of England'.

[82] PRO SP 16/400/7.

[83] For a complaint of innovation from an unexpected quarter, see *CSPD 1629–31*, vol. clxxiv, no. 64, and vol. clxxxvi, no. 107, John Howson Bishop of Durham to Laud, apparently supporting the dissident canon Peter Smart against the liturgical innovations introduced by John Cosin as Dean. See also Mervyn James, *Family, Lineage and Civil Society* (Oxford, 1974), 120, 168.

[84] *Winthrop Papers*, iii. 380–1.

[85] Knowler, ii. 119. For the events Wentworth was commenting on, see *CSPD 1637*, vol. ccclxiv, no. 68.

[86] *Winthrop Papers*, iii. 487.

Francis Seymour, a charge of 'popery' is straightforward: it means, as it does now, a simple, plain adherence to the church of Rome. By this definition, Laud was no papist, and it is worth noting that those who used this definition did not accuse him of being one. For others, the word had subtler meanings. For them, the real challenge was to understand the force of sin which had led most of the western world into apostasy for several centuries. They were always trying to identify the sins, and the spiritual principles, which had proved powerful enough to tempt so much of the world from its allegiance. It was these underlying spiritual principles which constituted the true forbidden fruit of popery.[87] For many, it seems that the Arminian belief that a man might do something to be saved seemed to be the true popish principle on which the apostasy had been based. When Sir Thomas Roe referred to the Palatinate as 'the only clear Protestant church of Germany', what he meant was that it was the only clearly Calvinist church of Germany.[88] For Peter Smart canon of Durham a key principle of popery was the belief in organizing worship to 'ravish . . . eyes'.[89] For John Dod, a key sin of popery was the belief that men could devise worship of their own invention. This, at least, was something Laud did believe, and if this was a correct definition of 'popery', then it would be right to call Laud a papist, and the King also. This definition is that of the man who was acting in 1637–9 as Pym's minister.[90] At the end of 1640, a group of Herefordshire and Shropshire ministers wanted to define papists to include all who would not take an oath against popery and Arminianism, or any who refused to subscribe to the doctrinal parts of the Thirty-Nine Articles, the Irish Articles of 1615, and the Lambeth Articles of 1595.[91] Again, if refusal to subscribe to the Lambeth Articles made a man a papist, it was perfectly fair to call Laud one. Perhaps, instead of dismissing charges of 'popery' out of hand, we ought to use them as a key to unlock the mystery of what each individual speaker meant by 'popery'. Not all charges of popery have any meaning, but some, at least, are perfectly correct according to their own lights. It is our task to discover what those lights were.

It would be wrong to paint too unrelievedly black a picture of the position of the godly gentry during the 1630s. They often enjoyed far better opportunities to worship as they chose at home than other

[87] I am grateful to Peter Lake for many interesting discussions of this question. See Lake, *Puritans*, pp. 171–80, from which our discussions began.

[88] *CSPD 1633–4*, p. 439. Roe, perhaps provocatively, was writing to Laud. See also John Dod, *Plaine and Familiar Exposition of the Ten Commandments* (1624), 20.

[89] Peter Smart, *Vanitie and Downfall* (Edinburgh, 1628), 8.

[90] John Dod, *Ten Commandments*, p. 12; Russell, 'Pym', 249 n.

[91] BL Loan MS 29/172, fo. 364ᵛ. I am grateful to Dr Levy, who discovered this MS, for helpful discussion of it. It is possibly one of the drafts from which the Ministers' Remonstrance of Feb. 1641 was put together.

people, in some cases because they owned the advowsons of their home livings, in some because, unlike lesser people, they could move to another house if it became impossible for them to worship where they were, and in others because of a plain seventeenth-century respect for rank. Sir Nathaniel Barnardiston, one of the leading gentlemen of Suffolk, succeeded in preserving the incumbent of his home living from deprivation by a long series of returns to the effect that, because of a great fall from his horse, he was unfit to ride to court. It perhaps shows something of the compromises which still held society together, that though Barnardiston saved his home vicar by these means, his nominee to another parish where he owned the advowson was deprived without any fuss. These two ministers were guilty of the same offence, which was refusing to read the Book of Sports in favour of Sunday recreation.[92] When the Barringtons were invited to move to Watertown, Massachusetts, the letter of invitation hopefully offered them the inducement of good hawking and hunting and fowling and fishing.[93] It is not the sort of letter which is written to the truly desperate. Had Barrington and his like been truly cowed, they would not have reacted in 1640 as authoritatively as they did. The particular reaction that came is a reaction to being on the losing side, felt by people who had not yet lost all the habits of mind resulting from seventy years of being on the winning one.

Nor should it be supposed that these godly gentry represented a united nation in 1637, any more than they did in 1642. The over-representation of the godly in surviving gentry collections of papers amounts to a serious distortion. We may perhaps get an opposite perspective from looking at literature, where the opposite distortion sometimes seems to apply. We can perhaps see a real shift in European ideas, and not just the influence of Charles and Laud, if we compare the thoughts on ordination of two personal friends, John Donne and George Herbert. Donne, writing sometime after 1618, greeted his friend's ordination to the *ministry*, and the key power he had gained was the power to preach:

> Mary's prerogative was to bear Christ, so
> 'Tis preachers' to convey him, for they do
> As Angels out of clouds, from pulpits speak,
> And bless the poor beneath, the lame, the weak.[94]

Donne, in a typical conceit, marries his Catholic background with a good Jacobean Protestantism which would have caused no anxiety to

---

[92] J. T. Cliffe, *Puritan Gentry* (1984), 176–7. See also *CSPD 1634–5*, vol. cclxxvi, no. 35 for John Hampden's success in coming to terms with the metropolitical visitation.

[93] *Barrington Family Letters 1628–1632*, pp. 183–4.

[94] John Donne, *Complete English Poems*, ed. A. J. Smith (1971), 331–2.

his patron Bishop Morton. In 1630 George Herbert was ordained, not to the ministry, but to the priesthood, and, as the title suggests, Herbert thought most of the power to administer the sacrament:

> But the holy men of god such vessels are
> As serve him up, who all the world commands:
> When God vouchsafeth to become our fare,
> Their hands convey him, who conveys their hands.
> O what pure things, most pure must those things be,
> Who brings my God to me.[95]

The change in Donne himself, as he grew older and moved more towards Arminianism indicates that this is a change in intellectual fashion, as well as a response to the new king and archbishop. In France, Holland, and Scotland, as well as in England, Calvinism no longer had the academic appeal of novelty. It was not only the sword of Tilly and Wallenstein that was threatening the cause, though that had a part to play too. Calvin had created a system so perfectly jointed and planned that it was not possible to move a piece in it without destroying it. Arminius, who began his work inside the Calvinist tradition, was one of those who discovered this. Stephen Marshall, preaching to the Long Parliament, said the country was reacting 'as if we were weary of the truth which God has committed to us'.[96] John Gauden, preaching at the opening communion service of the Long Parliament, made the point in a daringly novel use of a familiar image. From the earliest days of the Reformation, Protestants had been given to images of the sun, or light, of the Gospel. For early Protestants, it was rising, and dispersing the morning mists of popery and superstition. For Thomas Cartwright, it was the high noon of the Gospel. For Gauden, 'are not the lengthen and increase of ceremonious shadowes, a presage and signe of the shortning of our day and setting of our sunne, or diminishing of our light?'[97] The Gospel had had its day: this fear haunted the ageing generation which tried to revive it in 1642. Many of them took their chance, fearing it might be their last.

[95] Louis L. Martz (ed.), *George Herbert and Henry Vaughan* (Oxford, 1986), 145–6.
[96] Stephen Marshall, *A Sermon* (1641), 32.
[97] John Gauden, *Love of Truth and Peace* (1641), 31–2.

2

The British Problem and the Scottish National Covenant

I

Among Charles's three kingdoms, England was the most docile. The Scots were sometimes moved to complain of this fact, and Robert Baillie the Covenanter complained in 1639 of 'the obsequiousness and almost superstitious devotion of that nation towards their prince'.[1] English historians tend to forget that England was the last of Charles's three kingdoms to take to armed resistance, and the only one in which the King's supporters became a sufficiently large party to turn resistance into a large-scale civil war.

The outbreak of armed resistance to the King in three kingdoms within the space of three years suggests the possibility that their actions may have had some common causes. If there were common causes between the actions of the three kingdoms, their relations with each other are one profitable area in which we may search for them. It is now well established in the historiography of continental Europe that rule over multiple kingdoms was a common cause of political instability, and Professor Elliott has asked as long ago as 1953 whether the patterns they have found on the continent may perhaps apply to England too.[2] This question has been little explored. Scottish and Irish history are well-developed, if specialist, fields, but very few of those who work in them also work on English history, and the British dimension of these years has remained almost unexplored since the days of S. R. Gardiner.

The commonest causes of instability in multiple kingdoms were war and the distribution of offices, both fields in which outlying kingdoms often feared that their interests might be sacrificed to those of the leading kingdom. In Britain, there was some sign of developing tension in this area during the war years 1625–9. Secretary Coke, taking a leaf out of the Spanish book, drafted a plan for a union of arms.[3] This led to one Scottish regiment commanded by the Earl of Morton,[4] and to the

[1] Baillie, i. 204.

[2] H. G. Koeningsberger, Dominium Regale or Dominium Politicum et Regale: *Monarchies and Parliaments in Early Modern Europe* (London, 1975); J. H. Elliott, 'The King and the Catalans', *Cambridge Historical Journal* 11/2 (1953), 253.

[3] PRO SP 16/527/44.

[4] *RPCS*² ii. 37–8. On the Scottish consequences of Charles's war policy in the 1620s, see Maurice Lee, jun., *Road to Revolution: Scotland under Charles I 1625–1637* (Chicago, Ill., 1985), 13–37; *HMC Mar and Kellie*, pp. 133–4.

abortive political bargain represented by the Graces in Ireland.[5] There are some signs of traditional multiple-kingdom tension in the resentment at the effect of the wars on Scottish trade, but on the whole, this issue caused surprisingly little trouble in Britain until the government of William III made the first serious attempt to tap the wealth of Scotland in support of an English foreign policy.[6]

In Britain, the problem of multiple kingdoms seems to have been largely religious. There are only a limited number of parallels in Europe, and those not of the most fortunate. There are three cases of multiple kingdoms involving difference of religion: France and Béarn, Spain and the Netherlands, and the Empire and Bohemia. All the other rulers involved, Louis XIII, Philip II, and the Emperor Ferdinand, insisted without a moment's hesitation that neither their authority nor their consciences would permit them to preside over different religions at the same time. This should not be regarded as merely a case of pigheadedness. The enforcement of religion was so much the business of government, and the sanctification of government was so much the business of religion, that it was hard to imagine separating them. Moreover, as Philip II appreciated, the position of a ruler persecuting people in one dominion for believing what he allowed them to believe in another dominion was too vulnerable to be acceptable. Perhaps most of all, the attractions of an alternative model, tolerated by the same ruler in another dominion, were too great an invitation to instability. Of these three cases, that of France and Béarn was quickly disposed of, but the other two triggered off the two biggest upheavals in a century of European history. The reasons why this was so, of course, were not confined either to religion or to the Netherlands and Bohemia, but as precedents, they did show that the task of running multiple kingdoms with different religions was a dangerous one.

The kings of Britain had to achieve balance between the religions of three kingdoms, not merely of two. Their institutional base for tackling this task was not altogether satisfactory. Each kingdom enjoyed its own Privy Council and its own Parliament. In the case of Scotland, they were entirely legally independent, but in the case of Ireland, its Privy Council and Parliament were answerable to the English Privy Council, which had the right to approve Irish legislation under Poynings's Law, but they were not subject to the English Parliament. The English and Irish churches enjoyed bishops and Convocations, governed by a Royal Supremacy. In Scotland, on the other hand, such bishops as existed in 1603 amounted to little more than a Cheshire Cat. The Scottish Reformation, unlike the English or the Irish, had been carried through from

[5] Aidan Clarke, *The Old English in Ireland* (1966), 28–60.
[6] Rosalind Mitchison, *From Lordship to Patronage: Scotland 1603–1745* (1983), 123 ff.

below under a Catholic sovereign and therefore had not been in a
position to develop any theory of the Royal Supremacy. In Ireland, the
mythology of the Reformation was deeply linked with the English
attempt to 'civilize' the Irish, and it was therefore seen as essentially part
of the structure of English colonial power. In England, the mythology of
the Reformation was one of exaltation of the autonomy of the Crown
against the usurpations of a foreign bishop, and it was seen, even by
such profound critics of Charles as William Prynne or Henry Parker, as
essentially an exaltation of the powers of the Crown.[7] In Scotland, on
the other hand, the mythology of the Reformation glorified spontaneous
action by an autonomous kirk, and hence an ascending theory of power.
In its extreme form, this belief in an autonomous kirk developed into
the theory of the two kingdoms. As James Melville put it: 'thair is two
kings and two kingdomes in Scotland. Thair is Christ Jesus the king, and
his kingdome the kirk, whose subject King James the saxt is, and of
whose kingdom nocht a king, nor a lord, nor a heid, bot a member'.[8]
The key institution in this dream of a self-governing kirk was the
General Assembly, a representative body in which the magistrate had no
special powers. As the Covenanters put it:

No man will thinke that a republick, becoming a Christian kirk, should lose any
of her civile liberties, why then shall a kirk being in her self a perfect
republicke, although of another kinde, because she now lives under a Christian
magistrate, losse her priviledges, or suffer diminution in her Christian liberty,
whereof the holding of assemblies is a necessary part.[9]

In all three kingdoms, these mythologies of the origins of the Reformation had tended to fade into the background, and become considerably
less important with time, but in all three, they remained the ones on
which people fell back in moments of stress. In particular, General
Assemblies in Scotland seemed to have gone the way of Parliaments in
England; the last one had met in 1618. Yet Scottish General Assemblies,
like English Parliaments, seemed to have kept much of their place in
public sentiment, and even more their place in generally accepted
theories of obligation. What was not sanctioned by a General Assembly
in Scotland, like what was not sanctioned by a Parliament in England,
risked being regarded as not fully lawful. To the English, for whom the
Reformation had been largely an assault on the notion of an auto-

---

[7] Henry Parker, *Altar Dispute* (1641), 19–28; id., *Discourse concerning Puritans* (1641), 12, 30–3.
I would like to thank Dr J. S. A. Adamson for reminding me of these references.
[8] W. R. Foster, *The Church before the Covenants* (Edinburgh, 1975), 12 n.
[9] Anon., *Reasons for a General Assemblie* (s.l., 29 June 1638)(*STC 22054* Sig. B. 1). This should
not be taken as the view of all Scotsmen: a draft reply, by a Scottish bishop, says: 'I understand not
what he meanes when he calles the church a perfect republic': NLS Wodrow MS Fol. 66, fo. 75ʳ.
The author is clearly a bishop, since he refers to the bishops as 'us'.

nomous church, much Scottish thinking on this subject remained almost totally incomprehensible.

In making policy for any one of his kingdoms, Charles would take advice from the Privy Council of that kingdom. In the cases of Ireland and Scotland, where the king was not resident, the advice necessarily depended heavily on the wording of the question asked, yet advice was still available. Charles was much worse provided if, as often happened, he was making policy on a question which affected the relations of the three kingdoms with each other. In the Spanish monarchy, the Councils of Castile, Aragon, Catalonia, and Portugal were in theory held together by a Council of State which was capable of considering questions affecting the relations between them. The existence of such an institution in Britain would have made the task of handling a multiple kingdom very much easier. England and Scotland each had some honorary members on each other's Council: Laud, as a member of the Scottish Privy Council, had some theoretical *locus standi* in Scotland,[10] while some Scots had equivalent status in England. The Anglo-Scots, especially the Duke of Lennox, the Earl of Morton, and the Marquess of Hamilton, might give advice on the relations between the kingdoms, but their Scottish roots were not always seen as deep. The major weakness of the system was that the king was under no compulsion to take any advice on British questions at all: his advice came when and from whom he wanted it. In British policy, he enjoyed a freedom from institutional restraint such as he enjoyed in no other field, and such as, in prevailing theory, no king should have enjoyed in any field. In the drift to war between England and Scotland during 1638–9, it is an important part of the story that the English Privy Council, by convention recognized since 1603, had no right to give any advice on the Scottish policy which was leading to the war.

Charles occasionally took advice on British matters from Wentworth and Hamilton, and probably also from Lennox, but the only person with whom he seems to have discussed British matters consistently is Laud, who acted, as Gardiner put it, 'as if he had been the King's secretary'.[11] He enjoyed this position because he and the King were two like-minded people. There seems no sense in trying to apportion responsibility between them: he had acquired this position because he and the King shared a common outlook, and it seems fair to hold them both responsible for the resulting policy. Laud's responsibility seems to have always been confined to ecclesiastical matters, but since after 1629 there is little sign that Charles had any British policy on any other matters, save fishing, the restriction is perhaps not a significant one. It

---

[10] *CSPD 1633–4*, vol. ccxli, no. 7 (15 June 1633).
[11] Gardiner, *History*, viii. 309.

was Laud who involved himself with conveying the King's instructions on the management of the Scottish Chapel Royal, or in questions of ecclesiastical preferment in Ireland. He once wrote light-heartedly to Wentworth that 'I was fain to write nine letters yesterday into Scotland. I think you have a plot to see whether I will be *universalis episcopus*, that you and your brethren may take occasion to call me Antichrist'.[12] Even if Laud's political touch had been surer, and his knowledge of Scottish and Irish affairs deeper, than they were, this would hardly have been an adequate institutional base for a major policy.

If the handling of the multiple kingdoms of Britain was so peculiarly difficult, perhaps it is wise to ask, before condemning Charles's failures, why James managed to handle these issues for twenty-three years without any very dramatic results. The intensity of the fears expressed about the consequences of union in 1603–4 makes the lack of dramatic result all the more striking. For the Scots, the strongest fear of union was the fear of being junior partner, 'ane pendicle of thair kingdome, we to lose our ancient glorie forevir'.[13] It was a fear English Parliamentary speeches did nothing to discourage. For the Scots, it was necessary to accept junior-partner status in many things. The one field in which they would not do so was that of religion: many Scots responded, for reasons of patriotism as well as of piety, to David Calderwood's claim that no church had ever been as pure as the church of Scotland.[14] The Covenanters were playing an old tune when they claimed, at the end of 1638, that

this ancient kingdome, though not the most flourishing in the glory and wealth of the world, hath been so largely recompensed with the riches of the Gospel, in the reformation and purity of religion from the abundant mercy and free grace of our God towards us, that all the reformed kirks about us, did admire our happinesse. And King James himself of happy memory, gloried that he had the honour to be born, and to be a king, in the best reformed kirk in all the world.[15]

It was awareness of these emotions which led James to promise, before leaving Edinburgh, not to tamper with Scots discipline or doctrine, and also led the Scottish Parliament in 1604 to pass an act excluding the kirk from the scope of the commissioners for union. Yet they also provided an opportunity for English members of Parliament such as Sir Roger Owen to demand Scottish submission to English worship as

---

[12] Knowler, i. 271.

[13] Galloway, p. 53.

[14] *Quaeres concerning the State of the Church of Scotland* (s.l., 1638) (STC 4362), p. 3. The ascription to David Calderwood is from a pencil note on a copy in NLS. This may be the Presbyterian equivalent of ascribing earthworks of unknown origin to the Devil or Julius Caesar, but I see no reason to disbelieve it.

[15] *Answer* (Edinburgh, 1639), 3. This pamphlet replies to Hamilton's Declaration of Dec. 1638.

the price of naturalization. It was apparent by 1604 that the difference between the churches was a potential cause of instability.[16]

James handled this danger so cautiously that there is even room for dispute whether he had a British policy at all. In fact, it seems he adjusted each of his churches slowly and by very easy stages towards the others, and because the policy was pursued so slowly, and never entirely in one kingdom, it was possible for James's contemporaries to disagree about his ultimate aim. It was apparent in 1604 that one of the commonest grounds for accepting union was belief that the churches were united by a common agreement in true (that is, Calvinist) doctrine.[17] Since true doctrine was also the Ark of the Covenant to the more devout Presbyterian Scots, even more, perhaps, than to their English brethren, James had a strong British motive for his willingness to encourage doctrinal Calvinism. That James saw Calvinism as a ground of union between the kingdoms is suggested by his inclusion of a Scottish delegate in the British deputation to the Synod of Dort. That the delegate concerned was an ambitious careerist called Walter Balcanquall, who until 1638 consistently managed to back the winning horse, merely underlines the point about James's intentions. The Lambeth Articles of 1595, enshrining the most rigorous Calvinism, had been an embarrassment to Elizabeth, but were useful enough to James, who allowed them to be inserted, almost verbatim, in the Irish Articles of 1615.[18] Since the Plantation of Ulster, there had been a considerable increase in the number of Scots expected to worship in the church of Ireland, and to anyone familiar with Calvin's marks of the true church, a guarantee of true doctrine seemed likely to make them more willing to do so. The ban on anti-Calvinist writing in England under James blocked off the most important reason which might have led his Scottish subjects to accuse his English subjects of popery.

Yet James was not suspected of Scotticizing the church of England, since his vision of union involved a blend (modified in both cases) of Scottish doctrine and English government. James passionately disliked 'parity' in the church, and in its Melvillian form, was quite right in regarding it as a threat to monarchy. For James, bishops whom he appointed ('my bishops', as he called them) were, literally, a godsend. They were the means to make him a king in church matters, as he was in civil matters.[19] Perhaps no subject shows the depth of James's patience more clearly than his treatment of Scottish episcopacy. He was able to work with some public support from those who disliked the stricter

[16] Galloway, pp. 24–5, 106.
[17] Ibid. 6, 43.
[18] Tyacke, p. 155 and n.
[19] Michael Mendle, *Dangerous Positions* (University, Alabama, 1985), 75.

forms of Presbyterianism: as Dr Foster said, 'there was a considerable body of conservative opinion, to which James could and did appeal'.[20] Yet James never went too fast for this body of opinion, and his programme was carried through in easy stages over a twenty-four-year period from 1586 to 1610. Constitutionally, his procedure was impeccable, going through the General Assembly in any purely religious matter, and through Parliament in matters of the bishops' temporalities and Parliamentary membership. The fact that the programme was begun well before James's English accession (but not before he foresaw it) hid from all but the most sharp-sighted Presbyterians the possible motive of Anglicization.

In 1586 James secured a theoretical approval from a General Assembly for a severely modified form of episcopacy. In 1597 he took the next significant step, securing an Act of Parliament to give bishops back their seats in Parliament. After this, he waited five years before appointing any more bishops, and when he did, picked preaching ministers of good standing in the kirk. In 1606 he secured an Act of Parliament restoring to them the temporalities taken from them in 1587. Up to this date, his programme deserves Foster's comment: 'the episcopacy which James had revived was an almost purely civil office, and the new bishops had no significant status or authority in the kirk'.[21] A bigger milestone was passed in the General Assembly of Linlithgow in 1606, when bishops were made permanent moderators of presbyteries. He concluded his policy in the Glasgow Assembly of 1610, giving bishops power over the excommunication and deposing of ministers, the power of visitation, and control over presentations. Having done all this, he then revealed the underlying unionist assumption by sending three of his bishops to England for consecration, thus depriving the extremer English episcopalians of any chance to argue that the church of Scotland did not have a true ministry.[22] To prevent the episcopalian tide from flowing on to a point which would have taken it out of Scottish reach, he gave the Irish primacy, the Archbishopric of Armagh, to James Ussher, a believer in a severely limited episcopacy very like what had been approved at Linlithgow in 1606. That this was a British, and not just a Scottish, policy is underlined by the fact that James then turned his attention to his only remaining dominion where episcopacy did not exist: the Channel Islands. Even there, James chose to proceed, in typically Jacobean style, *one* Channel Island at a time, leaving Guernsey to be handled by Laud after his death.[23]

[20] Foster, *Church before Covenants*, p. 11.
[21] Ibid. 19.
[22] Ibid. 11–29.
[23] A. J. Eagleston, *Channel Islands under Tudor Government* (Cambridge, 1949), 100–28. I would like to thank my wife for drawing my attention to this reference.

The next item in James's British policy was the Royal Supremacy. In England, Ireland, and the Channel Islands, the Royal Supremacy was already an established fact, so it remained only to introduce it in Scotland. As an alternative to Melvillian two-kingdoms theory, it seemed to James profoundly attractive.[24] Again, the programme was begun before James's accession to the English throne. To enunciate the programme was one thing, and to make it effective another. The key to making it effective was control of General Assemblies. James encouraged those who wanted Assemblies to include lay members, having, through patronage, or as some said, bribery, more hope of controlling them than of controlling the ministers. The key to the whole struggle was James's claim to the power to call Assemblies, and to fix their place of meeting. It is no coincidence that some of the most famous Assemblies of James's reign met at places like Perth and Aberdeen, well away from the stronger areas of Presbyterian influence. In 1605, when the General Assembly was due to meet in Aberdeen, James prorogued it indefinitely, provoking a group of ministers who believed he had no right to do this to assemble without his permission. James, after a great deal of pressure, succeeded in getting them condemned for treason for denying his ecclesiastical authority and declining the jurisdiction of the Council.[25] In spite of this, James failed to get the next Assembly to recognize his right to call and prorogue it, and even the summoning of his leading opponents to England for instruction from the English bishops did not secure compliance. He did, however, manage to secure two clauses in the Acts of Parliament confirming the Acts of the Linlithgow Assembly of 1606 and the Glasgow Assembly of 1610. The first, in restoring the bishops' temporalities, called James 'soverane monarche absolute prince judge and governor over all persones estaittis and causis both spirituall and temporall within his said realme'. This brought James about as near the Royal Supremacy as Henry VIII had been in 1515. The 1612 Act granted James his claim to the authority to call General Assemblies, and included an oath to be taken by ministers on institution recognizing James as 'supreme governor'.[26] It was only after these Acts were secured that James expressed a hope to alter the General Assembly 'to the form of the convocation hous heir in England'. As a Royal Supremacy, this did not even amount to a Cheshire Cat: it was barely even a grin.

Having established his practical control of General Assemblies, James

---

[24] Mendle, *Dangerous Positions*, p. 75; *APS* 3. 292–3.

[25] Foster, *Church before Covenants*, pp. 120–7; Galloway, pp. 87–8.

[26] *APS* 4. 282, 469–70. I owe these references to [JRL] Crawford MSS 14/3/45, a paper probably compiled for Charles I's use about the time of the Pacification of Berwick. I would like to thank Dr J. S. A. Adamson for drawing my attention to these MSS. They are now transferred to the NLS.

then turned to the ceremonial front, and began a long campaign to secure what ultimately became known as the Five Articles of Perth of 1618. The most important of these upheld kneeling at communion, and the others supported the celebration of feasts including Christmas and Easter (or Yule and Pasch, as the Scots described them), private communion and baptism in cases of necessity, and episcopal confirmation. Having devoted an immense effort to securing the passage of these articles through a General Assembly, James then enforced them only briefly, and let them drop.[27] Was this a typical case of Jacobean laziness, or was there some useful purpose to be served by demanding subscription, and then not looking to see whether people had done the things they subscribed to? The frequency with which James used subscription in this way in England suggests that there was. Anyone who had subscribed the Five Articles of Perth did not necessarily have to kneel at communion, but he was estopped from saying that those who did so were damnable and unchristian. Subscription was incompatible with what Baillie regarded as a schismatic refusal to communicate with 'kneelers'.[28] Moreover, a Scot who had subscribed the Five Articles could not easily encourage English resistance on this issue: he could not describe kneeling as damnable or intolerable. If James was concerned about possible Scottish encouragement to the discontented in England, this may be seen as an important victory, and worth the effort James put into it. It is only if the Five Articles are seen in a purely Scottish context that they look like a case of wasted effort. With the passage of the Five Articles, James's ecclesiastical programme seems to have reached completion, and he is said to have given a promise in 1621, when he secured Parliamentary ratification of the Five Articles of Perth, that there would be no more innovation.[29] If so, there was one item which was left aside, and that was the suggestion of a Scottish liturgy. There is some evidence to suggest that James considered such a proposal, and rejected it. It is, indeed, because of this issue that he was said to have said Laud 'aimed to bring things to a pitch of reformation floating in his own brain', but before this story is believed, it should be remembered that it was told by Williams's biographer Hacket long after the event, and it is not above suspicion.[30] Be this as it may, James never introduced a Scottish liturgy. He had not achieved uniformity between his kingdoms, nor anything

[27] Gardiner, *History*, iii. 220–36. On the enforcement, see also Maurice Lee, *Road to Revolution*, p. 10.

[28] Baillie, vol. i, pp. xxix–xxx. It is perhaps the fear of schism which accounts for Baillie's striking lack of hostility to the Five Articles of Perth: ibid. 52, but also p. 68.

[29] Rothes, p. 91.

[30] Gordon Donaldson, *Making of the Scottish Prayer Book of 1637* (Edinburgh, 1954), 39; J. Hacket, *Scrinia Reserata* (1692), 64.

like it, but he had considerably reduced the differences, and had applied cosmetic treatment to those differences he could not remove. Above all, the common Calvinist theology, again confirmed in the Scottish Confession of 1616, immediately before the blow of the Five Articles of Perth, acted, in Dr Tyacke's famous phrase, as a 'common and ameliorating bond' between the kingdoms.[31]

That bond Charles promptly broke. James's cosmetic unity, like other cosmetic effects, depended on the light in which it was looked at. From the perspective of Archbishop Abbot, the Irish Articles of 1615 appeared more explicit than the English Thirty-Nine Articles, but very similar in the overall effect. To Charles I and his allies, the English Thirty-Nine Articles appeared to bear a meaning which put them into contradiction with the Irish Articles. Similarly, the Five Articles of Perth had appeared to some Jacobeans to bring Scottish practice within shouting distance of the English. To those responsible for the St Gregory's judgement in favour of altars in 1633, the gulf again appeared immense. While James had interpreted the church of England in the way which brought it closest to the churches of Scotland and Ireland, Charles interpreted it in a way which made it as different from them as possible.

Charles's Calvinist opponents spotted the point immediately. As usual in matters of Arminianism, John Pym was in the van. In his report on the case of Richard Montagu in 1626, he attacked Montagu's views on falling from grace on the ground that 'he opposeth the church of England to the church of Ireland, and the articles of either to other in the poynte'.[32] A Parliamentary bill of 1626, reintroduced in 1628, took up Pym's point by attempting to give statutory confirmation to the English and Irish Articles jointly, thereby making it a legal necessity to interpret them in a way which made them consistent with each other.[33] In 1628 Pym attempted to carry the appeal to the less ceremonial practice of Ireland into other areas, saying that the Irish subscription to the Book of Common Prayer asked far less than the English, and 'these islands are sisters'. In 1629 Rich joined in the appeal to the Irish Articles of 1615.[34] It is perhaps Pym and Rich who were responsible for showing Charles the risks inherent in contradicting, as Supreme Head of one kingdom, what he was busy enforcing in another. Charles seems to have taken the point at once, and in his Proclamation at the end of the

---

[31] Nicholas Tyacke, 'Puritanism, Arminianism and Counter-Revolution', in Russell (ed.), *Origins*, p. 121; Tyacke, pp. 228–9.

[32] *Debates in the House of Commons in 1625*, ed. S. R. Gardiner (Camden Society, NS 6, 1873), 181.

[33] Tyacke, pp. 154–5; *1628 Debates*, ii. 324.

[34] *1628 Debates*, iii. 515; *1629 Debates*, p. 119.

Parliament of 1626, he announced that the English Thirty-Nine Articles were to be binding in Ireland.[35]

This is perhaps the moment at which Charles's determination to achieve uniformity in his dominions was born, but pressure of events meant that major policies could not take shape until after the conclusion of peace in 1629–30. Meanwhile, events continued to illustrate the unwisdom of allowing major differences between his kingdoms. Peter Smart canon of Durham was one of those who were happy inside the Jacobean ecclesiastical establishment, but found the Caroline far beyond what he could tolerate. When he printed his sermon denouncing John Cosin's liturgical innovations at Durham, he did so in Edinburgh, thus evading English printing controls.[36] Above all, the existence of numerous areas under Charles's sovereignty where English liturgical practice and theological interpretation were not current meant that his critics enjoyed the constant encouragement of an alternative model.

Sometime between 1629 and 1633 Charles's mind seems to have moved on from the desire to rid himself of the embarrassment caused by the Irish Articles to a serious programme for uniformity among all those subject to his dominion. The first to be subjected to this programme were the Merchant Adventurers in the Netherlands: in a paper dated 1 July 1630 Laud expressed concern that they did not follow the set forms of prayer, and administered the sacraments in conceived forms of their own.[37] He wanted to bring them under ecclesiastical government, and to bring them to adopt the formularies of the church of England. The action which followed was intermittent, but was still in progress after the Pacification of Berwick.[38] By 1633 Laud had extended the programme to the regiments in Dutch service, and the implications for Scotland were spelt out in his insistence that clergy who did not use the ceremonies according to the Book of Common Prayer in England should not continue as chaplains to any English *or Scottish* regiments.[39]

The same line of thinking was applied to the French and Dutch churches in England. Here again, as with Scotland, the effect of perspective was vital. To Protestants like Archbishop Grindal, the Stranger Churches had appeared welcome refugees, differing in detail, no doubt, but standing for a religion which, in its broad essentials, was not incompatible with his own. To Laud, on the other hand, they appeared as 'an absolute divided body from the church of England

[35] Tyacke, p. 155; Larkin, pp. 90–3. I am grateful to Dr Tyacke for drawing my attention to the significance of this Proclamation.
[36] Peter Smart, *Vanitie and Downfall of the Present Churches* (Edinburgh, 1628).
[37] *CSPD 1629–31*, vol. clxx, no. 8.
[38] *CSPD 1639–40*, vol. ccccxxxvii, no. 59, and other refs.
[39] Laud, *Works*, VI. i. 23.

established', and he believed that 'their example is of ill consequence ...
for many are confirmed in their stubborn ways of disobedience to the
church government, seeing them so freely suffered in this great and
populous city'. He was well aware of the importance of the alternative
model.[40] In the Channel Islands, Charles and Laud prepared to complete the Jacobean programme of introducing episcopacy, and endowed
a number of scholarships to Oxford to ensure that the Channel Islands
should have ministers properly educated in the doctrine and discipline
of the church of England as they understood them.[41]

The Merchant Adventurers and the Stranger Churches were entirely
dependent on privileges, and one Channel Island was in no position to
resist what had already been imposed on the other. These were mere
preliminary exercises, and the real trial of strength was to be expected
when Charles and Laud tried their hand on the three major dominions
which did not accept English practice as redefined by Charles and
Laud. These were Scotland, Ireland, and New England. In New England, proceedings began in April 1634 with the appointment of Laud to
head a commission for the English colonies. This body was empowered
to set up ecclesiastical courts in the colonies, and, if Peter Heylin is to be
believed, contemplated sending out a bishop to New England. It began
its proceedings by ruling that no one should go to New England without
a certificate of conformity from the minister of his parish, and followed
it up by *Quo Warranto* proceedings against the Massachusetts charter.
Meanwhile, Governor Winthrop and his colleagues resolved 'to hasten
our fortifications'.[42] It seems to be in part a matter of chance that
Charles's personal rule ended with a riot in St Giles's kirk at Edinburgh,
and not with a premature version of the Boston Tea Party.

It would be interesting to know whether the Massachusetts colonists
were saved by their own visible determination to fight, by doubts in the
Privy Council, by fear of the Dutch, or simply because Charles and
Laud became preoccupied with the bigger fish of Scotland and Ireland.
For Ireland, the objective was enunciated in a letter to Laud from his
client John Bramhall Bishop of Derry on 10 August 1633. He asked for
both the articles and canons of the church of England to be established
by Act of Parliament. He received a sympathetic hearing.[43] The canons
seem to have been a common feature of the Caroline programme of
uniformity, which involved, in its fully developed form, a common

[40] Patrick Collinson, *Archbishop Grindal* (1979), 125–52. This judgement is not intended to
apply to every member of the Stranger Churches: Laud, *Works* VI. i. 25–6; also *CSPD 1637*, vol.
ccclxii, no. 24.
[41] Eagleston, *Channel Islands*, pp. 141–3.
[42] Gardiner, *History*, viii. 167–8; H. R. Trevor Roper, *Archbishop Laud* (1940), 257–62; E. S.
Morgan, *Puritan Dilemma* (Boston, Mass., 1958), 196.
[43] *CSPD 1633–4*, vol. ccxliv, no. 48.

acceptance throughout the King's dominions of the Thirty-Nine
Articles, a common liturgy, episcopacy, a Court of High Commission, a
body of canons for ecclesiastical discipline, and a common Royal
Supremacy. Different parts of the programme needed pressing in different places. For example, as Laud noted, the Irish did not need to be
forced to adopt the English liturgy, because they had it already.[44] The
High Commission was introduced in Ireland and reintroduced in Scotland, but was never extended to Massachusetts. New books of canons
were introduced in Ireland in 1634 and in Scotland in 1636, and the
visible unsuitability of the Scottish canons to Scottish conditions is in
part explained by the fact that large parts of them were copied from the
Irish canons.[45] The Thirty-Nine Articles were successfully introduced
by Laud and Wentworth in Ireland in 1634, in spite of a last-ditch
resistance from Archbishop Ussher,[46] but had not yet been produced in
Scotland in 1637. That the whole amounted to a common programme
was enunciated by the preface to the Scottish Prayer Book itself:

It were to be wished that the whole church of Christ were one, as well in form
of public worship as in doctrine, and that as it hath but one Lord and one faith,
so it had but one heart and one mouth. This would prevent many schisms and
divisions, and serve much to the preserving of unity. But since that cannot be
hoped for in the whole Catholic Christian church, yet at least in the churches
that are under the protection of one sovereign prince the same ought to be
endeavoured.[47]

The Ark of the Covenant of this programme was Charles's individual
Caesaro-papist version of the Royal Supremacy. This was originally an
English idea, but intended for export to the rest of the King's
dominions. As set out in the precedent book of Sir John Bankes, Charles's Attorney-General and later Chief Justice, Charles's version of the
Royal Supremacy depended on two ideas. One was a strict and literal
construing of the declaratory character of Henry VIII's Act of
Supremacy: the Act did not confer these powers of the King, but merely
recognized that he had them by right already. The other was a division,
so stern as to be almost a parody of Melvillian two-kingdoms theory,

[44] Laud, *Works*, VI. i. 354.
[45] The Scottish canons are printed in Laud, *Works*, V. 585–606. For the Irish canons, *Table of
the Church of Ireland: Constitutions and Canons Ecclesiasticall* (Dublin, 1653). The fact that the
Scottish canons were largely copied from the Irish helps to explain the fact, to which Prof.
Mitchison drew attention, that they 'bore no apparent relationship to the church as it existed in
Scottish law and practice': Mitchison, *Lordship to Patronage*, p. 38. Laud told Ussher that he would
similarly have preferred to have the English canons received in Ireland: Laud, *Works*, VI. ii. 418–19.
I would like to thank Martin Flaherty for this reference, for the text of the Irish canons, and for
much other help on Laudian policy in Ireland. He is responsible for the central ideas of this
paragraph, and I hope may print them in due course.
[46] Knowler, i. 329, 342–4; Laud, *Works*, VI. ii. 396–7.
[47] Tyacke, p. 253.

between the spheres of civil and ecclesiastical authority. Bankes wrote that:

the kingdome of England is an absolute empire and monarchie successive by inherent birthright, consisting of one head, which is the king, and of a bodye, which the law divideth into tow severall ptes, that is to say, the clergy and the laity; both of them next and immediately under God, subject and obedient to the head, and this kinglie head is instituted and furnished . . .

From here on, Bankes runs on in a verbatim recitation of the Act in Restraint of Appeals. The distinctive feature of this theory is the intense and equal stress on the notions of one head, and of two kingdoms. In his chapter of ecclesiastical or canon law, Bankes refers to causes 'the conusans whereof belonges not to the comon laws of England, and these matters ought to bee determined and decided according to the king's ecclesiastical lawes of this realme'. In this sphere, authority descended from the king to his bishops: 'the bishops of England are the immediate officers and ministers to the king's courtes'. This had always been the case: the Act of Supremacy of 1559 did not introduce a new law, but declared an old. In this theory of authority, an Act of Parliament might be used, as it was by the Scottish General Assembly, to provide a civilian rubber stamp and the necessary legal penalties. The tendency to avoid reliance on Parliamentary statute grew more strong with time, and can be seen in corrections Bankes made to his manuscript, probably after the passage of the Triennial Act in February 1641. He originally wrote that the title of Defender of the Faith was one to which the King had an undoubted right 'by authoritie of Parliament', but in his revisions, he altered this to read that the title 'appeareth by the statute of 35 H'. Erastian habits died hard in English lawyers: in discussing the Act of Supremacy, Bankes unthinkingly wrote that it 'doth abolish' foreign jurisdiction, and immediately altered the word 'abolish' to 'declare'.[48] It was by this theory of authority that Charles's Proclamation of 1626, for the peace of the church, had been made 'by the advice of his reverend bishops', instead of, as Proclamations usually were, by the advice of his Privy Council.[49] It was a theory which entitled the king, by the advice of bishops, whom he appointed, to govern the church as he wished, without any need for lay consent or consultation. In the hands of a king whose beliefs were unpopular, such a doctrine was provocative.

Contact with Scottish thinking forced the clericalist implications of this way of thinking to the surface, and it is much more explicit in Bankes's tract against the Solemn League and Covenant of 1643 than it

[48] Dorset RO, Bankes of Kingston Lacey MSS, vol. M, pp. 1, 17, 8, 7, 10, 9. Bankes corrected his MS for the Triennial Act, but the similarity of palaeography and ink falls short of proof that the other corrections were made at the same time.

[49] Larkin, p. 91.

is in his earlier writing. He refers bluntly to 'that part of the saide body called the spirituality, now being usually called the English church', and claimed that the Covenanters 'absolutely swear and covenant to take away from the King his ecclesiastical power and jurisdiction, which is exercised under his Majesty only by archbishops, bishops, chancellors, commissaryes, and other ecclesiastical judges and officers'.[50] The king's power, in fact, was bounded only by the law of God (as he interpreted it) and by the need to secure the consent of men whom he had appointed and might thereafter promote.

In May 1635 Charles obtained another brief on the Royal Supremacy from Lord Herbert of Cherbury. Remarkably, for a historian of Henry VIII, Herbert does not mention a single English statute anywhere in a memorandum of six pages: he chose to 'make use chiefly of the Old Testament, we having little extant in the New, as being written in a time when the Empire and priesthood were wholly dislocated'. He attempts to show by numerous examples that throughout the time of the kings of Israel, there was no change of religion which was not procured by kings' immediate power. He claims that 'they have thought it unfit that a subject should partake a supreme authority with them in ecclesiasticall affayres'. Making the application to kings of his own day, he says that 'whatsoever can be proved eyther in the Scriptures, codices, authentics, capitularibus or the lawes made by Constantine, Theodosius, Justinian, Charlemagne, to belong to kinges, may be thought their right'. This, perhaps, explains what was meant by the claim in the Irish canons of 1634 and the Scottish of 1636, that kings have 'the same authority in causes ecclesiastical, that the godly kings had among the Jews, and Christian emperors in the primitive church'.[51]

The point here is not merely the extent of the powers claimed, though in the case of Justinian, these were considerable enough to cause alarm. The real point is the source of authority: it is derived from God himself, and is claimed as inherent in all kings at all times and in all places. The declaratory clause in the English Act of Supremacy is taken literally: kings rightfully have these powers, whether any Act of Parliament recognizes them or not.[52] This means, then, that Charles thought his claim to be Supreme Head of the church of Scotland was in no way dependent on whether any such claim had ever been recognized in Scottish law: he had it, whether any Scottish law had ever recognized the fact or not. There was no need, then, for the elaborate machinery of consultation

---

[50] Dorset RO, Bankes of Kingston Lacey MSS, vol. L, pp. 3, 16.

[51] PRO SP 16/288/88. There is a note on the dorse of this document that it was shown to the Archbishop by the King's command.

[52] Irish canons, page 6: Laud, *Works*, v. 586. For a later use of a similar phrase by Laud, see Baillie, ii. 434. The phrase in question was not novel, being taken from canon II of 1604. Its English use was not novel, but its British use was: E. Cardwell, *Synodalia* (Oxford, 1842), i. 166.

laid down through General Assembly and Parliament: he could impose binding obligations on the Scottish church, as he did the canons, 'by our prerogative royal, and supreme authority in causes ecclesiastical'. When the Scots repeatedly claimed to be governed by their own laws, it was, by implication, this claim to a *jure divino* Royal Supremacy they were resisting. In public, they were careful not to challenge it too directly, for fear they might, in Hamilton's favourite phrase, 'irritate' the King. The difference between public and private reaction can be seen in the letters of the Covenanter Earl of Rothes. Writing officially to Hamilton, he said the King was making an attempt to constrain them 'beyond these just limitts of religious and lawfull obedience'. In private, writing to another Covenanter, he said the question was 'whither the civill magistrat sall have absolut power over the church to inbring or output either in doctrine or discipline at his pleasure'. This meant the same thing as the King's concern that he should be allowed his just authority.[53]

These two outlooks were encapsulated in an exchange, probably in September 1637, between Archbishop Spottiswoode of St Andrew's and Rothes. Spottiswoode said, albeit with some reluctance:

If the king wold turne papist, we behoved to obey: who could resist princes? When King Edward was a Protestant, and made ane Reformation, Queene Mary changed it; and Queene Elizabeth altered it againe; and so ther was no resisting of princes, and ther was no kirk without trubles.

Rothes, if his own account is to be believed, fastened on most of the weak points of this argument:

they gott it soon changed in England: the two professions were neir equally dividit: bot ther was few heir to concurr to such a change, all being reformed, and wold never yield: nixt, the reformatione of England was not so full as that of Scotland, and had not so much law for it: it was bot half reformed. And so speaking but slightlie of these maters, they sundered.[54]

This exchange was a clash of generations, as well as of ideas. Spottiswoode had become an archbishop in 1603, when Rothes was only three years old. In a country whose Reformation was considerably later than the English, he was still of the first generation, which had grown up before religion was established as a matter of choice. Rothes was no more a believer in choice, if it were ungodly, than Spottiswoode, but he had grown up with the conflict of hardened and inherited confessional loyalties, in which it was far harder than it had been in the England of the 1550s for a king simply to order people to believe something, and expect them to obey. For Charles, as for Spottiswoode, the powers which had been enjoyed by Edward, Mary, and Elizabeth ought to be

---

[53] Hamilton MS 1049; Crawford MS 14/7/45. These letters are of almost identical dates.
[54] Rothes, p. 10.

enjoyed by him too. He was claiming these powers in a very different world, where men were used to competing religions arguing for their allegiance. London and Edinburgh might not be, like Andrew Marvell's Amsterdam, 'staple of sects and mint of schism'[55] but they were towns in which religious monopoly, however much kings might regret it, was a thing of the past. In these circumstances, kings who wished to preserve their theoretical powers in religion intact had to be, like James, very cautious in their practical exercise. Charles, then, opened up a debate in 1637 on the extent of the powers a sovereign could enjoy in religion without the consent of his leading subjects, and that debate was conducted before an interested English audience.

II

In a book which is designed to tell the story leading up to the outbreak of the English Civil War, it is not necessary to tell yet again the chronological narrative of the struggle started by the Scottish Prayer Book of 1637. That task has been carried out in David Stevenson's *Scottish Revolution*, and is being revised in the light of further work by Dr Peter Donald. Gardiner's account, as always, remains well worth reading for a chronological outline. In the space available here, it is not worth attempting a full narrative which would make, at best, a few small corrections to these works.

The reasons why it is necessary to discuss the Scottish crisis as a preliminary to the English are different ones. First, it gives us an unrivalled chance to understand the mind of Charles I. In his reign, the summer of 1638, when his commissioner the Marquess of Hamilton was in Scotland negotiating with the Covenanters, is a rare time when the main outlines of policy were being formed by letter. Since Hamilton's archive seems to survive more or less intact, we are able to study the interaction between the King and some of his Councillors in a way which is not possible at any other time. Moreover, the Charles who experienced the English crisis had already lived through the Scottish, and on many subjects, most notably that of episcopacy, the Scottish crisis hardened ideas in Charles's mind, and those ideas in turn did a great deal to dictate the responses of his English, as well as his Scottish opponents. The points Charles regarded as negotiable and non-negotiable, as well as the demands the English made of him, were very heavily influenced by his experience in dealing with the Scottish Covenanters. Also, the Scots produced a large body of printed material, industriously and surreptitiously circulated in England throughout the

---

[55] Andrew Marvell, 'The Character of Holland', line 66.

years 1638–40. The ideas, the actions, and the sheer infectious force of their example all did a great deal to encourage the English Parliament and its supporters, as they did to terrify other people back into Charles's camp. Above all, it is impossible to understand the Scots' direct contribution to English politics after they crossed the Tweed in August 1640, without knowing something about the experience they brought with them when they came. It was because the Scots, like Charles, concluded that they were dealing with a British problem, to which only British solutions were possible, that they followed the English policy they did. In the Britain of Charles I, Calvinism in one kingdom was an impossibility.

Charles's decision to produce a new Scottish liturgy was not only a product of desire for British uniformity, but also of a deep disgust at Scottish methods of worship which is very much the mirror image of what many Scots felt for his worship. In 1633, when he was in Edinburgh for his Scottish coronation, he refused to take part in Scottish worship, and insisted on the use of the English Prayer Book at any service he attended. What seems to have offended him was lack of 'decency', always a key word in Charles's ecclesiastical policy. When left to themselves, it seems some leading Scottish churchmen did not, in effect, use a formal liturgy: the dislike for a 'reading ministry', which could be discharged automatically without faith or understanding, led to a cult of extempore prayer which was hard to combine with a set liturgy.[56] When the King's party was in Edinburgh in 1641, Sidney Bere reported that Henderson and another had the chaplain's places, 'but I cannot say, read prayers'. All was extempore, and the chapel 'fitted but after their fashion, without altar or organs'.[57] Charles's disgust at this sort of practice was eloquent:

that diversitie, nay deformitie, which was used in Scotland, where no set or publice form of prayer was used, but preachers and readers and ignorant schoolemasters prayed in the church, . . . sometimes so seditiously that their prayers were plaine libels, girding at soveraigntie and authoritie; or lyes, being stuffed with all the false reports in the kingdome.[58]

Charles's attitude to worship had much the same concern with order and form which characterized his court ceremonial and his taste in art, and the disgust he felt at plain worship such as many of his Scottish (and

---

[56] Donaldson, *Scottish Prayer Book*, pp. 42–3; *Large Declaration* (1639), 20. The *Large Declaration* was published in the King's name, but in fact ghost-written to his directions by Walter Balcanquall Dean of Durham: Baillie, ii. 429–30. The King (in his words) 'owned it from the beginning as his owne', and it seems to have expressed his sentiments: BL Stowe MS 187, fo. 9ᵃ. Charles's invocations of 'decency' are probably based on 1 Cor. 14: 40.

[57] PRO SP 16/483/68.

[58] *Large Declaration*, pp. 15–16.

English) subjects preferred was a genuine emotional force in the situation. It needs to be taken as seriously as the equally genuine disgust felt by many of those who protested that any appeal to the fancy and the senses in worship was, by definition, popery and a way of leading people to worship something other than God.

Charles and Laud were said to have originally wanted 'to take the English liturgy without any variation, so that the same service might be established in all his Majesty's dominions'.[59] They were persuaded by some of the Scottish bishops to adopt a distinctively Scottish liturgy, in order to avoid the charge of dependence on England. From then on, the service book evolved by correspondence between Charles and Laud in England, and a small group of rising Arminians among the Scottish bishops, notably Maxwell Bishop of Ross and Wedderburn Bishop of Dunblane. It seems to have been they who were responsible for some of the changes which led the service book's opponents, when it appeared, to say it was worse than the English one. Their appearance in the story underlines the point that there were Scots who might have been induced to support the service book. In 1634 the minister of Paisley had been severely rebuked for teaching 'that a man once justified, might possiblye fall away from justifiing faith'.[60] To him, as to an English Calvinist, closer conformity with the other kingdom might have appeared a way of achieving much-needed protection. The Scottish Covenanters themselves were alarmed by the strength of Arminian feeling among their countrymen. Robert Baillie, later one of the most distinguished Covenanting ministers, lamented in January 1637, seven months before the service book appeared, that many declared sundry tenets of popery and Arminianism, and showed no zeal for repressing papists and Arminians, or for redressing the afflicted state of Protestants abroad. Even many like Baillie himself, who were Calvinist to the core, and unwilling to accommodate 'popish rites, which the English wants',[61] were nevertheless far more moderate than they became later. Baillie, later a leading spirit in the Scottish drive to Presbyterianize England, believed up to 1638 in a modified episcopacy like that which had been agreed on at Linlithgow in 1606, and which was to be revived, to his derision, by Archbishop Ussher in 1641. He believed in 1637 that resistance to kings was under all circumstances a sin, and was prepared to accept the Five Articles of Perth, and to communicate with 'kneelers'. When he first considered the prospects for the service book, he feared not a general resistance, but a 'pitiful schism'.[62] One of the major

[59] Donaldson, *Scottish Prayer Book*, p. 41.
[60] Foster, *Church before Covenants*, p. 94.
[61] Baillie, i. 4–5.
[62] Ibid. 5.

mysteries in the Scottish story is the King's success in alienating, not only moderate opinion, but even many of those who should have been his natural supporters.

When the service book appeared in St Giles's kirk in Edinburgh on 23 July 1637, it had not been through any Scottish machinery of consultation. There had been no General Assembly and no Parliament, and it was imposed simply by Proclamation in virtue of Charles's putative Royal Supremacy. Whether it was popish or not, it was certainly a type of Protestant service which had not been seen in Scotland before except in a very few places under the King's direct and immediate influence. It probably had a closer resemblance to the Mass than to anything which Scots who had not visited England had ever seen before, and the Covenanter Earl of Rothes was probably right in his detached comment that the commons 'believed that service to be mass'. Rothes himself knew better, but he was surely right that the service book 'appeired, in the mater, to those of best understanding, and in the maner and forme, to the weakest, even to change the whole manner and forme of Gods publict worship formerly practised'. To Rothes, that appeared to be something which could not be done without law.[63] If Scottish law could be made by Proclamation in London, with the list of Scots consulted possibly still in single figures, Scots were entitled to express the fear 'that wee should no more bee a kirk or a nation'.[64] It was because this sense of Scottish constitutional and national identity became fused with the fear of popery that the Scots were able to produce such a formidable opposition to the service book.

To say this is not to suggest that the fear of popery by itself was anything other than a formidable force. It is not to be supposed that if Charles had succeeded, in his father's style, in arm-twisting a General Assembly into passing the service book, that it would therefore have become enforceable. Charles might, it is true, have been able to recruit a party in favour of the book, but whether that party would have been strong enough to prevail is more doubtful. That Samuel Rutherford should take the book for popery was not surprising: he had already been in trouble for a long time for his opposition to the Five Articles of Perth, and more recently for his assaults on Arminianism.[65] The reaction of a young lawyer called Archibald Johnston of Wariston, soon to become

[63] Rothes, p. 3. Rothes left a private note in his MS, which commented in Machiavellian tones that the book was not only against religion, but 'even against the rules of civile policie, which forbid any change in religione, without the appearance of some farr greater good, and people prepared to believe so, or very great force to compell their embracement, religion having greatest power of all things over the hearts of men, either in oppinione or really': ibid. 41.
[64] *Intentions of the Army of the Kingdom of Scotland* (Edinburgh, 1640), 5.
[65] Baillie, vol. i, pp. xxxiv–xxxv; Stevenson, pp. 24–5, 44, 56.

one of the Covenanters' leading men of business, is rather more significant. He was a good Calvinist, of much the same theological school as Oliver Cromwell, though of a less cautious temperament. He regularly read authors such as Dod and Perkins, and relied on the doctrine of Providence in much the same way as Cromwell. Before July 1637, he had shown no sign of being a religious trouble-maker: he listened to the sermons of Dr Fairlie, who became Bishop of Argyll in 1637, and even occasionally to the man who was to read the service book on the unfortunate day of its introduction. On 'that black doolful Sunday to the kirk and kingdome of Scotland', he seems to have encountered something right outside the limits of his tolerance, an 'Egyptian darknes covering the light of the Gospel schyning in this nation'. After two weeks, 'it come in my mind that, if we licked up this vomit of Romish superstition again, the Lord in his wrayth wad vomit us out. . . . The Lord ingraived in my mind that of the prophet, "thair is poison in the pot" '. To anyone who held the providentialist theory of divine intervention in earthly affairs, there was a point beyond which compromise was a gross political imprudence. That point Johnston reached almost at once.[66]

By contrast, Robert Baillie minister of Kilwinning took a great deal longer. When he was first asked to preach in favour of the service book, he declined on the very proper ground that he had not yet had time to read it, and it was not until October that he knew he must refuse. He feared popery, but it was not his only fear: he prayed at first that God 'would avert the poprie of one side, and the schisme of the other, and the bloodie sword of both'. When he finally made up his mind, it was not only because of the service book itself, but because of the innovations he feared to see following in its wake: 'no other way is left, bot either to swallow down all that the Canterburians can invent, or else to oppose them plainly in their lawless practises'. Baillie, who had the instincts of a scholar, had worked on the book, and on the Arminian literature which he saw coming behind it, and hoped he had been persuaded by what he read. Nevertheless, a small corner of Baillie's mind entertained the uncomfortable suspicion that he had been converted by fear. The minister who preached that sermon in favour of the service book which he had declined to preach was stoned by a company of women, and Baillie was distressed that 'no man may speak any thing in publick for the king's part, except he would have himself marked for a sacrifice to be killed one day'. Long afterwards, he continued to deplore the 'unhappie and ungodly violences' by which resistance to the

---

[66] *Diary of Sir Archibald Johnston of Wariston*, ed. G. M. Paul (Scottish History Society, 61, Edinburgh, 1911), pp. xvii–xviii, xix, 265, 267.

cause was silenced. Every time his Covenanter colleagues provoked Baillie's doubts, it was Charles who stilled them.[67]

The noblemen and ministers who came to the front of the resistance were careful to use the more decorous method of petitioning and lobbying the Council. For Lord Loudoun, who spoke to the Council for the petitioners on 21 December 1637, it was the close link between religion and law which was the heart of his case: he spoke for 'the defence of religione and the lawes of the kingdome, on which dependeth the weillfair of church and commone wealth, the deutie they owe to Almightye God, the alleadgence to their soveraigne lord and master the king, the conditions of lyff, libertie and fortune heire, and their happines heirafter'. This linking of religion, law, and allegiance was a conventional seventeenth-century case, and a powerful one. Alexander Henderson and the ministers of St Andrews presbytery asked for time to read the service book, claiming that 'in the maters of Gods worschip we are not bound to blind obedience, and complaining that the book was not warranted by the General Assembly, the 'representative kirk' of this kingdom.[68]

This was a powerful assortment of cases, with a wide enough intellectual range to explain the depth of the resistance. In the way of public support, there was little but a group of Edinburgh ministers who offered to trade reading the service book for a grant of adequate maintenance.[69] It is instructive, in assessing the lack of support for the book, to see what some of the Scottish Council were writing to Hamilton in London. The Earl of Traquair, Lord Treasurer of Scotland, said in his letter reporting the tumults that churchmen, who had the 'menaging of ye affaires of ye churche, and no small hand in ye disposing of what may concerne ye common weall, are not fitting for such great and weaghtie imployments'.[70] The Caroline version of the Royal Supremacy, in which church matters were handled by the king with the advice of his bishops, was as provoking to the Scottish Privy Council as to most other Scots. Traquair begged that 'his matie may be pleased to hear sume of the laytie', and predicted that otherwise there would be more trouble for the kingdom.

The Earl of Roxburgh, Lord Privy Seal, was responsible for rescuing the Bishop of Edinburgh from afternoon service on 23 July, and got stoned himself in the process. He protested against this 'barbarous tumult', but he was already complaining to Hamilton, before the service book appeared, of 'the violent prosidings of our bishops', and saying

---

[67] Baillie, i. 14, 20–1, 28, 23.
[68] Rothes, pp. 38, 45–6.
[69] *RPCS* vi. 514.
[70] Hamilton MS 1497 (undated, but clearly late July or Aug. 1637).

that the King should establish the church with a competence of money, 'but not to be masters over his pepill'. He blamed the riot in St Giles's kirk on the bishops' attempt to take sole responsibility for church affairs. He was particularly incensed that they had sent no official notification to the Privy Council of the public order problem they were about to create. He said they could have punished offenders 'if it had pleased our churche men ane little before to have consulted the Lords of his maties secrett counsell, or sent some members of them ane timely and carefull foresight'. He wanted the King to leave these matters to his Privy Council, 'which truly we have not ben remisse in since we were taken notice of, or thought to be concerned in that part of his Maty's service.'[71]

The first phase of the Scottish crisis ran from the reading of the service book on 23 July 1637 to the signing of the Scottish National Covenant on 28 February 1638. This phase was dominated by the attempt to work through the usual channels. In the usual channels, the key figures were the Scottish Council, notably Traquair and Roxburgh, in Edinburgh, and the Anglo-Scots Hamilton, Lennox, and Morton in London. The opponents of the service book addressed the Council, and the Council, by a succession of letters and messengers, tried to influence the Anglo-Scots to persuade the King to retreat. In addition, many of the noblemen among the protesters subsequently addressed the Anglo-Scots direct. During this phase, Traquair, as an old-style Councillor, continued to have private meetings and discussions with the leading protesters. The channels of communication, at least in Edinburgh, were still open. The message the Councillors passed on to Whitehall may not have been what the protesters wanted, but at least they called unequivocally for the withdrawal of the service book. Over and over again, they hammered home the message that 'that book will not settle here without much blode'. In February 1638 Traquair told Hamilton that 'it sall be as easy to establishe ye masse in this kingdme as ye service book as it is conceaved'. Traquair here understated the case: it might have been *easier* to establish the Mass, for there was an organized party for it. Though the King had potential supporters in Scotland, the service book went too far for them, and he picked up almost none of them until he had abandoned it. Meanwhile, Traquair was right that it was impossible to suppress the protests: 'I see not a probabilitie of power within this kingdome to force them'. The courtier language in which messages had to be conveyed to the King led to a fatal ambiguity. Traquair told

---

[71] Ibid. 382, 354. In the first of these letters, Roxburgh was discussing the complicated affair of the Abbey of Lindorres. In the second, he was not suggesting that the Council had been left in ignorance of what was well known to most of Edinburgh, but complaining that their responsibility had been usurped. On Roxburgh's rescue of the Bishop of Edinburgh, see Stevenson, p. 62.

Hamilton that the King must 'free ye subjects of y feares they have conceaved of innovacne of religione'.[72]

What Traquair meant, of course, was that the service book was an innovation. This message never reached Charles, who persistently replied, both directly and through Hamilton and others, that he expected the troubles to cease as soon as the protesters understood that the service book was not an innovation. At some date during 1638, Hamilton, Morton, and Lennox (doubtless well briefed) wrote back to three protesting lords that the King, not finding his answers

so clearlie understode as was wished and expected, his matie will be yet gratiouslie pleased further to explaine and declaire what his royall intentins are, and therby, no doubt free the hearts of his loyall subiects from any feares wche they might have apprehended, of innovation of religion, and ease your lp. of the truble rather of sending yr. supplications here.[73]

The very first time this happened, some of the protesters were taken in. The Earl of Roxburgh in November 1637 brought back the first of many declarations from the King promising that there would be no innovation. One at least of the protesters among Hamilton's Scottish correspondents took this as a hint that the King was ready to abandon the service book, and said it 'hath mightilie incouraged all thes who doth oppose the service book and uther unlawfull innovationes'.[74] It was a mistake which was not to be made again. Many times, both in Scotland and in England, Charles was to offer assurances that he would not support any innovation, but he always retained the confidence of his belief that what he had done was not innovation. The condemnations of innovation were aimed at his opponents. In most cases, there was enough ambiguity in the Jacobean religious heritage to make Charles' view excusable, if not defensible, but on this occasion, it must be said that he was plainly wrong. In the *Large Declaration* of 1639, Charles repeated the claim in a version which, to a Scottish ear, is of breathtaking insensitivity:

Disobedience to this our proclamation we had little reason to expect, because this service book was no new thing unto them: for it not differing from the English service book in any materiall point, and we supposing that the English liturgie neither was nor could bee displeasing to them, did likewise conceive that this book should be as little disliked by them.

These useless undertakings to avoid innovation, while not admitting he was guilty of any, are the first characteristic Caroline theme to

---

[72] Hamilton MSS 983, 982, 981.
[73] Ibid. 10829: Hamilton, Morton, and Lennox to Rothes, Montrose, and Cassilis, undated. They were answering a letter of 7 Mar. 1638: Rothes, pp. 83–4.
[74] Hamilton MS 394 (Loudoun to Hamilton, 25 Dec. 1637).

emerge in these months.[75] The second is Charles's great difficulty in absorbing the message that anything was impossible. Long after Traquair and Roxburgh had told him the service book could not be enforced, Charles was still commanding them to enforce it in the name of decency, order, and reverence. It is possible that Charles actually believed the case he argued in the *Large Declaration*, that the disorders were not about religion at all, but simply the result of discontent at the Act of Revocation of church property. If he believed, as he seems to have done, that he was not guilty of any innovation, he could well have believed this too. This lack of any sense of the impossible was a fault Charles showed on many other occasions,[76] but on this occasion, it was compounded by his inability to understand the force of conviction behind the complex of beliefs known to modern historians as 'Puritanism'. It is a weakness he has shared with others, but it has not helped any of them.[77]

The third characteristic Caroline theme to emerge in these months is Charles's readiness to take any dissent as a challenge to his 'authority'. This belief was very often a self-fulfilling prophecy. In December 1637 he complained of the 'foul indignity wherein his honour suffered' by the protests at the service book, which was true enough, but his persistence with the service book did not lessen the indignity. In February 1638 he told the Scottish Council that 'your course heerin hath been more derogatorie to our autoritie, then conduceing to the true quyet of the countrie. For we can never conceave that the countrie is truelie quyet when regall auctoritie is infringed'. They might, he told them, have a seeming settlement, but it could not continue where the king's true authority was not truly present. Making a mistake which he had made many times before, and was to make many times again, he thought to still trouble by taking personal responsibility for the service book, instead of allowing the petitioners to put the blame on the bishops. By staking his authority, Charles, like a losing gambler, merely endangered it further.[78]

Behind these exchanges lies a deeper question: whether a sovereign might accept a conditional allegiance. When the Covenanters in June 1638 offered to defend 'the religione, laws and liberties, the Kings Majesties persone and authoritie in preservatione thereof', they meant, though delicately, to spell out a condition.[79] It was the same condition

[75] *Large Declaration*, p. 19. See also *RPCS* vii. 33, 74, and other refs.
[76] See e.g. *CSPD 1639–40*, vol. ccccxxxvi, no. 41 (28 Dec. 1639). On this occasion, Charles ordered Traquair to arrest a Covenanter officer of the artillery in the midst of his own army, and to send him for trial in England for reconnoitring the fortifications of Berwick. I know no reply by Traquair.
[77] *Large Declaration*, pp. 1–16.
[78] *RPCS* vi. 546–7, vii. 15–16; Stevenson, pp. 80–1.
[79] Rothes, p. 149.

Loudoun had spelt out to the Privy Council in December 1637, when he argued that allegiance depended on religion and law. Charles was certainly entitled, in a period when almost any action might appear to some of his subjects to be against religion or law, to feel that a conditional allegiance was unsafe, and that any subject who offered only a conditional allegiance was potentially disloyal. This was one of the risks to which religious division had exposed any monarchy which continued the attempt to enforce religion. In 1639 Hamilton, speaking with his master's voice, wrote to Charles that 'they will condiscend to all sivill obediens, yet it is with this damnabill but, that your majesty most condiscend to the abolashing of bishops'.[80] In the *Large Declaration*, Charles savagely parodied this view: 'their meaning is, that they will continue obedient subjects, if we will part from our soveraigntie, which is in effect, that they will obey, if we will suffer them to command'.[81] The point is, in a sense, a fair one: the Covenanters' position was as Charles described it, and the threat he perceived was a genuine one. Yet, as James might have told him, it is a fact of political life in any century that most people's allegiance is in the last resort conditional, and political skill consists in so managing affairs that they are never moved to spell out the conditions, either to themselves or to others. It was because Charles did not admit the need for such skill that he was so frequently moved to perceive disloyalty among his subjects.[82] It underlines the point further that the authority which concerned Charles here was 'that churche government which our dear father of blessed memorye hath established'. He probably meant episcopal government, but it is likely that he also meant the Royal Supremacy, which the Covenanters were uninhibited about challenging because they did not believe it existed anyway.[83]

The second phase of the Scottish crisis runs from the subscribing of the Scottish National Covenant on 28 February 1638 to the time when the Glasgow Assembly dissolved itself on 20 December 1638. The Covenant itself was a response to one of Charles's Proclamations, condemning innovation and upholding the service book, both in the same breath. The final text, drafted by Henderson and Johnston with the assistance of several ministers, and revised by Rothes, Loudoun, and Balmerino, bound those who subscribed it to defend the true religion, and to 'resist all these contrary errors and corruptions according to our vocation, and to the utmost of that power that God hath put into our

---

[80] *Hamilton Papers*, ed. S. R. Gardiner (Camden Society, NS 27, 1880), 82. I am grateful to Dr Peter Donald for this reference.

[81] *Large Declaration*, p. 110.

[82] I am grateful to Dr R. P. Cust for allowing me to read an as yet unpublished paper on Charles I's published Declarations from 1626 to 1640.

[83] *RPCS* vii. 17.

hands, all the days of our life'. It told Charles, in barely veiled terms, that if he wanted to enforce the service book, he would have to fight for it.

The true religion which they bound themselves to defend was defined in terms of the Confession of Faith of 1580, printed with the Covenant. This roundly condemned, under the name of 'popery', all the doctrines which had since come to be known by the name of 'Arminianism', and also such popish ceremonies as 'calling upon angels or saints departed, worshipping of imagery, relics, and crosses; dedicating of kirks, altars, days, vows to creatures'. It condemned the Pope's 'desperate and uncertain repentance: his general and doubtsome faith'. Some of these things plainly enough condemned parts of the new liturgy. The preamble then repeated numerous Acts of Parliament, including the Act of 1604 exempting the kirk from the treaty for the Union, and used the coronation oath to emphasize the case that 'the true worship of God and the king's authority being so straitly joined, as that they had the same friends and common enemies, and did stand and fall together', and repeated the claim that new things in religion could only be established by the authority of a General Assembly and a Parliament. They bound themselves to 'the defence of our dread sovereign the king's Majesty, his person and authority, *in the defence and preservation of the aforesaid true religion, liberties and laws of the kingdom*'. The perception of loyalty as being owed to principles before it was owed to persons is one which was to be reiterated many times in the next four years. Time and experience did nothing to diminish Charles's conviction that such an attitude was inherently subversive.[84]

Thanks to Baillie's success in amending the draft, the Covenant did not contain any clear condemnation of episcopacy. His argument that such a clause would divide their supporters was unquestionably correct, and in the short run, it prevailed. Nevertheless, he said, the most part 'were peremptorily resolved not to indure any longer their lawless tyranny', and the story of the next ten months is in part the story of the slow conversion of the Covenanters into dogmatic Presbyterians.[85] In understanding the growth of a Covenanter case against bishops, nothing is more helpful than a study of Charles's case in favour of bishops. That he upheld them as a symbol of conformity with England was not a point in their favour, but it was even more important that he linked their existence so constantly with his 'authority'. At the end of 1639, when finally forced to accept that the Covenanters were abolishing episcopacy, he commented: 'now they ame att nothing but the overthrow of

---

[84] S. R. Gardiner, *Documents*, pp. 124–33: italics mine; *APS* 4. 264.
[85] Baillie, i. 50–4.

royall authoriti'.[86] Within his own definition, Charles was right: by his authority, he meant his ability, under the Royal Supremacy, to order the church at his pleasure. That was something to which bishops were an essential instrument. The bishops, having no equivalent to the English Convocation, were forced to reply to claims for the General Assembly by claiming to be 'the church'. One of them said that 'the prelates are the onlie representative church in this kingdome, for besides them non have place to sitt, or give voice in parliament and generall councels for the church, and they are the special office bearers in the same'.[87]

By February 1638 the Covenanters had realized, not only that Charles stood for liturgical and doctrinal beliefs to which they would not consent, but also that he stood for a theory of ecclesiastical government in which they need not consent. Like most other people, they tended to favour that theory of ecclesiastical government most likely to produce a church in which they found it congenial to worship. It was now clear to them that this meant a theory of ecclesiastical government in which the King's control was reduced to the bare minimum possible. So long as the King appointed bishops, this necessarily meant the abolition of bishops. If the King could hand-pick a 'church' to put through the measures he chose, success in riding out one crisis would give no more than a breathing space before the next. As Baillie put it,

the mischiefs are present, horrible, in a clap: will he [Charles] relent, and give way to our supplications, the danger is not past; we wot not where to stand; when the books of canons and service are burnt and away, when the High Commissione is doune, when the Articles of Perth are made free, when the bishops' authoritie is hemmed in with never so manie laws; this makes us not secure from their future danger: so whatever the prince grants, I feare we presse more than he can grant.[88]

In other words, the King could no more freely consent to the Covenanters' form of worship than they could freely consent to his.

In these circumstances, any concessions extorted from the King could only be made secure by constitutional arrangements which deprived him of the power to reverse them. This meant that Charles could no longer be allowed to rule the church through bishops of his own choosing. He was driving the Covenanters inexorably back towards a Melvillian two-kingdoms theory: it was the only way a godly kirk could be run under an ungodly sovereign. In this context, we should consider the hypothesis that bishops, in much of what the Covenanters wrote about them, were serving as whipping-boys for the power of the Crown: when

---

[86] Hamilton MS 1031 (Charles to Traquair, 1 Oct. 1639).
[87] NLS Wodrow MS Fol. 66, fo. 74[b]. The author is plainly a bishop, since he refers to the bishops as 'us'.
[88] Baillie, i. 48–9.

Rothes, for example, complained of their 'uncontrolable dominione',[89] what he in fact meant was the uncontrollable dominion the King exercised through them. When he wrote that the bishops and their civil allies 'wer grieved to find the course of blind obedience interrupted, and the subjects now to examine and consider what they wer urged to obey, and not to render such unlimited respect as they wer wont to those that wer sett in publict places, how unfitt soever, either by their conditione, or want of qualificatione', it can have taken little imagination in his readers to see the phrases as an attack on the King's control of the church. He summed up the whole Covenanter case when he accused the bishops of complying with the King, 'such complying being fitter for the servants of a persone than of a state'.[90] This cult of an impersonal state, in which the King's authority could be safely hidden, was one all Charles's opponents were ultimately driven to adopt, and it was one with which bishops appeared incompatible.

The other key development of the summer of 1638 was the King's conversion to the view that the best way to overcome Scotland was by an English conquest. Much of the debate on this issue was conducted by letter between the King and his commissioner the Marquess of Hamilton, who arrived in Scotland at the beginning of June 1638. Hamilton was of the blood royal, and deeply in the confidence of the King, who addressed him in letters as 'James'.[91] Hamilton's own religious convictions are not easy to discover, and his part in the story, both in 1638 and later, is not easy to analyse. It seems best to construe Hamilton as a fixer, one whose commitment to 'the art of the possible' was capable of overriding all his other commitments. Hamilton certainly felt a deep distaste for some Covenanter excesses, combined on occasion with some physical fear of Covenanter crowds in Edinburgh.[92] Yet it seems this distaste did not make him unable to negotiate with them, nor his fear turn him into a clear appeaser. Above all, Hamilton was a consummate courtier, and his picture of the art of the possible depended as much on what the King could be led to consent to as on what the Covenanters could be induced to accept. Because he was such a consummate courtier, his language in his letters to the King may be liable to misconstruction. Occasionally, the soothing language in which he wrapped up his message may have concealed that message from us. Perhaps, on occasion, it concealed it from the King too.

The King originally expected Hamilton to secure the acceptance of

[89] Rothes, p. 1.
[90] Ibid. 124, 70.
[91] Hamilton MSS 150, 160, and other refs. It is hard to gauge the significance of the form of address until we know whether Charles used it to the Duke of Lennox, who was also of the blood royal.
[92] Ibid. 325.2, 553, and other refs.

the service book and the giving up of the Covenant, which he regarded as a threat to royal authority. The Act Anent Bands, a Scottish Act of 1585 of which Charles was remarkably well aware, had forbidden oaths and associations entered into without the king's consent. The Covenanters were often hard put to it to answer arguments based on this Act. On 25 June, shortly after Hamilton's arrival in Edinburgh, Charles wrote to him about this 'damnable Covenant', exclaiming: 'by the heavenly God, so long as this covenant is in force . . . I have no more power in Scotland then as a Duke of Venice, which I will rather dye than suffer'.[93]

It is instructive to read this letter beside the letter of Hamilton's to which it was probably an answer. He had warned the King to prepare for the worst, since there was now no hope to prevail by treaty, and told him that if the King did not soon allow them to call a General Assembly, they would call one without his approval. He warned Charles that those best affected to him said there was no chance of securing the giving up of the Covenant: those he had spoken to would as soon renounce their baptism. He said most of the Council and the Court of Session 'and in a manner all the lawyers' did not agree with Charles that the Covenant was contrary to Scottish law. He said they and many Councillors urged the King to accept it. In the key passage of the letter, Hamilton wrote: 'tho I dare boldly affirm to your Matie ther are feu that doveth not conseave this the best and safest way, bot it shall never by my advyse, if your matie can cleeirlie sea, hou you can effect your end, without the haserding of your 3 crounes'. This is advice that Charles could not prevail without invasion, but is it advice in favour of invasion?

Hamilton's next paragraph suggests that it was not:

the conquering totallie of this kingdoume will be a difficult woorke, though ye were sertan of what assistans ingland can give you, but it feires me thatt they will not be so fourdwardt in this as they ought, nay that ther ar so manie malitious spereites amongst them thatt no souner will your bake be turned, but they will be redie to dou as we have doun heir, which I will never call by a nother name than rebellioun. Ingland wants not its owne discontents, and I feeire much help they can not give.[94]

For Charles to answer such a letter merely by saying that he would rather die than suffer it was a fine sentiment, and no doubt a sincere one, but it did not make life easy for his servants.[95] It did not help, either, that Charles, having sent Hamilton on what was, in effect a fact-finding mission, was prepared to disbelieve the information he was given if he found it uncongenial. In September Hamilton told Charles that many of the Scottish Council were now inclining in their hearts to

[93] Hamilton MS 10492.
[94] Ibid. 327.1, also 10484.
[95] Hamilton was in the end moved to tell the King that they would rather die too: ibid. 10491.

the abolishing of episcopacy. Charles, from the safety of Richmond, replied 'as for the danger that episcopall government is in, I doe not hould it so much as you doe, for I believe that the number of those that are against episcopacie, (wch. ar not in their hearts against monarchie) is not so considerable as you take it'. Hamilton, good courtier though he was, replied obstinately that he did conceive the danger episcopacy was in to be great, though he knew well that it was chiefly monarchy was intended by them to be destroyed.[96]

Having reached deadlock, Hamilton went back a second time to London to see whether personal contact with the King could induce more flexibility. He was not a Covenanter sympathizer: his complaints about how stubborn they were, and how difficult it was to content them with reason, were as bitter as Charles's own. He had come to tell Charles the limits of the possible. While he was in England, he unburdened himself in a letter of unusual frankness to Traquair. When he first reported to the King, 'I never found his looks to be such as they were that nyt'. He then attended again with Laud, and, at the King's invitation, outlined the measures necessary to build him a party, 'his answer was, that the remedy was worse than the disease'. The King then commanded him to speak no more of it:

and my Lord, when I tell you the deliverie upp of the covenante is his end, or least the gaining of so considerable a pairtie as to force them to it, you that knoweth how dear it is to them that hath subscreybet it, will think that I have reason to advise weall before I should undertake so hard and difficulte a taske. Yet such is my love to that poor miserable countrie, and the confidence I have in you and those that I pairted from at Broxmouth, as I am liklie to engage my self so farre.[97]

In the list of reasons why he was likely to engage himself so far, anyone familiar with courtiers' letters, or with Hamilton's own style, would have found one conspicuous silence: there is no mention of the love of his dear master as a motive for carrying on the work.

Yet, before we call Charles 'inflexible', or condemn him for being unable to listen to unwelcome advice we should remember that, twelve days after this letter, Hamilton was back in Scotland with full authority to pursue what was probably something like the policy the King had turned down with such contumely when he first heard of it. In a Proclamation issued on 19 September, and proclaimed on the 22nd, Charles announced a General Assembly and a Parliament, revoked the service book, canons, and court of High Commission, and suspended the Five Articles of Perth. He then issued the 1580 Confession of Faith,

[96] Ibid. 10503, 10505, and 10509.
[97] Ibid. 719 (5 Sept. 1638). Broxmouth was the Earl of Roxburgh's house: on the meeting to which Hamilton refers, see Donald, pp. 104–6.

with his own gloss on it instead of the Covenanters', as a 'King's Covenant'.[98] How Hamilton had persuaded the King to agree to such a concession is revealed by his next letter to the King: he said the Covenanters were trying to dissuade him from renewing the confession of faith, knowing well that it was the only means to work division among them.[99] As in England in the spring of 1641, Charles had retreated in order to gather a party.

During the second half of 1638, the attempts to gain Charles a party seemed to be on the edge of success. Once the Covenanters committed themselves at the Glasgow Assembly to strict Presbyterianism, they risked falling foul of the same impatience with clerical domination which had previously been turned against the service book. Among the nobility, who were Charles's chosen ground, he seems to have been making progress. A list of the Scottish nobility, labelled *pro rege* or *contra regem*, and probably drawn up at about this time, shows them nearly evenly divided. The list in the form in which we have it now, is clearly a corrupt copy, and not entirely trustworthy, but the overall picture it gives can be sustained from other sources.[100] The Hamilton Papers for the second half of 1638 contains expressions of support from two Marquesses, eight Earls, and one Lord, and this is clearly far from the whole. Recruits were nursed; the Signet Office was kept busy sending out letters thanking peers for their affection to the King's service.[101] The Earl of Airth, who was desperately in debt because the King had not paid him what he owed him, was secured by Hamilton's credit, and though no one was so crude as to spell it out, he understood that the King expected service in return for future favour. The resources of the Scottish monarchy were not large, but such as they were, they were deployed with skill and care.[102]

Among the ministers, we hear in the Covenanter accounts of those

[98] Gardiner, *History*, viii. 362–3; *RCPS* vii. 64–7.

[99] Hamilton MS 10502.

[100] Bodl. MS Nalson xix, fo. 11ʳ. This list, in its present form, is clearly the work of an ignorant English copyist, as shown by the spellings of 'Roxborough' and 'Southerland', and the typical English inability to cope with the title of the Earl of Airth. 'Lamberdale' appears to be a plain mistranscription of 'Lauderdale' and the inclusion of Viscount Falkland suggests the rote use of a list of the Scottish peerage available in London. Nevertheless, when the list is checked against other sources, enough of its information is accurate to suggest that the overall picture it gives is not significantly misleading. It is possible that further search in Scottish manuscript collections may reveal a more persuasive original.

[101] Hamilton MSS 448, 724, 431, 534, 453, 538, 643, 743, 744, 793, 726, and other refs. The peers concerned are the Marquesses of Huntly and Douglas, the Earls of Sutherland, Mar, Lauderdale, Eglinton, Airth, Kingorne, Nithsdale and Angus, and Lord Ogilvy. This list is far from exhaustive, and a complete list should include, among others, the Earls of Abercorn, Dunfermline, and Kinnoull, and Lord Sempill.

[102] Ibid. 281, 302, 305, 391; Napier, i. 248, 250, 253.

who suffered for opposing the service book, or feared they might do so. There is a considerable amount of information in the Hamilton Papers on ministers who petitioned for protection against the 'insolencies' they suffered for opposing the Covenant. By the spring of 1639 at least sixty-five 'deposed and distressed ministers' had gathered across the border at Berwick, receiving pensions out of the English Exchequer. These ministers are not only from the north-east, a notoriously anti-Coven-anter area where it seems unlikely that anti-Covenanter ministers at first suffered much distress. Those in trouble come from such Covenanter areas as Ayr and Kirkcudbright, among other places.[103] As early as Easter 1638 Baillie had reported division in Glasgow, where the kneelers and the non-kneelers took communion in different churches. A year later, on the eve of the First Bishops' War, he said, 'our dangers were greater than we might let our people conceave'.[104] Power was the Covenanters' enemy: it gave them opportunities to offend some of a body of people who had trusted them for a very miscellaneous set of reasons. Fortunately for them, it was only during the last quarter of 1638 that the King's attempts to recruit a Scottish party could be pursued with any real hope of success, and the time was not long enough. Before September 1638, the King's partisans faced the prospect of having to commit themselves to the service book, and the growth of his party when it was abandoned seems to confirm that the book was beyond the limits of tolerance of most Scots. In 1639 and 1640 the King's Scottish partisans had to commit themselves to supporting an English conquest of Scotland, and though Scots had done that before, it was a cause more likely to lose recruits than to gain any.

Charles's objective in allowing Hamilton to undertake the new policy had been the preservation of Scottish episcopacy. Announced in February, the policy might have succeeded, but in September it was too little and too late. Hamilton's message from the King, transmitted through the Scottish Privy Council, that 'his matie would never condiscend nor agree that the episcopall governement alreddie established withing this kingdome, shall be abrogat or dischargit or tane away',[105] seems to have fallen on very deaf ears. Hamilton seems to have at first hoped (perhaps on royal instructions) that the bishops would be able to attend the Glasgow Assembly, but the Earl of Lauderdale, who provided lodgings for them in Glasgow, reported that 'this will make me so odious among all those who now bear the swaye, as in their opinion I shall not in hast

---

[103] Hamilton MSS M/72/1 and 2; PRO E 351/1748. The most heavily represented diocese is Glasgow with 23 ministers, Edinburgh, with 16, comes next, and Aberdeen only produced 4.
[104] Baillie, i. 63, 194.
[105] Hamilton MS 714.

recover the name of a good Christian'.[106] It was of course difficult to report such news to Laud, whose reaction at finding the people 'so beyond your expression furious' that bishops were not safe in Glasgow was as might be predicted. After long attempts to be restrained, he finally exclaimed 'and for a nationall assemblye never did the church of Christ see the like', and commented on Alexander Henderson Moderator of the Assembly: 'truly my L. never did I see anye man of that humor yett but he was deep dyed in some violence or other and it would have bine a wonder to me if Hendershame [sic] had held free'.[107] In his next letter, Laud reported that the king was making all the haste he could with military preparations.

In abolishing episcopacy, and in refusing to be dissolved on Hamilton's orders, the Glasgow Assembly burnt its boats. From then on, what was under discussion was a proposed English conquest of Scotland. Those who embarked on this course knew its risks: Hamilton had already warned Rothes that if it were undertaken, he would never expect to see peace in this kingdom again. The Scots were well aware that England was the superior power, and that if it became a 'national quarrel', they would lose it. From the Glasgow Assembly onwards, it became the Covenanters' main objective to make common cause with their 'friends' in England.[108] Baillie recorded, for example, a decision to avoid looking for continental help, not only because their divines regarded Lutheran help as 'a leaning to the rotten read of Egypt', but also because foreign help would have made England their enemy: 'the evill in the world we most declyned, and our adversaries did most ayme at'.[109]

In attempting to make common cause with the English godly, the Covenanters were doing something many of them found congenial. Many of them had a strong sense of pan-Protestantism, and regarded the English godly, in particular, as fellow-sufferers in a common cause. As early as January 1637 Baillie said that 'it's our hearty prayer there might be a Parliament in England, which might obtain all misorders there redressed: this would be some hope for us also to be heard in our like grievances'.[110] This mixture of fellow-feeling and self-interest ran through all Covenanter dealing with England from the beginning. In December 1637 Thomas Ramsay, speaking to the Scottish Council,

---

[106] Hamilton MS. 453. See also Stevenson, pp. 113–14, 119; Gardiner, *History*, viii. 366, 369. Hamilton, especially in what he wrote to Charles, was speaking with his master's voice, and Charles's hostility to letting laymen judge ecclesiastical matters shines through everything he said. See e.g. the claim (Stevenson, p. 119) that the Assembly included many who were 'illiterate'—a word perhaps used in its medieval sense.

[107] Hamilton MSS 548, 549. 'Your' expression was Hamilton's.

[108] Rothes, p. 137.

[109] Baillie, i. 190–1.

[110] Ibid. 11.

applied his arguments to the English, as well as the Scottish, Prayer Book: 'he had been in Ingland, and had observed the great trouble it broght to the best and ablest ministers, and disturbance in the king-dome, thogh establisched by law, and what may be expected upone a worse without law?'[111] On occasion, the Covenanters had employed the threat of export of the Covenant to twist the King's tail. In June 1638, when Hamilton urged them to lay down the Covenant, they replied that they wished the King's subjects in England and Ireland had subscribed the like Covenant.[112]

In February 1639 they took this threat a step further, by publishing *An Information to All Good Christians within the Kingdome of England*, which argued that they and England were suffering from a common malady, involving the corrupting of doctrine, the changing of discipline, Arminianism, and Popery, and that the attempt to bring Scotland into conformity with England was the first leg of a journey intended to bring England into conformity with Rome. They said that if the Parliament of England were convened, and they could tell their story to it, they would be so far from censuring that they would be petitioners to the King for the Scots. They said the English would reap the fruit of helping the Scots one day, 'who knoweth how soon'.[113] Such books and pamphlets were distributed through the more adventurous parts of the English godly network.[114] As early as December 1637 a stationer was in trouble for printing the works of Prynne and Bastwick together with Scottish news, and later on, Samuel Vassall, later member of Parliament for the City, was found to be circulating large numbers of Scottish books.

As early as July 1638 the Covenanters were getting a response to such approaches. Sir John Clotworthy, an English settler in Ulster, and later member for Maldon in the Long Parliament, was writing to a Scottish contact reporting on the state of English preparations, and assuring the Scots of English sympathy: 'you will not believe how hartely yr cause is wisht to succeede, amongst ye nobilyty, gentry and commonalty'. He reported, with a touch of realism, that though the nobility had been trying to organize a society to petition the King, for removal of

---

[111] Rothes, p. 40. This type of argument may have tended to make Charles feel that he had been justified in imposing the service book. See *Large Declaration*, p. 174.

[112] Rothes, p. 122.

[113] *Information* (Edinburgh, 1639) (STC 21905). See also *Short Relation of the State of the Kirk of Scotland* (s.l., 1638) (STC 22039) and *Answer to the Profession and Declaration* (Edinburgh, 1639) (STC 22048), in which the Covenanters made the very considerable sacrifice of attempting to write in English spelling.

[114] *CSPD 1637–8*, vol. ccclxxiv, no. 13; PRO SP 16/428/48. See also *CSPD 1638–9*, vol. ccciv, no. 63; Bedfordshire RO St John MS J 1372; PRO SP 16/413/120 and 124; ibid. 16/414/82; ibid. 16/415/1 and 7; ibid. 16/418/99; ibid. 16/421/92 and 92.1. It seems improbable that Secretary Windebank uncovered all such cases, but it is not easy to guess how many more there may have been, nor how far the conversational ripples of each such case could spread.

grievances, 'ther cannot be gotten above 2 of ye nobility yt will ioyne in this businesse, you may guesse who they are'. He claimed, remarkably, that some forty or fifty 'leading persons' were considering finding 'an America in Scotland', thereby illustrating one of the King's reasons for insisting on uniformity between his kingdoms.[115] In another letter, intercepted by Secretary Windebanke, he appealed to the Scots not to make a peace without procuring the calling of an English Parliament.[116]

The next year Lord Brooke, probably one of the two peers alluded to by Clotworthy, was found in treasonable correspondence with the Scots, but Charles, after some hesitation, decided not to prosecute.[117] Later, after the Pacification of Berwick, Brooke was found entertaining Samuel Rutherford, one of the most radical of the Covenanters, in Warwick Castle.[118] The story, told much later, that Gualter Frost was carrying messages between the English and the Scots gains plausibility from the discovery that Lord Brooke in September 1640 was paying him travelling expenses.[119] In the spring of 1639 Anthony Lapthorne, a godly minister with a long record as a trouble-maker, and later a client of Francis Rous, was suspected of subversive contact with the Scots. When asked why he had gone three miles beyond Berwick, he replied 'to see the borders'.[120] It is hard to tell how big an iceberg this is the tip of, but it at least goes to sustain the proposition that the policy of the Covenanters during 1639 was heavily influenced by the desire to win English support. In May 1639 their committee of war accused the English ungodly of fear that 'our happinesse should emitt ye rayes of its example to our so nearlie intire and beloved neighbours'.[121]

The Scots' desire to make common cause with the English godly was

[115] NLS Wodrow MS Fol. 66, fos. 109–10. I am grateful to Dr Peter Donald, not only for the reference, but for the identification of the handwriting and the elucidation of the context. See Donald, pp. 180–8, to which this paragraph is heavily indebted.

[116] PRO SP 16/393/33. I am grateful to Dr Peter Donald for much help and advice with this letter also. On Clotworthy's ciphers, see *Winthrop Papers*, iii. 196, 193. I am grateful to Beryl Nash for this reference.

[117] PRO SP 16/413/20.

[118] Ann Hughes, 'Thomas Dugard and his Circle in the 1630s—A Parliamentary–Puritan connection?', *HJ* 29/4 (1986), 788. I am grateful to Dr Hughes for drawing my attention to this reference before publication. Dr Hughes has rightly treated this identification as tentative, but its probability is very great.

[119] G. E. Aylmer, *State's Servants* (1973), 254. Warwicks. RO, Warwick Castle MSS, John Halford's accounts, unfoliated, travelling charges and gifts. Another payment to Frost, listed under 'gifts', on a bill of 30 Jan. 1641, is made to him jointly with 'Dr. Ruterford'. If he is identical with the 'Scoch Dr.' who was paid £6 by Lord Brooke's command, he is probably Samuel Rutherford. I am grateful to Dr Ann Hughes for these references.

[120] PRO SP 16/412/58.1. On his preferment as lecturer at Minchinhampton Gloucs. (where he had been deprived in 1617) see *CJ* ii. 577, where he is described as 'an orthodox divine', and *PJ* ii.337. On the long and troubled career of Anthony Lapthorne, see K. C. Fincham, 'Jacobean Episcopate', Ph.D. thesis (London, 1985), 289–90. I am grateful to Dr Fincham for discussion of this case.

[121] Crawford MS 14/3/33.

influenced by logistical, as well as ideological, reasons: as war approached during the spring of 1639, they grew more aware, both of shortage of money in Scotland, and of the harmful long-term effects of the blockade of Scottish ports which was Hamilton's key contribution to the strategy of the Bishops' Wars. They were much better provided with arms than the English, and the war preparations recorded in the Crawford manuscripts show apparently wider private ownership of arms than in England.[122] Their two great shortages, especially in the border area, were money and food, and both led them to rely on English contacts rather than trusting to the success of their arms. It is interesting that the Earl of Holland, the general who reported the English army unfit to fight when the armies met at Duns, was being employed by the Covenanters a few weeks earlier as a 'mediator'. To him, they admitted to having written to many noblemen in England, and asked, shrewdly, for the differences to be settled by a conference of some of the nobility of England and some of the nobility of Scotland. The appeal from the English King to the English nobility was one they were to make again.[123]

When the armies met outside Berwick in June 1639, the Scots were willing to avoid fighting because they feared they might lose.[124] The English Councillors present were mostly willing to avoid fighting because they feared the consequences of any serious war between the kingdoms. The King himself, as he had told Hamilton some six weeks earlier, was prepared to make a cease-fire in order to recover control of the Scottish royal castles.[125] The Covenanters also probably feared that actual fighting, especially if it involved invasion of England, might lose them English support which could afford to be in the open so long as actual fighting had not broken out. For a variety of reasons, the parties agreed to negotiate rather than fight, and on 11 June 1639 the King and the Covenanters met face to face for the first time.

For the English, the negotiators were Arundel, Essex, Salisbury, Holland, Berkshire, Vane, and Secretary Coke, many of whom, according to one anonymous English report, 'were deeply tainted with a good opinion of their cause'.[126] In practice, the King and Hamilton did most

[122] Ibid. 14/3/14, 17, 19, 20, 22, and other refs. These documents give a remarkable picture of the extent of private ownership of arms in coastal Fife. But see PRO WO 55/1661, pt. II, unfol., 'Armes brought into His Majesties Magazine at New College', on the extent of arms ownership in England—I am grateful to Dr J. S. A. Adamson for advice on this question.
[123] Crawford MS 14/3/35 (25 May 1639). Such an offer was being reported in London by Apr. 1639: Altham MSS, vol. i, p. 43, no. 53.
[124] *Intentions of the Army of the Kingdom of Scotland* (1640), 9.
[125] Hamilton MS 10544 (20 Apr. 1639).
[126] PRO SP 16/423/119. On the charge the author makes, it is worth noticing the Civil War allegiance of the English negotiators. They were 4 Parliamentarians (Essex, Salisbury, Holland, Vane), 2 neutrals (Arundel and Secretary Coke), and 1 lukewarm Royalist (Berkshire). Secretary Coke's angle of neutrality was distinctly Parliamentarian.

of the talking. For the Scots, Rothes, Dunfermline, Loudoun, Teviot-dale, Henderson, and Johnston were the leading negotiators. The King's arrival at the beginning of the discussions seems to have been unexpected to the Covenanters, and, according to one account, 'did not a little daunt' them, though they nevertheless disgraced themselves in the ceremonious eyes of the English by not kneeling when the King came in. Loudoun, early in the proceedings, said that their desires were only the enjoying their religion and liberty according to the ecclesiastical and civil laws, to which the King, who probably thought this meant much less than it did, responded by asking him to put it in writing. In addition, they asked for the King to ratify the Acts of the Glasgow Assembly, for all ecclesiastical matters to be determined by a General Assembly, and all civil by a Parliament, for Parliaments and General Assemblies to be held at set times every two or three years because of the King's absence, and for Scottish 'incendiaries' to be returned for punishment.[127]

At Berwick, the King made a real attempt at a meeting of minds, but all that resulted was misunderstanding leading to widespread recrimination. Since Charles has been charged with bad faith over what he did at Berwick, it seems worth scrutinizing what happened for clues to how the misunderstanding arose. It appears that Charles made a real attempt to understand what was said, and revealed considerable and unexpected ability as a debater, but in the end, the gulf between the English and Scottish intellectual traditions was too wide to be bridged. On the first day, only a few preliminary exchanges took place. The King, after asking for the Covenanter terms in writing, set down his own, which involved a restoration of his sovereignty and the giving of civil and temporal obedience. A few explanatory remarks indicated where the difficulties were likely to arise. In reply to Loudoun's request to be governed by their own laws, Charles asked 'who shall be the judge of the meaning of those laws?', forcing Rothes to the caricature Protestant evasion that 'we desire to be judged by the written word of the laws'. A dispute about whether the Glasgow Assembly had been lawfully constituted moved the King to object to lay elders, and to say it was very agreeable to their disposition that every illiterate man might be judge of religion, 'for by that means they might choose their own religion'. At this point, Sir John Borough's journal records with relief that it was now one o'clock, and they adjourned for dinner.

The second meeting, on 13 June, tackled the difficult question of the authority of the General Assembly. Before that question was raised,

---

[127] PRO SP 16/423/92; BL Add. MS 38847, fo. 3ᵃ. I am grateful to Dr Peter Donald for drawing my attention to this MS.

there was a brief and unfortunate exchange about the service book, which Rothes described as containing the seeds of idolatry and superstition. The King replied 'if that bee idolatrie so is that of England'. It was a conclusion from which the Covenanters did not dissent, but one they could hardly spell out to the King's face, and Henderson diverted the debate onto the 'scandalous' lives of some of the bishops. The key question was raised by the King: 'whether do you hold the generall assembly independent or not?' This question seems to have been one of the General Assembly's independence from Parliaments, leading Rothes to horrify some of the English present by claiming that 'Parliaments have no power to make acts of religeon'. The King then raised his crucial claim to have a negative voice, as he had in English Parliaments. He presented a paper, asking whether they agreed that he could call and dissolve General Assemblies, that he had a negative voice, that he had a right to a 'competent number' of assessors in the assembly, and that a Parliament might disannul its acts. To all this the Covenanters answered 'either negatively or with restrictions'.[128]

The Covenanter replies showed clearly why the King thought their ideas were a challenge to his authority. Rothes, following Acts 5: 29, said they were bound to obey acts of the general assembly, 'though the king refuse in Parliament, it concerninge the worshippe of Christ'.[129] Henderson bypassed the challenge to the King's authority by retreating to a higher authority, and claiming the discipline of the church to be *jure divino*: 'both articles of faith and forme of government to bee determyned by the word and warranted by Scripture'. Charles followed up his advantage by asking Henderson what he thought of the Act of Parliament giving him power to call General Assemblies. Henderson replied that the Act was but 'cumulative and honorary', and that the General Assembly did not need the King's authority for its calling.[130] Henderson was using a claim to *jure divino* authority to override Scottish law in exactly the same style as Charles had done over the Scottish Royal Supremacy. This exchange illustrates the danger of putting too much weight on Covenanter rhetoric about law and consent. Law was a useful weapon while it was on the side of the angels, but in the last resort, it could not be pleaded against a direct divine command. By

---

[128] PRO SP 16/423/104.

[129] BL Add. MS 38847, fos. 11–13. For the English comment that the case against the power of Parliaments was argued 'but weakly', PRO SP 16/423/119. It makes a point of some importance that these claims to clerical autonomy symbolized 'popery' in the eyes of the English, almost as much as the service book symbolized it in the eyes of the Scots. 'Popery' was, by definition, what the Reformation had been against, and therefore was not the same target on the two sides of the Border.

[130] BL Add. MS 38847, fo. 12; PRO SP 16/423/119.

claiming *jure divino* authority for their respective visions of church government, Charles and Henderson had both taken up positions from which it was impossible to retreat without severe loss of face, or even something worse.

The King further exposed the difficulty of combining Covenanter ecclesiology with his authority by asking whether the General Assembly had power to excommunicate him, to which Rothes answered 'boldly, but as he thought, modestly',[131] by saying that Charles was so good a king he would not deserve it, but if he himself were king, the kirk would have power to excommunicate him. The King then asked whether he was accountable to any of his courts ecclesiastical or civil, or to any other than God, for his actions. Henderson answered that he was. The King said that then King David was mistaken in saying 'against thee only have I sinned', to which Henderson replied rather weakly by saying that the text meant 'against thee principally'. The account which records these words comments at this point that 'there is no hope of any good to be done upon them by treaty'.[132]

That agreement nevertheless was reached after this point suggests how desperate all parties were to avoid fighting. It is the more surprising since the key issue remaining was the abolition of bishops, without which, as Hamilton and Traquair both realized, no genuine peace was possible. It is on the question what was agreed about episcopacy that accounts of the Pacification of Berwick differ so sharply they have appeared irreconcileable. All accounts agree that the parties decided to refer this issue to a forthcoming General Assembly. The dispute is about how far the King had pledged himself to ratify the conclusions of the Assembly. Loudoun, author of the standard Covenanter version, which drove the King to a fury of denial, wrote that he had appointed the Assembly judge of matters ecclesiastical, and would ratify it in the ensuing Parliament. Loudoun subsequently sent copies of this document to Pembroke and Salisbury, appealing to them to confirm his recollection. There is no mention here of Charles's insistence that a settlement had to be faithful to 'established laws and constitutions'. The English account in BL Lansdowne MS 255 quotes Charles as saying that 'a free assembly lawfully called may do the same things if all agree', a phrase from which no clear conclusion is to be drawn.[133] The clue perhaps, is in Sir Edward Walker's account, which records Charles as promising to agree to whatever an assembly *lawfully constituted* shall

---

[131] PRO SP 16/423/119.

[132] Ibid. 16/424/113.

[133] BL Lansdowne MS 255, fo. 333; Donald, p. 266. For a fuller acount, see Donald, pp. 256–82.

determine. By this phrase, Charles almost undoubtedly meant, as he had done at Glasgow, an assembly including bishops.[134] On 6 August he instructed the Scottish bishops to protest against their exclusion from the General Assembly and from the subsequent Parliament. Yet the rough draft of this letter suggests that Charles, rather than engaging in deliberate duplicity, as Gardiner thought, was himself in doubt how far his concession should stretch. A vital correction in the letter reads: 'tho we doe may [sic] give way for the present to that which will be prejudiciall both to the church and our government, yett we shall not leave thinking in tyme how to remedy both'. If this reconstruction is correct, the Covenanters, by refraining from exploring the meaning of the phrase 'lawfully constituted', had decided to take the risk that the agreement might not prove watertight.[135]

Hamilton's understanding that Charles had perhaps agreed to abolish episcopacy is of some weight. On 8 July he wrote Charles a powerful letter expressing his reluctance to act as commissioner in the forthcoming General Assembly and Parliament. He said that the Covenanters 'can not but find that those particulars which I have so often sworne and said your matie would never condiscend to, will now be granted, therefore they will give no credit to what I shall say ther after, but will still hope and believe, that all ther desires will be given way to'.[136] The habit of saying 'never' and then retreating was one of Charles's worst political faults, and it made it very hard for his opponents to judge the limits of the possible.

Traquair, who acted as commissioner in Hamilton's place, seems to have read the King's intentions as Hamilton did, accepted a Parliament in which power was fundamentally altered by the absence of the bishops, and accepted an Act of the General Assembly declaring episcopacy unlawful. Charles's rebuke to Traquair provides evidence for both interpretations of Berwick. He said he had given Traquair power to consent to the abolition of episcopacy as contrary to the constitutions of the kirk of Scotland, but not to declaring it unlawful, for if he did, 'it may too probably be inferred, that the same callin is acknowledged by us to be unlawfull in any other churches of our dominiounes'. The phrase again illustrates how difficult it was to confine the consequences of the Covenant to one kingdom. Charles finally commented that 'all this gives fair occasion for a rupture'. He had by now recovered control

---

[134] BL Add. MS 38847, fo. 15ᵇ. For the King's support for the claims of bishops to sit in the Assembly, see Stevenson, p. 158.

[135] Hamilton MS 1030. For Gardiner's comments, see id., History, ix. 48–52. The full correction reads 'may doe may'—(sic).

[136] Hamilton MS 948. The same point about Charles's weakness for saying 'never' and then retreating was made by the Earl of Nithsdale: ibid. 883.

of the Scottish royal castles, which was probably the main thing he wanted out of Berwick, and was ready for a fight.[137]

Negotiation continued after this point, but there is little sign that any conclusion was likely to come from it. Indeed, the suspicion existed that the Scots were using the presence of negotiators in London during the Short Parliament to lobby for English support.[138] In practice, the Covenanters were preparing for war. In their next Parliament in 1640, they passed an Act for Triennial Parliaments, and set up a system for running a government by Parliamentary authority between Parliaments. This was the system, to be used throughout 1640–1, of the Committee of Estates. This was a body, like those familiar to many continental estates, in which Parliamentary authority was vested between sessions. When war came, it was divided between a body at Edinburgh and a body with the army. Later, it was further subdivided into a trinitarian body, one part at Edinburgh, one with the army at Newcastle, and one negotiating with the King in London. Any agreement needed the assent of the whole body, and no one member was allowed to commit the others without a collective decision. It was a cumbersome, almost Dutch, system, yet it worked, and, for the first time anywhere in the British Isles, turned Parliamentary government into an actual possibility.[139]

Before war came, the Scots had been much encouraged by the sight of an English Parliament in April and May 1640 refusing to grant the King supply for a war against them. This much encouraged them in the way of thinking to which they were already inclined. They said that this was an 'everlasting honour' to the English Parliament, and from then on, identified their cause with the strengthening of the English Parliament against the English King. In a short pamphlet of 1640, designed for circulation in England, they said their object was to have their grievances heard and redressed in an English Parliament. They argued, as the English were to do after them, that they were not engaging in rebellion, but only in self-defence, and argued that the wrongs done to them were no ground for a 'national quarrel', since the Parliament had disowned them.[140]

Two themes run all through the Scottish printed propaganda of 1640: one is the theme that they had no quarrel with England, but only with

---

[137] Hamilton MS 1031; Stevenson, p. 164. There are some differences of emphasis between Dr Peter Donald's account and mine. The failure of the Pacification is a subject on which confident interpretation is impossible.
[138] See ch. 3, below.
[139] APS 5. 268.
[140] Intentions of the Army of Scotland (1640), 5, 19; Lawfulnesse of our Expedition into England Manifested (Edinburgh, 1640), Sig. A. 3. The interpretation of the Short Parliament offered here was likely to be more congenial to Pym and Hampden than to Seymour and Hopton.

the faction of the 'Canterburians', by whom the English were as much vexed as they were. The other, reminiscent of Charles I, is that they could have no security for their own Reformation until they had reached its enemies among the English prelates. In a flysheet being distributed among the English troops in Essex in September 1640, they claimed that 'duty obligeth us to love England as our selves: your grievances are ours: the preservation or ruine of religion and liberties, is common to both nations: we must now stand or fall together'. They asked for 'the authors of all our grievances and yours' to be tried in Parliament. They remembered the help they had had from England at the time of the Reformation, and expressed a desire to return the favour.[141]

Their pamphlets of 1640 state, much more frankly than anything they had said before, what was to become one of the key themes of the next eight years: that Scotland could not enjoy its Reformation in peace until it had exported it to England. It was an exact mirror image of the reasoning which had led Charles to impose the Scottish Prayer Book. A remarkable providentialist passage in the tract on *The Lawfulnesse of our Expedition into England Manifested* explains that the Lord has followed the back-trade of our defection (or, as John Le Carré would have put it, he was taking back-bearings).

But so it is, that this back trade leadeth yet further, to the prelacy in England, the fountaine whence all these Babylonish streames issued unto us: the Lord therefore is still on the back-trade, and we following him cannot yet be at a stay.

In this pamphlet, the Scots were quite frank that, for reasons of their own security as much as of true godliness, they were coming to reform England. Their appeal, plain, partisan, and divisive, was for support from all Englishmen who would welcome such a reformation:

the reformation of England long prayed and pleaded for by the godly there, shall be according to their wishes and desires perfected in doctrine, worship and discipline; papists, prelates and all the members of the antichristian hierarchy, with their idolatry, superstition and humane inventions shall pack them hence; the names of sects and separatists shall bee no more mentioned, and the Lord shall be one, and his name one, throughout the whole island.[142]

In this passage, they committed themselves to as fully unionist a vision as that of Charles I himself. Like most seventeenth-century proposals for union, it proved divisive. When the Scots ultimately crossed the Tweed in August 1640, they brought into English politics a powerful polarizing force. For some, this prospect of godly reformation was inviting, indeed even an intoxicating draught of hope where there had been none for a very long time. For others, those who were invited to

[141] PRO SP 16/464/79.1.
[142] *Lawfulnesse*, Sig. A. 4.

depart bag and baggage, such an appeal was a cause for the most
profound fear. In fighting a superior enemy, the Scots' principal technique was to divide them, and they succeeded beyond their wildest
dreams. When they crossed the Tweed, the road on which they set out
led, not only to victory at Newburn, but also to the Westminster Assembly and the battlefield of Dunbar.

3

The Bishops' Wars and the Short Parliament

I The First Bishops' War

This chapter is designed to answer two questions. The first is why England lost the Bishops' Wars. Defeat at the hands of the Scots was not a common experience for the English: the last major defeat before the battle of Newburn in 1640 had been Bannockburn in 1314. Without the Scots' victory in the Bishops' Wars, the whole of the subsequent history of the years up to 1642, and indeed beyond, could not have happened as it did. It is therefore an essential part of the story of the coming of the English Civil War to explain why the English managed to lose to the Scots.

The other object of this chapter is to examine the effect of the Bishops' Wars on English public opinion. This is more difficult, since the sources, which are all too full on the first question, are dark and obscure on the second. Public opinion in wartime is notoriously hard to discover: the sources always tend to say either more or less than the truth. Even in the Short Parliament, the Scots were clearly perturbed by the silence of some of their supposed 'friends',[1] and it is hard to do better than Charles or the Scots did in reading behind the silences. Yet, in spite of all obstacles, the sources for 1639–40 are plentiful enough to allow some plausible conjectures. These are essential to the later story, since in November 1640 the Scottish war was the major recent event about which people might have opinions, and, indeed, the major unfinished political business.

No attempt is made here to retell the basic narrative of the Bishops' Wars. The main outline of events has been well established, and Gardiner's account stands the test of time. On military and logistical questions, it is to be brought up to date in a forthcoming book on the Bishops' Wars, and there is no need to undertake here the sort of detailed analysis which is to be the core of Professor Fissel's work.[2] In answering the question why the English lost, we suffer from too many explanations and from a course of events which does not make it easy to decide on their comparative significance. We also suffer from the added complication that there were two Bishops' Wars, and it is almost certain

---

[1] See e.g. NLS Wodrow MS Fol. 64, fo. 165 (no. 61) 'to a particular friend in the Parliament', warning him that if he should remain silent, God will do the work without him.

[2] Marc Fissel, 'Bellum Episcopale: The Bishops' Wars and the End of the "Personal Rule" in England 1638–1640', Ph.D. thesis (Berkeley, Calif., 1985). I am grateful to Prof. Fissel for many valuable discussions of these issues.

that the causes for failure in the First Bishops' War are not the same as the causes of failure in the Second. It is necessary to discuss the two wars separately, and to judge each failure by itself.

The weakness of the English financial and military system is now so fully studied, and so amply documented, that it is temptingly easy to use it to explain English defeat in *any* war.[3] The weakness of the system is a constant over the whole period from 1585 to 1640, and some explanations which can be invoked for the Bishops' Wars can be invoked for any war at any time in the period. The weakness of the English military machine was partly a weakness of an inadequate financial system, particularly visible in the tendency of equipment to be inadequate or to arrive too late. There is an intriguing contrast between the Scots, who had not yet gone through the major transition from private to public provision which marks the beginning of modern warfare, and were still relying on privately owned arms,[4] and the English, who had gone into that transition without the financial resources to carry it through, and fell uncomfortably between two stools. The absence of any Parliamentary supply compounded the financial weakness of the English system, but did not create it: there is no reason to suppose that even the most harmonious of Parliaments would have given the King enough money to fight a successful war. The Earl of Northumberland, probably one of the strongest supporters of a Parliament in the English Council, commented shortly before the Short Parliament that there was no hope of enough money, 'unless the Parlament be more liberall in their supplies to the King, than they have ever been since my time'.[5]

The other standing weakness of the English system was the price the King paid for his system of local government. An unpaid system of local government depended on the ability to run the counties through their own leading inhabitants, who expected to be able to advance their own standing with their neighbours as a result of the work they did. Since this was the price of their power to command obedience, the Crown normally co-operated with this outlook, but it did mean that the average Deputy-Lieutenant pressing men for the militia would think of what was best for Devon or Cambridgeshire, rather than of what was best for England. In the field of peacekeeping, this was an advantage, but in matters of revenue and military effort, it could be a disadvantage to the service. In the Bishops' Wars, this handicap operated as usual, and

---

[3] See L. O. J. Boynton, *Elizabethan Militia* (1967); T. G. Barnes, *Somerset 1625–1640* (Oxford, 1961), 244–80; Geoffrey Parker, 'If the Armada had Landed', *History*, 61/203 (1976), 358–68. The State Papers, Domestic for 1588 would be a much richer quarry for a historian explaining an English defeat than they can ever be for one who must explain an English victory.

[4] On Scottish arms, see Crawford MSS 14/3, *passim*.

[5] Alnwick MSS, vol. 15 (BL Microfilm 286), fo. 28ᵛ, 6 Feb. 1640. In this volume, I have used the foliation in the top right-hand corner.

occasionally, because of increased royal pressure, rather more than usual. A county's stock of arms, for example, was regarded by the county as designed for home defence, and 'home' meant the county, and not the country. Few of the things Charles I did during the Bishops' Wars caused more universal offence than his attempts to deal with an arms shortage by taking the counties' supply of arms, raised for the trained bands, and not supposed to go out of the county, for forces designed to go to the front. There is no need to believe the Deputy-Lieutenants of Cambridgeshire when they protested, in reply to this practice, that their country was 'the poorest county of England': the statement was a polite way of saying they were very angry indeed.[6] This anger lasted long enough to provide a clause in the Grand Remonstrance.[7] It was an area in which central and local priorities did not meet.

It is easy to multiply such cases. In May 1639 the Lords-Lieutenant of Essex wrote to the Council about the demand for twelve members of the trained bands to guard Tilbury Fort, saying they hoped the county was not expected to pay, for it never had done, and would object.[8] The attempt to insert officers into county forces who were not their regular officers was perhaps militarily justifiable, but it caused a further rise in the political temperature. In Durham, the attempt to provide officers from outside produced a vehement protest from Sir William Bellasis, a man in whom no political disaffection could be suspected. The officers, he said, complained of being not thought worthy of employment in his Majesty's service, and of being distrusted. Having concluded they were distrusted, they then complained vehemently about the cost. As a result, in a frontier county, at the height of the preparations, one of the Deputy-Lieutenants was sent to protest to the King.[9] Since local officers of the trained bands mostly had no military experience, it is easy to see the King's point of view, but again priorities did not meet: military gain carried political loss.

Such dilemmas were daily business for early Stuart governments. At no time during the early Stuart period was the gulf bridged between what was politically acceptable on the one hand, and what was viable in military or financial terms on the other. During the Bishops' Wars, these difficulties were compounded by the lack of any secure legal basis for the militia, or for the rates on which it was based. The Marian Act on which the militia rested had unwisely specified what types of weapon

---

[6] *CSPD 1639*, vol. ccccxvii, no. 64, see also no. 41. Cambridgeshire were equally concerned about the depletion of their supply of horses.

[7] Grand Remonstrance, clause 23: Gardiner, *Documents*, p. 211.

[8] *CSPD 1639*, vol. ccccxx, no. 40.

[9] Hamilton MS 690 (Bellasis to 'my Lord', 22 Feb. 1638/9). I am grateful to Prof. Marc Fissel for the point here made.

were to be provided, and by the end of Elizabeth's reign, these weapons were mostly obsolete. Whether for this reason or for some other, the 1604 Expiring Laws Continuance Act had allowed the militia statute to lapse.[10] When the 1624 Expiring Laws Continuance Act did the same for the Statute of Winchester, it seemed that there was no legal basis left for the militia except the prerogative. The issue was discussed in 1628, when Pym and Wentworth failed to get a new statute.[11] For whatever reason, the Parliaments of the 1620s had not left the King with any secure legal basis for impressment, military discipline, rates for raising arms, coat and conduct money for taking troops to the front, or for much else essential to the running of an efficient campaign. In the First Bishops' War, very little was heard of this issue, but this need not prove that people were unaware of it: Ship Money had encouraged the asking of the type of questions which would expose this weakness. When Pym chose to ventilate this issue in the Short Parliament, it should not have caused any great surprise.

It is hard to know whether legal issues or just plain reluctance (or both) lie behind the usual obstructions the war effort encountered: in Middlesex, the JPs protested at the 'very great' salary of £200 per annum for a Provost-Marshal for disciplining troops, saying it was a great burden, and his neglect of his duties made constables neglect their office.[12] In Devon, the punishment of muster defaulters seems for a while to have approached the limits of the enforceable. The Deputy-Lieutenants, who had duly reported muster defaulters to the Council, told Bedford, the Lord-Lieutenant, that this action had made them of 'ill savour' to their countrymen. They asked for the messengers of the Chamber, who were fetching defaulters to attend the Privy Council, to be withdrawn for fear they suffer too much disgrace to do his Majesty service.[13] If this situation had ever become general, a war effort of any sort would have become impossible. If we can believe so agitated a Laudian as Robert Sibthorpe, parts of Northamptonshire were also approaching this state. He complained in June 1639 that many of the pressed soldiers, including all three from his own village, had deserted, the constables would not report them to the Deputy-Lieutenants, and he dared not do so publicly himself, for fear of getting into trouble. He prayed for God to set a guard of heavenly angels about the King, and to

<hr />

[10] A. Hassell Smith, 'Militia Statutes and Militia Rates', in Peter Clark, Alan G. T. Smith, and Nicholas Tyacke (eds.), *English Commonwealth 1547–1640: Essays in Politics and Society Presented to Joel Hurstfield* (Leicester, 1979), 100. For the intention of someone in Crown circles to achieve a new military statute 'for the use of the moderne warres', see Huntington Library, Ellesmere MS 2616.

[11] Russell, *1621–9*, pp. 385–6, and sources there cited.

[12] *CSPD 1638–9*, vol. ccccxv, no. 17.

[13] Ibid., vol. ccccxiii, no. 65.

find him more faithful earthly attendants. If it should ever become generally recognized that it was possible to desert with impunity, the King would indeed need a guard of heavenly angels.[14]

At any time, the prevention of this sort of breakdown of obedience depended on ceaseless vigilance by the Privy Council. The summoning of defaulters before the Council was the driving force which made the whole system work, and the Council was suffering from the fact that it could not make everything top priority. Since 1634 the Privy Council had been giving top priority to the enforcement of Ship Money, and something had had to be sacrificed to create the time which was spent on censuring the constables of Paddington, Harrow, Pinner, Ealing, and Perivale, and innumerable other such figures. That something was probably often the militia. The militia system easily tended to rust in time of peace, and it seems likely that in the years 1634–9 it had been allowed to become even more rusty than usual: the number of muster defaulters recorded as appearing before the Council in these years is remarkably small.

If the Council tried to correct this imbalance, it only found it was paying another penalty instead: a drop in the yield of Ship Money when the priority given to that declined. In April 1639 the sheriff of Northamptonshire reported on his difficulties with Ship Money: 'I have been willing to deal with the constables in a more amicable way, in regard of their much trouble in raising men and money about the Scottish war, and the rather for that they are used as immediate instruments in that service'.[15] Sir Anthony Irby, the godly sheriff of Lincolnshire, was a man who could have been suspected of disaffection to the service, yet when he told the Privy Council in May that his Ship Money accounts were delayed because he had been busy with musters, the Privy Council could not deny the truth of what he said, and gave him more time.[16] The yields of Ship Money were already on a falling graph, which follows after, first, a 20 per cent rise in food prices, and second, the circulation of Hutton and Croke's judgements against the King. A further fall following a relaxation in pressure at such a key psychological moment was not going to help with the financing of war. There is perhaps no time in the century when it is clearer that the administrative system suffered from inadequate delegation: the Privy Council had too much to do even before it tackled any of its functions as a major policy-making body.

[14] Huntington Library, Stowe Temple MS 1876–96 (17 June 1639). I am grateful to Dr R. P. Cust for drawing my attention to this MS.
[15] CSPD 1639, vol. ccccxvii, no. 5.
[16] Ibid., vol. ccccxxi, no. 83.

Perhaps the most serious logistical failure in both Bishops' Wars was in the supply of arms. Here the trouble appears to have been not merely an immediate shortage of money, but a long-term lack of capacity in the English arms industry. Since 1604 industry had not grown to meet the sort of demands a war was likely to make on its capacity. In 1633 John Browne the gun-founder reminded the King that under James the musket-makers had emigrated to the Low Countries, where their skills were in more demand.[17] By 1639 it appears that not only muskets, but also pikes and many other sorts of arms, could not be made in sufficient quantity in the time available. In 1640 Lord Montague found his attempts to raise arms for the King's service were hampered by the fact that the armourers had been forbidden to work for anyone but the King,[18] and it is probable that other peers had similar difficulties in 1639. The English armourers' attempts to increase capacity are unlikely to have been helped by the fact that the Council's top priority was to keep down prices. The arms which were acquired from county stocks do not appear to have fitted the bill: the arms which were taken from Cambridgeshire were reported to be neither fashionable nor service-able, and some of the arms which reached the front were said to be of such poor quality that they could be pierced with a bodkin.[19]

The Ordnance Office was forced to buy the bulk of its arms from abroad. In June 1638 Charles reported to Hamilton that he had ordered arms from Holland for 10,000 foot and 2,000 horse, while Strafford, arming his Irish army, was also buying in the Netherlands.[20] These orders appear to have suffered from the lack of regular contacts with established suppliers. Many of these arms seem to have been grossly inadequate. In November 1639 Robert Thatcher the King's pike-maker submitted a bill for 36 days' works on imported pikes, made up of 5 days looking over coloured Dutch pikes, and binding them up, 16 days binding up the whole store of pikes, 2 days looking over defective long pikes to be made into short pikes, 8 days viewing Dutch pikes, 1 day viewing pikes brought back from the First Bishops' War, and 5 days sorting out pikes late from Hamburg. The account seems to show that Mr Thatcher lacked adequate resources to do the task in the time available.[21] The Ordnance Office seems to have done its best, but its ordinary estimate of £6,000 a year did not enable it to carry adequate stores in reserve. War budgets, depending on *ad hoc* supplementary

---

[17] *CSPD 1633–4*, vol. cclvi, no. 32. I am grateful to Dr Richard Stewart for much information on the armaments industry under James.

[18] *HMC Buccleuch* I. 282.

[19] *CSPD 1639*, vol. ccccxviii, no. 83; *CSPD 1638–9*, vol. ccccxiii, no. 89.

[20] Hamilton MS 10490; Bodl. MS Carte I, fo. 169.

[21] PRO WO 49/72, fo. 32ᵃ.

estimates, always left the office with a big problem in getting stores together soon enough.[22] Considering the difficulties under which it laboured, the Ordnance Office does not seem to have functioned particularly badly during the Bishops' Wars: its difficulties were those of mounting a sudden war effort on an inadequate peacetime budget. That the armourers had been very wise not to expand their capacity is illustrated by the attempt of the Privy Council, immediately on the news of the Pacification of Berwick, to stop payment on an order for which the tradesmen had already done the work. The Officers of the Ordnance protested vigorously that if this happened, they would lose their credits and reputations with the artificers, and not be any longer able to do the King service.[23]

This story is a reminder of the perennial problem of money behind Stuart war efforts. In the absence of a Parliament or of any major commercial source of credit, Charles financed the First Bishops' War largely out of anticipation and a massive series of loans from Privy councillors, prominent peers, and office-holders.[24] This appears to have served the turn for the First Bishops' War rather better than might have been expected, and shortage of money, though it is a permanent undercurrent, does not appear to have been nearly as serious a problem in the First Bishops' War as it was to be in the Second. When the King's troops reached Berwick, they were still in pay. Apart from the supply of arms, the other major logistical failure of the First Bishops' War appears to have been the commissariat, and especially the supply of drink. It is not clear whether this failure is due to lack of money, late delivery, limited resources of the north of England, or plain inefficiency.

The fleet blockading the Forth, which was an essential part of the plan, could be financed out of Ship Money. Its object was to deprive the Scots of money by exercising a stranglehold on Scottish commerce,[25] and thereby, perhaps, to force the Scots to take up the aggressor's posture by invading England.[26] This was one of the more successful features of the planning of the Bishops' Wars. The fleet suffered the usual complaints about inadequate arms and men not trained to use

[22] This point rests, both on my own analysis of the Ordnance Office records for 1639–40, and on Dr Richard Stewart's work on them in the reigns of Elizabeth and James.

[23] PRO WO 49/110, unfol. (17 June 1639). A note on the bottom of this copy says it was delivered to Secretary Windebank at his house, and that Windebank promised to deliver it to the King the same day.

[24] *CSPD 1638–9*, vol. ccccviii, no. 53, vol. ccccxiii, no. 137, vol. ccccxiv, no. 7, vol. ccccxv, no. 65; *CSPD 1639*, vol. ccccxvii, no. 3, and other refs; G. E. Aylmer, *King's Servants* (1961), 201.

[25] On the blockade, see Hamilton MSS 326.2, 850, 851, 1218; also Rothes, pp. 170–1.

[26] This conjecture is based on a careful reading of Hamilton MSS 711, 718, and other refs: if it is correct, it illustrates how far what was taking place was a trial at the bar of English opinion. This interpretation was directly expressed by Strafford on 24 Aug.; ibid. 1231.

them, but the biggest hazard to the fleet appears to have been smallpox, against which there were no adequate precautions to be taken.[27]

When the King decided to make peace at Berwick in June 1639, he was still at the head of a paid and undefeated army. His decision may have been based in part on awareness of the weaknesses of the system behind him, which seems to have surprised him more than they should have done. Windebank in March reported the King was 'finding the charges and troubles greater than he expected'.[28] It is impossible to say with certainty what impelled the King to make the Pacification of Berwick, since the fact that all the people involved in the decision were in the same place made it unnecessary to put the discussion on paper. However, it seems more likely that the reasons for making peace were political than that they were logistical or military.

One hope in which Charles can be proved to have been disappointed is the hope of entering the First Bishops' War at the head of a Scottish party. In a set of propositions he delivered to Windebank in October 1638, he expressed his hope of support from Huntly, Argyll, Nithsdale, and the Marquess of Douglas, and also said he thought no man would be so mad, when the King's army was in the field, as to hazard life and estate: he believed they would come in to the King if they could be received.[29] It was the same hope he had in Ireland in April 1642, and in England in May 1642: he believed his appearance in the field would be enough to bring victory, since his opponents would not take the risk of fighting him. These assumptions appear to have dominated English planning right up to the army's arrival at Berwick. In January 1639 he gave orders to sell arms to his party in Scotland.[30] In December 1638 Ashburnham expressed the hope that God would appease the rebellious Scots by dividing them among themselves.[31] At the end of March Secretary Coke was beginning to doubt both these assurances and the Scots from whom they originated. He said Douglas, Nithsdale, and Hay were in the King's camp at York, but the King would have to rely on his own power and wisdom to restore obedience in Scotland, and not on their private interest, 'whatsoever they give out of assurance of a great party'.[32] Charles seems to have remained more sanguine: on 25 April he issued a Proclamation drafted by Hay, which, among much else, discharged the Covenanters' vassals of paying rent to their lords. It offered pardon to those who submitted, and once again offered royal assurances that he would not permit any innovation of religion, but would maintain

---

[27] Hamilton MS 11147.
[28] *CSPD 1638–9*, vol. ccccxiv, no. 139.
[29] PRO SP 16/400/65.
[30] *CSPD 1638–9*, vol. ccccix, no. 207.
[31] Ibid., vol. cccciv, no. 117.
[32] PRO SP 16/415/65.

it as it was established by God's law and the laws and constitutions of his several kingdoms: he did not say what he would do if he believed that God's law and Scots law were in conflict.[33] By the middle of May the story of Scottish support was no longer commanding confidence. Edward Norgate, the signet clerk who was with the army, complained that the tales they were told in London that the Scots would disband and run away were 'every day disprov'd'. He said they were told that the King had a great party in Scotland, but nothing was more false. Reporting the startling defection of the Earl of Roxburgh's son to the Covenanters, he said: 'they know not who is sound'.[34] The Earl of Arundel, English Lord General, appears to have kept his hope of a Scottish party until he reached the Border: he wrote to Hamilton on 2 June, saying how strange it was that though the King had been there in person for a week, none had come out of Scotland to submit themselves. He was still saying hopefully that 'if the cheefe be with us, we shall reduce the rest by him', but he knew by then that it was not going to happen, and could console himself only by asking Hamilton to send him some good oysters from the Forth.[35]

It was this shock of discovering that the King's Scottish party had evaporated which was the immediate preliminary to the Pacification of Berwick. If it was also the cause of the Pacification, there was good political thinking behind it. Previous history had taught the English that it was much easier to conquer Scotland than to hold it. Moreover, since conquest had such potentially fearsome significance in seventeenth-century political thought, the prospect of holding down Scotland after an unaided English conquest was a daunting one. Successful English conquest depended on a Scottish party to whom power could be handed over once it was complete: like the Scots in England, the English in Scotland had to operate through their 'friends'. The King's friends, through the spring of 1639, were still professing loyalty to him, but were telling him things were worse than he had thought. Sir James Douglas in February warned Windebank that 'you will find all this will not easily settle', while the King's more loud-mouthed supporters, like Huntly and Nithsdale, were finding they were unable to make head against the tide. The failure of most of his Scottish friends to defend their own castles was a powerful warning to the King.[36]

The King also knew, by the time he came to Berwick, that three plans for foreign help had fallen through. The first of these was the plan for an Irish army, to be raised by the Earl of Antrim. This plan was suggested

[33] *CSPD 1639*, vol. ccccxviii, no. 50.
[34] PRO SP 16/421/34.
[35] Hamilton MS 1066.
[36] *CSPD 1638–9*, vol. ccccxiii, no. 101.

to the King by Hamilton in June 1638, and also leaked by him to the Covenanters as a threat to induce compliance in negotiation. Antrim, who was a Macdonnell in Ireland and a Macdonald in Scotland, had a claim to a considerable amount of Scottish land, in which he was already taking an active interest. The hope of occupying this land might enable him to recruit a force of his clansmen who could take the Covenanters in the rear.[37] The King in October 1638 was apparently relying on this plan, but its only actual effect was to drive Argyll, the other claimant to the Scottish land Antrim wanted, into the arms of the Covenanters. As Baillie reflected, the ways of Providence were indeed strange. The Covenanters' success in capturing the castle and harbour of Dumbarton was clearly one of the reasons why this plan fell through, but not all the reasons for its failure are clear.[38]

The second plan was for the help of a body of regular Spanish troops from the Netherlands, to be given in return for leave for the Spaniards to recruit soldiers in Ireland. The diplomatic threads of this plan were held by Secretary Windebank operating through Colonel Gage. The Spaniards politely declined, on the ground that they did not believe English army bread-ovens met the standards to which Spanish soldiers were accustomed. The seriousness of the English request is illustrated by a request in the State Papers for a report on bread-ovens. Once again, it tells us something about Caroline political methods that this highly provocative plan was communicated by Hamilton to the Covenanters, in the hope of bringing them to more flexibility in negotiation. The large number of leaks characteristic of Caroline plotting seems not to have been an accident: the usual object of these plots was to deter their potential victims, and it was only when the deterrent failed that the King actually had to contemplate using it.[39] A third plan, for Dutch help, was advanced by the King himself, and brusquely turned down by the Prince of Orange.[40]

By the time the King reached Berwick, he knew he would have to depend exclusively on the political loyalty of the English. From the beginning, the Council had realized that there could be a problem with the loyalty of the English: Hamilton had told the King so in June 1638,

---

[37] Hamilton MS 10488; see also ibid. 652 (Antrim to Hamilton, 14 Jan. 1638/9?). Antrim asked for arms and munitions for 2,000 men. For Hamilton's readiness to use the threat of this army as a diplomatic weapon, see Rothes, p. 137. See also Stevenson, pp. 99–100.

[38] PRO SP 16/400/65; Baillie, i. 192–3; Stevenson, pp. 128, 141.

[39] Hibbard, pp. 105–7; *Clarendon SP* ii. 19 ff.; *CSPD 1638–9*, vol. ccccxiv, no. 107; Baillie, i. 80. I am grateful to Prof. Hibbard for intriguing discussions of the sieve-like character of Caroline plotting. It must tell us something that while the Covenanters were told of the proposal, the Councillors were not.

[40] Groen Van Prinsterer, p. 144 (Prince of Orange to Charles I, 10 Mar. 1639, New Style). The making of almost simultaneous requests to the Spaniards and the Dutch illustrates an important point about Caroline diplomacy.

and in November 1638 a committee of the Council of War decided, 'for better preparing the hearts and affections of his Majesty's subjects to serve him in a business of so great importance', to call in a number of unpopular patents.[41] The King and Council knew they had a problem, not only with general disaffection, but also with a limited number of people whose sympathies were actively pro-Scottish. It is hard to assess the strength of this feeling, since much of it remained latent. What is perhaps not so easy to remember is that it was even harder for the King to make this assessment than it is for us. Seditious words, because they were punishable, were not uttered when the wrong people were thought to be listening. The King could not read a lot of private correspondence which is open to us, and Secretary Windebank, who worked tirelessly to penetrate the pro-Scottish network in England, could never know for certain in which cases he had failed. It is this perpetual uncertainty which made the English Council, during both the Bishops' Wars, liable to sudden losses of nerve and to regular looking over its shoulder for domestic opposition.

The Countess of Westmoreland, in an unsolicited letter to Secretary Windebank on 6 May, spelt out many of these points with remarkable clarity. After what may perhaps be taken as a ritual condemnation of the Scots, she warned him 'how uncertainly a warre wilbe maintained, wch is to be mantained out of prerogative, imposition and voluntarie contributions, they know our divisions, and the strength of ther own combination, and yt they have a party amongst us, and we have non amongst them'. After reminding him that English men and horses were unused to war, she argued that if the King continued the attempt to restore his honour 'the dishoner is likely to be increased, and the consequence the ruine to this kingdome; when things are brought to an ill passe, a bad composition is better than a wors'. There is surely an implied criticism of the King in the suggestion that they should employ 'temperate men of our own nation' to negotiate with the Scots, 'by wch it may appeere his matie intends to governe noe other ways but by the laws of yt kingdome'. Within the next two years, every prophecy in this letter had proved true.[42]

None of these doubts and fears should be held to imply any large amount of active disaffection among the peers and gentry who retained the formal responsibility for managing the war effort. Lords-Lieutenant and Deputy-Lieutenants, like modern Vice-Chancellors, accepted that co-operation was the price of dialogue. People who were to be at the

---

[41] *CSPD 1638–9*, vol. cccci, no. 59.

[42] PRO SP 16/420/70. The remark about horses being unused to war is a reminder that this was a general's daughter writing. She was daughter of Sir Horatio Vere, and widow of Sir Roger Townshend. Windebank, fortunately, ignored the Countess's injunction to burn the letter.

centre of the Scottish party in 1640–1 went on raising the militia, collecting coat and conduct money, and levying Ship Money with no more evident foot-dragging than anyone else. Indeed, it is possible, because they had to prove their loyalty, that such people worked harder at the war effort than anyone else, provoking the Scots to occasional fears that their 'friends' might prove a broken reed. The Earl of Essex, Lieutenant-General in the King's army, was to be one of the most dedicated pro-Scots in London from 1640 through to 1645–6, but when the Scots wrote to him, he forwarded their letter unopened to the King.[43] Sir Robert Harley, perhaps encouraged by the fact that his brother-in-law Lord Conway was commanding in the front line at Newcastle, appears to have done his best as Deputy-Lieutenant in Herefordshire. Among the Lords-Lieutenant, Bedford in Devon and Warwick in Essex were among the most effective as well as among the most potentially pro-Scottish. In Somerset, the war effort was being helped on by Sir Thomas Wroth, who had been expecting martyrdom in 1635. The King was bound to wonder how long the co-operation of such people might last, and the knowledge of their existence was a powerful incentive to avoid a long war.

The Countess of Westmoreland had drawn attention, by implication, to the absence of a Parliament. 1639 was the first occasion since 1323 when England had gone to war without a Parliament.[44] It was also the first occasion since 1629 when events had happened which, by established political convention, demanded the calling of a Parliament. It is likely that a lot of people who had assumed during the 1630s that another Parliament would be called when it became necessary suddenly began to wonder whether the absence of a Parliament might be intended to be something permanent. There is not much overt demand for a Parliament in 1639, since Charles in his Proclamation of 1629 had made it very plain that 'we shall account it presumption for any to prescribe any time unto us for Parliaments'.[45] Bearing in mind the risks of talking about Parliaments, we are perhaps entitled to treat what we find in 1639 as the tip of an iceberg. Lord Montague, in a note intended only for his own eyes, wrote: 'I would his Majesty had taken the advice of his common council before he had undertaken this war'.[46] Montague, an essentially middle-of-the-road man with a strong attachment to correct procedure, may have spoken for a considerable body of opinion.

[43] Baillie, i. 204. See ch. 2 p. 27 above for Baillie's comments.

[44] I am grateful to Dr J. R. L. Highfield and Prof. Michael Prestwich for advice on this point. The Scottish campaign of 1400 is an alternative candidate, but on this occasion, the absence of a Parliament arose only from Henry IV's promise not to ask for a subsidy.

[45] Larkin, p. 228.

[46] Esther Cope, *Life of a Public Man: Edward, First Baron Montagu of Boughton* (American Philosophical Society, 142, Philadelphia, 1981), 162.

An anonymous paper circulating late in 1638 probably spoke for many fewer people, but was more alarming. It complained that the ancient happy government by Parliament was altogether despised, and urged to make against the King's advantage. In a passage none the less plain for being oblique, it observed that had King Richard been as strong in the people's hearts as Duke Henry, he had never been deposed.[47]

Perhaps the most startling evidence is that two people took the risk of arguing for a Parliament to the King's face and in public. That both of them did so in the camp at Berwick can only have heightened the dramatic effect. The first was an imprudent Kentishman called Sir Thomas Wilford, who told the King he should have called a Parliament, and said that 'if you think to make a warr with yr owne purse, you deceive yourself'. The King restrainedly confined himself to observing that 'they were fools the last Parliament'.[48] The other was a much more significant figure: the Earl of Bristol. He spoke publicly in camp of the ground of the quarrel, and of a Parliament, and conveyed the startling information that most of the Lords in the King's camp, both Councillors and others, were resolved to petition for a Parliament. The King responded to this with a courtesy which perhaps shows how seriously he took the threat which it implied, and spoke privately to Bristol for an hour.[49] The next day he began negotiating for peace.

It would be wrong to portray the First Bishops' War as opposed by a united nation: it was not. Its tendency was to polarize the country between small groups of pro- and anti-Scots, and to cause acute alarm to a large middle group, of which Bristol and Montague could be taken as representatives. To them, whichever side they intended to occupy if polarization became established, it was the polarization itself which represented the real danger. Their object was to prevent it if they could. In making the attempt, they had to reckon with the feelings of the anti-Scots, as well as of the pro-Scots. A number of people, including Viscount Falkland, later a prominent Long Parliament member, had enlisted as volunteers against the Scots. Tom Elliot, one of the Grooms of the Bedchamber, was nearly led into a duel with the Earl of Roxburgh's son by his desire to maintain that Covenanters were all traitors.[50] Thomas Windebank, the Secretary's son was more verbose:

We have had a most cold, wet and long time of living in the field, but kept ourselves warm with the hopes of rubbing, fubbing and scrubbing those

[47] PRO SP 16/401/19.1. This document also took occasion to remember Felton. There is no clue to its provenance. See also W. Hunt, *Puritan Moment* (Cambridge, Mass., 1983), 278.

[48] PRO SP 16/422/65.

[49] Ibid. 16/423/67. Bristol had been restored to favour in Aug. 1637, and gave the credit to Holland: Plas Newydd MSS, Box XII (Bristol to Holland, 8 Aug. 1637). It is tempting to see the hand of Holland behind Bristol's intervention.

[50] *CSPD 1639*, vol. ccccxvii, no. 92, vol. ccccxx, no. 109.

scurvy, filthy, dirty, nasty, lousy, itchy, scabby, shitten, stinking, slovenly, snotty-nosed, logger-headed, foolish, insolent, proud, beggarly, impertinent, absurd, grout-headed, villainous, barbarous, beastial, false, lying, roguish, devilish, long-eared, short-haired, damnable, atheistical, puritanical crew of the Scottish Covenant. But now [*he concluded, in palpable disappointment*], there is peace in Israel.

Any attempt at a serious *rapprochement* with the Scots was likely to show up a good deal more such feeling, and it was a force with which any King had to reckon.[51]

There are not very many people of standing who can be clearly labelled as pro- or anti-Scottish in the First Bishops' War, but it is striking that among those who can be labelled, their attitudes in all cases correlate with their later allegiance in the Civil War. For example, it helps to explain the Parliamentarian sympathies of Secretary Coke, who was a good pro-Dort Calvinist, to discover that when he met Alexander Henderson at Berwick, he concluded that 'in all his speeches you may find as much devotion, wisdom, humility and obedience as can be wished for in an honest man and a good subject'. The Earl of Stamford, whose Parliamentarian allegiance has needed explanation, also decided at Berwick that Henderson and his colleagues were 'holy and blessed men, of admirable, transcendent and seraphical learning, and say grace longer and better than our campestral chaplains, that ride before our regiments taking tobacco'.[52] It is only necessary to compare this with the remarks of Thomas Windebank to see the Scots' capacity for polarizing English opinion.

Among the peers, who were summoned collectively to York to serve in the war, only Saye and Brooke refused. Their initial replies were a plain refusal from Saye, and a call for a Parliament from Brooke, but after consultation, they sent a second reply claiming that they were only obliged to serve the King within the kingdom of England, and not beyond the borders.[53] At least two other peers seem to have seriously contemplated refusal. Viscount Mandeville was only induced to go by his father's threat to disinherit him if he did not.[54] The Earl of Boling-broke was reported to have sent a joint reply with Saye, and probably only decided not to refuse at the last moment. His eventual reply, stressing his years, his infirmities, and the great burden on his estate, and saying he would come in such sort as the short time and his estate would permit, thus becomes a rare example where we can see behind

[51] *CSPD* 1639, vol. ccccxxiv, no. 50, also vol. ccccxxv, no. 46, and other refs.

[52] Ibid. vol. ccccxxiv, no. 28 (Norgate to Read, 19 June 1639).

[53] PRO SP 16/413/117. The military oath at York, which Saye and Brooke were ultimately committed for refusing, was devised by Hamilton. Hamilton MS 10531 (Charles to Hamilton, 2 Apr. 1639); 'for your military oath I lyke it extreme well'.

[54] Esther Cope, *Life of a Public Man*, p. 168.

the polite phrases in which peers and gentlemen replied to unwelcome requests from the Crown.[55]

Brilliana Harley, writing to her son at Oxford, could afford to be a little more frank, but did not have the confidence in the posts to be as frank as she wished. She wrote:

But if we fight with Scotland, and are ingaged in that ware, then a foren enimy may take his time of advantage. The caus is the Lords; and He will worke for his owne glorye. Deare Ned, you may remember I have offten spoken to you about theas times; and my deare Ned, would I weare with you one day, to open my minde more largly than I can by rwiteing.[56]

Brilliana did not say whose cause was the Lord's, but it is improbable that she meant the cause of Charles I. Thomas Smith, Northumberland's secretary in the Admiralty, wrote 'I beseech God to open his Majesty's eyes to know his friends from his foes'.[57] By contrast, Sir John Pennington, the recipient of this effusion, thought that 'there was never a greater rebellion heard of, or more unjust'.[58] In both cases, their stance on this issue is a good predictor for the course they took when they began to diverge on English affairs in the autumn of 1641.

The polarizing possibilities of this issue were increased by the divergence about whom to blame for the war. There was a general agreement in deploring the war, which made the question whether Laud or the Scots should be blamed for its outbreak the more divisive. A gentleman of Burnham, Bucks. was accused of saying that 'I care not for my lord of Canterbury, for he has been the occasion of this strife between the Scots and us, and I care not if he heard me'.[59] By contrast, Robert Sibthorpe the Laudian clergyman lamented the prospects 'if *bellum episcopale*, as the say some stile it, be not ended, and *rebellio Puritanica*, for soe I know it may be truly stiled, be not subdued, from which good Lord deliver us'. Sibthorpe was not alone in his tendency to turn to displacement aggression: just as he wanted to turn on the 'Puritans', as the local representatives of the cause which was provoking so much trouble, so his neighbours who belonged to 'the faction', set watches against a supposed plan by the papists to fire Kettering.[60] The emotions stirred by the Bishops' Wars were liable to turn Englishmen against each other.

In Exeter, when the King's Proclamation against the Scots was read,

[55] *CSPD 1638–9*, vol. ccccxii, no. 134; PRO SP 16/413/117.
[56] *Letters of Lady Brilliana Harley*, ed. T. T. Lewis (Camden Society[1], 51, 1853), 30.
[57] *CSPD 1639*, vol. ccccxxi, no. 142, also vol. ccccxiii, no. 56.
[58] Ibid., vol. ccccxxi, no. 128.
[59] Ibid., vol. ccccxxii, no. 113.
[60] Huntington Library, Stowe Temple MS 1876–96 (19 Apr. and 16 May 1639); also *CSPD 1638–9*, vol. ccccvi, no. 82, vol. ccccxiv, no. 17; *CSPD 1639*, vol. ccccxvii, no. 97, vol. ccccxxiii, no. 83, and other refs.

the Mayor and two Aldermen were charged with keeping their hats on. Two of them appeared, and said that they had taken their hats off at first, but had put them on again because the church was very cold, but the third, Ignatius Jordan, refused to appear before the Council or make any gesture of submission, sending only a medical certificate claiming that because he was eighty, he was too weak and infirm to attend the Privy Council.[61] In Hertford, a judge in an ecclesiastical court who said the Scots were traitors was answered by a local shoemaker: 'you shall answer for those words at the last day'.[62] At Ware, an anonymous libel proposed carrying Laud to the Scots, and expressed the fear of being eaten up with superstition and idolatry, and another claimed that England was fighting the Scots for not being idolatrous and having no Mass.[63]

At Kilsby, Northamptonshire, the vicar's attempts to preach obedience seem to have led to his usual misfortunes. When he spoke against the Scots' rebellion, he was interrupted by a parishioner saying the King must yield to them, and when he said to some neighbours that he hoped the King would quell the Scots, another said: 'perhaps the will of God is, that England's pride should have a fall'.[64] Clearly, the polarization between pro- and anti-Scots was generating a good deal of public debate, and some of it was taking alarming directions. At Kilgerran, Pembrokeshire, a man was charged with saying: 'King James was wise and learned, but King Charles wants a good headpiece'.[65]

Some of this debate seems to have centred on the most dangerous issue in early modern Europe, the proper limits of obedience to God and man. A certain Roger Moore of Middleton was accused of saying that if the King commanded him to turn papist, or do a thing against his conscience, he would rise up against him and kill him.[66] In Newcastle, where there seems to have been an organized body of Covenanter sympathizers, we get a rare glimpse of a debate over a pint of wine. One man said 'beshrew the Scots that stand out against the King, for they are likely to put us to a great deal of charge, and it is likely we shall all go and fight against them'. Another replied that 'they did nothing but in defence of their own right and maintenance of the Gospel, and did but defend themselves against those that would have brought in popery and idolatry amongst them'. He was asked, naturally enough, whether he was willing to fight against the Covenanters, and replied 'no, for unless his conscience moved him to it, he would not fight for any prince in

[61] *CSPD 1639*, vol. ccccxx, no. 157, vol. ccccxvii, no. 113.
[62] Ibid., vol. ccccxx, no. 138.
[63] *CSPD 1638-9*, vol. ccccxv, no. 100; *CSPD 1639-40*, vol. ccccxxxviii, no. 93.
[64] PRO SP 16/438/92.
[65] *CSPD 1639*, vol. ccccxxvi, no. 41.
[66] *CSPD 1638-9*, vol. cccciv, no. 64.

Christendom'.[67] These exchanges illustrate why governments had cause to fear religious division, and why Charles had cause to dislike the notion of conditional allegiance, but they also illustrate why attempts to enforce unity of religion were in the end bound to fail.

It is useless to attempt an estimate of the proportions of people adhering to each of these points of view: all the sources show clearly is that England was becoming a more divided country. The only source we have which approaches a controlled sample also offers us a pre-selected one: this is the replies by members of the peerage summoned to attend with horse and armour at York.

These replies, with two exceptions, stop short of outright refusal, but they indicate a remarkable lack of enthusiasm. If they were to be believed, the peers' replies would indicate an economic 'crisis of the aristocracy' graver than anything Professor Stone has ever alleged. Lord Willoughby of Parham, a future Parliamentarian, said that because of the shortness of time and the weakness of his estate, he could not be equipped as the King wished, but he would come. Lord Howard of Escrick, one of the most committed pro-Scots of two years later, said he would come with such equipage as his time and fortune would permit. Lord Montagu, who was seventy-six, was entitled to say that he could not come because of want of health and difficulty in getting arms, and offered £1,000 instead:[68] it is only from his private papers that we know he believed the cause of the war was the idolatry of the English.[69]

Yet not all of these reserved phrases indicate lack of sympathy for the cause of the war, since they come also from people whose political instincts were thoroughly anti-Scottish. Lord Herbert of Cherbury, for example, sent a reply which encapsulated the sense of ill-usage of a minor royal servant. He said the King still owed him £2,500 for his expenses as ambassador in 1624, he had been at great charge for writing the Rhé expedition in Latin and English, for keeping scholars and clerks for copying records for his history of Henry VIII, and for the debts of an unthrifty son—but he would come. Lord Maynard, a rare lay Arminian, felt a similar sense of grievance: he said the King had had £900 from him

---

[67] Ibid., vol. ccccxiii, no. 42.1, 42.2. The men accused denied the words. On Covenanter sympathizers in Newcastle, see Roger Howell, jun., *Newcastle upon Tyne and the Puritan Revolution* (Oxford, 1967), 97–107, and Hamilton MS 691. The more prudent Covenanter sympathizers caused more difficulty than the rash ones. Dr Robert Jenison, later a member of the Westminster Assembly, was 'something cool' when required by Sir Jacob Astley to preach obedience. He preached, as asked, on Rom. 13: 1, the famous non-resistance text, but he also preached on the victory of King Asa over the Ethiopians because he had cut down idols, and on Ps. 33: 16 'there is no king saved by the multitude of an host'. When challenged, he said he was only talking of man's weakness without God: *CSPD 1638–9*, vol. ccccxiii, no. 32; PRO SP 16/415/7 and 8.

[68] PRO SP 16/413/117 is Nicholas's calendar of the peers' replies. Nicholas sometimes edited out the peers' more colourful comments, for which see *CSPD 1638–9*, vol. ccccxii *passim*.

[69] Cope, *Life of a Public Man*, p. 163.

in three years, for which he was paying interest, he had served for twenty-eight years at continual yearly charge, and his fortune was far less than might be supposed—but he would come. Almost the only enthusiastic replies were from recusant peers hoping to recover their place in the sun, and in particular, hoping to recover the right to own their own arms. Lord Brudenell, for example, said his arms had been taken away, and continual rumours were spread of his disaffection, but if he could bring unarmed men, or would be allowed to buy arms out of the King's magazine or from the Netherlands, he would come. The chance given by the Bishops' Wars to the Catholics to take up the pose of the King's most loyal subjects was one many of them embraced with alacrity, but it did neither them nor the King much good.

The King's failure to command the enthusiasm of men like Herbert of Cherbury and Maynard, who should have been his natural supporters, is the key to the story of 1639–40. This was not because of disagreement with the King's religion or political bias: one of these peers was an Arminian and the other an Arminian sympathizer. Nor was it because of any sympathy for the Scots: both detested anything which savoured of 'Puritanism'. The absence of a Parliament may have weighed with some of these men, who were often as attached to legality as their more godly colleagues. It is perhaps more important that many of them still lived in a pre-party universe, and distrusted partisan courses liable to divide the body politic. The frankness with which the King was strengthening his 'party' in Scotland is likely to have alarmed many of them. They did not want this sort of polarization in England. Herbert of Cherbury was an old friend of Sir Robert Harley, and though their friendship had led to a welter of theological recrimination, they do not appear to have acquired a wish to harry each other out of the land.[70] Lord Maynard, even if with occasional difficulty, ran the Essex Lieutenancy in double harness with the Earl of Warwick and it was doubtful whether he could run Essex for long without Warwick's co-operation. This attitude was not confined to peers. John Altham of Gray's Inn, writing to his brother, said: 'the Scots are now wors than ever', but could combine this view with saying: 'but I could wish we were all friends'.[71] The pressure of good neighbourhood in the English countryside, even on political and religious opponents, was very strong indeed. The realization that the phrase 'adversary politics' meant exactly what it said was, for many of them, instinctive.

It is, perhaps, this reluctance to divide England into two opposed

[70] Jacqueline Levy, 'Harleys of Brampton Bryan', Ph.D. thesis (London, 1983), 50 ff.

[71] Altham MSS, vol. i, p. 45 no. 56, and p. 43 no. 52 (10 Aug. and 6 Apr. 1639 respectively). These MSS are still in the possession of the family. The present owner is Group Captain J. B. Altham, CBE, Ivy Cottage, 16 Whittlesford Road, Little Shelford, Cambridgeshire, to whom I owe thanks for permission to read these MSS and to quote from them. I also owe thanks to Dr J. E. Altham and to Mr Joseph Altham.

camps which made so many of the Council so eager to support the peacemaking at Berwick. They were tentative, even in exploring such ideas with each other. When Vane wrote to Hamilton in December 1638, he expressed the fear that the Scottish troubles might end in war, and added 'this puts [me] in mind of good King James and his *beati pacifici*'. It was a plain hint, but one to which Hamilton did not need to react.[72] By the time the Councillors had reached Berwick, they had had enough time to sound each other out to know that they wanted to move Charles to peace. They were, as always, careful of their master's honour, and appreciated that the issue of episcopacy in Scotland needed to be carefully wrapped up. Yet, whatever face-saving formulae might be reached, it is probable that most of the Councillors at Berwick (though not necessarily all of those in London) followed Hamilton and Traquair in believing that the abolition of episcopacy in Scotland was a necessary condition of peace. It seems that they succeeded in convincing Charles of the case for peace, but not of the case for abolishing episcopacy in Scotland.

In doing this, they achieved a worse policy than either they or Charles would have followed if left to themselves. If the King had died, leaving Hamilton and Traquair in control of policy, they would probably have left the Covenanters to abolish episcopacy, and allowed them the security of having no one to quarrel with but each other. They could then have waited, as Richelieu was later to advise Henrietta Maria to do, till the wheel of fortune turned, and the Covenanters had been in power long enough to create a reaction against themselves. This was the natural Jacobean line of policy, and it had considerable promise, if ever employed with enough patience. It would have caused some stirring among the godly of England, hoping to enjoy the same privileges as the Scots, but with no Parliament, and no Scottish army in England, it would have been hard for them to pursue these hopes.

If, on the other hand, Scottish episcopacy was to be preserved at all costs, there was no useful purpose to be served by the Pacification of Berwick. In 1639 the King was in command of an army still in pay, and better armed than it was to be again. If he was ever to fight the Scots, he would have had a much better chance of victory if he had fought them in 1639 than he was to have in 1640. If he had fought in 1639, he would have suffered for lack of a Parliament, but not nearly as much as he was to do the next year by fighting in the face of the refusal of a Parliament to finance the war. There was no useful purpose served by allowing a

---

[72] Hamilton MS 10799. It is interesting to compare this letter with Hamilton MS 10543 (Charles to Hamilton, 18 Apr. 1639), in which he said that he had shared Hamilton's dispatch with Arundel and Vane, for he dared trust no other. In 1642 these three people Charles trusted emerged as two neutrals and a Parliamentarian.

Parliament to give free publicity to all the grievances, if he was going to do nothing to meet them, and was going to obtain no supply. Office-holders' credit was a wasting asset, so if he was to fight a second time, he was much more likely to need a Parliament than he was the first time. Also, as Secretary Windebank perceptively remarked, the fact that all the drama of the first call to arms had led to nothing made people less eager to respond to the second. An unsuccessful Parliament was far worse than none. Similarly, Charles's habit of taking half a policy from his moderate Councillors, without carrying through the measures which would have made that policy consistent and workable, was worse than having no counsel at all.

II The Short Parliament

Attempts at peacemaking between Charles and the Scots continued for some while after the Scottish Parliament of 1639, but it was never likely that they would achieve much success, and those who conducted them did so more to discharge their consciences, or to place blame for break-down elsewhere, than because they really believed peace might be achieved. In July 1639 Holland wrote to Mandeville, one of the peers who had considered refusing to serve in the First Bishops' War, complaining: 'God forgive them that thus do advise our master to spoil and destroy this honourable and happy accommodation as he might have used it'.[73] It is hard to avoid the suspicion that Holland was trying to position himself so that he should emerge in the clear in an eventual inquest. Another visit to London by Traquair, in December 1639, resulted only in the agreement of the English Privy Council in favour of war. Traquair, because of the story he told on this visit, was ultimately cast by the Covenanters as the chief scapegoat for the renewal of Bishops' Wars in 1640, but he does not look very convincing in the part.

Only Wentworth, who frankly avowed the opinion that Scotland should be controlled by the English Privy Council as a dependency, seemed willing to volunteer for the part of scapegoat.[74] If the Scots knew of this opinion, it would go a long way to explain their later implacable hostility to him. Most of the Council accepted, though with increasing irritation, that since Scottish policy was *ultra vires* for an English Council, they could contribute nothing but logistical advice on how to suppress rebellion in Scotland: how to prevent rebellion from taking place was a question on which they were not competent to advise. Charles's scruples (or sense of shame) prevented him from so

---

[73] *HMC Eighth Report*, 1. 55.
[74] Stevenson, p. 100; Knowler, ii. 190–2. For a fuller narrative of these months than is attempted here, see Stevenson, pp. 162–82 and Gardiner, *History*, ix. 56–83.

much as discussing Scottish policy with most of them, and Northumberland said in September 1639 that 'the king is so reserved that unlesse it be to the Arch.bish [*sic*] or Hamilton he communicats nothing of the affares in Scotland, so that we are as great strangers to all those proceedings as if we lived att Constantinople'. He said he had learnt *by private letters* that they went on in rebellion.[75] This may be the ground of an intense but unexplained hostility which grew up between Northumberland and Hamilton. If so, it is ironic, since it seems likely that, had Northumberland known what Hamilton was doing, he would have approved of most of it.

The Covenanters themselves made one last attempt to send commissioners to England but whether to make peace, or, as Charles and Laud suspected, to encourage dissent in England, is not entirely clear. They were kept waiting over a month before they were allowed to see the King, who then only told them to give their demands in writing to Traquair. The Covenanters objected that they could only clear themselves by accusing Traquair, and provoked the King to reply that they were trying to give him the law when they should be taking it from him. He then walked out. The Covenanters, thinking he was taking counsel, waited, but when they finally went to look for him, they found him playing trictrac with Hamilton.[76] When they finally did obtain a hearing, it merely covered the same ground which had been covered at Berwick, with a few new disagreements added about the power to prorogue the Scottish Parliament. Loudoun again tried to 'distinguish between the church and state, this only in Scotland, a necessary distinction in Scotland', but Charles seems to have been even less interested than before in differences between English and Scottish institutions. The discouragement led to the rare event of Loudoun losing a debating point to Laud. Loudoun asked him not to meddle with the business of the kirk of Scotland, 'any more than they meddled with that of England', to which Laud replied, 'in some passion', that that request was easily granted.[77] Others seem to have sensed that Charles was reacting increasingly as a King of England. Ambassadors do not choose their titles at random, but the French Ambassador reported on 15/25 April 1640 that

il y a cinq ou six jours que le Comte de Morton et Traquair essayèrent de porter le Roy de la Grande Bretagne à quelque accommodement avec l'Ecosse; mais le Roy d'Angleterre les tesmoigna qu'il perdroit l'Angleterre ou qu'il les puniroit.[78]

[75] KAO De L'Isle and Dudley MSS U 1475 C 85/2.

[76] PRO 31/3/72, p. 53. Trictrac was an old form of backgammon. The Scots' presumption in going to look for the King is another example of their indifference to English standards of court ceremony.

[77] PRO SP 16/447/19 and 26.

[78] PRO 31/3/72, p. 112.

For practical purposes, the decision to renew the war had been taken well before this in December 1639. That decision led immediately to a discussion of how a new war should be financed. Northumberland, reporting the meetings of the relevant Council committee to his brother-in-law the Earl of Leicester, was careful to explain how limited their brief had been: 'to consider by what meanes the rebellious Scotts should be brought to obedience'. The alternatives, as the committee saw it, were only two: money could be raised 'by the ordinarie way of Parliament, or by extraordinary ways of power'. They agreed that the sum they needed was about a million pounds, a realistic estimate which, in the end, they overspent by some 5 to 10 per cent in the Second Bishops' War. 'To persuade a Parlament to furnish the King presently wth so much was conceaved a very unlikely thing'. On the other hand, when they examined the King's revenue, they found it so anticipated 'as little could be hoped from thence'. Others proposed excises, forcing each county to maintain a set number of men while the war lasted, and such ways, but these met with 'weightie objections'—probably taking the form of arguments that it would be impossible to collect the money. As a result, 'those Lords that were all this while most averse to Parlaments, did now begin to advise the kings makeing triall of his people in Parlament, *before* he used any way of power', and 'the King was soone gained'.[79]

This must have been a discouraging discussion: the strength of each case was in the impossibilities it pointed out in the other, and in this, each case was correct. It should be stressed that the King was not *consulting* his Parliament: he did not even intend to offer them the option of refusing. Like his contemporary Hobson, the King was offering the show of a choice. Windebank, writing to the Ambassador in Madrid the day after Northumberland's letter, made this crystal clear:

the Lords being desirous that the King and his people should meet if it were possible, in the ancient and ordinary way of Parliament, rather than any other, were of opinion his Majesty should make trial of that once more, that so he might leave his people without excuse, and have wherewithal to justify himself to God and the world, that in his own inclination he desired the old way: but that if his people should not cheerfully, according to their duties, meet him in that exigent when his kingdom and person are in apparent danger, the world might see he is forced, contrary to his own inclination, to use extraordinary

[79] KAO De L'Isle and Dudley MSS C 85/4: my italics. The estimate of spending is based on PRO E 403/2813, orders and warrants for payments on patents and privy seals, Michaelmas 1639–Easter 1640. It is not advanced with any confidence, since it is almost impossible to arrive at sensible criteria for inclusion and exclusion under the heading of war expenditure. In particular, criteria for inclusion or exclusion of naval expenditure are beyond anyone but a specialist naval historian. My own inclusions and exclusions are arbitrary.

means, rather than by the peevishness of some few factious spirits, to suffer his state and government to be lost.

As the French Ambassador more pithily put it, Charles intended to hold a 'Parlement à sa mode'.[80]

There is here a vital difference of perspective between a British King on the one hand, and an English Parliament and Council on the other. For an English Parliament, this was to be a request for subsidies to finance a foreign war, and though Parliaments did not normally refuse such requests outright, they did regard the propriety of foreign wars as a legitimate matter for discussion: they expected at least the ritual of consultation to take place. For the King, on the other hand, he was suppressing a domestic rebellion, and he saw no more need to take counsel on whether he should suppress it than Henry VIII had seen to take counsel on whether he should suppress the Pilgrimage of Grace. Any doubt about whether rebellion should be suppressed was potentially treasonable. The Council, who had never succeeded in crossing this gulf, were led along into speaking with their master's voice, while many of them probably hoped that a Parliament would be more successful than they had been.

Once again, they had sold Charles half a policy: there was a lot to be said for holding a successful Parliament, and as always, the strongest part of the case was in political, and not financial, terms. A successful Parliament would not finance the war effort, but it would make it appear an effort of the country as a whole. It would tar resistance with the brush of disloyalty, and would deprive the Scots of their strongest propaganda point: the appeal to English dissidents. The relief shown by the Scots, in their printed pamphlets, at the ultimate outcome of the Short Parliament is a measure of how much they had to lose if it had gone the other way. Yet, if the Councillors were to reap the benefits of calling a Parliament, they would have had to convince Charles that no Parliament ever responded to being asked to act in this way as a rubber stamp. After eleven years without a Parliament, there was a considerable amount of lost face, as well as a great accumulation of grievances, and no self-respecting member of Parliament could afford to agree simply to vote the King money and go home. A Parliament asked to vote supply without any redress of grievances, after an eleven-year interval, was likely to be an unsuccessful Parliament. As at Berwick, the Councillors had persuaded Charles of too little, or of too much.

Meanwhile, the news that there was to be a Parliament led, as could have been predicted, to a fall in the yield of Ship Money. The sheriff of Berkshire reported that 'I conceive the main ground of slackness at this

---

[80] Gardiner, *History*, ix. 76; *Clarendon SP* ii. 81; PRO 31/3/71, p. 154.

present more than heretofore is the expectation they have of the Parliament, that it will be reported to the King as a grievance, whereby they hope to obtain a remission thereof'.[81] This idea that Ship Money and a Parliament were alternatives was shared by others. Edward Nicholas, Clerk of the Council, said that 'the writs for levying Ship Money this next year are sent out, and shall proceed, notwithstanding the assembling of a Parliament, which is much marvelled at by many discreet and well-affected men'. From a loyal clerk like Nicholas, this was a very strong criticism indeed. On the prospects for the Parliament, he confined himself to saying: 'I pray God it may succeed as well for the good of the kingdom as the news of it is acceptable to all men in this kingdom'.[82] Sir Henry Vane, who succeeded to the Secretaryship when Sir John Coke was finally induced to retire, invited his correspondent Sir Thomas Roe to read between the lines: he said the King did not doubt of the 'particular contentment' he would get from the Parliament, notwithstanding rumours of the contrary by 'ill-affected persons'. Vane was telling Roe, between the lines, that the King had set a collision course, and regarded attempts to tell him so as disloyalty.[83]

It is not useful to attempt to take the political temperature in early seventeenth-century England by a study of elections: Professor Kishlansky is undoubtedly right that the major objective was normally to avoid a contest, and when we find a contest, we should be asking 'what went wrong?' In normal times, early Stuart elections were not primarily about policy: they were about status. There were many people who would have been perfectly happy not to sit, who nevertheless could not accept the loss of face in allowing their candidatures to go before their social inferiors and be rejected. The object of the leading gentry in most counties was not to secure the return of like-minded candidates: it was to ensure that there were no more candidates than there were seats. Professor Kishlansky is also right in identifying the years 1640–60 as the years in which this attitude suffered a sea-change in the face of partisan electioneering of the type we have since become used to.[84] In a society dedicated to achieving a show of unity, those who approached elections in a partisan way were fighting against opponents who had one hand tied behind their backs. Since it was often the godly who had the

---

[81] *CSPD 1639–40*, vol. ccccxlix no. 8, also no. 23, and vol. ccccxlv, nos. 1, 49, 52, 54.

[82] Ibid., vol. ccccxxxv, no. 64 (Nicholas to Pennington, 12 Dec. 1639). In this letter, Nicholas allowed himself one of his rare light touches: he reported that the Countess of Kent was so distressed at the death of her husband that Mr Selden (who had been her lover for many years) 'cannot comfort her'.

[83] Ibid., vol. ccccxlvi, no. 3.

[84] Mark Kishlansky, *Parliamentary Selection* (Cambridge, 1987), 5–6, 9–21, 105–111, and other refs. This was written before I had seen R. P. Cust, 'Politics and the Electorate in the 1620s', in id. and Ann Hughes (eds.), *Conflict in Early Stuart England* (1989), 134–67. Since both cases are rooted in evidence, it is essential to formulate them in a way which makes them compatible.

partisan political attitudes, the commitment, and above all the organization, necessary to mount political campaigns, they were the first beneficiaries of this shift towards partisan politics.[85] The possibility therefore
exists that, both in the Short and the Long Parliaments, the godly, with
disciplined congregations behind them, may have been somewhat over-
represented. However, it is doubtful whether the traditional pattern
broke in enough places for this over-representation to be significant,
and an occasional cross-check on the House of Lords, where the
opposite views are likely to be over-represented, will give us a corrective
to this possible bias. In the Lords, as their choice of preachers
throughout suggests, the dominant ecclesiastical strain was the middle-
of-the-road Jacobean outlook represented among the clergy by Archbishop Ussher and Bishop Williams. This was an outlook for which the
religion of the Scottish Covenanters and the religion of Archbishop
Laud were almost equally acceptable when out of power, and almost
equally unacceptable when in it. The dominant bias appears to have
been a desire to diminish the power of religious enthusiasts of all sorts
by a firm Erastian insistence on the power of Parliament to control the
church and the clergy.[86] In 1640, because the Laudians were still in
power, such attitudes worked in favour of the godly, and may have
helped many of them to secure nominations to the Commons by the
traditional machinery of uncontested elections.

Most of the counties where the traditional pattern of elections held
left, for that reason, no mark on the records, and are easily forgotten.
One fortunate exception is Somerset, where four candidates emerged,
and a straw poll of the gentry indicated no clear majority for either pair.
A study of this straw poll gives no indication that the two groups stood
for any identifiable political cause. This may have made it the easier for
the leading candidates to reach an agreement to cease labouring for
votes and not to attend the election. The gentry then agreed on an
indenture returning one candidate from each group, duly signed by the
leading partisans of both. This indenture was returned by Sir Thomas
Wroth, one of the godliest of sheriffs: the godly did not always behave
in a partisan manner.[87]

In some other places, there was a different story: in Norfolk, the

---

[85] Laudian clergy could be as partisan as the godly, if not more so, but they lacked the backing
needed for electoral organization.

[86] On this attitude, see J. S. A. Adamson, 'The Peerage in Politics 1645–1649', Ph.D. thesis
(Cambridge, 1986), 82–104, esp. his remarks on Northumberland and Saye.

[87] Bristol RO Smyth of Long Ashton MSS Nos. 57, 49, 50. I have taken the lists of 'Little Johns'
and 'Little Robins' as lists of those who 'plumped' for one of a pair of candidates. See also David
Underdown, *Somerset during the Civil War and Interregnum* (Newton Abbot, 1973), 24. I am
grateful to Prof. Underdown for helpful discussion of these documents, which were not available
when he wrote. He is not responsible for my interpretation of the 'Little Johns' and the 'Little
Robins'.

middle-of-the-road gentleman Sir John Holland faced a campaign against him based on his wife's Catholicism, and expressed in the slogan that 'there are too many religions in Holland'. Holland won the election in the face of this campaign, but so disliked the experience that he decided not to contest the county in the next election.[88] In Sandwich, Edward Nicholas found himself facing a rumour that he was a papist, and had not been to church for sixteen years. Nicholas lost the election and did not get a seat. Edward Partridge, one of the candidates on whose behalf this rumour was spread, did not get a seat either, but he did get one in the Long Parliament, where he proved to be one of its godly members.[89]

The two clearest cases of new-style electioneering are in Northamptonshire and Gloucestershire. In Northamptonshire, according to the hostile witness who tells the story, a plot was 'layed in London by persons of other countys, to have Sir Gilbert Pikering to be one of the kts'. The candidature was hastened forward, 'taking advantage of the modesty of other men (who would not thrust themselves forward to pretend for the place till they knew the resolution of some others whome they thought might as well deserve it'. This not proving enough, Pickering's supporters then gave it out that the rival candidate was supported by all the papists in the county, and then that he was liable to be questioned in Parliament for his conduct as a Deputy-Lieutenant. It is interesting that even in Northamptonshire, it was not the religious cry which ultimately won Pickering the election, but the cry of 'no Deputy Lieutenants'. When elected, Pickering was one of the group of associates waiting to present county petitions the moment Pym sat down.[90]

In Gloucestershire, the gentry appear to have believed they had reached an agreement to return Sir Robert Tracey and Sir Robert Cooke, only to find an organized godly attempt, in which Sir Robert Cooke may have been a party, to return Nathaniel Stephens, who had been removed from the commission of the peace for opposing Ship Money, and enjoyed 'an opinion of much zeal towards the zealous'. In this campaign, clergy appear to have been prominent, including Sir Robert Cooke's chaplain and Workman, the deprived lecturer from Gloucester who had prayed for the States General and the King of Sweden before he prayed for King Charles. The pro-Scots are particularly visible in this group: they included one Mr Baxter, 'who spares not

---

[88] Clive Holmes, *Eastern Association in the English Civil War* (Cambridge, 1975), 24–5. Holland sat in Nov. for the borough of Castle Rising. It is our professional good fortune that he did so, since he was an able and experienced Parliamentary diarist.

[89] PRO SP 16/448/33 and 54; Keeler, pp. 298–9. On Partridge's later career, see below, p. 439.

[90] Bedfordshire RO St John MS J 1369. I am grateful to Dr R. P. Cust for drawing my attention to this document. Cope, p. 157. See also below, pp. 108, 136 and n.

to excuse, if not to justify, the Scots in their holy proceedings', and two who had recently been investigated by Secretary Windebank for their Scottish contacts: Mr Whinnell, lecturer at Gloucester and a recent graduate of St Andrews, and Help-on-High Fox, son of a deprived clergyman, and recently back from a visit to Edinburgh. Stephens, like the godly candidate at Sandwich, was not successful in the Short Parliament but was in the Long, while Sir Robert Cooke, their other favoured candidate, was to emerge in 1642 as an extreme godly member. It serves to underline the reasons why so many people disliked political polarization that Cooke combined this extreme godly stance with being married to George Herbert's widow.[91] In the Gloucestershire election, we have a rare clearly documented continuity between the pro-Scots of 1640 and the Parliamentarians of 1642.

For those who were not pro-Scottish, such events increased the pressure for a successful Parliament which might put a stop to such division. A successful Parliament would necessarily involve a grant of supply to the King, but would have to involve reciprocal concessions towards legality. Something would have to be done about Ship Money and about the restoration of the principle of taxation by consent, and something would have to be done to ensure that it was not another eleven years until the next Parliament. Without some concessions on this front, members could not easily go home and defend a grant of supply. If a Parliament, after eleven years of unpopular policies, were simply to vote supply and go home, it would be denying all the reasons for believing Parliaments were worth having: it would be buying survival at the price of uselessness. Many members were eager to reach some settlement with the King, but could only begin to work for one if the King would accept the need for some substantial concession by him first. If any serious negotiation should begin, they would then have to face the problem of whether any sum they could expect the country to pay voluntarily would be big enough to justify the concessions the King would have to make to get it. The anxieties of moderate members were encapsulated by Sir John Holland, writing to his aunt:

I know Madam you now listen after this Parliamt. with as many feares as wee sitt in it. And I cannot lessen either, for wee are already streightened. The King is importunate for supply, and must have it move in the first place, or itt will bee unseasonable and soe nott acceptable. The trusts reposed in us are great. Our greevances many and wondrous heavy and cryes lowd for present releife even soe as time is now equally precious both to King and subject. How great are the difficultyes wee are in. Even soe great as if it please nott God to tutch

---

[91] PRO SP 16/448/79; *CSPD 1639*, vol. ccccxx, no. 153, vol. ccccxxix, no. 19.1; *CSPD 1639–40*, vol. ccccxl, no. 65; Keeler, pp. 141, 350–1. On Cooke's subsequent career, see below pp. 422, 492.

his Maties heart, with favour and grace towards us herein wee may all iustly feare the most on happy breach that ever befell this kingdome.[92]

Holland did not overstate his case. For the committed pro-Scots, on the other hand, priorities are likely to have been very different. Clarendon tells the story of Oliver St John, at the dissolution of the Parliament, allowing himself a rare cheerfulness, and thoroughly pleased that it had come about. It is likely that in this, Clarendon was more accurate than he has usually been given credit for being.[93] A successful Parliament could not happen without a grant of supply, and therefore the sacrificial victims of any reunion between the King and his Parliament would necessarily be the Scots. To Saye, Brooke, and 'some of that knott',[94] this is likely to have been an alarming prospect. This is not just because of ideological fellow-feeling for their co-religionists in Scotland; for some of them, Scottish success probably represented their last hope of being able to remain in England. Saye and Brooke had already contemplated emigration, and it is at least possible that Pym and Hampden had done so too. To one who believed, as Pym did, that all altars were *ipso facto* idolatrous, it was growing increasingly difficult to fulfil his obligation to go to church in Caroline England. He seems to have withdrawn from the parish where he had been living in Hampshire after Edward Nicholas's brother moved in in full Laudian panoply in 1634. His refuge in Richard Knightley's house in Fawsley, Northamptonshire gave him the spiritual ministrations of John Dod the Jacobean veteran, but Dod's death could not be far off, and it was doubtful whether any successor could continue to enjoy the blind eye of Sir John Lambe.[95] Pym's references in Parliament to those who 'had fledd into the desarte of another world' suggest that he did not find emigration an attractive prospect.[96] The Pyms and the Hampdens had both occupied the same estates since the thirteenth century, and might be understandably reluctant to abandon them. For them, as for the Scottish Arminians, the cause of greater conformity between the kingdoms was the only one which gave them any hope of remaining able to worship in peace in their own country. Charles's attitude to their beliefs must have been painfully clear by 1640, and only the Scots possessed the force to wring out of him a concession which would make his dominions safe for their sort of worship: it must have been clear that such a concession would never come voluntarily. Moreover, it was probably

[92] Norfolk and Norwich RO KNY 615. I am very grateful to Prof. Clive Holmes for sending me a transcript of this letter.

[93] Clarendon, *History*, i. 140.

[94] The phrase is William Montague's: *HMC Buccleuch*, 1. 278.

[95] Russell, 'Pym', p. 249 n; Donald Nicholas, *Mr. Secretary Nicholas* (1955), 103–4; J. T. Cliffe, *Puritan Gentry* (1984), 179–83.

[96] Cope, p. 155.

clear to them, as it was to the Covenanters in 1643, that if Charles were to win his current battle, their turn would come next.[97] Charles had been frightened by the amount of 'disloyal' pro-Scottish sympathy he had discovered during the Bishops' Wars, and if he should defeat the Scots, he would almost certainly move on to establish tighter control over their English co-religionists. For this group, hope could only come from a Scottish victory, or from a compromise settlement very much to the Scots' advantage, leaving them to secure acceptance on the Scots' coat-tails. To neither of these objectives could a successful Parliament contribute.

They thus had a very difficult tactical task. They could not openly work for the failure of the Parliament, since they needed the votes of men like Sir John Holland, who would be profoundly offended by any such suggestion. They thus had to appear to be working for the same objective as Holland—a bargain involving supply and redress of grievances. At each stage, they could hope to introduce one more grievance, or to express the grievance in more provocative terms, in the hope that Charles would find their proposals stretched beyond his willingness to bargain. To pursue this strategy successfully, they needed to confine themselves to grievances for which other members would also speak, while yet being careful not to pitch their demands so low that they became acceptable. This was a very difficult strategy to follow, and would hardly have withstood a determined attempt by the King to bargain: that would have forced them out in the open, and provoked the hostility of members who wanted a successful Parliament. Not for the last time, Pym and his allies had to hope that Charles would not prove too flexible, and not for the last time, Charles did everything they could have hoped from him.

It is hard to be certain how numerous the pro-Scots were in the Short Parliament. The list of those who can be proved with documentary certainty to belong to this group is small: Saye and Brooke in the Lords, and in the Commons, Sir John Wray, Sir Robert Harley, Sir Robert Cooke, Samuel Vassall, and Saye's younger son Nathaniel Fiennes, recently back from a visit to Scotland.[98] There are others whose inclusion in this group would seem overwhelmingly probable, Sir Walter Earle, the Earl of Bolingbroke, and Lord Mandeville, and Saye and Brooke's close associates Pym, Hampden, and Oliver St John. Behind

[97] Stevenson, pp. 255, 263, 290–1, and other refs.
[98] For Saye, Brooke, Bolingbroke, and Mandeville, see above, p. 84. For Vassall, above, p. 61. For Wray, see his speech of 2 May, below, p. 118, and for Harley and Cooke, their speeches of 4 May, below, p. 120. For Nathaniel Fiennes, Clarendon, *History*, i. 186, and for evidence that Clarendon was correct, P. H. Donald, 'New Light on the Anglo-Scottish Contacts of 1640', *Historical Research*, 62/148 (1989), 223 and n. For Earle, Pym, Hampden, and St John, the point is conjectural at this date, but rests on their records and their associations.

them was a group Clotworthy had probably estimated accurately at forty or fifty Lords and gentlemen — not enough to sway a Parliament on its own, but a powerful group so long as it was careful to keep in touch with its fringe sympathizers. As usual, Charles overreached himself, and probably won this group more sympathy by trying to deny Saye, Brooke, and Mandeville their writs of summons to the House of Lords. It is not known how Charles was persuaded to relent, but it is suggestive that on the day of the State Opening, Mandeville made a present of 'Bermoody orangs' to the Earl of Northumberland.[99]

The Parliament was certain to be very different from any which had met in the 1620s, because so many of the former leading members were dead or absent. In the Lords, the chief absentee was Pembroke, who had been succeeded by a brother who was not his political equal. In any informal negotiations, the absence of the Duke of Buckingham meant more than the loss of a lightning-conductor: it meant that Charles was deprived of a vital source of information. In the Commons, the three titans of the twenties, Coke, Sandys, and Phelips, were all dead. So were Sir Dudley Digges, Sir Nathaniel Rich, and Sir John Eliot. William Hakewill was no longer a member. Edward Littleton, who had chaired the Committee of the Whole during the Petition of Right debates, was Chief Justice, and Sir Thomas Wentworth, now Earl of Strafford, was free to indulge the anti-Scottish prejudices of a north-countryman in the House of Lords, where he and Saye became the two most effective debaters.

Among the twenty or so leading members of the Commons in the twenties, only two were still there: Sir Francis Seymour and John Pym. These two stood, and had always stood, for very different causes. Seymour had been opposed to the war with Spain, opposed to the Duke in part because of his support for the war, and never very much in sympathy with godliness. Seymour disliked papists, but held to what Pym would have regarded as the simplistic view that popery meant communion with the church of Rome. He was a Calvinist, but not of a particularly heated sort, and had joined late into the protests against Arminianism. By contrast, on the immediate issue of 1640, the House's right to give or refuse its consent to taxation, Seymour had always been one of the most sensitive members of the House: none could be expected to protest more loudly against any attempt to treat a Parliament as a rubber stamp.[100]

By contrast, Pym was an anti-Arminian first and foremost, and

---

[99] *CSPD 1639–40*, vol. ccccxlvii, no. 30.1; Alnwick MSS Y I 47 (BL Microfilm 390), unfol. Mandeville, like Hamilton, owed much of his political importance to the care with which he observed these courtesies.

[100] Tyacke, pp. 134, 136; Russell, *1621–9*, pp. 21, 34, 131, 152, 161, 173–4, 343, 398, 406–7, and other refs.

regarded Arminianism as partaking of all the qualities which made 'popery' so dangerous. For him, the rights and privileges of Parliaments were first and foremost a means of defending the true religion established by law, and by that he did not mean the religion of Charles I. While Seymour was an instinctive countryman, and ready to protest vigorously at any encroachment on local autonomy, Pym was a man without local ties, and an instinctive governor.[101] In the 1620s Seymour had been the more important and influential member of the two: it was he, and not Pym, who had been pricked sheriff to keep him out of the Parliament of 1626. That it was Pym, and not Seymour, who emerged as the leading political figure of the Short Parliament, is not just a tribute to his political skill. He had a great deal of skill, but in the absence of an atmosphere of crisis, his alarmism had always been capable of hitting a disastrously wrong note. Nor is Pym's prominence just a matter of his backing among the peerage: he enjoyed connections with Saye, Brooke, Bedford, and Warwick, but Seymour, the younger brother of the Earl of Hertford, had influential connections among the peerage too. That it was Pym and not Seymour who seemed to be saying what the Commons wanted to hear is also a mark of a significantly changed political mood.

There were other members with experience, but most of them not quite of the first water. Rudyerd was still the spokesman in the Commons for the house of Herbert, and since the politics of the Herberts seem to have been peculiarly influenced by an inherited clientage, he was still saying very much the same things. His line was still that it was worth granting supply, in order to ensure that there would be future Parliaments. Harley, Mildmay, and Fleetwood, the Duke's Calvinist credentials of 1626, were still there and as Calvinist as ever, but less effective without the voice of the Duke behind them. One minor client of the Duke who had some Parliamentary experience had been catapulted into prominence by the Ship Money trial: John Hampden. All these people had shown themselves Calvinist and anti-Spanish.

Those who had been against the Duke because they were opposed to the war with Spain were also still represented: Edward Kirton and Sir John Strangeways were Parliamentarians of experience and standing. Both had connections in the Lords: Kirton was the son of the Earl of Hertford's man of business, and Strangeways was an old friend and colleague of the Earl of Bristol. Bristol himself, the ablest member of this group, was still in the Lords, and more active than ever. None of this group were likely to feel any sympathy for the Scots, and though they were not Laudians, they were immune to many of Pym's more fundamental fears about religion. If the King were to reach an agreement with the Parliament, these were the sort of people with whom he

[101] Russell, 'Pym', passim; Tyacke pp. 130–1, and other refs.

would have to reach it, and the whole body of issues symbolized by Ship Money and the Petition of Right stood between them.

When the Parliament met on 13 April 1640, the new Lord Keeper was Sir John Finch, who had been Speaker in 1629 and Chief Justice in the Ship Money trial. He was an obvious enough candidate for Lord Keeper on the death of Coventry, but he was not, perhaps, the most appropriate person to bring the best out of a Parliament. His speech, however, tells us more about the King than about himself, for it represented a straight royal line with very little adornment of his own. He told them how fortunate they were to be 'graciously allowed' to discuss the weighty affairs of king and kingdom, recalling his remarks in the Ship Money trial about the holding of Parliaments being 'a lost privilege', and inviting a response that meetings in Parliament were a right and not a privilege. The statement that 'his Majestyes kingly resolutions are seated in the Arke of his sacred brest; and it were a presumption of too high a nature for any Uzzah uncal'd to towch it' was perhaps a warning not to enter into the rights and wrongs of the King's Scottish policy. If so, it was fair enough, but the image was more high-flown than those his predecessor Coventry had normally used. After a brief and oblique appeal to anti-Scottish prejudice, and a few remarks about the odiousness of the Scots' rebellion, he came to the point:

this summer must not bee lost nor any minute of time foreslowed to reduce them of Scotland left [sic] by protraction here they gaine more time and advantage to frame their projects with forreine states. His Majesty doth there-fore desire upon these pressing and urging reasons that you will for awhile lay aside all other debates, and that you would passe an Act for such and so many subsedyes as you in your hearty affeccions to his Majesty and to the common good shall think fitt and convenient for so great an accion.

If they did this, the King would call them back 'towards winter', when he would redress their 'just' grievances, and would also expect 'more ample supply'.[102] It was not a particularly inviting prospect. The phrase about 'just' grievances was one Charles had used regularly as far back as 1626, and members were entitled to expect that he would not regard very many of their grievances as 'just'. The promise of a second meeting after the summer was also a regular Caroline offer: there is no need to doubt its sincerity, since in 1628, the only time the Parliament had kept its side of the proposed bargain, Charles also kept his. However, the demand for a 'more ample' supply, necessary though it might be from the King's point of view, was hardly likely to add to the attractions of the offer. On Tonnage and Poundage, Finch said the King desired to claim it by grant of Parliament, and, applying the rubber-stamp

---

[102] Cope, pp. 115–21; *LJ* ii. 46–7. Variant readings appear to be only trivial.

principle literally, asked for a retrospective Act from the first year of the reign.

Finch also offered two other inducements to compliance. One was the example of the Irish Parliament recently held by Strafford, which had been induced to offer an ample grant of subsidies and a general declaration of support for the war. Strafford may perhaps have weakened the propaganda force of this Act by inserting into the preamble an eloquent tribute to the wisdom of his government as Lord Deputy. Since the operation of Poynings's Law prevented the Irish Parliament from amending bills without sending them back to the English Privy Council for reapproval, they had to accept this preamble as it stood or else reject the Act altogether.[103] It is probable that some cynics suspected the authorship of the preamble before it was revealed by the Irish Parliament the next year, and that Strafford only succeeded in turning a propaganda weapon into a boomerang. It was also unwise to recommend Irish practice to the English: the Scots, writing to 'a particular frend in the par.', tried to capitalize on this reaction: 'and so they that have been conquert by youre force, ar preparing to bring us all to ther condition'.[104]

Finch's other inducement was an intercepted letter from some of the Covenanter leaders to the King of France, asking for mediation. Finch and the King tried to interpret it as a direct attempt to put themselves under French sovereignty, which it clearly is not. Moreover, it was undated, and probably written before the Pacification of Berwick. Charles also lost the momentum of the letter by a procedural irregularity: he gave the task of presenting it to the Lords to Cottington, a new peer whose patent had not yet been read, and who therefore was not yet technically a member. By the time the Lords had decided to overlook Saye's objection to the irregularity, they seem to have had no impetus left to do anything further with the letter.[105]

In a Parliament dominated by supply, the Lords were often reduced to a secondary role, but they found several ways of expressing their feelings. On 16 April they refused a request to adjourn in order to allow the bishops to go to Convocation, saying the High Court of Parliament was not subordinate to any other court. On the 20th, this issue was revived, apparently by a remark by Laud referring to the bishops as a Third Estate in Parliament. This implied, in opposition to the controversial Lent reading by Bagshaw at the Middle Temple, that Bishops, like Lords and Commons, were an essential part of a Parliament, and

---

[103] PRO SP 63/258/73.
[104] NLS Wodrow MS Fol. 64, fo. 165.
[105] Esther S. Cope, 'Earl of Bedford's Notes of the Short Parliament of 1640', *BIHR* 53 (1980), 256; *LJ* iv. 55.

that it was impossible to hold one without them. The Lords refused to support Laud in this view.[106] A further dispute blew up on the 18th, over Roger Manwaring Bishop of St David's. He had been impeached by the Parliament of 1628, and declared, by the judgement of the Lords, incapable of any spiritual preferment, but nevertheless, had been subsequently made a bishop. His case was raised by the Earl of Essex, who declared bluntly that if Manwaring sat, he would not. This provoked Hall Bishop of Exeter to protest that 'if they dealt so with the bishopps they would show themselves to be like unto the Covenanters in Scottland'. This led Hall to be called to the bar on Mandeville's motion. The Scots were entitled to describe this as 'a notable shugg [sic] to the hirarchie', and to say that 'the upper house was much better than was expected, divers younge lords affecting the better parte'. The Lords do indeed seem to have been inclined to express their resentment at the Bishops' Wars (amongst other things) in the form of hostility to the bishops.[107]

Meanwhile, the battle about supply was to be fought out in the Commons. On the first day of business, 16 April, there was no sign of any member prepared to leap into the breach and move the grant of immediate supply. Windebank, who introduced the Covenanters' letter to the King of France, got no more reaction than Cottington had done in the Lords. He was answered by Harbottle Grimston, member for Colchester, putting 'a case of greater dainger here at home domesticall'. The danger he thought more serious was the neglect of Magna Carta and the Petition of Right. He made a few passing remarks about persecution of professors of the Gospel and about monopolists, but the sum of his argument was for observance of the law. He claimed that there were 'but few here that doe not experimentally know itt as badd as I have put it'. He was followed by Rudyerd, arguing that 'A Parliament is the seed of reconciliation betwixt King and people, and therefore it is fitt for us to lay aside all exasperations'. In an involved, and widely reported, image, he said that breaking a Parliament had left splinters in the body politic, which were hard to pull out, and said that the untimely breaking of this Parliament 'would be the breaking of us'.[108]

The proposals of this speech appear to have achieved little impact.

[106] *LJ* iv. 55; Cope, pp. 99, 235–6. On Bagshaw's reading and the issues it raised, see M. J. Mendle, *Dangerous Positions* (University, Alabama, 1985), 123–7, and other refs. I am grateful to Prof. Mendle for convincing me of the Scottish contexts of this and many other English issues.

[107] Cope, pp. 63, 99–100; NLS Adv. MS 33. 1. 1, vol. xiii, no. 7 (unsigned). The Scottish newsletter seems to show that it was Essex, not Saye, who was accused of savouring of a Scottish Covenanter. It seems that when the author of BL Harl. MS 4931 said that 'if I mistake not it was my Lord Say', his hesitation was justified. The Scottish newsletter is dated 23 Apr., and its comments on the temper of the Lords are therefore made before the debate on supply of 24 Apr. See also Cope, 'Bedford', p. 257.

[108] Cope, pp. 135–9.

He was followed by Sir Francis Seymour, who put an argument which was advanced many times against the voting of subsidies without any redress: 'our judgements may very well be questioned, and it may give the country (whom wee serve) cause to blame the men whom they have chosen as consenting to their sufferance'. This was the voice with which he had spoken in 1628, but he struck a newer note by describing the Parliament as the 'soul' of the commonwealth. This was an introduction to the grievance of the members condemned in 1629, and in particular, to the claim that since the Parliament was the highest court, judges in inferior courts had no jurisdiction over it. This speech contains a few remarks about religion, aimed at seminary priests and non-resident and non-preaching ministers, but it contains no attack on the main outlines of the Laudian church: the central attack is on those who tell the King 'his prerogative is above all laws and that his subjects are but slaves to the destruction of property'. It did not take much imagination to see Ship Money as the target behind these phrases. On past precedent, Seymour might refuse to bargain for Ship Money, and demand its abolition as of right before other matters were discussed. Whether he would now be prepared to bargain for it, and if so, how many subsidies he would rate it as being worth, yet remained to be discovered.

The next day, 17 April, the Speaker's report of the opening speeches by the King and the Lord Keeper again briefly raised the Covenanters' letter to the King of France, producing only a brief intervention by Pym to clear the French King of any suggestion of complicity in this letter.[109] Then came two major set-piece speeches by Pym and his stepbrother Francis Rous, speaking, as they had done in 1629, in tandem. Rous, who had already published against Arminianism, confined himself to the religious issue, and made the explicit and far-reaching charge that 'the roote of all or grievances I thinke to bee an intended union betwixt us and Rome'. One of his central pieces of evidence for this charge was a book published by Christopher Davenport, alias Franciscus a Sancta Clara, arguing that as the church of England sloughed off 'the old Calvinist man', its differences with Rome would diminish to vanishing-point. Significantly, it was to Parliamentary authority in religion that Rous turned for protection against this type of interpretation: he said Davenport 'undertakes to turn all or religion enacted in this house into an agreement with popery'. He complained of the widening use of the word 'Puritan' as an 'essential engine' in this work of reunion with Rome, 'for this word in the mouth of a drunkard doth mean a sober man, in the mouth of an Arminian an orthodox man, in the mouth of a papist, a Protestant. And so it is spoke to shame a man out of all

---

[109] Maltby, p. 7.

religion, if a man will bee ashamed to bee saved'.[110] He attacked the laying of 'illegal burdens' on ministers, especially deprivation or suspension for not reading the Book of Sports. To men like Rous, who took the sabbath literally, the Book of Sports was an explicit order to disobey a divine command, and therefore beyond the legitimate limits of obedience.[111] He then explained Ship Money as being designed 'to settle this work of parliament to be made needlesse': it was designed, as Rous saw it, to free the King from Parliamentary constraints in order that he or his advisers could pursue the intended work of reunion with Rome without Parliamentary interference.

The same synthesis was taken up by Pym, in a speech two hours long, which was perhaps the most successful of his life. It was so comprehensive in its attempt to cover all the issues which were concerning members that Rossingham the newsletter writer forwarded it in response to a request for the grievances of the Parliament.[112] At the same time, Pym succeeded in weaving all these grievances together into the same theological framework used by Rous. In sharp contrast to his line in 1629, Pym decided to begin, as Seymour had done, with Parliamentary privilege, and in particular with the arrests of 1629. It is his expressed reason for doing so that distances him from Seymour: he did it 'insomuch that verity in religion receives an influence from the free debates in Parliament, and consequently from the priviledges in Parliament': Parliaments were necessary *because* they were essential to the survival of the body of doctrine Pym defined as 'Protestantism'. Indeed, he defined the title to true religion as a form of property: 'that religion is possession whereof the laws of the land have placed us'.

He complained of the lack of execution of the laws against popery, and that papists had been admitted to 'great places of trust in the church and commonwealth (I crave pardon for the last slippe of my tongue)', of the presence of a papal nuncio, of the publishing of popish points in pulpits and Universities, 'and there maynteyned for sound doctrine', and of 'the introduction of popish ceremonyes, such I meane not as the constitucon since the Reformed Religion continued unto us; but we must introduce againe many of the superstitions and infirme cermenonies of the most decreppid age of popery, as the setting up altars, boweing to them and the like'. He also specified 'bowing towards

---

[110] Cope, pp. 145–8; Tyacke, p. 227 and n. Davenport was the brother of John Davenport, the founder of New Haven, Conn.

[111] On the drive for 'further reformation' see Francis Rous, *Oile of Scorpions* (1623), *passim*. For anyone looking for a long-term statement of Parliamentarian ideology, this work would serve better than most.

[112] Cope, pp. 148–56, 254–60. Aston, p. 7, seems to confirm that the bulk of this speech was actually delivered. On the texts of this speech, see Cope, pp. 299–302. For Rossingham, see *CSPD 1640*, vol. ccccli, no. 66.

the East, pictures, crosses, crucifixes and the like', comparing them to the dry bones in the Book of Ezekiel, which were brought together to make a man. He followed these points with the popular demand for the clergy to be allowed to enforce no more than was warranted by law, again implicitly denying Charles's notion of a separate sphere of clerical authority.

On civil matters, he began with Tonnage and Poundage, demanding by implication the reversal of the judgement in Bate's Case. He then ran through the issues of knighthood fines, monopolies, Ship Money, forest fines,[113] the use of the Star Chamber and Proclamations, and the military charges. He ended by blaming all those evils on the intermission of Parliaments, and quoted the laws in favour of annual Parliaments.[114] He ended by demanding that all these things be drawn together into a Remonstrance. It was an impressive performance, but it was hardly that of a man seeking compromise. Of all the issues he raised, the one which should perhaps be taken as the clearest example of a counsel of Achitophel,[115] designed to make the gulf unbridgeable, is the issue of military charges, coat and conduct money, rates for arms, and so forth. He described them as 'impositions against all lawe, which as they are very burthensome soe is the consequence very dangerous'. This point hit the King in his immediate preoccupation, the question of how to make war. He could not give up the military charges and finance an army, since they were the crucial means of transferring military costs to local, and not central, funds. If military charges were to go into a bargain with Ship Money, the sum Charles was likely to be offered would be far too little to compensate him for the loss of both. An Act of Parliament legalizing military charges, if it were acceptable to Charles, would demand a more constructive Parliamentary mood than the rest of Pym's speech suggested.

Pym and Rous both spoke from scripts, which were made available for copying.[116] Copies of their speeches were very widely circulated indeed, and we may wonder whether this was in fact the object of the exercise. An angry dissolution was likely to be followed by an attempt to resume the war without Parliamentary support. It was essential to Pym's strategy that any such attempt should fail, and this impressive exercise in focusing eleven years' resentments was more likely to contribute to

[113] On forest fines he was careful to clear the Earl of Holland, stressing that he had done nothing but as he was directed by the judges.

[114] On the precedents Pym was using, see Pauline Croft, 'Annual Parliaments and the Long Parliament', *BIHR* 59 (1986), 155–71.

[115] For the counsel of Achitophel, 2 Sam. 17: 21.

[116] Cope, pp. 298–300. Members were not supposed to use scripts, but the practice seems to have grown, rather than diminishing, during the Long Parliament. On some occasions, it may indicate a desire to address an audience outside the walls. The speeches which have found their way into Thomason Tracts and Rushworth were a self-selecting sample of those which used scripts.

that end than to any attempt to hold a successful Parliament. Pym had stopped short of repeating Rous's charge that there was a deliberate plan to reunite England and Rome, yet by providing so much supporting evidence immediately after that charge had been made, he encouraged people to fit his evidence into Rous's pattern, and popery was one thing good subjects knew they were entitled to oppose.

These speeches were followed by an exercise in Covenanter-style presenting of petitions, from Northamptonshire, Middlesex, and Suffolk the same day, and from Essex, Hertfordshire, Northampton town, and Norwich the next day. Both the identity of those offering the petitions, and the citation of the law for annual Parliaments in the petitions from Essex and Middlesex, suggest a considerable degree of co-ordination.[117] This suggestion does not, of course, deny that the petitions also represented a considerable body of public feeling. The political strength of the godly rested in the ability of like-minded people to make contact with each other at short notice, which is a more powerful force than the mere plotting of a few which was all that was perceived by their opponents.

The day ended with Edward Kirton, one of those who would probably have liked to bargain with the King, suggesting that Pym should quickly prepare a remedy for these grievances 'that soe wee might afterwards fall with more allacritye on the Kings affayres', and Alexander Rigby, one of the Lancashire godly, suggesting that, because these things would lose the King so much revenue, 'these may be supplyed by a constant revenue to be settled by us'. With this sweetening on the pill, the House resolved that the next day should be spent on discussion of grievances: Pym had won the first round.[118]

From then the Commons ran for a few days on normal lines. On 18 April Sir John Strangeways supported Pym in raising the grievance of the 1629 imprisonments, and Edward Hyde said Pym had left out the grievance of the Earl Marshal's court. A cursory attempt by Solicitor-General Herbert to call the House back to supply was ignored.[119] The 19th was a Sunday. Most of the 20th was spent on the Speaker's adjourning the House without its own consent in 1629, significantly misreported by the Scots as 'whether the power and will of the king be sufficient to dissolve a Parliament without the consent of both

---

[117] BL Harl. MS 4931, an account written by and for the godly, remarks 'of which petitions some before hand sayd, yt they wr ye Scottish Covenant wanting only hands'; Cope, p. 234. The petitions were presented by Sir Gilbert Pickering (Northants), Sir Gilbert Gerrard (Middlesex), Sir Nathaniel Barnardiston (Suffolk), Sir Harbottle Grimston (Essex), Sir William Litton (Herts), Alderman Atkins (Norwich), and Richard Knightley (Northampton). Sir Walter Earle defended their right to present them: Cope, p. 157; Maltby, pp. 11–12. For the texts of the surviving petitions, Cope, pp. 274–9; see also below, p. 136 and n.

[118] Maltby, p. 11; Cope, p. 157.

[119] Maltby, pp. 12–15.

houses'.[120] On the 21st, Harley presented a petition from Peter Smart of Durham,[121] and the records for Ship Money were sent for. Sir Walter Earle raised a new issue by pointing out that Convocation, for the first time since 1606, had a commission giving it power to make new canons.[122] There was an apparent indifference to bills such as had not been seen in any recent Parliament, but the miscellaneous raising of matters of complaint was going on very much as might have been expected. At this point, they were interrupted by a summons to attend the King, and were again addressed by the Lord Keeper, who 'made a speeche to excite the House to supply the king'.

On the 22nd, business was begun by Pym and Hampden taking up the cause of Peter Smart. Edward Kirton moved that they should take one more day to consider, and then take up the business of the Lord Keeper's speech. Pym seconded the motion to defer it to the next day, leaving the House free to return to the business of the commission for Convocation to make canons. Pym and Oliver St John both objected that the clergy could not bind the laity without the consent of the House of Commons. The day ended with a quarrel between Laud's secretary William Dell and Pym, in which Dell accused Pym of saying 'that the churches beyond sea were about to forsake us because wee did forsake our religion'. The House resolved that Pym had never at any time during the Parliament spoken unfitting speeches, and that no man had spoken this speech. Dell, grudgingly, 'does acknowledge he is mistaken, and will rest rather upon the sense of this house than his own'. As far as is possible to judge from surviving reports, Pym does not seem to have spoken precisely these words, but it is doubtful whether Dell was alone in believing he had.[123]

Business on the 23rd began with the choice of preachers for the Fast and the Communion. The choice is an interesting guide to the ecclesiastical temper of the House. They chose Ralph Brownrigg for the Communion, and Richard Holdsworth and Stephen Marshall for the Fast. The choice of members to go to ask the preachers gives a further clue to the quarters of the House the nominations were coming from. Pym was to go to Brownrigg, Seymour to Holdsworth, and Harley to Marshall.[124] All three of these preachers were impeccable Calvinists, but

---

[120] Ibid. 19–22; NLS Adv. MS 33.1.1, vol. xiii, no. 7.

[121] On Peter Smart and the issues raised by his case, see above, ch. 1.

[122] Cope, p. 164; Maltby, pp. 22–3. On the questions raised by Convocation's claim to make canons, see Esther S. Cope, 'Short Parliament of 1640 and Convocation', *JEH* 25 (1974), 167–84; Alistair Fox and John Guy, *Reassessing the Henrician Age* (Oxford, 1986), 206–19, and other refs. The history of the canons of 1640 is a clear illustration of Dr Guy's remark that 'the issues were not resolved during Henry VIII's lifetime'.

[123] Cope, pp. 168–9, 246; *CJ* ii. 8. It appears to have been Hampden's friendship which saved Dell from worse trouble.

[124] *CJ* ii. 9.

only Marshall was a great enthusiast for 'further reformation', and only Marshall was to be a regular preacher to the Long Parliament. Brownrigg and Holdsworth were both among the faction of establishment Calvinists who were at that time fighting a rearguard action against the Laudians in Convocation.[125] Brownrigg was a recent Vice-Chancellor of Cambridge, and Holdsworth a future one. Both were to be offered bishoprics in November 1641, and were to identify themselves with moves for a Jacobean-style compromise. Brownrigg had the further advantage of a family connection with Pym; he was married to Pym's niece, and during the 1630s they had both paid money to Samuel Hartlib which may have been a subscription for his newsletter.[126] These nominations suggest a House which, whether out of tactics or out of conviction, was much more moderate in ecclesiastical matters than its successor.

This done, the House went into Committee of the Whole to discuss whether to give the King's supply precedence over grievances. Rudyerd, always first on his feet, argued that they should, but was followed by 'a long pauze. Noe man speaking'. The silence was finally broken by Sir Ralph Hopton, in one of the key speeches of the Parliament. He argued, in a much-quoted image, that a servant pausing to pull a thorn out of his foot before obeying his master's command was not guilty of any delay or disobedience. His conclusion from this image was that 'the way of shipmoney and all unparliamentary supply not serviceable to the king profitable to the commonwealth only thornes'. It was a far-reaching demand, which on Hopton's own underestimates, would have cost the King something near £300,000 a year. Hopton gave no indication of willingness to replace this money, and Sir Thomas Jermyn Comptroller of the Household protested that 'wee doe not goe the way expected'. Seymour, who spoke next, discussed the argument that they should trust the King for future redress, and said that when they considered the Petition of Right, 'wee have cause to feare the woorst'. He argued that they should discuss grievances first, and then supply.[127] Strangeways expressed his approval of Hopton's image of the thorn, and drew attention to Ship Money on the traditional Parliamentary ground that they needed to be 'enabled' to give: their title to property had to be secure before they could freely grant it to the King. Edward Kirton, taking up the position he had been working towards since the beginning of the Parliament, argued that they should confer with the Lords on

---

[125] Tyacke, p. 240.

[126] PRO Wards 9.163, fo. 62. I am grateful to Prof. Roy Schreiber for this reference. Sheffield University Library, Hartlib MSS 23/11, fo. 4ᵛ, and 31/3/9. I am grateful to Mrs Turnbull and Sheffield University for permission to quote from these MSS. For a letter from Brownrigg to D'Ewes in favour of liturgical conformity, see J. T. Cliffe, *Puritan Gentry* (1984), 102.

[127] Cope, pp. 169–70; Maltby, pp. 36–8.

religion, property, and liberty in Parliament, and then they would be 'enabled' to do the King's business. Sir Harbottle Grimston, unusually taking over the role of family spokesman from his son, said that if they did not deal with Ship Money, 'wee shall have ill welcome home'. The debate ran on for a long time, but, except for a storm caused by Peard's calling Ship Money an 'abomination', little novel was added, and Kirton's motion was carried with very little sign of dissent.[128] The key speakers in this debate, Hopton, Seymour, Strangeways, and Kirton, were all to be Royalists in the Civil War: they were not irreconcilable opponents, but were indicating the minimum terms on which they could do business. It was doubtful whether, from the King's point of view, business was worth doing on these terms, but the reaction ought to have been expected, and there was no point in calling the Parliament if the King were not prepared to negotiate on such terms. The King, however, had clearly not expected this reaction, and called a meeting of the Privy Council that night. Northumberland's brother Henry Percy, who had done his duty by speaking for supply, reported that they were busy deciding to dissolve the Parliament.[129]

In the event, Henry Percy's fears were premature. 23 April turned out to be another partial success for the moderate Councillors. Charles agreed to keep the Parliament in session, but only in return for agreement to a proposal of Strafford's to take the issue of supply to the Lords.[130] There is still no sign that the King had taken the vital point that, after an eleven-year interval, he could not expect Parliamentary supply for *any* reason without doing something in return for it. The involvement of the Lords in issues of supply was always risky, since it was liable to provoke complaints of breach of privilege, but there were precedents in 1593, 1624, and 1626, of which only one had been entirely disastrous. It was a risky policy, but if the King had a major concession to offer, it would not have been *certain* to fail.

On the morning of the 24th, the King arrived unexpectedly at the House of Lords, giving them no opportunity to put on their robes. He complained that the Commons had put the cart before the horse, and repeated that 'my necessities are so urgent that there can be no delay'. He called on the Lords not to join in the 'preposterous course' of the House of Commons, and left the Lord Keeper to ask the Lords to reach a resolution during that day's sitting. In the ensuing debate, it seems that the Privy Councillors were under instruction to speak for the King: Strafford, Dorset, Arundel, Bridgewater, Cottington, and Laud duly

---

[128] Cope, pp. 171–4; Maltby, pp. 38–42; *CJ* ii. 10.
[129] *HMC De L'Isle and Dudley*, VI. 251–2; KAO U 1475 C 85/6.
[130] PRO 31/3/72, p. 136.

did,[131] but Holland, who had been told to speak for the King, went home to Kensington without speaking.[132] The group of Councillors was joined by two lay Lords, Northampton and Maynard, and one bishop, John Warner of Rochester. On the other side, only Saye took the risk of opposing the King's proposal outright, but Mandeville, Bristol, Southampton, Brooke, and possibly Manchester gathered round an alternative proposal by Lord Montague for an open-ended conference with the Commons. Cottington raised the spectre of the Covenanters offering the Crown of Scotland to the King of Sweden, but found no response. The key arguments against the King's course were put by Saye and Bristol. Saye warned that the Commons would so much resent it that it would bring them to a stand, and Bristol reminded them that 'it is not only monie will doe, but the harts must be had to with mony'. In time of danger, he argued, this was worth more than money, and to do that 'let the people be somewhat satisfied in the grevances'. The impression that this was less than an overwhelming demonstration of support was confirmed when the issue was put to the vote. There were three divisions, the first apparently on which question should be put first, and the votes against the King ranged from 25 on the first to 14 on the third. Some quarter of the lay peerage had voted against the King in public, from which it should be assumed that the proportion who were unhappy with his course of action was at least double that.[133] A list of dissenting Lords includes most of the obvious ones, but also a number the King should have been surprised to find there. The list is the Earls of Rutland, Southampton, Bedford, Hertford, Essex, Lincoln, Warwick, Clare, Bolingbroke, Nottingham, and Bath, Viscount Saye and Sele, and Lords Willoughby of Parham, Paget, North, Mandeville, Brooke, Robartes, Lovelace, Savill, Dunsmore, Deincourt, Montague, Howard of Escrick and Wharton.[134] The twenty-fifth appears to be the Earl of Newport, Master of the Ordnance, who claimed to have voted against the King by mistake.[135] Bristol, in spite of his contributions to debate, appears not to have risked snubbing the King with his vote.

On the 25th, the Lords delivered this conclusion to the Commons. It was introduced by the Lord Keeper, who brought a message from the King recalling them to what, as he saw it, was the real point of Ship Money: the need to be able to send out a navy: 'therefore think you of any other way, for guard and preservation of the seas, which, considering the naval preparations abroad doth so much import, that he may be able to maintain a navy, whereby he may be moderator and keep the

[131] *LJ* 66–9; Cope, pp. 66–79.
[132] PRO 31/3/72, p. 136.
[133] For the debates, see Cope, pp. 71–9, 110.
[134] PRO SP 16/451/39.
[135] PRO 31/3/72, p. 316.

dominion of the narrow seas; without which, it is impossible for you to subsist'.[136] In other words, the King could only afford to give up Ship Money if voted an equivalent revenue by Parliamentary means. The argument was as sound strategically as the argument of Seymour and Strangeways was sound legally, but there was no sign that the cases had met. Indeed, it was perhaps the key point against representative assemblies in early modern Europe that if they were truly representative, they could not afford to let such points meet. The amounts of money required for warfare were such that, except among the Dutch, whose enemy was visibly at their gates, consent for the sums thought strategically necessary was rarely likely to be forthcoming. That the ideal of government by consent should suffer in such circumstances was hardly surprising.

After the conference, the Commons adjourned, and when they met again on Monday the 27th, they briefly and improbably gave their minds to bills. Solicitor-General Herbert then reported the conference, and the debate on the Lords' intervention began. In the debate, no one spoke for the Lords except those speaking to a brief. The men briefed were Rudyerd, Peter Ball one of the Queen's counsel, Solicitor-General Herbert, and Sir Thomas Jermyn. Sir Henry Vane said he was not at the conference, and appears to have given no further opinion. On the other side, Harbottle Grimston made the point that the shortage of time was not their fault: if they had been called sooner, they would have come. The general cry of 'breach of privilege' came, as might have been expected, from Earle, Pym, St John, Glyn, and Hotham, but it also came from Charles Jones the judge's son, Robert Holborne, Edmund Waller, Sir Francis Seymour, and Sir Miles Fleetwood. It was almost a complete cross-section of the House. Having resolved to send Pym to complain to the Lords, the House went back to its grievances.[137]

Pym discharged this task vigorously on the 28th, leaving the Lords on the 29th to debate what he had said. Strafford immediately took the debate onto high ground by claiming free speech for Lords, while Saye unwisely reminded them that 'I did feare that this would be ye issue'. There was a general reaction of anger in the Lords: Arundel wanted to put the question whether the Commons had broken their privileges, Dorset asked 'let us be upon even termes with them', and Pembroke said that if they refrained from putting the question 'we are a poore

---

[136] *CJ* ii. 13.
[137] Maltby, pp. 66–76; Cope, pp. 177–80. On bills, see Cope, pp. 319–20. Three bills progressed as far as commitment in the Lords, and nine in the commons. Only the Queen's Jointure Bill in the Lords achieved a third reading in either house. The majority of these bills seems to have been veterans from the 1620s. For a brief debate on the bill for abuses in ecclesiastical courts, see Maltby, pp. 110–11. Most of these bills seem not to have generated great excitement: common recoveries by infants, like the poor were always with them.

house in my opinion'. On the other side, Bristol argued for accommodation, on the ground that the King's service mattered more than the privileges of the House, and Mandeville, Wharton, Hertford, and North argued for a conference before voting. The proposal for a conference was carried, but failed to head off the vote on the privilege issue, which was taken the next day. The Lords voted that they had not broken the privileges of the Commons by 80 votes to 2, a quite remarkable example of the willingness of a minority to force a division.[138]

On the 29th, the Commons took up ecclesiastical grievances, and began with what seems to have been a powerful discussion of the Laudian altar policy.[139] Hyde began it by saying 'that it is not contrary to the rubrick that the communion table stand altar wise', provoking Harley to reply that 'the forme of religion trenches upon religion. All our ancestors suffered for these words, *hoc est corpus meum*, and are not wee brought almost to idolatry, in bowing to that?' Harley was immediately supported by Francis Rous, Sir William Masham, Sir Edmund Moundeford, and Sir John Wray. Their intervention illustrated what was to be one of the major debating strengths of the godly through the next few years: their ability to produce an immediate team of speakers on any issue of collective concern to them, which, if their opponents were not equally quick and determined, could lead to their contributions being taken as the sense of the House when they were not. On this occasion, they were answered by one of the numerous Lloyds in the House, who argued that if it were put in the east end as the most convenient place, it was not against the Elizabethan Injunction, but if it were put there definitively, it was. This was a careful reading, subsequently supported by Convocation in its canons of 1640. The critics of current policy were then joined by three significant allies, Sir John Strangeways, Sir Ralph Hopton, and Sir Richard Dyott, one of the very few Arminians in the Commons.[140] Strangeways recalled the taking down of altars under Edward, and asked 'whether better reazons by those that have altered it, then those did it'. Dyott and Hopton appear to have followed the straight text of the 1559 Injunction, by which the table was to be kept at the east end, and moved into the body of the church at service time, though Hopton's speech is too imperfectly reported to permit certainty. Sir Henry Vane then reminded them that

---

[138] Cope, pp. 84–90. There is no evidence on the identity of the two, but the obvious guess is likely to be the correct one: the forcing of a division against such odds suggests concern for an outside audience.

[139] For the ecclesiastical debate of 29 Apr., Aston is a priceless and almost unique source: see Maltby, pp. 87–97.

[140] Ibid. 90. On Dyott, see Tyacke, pp. 140–2. His presence in this list is a striking illustration of Charles and Laud's ability to alienate their natural supporters.

in the King's chapel, it stood altarwise, and added the intriguingly reserved comment: 'as it goes generally I must say noe'. Edmund Waller provoked one of the first of his many personality clashes with Pym by asking why there should not be discretion in the authorities: 'if we allowe not that liberty to the governers of the church, what shall wee'. To Pym, this was a threat to the rule of law: 'rulers according to lawe, and not to rule us as they please and make rules, not execute those which are made'. Waller explained himself: 'wheere the rubric leaves a latitude sombody must prescribe a place els the parish divided among themselves'.[141] Sir Hugh Cholmely perhaps spoke for many gentlemen when he said 'hee cares not which way it stands, but to the matter of bowing to it, offence'. Finally, Pym, St John, Hampden, and Holles in quick succession demanded the question, and the existing policy was voted a grievance. This is a debate which should have caused some alarm to the King and Laud: it was not just the serried ranks of the godly who were arrayed against them, but it would seem that some half of those who were to be Royalists in 1642 were also. The cause of Strange-ways and Hopton, that nothing should be done in the church but what was warranted by law, was one to which the King was to come round in 1641, when it appeared the best way of thwarting the threat of a 'further reformation', but he would have to face the fact that it was a line of defence which failed to justify a lot of what he had been doing during the 1630s.

The following grievances caused less dispute: on Pym's initiative, they passed a rapid series of votes condemning images, crosses, and cruci-fixes, refusing of communion to those who would not come to the rails, enjoining articles at visitations without any authority save that of the bishop, and deprivations for not reading the Book of Sports. Sir Nevill Poole, who was not particularly interested in ecclesiastical questions, then exclaimed: 'enough of this already, moves to wave the rest'. After a technical exchange between Pym and Dr Eden, member for Cambridge University, about the limits to be permitted in University disputations, and an outcry about the prevalence of Mass, the debate wound to a close. It was a comprehensive condemnation of the Laudian church, and one which came from almost all quarters of the House. It was already clear that the godly by no means dominated the House, and that there was a lot of resistance to their view of ecclesiastical matters, but the King would have to retreat a long way before he could make common cause with this resistance.[142] He could not do so until Strange-

---

[141] Maltby, pp. 90–1. For what seems to be the first occasion on which Pym called Waller to the Bar, see ibid. 21.
[142] Ibid. 93–5.

ways, Hopton, and their like were more frightened of Covenants than they were of canons, and that could not happen until the Scots were a long way south of Berwick.

On the 30th, a long but uncontroversial debate on Ship Money was brought to a halt short of the point of condemnation by the persistent requests of Vane and Windebank that they should hear the King's counsel before condemning it. Pym, finding this request hard to resist, made a virtue of necessity by saying that 'I should thinke it an honor to this house to have them argue heare before us as iudges and it will countenance the iudgement of the house'. He turned the request into a concession of a point Charles had indignantly denied in 1629: the claim of the Parliament to be the highest judicial authority in the country.[143] The next day, Pym raised the case of another high-flown clergyman, Dr Beale, Master of St John's College, Cambridge. Beale had claimed that the King might make laws by himself, and that it was only of his 'royal benignity' that he admitted the consent of the Parliament. The King, he said, 'might command all wifes, children, estates and all', and 'we have property in nothing'. He said Tonnage and Poundage was absolutely the King's of inheritance, and that the Parliament, when it gave the King a subsidy or two, took away prerogatives worth two or three. He concluded, more picturesquely if less controversially, that 'the House of Parliament, both the Upper House and Lower House, cannot make a member, nay not a hayre, an excrment of a King'. There were two difficulties about sending for Beale: one was that he could claim privilege as a member of Convocation, and the other that he could claim it as the King's chaplain. Those who raised these notes of caution did not do so in order to defend him: Sir Thomas Jermyn Controller of the Household said: 'the King's Servant in ordinary if he gett out of the way. All that are of his opinion wishes wee were so rid of him.' A motion to defer his case was lost by 148 to 257, and an information asking him to appear was left at his lodging. The number of people voting, 405, is one of the two highest in any division between 1621 and the Civil War. It suggests that a large number of people were waiting with some anxiety for the King's response to their ignoring of his demands.[144]

On 2 May the reaction came, and the Parliament began its final series of debates. Vane opened the proceedings with an apparently uninformative message from the King, repeating that he needed supply, and that delay was as dangerous as denial. The sequel suggests, however, that

---

[143] Maltby, p. 104. This passage is a good example of the skills which made Pym such a successful Parliamentarian.

[144] Ibid. 112–14; Cope, pp. 185–6, 204–5. On Beale, see also Johann Sommerville, *Politics and Ideology in England 1603–1640* (1986), 119. Jermyn was probably typical of a larger body of the King's supporters than Beale.

there had been some effective backstage negotiation by Councillors.[145] After Price and Parry had supported Vane, and Pym had tried to obstruct him, Seymour at last opened serious bargaining, with the state- ment that 'if hee had sattisfaction for shipp money hee should trust the King with the rest'. Here was a proposal, tentative as yet, but one on which serious discussion could begin. Sir Roger North and 'divers of the House' immediately expressed approval. The beginning of negotiation, as might have been foreseen, left the godly and the pro-Scots exposed by their isolation. Strode immediately protested that 'if wee forgoe the service of God, wee had as good forgoe all as not adhere to all'. Hampden supported Strode. Vane took advantage of what looked like the beginning of a change of mood by approving of Seymour's motion, and observing that 'if a rupture should happen, he did believe that the country would not thank us'. One more speech for supply at this point might have set the mood of the House, but the man who caught the Speaker's eye was Pym, and he was not in favour of Seymour's proposal. He argued against leaving out the religious issue, but did not dwell on that point, on which he may have been doubtful of a majority. Instead, he attempted to improve the bargain by inserting military charges, an issue on which he could expect much wider support, and as intense resistance from the King: 'wee might be as much opprest by military charges as with shipp money hee would therefore have it published that no charges should bee laid upon the people without consent in Parlia- ment'. He then took a big risk by taking up the question of the Scottish war. He conceded that the King had power to make war and peace, that he had the power to judge the causes of war, and that he was not bound to take any counsel for the making or managing of the war. However, he argued that the Commons were equally not bound to engage themselves to maintain a war until its causes had been explained to them, and that they had a responsibility to the country not to enter into an open-ended commitment to maintain the war without some explanation: 'wee that are intrusted by our countryes ought not to engage our countreyes, our selves in the darke, but wee must have some light'. The prospect he opened up might or might not be attractive to the House, but it was certain to be highly alarming to the King. Jermyn 'said he expected not what was last spoken of'.

From then on, the debate suggests an almost equally divided House. Support for supply came from Serjeant Godbolt, Sir Robert Crane, Orlando Bridgeman, Sir Henry Mildmay, and probably from Falkland

[145] For this debate, see Maltby, pp. 120–7; Cope, pp. 187–93, 206–8. On the amount of subsidies to be asked for, there is an undated note by Vane on the back of a letter addressed to him from Rome on 7 Apr.: 'if the subsidies be smale, to put it off until his matie be spoken off. 6 subsidies offered to be refused'. This could date from any Privy Council meeting from 23 Apr. onwards: PRO SP 85/7, fo. 156ᵛ.

and Hyde. Suckling, Herbert, and Windebank, as official spokesmen, supported it. On the other side of the House, four different reasons for arguing against supply emerged. It is hard, in attempting to classify speakers, not to agree with the author of the Worcester College manuscript that 'many expressed themselves severall waies'. The first was the desire not to leave aside religious grievances, which was expressed by Strode, Hampden, Goodwin, Earle, and Glyn, and was probably behind Harley's proposal for a subcommittee. The second was the desire for a better bargain than Seymour had proposed. This was taken up by Edward Kirton, who supported Pym's call to secure 'the property of our goods in all things', by Sir John Hotham, who incurred the King's subsequent wrath by taking up the issue of military charges, by Sir Neville Poole, and by Sir Peter Hayman. Pym's demand for an explanation of the causes of the war was repeated, in very similar words, by Nathaniel Fiennes. It was also supported by Charles Jones chairman of the Committee of Privileges, and probably, though the reports are uncertain, by Digby. Sir John Wray, though he spoke in clichés which are hard to interpret, seems to have gone along with this argument. The fourth argument, developed by Charles Jones, was one of priority, that Ship Money should be abolished and *then* they should grant supply: 'if ship money taken wee may goe to supply'.

The atmosphere was growing similar to the last two days of the Parliament of 1614, when the Commons had also been considering supply with the pistol of dissolution at their heads.[146] As in 1614, the speeches indicated that the House was very nearly evenly divided. As in 1614, two procedural forces gave the opponents of supply a big advantage in an evenly divided House. One was the difficulty of deciding which question to put in a house which was divided along more than one line. The other was the strong political convention that, especially in major issues like supply, the House should not force things through by a bare majority, but should go on talking until something approaching unanimity emerged. As Sandys had said in 1614, it was against the King's honour to have any negatives in a vote of supply.[147] The point was especially telling in 1640, when any negative votes would be lovingly counted by the Scots. This procedural assumption gave the godly an advantage out of all proportion to their numbers, for while it was possible to convert Seymour to the view that a grant of supply would be too divisive to be worth it, it would never be possible, by any expenditure of time and effort, to convert men like Harley and Sir

---

[146] The parallel was made by Vane, who had been a member in 1614: Maltby, p. 132.
[147] See *CJ* i. 474. On reluctance to force close divisions on supply, see Russell, *1621–9*, pp. 40–1, 250–1, 258, 308. The last time such a division had been forced, in 1606, the King's majority of 1 vote had been too close for comfort.

Robert Cooke to the view that they should grant supply without redress in religion. On 2 May Solicitor-General Herbert, with the King at his back, jumped the gun by trying to force a vote on an open-ended question whether they would supply the King at all, only to be met by a rival question proposed by Hampden that they should vote on the question whether they were yet ready for a full resolution on the question of supply.[148] The House avoided the procedural trap of carrying both these resolutions, and instead decided to vote on neither. They then appointed Monday for 'an absolute answer to his Majestyes answer', and adjourned for what must have been an anxious Sunday.

The Councillors seem to have been busy during the Sunday, and on the morning of 4 May, Vane appeared with a final and precise offer: the King would give up Ship Money in return for twelve subsidies. The arithmetic of this offer is worth thought: twelve subsidies were worth £840,000 at the yield of 1621, or £660,000 at the yield of 1628. This was a good deal less than the estimate for the cost of the year's campaign: to raise the one million pounds needed for that, the King should have asked for fourteen or eighteen subsidies, depending on the yield he expected. He was offering to give up a regular revenue of some £200,000 a year in return for just over four times that, spread over three years. In other words, he was offering to sell Ship Money at something close to the going rate for sale of offices, of three-and-a-half years' purchase. From his point of view, it was a generous offer, so much so that a Lord Treasurer should have argued against it in Council. If his arguments had been overruled, it would have been for the political benefits, and not for the financial. Yet from the Commons' point of view, and even more from that of their constituents, the demand was awesomely large. It was nearly twice the amount raised by the two largest previous grants of 1606 and 1624, and it would mean their constituents would be escaping Ship Money only by paying a rather larger sum instead for the next three years. The sum was too little for the King, and too much for the Commons, but it seems to have been nicely judged: it represented the extreme outer limits of the possible for them both.

This offer, which was meant to expedite and clarify debate, in the event had the opposite effect. It mixed the argument for and against supply with another argument, between those who would have given supply on Vane's terms, and all those who would have offered supply on some other terms. Since this group may have included more than half

---

[148] Aston's diary goes a long way to revive the authority of Clarendon on the Short Parliament but Clarendon's chronology, as is common in memoirs, remains hopelessly confused. No diary confirms his report that some said the sum demanded was 'more than the whole stock of money in the kingdom amounted to', but it is credible. Clarendon, *History*, i. 136.

those who spoke, any crude classification of the House into those in favour of supply and those against is not possible. In practice, since Vane's offer was probably final, all those in favour of granting supply on any other terms should be counted as against. Yet since this was patently not the intention of a number of them, any such classification would do violence to the intentions of members, even while accurately recording the consequences of their acts. A further confusion results from a long argument over which question should be put to the vote. Hampden was now arguing for a question to be put that they needed to debate and vote on the legality of Ship Money before they could vote on supply. Solicitor-General Herbert finally recognized that the message had obscured, rather than clarifying, proceedings: 'because the king will out of his grace and favour hasten our business, his owne message has hindered his owne business'.[149]

Apart from official spokesmen, outright support for supply on Vane's terms seems to have come from Rudyerd, Glanvill,[150] Hyde, Falkland, Sir William Savill, and probably Sir Henry Slingsby. On the other side, the reasons were as they had been on Saturday, with two additions. The first was a direct attempt by Harley and Cooke to express opposition to the Scottish war, which appears to have attracted little public reaction. The other objection, coming significantly from Sir Francis Seymour, was that the sum demanded was too big: 'since 12 subsedyes were demanded, if hee must needes affirme yt without betraying the trust of that coutry hee could not doe it. Hee wished therefore an humble remonstrance to the King of the impossibility of it for his parte hee could not'. Holborne, who had been Hampden's counsel in the Ship Money case, also introduced a new argument: he pointed out that Finch, in his judgement, had said Ship Money was so inherent in the Crown that no Act of Parliament could take it away. The question therefore followed whether the bargain the King was offering could possibly be binding on him. This gave Hampden and St John an opportunity to press a case which commanded wide support, that the House should vote Ship Money illegal before they had voted any supply. Others pressed for more things to be included in the bargain: Gerrard, St John, Moundeford, Strangeways, Hoskins, and Hotham wanted to include military charges, and St John to include monopolies. Hampden, in passing, once again asked for the inclusion of religious grievances. Sir Nevill Poole and Henry Bellasis said that Ship Money was not enough, without specifying what else they would like to include. The debate ran

[149] For this debate, Aston is by far the fullest authority: Maltby, pp. 128–42. See also Cope, pp. 193–7, 208–10, and Hamilton MS 8253, a one-folio report by someone with a special interest in the Scottish War.

[150] Glanvill was able to speak because the House was in Committee of the Whole, where Lenthall was in the Chair.

on till six o'clock at night, and finally became lost in a welter of procedural interventions. It finally fell to Charles Jones chairman of the
Committee of Privileges to speak the lines which had fallen to Sandys in
1614, and put the case against going to a vote. 'The question of legality
wav'd because they would not have a question to which they must say
noe. Wee would have noe question put with which wee must say noe to
the King'.

The next morning Speaker Glanvill was warned not to attend the
Commons, and the Lords had due notice to put on their robes before
the King arrived to dissolve the Parliament. He praised the Lords,
proclaimed his loyalty to the religion of the church of England as he
believed it to be established, and expressed his determination to maintain propriety of goods as he understood it. For the Commons, he said
that 'I will not put the fault on all the whole House: I will not judge so
uncharitably: but it hath been some few cunning and some ill-affec-
tioned men, that have been the cause of this misunderstanding'.[151] In
relation to Pym, Fiennes, and the pro-Scots, this may not be an inaccur-
ate epitaph on the Parliament, but it is a grossly incomplete one. The
division of opinion on 2 and 4 May was not greatly different from the
division of opinion of August 1642, and Charles's great failure in the
Short Parliament was the failure to make common cause with men like
Seymour, Kirton, Hopton, and Strangeways, all of whom were to prove
beyond any doubt that they were not 'ill-affected'. This failure, though,
was theirs as much as his: Seymour's failure to rise to the offer of 4 May
was a missed opportunity for him, as much as for the King, and it was a
failure which did a great deal to show why Parliaments had been
brought to the verge of extinction. Throughout the Short Parliament, it
was Seymour rather than Pym who spoke with the typical voice of the
Parliaments of the 1620s. It was not a revolutionary voice: its outlook
was too local, and too non-governmental, for that. Seymour did not
want to take over power: he wanted to go home to Wiltshire and tell his
countrymen he had represented them well. For Seymour, a Parliament
was an instrument for limiting the power of government, not for exercising it. In this task, he was a great deal too successful for his own good.

Some of the voices around Pym may, by this stage, have been showing
an inkling of something different. Pym's speech of 17 April certainly
amounted to a full-scale alternative programme, and unlike Seymour, he
had a real appetite for power and was willing to pay for it. Among his
associates, Saye was already developing a theory of mixed monarchy
which put supreme power into the hands of the King, Lords, and
Commons together. The Lords, who held the balance, were likely to

[151] *LJ* iv. 81.

occupy the dominant position.[152] Lord Brooke, during the Short Parliament, once referred to the period between Parliaments by the startling name of 'interregnum'.[153] Some years earlier, the same group had replied to a letter from the Governor of the island of Providence, who was defending his 'prerogative', 'neither do we like the use of that horrid word'.[154] For the true godly, the purposes for which power was exercised were always more important than by whom it was exercised, and the temptation to transfer power into godly hands, wherever they might be, was always with them. It was a temptation from which Seymour was immune.

It is this temptation the Scots continually laid before them, and it is possible that Pym and his allies may have collaborated with them more closely than the public record suggests. Shortly before the end of the Parliament, an anonymous information alleged that some of the House of Commons had been having conferences with some of the Scottish commissioners, asking them to acquaint the House of Commons with their grievances. The Scots, it was said, replied that they had no warrant for this, but told them where to get their printed pamphlets, and said that if they were summoned to explain those, they would do so. He says that on Monday night (presumably 4 May) it was agreed that the book should be produced the next morning by Pym, who was to speak to it. The information said that one of the Scottish commissioners called Bartlett had often had conference with some of the Lower House on that business.

The Council investigated this charge, and intercepted a letter sent off on 5 May, under what was probably an assumed name, saying the House were 'this day about to petition his Majesty to hearken to a reconciliation with you his subjects of Scotland'. The most interesting evidence was the equivocal denial offered by Robert Barclay Provost of Irvine, the 'Mr Bartlett' of the information, who said he 'never had any direct conference or set meeting' with members of the Lower House.[155] This is a long way short of a total denial, and the speeches of Pym on 2 May, and Harley and Cooke on 4 May, give just enough supporting evidence to suggest that the story might be true. The decision to prevent Glanvill from taking the chair on the morning of 5 May could be, as was

[152] *Winthrop Papers*, iv. 266–7 (9 July 1640). The key phrase refers to the need for all degrees to be 'allwayes accomptable to Parliamentes consisting of all estates united yearly and havinge in that union *supremam potestatem*'. On the use Saye subsequently made of such ideas, see J. S. A. Adamson, '*Vindiciae Veritatis* and the Political Creed of Viscount Saye and Sele', *Historical Research*, 60/141 (1987), 45–63. I am grateful to Dr Adamson for showing me a draft of this article before publication.

[153] Cope, p. 112. It is perhaps even more startling that only Warner Bishop of Rochester appears to have reacted to the words.

[154] A. P. Newton, *Colonizing Activities of the English Puritans* (New Haven, Conn., 1914), 162.

[155] PRO SP 16/452/114, 115, 46, 102, 103.

commonly believed at the time, to prevent a vote that Ship Money was illegal, but it could also have been to prevent the raising of the Scottish issue.[156] If so, Charles made a bad political miscalculation. If Pym had raised this issue on the floor of the House, he would have lost. In November it was to be another story.

III The Second Bishops' War

Notwithstanding this dissolution, the King intends vigorously to pursue his former designes, and to leavie the same army of 30,000 foote and 3,000 horse. About 3 weekes hence, they are to be drawne together, but as yet I can not learne by what meanes we are certaine to get one shilling, towards the defraying this greate expence. What will the world iudge of us abroade, to see us enter into such an action as this is, not knowing how to maintaine it for one month. It greeves my soule to be involved in these councells; and the sence I have of the miseries that are like to insu, is held by some a disaffection in me.[157]

These were the views of Charles I's Lord General, the Earl of Northumberland, writing two days after the dissolution of the Short Parliament. His sense that Charles was once again setting out to do the impossible seems to have been widely shared, and not only by people who would have been natural opponents of another Bishops' War. This was the second time in his reign that Charles had angrily dissolved a Parliament without supply in time of war. The last time, in 1626, had precipitated a widespread sense of something very badly wrong. Yet the last time had been far less serious than the dissolution of May 1640. In 1626 the Commons had opposed the management of the war, but they had not opposed the war itself. Those with whom Charles had quarrelled in 1626 had included some who were unhappy about the war, and some who were strongly in favour of it, but if the Spaniards had actually landed in 1626 or 1627, there is little doubt that members would have been fighting by Charles's side. In 1640, on the other hand, there was the suspicion that many of the Commons were not merely against the war, but actually sympathized with the enemy: Secretary Windebank on 7 May complained that 'the Parliament . . . have clearly discovered that they like their courses so well that they would contribute nothing towards their suppression'.[158] This may have been accurate for Pym, even if it was a travesty for Seymour, but in the short term, what was believed mattered as much as what was true. The Council fought the

---

[156] Saye later claimed that the hasty dissolution was to prevent action on a motion by Nathaniel Fiennes, for a declaration that any money they raised should not be employed against their brethren of Scotland: William Fiennes, Viscount Saye and Sele, *Vindiciae Veritatis* (1654), BL E. 811(2), p. 43. Brampton Gurdon, writing to Winthrop, told a very similar story: *Winthrop Papers*, iv. 243–4.

[157] KAO De L'Isle and Dudley MSS C 2/42.

[158] *CSPD 1640*, vol. cccclii, no. 69.

whole of the Second Bishops' War with one eye over their shoulder for a fifth column. Others besides the Council could share such fears, and for them, the risk of further dividing England was a very powerful argument against the course the King was following.[159]

It was also a major difference between 1626 and 1640 that in 1626 the enemy was foreign, and safely on the other side of the Bay of Biscay. In 1640 the English were facing the only enemy with whom they had a common land frontier: they could not, as Phelips had once recommended, retire like the tortoise into his shell:[160] they had to make peace or stand and fight. With the common land frontier came an even more important difference: in 1626 Charles had been facing a foreign enemy, whom he could afford to leave alone if he chose. In 1640 he was facing a domestic rebellion. It seems likely that many of the English Council did not fully appreciate this distinction, since for them it was not true: for Northumberland or Vane, the struggle was with a foreign enemy, as it had been in 1626. It was only Charles who had to face the prospect that his authority might become a dead letter within one of his kingdoms. Moreover, since the Scots were his subjects, Charles had to consider the possible effects on his English subjects if he were to concede to them. Later, he was to find that concessions made to his Scottish subjects raised the appetite of the English to follow their example.[161] The notion that, if coerced hard enough, Charles might abandon bishops, Prayer Book, altars, kneeling at communion, and much else would be a heady wine for people like Nehemiah Wallington, who would become entitled to believe that the grass really was greener in the next field. Charles would also find, if he conceded these things to his Scottish subjects, that he had deprived himself of most of his best arguments for refusing them in England. He could not afford to convey the message that the door would open for those who pushed hard enough.

If Charles could not win, and could afford neither to lose nor to make peace, it is hard to see what he should have done next. There was, perhaps, one option still open, but one so surgically ruthless that no one seems to have dared to offer it to him. The Earl of Leicester, Ambassador to Paris, who thought of it, wisely kept it for the privacy of his commonplace book. This was that Charles should make one of his younger sons king of Scotland.[162] This would enable him to break the Union, and thereby to let the Scots have their own way without any acute danger to his rule in England. Since Scotland would then have a minority, the Covenanters would be left in control for long enough to

[159] See e.g. the views of Bristol, above, p. 112, and below, pp. 129–30.
[160] Russell, *1621–9*, pp. 83–4.
[161] See below, pp. 319, 406, 412, 464.
[162] KAO De L'Isle and Dudley MSS Z 47. I am grateful to Dr Blair Worden for drawing my attention to this part of the De L'Isle and Dudley collection, which is not calendared by the *HMC*.

build up their own enemies, and the career of Montrose suggests that the Covenanters were not without ability in that respect.

It was perhaps Charles's initial mistake to call a meeting of the Committee for Scottish Affairs the moment he returned to Whitehall, while still in the first flush of anger at the dissolution of the Parliament. This sitting down to counsel within minutes left no time for reflection. We are fortunate in having a record of the debates on this occasion. Since this record has been repeatedly questioned, it is worth saying that it is not unique: debates in the Privy Council had previously not normally been recorded, but from about 1638 onwards, quick scribbled notes by Nicholas, Vane, or Windebank became increasingly common. The existence of notes by Vane, then, is not necessarily the archival peculiarity it might appear. It also seems the balance of probability that the text of these notes, even if not their later interpretation, is substantially correct.[163]

These notes, studied with care, reveal one important point about Charles's relations with his Councillors. His habit of attending the Privy Council on any key occasion, and even more, his habit of spelling out when he did so the precise question on which he wanted counsel, seems to have done a great deal to inhibit freedom of debate, and even more to inhibit the raising of the more general issues. The first speaker, probably Vane himself, said that 'if his Majesty had not declared himself so soon, he would have declared himself for no war with Scotland'. This fits with Vane's later testimony that he had advised for a defensive war only.[164] The remark also contains a coded rebuke, but whether Charles had the ear to hear it is open to question. Northumberland also expressed doubts, but the mildness of his language compared with his vigour when writing to his brother-in-law two days later goes a long way to show what was wrong in Charles I's Council. He asked: 'if no more money, then what proposed? How then to make an offensive war, a difficulty. Whether to do nothing and let them alone, or go on with a vigorous war?' His speech and Vane's both seem to imply that the King had begun the meeting with a request for advice on how, not whether, to conduct an offensive war.

Laud and Cottington, of course, were on the other side. Laud told Charles that having tried all ways and been refused all ways, he was entitled to raise money 'by the law of God'. Cottington, in words later misquoted, said that 'leagues abroad they may make, and will, and

---

[163] PRO SP 16/452/31 (copy). The comments of Gardiner, *History*, ix. 120–33 and nn. are just. Northumberland, who was present, later possessed a copy of these notes: Alnwick MSS, vol. 15 (BL Microfilm 286), fo. 79[r–v]. It would be nice to know the issue on which the King was later angry with Northumberland, 'because he will not perjure himself for Lord Lieutenant Stafford': KAO De L'Isle and Dudley MSS C 2/45 (Northumberland to Leicester, 10 Dec. 1640).

[164] Gardiner, *History*, ix. 120 and n; Rushworth, *Trial*, pp. 546, 532.

therefore the defence of this kingdom'. Cottington, whose sympathies tended to be pro-Spanish, was playing on Charles's anti-French prejudices.[165] He said that in an 'unavoidable necessity' Charles was entitled to raise money, but does not appear to have said how such an entitlement could be made effective.

The key advice came from Strafford, and what we have of his speech should be quoted verbatim:

> Go vigorously on or let them alone, no defensive war, loss of honour and reputation, the quiet of England will hold out long. You will languish as between Saul and David, go on with an offensive war as you first designed, loosed and absolved from all rules of government, being reduced to extreme necessity, everything is to be done as power will admit, and that you are to do. They refused, you are acquitted towards God and man. You have an army in Ireland you may employ here to reduce this kingdom. Confident as anything under Heaven, Scotland shall not hold out five months. One summer well employed will do it. Venture all I had, I would carry it or lose all.

One of the most interesting, and least remarked, passages in this speech is the assertion that 'the quiet of England will hold out long'. In this statement, Strafford was almost certainly answering the principal objection, spoken or unspoken, on the other side, and in this, he appears to have been correct. The fears which sometimes swept over Windebank or Arundel, though fears to which most Tudor and Stuart gentlemen were subject, seem to have been exaggerated. England, however angry or disgruntled it might be, was not on the edge of revolt. The quiet of England held out another two and a half years from this speech.

Strafford, in spite of Laud's occasional jokes at the expense of his 'Puritan' upbringing, seems to have been totally immune from the emotive force of godliness. At the same time, and this is not coincidental, he enjoyed the sort of nationalistic detestation of the Scots which we used to be told was characteristic of all Englishmen. One of his major errors in 1640 was in assuming that most other people would share this emotion. The phrases about 'loose and absolved from all rules of government', especially if they do, as one might suspect, represent the *princeps legibus solutus* of the civil law, have an arbitrary ring which seems to sit oddly with the Wentworth of 1628. Yet even here, Strafford had a case. What was involved in 1640 was supply in wartime, and there were precedents for the view that 'subjects had a strict political obligation to grant taxation when circumstances required. Thus, in war, at least, the king bargained from a position of strength'.[166] From this perspective,

---

[165] It is always tempting to interpret divisions in the Council in terms of the pro-French members against the pro-Spanish, and perhaps the temptation should not be resisted.

[166] The words are those of Dr G. L. Harriss, in Kevin Sharpe (ed.), *Faction and Parliament* (Oxford, 1978), 88; see also p. 83.

there was justification for thinking, as Strafford did, that it was the 'frowardness' of the Commons which had brought affairs to the point of breakdown, and that once the King had been reduced to this point of necessity, he had to help himself as best he could.

The words which have gained most attention in this speech are: 'you have an army in Ireland you may employ here to reduce this kingdom'. It appears that Strafford did speak these words: the question is what he meant by them. He was attending a meeting of the Committee for Scottish Affairs, and speaking about Scotland. On pure textual logic, then, he should have meant Scotland by 'this kingdom'. On contextual logic, if he believed that 'the quiet of England will hold out long', he is unlikely to have wanted to bring an army to conquer it. And, to move from conjecture to evidence, it is plain that Strafford meant to employ the Irish army to subdue Scotland.

The plan was not, as it had been in the First Bishops' War, to use a collection of clansmen under the control of Antrim: it was to use the new Irish army of 8,000 men, largely Catholic, and paid out of the English Exchequer. As king of three kingdoms, Charles was as entitled to use the Irish as to use the English to repress his rebellious subjects of Scotland. Strafford, with a discreet subliminal reminder of his success in getting subsidies from the Irish Parliament, was telling Charles that if England would not help him to conquer Scotland, Ireland would. The new Irish army, being largely Catholic, was likely to be immune from any sympathy with the Scots' cause, and Strafford believed he had contained any attempt to whip up sympathy for the Covenanters among the Scots in Ulster. If they should stir, a Catholic Irish army marching across their territory on the way to St George's Channel would be unlikely to object to official orders to fight against them.

The most unambiguous evidence of Strafford's intentions is his letter to Hamilton of 24 March 1639/40, telling Hamilton he intended to be ready to 'enter Scotlande by the last of June'.[167] The papers of the Earl of Ormond, Lieutenant-General of the army, are almost equally clear. The officer list is endorsed 'this army was the 10,000 men raised for the expedition into Scotland'. This may be dismissed as a later note, but the same cannot be said of the two sets of notes on plans for landing at Dumbarton, nor of the repeated notes of plans to get the army to Carrickfergus and get boats to meet it there: Carrickfergus was a good port to use for Scotland, but an extremely foolish one for England. A landing in England from Carrickfergus could only be meant, as another plan in Ormond's papers suggests, to make a junction with the King at Berwick. In fact, an advance party of 500 was sent over, and added to the garrison of Carlisle. Though, as a point of strict pedantry, Carlisle is

[167] Hamilton MS 803.

in England, there seems to be no doubt that an enemy to be faced from Carlisle was Scottish.[168]

In the long term, Strafford's plan deepened an already existing Scottish interest in securing the Protestant supremacy in Ireland. In the short term, however, Strafford had a perfectly practical plan. His army was in pay from the English Exchequer,[169] and the question is why his plan was not executed. Strafford's own answer, supplied at the Council of Peers in September, was lack of ships.[170] Perhaps, though, a likelier answer is the one supplied by Lord Ranelagh at Strafford's trial, which is failure to obtain enough arms.[171] The notes of the Irish Council of War record that they were to buy their arms, tents, and horses in England.[172] We know that the tents were not yet available on 13 June,[173] and the shortages of both arms and horses in England were even more serious than in the First Bishops' War. Not only were they in short supply, but the supply that was available was extremely late, so if Strafford was relying on English arms supplies, it is likely that they did not appear until the war was over. If Charles had either sent the arms to Ireland, or kept in England the money he was sending to Ireland, he would probably have done much better by concentrating his resources than he did by dissipating them.

If it is so clear that the Irish army was meant for Scotland, it must be asked how the belief got abroad that it was meant for England. For this, it seems Charles and Strafford had themselves to blame, for the rumours that the Irish army was intended for England started within the court, and were duly picked up by the French Ambassador.[174] It seems to be the usual story of Caroline diplomacy by threat: the threat was intended to induce compliance, not to be executed. Instead, it was believed, but did not induce compliance. Strafford might well have paraphrased his own remark about the trial of Prynne: 'a prince that loseth the force and example of his army, loseth withal the greatest part of his dominion'.[175] The threat, at least in an oblique form, can be taken even closer to Strafford. Immediately after the Short Parliament was dissolved, his brother Sir George Wentworth, talking to, of all people, Sir Thomas Barrington, said 'this commonwealth is sick of peace, and will not be well till it is conquered again'.[176] This remark can only have been

---

[168] Bodl. MS Carte 1, fos. 187ᵛ, 225, 337, 177–80, 194, 228–30; *CSP Ire. 1633–47*, vol. cclviii, no. 38; J. C. Beckett, *Making of Modern Ireland* (1966), 75; *CSP Ire. 1633–47*, p. 306.

[169] PRO E 405/285 Mich. 1639, fos. 36ᵛ, 37ʳ; ibid. 403/2813, fos. 48ᵛ, 56ᵛ, 57ʳ, 58ʳ, 65ᵛ, 74ᵛ.

[170] *HMC Tenth Report*, VI. 137.

[171] Rushworth, *Trial*, p. 540.

[172] Bodl. MS Carte 1, fos. 179–80.

[173] *CSPD 1640*, vol. cccclvii, no. 1.

[174] PRO 31/3/72, pp. 142, 255; Gardiner, *History*, ix. 123 and n.

[175] See above, p. 23.

[176] Rushworth, *Trial*, p. 540.

intended to deter Barrington from too close co-operation with the Scots. Vane must undoubtedly have known that the Irish army was intended for Scotland, and clearly allowed himself to be used to give a false impression. What Vane knew, Pym probably knew also, but if they set out to deceive, Charles and Strafford were their chief allies in the deception.

This was not the only plan to gain help from outside England. Shortly after the Parliament was dissolved, negotiations began on a plan to gain armed help from Spain. This plan was not, as might have been thought, a mare's nest: the Spaniards wanted naval protection through the straits of Dover. Above all, they wanted to recruit men. The crisis of the Thirty Years' War was accompanied with an acute shortage of European manpower, and the British Isles were one of the few areas not yet depleted. For the Spaniards, Ireland in particular was a promising source for recruits, and the short-term use of some veterans might have been usefully recompensed by a supply of new Irish recruits. There were, of course, snags in the way, and before they could be overcome, Spain was diverted by the Revolt of the Catalans, and unable to give any help if it chose.[177] From then on, Charles was dependent on English resources, and they did not look promising.

The day after the Parliament broke up, placards were put up inviting apprentices to join in hunting 'William the Fox' for breaking the Parliament. A guard of trained bands deterred them for a time, but on 11 May they succeeded in mounting an attack on the Archbishop's palace at Lambeth. Laud had warning, and escaped, but the rioters, three days later, succeeded in breaking open the prisons. The general alarm was measured by the judges' decision that the rioters had committed treason. Archer, the supposed ringleader, was the victim of the last judicial use of torture in English history, and the warrant under which it was done was in Charles I's hand throughout. The root of Charles's concern is perhaps shown by his decision to place an extra guard on his children.[178] Ever since the death of Buckingham, Charles had been exceptionally liable to take fright at violent crowds, and this was to be a serious weakness during the next two years. Bristol, who had opposed the break-up of the Short Parliament on the ground that it would lead to 'fractions' at home, told Strafford the riots were the result of the breach

[177] KAO De L'Isle and Dudley MSS C 87/6; Bodl. MS Nalson xii, fo. 1; J. H. Elliott, 'Year of the Three Ambassadors', in Hugh Lloyd-Jones, Valerie Pearl, and Blair Worden (eds.), *History and Imagination: Essays in Honour of H. R. Trevor-Roper* (1981), esp. pp. 173–6; J. H. Elliott, *Count-Duke of Olivares* (New Haven, Conn., 1986), 574–7.

[178] Gardiner, *History*, ix. 133, 141; Pearl, p. 108 and n; PRO SP 16/454/39; *CSPD 1640*, vol. ccccliii, no. 63. It should be said that this last order was not issued till 15 May. The hand is identified by the editors of *CSPD*.

of the Short Parliament.[179] In fact, it seems these riots were less serious than they were feared to be: the French Ambassador had them more in proportion when he called them 'choses fort étranges en un état paisible comme celuy d'Angleterre'. They were indeed strange, and cause for concern, but they did not mark the end of England's status as an 'état paisible'. The French Ambassador, whose perspective on this subject is a valuable one, was still surprised by English peacefulness as late as New Year's Eve 1641.[180]

A more serious cause of trouble, even if a cause of less immediate apprehension, was the decision to put off the rendezvous of the troops who were being pressed, first from 1 June to 10 June, and then to 1 July. This decision was the result of shortage of money: the troops remained a charge on their counties and not on the Exchequer until they were transported across the country boundaries. Shortage of money also delayed supply of arms, powder, beer, butter, and other necessities, and led to much of what had been provided going bad before it could be used. Thus, as was normal with Stuart warfare, lack of money, by causing delay, led to extra expenses. It also led to increased discontent in the counties, since they had a problem of deciding what to do with large numbers of pressed men. The men could get no work from employers who knew they could not stay with any job they might take.[181] This meant, either a great charge on the county, or that the men would become disorderly through desperation. As the sheriff of Somerset reported, it was dangerous to bring so great a body together.[182] Conversely, if they were allowed to disperse, they would desert.[183]

In Lincolnshire, Deputy-Lieutenants complained that the pressed men were rebellious, and unless some of them were punished, they themselves would not be able to serve the Crown in this kind again. It makes an eloquent point that, in a society dominated by the pursuit of office, the Crown had to give out that Deputy-Lieutenants were not to be allowed to resign without special licence.[184] Strafford and the French Ambassador might be right that the English were not on the verge of revolution, but they were on the verge of total non-co-operation, which can sometimes be much harder to punish or control.

If Pym's objections to the legality of military charges had been designed to weaken the war effort in a Second Bishops' War, they were successful. The heaviest resistance in the Second Bishops' War seems to have concentrated on the issue of coat and conduct money, raised

---

[179] Cope, p. 90; Rushworth, *Trial*, p. 542.
[180] PRO 31/3/72, p. 148; below, p. 454.
[181] *CSPD 1640*, vol. cccliv, no. 99.1, vol. ccccclvi, no. 14.
[182] Ibid., vol. ccclvii, no. 50, vol. cccliv, no. 85.
[183] Ibid., vol. ccclii, no. 62; Bedfordshire RO St John MS J 1414.
[184] *CSPD 1640*, vol. cccliv, no. 49, vol. ccclvii, no. 104.

locally by county rates to clothe the troops and feed them on their way
to the rendezvous. It seems to have been rare for refusers to avow that
their refusals were based on grounds of legality, though some did. One
refuser in Norfolk asked 'what authority the lieutenant hath to impose
his charge upon the country; seeinge that every lieutenant hath a lawe by
himself, wisheing all those were charged that will paie money otherwise
than by course of lawe'. Yet, even in the same sample of refusals, this is
balanced by the man who said 'it were fitter the coats should be pulled
of rich men's backes, then the skin over his eares'. Curiously, this man
was a gentleman. The same sample also includes the ultimate in local-
ism, the constables of Hingham, who were accused of spending all their
coat and conduct money on the troops from their own village, not on
those from the hundred.[185] In Essex, the collectors raised £540 out of
£2,400 and reported that they despaired of the rest, and in the hundred
of Brixton, refusal appears to have been almost total.[186] Similar refusals
came from all round the home counties, and the lack of similar complaints from the remoter regions need not prove that they were more
compliant.

Similar troubles affected the pressing of troops. In Wiltshire, the
troops tumultuously released the coat-and-conduct-money refusers who
had been imprisoned.[187] This was a significant action, since troops were
upholding those who were refusing to pay money for their own
sustenance. In Hertfordshire, the trained bands raised an issue of
principle, by claiming that they were *ex officio* not obliged to serve
outside the county.[188] Lord General Northumberland said that London,
Kent, Surrey, Essex, Hertfordshire, Buckinghamshire, and Bedfordshire were so 'restive' that they would not get nearly the required
number of men from them.[189] Writing privately to his brother-in-law, he
was more explicit: he said 'so generall a disaffection in this kingdome
hath not been knowne in the memorie of any'. He complained of men
being mutinous and running away, and expressed the fear that those
who remained would be readier to draw their swords against their own
officers than against the Scots.[190] In this last fear, Northumberland
exaggerated, but it is a good example of the extent to which the Council
fought the Second Bishops' War with one eye over their shoulders. He
was, though, entitled to his view that 'there hath beene a great failing in
the laying of this designe'. It was already clear that if England lost the
war, defeat would lead to powerful demands for an inquest.

[185] PRO SP 16/460/29.1.
[186] *CSPD 1640*, vol. cccliv, nos. 45, 70.
[187] Ibid., vol. ccclvi, no. 44.
[188] Ibid., vol. ccclvii, no. 36; PRO SP 16/466/42, fos. 13–18.
[189] *CSPD 1640*, vol. ccclvii, no. 5.
[190] KAO De L'Isle and Dudley MSS C 85/16 and 17.

In the collection of Ship Money, the story is similar, and we have still not advanced much on the sheriff of Flint, who said he did not know whether to blame poverty or the dissolution of the Parliament.[191] It is true that 1640 was a depressed year for trade, and seems to have produced one of the shortages of coin which periodically added to the difficulties of English tax collection. Our loudest complaints to this effect come, probably enough, from the Stour Valley, an area in which short-term economic trends could easily cause real hardship in the clothing industry. Yet it is equally suggestive that the sheriff of Suffolk who so plaintively addressed these complaints to 'your imperial Majesty' was Sir Symonds D'Ewes, who was soon to emerge for all to see as a firm principled opponent of Ship Money.[192] One of the worrying signs was the number of refusals by local officials to take part in collection. The bailiff of the Chiltern Hundreds was one of the first in trouble for this, and it may not be a coincidence that he came from John Hampden's home area, where the godly community was unusually strong.[193] It was more serious when the parish constables, the base of the whole administrative pyramid, refused to make rates for Ship Money. Such reports came, among other places, from Hertfordshire, Worcestershire, Buckinghamshire, Bedfordshire, and Somerset.[194] In Worcestershire and Somerset, disciplinary action against the constables also failed. In Worcestershire, many preferred to stay in prison rather than submit and resume collection. In Somerset, they confessed frankly that they were more frightened of their neighbours than of the Crown: they said they were threatened with lawsuits, bills, and stones, and that they would rather fall into the hands of his Majesty than the hands of 'resolute men'. The threat of violence remained sporadic, but it was there. In Cheshire, Thomas Stanley of Alderley, a rare case of a JP willing to have recourse to violence, threatened to shoot anyone who distrained his goods for Ship Money.[195] The sheriff of Cambridgeshire reported that some of his men were grievously wounded trying to distrain for Ship Money, and when he tried to prosecute the offenders, the Grand Jury found 'ignoramus' and dismissed the case.[196] These outbreaks of violence, though they made headlines, seem to have remained rare. The Crown was in fact at much more risk in cases like that of the taxpayers of Odiham and Alton Hundreds in Hampshire, who reported that, since previous refusers had not been punished, they

[191] *CSPD 1640*, vol. cccclvii, no. 78.

[192] Ibid., vol. cccclvi, nos. 31, 41.

[193] Ibid., vol. cccclv, no. 115.

[194] Ibid., vol. cccclvi, no. 49, vol. cccclvii, no. 22; PRO SP 16/463/86.1 and 86.2; ibid. 16/464/23.

[195] *CSPD 1640*, vol. cccclix, no. 21.

[196] Ibid., vol. cccclvii, no. 55; PRO SP 16/463/43.1 and 43.2.

would refuse also.[197] In this, as in other areas, when refusal exceeds the capacity of authority to punish it, the point of breakdown has been reached. In the summer of 1640 this point looked uncomfortably near.

It is very difficult indeed to analyse this sort of evidence by individual example: we have no figures for proportions of coat and conduct money collected, and since the Ship Money figures did not benefit from a full year's collection, apparently disastrous figures are hard to compare with any other year. It is also hard to know how far our picture is influenced by the exceptional richness of State Papers, Domestic for 1640: do we know of more refusals because we have a greater total bulk of evidence? Yet when all these qualifications are made, the scale of tax refusals was enough to deserve to be taken seriously, and a necessary reminder that, whatever theories might say, there is a residual sense in which all seventeenth-century government was by consent. It is even harder to analyse the motives of these refusals: were they a matter of general resentment at paying, or simply of hope that they might get away with it? Or do they measure a growing sense of unwillingness to pay illegal taxation, or sympathies which were on the Scottish, rather than the English, side? If, as is most probable, they represent a mixture of all of these, what are the proportions in the mixture? These, in the end, are matters of conjecture. Rather than pursue them vaguely across the country, it may be better to look cursorily at a sample of refusers thorough enough to be worth study: the coat-and-conduct-money refusers for Middlesex. The list of these was collected by three local JPs. One of them, to judge from his later record, may well have been pro-Scottish, but since he was also a Clerk of the Council, he had to cope with the consequences of failure to collect the money. The JPs, in their introductory comments, adopted a distinctly sympathetic tone, being 'much moved with the complaints of most of the meaner sort, who were not only destitute of money, the chargeable time of reaping their crops being now at hand, but also of men, their servants being pressed away for the northern expedition, and the country so unfurnished of mowers and reapers that they feare to have the corne shed upon the ground for want thereof'.[198] They claim that many will be able to pay when the harvest is over and they have sold their corn. From the King's point of view, this was of course a way of saying they were able to pay when the campaigning season was over. It is worth wondering how consistently this conflict of priorities handicapped seventeenth-century warfare.

The list of refusers immediately reveals the names of three of those

---

[197] *CSPD 1640*, vol. ccccliii, no. 23.
[198] PRO SP 16/461/103, fo. 182. What follows is taken from this survey, which deserves more thorough analysis than it is given here. I am grateful to Dr J. S. A. Adamson for drawing my attention to the absence of Essex from the list of refusers.

who were to sign the Petition of the Twelve Peers, the major protest against the war. In St Clement Danes, the Earls of Salisbury and Rutland were out of town, and their stewards said they had been given no direction to pay. This evidence could mean anything, but we are on firmer ground with the Earl of Mulgrave, in Kensington. He evaded an assessment of £1 by pleading poverty. It is true that Mulgrave's estates had been occupied by the Scots, but it is very difficult to believe that his credit did not extend to £1. In Greenford, Brampton Gurdon was one of many who complained that the assessment was unequal and unfair. He may well have been right, but since he was a conspicuous opponent of the war and a close friend of John Winthrop, it is hard not to suspect political disaffection.[199]

Most refusers, of course, come from much lower down the social scale: direct refusal was not the political style of peers and gentlemen, and most of them appear to have gone on paying, and working, in the hope of being able to exert influence against the policy. The ambiguity of the gentry's position is well illustrated by the returns from Harrow-on-the-Hill. Sir Gilbert Gerrard, the resident gentleman, was a Ship Money refuser, a member of the Providence Company, and later a pro-Scot and Parliamentary Treasurer at War. In the Short Parliament, he had spoken against military charges. Nevertheless, he paid the 18s. he was assessed to pay for coat and conduct money in Harrow-on-the-Hill, but he was the only taxpayer in the parish who did so. The others returned a collective reply, and 'all say they have it not to pay'. If the Council suspected that Gerrard's lack of enthusiasm for the service was behind this return, its suspicion can only have been heightened by finding a similar pattern repeated from Gerrard's other lands in Sudbury and Pinner.[200] Even the collectors pointedly refrained from endorsing the taxpayers' claim that they did not have the money.

They took a very different line in some other cases, of which the most conspicuous is Uxbridge. There, thirty-three made a collective answer that they could not maintain their poor, for they had lost their market and their trade was decayed, and they could not pay. Here, the collectors said that 'wee finde it to bee a towne very much chardged with poore, and the inhabitants for the most pte tradesmen and innkeepers of meene habylytye'. They said they could not hope to receive more than half the sum assessed on the town. Among twenty-two defaulters in

---

[199] *Winthrop Papers*, iv. 243–4, and other refs.

[200] For evidence that this suspicion was entertained, see *CSPD 1640*, vol. ccccliii, no. 54. There is perhaps an example of the importance of the main resident landlords in the remarkably successful return for Fulham, which collected £23 7s.8d. out of a total of £25 (ibid., fo. 216). The principal landowners there were the Bishop of London, Lord Treasurer, and Sir Nicholas Crispe the Customs Farmer, one of the King's principal creditors. On land ownership in Fulham, see House of Lords RO, Original Acts, 16 Car. I, cap. 32.

Hornsey, they carefully distinguished between five who 'cannot pay' and seven who 'hath not money'—presumably a credit problem. The formula 'saith he cannot pay' indicates a suspicion that the case was one of reluctance and not of inability. In Ruislip, where thirty-three sent in a collective protest that the parish was over-assessed, the collectors carefully expressed their agreement with the protest.

They prudently made no comment on the protests of the constables of Harmondsworth, Ickenham, and Kensington, who said they had made up the shortfall of the previous year's coat and conduct money out of their own pockets, and would pay when repaid. They made no comment, either, on the large number of cases who pleaded privilege as royal servants. Dr Mayerne the King's doctor, in Chelsea, had every right to do so, but some of those who helped to make up the total of ninety-three refusers in Enfield were rather more doubtful cases. Enfield, which seems to have been a contentious parish, produced the only refuser who made an explicit plea of legality, but even so only in the cautious words that 'he doth not deny it soe it may appear lawful'. In Hillingdon, twenty-six, in another collective reply, said they would pay as soon as they could raise it 'upon sale of some commodities', presumably meaning after harvest. We can only speculate on how much reluctance this reply may have covered. One refuser, again in Enfield, made the point Ship Money refusers were beginning to make, that last year's refusers had escaped, 'and therefore he doth now refuse to pay till they have paid'. In Tottenham, Sir John Coke, recently dismissed from the Secretaryship on the ground of old age, was 'in Darbishire, and not spoken with'.

Other refusers argued that the sum was too much, especially in the context of other taxes being raised at the time. The vicar of Perivale, in words which must have haunted him whenever tithe was to be collected, pleaded that he could not pay this: it was far too heavy, being a tenth of his income. At 'Weale hamlet' (probably Wealdstone) the constables refused to make a rate, and 'replyed that the heavy taxation of coate and conduct money and shipmoney both concurringe at one tyme, would so disable them to make any payment, that they thought fitt rather to make noe assessment at all then after they had made it not to be able to pay the sume assessed'. In St Leonards Shoreditch, a number of refusers replied explicitly 'not so much', and were joined by others who 'will not pay at all'. One, like the proverbial bells of Shoreditch, said he would pay 'when he hath money'.

This survey seems to give weight to all the commonly alleged motives of refusal, and, by giving weight to all, gives us no clear lead between them. It does show an articulate and able body of taxpayers, able to choose grounds of refusal with some subtlety, and with some skill, in many cases, at making the system work to favour them. The collectors' responses illustrate how much better the prospects were for those who objected to their rates than for those who objected to the levy outright. The clearest message, as might be expected from the nature of the source, is of the sheer weight of taxation involved. One taxpayer at Northolt underlined the point by saying that at the rate he had been assessed at in 1628, his Ship Money and his coat and conduct money together came to twenty-one subsidies.[201] It was a fair point, but it would have been legitimately possible to answer it by arguing that it only illustrated that the Parliamentary subsidy had got too low. What really emerged was the difficulty of financing wars by consent at the costs prevalent in 1640. Taken as a whole, the survey indicates an administrative problem too big to be solved with the resources available.

This might have appeared a good time for avoiding unnecessary trouble, but the King nevertheless decided to precipitate another storm of ecclesiastical criticism in the midst of the difficulties over money and troops. Convocation was normally dissolved at the end of a Parliament, but the King, apparently on his own responsibility, decided that he would continue it. His immediate motive may have been the desire to complete the grant of clerical subsidies which was in the pipeline, but he justified his decision to the Privy Council on the ground of his desire to take into consideration the 'just grievances' complained of in Parliament, 'and to remedy so many of them as he should find to be real'. The Council, after a 'serious debate', 'unanimously approved and commanded that a memorial of this his Majesty's care in continuing the Convocation for the quiet of the church' should be entered in the register.[202] It was, of course, the effect of such an entry to record that the Council were not responsible for the decision. Five days later, the King instructed Laud, in the course of drawing up new canons, to provide a new oath, to be taken by all the clergy, binding those who took it to renounce popery and adhere to the doctrine and discipline of the church of England.[203] With this official encouragement, Convocation

---

[201] PRO SP 16/461/103, fo. 251. This taxpayer, Henry Arundell, had been involved in the preparation of the Middlesex petition to the Parliament, and had given it to Sir Gilbert Gerrard, who owned land in his parish: *CSPD 1640*, vol. ccccliii, nos. 52–5. That there was prearrangement between Gerrard and Arundell seems likely enough, but this individual reply suggests that Arundell was more than a cats-paw. According to Arundell's account, the petition (which does not now survive) made the same requests as the others; against Ship Money, against innovation in the church, and in favour of annual Parliaments. See above, p. 108.

[202] Gardiner, *History*, ix. 142–3; *CSPD 1640*, vol. ccccliii, no. 14.

[203] Ibid., no. 102. It is a good example of the difficulty of disentangling the respective responsibilities of the King and Laud that this letter from the King to Laud survives in the form of a draft in Laud's hand. It is perhaps best to assume they were jointly responsible except where there is concrete evidence to the contrary.

completed a new set of canons on 29 May, which, after the necessary rubber-stamping by the Convocation of York, were duly printed and published.

The reasons for making these canons are probably accurately set out in the preamble, which, whoever may have written it, probably accurately expresses the King's mind.[204] It expresses his horror 'that many of our subjects being misled against the rites and ceremonies now used in the church of England, have lately taken offence at the same, upon an unjust supposal that they are not only contrary to our laws, but also introductive unto popish superstitions'. It is claimed that 'it well appeareth *unto us*'[205] that the ceremonies in question continued back to the days of Edward VI and Elizabeth, although they had since 'begun to fall into disuse, and in place thereof other foreign and unfitting usages by little and little to creep in'. The authors of jealousies about ceremonies, it was said, 'though they colour the same with a pretence of zeal, and would seem to strike only at some supposed iniquity in the said ceremonies; yet, as we have cause to fear, aim at our royal person, and would fain have our good subjects imagine that we ourself are perverted, and do worship God in a superstitious way, and that we intend to bring in some alteration of the religion here established', although 'we assure our self, that no man of wisdom and discretion could ever be so beguiled, as to give any serious entertainment to such brain-sick jealousies'. In other words, Charles was passing the canons in order to clear himself of the charge of religious innovation. Perhaps only those who have studied his reaction to the charge of innovation in Scotland will find this explanation believable.

The first canon upheld the King's power, asserting that 'the most high and sacred order of kings is of divine right, being the ordinance of God himself'. This said something more than the conventional belief that 'the powers that be are ordained of God': it argued that God had specifically established monarchy as the correct form of government. It was not a new belief, but it was not universally accepted. This canon also upheld Charles's belief that the Royal Supremacy was founded in Scripture, assimilated the General Assembly to the Pope by condemning 'any independent coactive power either papal or popular', and asserted that taxes were due 'by the law of God, nature and nations'. To some people, this appeared to be an altogether improper attempt by the clergy to meddle with the professional legal question of the lawfulness of Ship Money.

[204] For the text of the canons, see Laud, *Works*, v. 608–33. What follows is taken from there unless otherwise stated.

[205] My italics. On the issues involved in Convocation's claim to legislate for the church, see J. P. Sommerville, *Politics and Ideology in England 1603–1640* (1986), 203–16; above, pp. 15–16 and 39–41; and below, pp. 231–4.

The canons against popery and Socinianism were relatively uncontroversial, but the canon against sectaries took in a great many who would not normally have been regarded as sectaries. It condemned as such all who did not regularly attend their parish church, including those who attended the sermon but not the service, and condemned all books against the discipline and government of the church of England. The largest public controversy centred on the canon the King had required enforcing an oath against innovation. The oath committed those who took it to approving the doctrine and discipline of the church of England as containing all things necessary to salvation. The most controversial clause was: 'nor will I ever give my consent to alter the government of this church by archbishops, bishops, deans and arch-deacons, etc, as it stands now established and as by right it ought to stand'. As many critics pointed out, this appeared to bind them to oppose any lawful Act of Parliament in which King and Parliament might enact the contrary. As a group of Northamptonshire ministers tellingly pointed out 'the whole clergie [sic] is filled with so many ambiguities that we dare not take it'.[206] This ambiguity was highlighted by the canon on ceremonies, which justified, by carefully reciting *half* of Queen Elizabeth's Injunction,[207] the permanent placing of the altar at the east end, and said that though this 'doth not imply that it is or ought to be esteemed a true and proper altar, wherein Christ is again really sacrificed, but it is and may be called an altar by us, in that sense in which the primitive church called it an altar and in no other'. In many parts of the canons, Charles was entitled to claim that his opponents were innovators, and in many others he was entitled to claim that the rigour of literal interpretation was on his side, even if normal practice was not. In the defence of bowing, for example, the canon conceded that it had passed out of use, and had to be defended by 'the most ancient custom of the primitive church in the purest times', rather than by Jacobean practice. The case of the altar, on the other hand, shows that Charles was quite as capable as his opponents of using an expressed dislike of innovation as a cover for what was really theological partisanship.

That these canons should produce protests from the godly ministers of London and Northamptonshire was no great cause for surprise. It was not wise, at this stage, to remind such people of their reasons for hoping for a Scottish victory, but their protests need not be held to symbolize widespread public disaffection. It was altogether more serious to find a petition of protest being organized at the Devon assizes,

---

[206] PRO SP 16/461/88 and 90; ibid. 16/461/87.
[207] For the full text of the Injunction, see Tyacke, pp. 200–1. For the issues involved, ibid. 198–216, and other refs.

with the support of such impeccable friends of the church as the Earl of Bath.[208] This petition took its stand on the good Whitgiftian ground that discipline contained nothing necessary to salvation, and said they could not be tied never to alter discipline even if the King and 'state' should enjoin them to. The campaign to enforce the Etcetera Oath invited resistance, and provided an occasion for organization. In August a meeting of London ministers for co-ordinating opposition included Dr Downame (John Downham, or possibly Salisbury's chaplain Calybute Downing), Cornelius Burges, Edmund Calamy, John Goodwin of Coleman Street, Mr Jackson, Mr Browne, and Offspring of St Antholin's. This list shows a clear continuity between the Feoffees for Impropriations of the early 1630s, and the organization of pro-Scottish ministers of 1641. Sir John Lambe, who detected this meeting, believed it was engaged in potentially treasonable correspondence with the Scots.[209] His evidence falls short of proof, but his suspicion is likely enough. By September, so good a conformist as Robert Sanderson was advising Laud that the oath was causing such distaste among those 'otherwise every way conformable' that it should be abandoned.[210] The oath, and the canons generally, were probably intended to isolate and reveal the pro-Scots, but instead had the effect of bringing them much extra support.

For much of the Second Bishops' War, the pro-Scots seem to have prudently concentrated their protests on issues on which they enjoyed wider public support, but occasional incidents show that the polarizing power of the Scottish issue was unabated. One of them took place in the Green Dragon tavern in Bishopsgate Street, where two Dedham clothiers fell into conversation over dinner with two officers about to go off to fight the Scots. The clothiers seem to have taken the risk of expressing pro-Scottish sentiments, leading one of the officers to rail against 'Puritans'. The clothiers then asked him what a 'Puritan' was, 'whereat he flew into such a rage he threw a trencher', and then hit one of the clothiers on the head with the flat of his sword. It was the clothiers, not the riotous officer, who were imprisoned for this incident.[211] A meeting of Northamptonshire clergy at the Swan in Kettering, detected by the ever-vigilant Sir John Lambe, appears to have had before it a letter from the Scottish army, claiming that they came only to reform some abuses, among which they named Laud and Strafford.[212] Thomas Triplet, equally vigilant, reported that his enemy

[208] PRO SP 16/461/87.
[209] Ibid. 16/463/54.
[210] Ibid. 16/467/56.
[211] Ibid. 16/466/112–16; ibid. 16/467/14, 15, 17.
[212] Ibid. 16/465/8, 44, 45.

George Lilburne 'sure is a Covenanter, if we could discover him'.[213] Only the event was to prove Triplet right. A rumour that Cornelius Burges had been in Scotland is perfectly possible, but cannot be confirmed. A search of both his town and country houses on the same day failed to reveal any incriminating evidence.[214] As in the case of George Lilburne, only time was to show that these suspicions were correct. It seems probable that the organized pro-Scots were keeping their powder dry until the Scots should cross the Border. Meanwhile, Scottish books continued to circulate as far afield as Lewes.[215] A report came from so improbable a place as Naworth (Cumberland) that 'our country is extremely factious, and generally inclined to the Scots'.[216]

This feeling was supported by a steady trickle of seditious words, sometimes involving the charge that Archbishop Laud was a papist. A Devizes clothier, talking on the road, was told 'it was bishop Laud who was the cause of the suffering of all this army, and said that the King was ruled by him'. The other man said he did not know who Laud was, and the clothier had to explain to him that he was bishop of Canterbury, and that it was common knowledge that he had turned papist.[217] A man at Lutterworth, doubtless picking up a magnified report of the searching of Saye and Brooke's studies after the Parliament, said that 'the best men of the kingdom, Saye, Brooke and Warwick, are imprisoned by the King'.[218] The vicar of Pepper Harrow, Surrey, refused to pray against the Scots. A certain Mrs Chickleworth of Aldgate reached higher, by reporting that the King went to Mass with the Queen. Another added that the Prince had been found to be very 'pensive', and when asked why, replied 'my grandfather left you four kingdoms, and I am afraid your Majesty will leave me never a one'.[219] These words show that an alternative structure of blame remained available: those who wished to blame court papists, rather than Scottish Puritans, for the war, knew it was a current explanation.

It was not a promising atmosphere in which to march out to war. Vane may well have exaggerated in saying that the army took it for orthodox that the rebels were the redeemers of their religion and liberties,[220] but there was no reason to think the army immune from the pro-Scottish sympathies to be found elsewhere. The problem of money

---

[213] PRO SP 16/458/19.

[214] Ibid. 16/467/92, 93, 96, 100.

[215] Ibid. 16/465/60.

[216] CSPD 1640, vol. ccclix, no. 42 (Sir William Howard to Conway).

[217] PRO SP 16/461/46.1; CSPD 1640, vol. ccclvi, no. 36. It is worth noting that both these informations came from the same informant, and it was he who had professed not to know who Bishop Laud was.

[218] CSPD 1640, vol. ccclviii, no. 110.

[219] Ibid., vol. cccliv, no. 42; PRO SP 16/470/102.

[220] PRO SP 16/466/76.

grew more acute, and the army was out of pay before it met the enemy. Attempts to raise money, as in the First Bishops' War, had been reduced to attempts to raise loans from the City and from officeholders. The City proved so resistant that Strafford threatened to hang some of the Aldermen, leaving his friend Christopher Wandesford to express the fear that his ill-health had affected his reason.[221] An attempt to raise a scutage in traditional style raised only £746 16s.8d.[222] Apart from pay, the shortage of money showed up in poor commissariat, and above all in a disastrous shortage of arms. Conway, commanding at Newcastle, was protesting from early in the summer about the poor quality of arms that reached him.[223] The army were further handicapped by the Petition of Right, which prohibited martial law and billeting. The commanders were chary of executing martial law, but the Privy Council refused to recognize the existence of any law against billeting, telling the Council of the North that 'neither his Matie. nor wee ourselves have seene or read any such law to prohibit it. Nor was it ever in the thought of his Matie. to devest the Crown of that necessary power, wthout which expedient it is impossible for armyes to march'.[224] Northumberland, at the last moment, was prevented from serving as Lord General by what seems to have been an attack of malaria.[225] Suspicions of diplomatic illness seem to be unjustified, since it was over a year before he was fully restored to health. Strafford, in desperately poor health himself, had to deputize at the last moment.

The troops also arrived in the north shaken by a series of mutinies, mostly aimed against supposedly Catholic officers. The Essex soldiers, rioting for a wage of 12d. rather than 8d. a day, illustrate Professor Parker's dictum that army mutinies are a chapter in the early history of collective bargaining.[226] Others showed more theological concerns: a widespread mutiny and desertion at Daventry was justified by assertions of determination not to fight against the Gospel, and not to be sent to sea or commanded by papists.[227] The men from Devon and Dorset each

[221] Pearl, pp. 99–103. Bodl. MS Carte 1, fo. 197 (Wandesford to Ormond, 26 May 1640): 'I am not satisfied that these great distempers of his body came without some strong and violent operations of his mind'. Wandesford added that 'if you did not love this man well of whom I speake', he would not have mentioned it.

[222] PRO E 405/285, Eas. 1640, unfol.

[223] CSPD 1640, vol. ccccliv, no. 30, vol. cccclvi, no. 43.

[224] PRO SP 16/464/17.

[225] KAO De L'Isle and Dudley MSS C 85/18 and 23. PRO SP 16/478/10 (2 Mar. 1642), and PRO SP 16/483/88 (25 Aug. 1641), where he says he has 'beene all this summer wandering from place to place seeking remedies for the recoverie of my health'. His full recovery was noted by Edward Nicholas on 7 Oct. 1641: Guildford MSS 85/5/2/10a.

[226] CSPD 1640, vol. ccccix, no. 36; Geoffrey Parker, Army of Flanders and the Spanish Road (Cambridge, 1972), 187–8.

[227] PRO SP 16/460/5. On the 'miseries and deaths' troops believed they faced at sea, see also CSPD 1640, vol. ccccliii, no. 40.

actually murdered one of their officers. The Devon men appear to have been correct that he was a papist, since they succeeded in taking a crucifix from his dead body.[228] This sort of action shocked all shades of respectable opinion: Bedford, as Lord-Lieutenant of Devon, vigorously lent his name to tracking down the murderers, and Nathaniel Fiennes, in an unsigned newsletter, loudly condemned the 'west countrie clownes' responsible.[229] Before any attempt is made to deduce general political sympathies in the army from these mutinies, it should be recorded that Fiennes also reports a meeting between some soldiers and the Covenanter Lord Loudoun, when they nearly pulled him to pieces 'so much were they enraged against this Lord for noe thing els but because hee was a Scott'.[230] It would seem that soldiers were capable of turning against anyone they could blame for their predicament: whether received opinion would, in the end, blame the war on the papists or the Scots perhaps waited to be determined by the fortunes of battle. Other soldiers showed an appetite for altar rails, and were duly disciplined by the earl of Warwick. Again, we should be careful not to take it for granted that those who attacked rails were 'Puritan'.[231] One of those convicted for the offence in Essex had a record which included absence from church, fornication, and committing adultery with the same woman as his father. As Dr Sharpe concludes, 'not even in the most elastic definition of that much-stretched word can Ayly be described as a Puritan'.[232] Rails seem to have provoked a straightforward impatience of restriction, as well as a desire for fuel, and attacks on rails, without supporting evidence, should never be used to prove political or religious affiliation.

It added considerably to the general demoralization that, as this army approached the enemy, much of it had still not received its arms. The Ordnance Office tried to minimize the risk of riot (or of troops selling their arms *en route*) by sending the arms by sea to Hull, for the troops to pick them up at the end of the march. Many of the arms arrived after the troops had passed the collection-point. We have an official dispatch sheet only for the artillery, which shows that much of it did not leave London till 10 August or later, while the Scots crossed the border on the 20th. Seventeen ships carrying small arms did not leave London till 1 September.[233] The battle of Newburn was fought on 28 August.

[228] PRO SP 16/463/88.

[229] Huntingdon RO Manchester MS 32/5/17. He stated that Astley had 'not yet thought it fitt' to arm the troops who had reached the rendezvous.

[230] Ibid. On Loudoun's release from the Tower, and possible reasons for it, see PRO 31/3/72, pp. 180, 215; Hamilton MS 1218; Donald, pp. 343–8.

[231] *CSPD 1640*, vol. cccclxi, nos. 24, 25.

[232] *Crime in England 1550–1800*, ed. J. S. Cockburn (1977), 105 and n.

[233] Staffs. RO Dartmouth MS D 1778/1/i/5.

Another report tells us that the great guns to defend Newcastle arrived there after the Scots.[234] On 18 August young Francis Windebank reported to his father that none of his men had any arms, and that they would be much braver in the face of the enemy with them than without them.[235] The next day William Ashburnham reported to Nicholas that a third of the army was without arms.[236] On the 20th, Strafford reported receiving an estimate from Sir Jacob Astley that almost a quarter of the army was without arms.[237] It seems likely that delays in finding money had a lot to do with this situation.

Meanwhile, as intelligence reports had been suggesting for some time, the Scots decided they would not wait on the Border, as they had done in the First Bishops' War, but would invade England. It is possible that the English had not wanted to discourage them from invading: the decision to group forces around Newcastle, rather than Berwick, had the effect of leaving the Border invitingly unguarded. It is possible that Charles and Strafford hoped that an actual invasion would have the effect of rousing the English to an outburst of anti-Scottish feeling. If so, this feeling balanced a frequently expressed sense that the Scots would not dare invade unless England were internally divided.[238] Intelligence constantly stressed Scottish awareness of disorders in England, and Northumberland, writing to his sister on 2 July, said the Scots would not dare invade without internal troubles in England. It is also possible that the Scots were encouraged to invade by intelligence of the disorder of English military preparations. It seems that they invaded with expectations of a party in England, but that they may have hoped for more support than, in the event, proved to be available.

The Scots themselves gave the English naval blockade as a reason for their invasion, claiming that it had created such a shortage of food that they were left with no choice in the matter.[239] This may be true, and it is probably one of the reasons for which Hamilton had originally recommended the blockade. It is a strategy which strengthens the suspicion that the English wanted the Scots to invade. Yet, though the Scots' story about the blockade is inherently probable, we should not take their word for it, since they had an ideological motive for telling it. Some Scots, such as Baillie, shared the English horror of resistance, though others had been emboldened by the study of Knox and Buchanan to

---

[234] Staffs. RO D 661/11/1/5 (Richard Dyott to his father, 7 Sept.). He claimed, in some indignation, that the Scots had intelligence of the delay of the English artillery. Also PRO SP 16/465/52.

[235] PRO SP 16/464/26.

[236] Ibid. 16/464/44.

[237] Hamilton MS 1229.

[238] *CSPD 1640*, vol. ccccliv, nos. 51, 98, vol. cccclvi, no. 43.1.

[239] Hamilton MS 1217, and other refs.

take a more generous view of it. They did know, however, that it was a vital part of their public relations to convince the English that they were not rebels, or at least to give their friends an excuse for pretending they were not. Their marching pamphlet, *The Lawfulnesse of our Expedition into England Manifested*, begins with a heavy stress on the blockade, leading on to the one justification of resistance which was generally acceptable: the argument of self-defence.[240] In 1640, as in 1642, it was ideologically vital to establish that the King was the aggressor, and the King, who did not number patience among his primary virtues, duly obliged. It seems likely that the hope of an English party did more to encourage Scottish intervention than the blockade did, but the blockade provided both an extra reason and a vitally necessary excuse.

By deciding not to defend the line of the Tweed, the English army laid upon itself the necessity of defending an inferior position. Most positions between the Tweed and the Tyne would have been dangerously liable to outflanking, and it was impossible to abandon Newcastle without abandoning to the Scots control of London's coal trade. Since control of the coal trade would enable the Scots either to freeze London into submission, or to finance a war effort off the resultant customs duties, Newcastle had to be defended. This need more or less dictated to the English a need to defend the line of the Tyne. The Scots, commanded by Leslie, who was a seasoned general with continental experience, approached the Tyne at the ford of New-burn, a place where higher ground dominates the north bank, and flat, low ground stretches some way back from the south bank. Leslie, of course, set up his artillery on the hill, where they had free fire down-wards into the English infantry. The English, meanwhile, were firing upwards at well-entrenched positions. The English, as Gardiner said, occupied 'an indefensible position'. He commented: 'I do not think it presumptuous in one without military knowledge to speak strongly on this point. In the summer of 1880, I visited the spot, and the impossi-bility of resistance appeared to me to be evident even to the most unpractised eye'.[241] This judgement estops a verdict on the manifold other reasons why England might have lost the Second Bishops' War: inadequate money, unwilling troops, political disaffection, and inadequate arms all could easily have led to English defeat. In the event,

[240] *The Lawfulnesse of our Expedition into England Manifested* (Edinburgh, 1640), Sig. A, 2, 3.
[241] Gardiner, *History*, ix. 192–5 and n. Dyott's account of the battle, which was unknown to Gardiner, confirms what he says. My own impression of the ground in the summer of 1988 confirms Gardiner's. The advantage of the ground to the Scots seems slightly less overwhelming to me than it did to him, but it is clearly considerable. The role played by the Scottish artillery at Newburn is unusual, but it is hard to say whether it indicates exceptional Scottish skill, exceptional Scottish good fortune, or exceptional English willingness to run away. I am grateful to Prof. Sir John Hale for advice on the ballistics involved.

they drew up for battle in a position where even the best of armies would have been likely to lose.

When the battle began, it progressed as might have been expected. The play of the Scottish cannon forced the English foot to turn and run, and the few English horse who fought bravely as the Scots crossed the river were unable to stop them. Those few people who fought bravely at Newburn, including Comissary Willmott and Colonel Lunsford, retained for ever after a special hold on Charles's affections.

Newcastle was indefensible with the Scots on the south bank of the Tyne and Gateshead unfortified, so it was hastily evacuated, leaving the Scots control of the City, the food and munitions stored there, and the London coal trade. The English withdrew, looking for a more defensible line, and the Scots swept on to occupy Durham. When they arrived there, the Scots illustrated their capacity to polarize English politics by their treatment of Bishop Morton, who would have been a key figure in any compromise settlement in England. We are told by Richard Dyott that General Leslie told Morton 'that though he had written much against the papist, yet being a byshop, he must downe with the rest. Which I had from his lordship's owne mouth'.[242] For so small a battle, leaving only 26 horse and 300 foot dead on the losing side, the battle of Newburn settled a remarkable number of things. In the internal history of Britain, perhaps only Bannockburn, the Boyne and Culloden have settled as much.

Newburn determined, first, that Scotland would not be Anglicized in religion: the Covenant, and the cause it represented, were there to stay. From this followed that any ultimate Act of Union could not be simply on terms of perfect union, but would have to allow for some form of unity in diversity. Newburn settled that Scotland would keep a distinctive identity within a British union. In the longer term, the pressure to protestantize Ireland was likely to grow stronger, in order that it should become impossible to use Irish power as the sort of threat it had been in the eyes of Strafford. Newburn is an important event in the history of Ulster, as well as of many other places. Immediately, Newburn determined that the Scots would become a force in English politics. As such, they provided the two crucial characteristics of an opposition: an alternative political model, and an alternative power-base. Without those things, no opposition could effectively operate, and the Scots conferred both on their English friends. No longer was the King the sole effective source of power. For the first time since 1485, parties in England were now an established fact, though one to which the English would adjust extremely slowly.

Immediately, Newburn restricted Charles I more effectively than any-

[242] Staffs. RO D 661/11/1/5 (7 Sept.).

thing the English had ever done to him. The defeat brought into the open all those who believed, like Northumberland, that there had been a great fault in the laying of this design. To go to war in the face of a Parliament and half the Council is a decision which only success can justify, and success had not come. Such defeats demanded scapegoats, and the Scots were already suggesting Strafford and Laud as the obvious candidates for the part. Scapegoats might save the King's honour, but they were also needed to protect him from himself. Kings who lost quite so discreditably could expect to have their power reduced, and Newburn, like Bannockburn and Radcot Bridge, meant that the King who lost it could never hope to recover all the power he had had before. Kings who proved themselves so incapable tended to be hedged around with restrictions. The commonest form of restriction was an afforced Council, semi-compulsory additions to the King's Council to ensure that he was subjected to good advice. In bringing such a result about, a Parliament was normally regarded as an indispensable instrument. So far, the precedents which every political Englishmen knew were clear enough. What the precedents did not say, since the union of England and Gascony had never been close enough to make the problem arise, was how to solve the problem of another kingdom, subject to the same king, claiming an interest in the political settlement of England. It made the problem harder that there was a third kingdom across the Irish Sea, and every measure to unite England and Scotland would have the effect of further alienating Ireland from them both. What needs explanation is why the journey from Newburn to Nottingham was to take another two years.

4

The Treaty of London: Anglo-Scottish Relations

SEPTEMBER 1640–MAY 1641

I

The Scottish victory at Newburn generated more alarm in London than it did at the front.[1] When the news reached London on 31 August, the Council immediately ordered out the Gentlemen Pensioners to guard the King's wife and children, and gave orders for placing guns and a garrison to defend Whitehall, presumably against frontal assault.[2] Arundel, as Earl Marshal, and Cottington, as Constable of the Tower, issued orders for a supply of spades and pickaxes for building earthworks to defend the Tower, for gun platforms for mounting new guns, and placed orders for new ordnance.[3] Windebank on 5 September wrote to the Ambassador in Madrid that the preservation of the monarchy was at stake, and 'I hope in God we shall overcome this danger, which I believe the greatest that hath threatened this state ever since the conquest'.[4] In practical terms, this was somewhat alarmist: London was not about to break out in revolt in September 1640, and there was no likelihood of an armed assault on Whitehall Palace. In part, this reaction measures a process common in wartime, whereby disasters grow in the telling. Yet it also underlines the fact that Newburn was a political, far more than a military, defeat. This capacity for hysteria because of domestic dissent had been latent in the council since the Lambeth riots of May, if not longer, and one of the reasons why defeat was serious was that it was likely to force this hysteria to the surface. Yet, even if the hysteria is discounted, the practical fact remains that England had gone into war with a divided country, and every attempt to persist in the war in the face of defeat was likely to deepen the division. This was the rational basis of the Council's alarm.

At the front, the immediate retreat was precipitate, because the English army needed to establish a safe position. The Scots, according

---

[1] This chapter should be read in conjunction with Donald, ch. 6. Our findings are very similar, but each has some distinctive pieces to add to the jigsaw.

[2] PRO SP 16/465/55 and 56.

[3] *Clarendon SP* ii. 114–15; PRO WO 49/72, fos. 49ª, 50ª, 52ª, and other refs; ibid. 55/455, pp. 71, 73.

[4] Bodl. MS Clarendon, vol. 19, no. 1418.

to Sir Richard Dyott, 'mad great hast in their march, to be at York before the Kings army can be in a readiness'. The line of the Tees is not defensible, so the only way the King's army could adopt a secure position was by retreating all the way to York, where the open ground of the Vale of York would ensure that the Scots did not surprise them or outflank them. The case for retreat was underlined by rumours that the Earl of Argyll was going to invade by the West Marches, with the army which had been kept back to protect the west coast against the Irish.[5] Once the army was back in York, and regrouped, it was able to gather its courage. To those immune from political doubts about the war, it might appear possible to go on fighting. Sir Richard Dyott reported on 7 September that 'the King is preparing a good army, and when it is reddy, intends to march towards them. The Lord speed him'. On 11 September Vane reported that the King still had an armed force of 16,000 foot and 2,000 horse,[6] and though this was now an inferior force to the Scottish, it was not disastrously so. An order had already gone out for all those who held land by feudal tenures to do the military service their tenures commanded, and on 11 September Charles sent out orders for all trained bands to be ready to come to the north.[7] If there were to be a real outburst of national solidarity producing a desire to fight with a will and without too much regard for legality, the day might yet be saved. For Dyott, the trouble appeared to have come from 'the incredulity of his subjects, who could not be induced to believe (notwithstanding the frequent advertisement from those points) that the Scots would invade us. And those persons were backward and unwilling to arm until the blow was given'. Now, he hoped, the country would repent 'our causeless divisions at home, disabling the King for want of money, to doe in time what was necessary and by him desired'.[8]

Dyott wrote from an Arminian perspective, and for those who did not, divisions seemed less 'causeless' and a good deal more serious. Vane, two days after the battle, wrote that 'it is strange to see how Lesley steales the hearts of the people in these northerne partes; you shall do well to thinke of timely remedies to be applyed, least the disease

---

[5] Staffs. RO D 661/11/1/5 (Dyott, 7 Sept.). These letters, which survive only in a copy, are unfoliated, and are therefore referred to by the dates of the three letters included, 31 Aug., 7 Sept., 25 Sept. The divisive potential of Scottish news is illustrated by the results when Dyott's son read what must have been the letter of 31 Aug. in public in London. Richard Bateman denied the authenticity of the letter, claiming it was written by 'some Jesuit' and said the King was set upon a dishonourable action, and whoever set him against his subjects of Scotland deserved to be hanged. PRO SP 16/466/91, 92, 116.

[6] PRO SP 16/467/28.

[7] Larkin, pp. 731–2; PRO SP 16/467/28.

[8] Staffs. RO D 661/11/1/5 (Dyott, 31 Aug.). For the remarks about 'causeless divisions', ibid. (7 Sept.).

grow incurable'.[9] By 3 September Vane's sense that they were at the end of their tether was heightened by exhaustion: he wrote to Windebank at three in the morning, complaining he could scarce keep his eyes open: his next letter is dated at five the same morning.[10] Vane was not in favour of resuming the war, though it was not until 20 September he allowed himself to become explicit by saying there was now no danger of venturing all of a day.[11]

The King, by contrast, could see no problem except the lack of money, and Vane's letters make an intriguing mixture of his own political doubts and the King's insistent demands for money which London could not send. It seems to have been a simple recognition that he could not keep his army together without money, rather than any dawning comprehension of the political arguments against the war, which convinced the King he could not fight for the time being.[12]

The political arguments for peace were highlighted by the presentation of the Petition of the Twelve Peers, which was signed on the same day as the battle of Newburn. The Petition was drawn up at a meeting in Bedford House in the Strand, where those present included, to Secretary Windebank's knowledge, the Earls of Bedford, Essex, and Warwick, Saye, and Brooke, Bedford's son Lord Russell, and Pym and Hampden.[13] It was subsequently said to have been written by Pym and St John,[14] both clients of the Earl of Bedford,[15] but the task of signing it was left to peers.[16] The signatures obtained were those of Bedford,

---

[9] PRO SP 16/465/50.

[10] Ibid. 16/466/30 and 31.

[11] Ibid. 16/467/120.

[12] This is the impression given by a careful reading of Vane's letters from the north, and it is confirmed by the King's speech to the Council of Peers, ibid. 16/468/1. On 4 Sept. there was £1,037 left in the Exchequer: ibid. 16/469/72.

[13] Ibid. 16/464/45.

[14] 'Papers relating to the Delinquency of Lord Savile', ed. J. J. Cartwright, *Camden Miscellany*, 8, 1883), 2.

[15] Alnwick Castle MSS Y III (2) (4) envelope 7 shows Pym acting as Bedford's agent in trying to resolve a dispute with Robert Scawen about his terms of employment, and Oliver St John acting as Bedford's counsel. Ibid. Y III (2) (3) envelope 5 shows that Bedford paid St John's commons at the Inns of Court. Not all relationships between gentlemen and peers are properly described as the relations of patron and client, but in these particular cases, the terms appear to be exact. Alnwick MSS Y III, which is not included in the BL microfilm, is a collection of Russell papers which were in the possession of Robert Scawen when he left Bedford's service for Northumberland's. Most of them relate either to Covent Garden or to the draining of the fens. I am grateful to Prof. David Underdown for bringing the collection and the first of these references to my attention, and to his Grace the Duke of Northumberland for allowing me to see them.

[16] For what are probably the printing instructions for the Petition, see Lancs. RO Hulton MSS DD/HU 46/21. I am grateful to Christopher Thompson for this reference. The instructions are sent from Pym, writing from Warwick's house at Leighs on 3 Sept. 1640 to William Jessop Secretary of the Providence Company. Pym does not specify the document which is to be printed, but at this date, there is no likely alternative. Distribution was entrusted to Sir John Clotworthy and Mr Sterry, possibly Dr Peter Stirry, chaplain to Lord Brooke and later to Lord Protector Cromwell.

Hertford, Essex, Warwick, Rutland, Bolingbroke, Exeter, Mulgrave, Saye, Mandeville, Howard of Escrick, and Brooke.[17] The most significant coup for the petitioners was the signature of Hertford, probably drawn in by his brother-in-law Essex. Apart from being outside the usual knot of godly peers, he was well known and liked, and carried the potential threat implicit in being the son of Arabella Stuart and the grandson of Catherine Grey.

The Petition itself began by complaining, in various oblique ways, against the war, demanded better repression of recusants, took note of rumours that the Irish army was to be brought to England, and complained of innovations in religion and of monopolies, and called on the King to summon a Parliament. This, they hoped, would lead to the punishment of those responsible for grievances, and to the composing of the war 'without blood', 'ye comfort of your people, and uniting of both your realms against ye common enemies of ye reformed religion'.[18] Sir Richard Dyott was ready to take offence at the Petition:

Many doe wonder, that at such a season, when the Scotts had gott such footing in the land, and the King had bin at soe immense a charge in raising, furnishing and paying soe great an army, such a peticon should be offered; whereby this intended action should be retarded, discountenanced and indeed overthrowne. But we must not image that the intencon of such noble lords was other then honorable as tending to the weale of both kingdomes.[19]

It is tempting to wonder whether Dyott knew his *Julius Caesar*.

The Venetian Ambassador reported a story that if the King did not summon a Parliament, they would do it themselves.[20] This looks, at first sight, like another Venetian tall story, but it is worth putting it beside an entry in a volume of legal notes by Oliver St John, one of the two likely authors of the Petition. This records, in the course of a discussion of names given to Parliaments, a reference to the Parliament of 1258, which had 'erected' the Twelve Peers. This notion of peers as a sort of

[17] There are discrepancies in the lists of signatures. I have followed PRO SP 16/465/16, confirmed by Crawford MS 14/3/71, which is probably taken from the Scots' presentation copy. See below, p. 155 and n. 33. Gardiner (*History*, ix. 199) is not justified in his claim that 'behind these names was England itself': when the Civil War came, they divided into 1 Royalist (Hertford), 1 dead (Bedford), and 10 Parliamentarians. They were more than a clique, but they were considerably less than 'all England'.

[18] For the text, I have used PRO SP 16/465/16, checked against Pym's personal copy, Yale University, Beinecke Library, Osborn Files, Pym. There are no significant discrepancies between the two. Pym's copy is not in his hand, but he would have been unlikely to preserve an incorrect text.

[19] Staffs. RO D 661/11/1/5 (Dyott, 7 Sept.). For a description of the peers as a 'company of Puritan rascalls' see MP 9 Mar. 1641. It shows how the world had changed that these had by then come to be regarded as seditious words.

[20] *CSP Ven. 1640–2*, p. 77.

caretaker government was one to which some of them easily returned.[21] This is not enough to make the Venetian's story true, but it is enough to prevent it from being incredible.

What can now be taken as fact, and not conjecture, is that some, at least, of those involved with the Petition were working in collusion with the Scots: Dyott's scepticism about their honourableness was entirely justified. The letter from which this is known to us survives in a copy taken by Balfour of Denmilne, Lyon King of Arms in Scotland, probably from the papers of the Committee of Estates in Edinburgh.[22] This letter bears the signature 'N.F.' for which the only plausible candidate is Nathaniel Fiennes. The argument of the letter, that the Scots staying at Newcastle would give their friends an opportunity to make a better peace for them, is intriguingly close to the summary later given by Fiennes's father Saye of what the Scots 'knew' at this time.[23] The Petition itself, which is announced in the first paragraph of this letter, survives in a Scottish copy, probably also taken from the papers of the Committee of Estates.[24]

Part of this letter might lead us to share Baillie's suspicion that the Scots' friends tended to promise more than they could perform. They claimed that nine colonels in the King's army had given assurance that they would join with the Lords. If this refers to any explicit pro-Scottish commitment, it is highly unlikely, but it is more probable that nine colonels may have shared Vane's fear of the dangers of 'venturing all of a day', and may have wanted some form of cease-fire. The letter also announces that the Petition was meant to be the signal for a petitioning campaign from the City of London and the gentry. In this, they promised more than they could perform, but not more than they attempted.

[21] BL Add. MS 25266, fo. 113ᵛ. These are a series of working legal notes on medieval records, and it makes an important point that St John's constitutional precedents arise naturally in the middle of notes on such matters as dower and waste, which were his daily legal bread and butter. St John's likeliest source, since many surrounding notes are from the Patent Rolls, is *Calendar of Patent Rolls 1247–58*, p. 626. Another possibility is 'Dunstable Annals', in *Annales Monastici*, ed. H. R. Luard (Rolls Series, 36, 1886), iii. 208–9. I am grateful to Dr David D'Avray, Dr M. T. Clanchy, and Prof. R. C. Stacey for advice and help on this point. St John's notes cannot be dated, but were probably taken during the 1630s.

[22] NLS Adv. MS 33.1.1., vol. xiii, no. 28. Dr Peter Donald and I discovered this document independently, though he found it first. He has since found another copy, with a securer provenance and a less corrupt text. I am very grateful to him for generous help with the identification and transcription of this document. See P. H. Donald, 'New Light on the Anglo-Scottish Contacts of 1640', *Historical Research* 62/148 (1989), 221–9.

[23] William Fiennes, Viscount Saye and Sele, *Vindiciae Veritatis* (1654), BL E. 811 (2), p. 29, and also p. 43 on the closeness of Nathaniel Fiennes's relations with the Scots at this time. On the authorship of the *Vindiciae*, see J. S. A. Adamson, '*Vindiciae Veritatis* and the Political Creed of Viscount Saye and Sele', *Historical Research*, 60/141 (1987), 45–63.

[24] Crawford MS 14/3/71. The Scots seem to have used the Committee of Estates, as the English were later to use the Clerk's table, as a source of papers for copying. A comparison of e.g. NLS Wodrow MS Fol. 66 and NLS Adv. MS 33.1.1, vol. xiii will quickly prompt the suspicion that their authors were copying from a common repository.

The City ministers delivered a petition, taken by 'one Dr Burgess, a clergyman, but of the tribe of the Covenant, and one that hath been in Scotland'.[25] The City petition, according to Vane, was said to be signed by 4 Aldermen and above 10,000 others, and was said to have been delivered by Warwick's ally Maurice Thompson.[26] All that survives from other counties, however, seems to be occasional correspondence about the circulation of a petition in draft. In effect, the Crown seems to have been facing an alliance between a group of peers and the leading City ministers, with the gentry sympathetically keeping their powder dry.

This letter also gave the Scots a great deal of intelligence and advice. It told them the King's forces were running out of money, and that he would not be able to keep them together long. It also told the Scots it was necessary for their friends to know what the Scottish army was going to do, for fear they might accidentally cross their proceedings. Their advice to the Scots was to 'facilitate' the King's answer to the Twelve Peers by instantly submitting a humble petition for a treaty of peace. The Scots took this advice on 4 September, three days after the letter was written, and a copy of their petition now survives in Pym's papers, where it is filed with his copy of the Petition of the Twelve Peers.[27] The Scots, as often, were slightly bolder than their English allies; where N.F. had advised them to petition for a committee to conclude a treaty, they petitioned for a treaty 'wth ye advice of ye estates of ye kingdome of England contained in a Parliament'. With this, Balfour of Denmilne has copied a further letter of 5 September. This expresses approval of the Scottish petition (of which the English had probably had an advance copy), reported the King's reception of the Petition of the Twelve Peers, explained that it was 'impossible' for them to send the Scots money and victual, and advised them to gain the King's goodwill by releasing Commissary Willmott, who had been taken

a [25] *Clarendon SP* ii. 117. It is interesting that the belief that Burges had been in Scotland, which had recently only been suspicion (above, p. 140) is now treated as fact.

[26] PRO SP 16/467/111 and 135. For the text of the City Petition, see Yale University, Beinecke Library, Osborn Shelves b. 297. It differs from the Petition of the Twelve Peers mainly in the stress on the effect of monopolies on the decay of trade, and in the complaint that, in spite of Ship Money, Turkish and other pirates were still taking merchants captive. For the link between Warwick and Maurice Thompson, see PRO WO 55/456 (23 Feb. 1640–1), delivery of 36 barrels of powder for ships to Thompson 'for ye Earle of Warwicke'. Dyott (Staffs. RO D 661/11/1/5 (25 Sept.)) also records the presentation of a petition from some Yorkshire ministers on 24 Sept. but says nothing of its contents. For an attempt to organize a petition in Northamptonshire, see Bedfordshire RO St John MS 1403 (unsigned) and perhaps also MS 1401 (Gilbert Pickering to Sir Rowland St John), though this could refer to the petition to the Short Parliament.

[27] PRO SP 16/466/36; Yale University, Beinecke Library, Osborn Files, Pym. There is no proof of when this document came into Pym's possession, and it could have been a few weeks later, during the Treaty of Ripon. It is suggestive that Pym's copy of the Petition, of the Scots' demands, and of Lanerick's answer of 5 Sept. are all in the same hand, which might be compatible with a copying date around 8–10 Sept.

prisoner at Newburn, unless they thought he might 'discover your weaknes'.

This is enough to indicate a very substantial degree of collusion on the part of at least some of the Twelve Peers. The amount of information available to the Scots goes a long way to explain their political sure-footedness, and the extent of Scottish military backing for the Twelve Peers goes a long way to explain their political boldness. It also indicates that the Council's misgivings about the strength of the 'tribe of the Covenant' in England were largely justified. This story also shows what a big political risk the Twelve Peers and their allies were taking. N.F.'s letter comes under the heading of giving aid and comfort to the King's enemies in time of war, and therefore was legally treasonable. With the greatest care in the world, it was impossible to be certain that such dealings would remain permanently secret: the King already had evidence against Lord Brooke,[28] and since there was no limitation of actions on treason, he would use it whenever the wheel of fortune turned far enough to make it advisable to do so. The Scots seem to have never fully understood the need for discretion in English politics, since they did not understand how dangerous such conduct might be. Sir William Berkeley soon told Secretary Windebank information about English Lords which he had got from General Leslie. This is probably the same information he was giving out a few days later at York, that the Scots had been invited to invade by thirty-seven peers. Windebank had some reason for telling Charles that it would be easy to discover such as held intelligence with the rebels and invited them into England. Charles's marginal comment: 'it shall not be forgotten' was chilling in its economy.[29] From this point on, if not before, the Parliamentary leaders' willingness to trust Charles must have been severely limited by their knowledge that they had themselves committed treason, and by their fear that Charles knew it. Charles's 'untrustworthiness', which was the theme of so much later trouble, was a real phenomenon, but it is hard for anyone to trust those against whom they have committed treason. From this point onwards, the inner ring of the Twelve Peers could not afford any settlement which gave them less than total success.

The Privy Council's response to Newburn probably owed as much to the Petition of the Twelve Peers as it did to the battle. Windebank on 3 September reported to the King the sum of a good deal of discussion in

---

[28] Above, p. 62. See also PRO SP 16/464/45.

[29] *Clarendon SP* ii. 120. PRO SP 16/468/23 (Vane to Windebank, 24 Sept.) reports that Bristol, at the Council of Peers, demanded justice on Sir William Berkeley for this report. Thirty-seven peers sounds an incredible number for support for the Scottish invasion, but thirty-seven Lords against the war is entirely possible, and the Scots' friends would have been capable of inflating the one into the other.

Council.[30] True to their character as consensus politicians and as Englishmen the Council gave priority to the restoration of unity in England, rather than to the defeat of the Scots. They asked whether some noblemen should be called to Council 'if it be but to engage them'. Their main objective was 'the uniting of your Majesty and your subjects together, the want whereof the Lords conceive is the source of all the present troubles; and they are confident, if your Majesty and people had been well together, the rebels durst not have thus insolently affronted your Majesty and the nation'. They hinted tentatively at the calling of a Parliament or a Council of Peers, and warned the King that without some such 'sweetening', money would be raised 'very coldly and slowly'. Without voluntary assistance in both, they said, the kingdom would be in danger, 'for to force supplies of either in this conjuncture is not held practicable'. Windebank anxiously assured Charles that he only had 'the ministerial part' in relaying this advice. He might well do so; the Council were telling Charles that co-operation between him and his subjects had broken down so far that they were no longer prepared to fight for him against invasion.

With these questions in mind, the Council held a meeting with Bedford and Hertford, as spokesmen for the Twelve Peers on 7 September. Hertford, who acted as speaker,[31] said that if the Council did not join them, 'they and the rest must wash their hands from those mischiefs that were otherwise like to fall upon the state'. The Council then appointed Finch, Arundel, Cottington, and Windebank to confer with them. They charged them with siding with the rebels, 'whom yet they had not termed rebels, but the Scotch army'. Arundel convinced himself that they seemed to care that England should be 'conquered by so poor a nation as that of the Scots', and from this disadvantageous footing, the peers came to the case for a Parliament, where they seem to have given the Council the impression that calling a Parliament would so win the people's hearts 'that they would come in to his Majesty in this action' — in other words, that a Parliament might support the resumption of the war. Hertford may perhaps have believed this, but Bedford surely did not. The Council opened up daylight between the peers by asking whether they knew of any Covenant to be sworn in England like that in Scotland; Hertford said he knew of none, and detested it, and Bedford denied knowing of any, but 'more faintly'. The time had not come to exploit the division, but it was doubtless noted for future use.

Over the next few days, the Council reassured themselves by discovering that Bristol and Sir Francis Seymour would have no truck with

---

[30] *Clarendon SP* ii. 97–8, summarizing PRO SP 16/466/5 and 11.
[31] *Clarendon SP* ii. 110–12, summarizing PRO SP 16/466/75.

the Twelve Peers,[32] but on the 18th, they reported their 'great wonder' that in spite of the loss of Newcastle more peers had signed the petition. The likeliest candidates for the extra signatures are North, Willoughby (presumably of Parham), Saville, Wharton, and possibly Lovelace.[33]

The Privy Council had already on 2 September advised Charles to call a Great Council of Peers, having apparently been convinced by Cottington's argument that they should leave the Council of Peers to take the risk of advising Charles to call a Parliament.[34] On 16 September, shaken by their failure to prevent the City from petitioning for a Parliament, they advised the King, on Arundel's motion, to call a Parliament 'that he may have the honor of it himself', or in other words, to call one before he was forced to.[35] It was not clear exactly what problems the calling of a Parliament was meant to solve: Vane, the same day as the Council's resolution, remarked: 'which word is thought sufficient, not only to put the Scots out of the kingdom, but a balme to cure all our soares'.[36] The French Ambassador was clear that a decision to call a Parliament was tantamount to a decision for peace, but Vane, at his master's side, was not so convinced, at least in his official capacity; Charles continued to hope that he might win Parliamentary support for resuming the war.[37] Even if a Parliament were to be convinced that the Scots' terms were impossible, it is hard to see how a resumption of war could be combined with a Parliamentary devotion to a legality which meant that no wars could be afforded. A resumed war without Ship Money or coat and conduct money would not be practical politics.

In fact, the real problem facing Charles's advisers after Newburn was not that of persuading him to call a Parliament: it was the problem of persuading him that he had to give in to the Scots. After Newburn, Charles's options were only to give in to the Scots, or to persuade the English to fight them. It took him four months to face the fact that since he could not do one, he had to do the other. Charles saw first the Council of Peers and then the Parliament as opportunities to persuade the English to fight the Scots, while most of the council, again adopting

---

[32] *Clarendon SP* ii. 114.

[33] PRO SP 16/467/88. The list of names is based on a comparison of the list on Pym's copy with the list in ibid. 16/465/19. Pym's list includes Bristol, who refused, and should therefore be taken as a list of those who were asked to sign, rather than of those who did. Those listed here were on Pym's list and in the list in ibid. 16/465/19. North, Willoughby, Savill, and Wharton are all probable enough, though Lovelace's later record must raise questions. The names on Pym's list but not on the other are Bristol, Bath (who presumably both refused), and Lincoln, whose absence from the list of signatories remains mysterious. See also Northants, RO Finch-Hatton MS 2619. I am grateful to Dr J. S. A. Adamson for this reference.

[34] PRO SP 16/466/11, see also no. 12.

[35] Ibid. 16/467/75.

[36] Ibid. 16/467/76.

[37] Conrad Russell, 'Why did Charles I call the Long Parliament?', *History*, 227 (1984), 375–83.

a purely English perspective, probably saw them both as opportunities of sharing the responsibility of persuading the King to give in.

From the Scottish end, Loudoun warned Hamilton on 8 September that delays in serious negotiations for peace would only make it harder: 'difficulties will intervein on all sides, and matters will daily grow wors and wors'. The delay tended 'to beget a suspition that his Matie doth not yet intend a reall peace'. This is why the Scots wanted 'peace concludit wt. advyse of the Parl. of England, without wch it is conceived noe peace can be secure and durable'.[38] In other words, the Scots feared that Charles was so reluctant to make peace with them that they could trust no peace unless Charles were deprived of the power to break it. This meant that they would have to change the structure of power in England, in order to protect their own position in Scotland. What Loudoun was telling Hamilton was that the longer the King delayed, the less negotiable this demand would become. Vane, reporting the Scots' demand for peace terms to be confirmed by a Parliament to Windebank two days later, said: 'by this you may judge of the rest'.[39]

The official Scots' demands were addressed to Lanerick, Hamilton's brother, who was now Secretary for Scotland, on the same day as Loudoun's letter. They demanded royal confirmation of all the Acts of their last Parliament, including the abolition of episcopacy, Scottish control of Edinburgh castle, that Scots living in England and Ireland should not be punished for subscribing the Covenant nor made to take oaths against it, that the 'common incendiaries' responsible for the war should be punished, that their ships and goods should be restored, reparations paid for their losses, and declarations against them recalled.[40] What was later to be their eighth article concerning the securing of the peace, which contained their most fundamental demands for change in England, had not yet appeared, but the third and fourth both had English implications. Allowing Scots resident in England or Ireland to take the Covenant was a body-blow at Charles and Laud's policy of British uniformity, and by 'common' incendiaries, the Scots did not intend a social sneer: they meant common to both kingdoms, and therefore specifically intended to include Laud and Strafford. These two demands Charles, King of England could not easily have conceded. Conceding the rest would have been tantamount to a temporary breach of the Union, since it would have rendered the King's control of Scotland a dead letter. However, since the King's control of Scotland was a dead letter already and the Scots' presence in England was an even more urgent threat to his English authority than the loss of British uniformity

---

[38] Hamilton MS 1216.
[39] PRO SP 16/467/5.
[40] Ibid. 16/466/42.

could be, the Machiavellian thing for Charles to do would have been to concede all the Covenanters' purely Scottish demands. He could then, like Richard II after 1388, have waited for their unity to break up before drawing on new Scottish allies to exact his revenge. If he could not do this, he should have adopted Leicester's suggestion and made his younger son King of Scotland. What he attempted, however, was the one thing he could not do: to restore his Scottish authority on his own terms and by force.

When the King met the Great Council of Peers at York on 24 September, he immediately announced that 'I have of myself resolved to call a Parliament', and forced the Lord Keeper to backdate the writs by summoning it for 3 November, exactly forty days later. He made clear, however, that his object was not to make peace: 'an army of rebels lodged within this kingdome, I thought it most fitt to conforme myself to the practise of my predecessors in like cases, that with your advice and assistance wee might ioyntly proceed to the chastisement of these insolencies'. With his usual habit of trying to limit counsel to a very specific point, he asked their advice on how to raise money to keep his army together until the Parliament met, for he thought, he said, that none of them would counsel him to disband his army while the Scots were armed and in the field.[41] Most of the morning then passed on the reading of briefing papers, of which written copies were then distributed.[42] The King then asked whether the Peers would like him to be present at their debates, to which Bristol bravely replied that 'it would be more for the King's service, and more agreeable to the course of councells, that when his Maty. had stated the buisness to them, he should not trouble himself with being present at their debates'. It was Bedford who replied, to the strong approval of Richard Dyott, that he would think that man unworthy to live, who in the King's presence would be afraid to speak anything, so the King stayed.[43] Since this speech contradicts the view Bedford expressed in the privacy of his commonplace book, it should be taken to represent the revival of that Jacobean creature, the Calvinist courtier.[44]

In the afternoon, Bristol began proceedings by moving to appoint a committee to negotiate with the Scots and hear their grievances. Strafford protested that it was not for the King's honour to negotiate in such

[41] Ibid. 16/468/1. Seventy-six peers attended: ibid. 16/466/42. For the need to backdate the writs, see ibid. 16/468/16; the King had omitted to allow for the post time between London and York.

[42] Kenelm Digby. I am very grateful to Mr James Robertson for his generosity in lending me a transcript of this MS.

[43] Bristol's speech is from Kenelm Digby, and Bedford's from Staffs. RO D 661/11/1/5 (Dyott, 25 Sept.).

[44] Bedford MSS vol. XI i p. 44.

sort with rebels, to which Bristol gave the coolly realistic reply that 'they
are not to be looked upon as rebels, since his Maty hath not power to
punish them as such'. He spelt out the point by saying they were on
terms to measure length of pikes with the King, and the treaty must be
between an army at York and an army at Newcastle. Having thus got
the peers to face facts, he moved for 'some lords they could not except
against' to be appointed to treat with them.[45] This was done, and the
Peers appointed the list of commissioners who were to hold responsibility for negotiating a treaty with the Scots for the next eleven months.
The manner of their appointment was vital, since in the first instance
they were answerable to the Lords, rather than to the King. The list was
indeed such as the Scots could not except against: it was Bedford,
Hertford, Essex, Bristol, Berkshire, Holland, Salisbury, Warwick,
Paget, Mandeville, Howard of Escrick, Dunsmore, Wharton, Poulet,
Brooke, and Saville.[46] Seven of the twelve peers had been included in a
list of sixteen. The list was neatly balanced between the two factions of
the autumn of 1640, well defined by Francis Read as the favourers of the
Scots and those who did not oppose them,[47] but even here, the Scots
were to have an advantage. When this division came into the open,
during the Parliament, ten of these Lords were to emerge as favourers of
the Scots, and only six not.[48]

They then passed on to discuss an exchange of prisoners taken at
Newburn, which the King welcomed, since English prisoners had
behaved so gallantly 'where soe many others failed of their duty'. The
King then raised the question of the Scots imprisoned in England for
refusing the Oath of Supremacy. Bristol, after warnings of the danger of
following the course of the King of Spain with the Hollanders or the
King of France with the Huguenots, told the King he should not
imprison them for refusing the Oath of Supremacy, 'that their religion
permitted them not to take it, it being contrary to the very grounds of
their doctrine and faith'. He explained that if the King should stick to
his ground, it would be tantamount to forbidding them to come into
England. 'It was then ordered, those prisoners should have liberty.'[49]

The King then asked the Lords to declare that the war had been justly
grounded, and to consider some way of raising money to keep the

---

[45] All this is from Kenelm Digby.
[46] PRO SP 16/468/6.
[47] Ibid. 16/470/17.
[48] The pro-Scottish commissioners were Bedford, Essex, Holland, Salisbury, Warwick, Paget,
Mandeville, Howard of Escrick, Wharton, and Brooke. Hertford, Bristol, Berkshire, Dunsmore,
Paulet, and Savill did not favour the Scots. For the evidence for this judgement, below *passim*,
index under names. Only for Salisbury does this classification include an element of conjecture.
Bedford, had he lived longer, might possibly have switched camps.
[49] Kenelm Digby.

English army together until the Parliament. This, being a large issue, was deferred to the next day.

It is worth remembering, when we look at the debate on money the next day, that in calling together the Peers, the King was assembling his creditors. He had borrowed such large sums from Councillors, office-holders, and other categories among whom peers were heavily represented, that it is likely he may have owed money to the majority of those present. In some cases, the sums involved were very large indeed, and though in many cases the peers had themselves borrowed the money, and relied on a royal protection to keep their own creditors at bay, peers' desire to recover their money is likely not to have been a negligible force in the politics of the next few years. It is, in the nature of the case, hard to trace the influence of these debts, since peers would be unlikely to impeach their credit by avowing it and it is not easy to see until well into the war years, when some of these peers were in charge of the Parliamentary committee for the King's revenue.[50] The likeliest way for debt to influence the peers was towards demands for a Parliament, not only because Parliamentary supply was the only thing ever likely to repay these debts, but also because, pending repayment, Parliamentary privilege was a very valuable weapon for debtors.

It is not fanciful to see the influence of the King's debts to them on the peers' visible reluctance when they were asked for more money. Mandeville and Savill expressed surprise that the King had entered a war 'without knowing how to defray the charges of it for some time'. The declaration that the King needed £200,000, the first £50,000 within a fortnight, is not likely to have cheered the Lords. Lord North, even while offering to give the equivalent of eight subsidies for himself, exclaimed: 'one word of four syllables, Parliament, like the dew of Heaven'. They finally agreed, no doubt with some reluctance, to ask the City to lend money, and to offer themselves as security for the City's repayment. It was hoped that the decision to call a Parliament might persuade the City that there was some hope of their loan being repaid, and a balanced committee, dominated by Strafford, Bristol, and Bedford, was named to draft a letter to the City.[51]

The letter came back from committee later that afternoon, and, by its antiphonal character, illustrates both that it came out of a balanced committee and that the disagreements in the committee had not been resolved. They rehearsed that a Parliament was to meet, and negotiations with the Scots were to begin,

---

[50] On this issue during the war years, see J. S. A. Adamson, 'The Peerage in Politics 1645–1649', Ph.D. thesis (Cambridge, 1986), 47–53.

[51] Kenelm Digby; *Hardwicke SP* ii. 210. Kenelm Digby makes clear that the speech about the word of four syllables was delivered by North, and not, as Hardwicke improbably has it, by Northampton. See BL Harl. MS 456, fo. 2, which has '3 sillables'.

wherein as we rest most assured that his Matie will be no way wanting in his grace and goodnesse to listen to the just and reasonable demands of his subjects of Scotland; so if they shall insist upon termes dishonorable for his maty and ye English nation to condiscend unto wee should all hold our selves obliged in honner and duty to preserve and defend this kingdome from all invasions and spoyles by any kind of enemy whatsoever.[52]

It is easy to imagine that Bristol wrote the first half of this sentence, and Strafford the second. Once again, all that had been produced by the interaction of Charles and moderate Councillors was a fudge: Windebank later thought this formula proved the peers were 'firm to his Majesty for the repulsion of the Scots',[53] whereas most of the peers probably thought the phrase was a piece of padding designed to save the King's face. On the actual question of war or peace, the Peers dodged the issue: 'till by ye happy successe of this treaty, or ye great wisdome of ye Parliamt. some course might be taken for a firme peace, or a just warre'.

On 26 September, in discussing the instructions for the peers who were to treat with the Scots, the Peers had some opportunity to continue the King's political education.[54] The King, regardless of what had happened since, tried to make the Pacification of Berwick the rule of negotiation, and met awkward questions from Savill and Berkshire about whether or how the Scots had broken the Pacification. The King, in reply, 'desires to be understood'. The King continued to insist, even in the face of rare dissent from Finch, that it was dishonourable to go further than the Pacification. Holland, saying that they would urge oaths, received the potentially equivocal reply that 'the King never swore to the Pacification'. Once again, the King returned to his basic point: 'they are now in rebellion, but when they are reduced, then he will consider of matters of grace'. Bristol again had to spell out to the King that he had lost: 'We must now speak of the business, as to men that have gotten these advantages'. After a few more such exchanges, the King asked the revealingly utopian question: 'whether they will take it in the state we are in, or in justice and right'. Bristol produced the face-saving formula that the Pacification should be the rule, but that for

---

[52] West Devon Record Office, Drake of Colyton MSS, 1700/M CP 17. The names of signatories on this document appear to constitute an attendance list. At 57, it is well down on the previous day's 76, but this was the last item of business of the day. (For an initial attendance list, see Bodl. MS Clarendon, vol. 19, no. 1431). The absence of Saye and Sele is surely confirmed by his otherwise inexplicable silence.

[53] Bodl. MS Clarendon, vol. 19, no. 1437. See also PRO SP 75/15, fo. 478^r (30 Oct./10 Nov.) where the resident in Denmark thanked Windebank for telling him that 'the nobilitie are united in such dutie, loialtie and vigour, to sett themselves against those Scots rebells'. Also Bodl. MS Clarendon, vol. 19, no. 1430.

[54] *Hardwicke SP* ii. 219–25.

'second thinges', the commissioners should have power to represent to the King what they said.[55]

On the 28th, there was a brief but uncomfortable moment when the Scots refused to negotiate unless given a safe conduct from the peers as well as the King: they were probably thinking of the imprisonment of Loudoun in the spring. Bishop Curle of Winchester thought his way round this problem by invoking the model of witness-lists to medieval charters, and the peers duly witnessed the King's safe conduct. The issue also provoked the first of many debates on whether they could risk a breach, and Strafford for the first of many times, argued that they could. He said that they had not been able to fight because they did not have their arms, but now they had them, they could if they had money.

The issue was passed over while the commissioners negotiated privately with the Scots at Ripon. The King almost certainly hoped that he might secure a quick peace at Ripon, so that he could conclude a treaty before the Parliament met, and before the Scots negotiators came to London.[56] The Scots, by insisting on negotiating for maintenance for their army before discussing any of the substantive issues, put paid to this hope. Since few on the English side were prepared to risk renewing the war, the Scots could afford to be as obstinate as they liked: the effect would only be to make the King and Strafford more obviously isolated. The English commissioners succeeded in reducing their financial demands, but not in shaking the basic principle. On 6 October Hertford, for the commissioners, reported back from Ripon to this effect: 'either we must drive them out, or a competency to be allowed, for maintaining their army'. The King for a while hoped to draw advantage from this situation: 'a shock of Parliament to give invaders or rebels money.' He hoped, as Clarendon later put it, that a Parliament might be more sensible of his honour than the peers seemed to be:[57] that he might be able to appeal over the heads of his peers and Councillors to the presumed anti-Scottish sentiments of his Parliament. In the ensuing days' debate, he had the support of four peers apart from the inevitable Strafford: Northampton, Huntingdon, Herbert of Cherbury, and Maynard. The last two, though they had both been reluctant in 1639, had reacted to invasion as Charles expected: as Maynard put it, 'the giving them any thing, a hard morsel to digest by any Englishman'. Both peers were Arminians, and it is not a coincidence that it was such peers

---

[55] BL Harl. MS 456, fo. 12[v]. I would like to thank Dr Peter Donald for drawing my attention to the fact that Hardwicke inadvertently turned over two folios of the manuscript together: *Hardwicke SP* ii. 227–34.

[56] *CSP Ven.* 1640–2, pp. 86–7; *Hardwicke SP* ii. 263. Mandeville's alarmed protest against the idea of reaching agreement before a Parliament is revealing. On the Treaty of Ripon, Dr Peter Donald's account (Donald, pp. 376–90) is considerably fuller than mine.

[57] Clarendon, *History*, i. 159.

who reacted in a way Charles found comprehensible. It is a good example of the way religion influenced perceptions of many apparently secular issues. Strafford, beginning to talk in Charles's style, protested that 'to grant them any dishonourable terms, he will first die'. It was again Bristol who faced facts, and pointed out that if they would not give the Scots maintenance, they had the means to take it, and could occupy two provinces more. The King, not yet persuaded, asked hopefully 'whether you would have the treaty put to an end before a Parliament', only to be told by Savill that even if he granted them all they required, they still desired something which must be ended by Parliament. The next day the King asked what would happen if they refused to treat until their maintenance was settled. He clearly hoped this was a leading question, leading to the answer that they should break off negotiation. The Lords did not answer. For once, this actually constituted a stern reply.[58]

On 17 October the commissioners brought the final terms from Ripon, which involved paying the Scots £50,000 over two months, or £850 a day, beginning, to the Scots' eloquent disappointment, only from 16 October.[59] Bristol declared that though these terms were not as honourable as he could have wished, they were acceptable. Strafford dissented vigorously, and the next day, probably signed his death warrant by offering to bring over the Irish army at two days' notice if someone would give him ships.[60] The atmosphere seems to have been growing heated. Finch called it a 'hopeful treaty', to which Strafford objected. Finch explained himself, and Strafford said 'he differs wholly from him'. Bristol said they were most to blame who had led the King to believe he could have three armies in Scotland, when in fact they had one in England.[61] Strafford 'answered that he could not but see he was pointed at', and the King said the design was not to be blamed because money had failed. Bristol 'replied that wise men ought not to enter into an undertaking without equal certainty of the means'. It begins to be possible to see the tensions which were to lead to the impeachment of Strafford a few weeks later. On this occasion, however, the incipient storm was stilled by Bristol pressing Strafford to tell them whether they really had the option of a battle. Strafford, reluctantly, 'would not answer for the success', and with that answer, the last chance that the Lords might be induced to support fighting the Scots was gone.[62] On 23 October it was agreed that the treaty should be remitted to the Parliament, and the Scots should send delegates to London. The Scots, at last,

[58] *Hardwicke SP* ii. 241–74.
[59] PRO SP 16/470/1.
[60] *Hardwicke SP* ii. 284.
[61] For these exchanges see *HMC Tenth Report*, vi. 137.
[62] *Hardwicke SP* ii. 288; see also Rushworth, *Trial*, p. 530.

had achieved their major objective, of negotiating a treaty with an English Parliament instead of with Charles. They may have been helped in achieving this aim because a good many English peers probably also welcomed the chance to take Scottish policy out of Charles's hands, where it had not been managed with conspicuous success. In the slow struggle to kick Charles upstairs to the honorary status of a Merovingian king or a Japanese emperor,[63] the Treaty of Ripon was a first major success.

To the pro-Scots, who had kept their heads down and left the others to do most of the talking, the result was a triumphant success. For those who did not oppose the Scots, like Bristol and Hertford, the results were more complex. They were secured against a further battle, which was their immediate objective. What they probably did not yet realize was the extent to which they had merely moved into another round of the struggle for British uniformity. Having defused an attempt to Anglicize Scotland, they were now faced with a major attempt to Scotticize England, and that was to prove even more divisive than the previous round had been.

Saye, Brooke, Pym, and their fellows may have been a tightly knit group, but they were able to draw on a considerable body of feeling in the country as a whole, some of which was becoming alarmingly articulate. A man accused of seditious words in Southwark at the end of September confessed to saying 'that there were in London a great many of religious men, which if the Scots were here would take their part rather than the King's'. The words to which he confessed were probably more seditious than the words with which he was charged. The King's shoemaker was accused of saying the Scots were honest men, and that they lied who said they were rebels and traitors.[64] If the King could be given the lie by his shoemaker, his authority had been brought alarmingly low. It was becoming necessary to take seriously people who, a year earlier, would have been dismissed as a 'lunatic fringe': the main stream of political opinion was shifting. In Bristol, Mr Hazard, whose wife was soon to join in founding a Baptist church, left out of the liturgy the words of the prayer against the Scots: 'especially against those his trayterous subjects, who having cast of all obedience to their anointed sovereign, doe at this time in rebellious manner seek to invade the realme'. Instead he put in his own words: 'and now and evermore detect and reveale unto him all those trayterous enemies in this kingdome that disturbe the peace of the realme, and that vex and molest the hearts of

---

[63] I owe the parallel to the Japanese emperor to an unpublished paper by Prof. E. S. Morgan. I would like to thank him for permission to refer to it.
[64] PRO SP 16/468/89 and 97.

thy church and faithful people'.[65] It was soon to be a question which of these formulations was mainstream, and which was lunatic fringe.

Sir Robert Harley, of course, acted as a magnet for many pro-Scots with hopes for the ensuing Parliament. William Bourne of Manchester College wrote to him complaining of organs, altars, gestures, vestures, Crosses, etc., and urged him to follow the Apostles, as in France, Geneva, and Scotland, and unite the kingdoms.[66] A draft, perhaps drawn up by the ministers of Hereford diocese for the Ministers' Remonstrance, asked 'if the Scots will not be as us, shall we kill them all or be excepting what might be excepted as they are?'[67] It seemed a simple question, but in a year's time, many were to find it rather less simple than it seemed. When the Scottish commissioners arrived in London, the Venetian Ambassador reported that they were greeted by the cheers of 'this libertine populace'.[68] To Charles, this probably seemed the ultimate indignity. If he had been a far-sighted politician, he should have been rubbing his hands, for the Scots in London were to prove far more successful in giving Charles a party than he by himself could ever have hoped to be.

II

The Long Parliament, from the day of its meeting, was different from any Parliament since the heyday of Richard, Duke of York. This was because, long before the Act restricting it, the King had lost control of the prerogative of dissolution. It had been the central fact of all previous Stuart Parliaments that they sat so long as the King thought it was in his interest that they should do so, and not a day longer. In a sense, this was still true, but the fact that the most powerful military force in England was no longer under the King's command meant that his judgements of his interest could not be too much influenced by whatever actions the Parliament might take. The French Ambassador had appreciated this well before the Parliament met: 'ce Parlement doit avoir une fin [*sic*] differente de celle qu'ont eue tous les autres que le Roy de la Grande Bretagne a tenus jusques icy, puisque le Roy de la Grande Bretagne ne le peut rompre sans hazarder l'Angleterre'.[69] He explained that to get the

[65] PRO SP 16/467/147.

[66] BL Loan MS 29/119 (8 Jan. 1640/1).

[67] Ibid. 29/172, fo. 363[v]. See Jacqueline Levy, 'Perceptions and Beliefs: The Harleys of Brampton Bryan and the Origins and Outbreak of the First Civil War', Ph.D. thesis (London, 1983), for the identification of the hand as that of William Voyle curate of Llanfairwaterdine. I am grateful to Dr Levy and Dr Peter Donald for helpful discussions of this document.

[68] *CSP Ven. 1640–2*, p. 97.

[69] PRO 31/3/72, p. 282.

money he needed to pay the armies, the King must give his people at least the appearance of satisfaction, and the Scots would not give up what they had got without good reasons. It was on this understanding, that he was now dealing with a Parliament as a lasting feature of a body politic, that he advised his government to respond to Pym's overtures for a Parliamentary–French alliance.[70]

The Venetian Ambassador, who showed a good grasp of the progress of Anglo-Scottish relations, reported ten days after the Parliament had met that its members were already planning to institutionalize this bar on dissolution, and ensure that it should meet every year. A week later, he reported that 'it is the common opinion that these [the negotiations] will proceed slowly, the English conspiring tacitly at the sojourn of a hostile force in their country until the fabric of their far-reaching designs has reached perfection, all alike opposed to the true worship of God and to the rights of the royal sovereignty'.[71] The Venetian's opinion that the English wanted the Scots to draw out their negotiations, in order to prolong the Parliament, is confirmed by Robert Baillie. He wrote on 2 December that

nothing frayes all here so much as our quick agreeing with the king, and the disbanding of our armies thereupon. Under God, they all every where professe that they are aughtin to that armie their religion, liberties, Parliaments and all they have; that if we take conditions for ourselves, they say they are undone. Much fair speech they give us, but for their deeds we yet see naught.[72]

As this passage indicates, the relations of the Scots and their English friends were never free of mutual suspicion and misunderstanding: the meeting of cultures involved in their encounter is often exciting, and may often have been a fertile source of new ideas for the English, but, as the sequel shows, it was never entirely founded on mutual understanding. The Scots and their English friends were bound together by the fact that they needed each other urgently for survival, more than they ever were by any deeper common purpose: they were, in Christopher Thorne's famous phrase, 'allies of a kind'. To understand such a relationship, it is necessary to see it from both sides.

The changed political climate, the presence of Baillie in London, and the need to discuss Scottish affairs in Parliament, all make it easier than before to identify the Scots' political friends. On the whole, the list of the inner ring is as might be expected. In the Lords, it is of course headed by Saye and Brooke, and Brooke's household accounts record

---

[70] Ibid., pp. 295, 300–1.
[71] *CSP Ven. 1640–2*, pp. 96, 97. The Venetian Ambassador showed an unusual understanding of the issues involved in the treaty, which may be explained by the fact that his regular informant was Feilding, who was Hamilton's brother-in-law.
[72] Baillie, i. 275–6; PRO 31/3/72, p. 354.

expenditure on tobacco 'when the Scoch lords supped here'.[73] With them came Mandeville, apparently one of the most committed pro-Scots, Warwick, Paget, Wharton, and Holland. In the Commons, the list included most of the inner ring: Pym, Hampden, Nathaniel Fiennes, the younger Vane, Holles, Earle, Strode, and St John. This group enjoyed vocal support from committed adherents of godly reformation, such as Francis Rous, Sir Miles Fleetwood, Sir John Wray, George Perd, Alderman Penington, Sir Symonds D'Ewes, and William Purefoy, and at first from a few fair-weather friends such as Sir Edward Dering and Sir Henry Anderson. In addition, the Scottish commissioners enjoyed very close relations with a group of London ministers, probably much the same group Lambe believed had been in correspondence with them in September. Of these, Baillie picked out Cornelius Burges and Calybute Downing vicar of Hackney for the special honour of a mention in dispatches.[74] Behind them in turn seems to have been the national network on which godly ministers could always call when the Gospel stood in need. It seems, with a few necessary additions and subtractions, that in the Commons the pro-Scots of 1640, the enthusiasts for further reformation of 1641, and the Parliamentarians of 1642 are three names for the same body of people. In the Lords, it was to be another story, but in the Commons, the evidence is clear enough to suggest that pro-Scottish sympathies were the result of a common allegiance to the cause of godly reformation. There are, of course, exceptions: Paget and Dering are two pro-Scottish Royalists who were widely recognized at the time as having changed their alliances. Selden is a rare example of an anti-Scottish Parliamentarian.

For some of the pro-Scots, notably Harley, Rous, and Penington, heart and head may have gone together. For some others, it seems to have been much more a marriage of convenience. Oliver St John, for example, went along with the strategy of the group to which he belonged, but appears to have retained deep English nationalist feelings underneath his immediate position: in June 1641 he shocked D'Ewes by speaking 'verie unseasonablie' in favour of English claims to suzerainty over Scotland. When he did his duty by speaking in favour of the Scots in the debate on the Brotherly Assistance on 3 February, he did so with such a notable lack of enthusiasm that he might have been wiser to stay silent.[75] It would be fascinating to know, at this date, to which category Saye, Fiennes, and the younger Vane belonged. There are also some conspicuous absentees in the list of prominent Parliamentarians who

---

[73] Warwick Castle MSS, Halford's Accounts, vol. i. The entry is undated, but the nearest dated entries appear to date from the spring of 1641. The tobacco cost 1s. 1d.

[74] Baillie, i. 274, 290, 306.

[75] BL Harl. MS 163 fo. 334ᵃ (19 June 1641); Peyton, fo. 79ᵛ. For similar sentiments from Speaker Lenthall, see D'Ewes (N.), 274.

spoke in favour of the Scots, among whom Oliver Cromwell is perhaps the most noteworthy. The Scots, even at this early date, looked automatically to 'independency' to explain their tensions with their English allies. What they never seem to have understood is the depth of the tension between Scottish claims to church autonomy and English devotion to the control of the church by statute and common law. Attitudes to the Scots, as they became clearer over the next few years, might help to sort those Parliamentarians who were first and foremost enthusiasts for the Gospel by any means, like Rous, from those like Selden, St John, or Saye, for whom the non-Scottish ideal of Parliamentary control of the church may have mattered as much as the creed expressed.

For the time being, however, men like Saye and Brooke were good enough politicians to realize that, since their immediate dependence on the Scots was total, any doubts they might have about the Scots' aims had to be subordinated to the immediate objective of controlling a very angry King. Any time the Scots chose to make terms and go home, their friends' days would be numbered. How far, left to themselves, the English Parliamentary leaders would have gone along with the Scots' demands is a question to which we will never know the answer. They were aware that, left to themselves, they would not have been sitting in Parliament at all, and the question is therefore entirely theoretical.

It is therefore necessary, in order to understand the situation with which the English were dealing, to see the first six months of the Long Parliament from the Scottish point of view, as a chapter in Scottish history, told from Scottish sources.[76] This is an important enough topic in its own right, but it is also a topic without which the history of England during these years cannot be understood. The Scots were, in the first instance, concerned with the security of what they had done already. Seven of their eight negotiating articles concerned the confirmation of what had already been done in Scotland. Beyond that, the Scots were concerned with their obligations to their English allies who had frustrated the King's hopes for the Short Parliament and the Second Bishops' War, and who had probably made a bigger contribution than is now apparent to the Pacification of Berwick. Yet gratitude is not one of the more durable political emotions, and Scots' trust in their allies needed constant renewal. For Johnston or Henderson, who believed presbytery was *jure divino*, there may well have been a missionary motive of some substance. Yet to the Scottish commissioners as a whole, especially to such able politicians as Rothes and Loudoun, the dominant issue was probably always one of Scottish security.

[76] Dr Stevenson (pp. 214–42) has already told the purely Scottish story, and I have not improved upon his work. The aim of this chapter is to recount the interaction between the Scottish and English stories, as seen from the Scottish point of view.

The Treaty of London was not the first time the Scots had reached an agreement with Charles I, and they had been dealing with him for long enough to appreciate that they were asking for things he could never grant with a quiet conscience. Baillie, not the sharpest politician among the Covenanters, had reached this realization as early as 1638.[77] The biggest deterrent to simply reaching a Scottish agreement and going home, leaving their English allies in the lurch, was not either gratitude or missionary zeal, but simply concern that whatever settlement they reached should last. Since they believed it was beyond the limits of Charles's power or of his conscience to adhere voluntarily to any settlement they found acceptable, they had to fortify their settlement with such changes in English affairs as should put it beyond Charles's power to attack them again. They were well aware that England was militarily the superior power. They had been fortunate beyond measure that twice in a row, English discontents had made the country unwilling to help Charles to subdue Scotland. They could not count on such good fortune a third time. They therefore had to rely on their English friends to drive through changes in English government and religion which would extinguish both the King's power to start a war without Parliamentary consent, and the religious cause in whose name the King had made war on them. Having carried through these changes, they then needed to make them irreversible. Their insistence on negotiating with an English Parliament was not only based on the desire to get more favourable immediate terms: it was also based on the desire to make the English Parliament the guarantor of whatever settlement they might reach. Since they had been threatened by an Irish army, and had a strong interest in the Scottish plantations in Ulster, their demands were also bound, from the beginning, to have an Irish dimension which, in the long term, was to prove one of the most explosive things about them.

In the pursuit of these objectives, the Covenanters soon showed that they had been entirely convinced by Charles I's case for the full uniformity of the kingdoms: they simply accepted it, and put the boot on the other foot. On 12 December Baillie told his wife that they had 'good hopes to get bishops, ceremonies and all away, and that conformitie which the King has ever been vexing himself and us to obtain betwixt his dominions to obtain it now, and by it a most heartie nation of the kingdomes'.[78] In the process, they had to eradicate the religious creed which they described, in a nice exercise in partisan precision, as 'Canterburian popery, and Arminianism'.[79] They also believed that episcopacy

---

[77] Above, p. 54.

[78] Baillie, i. 278.

[79] Rushworth, *Trial*, p. 770. The immediate target of this phrase was John Bramhall Bishop of Derry, a man specially disliked by the Scots, but Baillie, who was largely responsible for this document, almost undoubtedly intended the phrase to be applied to the Laudians as a whole.

itself was a root of the quarrels between the kingdoms. They recounted, in their charge against Laud, that from the first reformation of the kirk of Scotland, even before James's coming to England, 'the prelates of England have been by all means uncessantly working the overthrow of our discipline and government'. They then turned to the instinctive desire of the hotter sorts of Protestant to identify the spiritual principle which was the root evil of popery, and concluded they were handling 'an evil therefore which hath issued, not so much from the personal disposition of the prelates themselves, as from the innate quality and nature of their office, and prelatical hierarchy, which did bring forth the Pope in ancient times, and never ceased till it brought forth popish doctrine and worship'.[80] Similarly, they had to eradicate the power of popery in its overt and Roman form. This involved the disarming of papists in England, but even more the disarming and disbanding of the new army in Ireland.[81] Indeed, it was so essential to the Scots' purposes to secure the Protestant ascendancy in Ireland that it is necessary to ask whether it was really by misunderstanding that they repeatedly referred to Ireland as being subject to the English Parliament, or whether this was really a concealed item in a programme for the security of Protestantism.[82]

It should then be apparent that the Scots' programme involved far more than could legally be included in the negotiating of an Anglo-Scottish treaty. The treaty could, for example, provide that Laud and Strafford be tried by the English Parliament, but only their English friends could make a trial effective. The Scots could not, either, go too far towards imposing Scottish religion in England without risking the reaction Charles had met in Scotland in 1637. On the other hand, though the demand had to come in the first instance from their English friends, it was only if it came in conjunction with the treaty that there would be the remotest chance of securing its passage through the House of Lords. The Scottish programme of godly reformation consistently commanded the support of some 130 votes in the Commons, which, on an average attendance and with Charles's co-operation in recruiting a few extra votes, could just become a majority. In the Lords, on the other hand, it was doubtful whether such a programme could muster more than some 15 votes at most. Unless the King should become so provoca-

[80] Rushworth, *Collections*, III. i. 118. It was in pursuit of this line of thought that the Covenanters later described the Five Articles of Perth as 'five articles of conformities with the church of England': NLS Adv. MS 33.4.6, fo. 144ᵛ. It is worth remembering in this context that Rothes, then newly of age, had been among those who opposed the Five Articles of Perth when they first came before the Scottish Parliament in 1621: Maurice Lee, *Road to Revolution* (Chicago, Ill., 1985), 10. On the excision of these passages, to avoid inflaming the susceptibilities of the Lords, see Donald, pp. 402–3.

[81] Rushworth, *Collections*, III. i. 372.

[82] BL Stowe MS 187, fo. 54ʳ: Scottish Record Office, PA 7/2, no. 78B.

tive that the less godly of the lay peers became determined to take control of religion out of his hands, there was little prospect of turning this into a majority, especially since the bishops could be counted on to provided a block vote against their own abolition. It was only as a sacrifice demanded for the conclusion of a British peace, or possibly even as the price of a full Act of Union, that the Lords could ever have contemplated agreeing to such a programme.[83] Even if the Scots did not appreciate this fact, Saye, Brooke, Mandeville, and Holland undoubtedly did, and were in a good position to tell the Scots so. Since the King could be expected to resist tooth and nail what was in effect a proposal to take control of the church out of his hands, this part of the Scottish programme had to be seen as a concerted effort between English Commons and Scottish commissioners.

It was a wildly ambitious programme, undertaken only because the Scots could see no security for their own church in anything less. In that, the history of the next sixty years suggests that they were right: the 1707 solution, allowing two churches within one United Kingdom, was one which was not conceptually possible in the middle of the seventeenth century. In agreeing to delay the treaty in order to let their English allies pursue a settlement, the Scots made the assumption that time was on their side. In this, they seem to have been wrong. This was not only, or even principally, because the English were capable of a rapidly growing impatience when some of them began to perceive the Scots as a reason why the political crisis was prolonged. It was also because of the remarkable financial burden laid upon England by the Treaty of Ripon. The English had to find money to maintain both armies, at a cost estimated by Bristol at some £60,000 a month.[84] This was a very heavy strain, not only on the taxpayer, but even more on an undeveloped system of credit. The financial burden was sooner or later likely to make the English, and even the Scottish army themselves, desperate to conclude the treaty on any terms. The Scots' power in England was temporary, because it arose from the unwillingness of the English to fight them. Whenever this unwillingness should cease, either because of the unpalatable character of the Scots' demands, or because of the financial burden of supporting them, the Scots' power in England would cease with it. The King, it seems, expected that point to come very much sooner than it did, and indeed, seems to have been surprised that it had not come by November 1640.[85] In his opening speech to the

[83] For the Scots' occasional temptation to union, see BL Stowe MS 187, fo. 47ᵛ, and NLS Adv. 33.1.1, vol. xiii, no. 72, recounting that they wished to have Southesk in London because he had been at the last treaty of union in 1604. Some of the heads of the Scots' art. 8 also have a distinct unionist flavour. See also PRO SP 16/480/18 and *LJ* iv. 153.

[84] D'Ewes (N.), p. 318.

[85] MP, 18 Nov. 1640; Russell, 'Why did Charles I call the Long Parliament?', pp. 375–83.

Parliament of 3 November 1640, he was still speaking optimistically of
chasing out the rebels. However, when he faced the fact that the time
had not come, he did not lose hope that it would come. He was waiting,
as the Venetian Ambassador reported, 'until time affords him the means
to restore his failing fortunes'.[86] It remained true that in any contest
between a king and a parliament, the biggest weapon on the King's side
was time. This Charles appreciated far more clearly than his opponents
did. It was his only card, but it is not always appreciated how nearly it
won him the game.

With this said, the formal negotiation of the treaty can be considered
as what it was, one part of a story some of which was taking place
elsewhere. The Scottish commissioners appointed to negotiate on behalf
of the Committee of Estates were Rothes, Dunfermline, Loudoun, Sir
Patrick Hepburn of Wauchton, Sir William Douglas of Cavers, Drummond of Riccarton, Wedderburn, Smyth, and Kennedy, with Henderson and Johnston to represent the General Assembly. Of these, Rothes,
Loudon, Henderson, and Johnston seem to have been by far the most
important. They also brought with them four chaplains, who took no
formal part in the negotiations, but who were deeply involved in preaching in public, in negotiations with the English godly, and later in the
writing of books. They were Robert Blair, who, we are told, was chosen
to satisfy those in England who liked the New England way better than
Presbyterianism, Robert Baillie for convicting the 'prevalent faction' (of
Arminians), and George Gillespie for crying down the English
ceremonies, and John Smith, whose precise function we are not told.
On 15 November the Scottish negotiating team had reached Ware, and
broke their journey because it was the sabbath. They went to church,
and 'after we were warned of the ending of the service', heard the
minister preach two good sermons. When they arrived in London the
next day, they were immediately greeted by the Earl of Warwick and
other Lords, reporting the Parliament's agreement to finance their army
for the time being. Within two days of his arrival, Baillie had seen the
text of the London Root and Branch Petition, which was not to be
presented for another three weeks.[87]

We are fortunate to possess the Scots' negotiating instructions, with
the negotiators' requests for clarification and the Committee of Estates'
replies. They were told to enter a protestation, as they later did, that in
negotiating with commissioners appointed by the English Parliament,
they were not recognizing its authority over Scotland, to secure money
to pay the army, and to ensure that if the treaty broke up, there should

---

[86] CSP Ven. 1640–2, p. 96.
[87] Baillie, i. 269, 271, 273–4; Stevenson, p. 214.

be a period of warning before hostilities were resumed.[88] They were to insist that the last Parliament of Scotland had power to prorogue itself. A query from the negotiators on this got a firm answer: discharging the continuance of the Parliament by the King's sole power 'is not to be assented unto'. This idea of a self-governing Parliament, whose sittings were to be ended by its sole authority, is likely to have been an infectious one in England, and may be part of the intellectual origins of the later Act against dissolving the Long Parliament without its own consent. They were told to refuse to negotiate with any who did not enjoy a commission from both King and Parliament. On this, the negotiators asked what to do if the English would not negotiate on these terms, and were told to do as the English Parliament or those 'weel affected therein' should advise. A succession of instructions directed them to make no concessions of form or matter on the confirmation of the Scottish Acts of Parliament, because 'the King *de pacto* is obleidged to assent to what the Parliament finds'. There is no clue in the text to whether this is a far-reaching piece of contractual thinking, or merely the Scottish reading of the Pacification of Berwick. They were instructed to ensure that Scots in other parts of Britain were not to be made to take oaths contrary to Scottish laws: there was to be no more swearing to the Royal Supremacy either in England or in Ireland. The 'incendiaries' responsible for the Bishops' Wars were to be tried by the Parliaments of their own kingdoms, and Scottish castles restored to Scottish control. They were to secure reparation for Scottish losses, and were told, when they asked what was the lowest acceptable figure, to use their discretion. Berwick and Carlisle were not to be fortified without the consent of the Parliament of England.

These basically Scottish points were followed by the article 'for the securing a setled peace', which was to become the Scots' article 8, the widow's cruse of the negotiations. Baillie was quite right in his prophecy that it 'will not faill to draw long; for here will fall in a number of articles of most weightie consideration. The English, of purpose, would be glad to draw all out to the full'.[89] The method of article 8, the production of a number of general headings, each of which could be divided into as many subheadings as were needed, was ideal for the purpose. In the form in which it appeared in the instructions, the article began with a

---

[88] PRO SP 16/472/22, and 22.1. The most intriguing question is why these instructions are in the English State Papers. Without information on when they came there, it is hard to be certain, but if their arrival is contemporary, there are several serious possibilities. Dunfermline and Montrose had both already given intelligence to the King (Hamilton MSS 1273, 1096; Baillie, i. 262). There is the further possibility that this is part of the traffic through the Hamilton–Loudoun pipeline. On this the question remains open whether the pipeline worked to the advantage of England, of Scotland, or of peace.

[89] Baillie, i. 285.

demand for an Act of Oblivion in both kingdoms (to which Ireland was later added).[90] Parliaments in both nations should be held 'every two years or three years at furthest', and these Parliaments should try wrongs done by either kingdom to the other. Between Parliaments, there should be a body of 'constant and select commissioners' of both nations, called *Conservatores Pacis*, who were to try wrongs done by either kingdom to the other. The Venetian Ambassador was surely right in his comment on this proposal, that it 'would constitute a tribunal which would always represent the majesty and authority of Parliament, to the total exclusion of that of the king'.[91] With this came the proposal that neither kingdom should make war on the other without the consent of the Parliament. There was to be no blockade, even by freebooters, without the consent of the Parliament of the kingdom undertaking it, a proposal which surely confirms the Scots' earlier assertions about the effectiveness of the English blockade. Neither kingdom was to undertake foreign wars without the consent of the other. The Prince was not to marry without the consent of both kingdoms, and Scots were to have places about the King and the Prince. There was to be a common Confession of Faith and a mutual obligation to defend it. All papists were to be removed from the Prince, and sufferers for the Scots' cause in other kingdoms (meaning mainly in Ulster) were to receive reparation. A final demand was that membership of the Scottish Council and Court of Session should be confined to 'such as may stand with our religion'. It is a good example of the exigencies of dealing with Charles that, when translated into practical terms, this became a proposal for Parliamentary nomination.[92] The Scottish negotiators naturally pointed out that this would be displeasing to the King, and asked how far they might push it. They were told to dispute it to the full, but not make a breach on it.

Since the negotiators did not ask this question about the other heads of the article for a settled peace, it is hard to be certain which of the others the Scots intended at this stage to insist on, and which were to help the English gain time. The procedure suggests that the Scots were prepared to consider half a loaf. They were to negotiate on each article in turn, concluding each before they went on to the next, and the seven purely Scottish articles were put before the unionist article 8. Also, though Baillie at this stage clearly expected the Scots to press for the abolition of episcopacy in England, the formal demand in the instructions confined itself to the call for a common Confession of Faith, which

[90] BL Stowe MS 187, fo. 40ᵛ; BL Harl. MS 162 fo. 174ᵃ.
[91] *CSP Ven. 1640–2*, pp. 133–4.
[92] The Scots, apparently, had been discussing such a proposal as far back as Oct. 1639: Alnwick MSS, vol. 14 (BL Microfilm 285), fo. 235ʳ⁻ᵛ.

would rule out Arminianism but not episcopacy. Though Baillie clearly disliked Ussher, Holdsworth, Brownrigg, Ward, Featly, Prideaux, and such 'rabbies', the instructions carefully refrained from blocking a deal with this Calvinist episcopalian group.[93]

Before the negotiators first met on 19 November, both Houses made their support for negotiations clear. The King's call for war, in his opening speech, had been brushed aside and ignored, and in the Commons, when Sir William Widdrington member for Northumberland called the Scots rebels, he was brusquely forced to withdraw by Glyn and Holles.[94] On 12 November Bristol had made a long report at a conference on the Treaty of Ripon, which had been 'of hard digestion to his Majesty'. He explained that the settlement had been necessary: 'he durst not say that the Scots would come forward, but that it was in their power, if they would'. He said the commissioners would not look further back than their own employment, would not lay the fault upon any man, would not ask why the Scots entered the kingdom, nor why, when service was to be done, the King's army was out of the way.[95] This, no doubt, was essential to their status as negotiators, but the House of Lords as a whole was less abstemious, and set up a committee under the Earl of Dover, to investigate responsibility for the breach of the Pacification of Berwick. This committee gathered a considerable file before it was overtaken by the impeachment of Strafford and Laud.[96] The Lords also made their feelings clear by punishing for seditious words someone who had called the Lords at Ripon 'base Covenanting Lords', and for good measure punished two people for seditious words against the Twelve Peers.[97] When the conference was reported to the Commons, Pym moved for thanks to the Lords for their efforts in the treaty, producing a pained demand from Sir Thomas Jermyn 'first that his Majesty should have thankes'. Both motions were accepted but Strode's and Clotworthy's for thanks to the Twelve Peers was for the moment left aside.[98] Strafford had been impeached and sent to the Tower on 11 November, and was in no position to use his tongue against the Scots when they arrived.

The Scots' first day in town was the day of the Commons' public Fast,

---

[93] Baillie, i. 275.

[94] CJ ii. 25; Peyton, fo. 9; Palmer, fo. 28. See also Peyton, fo. 7, for the speeches of Holles and Wray on 9 Nov. Holles, perhaps not yet certain of the temper of the House, took refuge behind the wording of the York communiqué, while Sir John Wray, more boldly, argued for the unity of the three kingdoms.

[95] MP, 18 Nov. 1640 (Roe's report).

[96] LJ iv. 91; MP, 14 Nov. 1640 [?1638], 26 Jan. 1639, 13 Apr. 1639, Apr. 1639 (the military oath), and other refs.

[97] LJ iv. 90, 96, 105. Yale University, Beinecke Library, Osborn Shelves fb 161, no. 194 has Browne's notes of the first of these cases. See also MP, 25 Nov. and 8 Dec. 1640.

[98] D'Ewes (N.), p. 41.

addressed by Burges, who had been described as 'of the tribe of the Covenant' back in September, and by Stephen Marshall, also among the Scots' friends. These two launched a call for further reformation which must have warmed the hearts, not only of the Scots but of all those English people who believed that since 1559 they had lived in a church 'but halfly reformed'.[99] Burges, preaching on the delivery of Israel from Babylon by an army coming from the north, made it his central theme that the only proper response to such a deliverance was to make a covenant with God.[100] Any one of these references could, and probably did, refer to the Covenant of Grace, but overall impression must, to put it no higher, have been suggestive. Both preachers called for the punishment of idolatry, and Burges pointed out, perhaps to Henrietta Maria's alarm, that even a wife was to be punished for it.[101] Marshall called for the suppression of Arminianism and for the enforcement of the sabbath, and also, no doubt to the Scots' utter delight, for discipline and the abolition of 'promiscuous communion', to which every sinner was admitted.[102] Burges warned them firmly that those who hoped for golden days by the punishment of those who invaded their laws and liberties would be disappointed if they stopped there:

Oh brethren!, deceive not yourselves. If this be all you look at; if, upon opening this doore of hope, this be all you ayme at, to make use of the time to secure your selves against oppressors, and never thinke of closing with God; but thinke of it; you may perhaps goe farre in pursuit of your owne designes, in providing against the evils you sigh under; and, this Parliament may do great things this way: but let me tell you from God, that this will never do the deed, till the covenant we have been all this while speaking of, be resolved on and solemnly entered into by all those that expect any blessing from that High Assembly.[103]

With this encouragement behind them, the Scots went in to their first meeting on 19 November, to be faced with the King in person. Rothes and Henderson, who do not seem to have expected him, asked whether the commissioners' commission ceased in his presence. In this, they

[99] P. Collinson, *Elizabethan Puritan Movement* (1967), 29 and *passim*. The point is about perception of the Elizabethan Settlement, and is not altered by Norman Jones's reconstruction of how that Settlement was arrived at: Jones, *Faith by Statute* (1982). Burges, preaching his opening sermon to the Long Parliament on 17 Nov. 1640, made it a point that he was speaking on the anniversary of the day when reformation was *begun* by Queen Elizabeth: Peyton, fo. 18.

[100] C. Burges, *First Sermon* (1641), 6, 8, 10, 13, 15, 22, 24, 27, 34; and other refs; Stephen Marshall, *Sermon* (1641), Epistle, pp. 10–11. The committee which chose the preachers consisted of Roe, Earle, Fleetwood, Mildmay Barrington, and Pym, a group in which the allies of the Twelve Peers had a majority. The invitation to preach was taken to Marshall by Harley (not a member of the committee) and to Burges by Pym: *CJ* ii. 20, 24.

[101] Burges, *First Sermon*, pp. 10–12, 15; Marshall, *Sermon*, pp. 33–4.

[102] Marshall, *Sermon*, pp. 22–31, 32, 33, 35.

[103] Burges, *First Sermon*, p. 43.

were supported by Bristol, and when the next meeting began without the King, Bristol allowed himself to observe that 'there will be no doubt so long as the King was absent'. It was becoming an increasingly common attitude to Charles.[104] Henderson then asked whether the negotiators were empowered by the King and Parliament, and was told by the King, apparently claiming to supersede the Ripon commission, that 'the commission is now only from me, not from the Parliament': 'the Parliament never joynes', to which Rothes bluntly replied that 'they have no power to treat unless the Parliament joyne'.[105] The 'well affected' must have advised them that they could safely insist on this point.

On 20 November both Houses gave a commission to the negotiators, while reserving the right to approve of their conclusions, and on 21 November negotiations began in earnest, and the Scots moved on to their first demand, that their Acts of Parliament be published in the King's name.[106] The King's absence made it necessary to proceed by written papers. The King first offered to confirm all the Acts except the first, but since it was the first that enacted that the others were passed in a lawful Parliament, the concession was not of as much substance as it appeared to be. On the 26th, the English commissioners gave in a number of papers in the King's name, objecting to particular Acts 'all written, as was supposed, by Sir John Hay', the Scottish Clerk Register.[107] Hay was one of the more fiery spirits among what was the nucleus of a Scottish government in exile in London, involving Traquair, Sir Robert Spottiswoode the Archbishop's son, Walter Balcanquall, and the bishops of Ross and Brechin. With the exception of Traquair, who seems to have joined Hamilton in his efforts at mediation, these people constituted a strong anti-Covenanter influence on the King. In fact, it is doubtful whether the Scots were right about authorship of these papers. One, attempting to hold the Scots to the Berwick terms, and reciting the paper by Loudoun which had begun the Berwick negotiation, is almost verbatim in terms the King had used at Ripon and before. The objection to the Act against the *Large Declaration*, which had accused that work of 'lies', made the obvious point that they could not expect a gentleman, much less a prince, to belie himself, and anyone might have written it. The objection to the Scottish Triennial Act, that it defrauded the King of the means of expressing grace to his subjects, and communicated an incommunicable prerogative, is suggestively like some of the things

---

[104] BL Harl. MS 457, fos. 3^r, 4^{r-v}, 8^v.

[105] Ibid., fos. 3^v, 4^r, 6^v.

[106] For the Acts involved, see *APS* 5. 259–99. In addition to major items of policy, they included such measures of godly reformation as the prohibition of salmon fishing on the sabbath.

[107] BL Stowe MS 187, fos. 7^r, 9^r. BL Harl. MS 457 is the English minutes, and BL Stowe MS 187 the Scottish minutes.

Charles later said about the English Triennial Act. The objection to the
Act on Scottish forts, that it deprived the King of what the meanest of
his subjects enjoyed, 'to wit the proprietie of his owne' is so like his later
reply to the English Parliament on Hull that it seems probable they were
the work of the same royal author.[108] As always, the study of Charles in a
British context makes it harder to lay responsibility on his ministers:
when such closely similar policies and arguments proceed from two
separate groups of ministers, there is an acute temptation to place
responsibility on the master both groups served. This is a conclusion the
treaty negotiators may have drawn. At last, on 28 November the King
retreated on the substance of this demand. The Scots, as instructed,
spent a few more days ensuring that the manner of publishing the Acts
did not call the last Parliament's legitimacy in question.

While these issues were in progress, the Commons met one Scottish
fear by ordering the cashiering of popish officers from the King's army,
to the extreme indignation of a young Irish officer called John Barry:
'the Parliament house are taking an order to cashier all papist officers,
and among the rest myself'. 'They fall out bitterly against us all, and
begin to banish us out of town, and to remove us from court; what will
become of us I know not, but we are in an ill taking at present'. Barry
vigorously protested his loyalty: 'Sir, I was never factious in religion, nor
shall ever seek the ruin of any because he is not of my opinion'.[109]
Barry's prophecy was premature: he was to be one of the leaders of the
Irish Rebellion. Already, it was being shown that Scottish proposals for
strengthening Protestantism were capable of producing an Irish back-
lash. A proposal by Pym on 23 November, that papists should be made
to dress with a distinguishing mark like the Jews in Italy, is unlikely to
have eased these anxieties, even though the French Ambassador assures
us it was rejected by 'tout le monde'.[110] On the 24th, Hotham proposed
cashiering the regiment in the King's army commanded by the Scottish
Earl of Crawford, which was duly done. The reason given for these
reductions in the army was the perfectly genuine one of saving expense,
but it is unlikely to have escaped the Covenanters' notice that all those
most likely to be willing to fight them were being deprived of the means
to do so. We have also, perhaps, part of the explanation of why the Earl
of Crawford's resentment against Hamilton, who was widely held
responsible for the policy of concession to the Covenanters, grew to the

---

[108] BL Stowe MS 187, fo. 12ʳ. For the King's argument on Hull, see Rushworth, *Collections*, III. i.
572.

[109] *HMC Egmont*, I. 122. Barry was writing to Sir Philip Percivall, Clerk of the Parliaments of
Ireland.

[110] DO, vol. i, fo. 10ʳ; PRO 31/3/72, p. 341. The comparison to the Jews in Italy was made by
the French Ambassador, not by Pym.

point where it later triggered off the Incident before the King was ready
for it. The Covenanters, however, remained anxious. On 7 December
the committee at Newcastle with the army said that 'our enemies are
bussy on all handes, and wee assure you they are not wanting in Scotland, yea even at this time'. They also observed anxiously that the
English had carried a great stock of ammunition to Carlisle, and were
working on the fortifications of Berwick.[111]

There was a mine here the King was later to try to spring, but in
London, responsible middle-of-the-road English opinion, as represented by Bristol, was still too set on concluding peace for any such project
to be possible. Baillie was still being assured on 2 December that two
thirds of the Commons were their friends, which probably meant no
more than that they wished to conclude a peace. He was also being told
that the English wanted to defer the issue of Root and Branch until the
trial of Strafford had progressed further.[112] In the formal negotiations,
article 2 was passed over since it was included in one of the Acts of
Parliament confirmed by article 1. On 8 December the Scots presented
their third demand, that Scots outside Scotland should not be made to
take oaths unwarranted by their laws. This met an instant written reply
that Scots 'as of Scotland' should not be made to do anything contrary
to the laws of Scotland, but Scots who transplanted themselves to
England or Ireland should be subject to the laws of those countries, and
to the oaths established by those laws. This was less than the Scots
wanted, especially in relation to Ulster Scots, whom the Scots always
wanted to be able to continue to behave as Scotsmen, but they instantly
accepted it.[113] The position was perhaps too reasonable to be easily
argued against, and the King does appear to have conceded the immediate demand that Scots travelling in England should no longer be forced
to swear to the Royal Supremacy.

The Scots then passed on to their fourth demand, for the trial and
punishment of incendiaries, and again met a reply the King was to use
again: 'his Majesty conceaveth he hath none such about him'. Charles's
resistance to the punishment of his servants was a deep conviction
which went back to 1626, but it never did his servants much good. Since
what was wanted, in the demand for the punishment of a royal servant,
was that the King should abandon the policies for which the servant
could be held responsible, the harder the King defended a threatened
servant, the more savagery against him was needed to ensure that the
policies he represented should be seen to be abandoned. Thus, the more

---

[111] NLS Adv. MS 33.1.1, vol. xiii, no. 42.
[112] Baillie, i. 275; NLS Wodrow MS Quarto 25, 117ʳ–18ʳ.
[113] BL Stowe MS 187, fos. 15ʳ⁻ᵛ. On the Scots' wishes, see *APS* 5. 300 and Baillie, i. 279.

Charles defended his servants, the more at risk they were, and the convictions which did him credit as a gentleman did him no good as a politician. In particular, the King was determined to defend the Earl of Traquair for his actions as King's commissioner in 1639. Traquair appreciated the risks to himself, and was doing all he could to be conciliatory, but the King's defence of him nearly turned him into the Scottish Strafford. The delivery of the Scottish charges against Laud and Strafford can have done nothing to sweeten the atmosphere. That against Laud held him responsible for the introduction of the Scottish Prayer Book, and argued with some force that episcopacy was a principle which divided the kingdoms. That against Strafford accused him of provoking the Bishops' Wars for no reason they could under-stand except his contempt for the kirk of Scotland. They accused him, perfectly correctly, of intending to take the Irish army to Scotland, and said, in words which raise the suspicion that they might have seen Strafford's letters to Northumberland, that he wanted to make Scotland a 'conquered province'.[114] A further tension is hinted at in a note in the English minutes: 'the Scots excuse sermons charged to be preached by some of theirs, especially of one Mr. Blair'.[115] Some hint of what was behind this emerges from the English minutes for the next day: the English commissioners read the end of the Scottish charge against Laud, 'saying that this was not a particular charge upon the Archbishop of Canterbury, but against episcopacie in generall, and therefore desire it might be omitted'. After a short recess, Alexander Henderson 'sayeth they do not presume to prescribe to the Parliament what to do concern-ing episcopacie, though in their own experience they found it prejudi-call etc'.[116] If this is compared with the uncompromising *jure divino* Presbyterian position Henderson had taken at Berwick, it indicates a retreat big enough to be a sign that the Scots were encountering very considerable resistance. This resistance tended to centre on the charge that the Scots were 'prescribing' to the English what to do, and drew on some of the same emotions the Covenanters themselves had exploited in 1637. It was at about this date that Sir Thomas Knyvett, a good political weathercock precisely because he was not a political animal, exclaimed

God a marcy good Scott! But mustris marke the winding up. Scott is not gone yet. Behould I doubt we must be acquainted with Mr Knocks aswell Buchanan and Mas. Henderson before we be ridd of them. Some heads may perhaps

---

[114] Rushworth, *Trial*, pp. 770–1; Knowler, ii. 189–92. Baillie (i. 180) reports that 'our friends in the lower house' had considered these charges before they were made public. For the Scots' agreement to suppress some of their criticisms of episcopacy in England, see Donald, p. 402, and BL Harl. MS 457, fo. 31^r.

[115] BL Harl. MS 457, fo. 30^r.

[116] Ibid., fo. 31^r.

satisfye both kingdomes, but thay must have better braines yo do'te with out losse than any I beleeve are amongst them.[117]

Under these circumstances, it was a tactical necessity for the Scots to be able to work behind a front of English allies. They had always felt the need for such a front, and on the issue of church government in England, it was more acute than on any other issue. We may then wonder, as Charles almost undoubtedly did, what the Scots' role was in the presentation of the London Root and Branch Petition on 11 December. This was the Petition Baillie had seen as far back as 18 November, but on 2 December his Parliamentary friends were still urging that it should be deferred until the trial of Strafford had advanced further. There is no reason to believe they had changed their minds before 11 December, and Baillie's claim that the Petition was presented because 'the people's patience could no longer in' could be suspected of being disingenuous.[118] On the morning of 11 December Pym was summoned to see some of the Scots commissioners, and told that, because money was coming through too slowly, they were in great distress and 'the verie cloathes of many persons were ragged and worn out'. We may well wonder *which* people's patience Baillie thought would no longer in.[119]

The Petition itself was almost undoubtedly organized through the City ministers, but these were probably the very people in London who were, of all others, closest to the Scots, and they too, as they regularly reminded the Parliament in their sermons, were capable of feeling impatience at the slow progress of the Houses towards reformation of religion. The Petition itself, with its heavy anti-Arminian stress and its vigorous attack on Laudian ceremony, covers ground the Scots and the City ministers had always had in common. There are only two clauses which show signs of a more distinctive Scottish influence. One is the last clause:

the present wars and commotions happened between His Majesty and his subjects of Scotland, wherein his Majesty and all his kingdoms are endangered, and suffer greatly, and are like to become a prey to the common enemy in case the wars go on, which we exceedingly fear will not only go on, but also increase to an utter ruin of all, unless the prelates with their dependencies be removed out of England, and also they and their practices, who, as we, under your honours' favours, do verily believe and conceive have occasioned the quarrel.

---

[117] *Knyvett, Letters*, p. 97. Knyvett's two opening sentences, mysterious in isolation, probably refer to a now missing enclosure of the poem 'Gramercy, Good Scot', for which see NLS Adv. 33.1.1, vol. xiii, no. 69, and *Diary of John Rous*, ed. M. A. E. Green (Camden Society, 66, 1856), 110–11.

[118] Baillie, i. 273–4, 275, 280.

[119] D'Ewes (N.), p. 141. This meeting was arranged by 'some' of the English Lords Commissioners. It would be nice to know their names, and also whether this was the first moment at which Pym knew the Root and Branch Petition was to be presented that day.

This is remarkably like the conclusion of Baillie's paper against Laud, and we may wonder whether the key point in the timing of the Root and Branch Petition was to give English cover to that paper, which was presented to the commissioners one day after the Root and Branch Petition. The other clause, singled out with some shrewdness by Secretary Vane, was the inclusion of kneeling at communion among popish ceremonies. This was by no means a unanimous view among the English godly, and their public position tended to confine itself to claims for liberty for those who did not kneel, rather than condemnations of those who did. For the Scots, on the other hand, 'kneelers' represented the insidious Anglicization of the Five Articles of Perth, and the wording of the clause suggests that its authors were more sensitive to Anglo-Scottish union than to the internal union of the English godly.[120]

When the Petition reached the House of Commons, it was presented by Alderman Penington, member for the City, and was said to come with 15,000 signatures. Support from Alderman Cradock, the former Governor of the Massachusets Bay Company, was hardly unexpected, and he is likely to have been involved in its presentation. Among the leading group, Strode and Fiennes, always two of the most eager, spoke in favour of the Petition.[121] Among the group who were later to be known as the anti-Scots, Digby and Falkland seemed chiefly concerned to prevent a snap vote. As in many debates, the interesting speeches were from those whose line was less predictable. Sir Miles Fleetwood, the Duke's old client, said that religion was the chiefest pillar of their happiness, and if they did not look to it, they were undone, and used this impeccably godly sentiment to cover the rather lame conclusion that 'many parts' of it were worthy of consideration. D'Ewes, in very similar terms, insisted that 'if matters of religion had gone on but 20 yeares longer as they had done of late yeares, ther would not in the issue soe much as the verie face of religion have continued amongst us but that all should have been overwhelmed with idolatrie, superstition ignorance profanenes and heresy'. His conclusion, however, was 'to advize of the saied petition before us with such moderation as his royall Majestie himself might not misinterprett it'. His distinction between 'ancient and godlie bishops' and 'ther baronies and temporall employments' indicated one promising line for such moderation to take. Sir Nevill Poole, one of the few in the Commons who became Parliamentarians in 1642 without any visible devotion to godly reformation, com-

---

[120] Gardiner, *Documents*, pp. 140, 144; Northcote, pp. 51–2. Vane is like to have had a sharp eye for issues involving kneeling, since it had been a sore subject in his own household, being the issue on which his son had temporarily departed for Massachusetts.

[121] For the debate, Northcote, pp. 51–3, and D'Ewes (N.), pp. 139–41.

plained that many parts of it were scandalous, but the most ominous speech from the Scots' point of view was that of the godly, but possibly anti-Scottish, Lord Fairfax, who proposed that the petition should follow the Book of Canons.[122] This debate did not suggest the existence of a spontaneous majority for Root and Branch. The strand of opinion represented by Fleetwood and D'Ewes was one without which a majority could not easily be constructed, and their view, at this stage, seems to have been that they did not regard Root and Branch as worth the political divisions it would undoubtedly cause. The Scots, if their English political ear was yet well enough trained, should have been sadder and wiser men the next day.

This resistance makes an instructive contrast with two other measures on the Scottish shopping list which went through without question in the next eight days. The impeachment of Laud was moved by Pym on 18 December, immediately on the report of the conference at which the Scottish commissioners' charge against him was read to the Commons. It was carried through without a murmur of opposition. There is here no suggestion of complaint at the Scots meddling in English matters, and it would be very nice to know whether this was because the Scots were thought to have suffered enough from Laud to be entitled to complain, or because the impeachment of Laud was so generally popular that no one imagined that it was being done in response to Scottish pressure. Harbottle Grimston quoted the Scots' charge with approval, saying that 'we do all know he is guilty of the same, if not more, here in this kingdom'. The presence of Grimston here is significant: his persistent and eloquent devotion to the Book of Common Prayer makes him a representative of the same moderate strand as Fleetwood and D'Ewes: he was godly, but no advocate of a New Model church. Yet there is no suggestion of moderation in Grimston's attack on Laud: 'look upon him as he is in his highness, and he is the very sty of all pestilential filth, that hath infected the state and government of this commonwealth'. He accused him of preferring 'popish' bishops, such as Wren, 'the least of all these birds, but one of the most unclean ones', and concluded that 'like a busie, angry wasp, his sting is in the tail of everything'.[123] The next day, a committee undertook the task of trying

---

[122] The parallel to the canons was not made at random. They had been condemned (*CJ* ii. 52) because they 'do contain in them many matters contrary to the King's prerogative, to the fundamental laws and statutes of the realm, to the property and liberty of the subjects, and matters tending to sedition, and of dangerous consequences'. This was precisely the same as most English laymen's objection to the jurisdiction of General Assemblies: Fairfax was saying they were 'but old priest writ large'. See also J. T. Cliffe, *Puritan Gentry* (1984), 229.

[123] D'Ewes (N.), p. 169; Rushworth, *Collections*, III.i. 123–3. D'Ewes's report of Grimston bears a recognizable resemblance to the printed text.

to ensure a preaching ministry in every parish, one which had been dear to godly reformers since Elizabeth's reign, but which would also have the effect of bringing the ministry very much nearer the Scottish ideal. It is suggestive that proceedings were started by a petition from the parish of Hughenden, much of which belonged to John Hampden.[124] Taken together, these responses suggest a House which would be perfectly happy, as its predecessor had been, with the sort of religion represented by Holdsworth and Brownrigg, but which was frightened of the divisive powers of the sort of godly reformation the Scots wanted.

Meanwhile, the Scots were left with the issue of the incendiaries still on the negotiating table. Since they had succeeded in bringing the cases of Strafford and Laud before the English Parliament, they were left debating only the issue of the Scottish incendiaries, and especially that of Traquair. The King on 23 December thought he had conceded this article by agreeing that he would not hinder any of his subjects from being tried and judged by the Parliament of the kingdom to which they belonged. To his dismay, he found this was not all the Scots were asking: like the English prosecutors of Strafford afterwards, they were trying to deprive Charles of the prerogative of pardon. The Scots insisted that this was necessary, lest the incendiaries 'interpret his Majesty's dealing to be ane approbation of what they have done, and ane emboldening of them and others to the lyke attempts hereafter'. By no lesser means could it now be made clear that Charles was not hereafter to be served in this manner. It is no wonder that Charles protested that 'it were to prelimitate his justice and mercy if he should declaire any further'.[125] On 24 December the Scots asked the English commissioners 'to represent to his Matie. that this reply is not satisfactory, and to propose it to the Parliament'. Baillie said that the appeal to Parliament was 'our last and sure refuge', and that the Lords told the King that 'doubtles all there would be for the Scotts demand'.[126] At this point, to the Scots' irritation, proceedings were interrupted by 'there Christmas'—another reminder that the meeting of the English and the Scots was a potential conflict of cultures, as well as of creeds. Even so godly an Englishman as Lord Brooke celebrated the season, and his household accounts show payments for minstrels at 'Christ-tide'. There were some among the English godly who did not celebrate even at Christ-tide, but the Scots' perplexity at finding negotiations interrupted

---

[124] D'Ewes (N.), pp. 170–1; CJ ii. 54. For Hampden's ownership of land in Hughenden, see PRO Wards 2/30. Hampden was a member of the committee set up to deal with the matter.

[125] NLS Adv. MS 33.4.6, fos. 99–100; BL Stowe MS 187, fo. 26ʳ⁻ᵛ. Baillie (i. 284) says that though Strafford was not formally involved here, it was the King's concern with his case which made him so insistent on the principle involved.

[126] Baillie, i. 285; BL Harl. MS 457, fo. 39ʳ.

by 'there Christmas' gives a strong suggestion of two nations divided by a common language.[127]

After the holiday, a meeting on 28 December was inconclusive, and another on the 29th grew uncomfortable. The Scots' suspicion showed raw in their objection to a phrase that the King commanded the Lords 'at this time' to promise it, 'as if after the distractions the king would not condiscend'. A query from Bristol about who were incendiaries drew from Rothes the definition that they were 'such . . . as are clearly convicted of incending the King'. The fiction of blaming the minister was growing increasingly difficult to sustain. On the 30th the King finally gave in totally, agreeing to an answer dictated verbatim to him by the Scottish commissioners, from which he deleted only the words 'out of our goodness and justice'.[128] If the Scots feared that they had not yet heard the last of this issue, they were right.

While this was going on, an important series of private meetings seems to have been taking place between the Scots and their Parliamentary friends. These meetings seem to have left Baillie alternating between hope and fear. On 12 December he said that 'God is makeing here a new world; no fear yet of raising the Parliament, so long as the ladds about Newcastle sit still'. Yet in the next breath, he complained that 'all the happiness may soone vanish; a gloom of the king's brow would disperse this feeble people, for anything yet we see, if the terror of God and us afrayed not their enemies, if help from God and us did not continue their courage'.

On 28 December he recorded a great deal of collaboration. He said that the Scots' paper on the article on their losses was now in the hands of 'the English, our friends' to be improved. In return, the English wanted them to draw out their eighth article to the full, for they had much to do, including the overthrow of episcopacy and 'the planting of the court'—a revealingly Ulster phrase for Bedford and Pym's plan to take over key offices. For all this, the English had told them, 'long tyme is requyrit'. Yet at the same time 'their great charges, fiftie thousand pound in the moneth for the armies, will force them to close one session, and end the most of their greatest affaires, that both armies may be dismissed; bot this cannot bee in haste'. Most important of all, he revealed advance Scottish involvement in drafting the text of the Root

---

[127] NLS Adv. MS 33.4.6, fo. 98ᵛ; Warwick Castle MSS Halford's Accounts, vol. ii, Gifts. For English godly who did not celebrate, see *Records of Bucks.*, ed. W. H. Summers (Aylesbury, 1897), VII. ii. 108; *Records of a Church of Christ at Bristol*, ed. Roger Hayden (Bristol Record Society, Bristol, 1974), 85.

[128] BL Stowe MS 187, fo. 26ᵛ; BL Harl. MS 457, fos. 44–5. It is doubtless relevant to the King's climb-down that Sir Jacob Astley, writing from the army on 23 Dec., firmly expressed the hope that peace would be concluded: PRO SP 16/473/87.

and Branch Bill. His words should be quoted verbatim, since it is almost possible to imagine the dialogue they report:

The farr greatest part are for our discipline; for all the considerable parts of it, they will draw up a modell of their owne, with our advyce, to be considered upon by commissioners of the church, and others appoynted by Parliament, and if God shall bless this land, by these commissioners to be settled in everie congregation at this extraordinarie tyme, till afterward, the church being constitute, a Generall Assemblie may be called to perfyte it. At this tyme a Generall Assemblie would spoyle all, the farr most of their clergie being verie corrupt. If all this were done, we might be gone.[129]

The entrusting of enforcement to Parliamentary commissioners, though it could be derived from the Act appointing the Scottish Committee of Estates, was a notion the Scots would not voluntarily have applied to a well-established church, since they believed in true Hildebrandine style, in the autonomy of the church. It was, on the other hand, a congenial idea for Pym, who had recommended it for the enforcement of the recusancy laws as far back as November 1621.[130] In 1641 it suited the needs of the moment, and was used for Penington's bill for abolishing superstition and for the bill for scandalous ministers, as well as for the Root and Branch Bill. The church to which this pointed was the Cromwellian church of the Triers and Ejectors, not the Presbyterian church of which the Scots dreamed.[131] In assuring the Scots that 'a Generall Assemblie would spoyle all', their English allies no doubt spoke the truth. Yet if they led the Scots to believe that they later intended to call a real General Assembly, and not the state-nominated body which later met at Westminster, they must at least have been guilty of being economical with the truth. If Saye, for example, was a party to giving the Scots any such assurances, and the Scots believed them, understanding between the cultures was still very limited indeed.[132]

While these talks were going on, the formal negotiations turned to the

[129] Baillie, i. 283, 285–7.

[130] *Commons' Debates in 1621*, ed. W. Notestein, F. H. Relf, and Hartley Simpson (New Haven, Conn., 1935), ii. 464, vi. 207. This is a good example of a speech made in the 1620s which has an importance with hindsight which it did not have in the context in which it was delivered. Both perspectives are valid in their proper place. On the European context of such proposals, see Russell, 'Monarchies, Wars and Estates', *Legislative Studies Quarterly*, 7/2 (1982), 206–7. On this issue, Scotland may have acted as a channel for the transmission of ideas from France to England.

[131] On the Long Parliament's use of commissioners for law enforcement, see House of Lords Record Office, Original Acts, 16 Car. 1 cap. 1; D'Ewes (N.), pp. 270–1; *CJ* i. 72, 109; DO, vol. i, fo. 42ʳ. For Vane's text of the Root and Branch Bill, which is much as described here, see PRO SP 16/539/59.

[132] For Scottish belief, admittedly at the safe distance of Newcastle, that there were 'great houps' of one confession of faith, one Directory for worship, and one catechism, as well as one form of church government, see Alexander Balfour to Sir James Balfour, 29 Dec. 1640, printed in Baillie, vol. ii, App., p. 473.

issue of the Scots' losses and their claims for reparation. This was an
issue on which the King appears to have hoped for a breach:[133] as at
Ripon, he probably hoped that the notion of paying Danegeld to an
invading army would inflame English sense of their own honour.
Because the issue demanded money, and money had to come from the
Parliament, the negotiators' importance on this issue was less than
usual. They agreed a paper on what the losses were, and reported it to
the Parliament on 12 January. At this meeting, Bristol did not take the
opportunity to break with the Scots: his report was 'very favourable',
and was assisted by Paget and Wharton 'our good friends', and by
Mandeville reading papers 'in the best toone he could'.[134] Bristol's
report is so good an indication of his evolving position that it is worth
discussing at length. He said it should not be thought a dishonour to
relieve an invading army 'as the case nowe standeth', because the dishonour should fall on the 'ill instruments' whose 'improvident counsells' had brought them to such an unhappy condition. As at York, he
was placing the blame squarely on those who had led the King into the
Bishops' Wars. He said their condition was like that of Rome after the
Battle of Cannae, 'as I do remember', and in these conditions, it was a
great honour to buoy the state up again. He wanted to replace the ill
counsels which had brought them to this condition with 'wise, prudent
and settled counsels', and reminded them that England could not have
been brought to this condition 'were itt not for want of unitie and
discord amongst our selves'. Bristol perhaps deserves more credit than
Hyde for the creation of the new constitutional royalism of 1641. When
once unity was restored, he had a Shakespearian prescription: that they
should see what these great armies, united together, could do abroad.[135]
We have an early hint of the scheme Bristol was backing in August, to
divert the Scottish army to the recovery of the Palatinate.

Action on this report was the responsibility of the Commons, since it
involved the provision of money. The Scots had computed their losses at
the startling sum of £514,000, but were not claiming the whole of this,
and, no doubt on the advice of their English friends, scrupulously
refrained from asking for any particular sum, confining themselves to
saying that they hoped the English would partake of the charge, as they
had partaken of the benefit. The French Ambassador believed they
would accept half the sum.[136] After some delay, the Commons came to
consider the issue on 22 January. Jermyn and Vane, no doubt speaking

---

[133] Baillie, i. 289; NLS Adv. MS 33.4.6, fo. 115r.

[134] Baillie, i. 290.

[135] Bodl. MS Nalson XIII, fo. 12r–v. The classics, as well as the Bible, could provide a coded
language, and in citing Rome after Cannae, Bristol was making a Fabian invocation of the virtues
of delay. It is, in fact, a neat summary of the strategy he induced the King to adopt.

[136] D'Ewes (N.), p. 247; PRO 31/3/72, p. 406.

to a brief, opposed the Scots' demand with the help of John Selden, who
was becoming one of the leading anti-Scots in the House and of Dr
Turner, who had proposed the Queries against Buckingham in 1626.
Grimston, Perd, D'Ewes, and, cautiously, Rudyerd were in favour.[137] Sir
John Wray, one of the Scots' most faithful friends, argued that 'the
boute feux of this prelaticall warr' should be made to pay the shot for
their activities, and should not be allowed to divide 'us' from 'them who
worship bot one God and serve but on maister with us'.[138] With careful
procedural guidance from Pym, the House then voted on the question
of principle that they should give assistance to the Scots, and would in
due time consider the matter and manner of it. In this very anodyne
form the question was carried without a division.

On 3 February the issue came up for debate again, and the sum was
to be decided. Sir John Strangeways and John Selden attempted to
reverse the principle of assistance and Selden hinted that it might be
treasonable to give money to those that came into the realm with swords
in their hands. Kirton, another of the consistent anti-Scots, supported
him, and was answered by a long disquisition from D'Ewes to the effect
that the English and the Scots were one nation. At this point, as so
often, D'Ewes's own speech meant that his notes broke down. He
records that Holles and Earle spoke, and though we may well guess
what they said, D'Ewes does not tell us. Marten proposed £300,000;
Strangeways, presumably with extreme reluctance, agreed to go as high
as £200,000; and the House finally fixed on £300,000, to Baillie's great
relief.[139] The Scots were even more relieved, or so they said, that the
money was to be given under the title of a 'Brotherly Assistance', thus
allowing them the status of brethren. The title, however, provoked
others. Thomas Triplet wrote to his friend Edward Hyde, and reported
a rumour that the money for the Brotherly Assistance was to be raised
by fining Alderman Abell the wine monopolist, 'and so lett Abell pay
Caine'.[140]

While this issue was on the table, others were going forward on which
the Scots had to act through their English allies. At the beginning of
January another month's cessation of arms was agreed until 16 Febru-

---

[137] D'Ewes (N.), pp. 268, 272–5.

[138] PRO SP 16/476/68. The spelling 'bot', especially when used in one place but not the next,
and perhaps also the handwriting, suggest a Scottish copy. This would not cast any doubt on the
speech, since Sir John Wray seems to have been a regular user of scripts, and is very likely to have
given a text to his Scottish friends for copying. What would be nice is to know how, if it is a
Scottish text, it came to be in State Papers.

[139] D'Ewes (N.), pp. 137–20; Peyton, fo. 79ᵛ; Baillie, i. 297. John Pyne, a pro-Scot who was
much worried by the strength of the pro-episcopal party in the House, correctly predicted the sum
to be voted the day before the debate. Bristol RO Smyth of Long Ashton MS 139(b).

[140] Bodl. MS Clarendon, vol. 20, no. 1514. For the speech by Pym which could be the source of
this idea, see D'Ewes (N.), p. 351.

ary, 'if the treaty shall last so long'. The Commons also turned their attention to an issue essential to Scottish security, but one they could not easily make out to be under their jurisdiction: that of the Irish army. The King, right up to the last moment, was insisting that the Irish army should not be disbanded before the Scottish, while the Scots felt it vital to their security that it should be.[141] The issue was raised in the Commons on 4 January by Earle, Clotworthy, and Fiennes, all of them safely identifiable as among the Scots' friends. From then, through February and March, the issue was constantly raised, and normally by Earle, who seems to have made it his own. He was supported, at various times, by Clotworthy, Strode, D'Ewes, Whistler, Holles, Sir Hugh Cholmeley, and Reynolds.[142] Speakers on the other side were scarce. Since few members had any great liking for the Irish army, but the King was determined to keep it, the issue is a good one on which to look for covert recruits to the royal service. Five members certainly spoke against its disbandment.[143] Of these, Jermyn and Vane were Privy Councillors, Sir Frederick Cornwallis was a Gentleman of the Privy Chamber, and it raises speculation to find that the others were Sir John Culpepper and Sir John Strangeways. We should perhaps add Robert Trelawney who later combined Irish interests with Royalist sympathies so intense as to get him expelled from the House in March 1642.[144]

As the Scots anticipated, their seventh demand, concerning the recalling of the hostile declarations against them, was rapidly agreed, and they were coming very near the point of presenting their eighth and final demand. This was both the one they needed to spin out, and the one on which they were likely to be justly accused of dictating the settlement of England. As with the charge against Laud, their proposals were heralded by a flurry of English demands for the same things. One of the Scottish newsletters tells us that the revival of the Root and Branch Petition, the Ministers' Remonstrance, and the presentation of a series of county petitions against bishops were timed to come together.[145] We are not explicitly told that they were planned to precede the presentation of the Scots' eighth demand on 10 February, but the fact that this information is in a Scottish source would alone suggest it. This time, the Root and Branch Petition came before the Commons two days ahead of the Scots and not one. The Ministers' Remonstrance on 23 January

---

[141] For the King's desire to keep the Irish army, see PRO SP 63/258/70, 74, 85, 96, and other refs. For the Scots' desire for its disbandment, see BL Stowe MS 187, fo. 55ᵛ, and Rushworth, *Collections*, III. i. 372, dated by *HMC Salis.* XXII. 351.

[142] D'Ewes (N.), pp. 213; 229–30, 325, 346–8, 357, 359, 454, 461, 482, 484–8, 498; *CJ* ii. p. 62; *Two Diaries*, p. 7.

[143] D'Ewes (N.), pp. 229–30, 350, 484 n; BL Add. MS 6521, fo. 68ʳ⁻ᵛ; *HMC Cowper (Coke)*, II. 274.

[144] Keeler, pp. 363–4.

[145] NLS Adv. MS 33.1.1, vol. xiii, no. 60.

came well ahead, to allow time for debating in the Commons' very crowded timetable. It was presented by Sir Robert Harley, with a supporting remonstrance from the diocese of Peterborough from Sir Gilbert Pickering. It was later avowed to the House by Burges and Downing, both among Baillie's familiar friends.[146] There is no need for such conjecture, since Baillie said on 12 December that those drafting the Remonstrance 'meets with us' on it.[147] The preparation of the county petitions was known to Baillie on 12 December, and probably as early as 18 November.[148]

We are given a very rare glimpse of the advance planning behind these petitions, and also of the irritation Scottish pressure could cause for their English friends, in a letter written by Howard of Escrick, one of the two who had presented the Petition of the Twelve Peers to the King. Writing on 7 January to Sir Thomas Smyth, who was about to become Root and Branch candidate in the Bridgwater by-election, he recounted a letter to Lord General Northumberland, saying the English army was running out of credit, and must consequently disband, while, 'on the other side', he said Argyll was making great preparations in Scotland, 'inas much as beeing att my wits end the olde proverb comes accidentalye into my heade *quos Jupiter vult perdere hos dementat*'. The target of this unflattering proverb appears to be the Scots and not the King. In London, he said there was great apprehension of the breach of the Parliament, and

theyre ar divers petitions alreadye come upp and more ar daylie expected, earnestlye praying that episcopacye may bee utterlye abolished and heare will bee the fountayne of goode or evill for I am crediblye informed his magestye can never consent too it and then yt must necessarylie put us all upon desperate courses.[149]

---

[146] D'Ewes (N.), 277, 314; Peyton, fo. 73.

[147] Baillie, i. 282. He also records (i. 291) that he had sent a copy of the Ministers' Remonstrance to Scotland before it was given in. The text of the Ministers' Remonstrance is now lost, being presumably a casualty of the House of Commons' fire. Some idea of its contents can be gained from the heads and notes of discussion in *Verney's Notes*, pp. 4–14. The charges against the bishops included their composition of prayers 'against the honest Scotts'. For what may be the draft for the Remonstrance submitted by the ministers of Hereford diocese, see BL Loan MS 29/172, fos. 363–6. I am grateful to Dr Jacqueline Levy for the identification of this MS, and to her and Dr Peter Donald for helpful discussions of it.

[148] Baillie, i. 280, 273–4.

[149] Bristol RO Smyth of Long Ashton MS 137(b). The date of 7 Jan. 1641 appears to be Scottish style. It is worth remark that Howard broke the flow of his letter to express his confidence in the messenger. On the Bridgwater by-election, and Smyth's presumed Root and Branch sympathies, see ibid. 139(b) (John Pyne to Smyth, 2 Feb. 1641). Smyth's sponsors for the seat were Pyne and Robert Blake, son of one of Pym's tenants, and future Commonwealth Admiral. Blake was threatening, if not sufficiently reassured on Smyth's Root and Branch sympathies, to stand himself. If Pyne was in fact correct about Smyth's views, he is an almost unique example of a Root and Branch Royalist.

In a postscript, he asked 'praye lett mee know what sence you have in the countrye of these things and whether Somersetshyre prepare any petition or no'. In the event, petitions came from Kent, Essex, Suffolk, Hertfordshire, Bedfordshire, Sussex, Surrey, Cheshire, Warwickshire, Cambridgeshire, Gloucestershire, Buckinghamshire, and Norfolk, but not from Somerset. The conclusion seems to follow that central prompting, though present, was not a sufficient condition for the presentation of a petition, and that they only emerged from counties where there was enough spontaneous feeling ready for organizers to call it into action.[150] At the same time, this letter shows the English Parliamentary leaders as increasingly reluctant followers of their Scottish allies, who, having given them the opportunity to hold a Parliament, were rapidly depriving them of the opportunity to make a success of it. It was the need to retain his Scottish allies, not revolutionary fervour, which was putting Howard of Escrick upon desperate courses.

When the Ministers' Remonstrance came before the Commons on 1 February, the divisive power of these issues was becoming apparent. Digby, Strangeways, and Selden involved themselves in an unsuccessful attempt to discredit the Remonstrance by pretending it did not represent the intentions of its signatories.[151] Speeches by Hampden, Pym, and Holles, and testimony by White of Dorchester, Marshall, Calamy, Burges, and Downing defeated this effort, but did not answer Culpepper, who said that because the bishops were 'maine columns of the realme', they should not refer the Remonstrance to any committee whatsoever. Sir John Coke was surely right that 'the heat in the lower House increases'.

As the temperature rose, both sides appealed more loudly to the public. Alexander Henderson, under the diplomatic cloak of pretending to be an English observer, published *The Government and Order of the Church of Scotland*, a sober factual description of how Scottish government worked.[152] He complained that in England 'many of the godly [were] much wearied of the prelacy, who yet bow their shoulder to bear and couch down between the two burdens'. As always, English attachment to the supremacy of the state over the church was unintelli-

---

[150] Somerset feeling seems, at this stage, to have been channelled into attempts to reverse the Beckington case and to secure the impeachment of Bishop Piers, rather than into the more general issue of episcopacy. Smyth of Long Ashton MS 139(a) (Pyne to Smyth 17 Dec. 1640). It would be nice to know Pyne's reasons for being determined to prevent the return of Sir Thomas Wroth at the Bridgwater by-election.

[151] *HMC Cowper (Coke)*, II. 272; D'Ewes (N.), pp. 307–10, 313–15.

[152] Wing 1432. The use of an English cover is perhaps a measure of Charles's resentment at Scottish interference in English matters, and was probably designed to protect Henderson against a legal charge, rather than to deceive. On Charles's lasting resentment at Scottish intervention in English affairs, see Guildford MSS 52/2/19(8) (Nicholas to Charles, 18 Aug. 1641). I am grateful to Dr J. S. A. Adamson for bringing these MSS to my attention.

gible to the Scots. Henderson tried to answer this by pleading the example of all the reformed kirks, and allowed a hint of *jure divino* beliefs to appear in the plea to follow them as they followed Christ. *The Unlawfulnesse and Danger of Limited Prelacie*, possibly also by Henderson, allowed its *jure divino* position to emerge much more plainly. It argued that in the government of the church all offices must be set up by God and not by man, and 'we are forbidden *praecepto negativo* to governe the church by humane wisdom'. The author argued, like the Exclusionists of 1680, that limitations were too weak to control a bishop: although even the best of papists believed the pope should be under the Council, this was how Antichrist had mounted up. In an unusually plain threat, the author said that such an institution would cause a shameful schism with all the reformed churches, especially that of Scotland.[153]

On the other side, Ussher was working on a scheme for limited and modified episcopacy, which was published in a pirate version without the author's permission.[154] It may be this that *The Unlawfulnesse* was meant to answer. The most powerful voice raised in public was that of the King. On 23 January, the day when the Ministers' Remonstrance was presented, he told the Lords he would never consent to the abolition of episcopacy nor to the removal of bishops from the House of Lords. D'Ewes commented that 'this speech filled most of us with sadd apprehensions of future evills in case his Majestie should bee irremovablie fixed to uphold the bishops in ther wealth pride and tyrannie'.[155] There is no trace here of the concern for the King which he had felt on the presentation of the Root and Branch Petition on 11 December. In the contest between the King and the Scots, there were a good many on the Parliamentary jury whose sympathies would turn against whichever party seemed to them to be most intransigent.

All this heightened the tension when the Root and Branch Petition again came before the Commons on 8 February. This time, it is not possible to say by whose initiative the matter was brought forward at that time. What is clear is that a number of members, including D'Ewes, had not expected a full-dress debate on the principle of episcopacy. D'Ewes thought that 'the onlie question was whether that should be committed with the Remonstrance of the ministers. But divers mistaking the question fell into other long and large disputes'.[156] As usual D'Ewes

---

[153] BL E. 206(5), pp. 2, 8–9, 12. For Baillie's earlier positions, see Baillie, i. 52–3, 156–7, and 171.

[154] D'Ewes (N.), p. 343. This work does not appear to survive in print, but for what is possibly an MS text of it, see CUL Add. MS 44/6, fos. 1–2. I am grateful to Dr J. S. A. Adamson for this reference.

[155] D'Ewes (N.), p. 281.

[156] Ibid. p. 335.

did not recognize what was going on under his nose. Baillie understood much faster: 'my Lord Digbie and Viscount Falkland, with a prepared companie about them, laboured, by premeditat speeches, and hott disputes, to have that petition cast out of the House without a hearing'. What the opponents of the Petition were trying to do was close the issue of episcopacy by taking a snap vote in its favour. 'All that night our party solisted as hard as they could',[157] and in the end, the debate produced a parade of godly speakers unprecedented in its completeness. This was not enough to avoid the appearance of a deeply divided House. Rudyerd, who began the debate, was against abolition, essentially because he liked to avoid confrontations. His patron Pembroke had been gathering signatures for a pro-episcopal petition in the City.[158]

The two speeches which seem to have made the deepest impression, both of them later available in a printed form, were by Digby and Fiennes. Digby, like every other opponent of Root and Branch, found it necessary to begin with a vigorous condemnation of the Laudian clergy, in order to establish his claim to a hearing.[159] He then neatly capped his own image by calling the petition 'a commet or blazing star, raised and kindled out of the poysonous exhalation of a corrupted hierarchy', and then adding that the comet had a terrible tail which pointed to the north. He played for a while on gentlemen's fear of the multitude, and picked up the attack on 'lascivious, idle and unprofitable books' in clause 8 of the Petition: 'did ever any body think that the Gayeties of Ovid, or Tom Coryat's Muse, should by 15,000 have been presented to a Parliament as a motive for the extirpation of bishops?'[160] This fear of moral reformation may have had more influence than its limited prominence in the debates indicates. The hub of Digby's argument centred on the proposition that episcopacy, like alcohol, was subject to a distinction between use and abuse: 'Christ's discipline hath been adulterated, this true, the whole church inebriated by the prelates, therefore infer our petitioners; let not so much as the chast, the sober use of them be suffered'. He argued, as all defenders of episcopacy did, that they should be very careful of allowing petitions against a law established, and argued that he would not vote for abolition till shown a form of government not liable to similar inconveniences, and convinced that such a 'utopia' was practicable. He wondered why a reform of government which had been continued since the Apostles' times, and had been

---

[157] Baillie, i. 302.

[158] Ibid. 296.

[159] For the text of Digby's published speech, see Rushworth, *Collections*, III. i. 170–4. Drake's notes (*Two Diaries*, p. 2) were taken in the House, and seem to establish that Digby delivered something resembling his printed text. D'Ewes (N.), p. 335 captures the attempt to force a snap vote, which has been obscured in the published text.

[160] See Gardiner, *Documents*, p. 139 for the clause Digby was attacking.

accepted by the 'learnedest' of the reformed churches abroad, should suddenly 'at the fag end of 1640' be discovered to have such a devil in it as no law could restrain, and said that triennial Parliaments could keep many a worse devil in order. He raised the spectre, common to anti-Presbyterians, of a bishop in every diocese being replaced by a pope in every parish, and the further spectre of a General Assembly claiming to excommunicate kings. It was a fine rousing performance, well cal-culated to appeal to his hearers' prejudices.

It was promptly followed by another prepared speech from Falkland, who apologetically spent more of his speech condemning the Laudian bishops than in defending episcopacy.[161] He reminded them, as most supporters of bishops did, that the Marian martyrs had included bishops. He described episcopacy as an 'ancient tree', which had grown for 1,600 years, and suggested that they prune its branches, rather than rooting it up, in order to see whether there was enough sap left for it to grow again. He argued, as many others were to do, that the proper way to control bishops was to subject them to Parliaments.

The opposition of these two might have been expected, and it should have alarmed the Scots more to find them joined by Harbottle Grim-ston, who spoke so eloquently for the impeachment of Laud. He warned that 'it may be that the new government, which is so much desired, if it be brought in upon the grounds and foundations that some would have it, it will be out of our powers ever to master it again'. Under the existing government, on the other hand, if the clergy exceeded their bounds, they might fall into a praemunire, 'and if that be not sufficient, we have yet another hank upon them, for our Parliaments have continually a command over them'.[162] It emerges very clearly from this speech how instinctively the English assumed that their problem was of how to control the clergy: the Scots made no such assumption, and indeed assumed the opposite, that the problem was how to ensure that the state did not control the clergy.

Fiennes, the first Root and Branch supporter to get into the debate,[163] fully shared English assumptions, and was pushed into answering several of Digby's arguments by leaking the current draft of the Root and Branch Bill: he said that if the proposal were for General Assem-blies able to excommunicate kings, 'I shall never give my vote, nor

[161] Rushworth, *Collections*, III. i. 184–6. Drake (*Two Diaries*, pp. 2–3) captured two of Falk-land's images, but altogether failed to reproduce the structure of his argument. For Falkland's remarks on the Laudians, see above, ch. 1 pp. 16–17.

[162] Rushworth, *Collections*, III. i. 187. D'Ewes confirms the overall thrust of the speech, but does not reproduce any of the argument.

[163] Ibid. 174–8. Drake and D'Ewes each reproduce one of Fiennes's points. Rushworth's texts seem, on the whole, to be reliable in this debate, though there is a probability that his texts had been touched up after delivery. On the order of the speeches, however, he is not a good authority: *Two Diaries*, p. 3; D'Ewes (N.), p. 336.

consent thereunto as long as I live'. In forcing him to this declaration, Digby had struck a very powerful blow at the Anglo-Scottish alliance. Instead, Fiennes said,

by the law of this land not only all ecclesiasticall jurisdiction, but also all superiority and preheminence over the ecclesiasticall state, is annexed to the imperial crown of this realm, and may be granted by Commission under the Great Seal, to such persons as his Majesty shall think meet: Now if the King should grant it to a certain number of commissioners, equal in authority, as he may do, this were an abolition of episcopacy, and yet no diminution of monarchy.

He tried to trump Digby's argument that episcopacy logically went with monarchy by claiming that the civil government under the King was 'aristocratical', whereas the clerical was monarchical, indeed papal. Yet this only drew attention to the real substance of Digby's claim, which was that under a monarchy the church could not be governed in a way fundamentally unacceptable to the King. The rest of Fiennes's speech was a long disquisition on the theme that power corrupts, but he did not develop a clear argument to show that episcopal power corrupted worse than any other power.

Sir John Wray, following him, said he did not see why they should not as well meddle with bishops as Henry VIII had done with abbeys. It seems a fair reply, yet it never effectively silenced the argument against changing established laws. Holles 'spake verie patheticallie' against bishops, but he apparently used no script, and D'Ewes does not tell us what he said.[164] Bagshaw, another telling recruit to the anti-Root-and-Branch cause, quoted references to bishops in Magna Carta, and trumped one of the Scots' main arguments by saying that the only reason why Scotland and other reformed churches needed to go Presbyterian was because they could not rely on the common law to protect them against popery.[165] William Pleydell, the most free-spoken supporter of episcopacy in the House, disowned the Laudian bishops in a somewhat cursory way, and reminded the House that the King had expressed himself.[166]

For the rest of the debate, we are forced back on D'Ewes, since the other speakers did not use scripts, and Drake, Peyton, and Verney soon became exhausted. Drake gives us an important speech by Pym, who seems to have argued for the abolition of episcopacy in order to use the bishops' lands to solve the King's financial problems.[167] Beyond this, we are told only which side people were on, and since there were two

---

[164] D'Ewes (N.), pp. 336–7.
[165] Rushworth, *Collections*, III. i. 186–7; D'Ewes (N.), 337 n; Peyton, fos. 81–2.
[166] Rushworth, *Collections*, III. i. 186–7; *Two Diaries*, p. 3.
[167] This is my reconstruction from Drake's rather confused note; *Two Diaries*, p. 3.

questions, whether to commit the Petition, and whether to abolish
episcopacy, it is not always easy to tell opinions on both questions. As
far as we can tell, there seems to have been a clear party line-up, in
which the pro-Scots and future Parliamentarians were on one side, and
the anti-Scots and future royalists on the other. Hyde, Culpepper, Hopton, Waller, and Strangeways spoke against Strode, Hampden, Earle,
Mildmay, Vassall, Rigby, Cromwell, and Crew. The debate ran on for
another day, but reached only the inconclusive ending that the London
Petition should be referred to a committee, but the question of episcopacy should be reserved to be considered by the House at a time to be
determined. Having scrupulously refrained from dividing on any of the
main questions, they then relieved their feelings by dividing on the
question whether to add six more members to the committee for the
Remonstrance, to which the Petition was referred, but it is not easy to
see this as a party division or to draw any firm conclusions from it.[168]
What was clear at the end of this debate was that the avoidance of
adversary politics could not survive much discussion of this issue, or of
the general demand for 'further reformation' which lay behind it. Since
the Scots knew that all parties were anxious for an end, they would have
been wise to pick this point to draw back. In the Lords, Berkshire,
Dorset, and Bristol, later joined by Hertford, Savill, Dunsmore, and
Poulet, began to call for the final conclusion to the treaty, and such a
call was likely to find hearers.[169]

Instead, the Scots passed on to their eighth demand. Since the eighth
demand was a widow's cruse, it is not always easy to be certain which
parts of it surfaced at which time. The first version produced a surprised
reply from the English commissioners on 9 February, that they 'resolve
of no answere, but will acquaint the king and the kingdome therewith,
being of this nature'. It also sent Sir John Borough, secretary to the
English commissioners, to look up the treaty of union of James's first
Parliament.[170] They asked, then and later that the fortifications of
Berwick and Carlisle be dismantled, and went on to claim that some
Scots should attend about the King, Queen, and Prince (the Queen had
been added since November). They asked for Scottish Councillors to be
chosen in Parliament, for freedom of trade, which subsequently
transpired to include the right to trade with the English colonies, for

[168] *CJ* ii. 81. See Gardiner, *History*, ix. 287; Baillie, i. 302. Gardiner's reconstruction is conjectural, and, to me, unconvincing. Baillie's comments probably represent what his friends told him,
and they badly needed to reassure him. The division seems to me more likely to have been used as a
safety-valve in a House which had just avoided voting on a major question of principle than as a
settled party division.

[169] BL Harl. MS 6424, fos. 23ᵛ–4ᵛ; NLS Wodrow MS Quarto 25, fo. 152ʳ⁻ᵛ.

[170] BL Harl. MS 457, fos. 65–6. On the Scots' concern with Union, see NLS Adv. MS 33.1.1,
vol. xiii, no. 72.

neither kingdom to make war on the other without the consent of the Parliament, for neither to make a foreign war without the other's consent, for the triennial Parliaments of both kingdoms to try quarrels between the kingdoms, and for mutual recognition of each other's court judgements.[171] This was enough to make Sir John Coke fear that the treaty would be going until midsummer,[172] but the crucial issue of English conformity to Scotland remained quiet for a few days longer.

The issue was forced to the surface again by one of the most mysterious events in the story: the decision of many in the City to withhold the money they were being asked to lend to pay the armies until they should obtain justice on the Earl of Strafford.[173] Penington, who is the only person who appears as a front for those refusing to lend, appears to have first thought of this device in the dispute at the end of January about the reprieve of Goodman the priest, which was felt by many to be a possible test case for the reprieve of Strafford. Sir William Uvedale, treasurer of the army, noted such moves with dismay, since they risked making his job impossible.[174] In the Commons, Marten, Earle, Arthur Goodwin, and Strode showed signs of supporting such moves,[175] yet Pym and Saye equally clearly opposed them. Saye on 23 March said such things might be done by 'mistakes', and Pym on 20 February scandalized Sir Thomas Peyton by proposing that they assume a legislative power to compel the Londoners to lend.[176] If the refusal of money was indeed designed to achieve the sort of political ends pursued by Alderman Penington, it backfired disastrously, for its chief effect was to destroy the Scottish army as a fighting force, thereby making Root and Branch and the execution of Strafford far less likely.

It is important, in any City matter, to remember the reminder Recorder Gardiner gave to the House on this issue on 30 March, that the City were not all of one mind. It is perfectly possible that not all those who refused to lend their money did so for the same reasons. Recorder Gardiner invoked a flight of 'hot money' to the Netherlands, and the City petition for justice on Strafford alleged that foreigners had looked on the state as in an unsettled condition ever since the breach of

[171] PRO SP 16/478/70.

[172] HMC Cowper (Coke), ii. 274.

[173] Pearl, pp. 198–207. I am grateful to Prof. Pearl and to Prof. R. S. Brenner for discussions of this question over a period of years. This account adds to Prof. Pearl's only in the Scottish evidence, yet the story still leaves unanswered questions.

[174] PRO SP 16/479/58 and 480/11; D'Ewes (N.), p. 371.

[175] D'Ewes (N.), pp. 371, 514.

[176] CJ ii. 111; Peyton, fo. 89ᵛ. See also LJ iv. 194 for the Lords' attempt, probably inspired by Bristol, to follow Penington's example and impose an explanation on the delay of money which would suit their own political advantage. The Lords suggested that the failure to lend money was due to impatience at the delay in concluding the Scottish treaty. See also Two Diaries, pp. 26, 28. In calling the Brotherly Assistance a viaticum for the Scots, Bristol was making a strong appeal to those who thought this way.

the Pacification of Berwick, and had therefore called in their money.[177]
All this may well have been true, and it was certainly true that since 1639
the City had faced so many demands for loans that they were entitled to
feel a good deal of irritation. Baillie, whose City sources were good, if
limited, believed in a political explanation. He thought rumours were
being spread, he believed by Scottish exiles in London, that the Scots'
former zeal had been broken, and they would abandon Root and
Branch and the execution of Laud and Strafford, and quietly go home.
He claims that the money the Londoners were withholding had already
been collected, and was being withheld for political reasons. The preferment of seven new Councillors, most of them ambiguously described by
Baillie as 'our old friends' on 19 February, encouraged the idea that
some form of settlement was near, which, if true, must exclude Root and
Branch.[178]

Right or wrong, this was the Scots' analysis, and they acted on it. They
instructed Alexander Henderson to write the 'little quick paper' of 24
February, which initiated one of the worst moments of the whole negotiation. This paper denied that they were become remiss in their zeal
against prelacy, 'the cause of all our broyles', and denied their desire to
be reconciled with those who upheld it. They also demanded almost the
only thing Charles was less willing to grant than the abolition of episcopacy: the execution of Strafford: 'better one perish than unitie'.[179]

The paper was designed to be presented to the Parliament, as well as
to the commissioners, and in the process, by means still not entirely
clear, it found its way into print. Baillie claims it was 'put in hand' 'by
Holland, our good friend, mynding, as we know all, no evill to us'.
Whether the printers of the paper intended ill to the Scots or not, they
certainly did ill to them, for the paper put the King in such a rage that
Johnston of Wariston undiplomatically said that 'the king hes run starke
mad'. Charles claimed it was a seditious libel, that they had forfeited
their privilege as ambassadors, and that they deserved hanging.[180] The
Scottish commissioners' report to their colleagues at Newcastle indicates that they were more willing to stand their ground than their
English friends were.

[177] BL Harl. MS 162, fo. 379ᵃ; PRO SP 16/478/86.
[178] Baillie, i. 305–6.
[179] On this paper, see Donald, pp. 415–19; BL Stowe MS 187, fo. 38; BL E. 669, fo. 3(4).
Between these texts, there are only the most trivial variations in wording, but someone has altered
the Scottish spelling of the manuscript to the English spelling of the printed version.
[180] Stevenson, p. 219; NLS Wodrow MS Fol. 66, fo. 107. I am grateful to Dr Peter Donald for
the latter reference. See also NLS Wodrow MS Fol. 66, fo. 174 (Maitland to [?Loudoun]) for the
claim that the paper had, in fact, induced the City to lend money. The report seems to have been
premature: Pearl, pp. 204–5; D'Ewes (N.), p. 433. However, it does tend to show the Scots'
sincerity in their explanation of their paper. Baillie, i. 306.

And such as favour prelacie (who are very many here) labor to give hard impressions against us, taxing us of presumption, as if it were presumption to give directions to reform them and evert their lawes. . . . The next paper anent episcopacie wilbe the remonstrance of it as a spetiall mean of union betwix the two nations, which we shall press with all the force of arguments. The English, yea, many of our friends, doe ask if we will so stand upon it, as not to make a peace until wee get episcopacie removed in England, which they thinke is too muche for us to doe, and will never compert that wee should force them to make any alteration in there religion, lawes or church discipline at our pleasure.[181]

They anxiously advised Newcastle to keep the army together, and said they could not tell what would be the issue of the treaty until the cases of Strafford and episcopacy were decided. Clearly, they were prepared to contemplate a breach on this issue. Their determination was abruptly diminished a week later, when Newcastle replied that the Scottish army could not and would not march unless its arrears were paid.[182] Since Charles held intelligence with Montrose, who was a member of the committee at Newcastle, it is possible that he knew of this reply as soon as the Scottish commissioners did. If so, he realized that the wheel of fortune was at last turning in his favour, and for the first time since Newburn, he was no longer negotiating under armed threat.

On 26 February the King called a meeting which was probably a meeting of the English commissioners for the treaty, though it is not recorded in the minutes. The note in Mandeville's papers begins: 'The King: Itt is ye base proceedings off ye Scoch commissioners that makes mee call for you'.[183] In the Commons, the Scots' friends were forced to defend the paper against an attempt on 27 February to have it called in and condemned. Hyde, Capel, Hopton, and Strangeways led the attack on the paper, and Hampden, Gerrard, Maynard, Rudyerd, Penington, and Sir Hugh Cholmeley tried to oppose them. Their performance was very much that of men on the defensive, and when Hyde challenged Hampden to state his opinion on episcopacy, Hampden could only reply that 'we are all of a mind in desiring what is best'. D'Ewes and Drake both remarked that there was 'much heat', and D'Ewes said it 'raised one of the greatest distempers in the House that ever I saw in it'. Once again, the Scots' power to polarize English politics was very much in evidence. The House, in the end, laid the issue aside, but it remained live.[184]

The Scottish commissioners, as they had told their colleagues at

---

[181] NLS Adv. MS 33.4.6, fos. 129–30.
[182] Ibid., fo. 134ᵛ.
[183] Huntingdon RO Manchester MS 32/5/23.
[184] D'Ewes (N.), pp. 417–8; *Two Diaries*, pp. 12–13. For a Scottish report of this debate, see NLS Wodrow MS Quarto 25, 151ʳ–2ʳ and NLS Adv. MS 33.1.1, vol. xiii, no. 71.

Newcastle, were preparing another paper. They first offered a small apologetic paper on 1 March, which stood their ground on episcopacy, while not mentioning the case of Strafford.[185] The paper of 10 March, which returned to the issue of episcopacy,[186] was the Scots' major statement on this theme, and argued forcibly and at length the case that Charles had formerly argued, that two kingdoms under one king could not live peaceably together unless they had the same religion. They claimed that 'all the question is whether of the two church governments shall have place in both nacons'. They said they were not acting out of desire to reform England, but because, if they did not, 'our reformacon wch hath cost us soe deare, and is all our wealth and glorye shall agayne be spoyed and defaced from England'. Once this conformity was achieved, they hoped, 'the church shall be peaceably governed by comon consent of churchmen in assemblies', and the King would become head of all the Protestants in Europe.

The English Lords Commissioners did not appear impressed by this argument. They told the Scots not to intermeddle with the reformation in England, but to leave it to the King and kingdom, and not to publish or divulge any discourse against the established laws of the kingdom. The Scots replied that without this, they thought the peace would not be durable, as they hoped it might be, and played what had been their trump card over the incendiaries: they asked the Lords Commissioners to show their paper to the Parliament. To this, Bristol and Essex gave two very different replies: Essex asked them to defer it, for fear of prejudicing the trial of Strafford, and Bristol, with the seasoned diplomat's ability to seize the moment of advantage, said that if they gave the paper to the Parliament, 'the king will give it with the king's reasons against it'. Since even their friends were advising them that they now stood to lose such a contest, the Scots retreated. Rothes, in announcing the Scottish retreat, carefully, if probably inaccurately, ascribed it to Essex's reasons and not to Bristol's.[187]

Meanwhile, impatience in Parliament for the conclusion of the treaty was growing. Bristol on 3 March moved for the Scots to set down all their demands at once, since the kingdom could no longer bear the charge. It was, significantly, Hyde and not one of the Scots' friends, who reported the Commons' agreement with this demand.[188] A division of 5

---

[185] For a printed text of this paper, see Scottish Record Office, PA 13/1, p. 1.

[186] NLS Adv. MS 33.4.6, fos. 142–7: there is another text in Yale University, Beinecke Library, Osborn Shelves fb 161, fos. 57–66. See also NLS Wodrow MS Quarto 25, fo. 152ʳ, for the point that the Scots could not conform to episcopacy, since they had abjured it. This paper was printed both in London and in Edinburgh: *Arguments given in by the Commissioners of Scotland* (BL E 157(2)): *The Scots Commissioners their Desires concerning Unitie in Religion and Uniformitie of Church-government*, printed by James Bryson (Edinburgh, 1641) (Aldis 1020).

[187] BL Stowe MS 187, fos. 46–8; BL Harl. MS 457, 78–9.

[188] *LJ* iv. 175, 178.

March, confusedly reported by *Commons' Journals* and one of the Scottish newsletters, indicates a tension over the Scots' article 8 in the Commons. The clearest account of this division is Sir Robert Harley's. The debate was on a paper of Arundel's from the Lords, which demanded an immediate conclusion to the Scots' eighth article. It was, in effect, a proposal to send the Scots home, and was what the King had been waiting for ever since Ripon. The anti-Scots simply wished to agree to this proposal, while the pro-Scots took refuge behind a neutral motion to send the paper to a committee. On this neutral motion, the pro-Scots, with Holles and Irby as tellers, mustered 213 against 107 for the anti-Scots, with Sir Frederick Cornwallis and Ashburnham as tellers. Harley commented that the distempers in the House were so high that the disparity of voices was a 'special providence'. The 107 in the minority, with 2 of the King's known associates as tellers, should be regarded as a nucleus of a future Royalist party.[189] In the Lords on 6 March Bristol expressed the fear that the Scots might summer in England. His calls for haste were opposed by Saye, and supported by Seymour (recently raised to the peerage), Berkshire, and Saville. Essex, Holland, and Paget tried to sidetrack Berkshire's speech by accusing him of censuring the commissioners while being one of them himself. On the same day, Saye's speech against the liturgy led to a vigorous exchange with Bristol about whether this was the season to alter matters by law established. Dunsmore and Poulet joined the resistance to the Scots' demand on uniformity of church government.[190] When the cessation of arms came up for renewal on 9 March, Sir William Uvedale allowed himself the words: 'which wee all hope wilbe the last'.[191] The Scots' friends in the Commons were busy with the less explosive, if still provocative, business of the Ministers' Remonstrance, the bill against pluralism, and the Bishops' Exclusion Bill, but these, and even Penington's bill to abolish superstition (later to be the Commons' order of 8 September) were better designed to the contenting of the English godly than to the cementing of a firm league with the Scots, for whom such measures, if necessary, were still incidental. Only in their desire to secure the disbandment of the Irish army before they went home were the Scots still securing wholehearted support in the Commons.[192] On 13 March the Scots seem to have meekly accepted without comment the King's objection to the setting up of conservators of the peace, which he called keeping up their tables under another name. They thereby back-

---

[189] BL Loan MS 29/46/3; NLS Wodrow MS Quarto 25, fo. 152ʳ. *CJ* ii. 97 reports the issue of the division correctly, but has the tellers back to front. The report in D'Ewes (N.), p. 445 can be seen to be correct once the full story is known, but is too elliptical to tell the full story alone.

[190] BL Harl. 6424, fo. 46ʳ; NLS Wodrow MS Quarto 25, fo. 152ᵛ.

[191] PRO SP 16/478/27.

[192] D'Ewes (N.), p. 454; BL Add. MS 6521, fo. 68ʳ⁻ᵛ.

tracked, for the time being, on something as vital to their English friends
as Root and Branch was to them. The Scots seem to have been hanging
on to secure the condemnation of Strafford, but without great hope that
they could secure much more.[193] On 9 April a division on the next
month's cessation again indicated that the Scots were on the run. A
motion was put for a cessation for the impractically short time of a
fortnight, which was carried by 167 to 128. Holles and Sir Edward
Hungerford were tellers in the minority. The Lords, through Bristol,
had to interfere the next day to secure the necessary month.[194] On 14
April the Committee of Estates at Edinburgh who were not up to date
with the swing of opinion in London, told them to persist with their
paper of 10 March,[195] but Bristol's report of article 8 to the Lords the
same day showed plainly how much resistance such an attempt was
likely to meet.[196] On 20 April the King repeated his objection to the
proposal for Conservators, and asked that the Act of Oblivion for which
the Scots were asking should be made reciprocal.[197] This was a brilliant
proposal, since it sounded so reasonable it would be hard to resist, yet it
had the effect of withdrawing the King's hard-won agreement to article
4, on the incendiaries. Since the Scots had always insisted that no
agreement should be final until all the articles were concluded, they
were in no position to object to this withdrawal of a concession. They
were thus left with the prospect of spending the summer winning back
the concession they had already won once.

Having secured possession of the stick, the King the next day offered
the carrot. He met the Scottish commissioners privately at Whitehall,
and gave them back their paper on the choice of great officers in
Scotland with a favourable answer. It was not, as it at first appeared to
be, a full acceptance, but it was a promise of serious negotiation. At the
same time, the King offered to come to Edinburgh to conclude the
treaty himself.[198] This offered two things, and it was perhaps for the
Scottish commissioners to choose which was intended. Either it meant
that the King was coming to Edinburgh in order to concede their purely
Scottish demands in return for the abandonment of their claims to settle
England, or else it meant that he was coming in order to appeal behind
their backs for the support of the anti-Covenanter Scots. Baillie took the
worse interpretation: 'our unfriends are the authors of these coun-

[193] PRO 31/3/72, p. 213; Groen Van Prinsterer, p. 417.
[194] *CJ* ii. 118; PRO SP 16/479/27; Baillie, i. 346. See EUL MS Dc 4.16, fo. 94ʳ, for an English
threat that if the Scots continued to press their paper of 10 Mar., they would not recommend any
cessation at all.
[195] EUL MS Dc 4.16, fo. 94ᵛ.
[196] PRO SP 16/478/70; BL Harl. MS 6424, fos. 55–6; *LJ* iv. 216.
[197] EUL MS Dc 4.16, fo. 95ʳ.
[198] NLS Adv. MS 33.1.1, vol. xiii, no. 80; NLS Wodrow MS Quarto 25, fo. 160ᵛ; BL Harl. MS
457, fo. 80ʳ.

sels',[199] but even if Baillie's interpretation, which was probably the right one, was accepted, it did not mean the Covenanters could ignore the King's offer. They could not prevent him from visiting Edinburgh if he chose, and their only way of preventing him from agreeing with their opponents was to offer him as much as they could themselves. It was painfully clear that the price they would have to pay to prevent the King from undermining them in Scotland was to cease to undermine him in England. The French ambassador reported that he had offered them 'qu'il leur donneroit là toute sorte de contentement, qu'ils pourroient cependant retirer leur armée d'Angleterre, et de ne se point mesler des choses qui s'y passeront'.[200]

The Scots took the hint and on 1 May they submitted an eloquent paper on their need to go home: 'the expense of the king and kingdoms for maintenance of armies within their own bowels is vast': 'many of the nobility and gentry, to their great loss, are detained from their weighty affairs and families': 'our army in danger either to starve or provide for themselves in other places'.[201] The emotion was sincere, and from this point onwards, the Scots in English politics were, for the time being, a spent force. The treaty dragged on until August, but the biggest delay was now in the House of Commons' efforts to provide money, and the somewhat desultory negotiation which continued was mostly about purely Scottish issues such as the appointment of Scottish great officers and the terms of the Act of Oblivion. The Scottish party in England, without the prospect of future protection from the Scottish army, might view the future with apprehension, and the King's initial confidence that time was on his side had been triumphantly vindicated.

A number of conclusions emerge from this story. One is that the Scots' power depended on a situation where they were prepared to fight, and the English were not. The Council had been quite right in its initial analysis that the collapse of English power had been the result of English divisions. As soon as the Scots, rather than the King, came to seem the divisive force, Bristol and his fellows could afford to refuse their demands with impunity. That point seems to have come when, instead of claiming their own religion and liberties, they appeared to be dictating a settlement to England. The creed of British uniformity seemed to be as divisive in their hands as it had been in those of Charles I in 1637.

Another conclusion which seems to follow from the material here recounted is that it is not true to say, as is usually said, that the Long Parliament was united at the beginning, and subsequently became

[199] Baillie, i. 350.
[200] PRO 31/3/72, p. 538 *bis*.
[201] *LJ* iv. 231–2.

divided. Whether the Long Parliament was united or divided always depended, not on the time, but on the issue under discussion. The issues raised by the Scots, involving a demand for further reformation of religion, split the Parliament very much along the same lines as it was to split in 1642. The Scots lined up Pym, Holles, Hampden, Earle, Fiennes, and Strode against Digby, Strangeways, Hyde, Falkland, Culpepper, Hopton, and Waller. The line-up is a familiar one, and seems to represent a line of division which was deep and long-lasting. The attack on the Laudian church did not divide these people, as Digby and Falkland tried very hard to make clear during the debate on Root and Branch. The division between them was, as Dr Morrill has summarized it, between those who wanted to go back to the church of James I, and those who wanted a large measure of further reformation.[202] For many of them 'further reformation' meant first and foremost the purging of idolatry and Arminianism, and they wanted Root and Branch, if at all, more as a means to the end than as an end in its own right.

The conflict which produced this line-up was the one which had come to a head in 1637–8, and which remained the central conflict in the British crisis of 1637 and after. The conflict between the King and the Covenanters was, far more than any other conflict except the less infectious one between the English and the Irish rebels, a clash of irreconcilable ideas. Between Alexander Henderson and Charles I lay many of the same issues which had divided Gregory VII and the Emperor Henry IV, and the conflict was deepened by the fact that two different theories of authority were being used to uphold two different religions. The Scots inherited a culture in which resistance came far more easily than it did to the English. Between Charles and the Covenanters, no lasting reconciliation was possible. It was on the back of this irreconcilable conflict that Pym and his allies hoped to ride to power, not by a violent coup, but by a political settlement. In staking their future on a political settlement between the King and the Covenanters, they became the heirs to all the agonies Hamilton had suffered in 1638. In the end, they suffered all Hamilton's political failures, and for the same reason: they were trying to reconcile the irreconcilable. The Scottish conflict had broadened out to involve the English, and since the English could not mediate in it, they slowly learnt, Bristol as much as Pym, that the only alternative was to take sides in it.

The debates, and even more the reluctance privately expressed to the Scots by their friends, suggests that most of the English did not want a

[202] J. S. Morrill, 'Attack on the Church of England in the Long Parliament', in Derek Beales and Geoffrey Best (eds.), *History, Society and the Churches: Essays in Honour of Owen Chadwick* (Cambridge, 1985), 108.

further reformation badly enough to risk a civil war for it. A few did: Clarendon may well be right that Nathaniel Fiennes was among them[203] and Strode is another serious possibility. In the City, some of the ministers, whose providentialist theory of causation did not encourage attention to common prudence, may have been prepared to take the risk of pushing ahead with a new reformation at any price. In the Commons, some of the hotter members, such as Cromwell, Penington, or Rous, may have been prepared to do the same. This, though, was something less than a revolutionary head of steam. The reaction of the crucial moderate godly members, such as D'Ewes, Fleetwood, Grimston, Rudyerd, and Bagshaw, suggests that the majority of the Commons had still set their faces against adversary politics. They were prepared to accept half a loaf rather than divide the country at the risk of civil war. If men like Bristol, Savill, and Holland, who shared the same reluctance to divide the country, could gain control of Charles's ear, the prospects for peace might be good.

It was the Scots' special contribution to this situation that they constantly forced the divisive questions to the top of the political agenda, and therefore forced the English to choose sides about them. Since their English friends owed their power to the Scots' army, they were in no position to resist such pressure, however hard they may have protested privately against it. Moreover, their English friends took political risks which made retreat very difficult indeed. This was not only a matter of treason committed during the Bishops' Wars, though that threat could not be ignored. It was also that the Scots had whipped up hopes which were not easily stilled. It was the Scottish troubles which set a member's young chaplain called Christopher Feake to the reading of the prophecies of Daniel and Revelation, and once he had read them, he did not find them easy to forget.[204] In a lower key, the same process happened to people like Burges and Marshall, or Harley and Rous. After a long period of near-despair, a deep draught of hope is inebriating in its effect, and is not easily made to go away. It was the Scots who unleashed this hope that the world of the godly could be different, and, even after the Scots' departure, that hope changed the political balance irreversibly. The last time the English godly had experienced such an abrupt transition from despair to hope was 17 November 1558, a parallel D'Ewes and Burges, among others, were eager to keep in members' minds. Then, as in 1640, much of the hope raised had been disappointed. It was not for nothing that the Long Parliament's daily prayer concentrated on the Lord's great deliverances for England in 1588 and 1605. Members believed they were experiencing another, and one of the

---

[203] Clarendon, *Life*, pp. 74–5.
[204] J. T. Cliffe, *Puritan Gentry*, p. 207.

clearest rules of divinity was that the surest way to lose the benefit of
such a deliverance was to be unthankful or half-hearted in the
acceptance of it. All these forces made the English godly very much less
willing to compromise in 1641 than they had been in 1640. Their hopes,
together with the fears of Pym and his allies that they might be prosecuted for treason, were to make a highly volatile emotional mixture. It
was an atmosphere in which Cromwell was to find it easier to hit the
right note than Falkland. By generating such an atmosphere, the Scots
raised a threat to the peace of England which was to last long after their
departure. At just the moment when the temperature might have been
expected to drop if it was going to, the King, having done so well up to
that point, raised it to fever pitch by undertaking the Army Plot, and
promptly throwing away all the political capital he had gained by his
patience in the long struggle with the Scots. While Bristol had guided
him through the treaty, he had been successful. On the trial of Strafford,
an issue too personal to allow anyone to take him in hand the way
Bristol had done over the treaty, he threw all his advantage away. It was
a pattern he was to repeat.

5

The Long Parliament: The Opening Months

NOVEMBER–DECEMBER 1640

In the archival history of England, 3 November 1640 is a date of major significance. The change is clearest in the biggest archive, that of State Papers, Domestic. Up to 3 November it is a government archive, recording the taking of decisions. On the day the Long Parliament met, it ceases to be any such thing, and becomes instead something much closer to a diplomatic archive: it records, with a stark absence of comment, actions taken elsewhere, in the two Houses of Parliament. The majestic series of royal Proclamations ceases totally from 18 November to 8 March. Declared Accounts are no longer declared: Acts of the Privy Council and the Signet Office docket book, though they continue, show a sharp drop, both in the volume and in the importance of business. If we wish to look for records of the taking and execution of decisions, we should look at the *Lords' Journals*, the House of Lords Main Papers, and the *Commons' Journals*.

In part, this drastic archival change measures the effects of the summons of a Parliament the King could not dissolve: some part of the story it tells is that of a real shift in power. Yet this impression is in part illusory, and also temporary: from January 1641 onwards, the State Papers again record a slow increase in the activity of those who owed their power to royal appointment, though not back to the level of October. The King's apparent powerlessness in November and December 1640 was in part the consequence of defeat, which was real enough, but could come to seem less immediate with the passage of time. It is also the result of the King's entire lack of policy for the situation in which he found himself. He had agreed to call a Parliament, but he had not yet absorbed the lesson that the country would not help him to prosecute the Scottish war. His opening speech, after mentioning his need for 'support', offered the Parliament an agenda of chasing out the rebels, and *then* redressing their 'just' grievances.[1] He was asking for exactly what he had asked for in the Short Parliament, and, indeed, even expressed the conviction that if he had been believed in the Short Parliament, none of the intervening trouble need have happened. He

---

[1] MP, 3 Nov. 1641. The word 'support' had become recognized in 1610 as the appropriate term for a permanent addition to the Crown's income. There is another text in PRO SP 16/471/13.

was still insisting on supply before redress of grievances, and it is
perhaps this adamantine determination to give priority to his own
agenda which made the Commons in his reign show a determination
which they had not shown under James to insist on redress before
supply. On 5 November he was induced to come back to the House of
Lords and explain himself. He now partially withdrew his description of
the Scots as 'rebels', but his new programme was to offer them terms
such as they had refused before they had won, and chase them back to
Scotland if they refused.[2] As a political agenda for November 1640, this
was not in the real world, and when Secretary Vane was asked a few
weeks later for a copy of the King's opening speech, he said he had lost
it.[3]

When the King realized that his policies did not fit the world of
November 1640, he still continued to hope that the world would change
again. Baillie is probably right that he continued to hope for a reaction
against Scottish invaders until, to his surprise, the Houses agreed to give
the Scots reparation for their losses.[4] It was thus not until January 1641
that the King had any policies for the situation in which he found
himself. His surprise at finding his subjects were prepared to support an
invading army of Scots is legitimate, but until he had faced the fact that
this was actually the case, he had policies only for an imaginary world.
When he recovered his touch and began to find policies for the actual
situation, he found he had a great deal more power left than was
apparent in November and December 1640. In terms of political power,
the last two months of 1640 constitute something very like a royal
minority, and like other royal minorities, it gave many people a taste of
power they were reluctant to abandon when the King was back in
action.

There had perhaps not been an equally dramatic case of a King
committed to an unviable policy since Henry III's attempt to continue
the Sicilian Business in 1258. As that case suggests, English history
supplied a well-worn tradition of precedents for handling a situation in
which a King became committed to unviable policies. A Parliament, to
share the responsibility as widely as possible, was an essential part of the
remedy, but it was to be used more as a forum than as an agent. The
central responsibility in such a crisis, as men like Bedford and Saye
knew perfectly well, tended to rest with the peerage.[5] It was their
responsibility to find a new political line which could reunite the

[2] MP, 5 Nov. 1641.
[3] HMC De L'Isle and Dudley, VI. 370–1. Vane strained credulity when he claimed that no other
copy could be had.
[4] See above, p. 186.
[5] On Bedford, see Russell (ed.), Origins, p. 111 and n. On Saye, see Bodl. MS Tanner 88*, fo.
203^{r–v}.

country. To signal the change of policy, punishment of ministers who could be held responsible for the old policy was essential. With rulers who understood the rules well, like Henry VIII, a minister might even hope, like Wolsey in 1525, to receive a royal rebuke for his master's policy, and remain in office afterwards.[6] The extreme cases, in which the minister suffered exile or even death, had often been those in which the King had either refused to let him go, or refused to renounce responsibility for the policies he had represented. If the victim, like Thomas Cromwell, was low-born and had offended many of the higher nobility, he was the more at risk. When Richard II in 1386 had told his Parliament that he would not dismiss a scullion or a kitchen boy at their request, he had contributed significantly to the death of the ministers impeached in the next Parliament of 1388. Seen against this background, Charles's determination to defend his servants was a considerable threat to their safety.

   After the punishment of old ministers came the appointment of new. This was to provide the King with an afforced Council, designed to ensure that he heard the opinions of those to whom he had previously preferred not to listen. This was also intended to bring in those who had been out into the range of office and patronage, but it was above all intended to signify the abandonment of unpopular policies. There was, however, a major difficulty about reforming Charles I by means of an afforced Council: he had an 'advised council' already.[7] Many of his existing Councillors, such as Pembroke, Holland, Northumberland, and Hamilton, were capable of giving his advice which went against his political inclinations. On many occasions, they had done so, and had persuaded him. The difficulty, as Charles's opening speech painfully illustrated, was that when persuaded, Charles never absorbed the implications of the case of which he had been apparently persuaded. Saddling him with an advised council, then, was only likely to lead to another instalment of the sort of problems the country had experienced already. Beyond an advised council, there was the possibility of Parliamentary appointment of great officers, and therefore of the carrying on of government in the King's name in ways he could not personally be persuaded to agree to. This, as Simon de Montfort and the Lords Ordainers had found, was an unstable solution, and tended to lead to war. Beyond that lay only deposition, and the experience of the fifteenth century seems to have established a tradition in English mythology that deposition caused more trouble than it was worth. It was, moreover, well known to be theologically a sin, and therefore was

---

[6] The scene played between Henry and Wolsey on the abandonment of the Amicable Grant was surely collusive.

[7] I am grateful to Prof. R. C. Stacey for this point.

difficult to justify in the name of a movement designed for the reformation of religion.

In 1640 to 1642 there was the further obstacle to deposition that there was no serious candidate in whose name the deed could be done. Hertford, Hamilton, Huntingdon, and Lennox could have pretended, though in Hamilton's case only to the Scottish throne, but it was very clear that none of them would make the attempt. The Elector Palatine, Charles's nephew, would have been a serious candidate if he had been willing, and it is at least possible that the repeated rumours of English intervention in the Palatinate which were spread during 1641 were designed to ensure that he remained unwilling. In this, Charles succeeded, perhaps with some assistance from the Elector's mother Elizabeth of Bohemia.[8]

Without a satisfactory pretender, the only possible target for serious politicians was, and had to remain, a settlement with Charles. This fact alone was to give him very considerable power once he came to terms with the fact that a new settlement was needed. So long as he lived, he retained a veto over any final resolution of the crisis, since the only stable title to power which most of his critics could envisage continued to be by his grant. Moreover, whenever Charles began to negotiate, he would find that, in a long-drawn-out crisis, the King retained very considerable advantages. Once he conceded power to his opponents, they would find that power carried with it its own penalties of unpopularity, and they would be bound to disappoint at least some of the expectations which had brought them into office. It was always possible that those who won power by this route would fall out among themselves, as the Earls of Leicester and Gloucester had done under Henry III. Henry's own comeback after 1258 could serve as a paradigm for any of his successors reduced to similar straits. In this pattern, the King could exploit his opponents' diminished popularity in order to raise a party against them, and could come back almost as a rebel against the government being carried on in his own name. If he were to plan any such comeback, Charles would enjoy two advantages which most of his predecessors in similar straits had not. One was that this was the first such crisis (with the possible exception of 1539–40) since the country had become divided in religion. This made it much easier to hope that the King's opponents, if they should enjoy power, would

<hr />

[8] PRO TS 23/1/11 and 12. I am grateful to Dr J. S. A. Adamson for this reference. The Elector's arrival in England at the beginning of Mar. 1641 was unexpected and unwelcome to Charles: *CSP Ven. 1640–2*, p. 130. See Baillie, ii. 473 (Alexander Balfour to Sir James Balfour, 29 Dec. 1640) for a report that he had been sent for *by the Parliament*. It is not necessary to believe this report, which comes from Newcastle and not from London, but Balfour may not have been the only person who believed it. The French Ambassador's suggestion that he came because of concern at the Dutch marriage negotiations is more likely to be right: PRO 31/3/72, p. 485.

breed their own opposition. The flow of seditious words reported to the
Long Parliament was a constant reminder that such a strand of opinion
existed to be called on. On 6 January 1641, for example, a Kentish
parson was reported to have said that 'if the Parliament went on to taxe
such men as they had begunne, ther should bee such a blow given
before Easter next, as that the rebels of Scotland and the puritans of
England should be slaves for ever'.[9] Religion, in fact, presented Charles
with the means of raising a party, for Pym was no more capable of
speaking for England in religion than Laud had been.[10] He enjoyed, it is
true, a larger measure of support, but if he were to initiate a real
programme of religious reformation, he would find that he faced an
equally powerful resistance. It could accentuate the point that this was
the first political crisis since 1216 in which the King's enemies had relied
on a foreign army, and that too could provoke a very powerful reaction.

These dangers were considerable, and the task of avoiding them
depended in part on pressing the King to make a settlement quickly.
The more rapidly his concessions were made, and the more apparent
political goodwill they came with, the less dramatic they would need to
be.[11] A stable settlement also depended on inducing the King's enemies
not to ask too much, since it was essential to the stability of any long-
term settlement that the King should, however reluctantly, be able to
consent to it. His opponents might perhaps force him to accept a
settlement to which he could not really consent, but if so, they would
risk finding, as the Lords Appellant had done after 1388, that they were
at risk from a royal vengeance no less severe for being delayed.

The House of Lords had behind them a long tradition of political
compromise, and seem to have found, with unerring accuracy, the new
political centre of gravity on which any new political consensus would
have to rest. As a House, they covered a very wide spectrum of opinion,
ranging from the recusant peers Viscount Montagu and Lord Brudenell
on the one hand to Saye and Brooke on the other. Many of the members
of the Lords were intensely partisan, and willing to pursue partisan
objectives in alliance with friends in the Commons or at court. Yet the
House collectively seems to have been capable of achieving at least a
working illusion of consensus. For a House in which Saye sat with
Bishop Warner of Rochester, this was a considerable achievement, and
one which tends to suggest that in November 1640 the English body
politic was not yet irreconcilably divided unless the King and the Scots
should choose to make it so.

[9] D'Ewes (N.), p. 222. This is one of many such examples.

[10] See BL Loan MS 29/172, fo. 363ʳ, for the realization among some of the godly that there was a case for deferring religious issues because they were more divisive than civil ones.

[11] On the advantages to be gained by concession, see Sir John Suckling in PRO SP 16/478/82. This was perhaps wiser advice than Gardiner (*History*, ix. 311–12) suggested.

The Lords were asking Charles to make very considerable sacrifices. They accepted the conventional analysis that in a crisis of this sort, ministers had to be charged as scapegoats. On 11 November they committed Strafford to the Tower at the Commons' request. A few days later, a request by Lord Goring to bail him because it would be 'pleasing' to the King and Queen was brusquely turned aside by a speech from Lord Paget, saying it would be against the law of the land and the privileges of their House.[12] Laud, being less physically dangerous than Strafford, was treated rather more mildly, and committed only to the Gentleman Usher. They agreed on 21 November to the Commons' request that peers should be examined on oath in the preparation of the case against Strafford, thereby making it possible to examine the Privy Council on oath on the proceedings of the Council table.[13] At the very beginning of the Parliament, they spelt out the fictional element in the doctrine of ministerial responsibility in an unusually plain way. Sir William Beecher Clerk of the Council was before the Lords for a breach of privilege for searching the studies of Saye and Brooke after the dissolution of the Short Parliament. Beecher pleaded the King's command as his justification, and was told that 'it aggravates his offence, in using his Majesty's name, when he might have put it upon the Secretaries'. He was sent to the Fleet, but released after a symbolic imprisonment of two days.[14] On 18 February, when they asked the Commons to join them in moving that Strafford's places be sequestered, they were begging the King to accept that ministerial responsibility was a necessary fiction. On this occasion, the request enjoyed the support of Strafford himself. He wanted the King to deprive him of his office, believing that it would be some advantage to him if the King would make it clear that he did not want to keep Strafford in his service. The King, who wanted to keep Strafford in spite of the Earl's reluctance, refused.[15]

The Lords also made it clear what sort of policies they hoped would be followed after the necessary scapegoats had been sacrificed. They firmly upheld the Petition of Right, and a committee on imprisonment, chaired by the Earl of Dover, condemned varous imprisonments it reported as being contrary to the Petition of Right. The Lords were having no truck with the King's arguments that it was not a statute.[16]

[12] DO, vol. i, fo. 6^{r-v}.

[13] LJ iv. 95.

[14] Ibid. 87; PRO 31/3/72, p. 327.

[15] LJ iv. 166; HMC De L'Isle and Dudley, vi. 350 (KAO U 1475 C 129/11), Lucy Carlisle to Lady Leicester, 17 Dec. 1640. For an oblique attempt to explain to Charles how his servants might suffer from his support, see the conversation between Hamilton and the King repeated in Clarendon, History, i. 153.

[16] LJ iv. 101, 100, 119.

They condemned Ship Money without a dissentient voice, and on 26 February instructed that their resolutions against Ship Money were to be publicized by the judges on circuit.[17] They also conveyed to the King that they thought he had unduly diminished the independence of the judiciary by asking him to change the judges' tenure from during pleasure to during good behaviour, which the King granted. As a practical measure, the change may have been more symbolic than real, but it conveyed a message to the King in a plain but discreet manner, and on this occasion, the King heard it.[18]

On religion, the Lords made their position plain at the very beginning, in their choice of preachers for the Fast. They named Morton Bishop of Durham and Potter Bishop of Carlisle. Potter was named by Baillie as one of the 'most innocent' bishops,[19] and Morton was famous as, among much else, the Calvinist spokesman at York House in 1626. The Lords, throughout the first year of the Parliament, adopted a collective position which was firmly Calvinist episcopalian, without attempting to reduce Arminians lower than they had been under James. They condemned some of the minor and more extreme Arminians, such as Reeve and Pocklington, and gave the Calvinist bishops Morton and Davenant what must have been the congenial task of drawing up recantations for them.[20] At the same time, these and other actions carried a message of restraint for the hotter religious reformers. On 30 November the Lord Keeper at the King's command referred to the Lords a particularly striking anti-Prayer-Book riot at Halsted in Essex. The rioters had knocked the Prayer Book out of the clergyman's hand as he was baptizing a child, and kicked it up and down the church. They had taken him by the throat and torn his surplice and his hood in pieces, while calling, rather alarmingly for 'Scotch blades'. The Lords condemned them for their attacks on the Prayer Book 'established and confirmed by Act of Parliament', but sentenced them, no doubt to Charles's disappointment, to nothing worse than a submission.[21] This judgement, with its reliance on the slogan of 'by law established', used what was rapidly becoming the coded signal for those who wanted a return to James's reign rather than any further reformation. Later on, the Lords spelt this message out rather more plainly by directing that the rails at St Saviour's Southwark should be restored as they had been the last fifty years, and not as they had been the last four or five.[22] They underlined this middle-

[17] *LJ* iv. 173.

[18] Ibid. 130, 132. On questions of tenure, see G. E. Aylmer, *King's Servants* (1961), 106–25.

[19] Baillie, i. 274.

[20] *LJ* iv. 170; MP, 16 Jan. 1641. In a long list of Reeve's errors, the Arminian ones were selected for a prominent place in his condemnation: *LJ* iv. 170, 131, 180, 183, 174.

[21] Ibid. 100, 109, 113; MP, 10 Dec. 1640.

[22] *LJ* iv. 277.

of-the-road message in an important order on 16 December, in which they ruled, on the petition of Viscount Montagu, that privilege of Parliament was a good bar to an action for recusancy, and spelt out that peers' wives, children, and servants enjoyed protection as well as themselves.[23] There was to be no co-operation with Pym's attempts to force recusants into the wilderness. The Lords' concern with the privileges of their order was not merely a piece of self-importance; it was also a very useful device for preserving a show of consensus across a very wide spectrum indeed.

These positions, as sketched out by the Lords in the opening months of the Parliament, had something for everyone. They were not congenial to the King, but they were a lot more congenial than other things his resistance forced him to accept later. They were probably not congenial to religious reformers like Rous and Harley, but they represented a position with which such men had lived before, and might possibly live again. The Lords' judgement, that it was James's reign which had struck a political and religious centre of gravity, is one which modern historians have increasingly come to share. If Charles had adopted these policies immediately in November 1640, there is no reason to believe that they would have divided the country to the point of civil war, especially since resistance to them would have come from groups at opposite ends of the spectrum, who could not easily make common cause with each other. It was, however, one thing to see the lines of a potential settlement, and quite another to sell them to the Commons, the Scots, and above all to the King.

In the Commons, proceedings were dominated by the need to spell out to the King that he could not expect co-operation in returning to the world of the 1630s. The message was the more urgent for the fact that the King appeared not to have absorbed it. The Privy Council had expected that the King would prepare for the Parliament by announcing the abolition of Ship Money before he was forced to it, but when the Parliament met, no such concession had been announced.[24] The King's failure to announce any concessions therefore left the Commons to make most of the running. In the process, the Commons showed a very large degree of unanimity in what they wanted, though rather less unanimity when it came to expressing a priority between their different desires.

William Lenthall, in his opening speech as Speaker, put the emphasis on the restoration of Parliaments and liberties, and, according to the French Ambassador, succeeded in displeasing the people by saying their purses were the King's treasure, and the King by saying only a Parlia-

[23] Ibid. 110.
[24] PRO SP 16/468/17.

ment had the key to it. He reminded the King of attachment to the Petition of Right: 'looke but a very little backe, there shall we see our just libertyes gratiously declared by our sacred Majesty, and is our happiness shut upp in ye remembrance of times past only noe'. He told the King with undiplomatic plainness that he would have to co-operate with Parliaments in future, expressing his intention 'to endeavour a sweete violence which may compell (pardon dread sovereign ye word compell) your Majestie to ye love of Parliaments'.[25] It would be nice to know who, if anyone, briefed Lenthall to speak in this very unusual manner. Secretary Vane, who nominated him, would appear an obvious possibility, since the speech so closely resembled Vane's conviction that it was 'high time' the King relied on the counsel of his people.[26]

As always, much of the first full day of business on 6 November went on such routine business as setting up Grand Committees and making interim rulings on double returns, but some business was conducted. In an important constitutional innovation, the House claimed a right to handle Irish affairs, and set up a Grand Committee for the purpose. Some people seem to have expressed surprise, on the ground that Ireland had its own Parliament, but others overruled them by claiming as a parallel that a writ of error from Ireland lay in the King's Bench in England. In the short term, this move suited the interests of the Irish Parliament, which hoped to make common cause with the English Parliament against Strafford, but it was a precedent which was to lead to trouble later. Earle and Sir John Clotworthy, who had been found a seat by the Earl of Warwick, appear to have initiated the move, but it did not go entirely as they planned. They had intended to refer Irish affairs to a select committee, but on a division, the House overruled them by the narrow majority of 165 to 152, and decided to refer Irish affairs to a Committee of the Whole House. Clotworthy and Sir Henry Mildmay were tellers for the minority.[27]

Sir Benjamin Rudyerd, clearly speaking, as usual, from a script, offered a major speech. Peyton called it an 'elegant speech', and wrote 'this speech gett a good copy of'. Apart from the printed version, there are no less than five manuscript copies of this speech in State Papers.[28] The number of copies suggests that this speech may have been circulated around the court as a memorandum of what they had to come to terms with. In one way, Rudyerd's importance was diminished compared with what it had been in the 1620s, since he could rarely speak for

[25] MP, 5 Nov. 1640; PRO SP 16/471/25.

[26] PRO SP 16/468/116.

[27] CJ ii. 21; Palmer, fo. 7; Holland, vol. i, fo. 1; also D'Ewes (N.), p. 3. There is a note at the end of Palmer's diary (fo. 185ᵛ): 'Irld. a distinct dominion but being by conquest may by expss. words be bounde by Pliamts. here'. This seems to be part of his notes for art. 15 at the trial of Strafford.

[28] Peyton, fo. 3; PRO SP 16/471/38–41B; Rushworth, Collections, III. i. 24–6.

a united Pembroke clientage. On a few issues, such as the disputed election of Pembroke's secretary Michael Oldsworth, his clientage continued to function as a united and therefore powerful force.[29] On many other issues, growing polarization tended to dissipate what had always been a centrist force. It makes the point that Pembroke's clients in the Long Parliament included Edward Hyde and John Glyn,[30] whose political lines diverged steadily as the Parliament went on. On the other hand, Rudyerd, unlike many of the newer members, was a known quantity, and his close personal friendship with Pym, for whom he was a feoffee to uses, could be presumed to make him privy to the thinking of the circle for which Pym spoke.[31]

Rudyerd's speeches were written to a formula, and at first glance, this appears to be the standard Rudyerd speech, pressing for restoration of unity through concessions of policy by the King, and on money by the Commons. Yet, the very existence of the standard model draws attention to the divergences from it, and confirms Rudyerd's own judgement that 'I have gone in a way much against my nature, and somewhat against my custome heretofore in this place'. In giving reasons for his changing outlook, he gave clear priority to the new religious policy of the 1630s: 'wee know all what disturbance hath been brought upon the church for vaine pettie trifles, how the whole church, the whole kingdome, hath ben troubled where to place a metaphor, an altar'.[32] 'They would evaporate and dispiritt the power and vigor of religion by drawing it out into some solemne spetious formalities, into obsolete antiquated ceremonies new furbished up'. Yet at the same time he aligned himself with the moderate position of the House of Lords by censuring prosecutions of ministers, not because they were done 'against religion', but because they were done 'against law'. He complained of the Laudian redefinition of the word 'Puritan', so that 'under the name of Puritans all our religion is branded'. He explicitly agreed with Pym, St John, and Rous that the civil troubles were the result of a design to alter religion: 'they who would introduce another religion into the church, must first trouble and disorder the government of the state, that soe they may hide, and worke their ends in a confusion; which now lies at the door'.

He was insistent that there must be punishment of guilty ministers,

[29] D'Ewes (N.), p. 432.
[30] Birmingham Reference Library, Coventry MSS, Grants of Offices, nos. 337, 601. In Hyde's case, he should perhaps be described as a disappointed client. See Clarendon, *History*, i. 59.
[31] Somerset RO DD/BW Pym MSS, nos. 232, 239, see also nos. 224 and 227.
[32] Rudyerd seems to be making fun of the words of the canons of 1640: 'this situation of the holy table doth not imply that it is or ought to be esteemed a true and proper altar, wherein Christ is again really sacrificed; but it is and may be called an altar by us in that sense in which the primitive church called it an altar, and no other'. Laud, *Works*, v. 625.

and complained of evil counsellors casting responsibility on the King: 'they have unmannerly and slubberingly cast all their projects, all their machinations, upon the King, which no wise or good ministers of state ever did, but would still take all harsh, distasteful things upon themselves, to cleere, to sweeten their masters'. He was somewhat surprised at himself, since, as he rightly said, he was not 'vir sanguinis', but he could see no other remedy. He insisted that no more money should be voted until the King changed his counsels: 'more money without other counsels will be but a swift undoing'.

So far, as Peyton's reaction suggests, Rudyerd was probably speaking for almost the whole House, but the speech included a constructive side, which, as always, was almost totally ignored by the House. He knew that, to implement any of his programme, he had to induce the House to win the King's trust, and above all, that they must make it possible for the King to be solvent while holding Parliaments. He said the King had put himself in their hands, 'but if he prosper not better in our hands, than he hath done in theirs who have hitherto had the handling of his affairs, wee shall for ever make ourselves unworthy of soe gratious a confidence'. He realized that 'it hath been said too of late, that a Parliament will take away more from a King than they will give him', and warned them that they could only refute this argument by being 'more free of our purses'. It was a very necessary warning.

Pym's major speech followed on 7 November. It lasted some two hours,[33] and covered all the same ground he had covered in the Short Parliament. On some points, he was more explicit than he had been in the Short Parliament.[34] He committed himself firmly to the proposition he had left to Rous in the Short Parliament, that the root of the trouble was a design by papists to alter the country's religion, which they could only pursue by attacking the law which protected true religion. He repeated what Rudyerd had said, that money would depend on the King's changing his counsels: 'if he will change his counsel and course, we shall see him as flourishing as any of his predecessors'.[35] He classified two other groups as allies of the papists. One was 'a corrupt part of the clergy', that 'finds a better doctrine in papists to serve ther turnes better than that of our church'.[36] By this he surely meant to imply that Arminians agreed with the papists on the crucial doctrines of justifica-

---

[33] *HMC Leeds (Strange)*, p. 98.

[34] The best reports in the House appear to be Palmer, fos. 15–18 and Holland, vol. i, fos. 5ʳ–7ᵛ. In the light of these, the best full text appears to be Bodl. MS Clarendon, vol. 19, no. 1448, though occasional palpable errors in this text need correcting in the light of the text in PRO SP 16/472/45. Rushworth became confused between this and Pym's Short Parliament speech. D'Ewes (N.), pp. 7–11 is reporting the right speech, but less competently than the sources cited above. Quotations used here are from the text in Bodl. MS Clarendon, vol. 19, no. 1448 unless otherwise stated.

[35] This passage is from Palmer, fo. 16. It was not in Pym's script.

[36] Holland, vol. i, fo. 5ᵃ. Palmer's wording is 'those yt come near papists', fo. 15.

tion and election, and therefore, on the issues which mattered, were not on the Protestant side. The other group, by which Pym was always particularly bewildered, were those who, though not papists themselves, did not particulary mind popery, and in Laodicean style, were willing to work with it when occasion demanded. 'Those yt thinke off there own pferment and pfitt and further proiects and illegal courses. These would lett in poperie Turcisme too'.[37] In this passage, it is likely that he had Strafford in mind. In pressing, as he did for most of his speech, for Parliamentary privilege, frequent Parliaments, and the rule of law, Pym was asking for the same things as most of the other members who spoke in the opening debates, but analysis of the speeches would soon show that he was asking for them for very different reasons from many of the others.

It was soon to become clear that the Laudian church had no avowed defenders in the Long Parliament. Pym's attacks on it did not differentiate him from other members. What did differentiate him and his allies from other members was their explicit and avowed belief that the Laudian church was designed to reintroduce popery, in contrast to such men as Sir Edward Dering, who believed that Laud had gone only to 'the brink' of popery.[38] It would be wrong to treat this charge of 'popery' simply as an exercise in self-delusion or in unscrupulous propaganda. Unscrupulous politicians in the Long Parliament came in all theological persuasions, whereas the charge of popery against the Laudians was made only by politicians of one theological persuasion: those who had a long established record of regarding Calvinism as being of the very essence of Protestantism. When these people called Laudians papists, they were making a statement about their own definition of popery. Within that definition, what they said was perfectly sincere, and even accurate. The other peculiarity of Pym's allies was their willingness to claim, as Pym and Rudyerd did in the opening debates, an exclusive priority for religion above other issues.

Other members, speaking about very much the same grievances, wove them together into a very different sort of web. Edward Bagshaw, who also spoke on 7 November, came from much the same social circle as Pym, and also argued that religion and law were indissolubly associated, but the conclusion Bagshaw drew from this association was that 'justice is to the civil body, as food to the natural'.[39] He turned, when

---

[37] Palmer, fo. 15. On the church of Laodicea, see Rev. 3: 14–16. The immediate target of this passage is likely to have been Strafford. I am grateful to Prof. Caroline Hibbard for several interesting discussions of it. See Hibbard, pp. 169–71.

[38] S. P. Salt, 'Origins of Sir Edward Dering's Attack on the Ecclesiastical Hierarchy', *HJ* 30/1 (1987), 38. I am grateful to Mr Salt for lending me a proof of this article.

[39] Gawdy, vol. i, fo. 4ᵛ; Holland, vol. i, fo. 7ᵛ; Rushworth, *Collections*, III. i. 26–7; PRO SP 16/471/63.

looking for the root of evil, to what he saw as the failure of the judges to do justice, and proposed that violation of the Petition of Right or the Statute of Monopolies be made praemunire. A version of this speech in State Papers includes a passage missing from the printed version, expressing hostility to the Scots. 'And are not our lives in danger, whilst an enemy disguised like a friend is provoked, and as it were suffered, because indirectely and in vaine resisted, to come almost into our very bosomes, and to rifle some of their goods, and others of their loyalty'. The contrast with Pym, who had presented the Scots as fellow-sufferers from Laudian innovation, was stark. To many of Bagshaw's pro-Scottish friends, it may have been also alarming. Harbottle Grimston, as might be expected, was impartial in any division between those who put law first and those who put religion first: he claimed that 'the judges have overthrown the law, and the bishops the Gospel'.[40] In this phrase, he was highlighting the Parliament's chief professional rivalries: since the Parliament of 1628–9, members had been increasingly concerned to establish the claim of Parliaments to be the supreme interpreters of both, while the King had been increasingly concerned to assert the professional claims of bishops and judges as supreme interpreters in their own spheres. In the process, he had simply succeeded in casting grave doubt on their professional autonomy, and strengthening the Parliamentary claim to be supreme judges in law and supreme authorities in religion.[41]

On Monday 9 November the Commons began with a report of the King's speech of 5 November, recanting his description of the Scots as rebels.[42] The report also produced an angry reply by Edward Kirton to the King's remark in his first speech that if he had been believed in the last Parliament, the subsequent troubles would not have happened: he said that some ill-willers to the state must have put such an insinuation into the King's breast.[43] Kirton was always a convinced anti-Scot, and his speech shows that, even for the most dedicated anti-Scot, the opportunity to hold a Parliament was a chance to vent so many frustrations that the occasion was not to be wasted on a tame acquiescence in the King's anti-Scottish plans. Cradock and Penington, members for the City, also took the chance to protest against the fortification of the Tower, and Pym called for a committee to remove papists out of town.[44] On both these issues, the King chose to give way. The major set-piece performance of the day came from Sir John Culpepper, reporting the

---

[40] Gawdy, vol. i, fo. 3ᵛ; Rushworth, *Collections*, III. i. 26.

[41] On the history of this issue, see Russell, *1621–9*, pp. 348–58, 409–12.

[42] Palmer, fo. 22. *CJ* ii. 23 included an order for members to have copies of the report, but the speech itself is not entered.

[43] Peyton, fo. 7.

[44] Holland, vol. i, fo. 20ʳ; Palmer, fo. 24; Peyton, fo. 8.

grievances of Kent.[45] He complained of the great increase of papists (by which he probably meant Roman papists), and of new ceremonies, such as placing the communion table altar-wise 'and bowing and cringing too, towards it'. The addition of the word 'cringing' establishes Culpepper's credentials as a good anti-Laudian Protestant, but stops well short of Pym's belief that this was idolatry. Like the petition from Hertfordshire presented on 7 November, he raised the issue of military charges, though he did not repeat Hertfordshire's demands for a new law to settle obligations in military matters.[46] It is well worth remembering that the uncertainty of existing law made legislation on the militia a necessity from the very beginning of the Long Parliament. Culpepper also raised the special Kentish grievance of their arms taken away from them for use in the First Bishops' War, and not yet restored.[47] His next grievances were ones which were to become the central issues of the opening months: the canons and Ship Money. His complaint of the canons was the strictly constitutional one that the clergy 'have assumed to themselves power to make laws', which 'in this age, when the second ill president becomes a law, is full of danger'. His complaint of Ship Money was the obvious one that it took away title to property, and 'we owe all that is left to the goodness of the King, not to the law; Mr. Speaker, this makes the farmers faint, and the plough to grow heavy'. He complained of the decay of the cloth trade, which he blamed (wrongly) on impositions, and offered a proposal that customs should be diverted to put the weight on imported superfluities. He ended with an assault on monopolists which was among the great pieces of oratory of the Parliament:

these, like the frogs of Egypt, have gotten possession of our dwellings, and we have scarce a room free from them: they sipp in our cups, they dip in our dishes, they sit by our fires, we find them in our die-fatt, wash-bowle and powdering tubb; they share with the butler in his boxe, they have marked and sealed us from head to foote. Mr. Speaker, they will not abate us a pinne.

It was, naturally enough, this final passage which led to immediate action, in the form of a proposal from Seymour and Strode that all

---

[45] Rushworth, *Collections*, III. i. 33–4; SP 16/471/63; Holland, vol. i, fo. 13ᵛ. *CJ* ii. 24 records Culpepper's oral presentation of the Kentish petition, but there is no mention of his speech in the diaries. This must raise the possibility that Culpepper did not deliver the speech, but merely deposited a script with the Clerk. However, the fact that the order to expel monopolists followed immediately on the time when Culpepper is supposed to have delivered it suggest that it is the balance of probability that he did. So much more happened in the Long Parliament than any of the diarists recorded that it is always difficult to ground arguments on their silence. See JRL Crawford MS 14/3/76, which appears to allude to the speech.
[46] Peyton, fo. 3.
[47] Above, p. 73.

monopolists should be expelled from the House.[48] Overall, the speech went to show quite how far the King would have to retreat before he could see the daylight between Culpepper and Pym. There is no reason to believe that Culpepper ever changed his mind about the beliefs he expressed in this speech, and his behaviour later in the Parliament should be explained in terms of changed circumstances, and not of changed convictions.

On 10 November Digby assaulted many of the same targets in what Peyton describes as 'a most excellent speech'.[49] He dwelt, like Culpepper, on Ship Money and monopolies, military charges and impressment, but reserved his heaviest fire for the new canons of 1640. Like Culpepper, he concentrated on the constitutional issue of the clerical claim to legislate: 'doth not every Parliament man's heart rise to see the prelates thus usurp to themselves the grand preheminence of Parliaments?' He was particularly incensed by the requirement in the Etcetera Oath to swear never to alter things which might be legally altered by Act of Parliament. As time was to show, Digby never wished to alter the government of the church by archbishops (or 'arch things', as he called them on this occasion). His indignation was at being asked to swear an oath against the legislative supremacy of Parliament: 'it is a covenant against the King, for bishops and the hierarchy; as the Scottish Covenant is against them, only worse than the Scottish, as they admit not of the supremacy in ecclesiastical affairs, and we are sworn unto it'.[50] Like most other members, he was instinctively interpreting the Royal Supremacy as a legislative supremacy of King in Parliament. This cannot have made good reading for Charles, but his comparison of the Etcetera Oath to the Scottish Covenant had no more comfort to offer to Baillie than it did to Laud.

These opening speeches indicated the possibility of an agreed programme of action, but also showed, on careful study, that the agreement was highly superficial, because similar views were held for such highly different reasons. There is, for example, no suggestion in Digby or Culpepper that they thought the canons were ushering in popery or idolatry: Culpepper's reference to 'cringing' is the only hint in that direction, and that is probably more evidence of anticlericalism than of a hotter sort of Protestantism. Nowhere did they suggest that the Laudian church was popish, and nowhere did they suggest that Ship Money represented any evil more insidious than the arrogance of

[48] Palmer, fo. 27; Holland, vol. i, fo. 13ᵛ; D'Ewes (N.), pp. 19–20; CJ ii. 24.

[49] Peyton, fo. 9; Palmer, fos. 28–9; Rushworth, *Collections*, III. i. 31–2. Digby, as the son of Bristol and the son-in-law of Bedford, was under a variety of influences during these months.

[50] Something resembling this passage was delivered: see Peyton, fo. 10: 'a covenant of ye hierarchy against regall power'. Also Palmer, fo. 29.

power: there is no mention in their speeches of a grand design to change the country's religion.

In the short term, however, these speeches did indicate to a considerable agreement on immediate objectives, and there were enough of these to keep the House busy for some time. The impeachment of Strafford came first. It was hinted at by Earle, Clotworthy, and Kirton on 6 November,[51] and formally moved by Pym on 11 November, the day Strafford arrived in town from Yorkshire. He was immediately sent to the Tower, and a committee continued to prepare the charge against him, much assisted on 19 November when Pym got possession of a copy of the Remonstrance of the Irish Parliament.[52] Nevertheless, the prosecution of Strafford continued to hang fire, and was not ready to begin until March. The delay cries out for explanation, but none is immediately susceptible of proof. Perhaps the likeliest is that the prosecution was hanging fire in the hope of some concession by the King. It was well known to be displeasing to the King, and the immediate objective of the English, if not of the Scots, was probably to disgrace Strafford and put him out of office, rather than to bring about his death. It seems to have been only the King's resolute determination to defend Strafford which turned his prosecution into a fight to the death, and it is perfectly possible that such men as Bedford and Saye allowed the trial to be delayed in the hope that a fight to the death could be avoided.

These months also showed an obsessive determination, which perhaps took up more Parliamentary time than almost anything else, to reverse the judicial proceedings of the 1630s. Over and over again, a detailed hearing of some minor case ended with the judges turned into delinquents, and the delinquents into martyrs. The process began when Pym presented petitions from Mrs Burton and Mrs Bastwick to reverse the sentences on their husbands.[53] A petition from Prynne's servant presented by Rous soon followed, joined by one from Oliver Cromwell on behalf of John Lilburne. They seemed later a strange pair of bedfellows, but the issues involved in the attack on the Laudian hierarchy were ones on which Cromwell and Lilburne continued to agree as long as they both lived. The Councillors present, Vane and Roe, expressed doubts about the programme of sending for these people to hear their complaints, and Vane asked for them to hear the King's counsel first. The House entirely ignored these objections, and the proposal to send for them was explicitly supported by a member as little addicted to godliness as Sir Francis Seymour.[54]

[51] Peyton, fo. 5.
[52] BL Harl. MS 541, fo. 64ʳ. On the Irish Remonstrance and the English Parliament, see Russell, 'British Background to the Irish Rebellion of 1641', *Historical Research*, 61/145 (1988), 166–82.
[53] D'Ewes (N.), p. 4; Holland, vol. i, fos. 2, 10–12.
[54] D'Ewes (N.), p. 5: Palmer, fo. 11; Peyton, fo. 3; *CJ* ii. 22.

Seymour is likely to have regarded the proceedings against Prynne as an example of arbitrary government: there is no reason to suppose he felt very much theological sympathy with Prynne and his fellows. To others, it was a different story: when Burton and Prynne entered London on 28 November, Robert Woodford steward of Northampton wrote in his diary:

oh, blessed be the Lord for this day! This day those holy living martirs Mr Burton and Mr Prynne came to towne, and the Lord's Providence brought me out of the Temple to see them. My hart rejoiceth in the Lord for this day; its even like the returne of the captivity from Babilon. There went to meet them about 1,500 or 2,000 horsemen, and about 100 coaches, and the streets were all thronged with people, and there was very great rejoicing.[55]

This missionary attitude extended to at least one member of the committee which handled these cases and that of Alexander Leighton. On 11 November this member wrote to the Scottish Earl of Lothian, saying brave spirits in the House had already struck at the root of all our miseries; 'the hierarchie shakes, and if this Parliament continue, they are gone roote and branch'. He acclaimed the courage of many sons of God in both kingdoms who were raised up to this work, which sounded out the downfall of Babel, and expressed the hope that all papists would be confined, and there would be no more use of 'laymen's books' (images). On 24 November he wrote again, saying there were plans to attack Laud, and praising Denzil Holles, 'a good commonwealthsman' for his attack on Widdrington's speech calling the Scots rebels. It would be nice to know which member of the committee was responsible for this letter. The possibilities include Hampden, Strode, Penington, Perd, Sir Edward Hungerford, Rous, and Pym.[56] Whoever it was, he clearly regarded these individual cases as stage-setting for something which was to be much more far-reaching.

The individual cases continued, and became so numerous they threatened to choke the Parliament. Many of them were such clergymen as Dr Layfield vicar of All Hallows Barking, who had decorated his church with such a profusion of images that they were taken down by Dr Duck Chancellor of the diocese of London.[57] Dr Clarke, hammer of the godly of Northampton, made a good showing before the committee

[55] *HMC Ninth Report*, II. p. 499.
[56] Crawford MSS 14/3/76 and 77. As with most letters from a Scottish provenance, these are copies, and there is no possibility of a palaeographical identification. The first letter, though dated 18 Nov., is, on internal evidence, clearly written on 11 Nov. For the list of the committee of which this author was a member, see *CJ* ii. 24. There is no further ground to identify the author save hunch, but on that ground alone, it might be possible to suggest Francis Rous.
[57] BL Harl. MS 541, fos. 70ᵛ–1ʳ; DO, vol. i, fo. 8ᵛ.

of religion, but spoiled the effect when 'ere hee was aware he called the wine sacred wine after the communion was ended'.[58] The majority of these cases, in both Houses, originated from local petitions, and gave the opportunity for settling some old scores. In the Lords, where some original petitions survive, they often give the impression that the vicar's idolatry or Arminianism had not annoyed his parishioners as much as some other habits, usually an addiction to drink or litigation. The vicar of Kensington, who was taken home in a coach because he was drunk, would probably have annoyed his parishioners whatever his theological persuasion had been.[59] Yet, even if it was personal failings which produced the petitions, it was the theological charges which did the damage. Some, at least, of the clergy understood this very well. A certain Jonathan Skinner, of Wolverstone in Suffolk, was accused of such things as beating a woman to death, and isolating another by excommunication until she died of starvation. When brought before the committee, Skinner insisted that 'he did not alwaies adore or bow to the table, and never to the bread or wine; but for all other particulars, he did upon the manner confes them'.[60]

Most of these were small fry, and their cases tended to languish because the House did not get round to finishing them. Some others were more important: Peter Smart, who enlisted the aid of Edward Bagshaw, at last succeeded in turning the tables on John Cosin former Dean of Durham, now Master of Peterhouse. Two bishops, Wren of Ely (formerly Norwich) and Piers of Bath and Wells were impeached. The charge against Bishop Piers, it is interesting to notice, was supported by Sir John Stawell, soon to be the most passionate Royalist in Somerset. It was Stawell who presented the original petition against him, Stawell who moved to secure him in case he fled, and Stawell who hastened the sending up of the case to the Lords. In the process, he gave a hint that he may have opposed the bishop on the vexed Somerset issue of church ales. Stawell, whose fear of the lower orders was perhaps even more obsessive than his hatred of Puritanism, was just the sort of man who might have opposed the merriment of church ales for simple reasons of public order, without any religious motives whatsoever.[61]

By contrast, the record of both Houses suggests that they were unusu-

---

[58] D'Ewes (N.), p. 82.
[59] MP, 13 May 1641. See also MP, 10 Dec., 15 Dec., 5, 13, 16, 21 Jan., 6, 9 Feb., and other refs.
[60] D'Ewes (N.), p. 201.
[61] Ibid., app., p. 542; Northcote, pp. 101, 111; Stawell's reported words, 'whether not preach twice upon Michaelmas day to hinder church ales', are not by themselves clear, but in the context of his undoubted hostility to Piers, and apparently to the Book of Sports, the meaning given here is the likeliest. On the Somerset Church Ales, see T. G. Barnes, 'County Politics and a Puritan Cause Célèbre: Somerset Churchales/1633', *TRHS*⁵ 9 (1959), 103–22.

ally uninterested in the passage of bills. In the first two and a half months, up to 23 January, ten bills were introduced in the Lords, and twenty-six in the Commons. The bills before the Lords were four public bills and six private bills. Of these, only one of each had completed its passage through the House before 23 January. One was a private bill to allow one of their members, the Earl of Winchilsea, to sell lands.[62] This ultimately became a statute. The public bill was the bill for the Queen's jointure, the only one clearly enjoying royal sponsorship. This was sent down to the Commons on 5 December, with a request for expedition. The Commons, however, appear to have used it as a minor bargaining counter in the struggle for a settlement. On 17 February, the day after the King's assent to the Triennial Act, it was read a second time and committed. On 19 May, a week before the Root and Branch Bill, there was an order for the committee to sit 'tomorrow'. On 20 July, the day the Queen gave in to Parliamentary pressure not to go abroad, it was ordered to be reported 'tomorrow'. It was, but when reported, it was promptly recommitted, and nothing more was heard of it.[63] Two other private bills from this list ultimately reached the statute-book. One was a bill allowing the Marquess of Winchester to sell lands.[64] The other was a bill confirming an exchange of lands in Fulham between the Bishop of London and Sir Nicholas Crispe the customs farmer. It was sent to the Commons on 22 February, and was carried by the narrow margin of 76 to 68 on 27 July. The resistance was probably because it was in favour of two people who were widely regarded as delinquents. It finally received the Royal Assent on 7 August.[65]

Of the other public bills considered by the Lords before 23 January, the Arms Bill was read once, and nothing more was heard of it.[66] The bill for bringing water from the River Colne was sent to committee on 6 February, and nothing more was heard of it. It probably fell victim to a memorandum from the New River Company, which argued that the Colne water was polluted. It also defended the view that water is a natural monopoly by arguing that if there were two lots of pipes, no one would know which to dig up in an emergency.[67] The bill for dyed and dressed cloth lapsed in committee,[68] and the bill for hospitals was sent

[62] *CJ* ii. 100, 103, 106, 116, 141; *LJ* iv. 150, 152, 168, 169, 172.
[63] *LJ* iv. 88, 90, 105; *CJ* ii. 50, 87, 218–19; BL Harl. MS 163, fos. 589, 795[b]. Palmer, who reported the bill, received an annual fee of £2 as the most junior person on the list of the Queen's counsel. NLW, Wynnstay MS 168, fo. 188.
[64] *CJ* ii. 57, 91, 93, 96, 113; *LJ* iv. 243, 258.
[65] *CJ* ii. 90, 106, 215, 225; *LJ* iv. 330, 349.
[66] *LJ* iv. 129. On the previous history of this bill, see Russell, *1621–9*, pp. 45, 48 n, 77, 91–2, 120, 132, 217, 222, 274–5.
[67] *LJ* iv. 148, 163; MP, 30 Jan. 1641.
[68] *LJ* iv. 84, 86.

to committee on 6 August, and did not emerge.[69] Two naturalization bills completed their passage through the Houses during the summer of 1642, but seem never to have been presented to the King.[70] The third was delayed in July 1642 when the Commons sent it back to delete the words 'spiritual and temporal' from the reference to the Lords in the enacting clause,[71] and nothing more was heard of it.

In the Commons, twenty-six bills were introduced, not counting the protean subsidy bill, which kept changing its title. Of these, only one, the bill for Triennial Parliaments, completed its passage through the Commons within the first three months. When introduced by Strode and Cromwell, it was a bill for annual Parliaments, but the committee expunged all but a few lines, and replaced it with a new bill for triennial Parliaments.[72] This was then taken over by Prideaux, and sent to the Lords on 20 January. When it passed the Commons, William Davenant was indignant that 'no man presumed to resist, or dispute, against the body of the bill, but many very wisely against particular clauses of it'.[73] This probably indicates that it was already known that the King would take up the position he announced on 23 January, of accepting the principle of the bill while opposing its details. In the form in which it left the Commons, the bill provided, if the King did not call a Parliament when required, for the task of doing so to pass directly to the sheriffs, and then to the electors themselves. The Lords, with rather more concern for order, inserted the Lord Keeper and twelve peers between the King and the sheriffs.[74] This was accepted by the Commons, and the bill received the Royal Assent on 16 February, followed by bell-ringing at St Margaret's Westminster.[75]

By contrast with this unseemly haste, the funereal pace on other bills is all the more striking. Three other public bills introduced before 23 January ultimately reached the statute-book. Two, the bill to regulate the Clerk of the Market[76] and the bill for the Abbreviation of Michaelmas Term, were veterans from the 1620s, and indeed, the bill to

---

[69] Ibid. 85, 86, 122, 129, 152, 282, 344. The original bill (or one of them?) is in MP, 2 Jan. 1641. It restricts the making of long leases.

[70] *LJ* iv. 130, 154; *CJ* ii. 114, 119, 211, 524, 687; *LJ* iv. 135, 141–2, 154, 168; *CJ* ii. 121, 130, 211, 687.

[71] *LJ* iv. 120, 122, 123, 127; *CJ* ii. 65, 114, 119, 211, 687.

[72] *CJ* ii. 58, 60, 70; BL Harl. MS 476, fo. 179ʳ; D'Ewes (N.), pp. 196–7; DO, vol. i, fo. 27ᵛ; *LJ* iv. 136, 139, 145, 147, 150, 152, 160; *CJ* ii. 79, 80, 85; *LJ* iv. 161, 162, 163, 164.

[73] Staffs. RO D 1778/I/i/12 (Davenant to Legge).

[74] Bl Harl. MS 6424, fo. 12ʳ. MP, 28 Jan. 1641, shows that the insertion of the Lord Keeper was in a list of heads approved by the King. For the insertion of twelve peers, the Lords themselves appear to have been responsible.

[75] Westminster City Library, E 23, St Margaret's churchwardens' accounts, 1640–2. The bell-ringers were paid 5s.

[76] Russell, *1621–9*, p. 103 and n.; *CJ* ii. 36, 75, 160, 165, 184; *LJ* iv. 302, 313, 326, 356. For the content of the bill, see D'Ewes (N.), app., p. 542.

abbreviate Michaelmas term had been going since the 1580s.[77] It may have been the easier to make progress on them because they had already received committee scrutiny in other Parliaments. The third, the bill to restrict the Stannary Courts, was introduced on 24 December, sent to the Lords on 6 July, and received the Royal Assent on 7 August.[78] Of the others, the only one of the first importance is D'Ewes and Penington's bill to abolish idolatry and superstition, which was scheduled on Sunday 8 August to be reported 'tomorrow'.[79] It was a bill it would have been useless to send to the Lords before 1642, and it finally turned into the Commons' order of 8 September.[80]

Of the others, the bill for giving representation to County Durham ran into the usual disputes about how many boroughs should be included. It reached the Lords, where it had a first reading on 18 April 1642, but that was the last that was heard of it.[81] The bill to restrict the export of wool, encouraged by Sir Arthur Ingram, was sent to the Lords on 2 March, with a request for expedition, but it never progressed beyond commitment in the Lords.[82] A bill on enclosures, to apply a procedure like that of the Informers Act, whereby offenders had to be prosecuted in the counties, was given a first reading on 7 November, but it never advanced as far as a second. This does not suggest that enclosures were a priority issue for the Long Parliament.[83] The bill for reformation of abuses in ecclesiastical courts was presumably rendered potentially redundant by Root and Branch, and nothing more was heard of it after a second reading on 27 April.[84] A bill on elections disappeared in committee,[85] and so did a bill to declare the common law on salt marshes.[86] The major public bills of the Long Parliament did not appear until the summer, when the limits of the politically possible had become clearer. Without them, this is not a particulary distinguished list of bills.

[77] Russell, *1621–9*, pp. 42–3, 187, 234, 307; *CJ* ii. 68, 73, 101, 108, 141; *LJ* iv. 243, 246–7; *CJ* ii. 144, 145; *LJ* iv. 247. I am grateful to Dr Victor Morgan for the information that this bill goes back to the 1590s and not merely to 1601 as stated in Russell, *1621–9*, p. 43. For an even earlier appearance of the bill, in 1581, see *CSPD 1581–90*, vol. cxlviii, no. 25.

[78] *CJ* ii. 58, 83, 194; *LJ* iv. 302, 311, 316, 322, 338, 349. The Lords heard counsel for the King and the Prince, but, having done so, passed the bill without further alteration.

[79] D'Ewes (N.), pp. 271, 327, 356; *CJ* ii. 183, 191, 199, 246; BL Harl. MS 164, fos. 816[b], 818[a].

[80] For the content of the bill, DO, vol. i, fo. 42[r–v]. For the Commons' order, Gardiner, *Documents*, pp. 197–9. Bowing, the sabbath, and the Book of Sports are additions to Penington's original bill.

[81] *CJ* ii. 38, 40, 61, 219, 491, 515; D'Ewes (N.), p. 88; Northcote, p. 18; BL Harl. MS 163, fo. 795[a]. This last sharply contradicts the *CJ* entry for 21 July. The subsequent history of the bill shows that D'Ewes was right: *LJ* iv. 713, v. 3.

[82] *CJ* ii. 69, 77, 456, 466; *LJ* iv. 625, 629, 658.

[83] *CJ* ii. 21. For the content of the bill, see Palmer, fo. 10.

[84] *CJ* ii. 40, 128.

[85] Ibid. 58, 114.

[86] Ibid. 68, 73. This bill was presumably concerned with concealments and defective titles.

The private bills introduced in the Commons before 23 January, none of which progressed particularly rapidly, and none of which became statutes, are also a rather insignificant lot. There are six naturalization bills, three bills to enfranchise copyholders, three to sell lands, one to reverse a Chancery decree, and one concerned with a salt marsh, which is probably designed to settle a concealment dispute. The one peculiarity in the progress of these bills is that the three bills to sell lands were all rejected.[87] This perhaps suggests, like the development of the strict settlement, that resistance to the breaking of entails was becoming somewhat stronger. There were, of course, other bills introduced during the first two years of the Long Parliament, but the time from 3 November to 23 January is quite long enough for most of the proposed bills waiting from the eleven years without a Parliament to be brought into the open. As a harvest of eleven years, this is a strikingly slim one, and it gives the impression that there were not very many things people had wanted to do during the 1630s which they had been prevented from doing because they required legislation.

This list, in fact, suggests that naturalization was almost the only thing the lawyers had found themselves unable to achieve without statutory assistance. One should perhaps add the changing of parish boundaries, on which numerous bills surfaced later in the Parliament. This suggests that it would be worth the effort of investigating alternative ways of doing things developed by the lawyers during the 1630s. The collusive action could do many things, including changes of title to land. The King could do many others through Proclamations grounded on the broad categories of common law offence such as fraud and nuisance.[88]

If the need for Parliaments to pass bills was atrophying as fast as this list suggests, it becomes more challenging to explain why in 1640–1 the desire to recover regular Parliaments was so widespread, so strong, and so urgent. The people who cried out for triennial Parliaments do not seem to have wanted them in order to pass bills. The function of giving consent to taxation appears to have been vital to all those who demanded regular Parliaments, and the debates on Ship Money produced a lot of the demands for frequent Parliaments. Yet it seems in 1640 to have been the counselling function of Parliaments which was held to be most urgent: they were seen as a way of making it impossible, or at least extremely difficult, for the King to follow policies intolerable to the majority of the nobility and of the gentry. What was being complained

[87] Ibid. 86, 91, 222.
[88] On the collusive action, see R. Buchanan Sharp, *In Contempt of All Authority* (Berkeley, Calif., 1980), 135–51, and other refs; T. G. Barnes 'Prerogative and Environmental Control of London Building in the Early Seventeenth Century: The Lost Opportunity', *California Law Review*, 58 (1970), 1332–63.

of was Charles I's tendency to go his own way, and expect everyone else to follow, rather than take part in any meaningful exchange about what should be done. It was perhaps Bulstrode Whitelocke who summarized the point most neatly. Speaking on 21 December in favour of the impeachment of Lord Keeper Finch, he complained that 'he devised a way that the King should not need us'.[89] What members were constantly stressing was that there was an interdependence between the King and the gentry, and therefore that there had to be institutionalized means of getting him to listen to them. They knew this would not come easily, and that is perhaps why, after the counselling function, it is the function of Parliaments in punishing delinquents which was most stressed. For people like Digby and Bagshaw, speaking in the Root and Branch debate, it was the ability of Parliaments to control delinquent clergy which would make it safe to continue to have bishops.[90] It is a line of argument which indicates a considerable distrust of the King, and, on occasions, of power itself.

In the short term, there were three major political issues on which all members seem to have wanted action. One was the control of recusants, on which future Royalists like Seymour and Culpepper were as insistent as others. As always, what sorted the godly from the ungodly was the question whether restrictions should be confined to *convicted* recusants. As an issue, that of unconvicted recusants was ideally designed to sort members whose first attachment was to the rule of law from those whose first attachment was to the creation of a godly commonwealth. The King's Proclamation banishing recusants from London deeply disappointed Alderman Penington because it applied only to convicted recusants.[91] On 3 December Maynard moved 'that ther might bee an act drawn to convict them without any further formall or legall conviction'.[92] It is worth remembering that this speech was the work of a Serjeant-at-Law. On 6 March there was an interesting exchange between Selden and D'Ewes about the case of Dr Cosin. The draft articles against Cosin had accused him of employing a glazier and painter who were popish. Selden moved that this article be omitted, presumably because it was not actually against law to employ Catholic glaziers and painters. D'Ewes disagreed, 'because these men did performe that service which a good Protestant would not have undertaken; and ther are many secrets in framing popish Images which is not yet

---

[89] Northcote, p. 97.
[90] Above, pp. 193–4.
[91] D'Ewes (N.), p. 37.
[92] Ibid. 99; Northcote, p. 26. Maynard is not responsible for the wording of D'Ewes's report, and Northcote's report suggests that he wished absence from church to be prima-facie evidence of guilt. This still suggests a presumption of guilt.

knowen among us'.[93] On this occasion, Selden had the better of it, but only in order to save time. In general, this type of issue split the House roughly down the middle.

In the short term, the bulk of the business on recusants was in the hands of a committee chaired by John Glyn. Glyn is one of those members whose godliness is hard to estimate: he always worked with the godly faction in the House, but without ever expressing himself in the sort of zealous language characteristic of Francis Rous. In August 1642, when D'Ewes was feeling more than usually cantankerous, he described him as 'a swearing, profane fellow, yet now temporizing with the fiery spirits'.[94] Without taking D'Ewes's judgement too seriously, it might be wise to include Glyn in a category of the 'politically godly', which is all his Parliamentary record proves.

The report of this committee on 1 December revealed a systematic use of the dispensing power of the Crown to protect priests from the rigour of the laws. It was short of a suspending power, yet was exactly what was intended by the famous phrase of 1689, 'the dispensing power as it hath been exercised of late'. Seventy-four individual cases were proved, and the ministerial part had been done by Secretary Windebank. This was a case in which the King, and even more the Queen, were clearly behind the minister, but it was most unlikely that this would serve to protect the minister.[95] Behind the complaints there was also John Pulford, receiver of recusant revenues in the south, who was highly concerned about the failure to gather adequate revenue from recusants' estates. Since he had provided lodgings to Pym during the Parliament of 1628, he presumably was able to gain a hearing in high Parliamentary places.[96]

This report appears to have united the House: Pym, Hopton, Harley, and Culpepper immediately spoke against the growth of popery. A proposal to remind the King of his protestation on his marriage 'that notwithstanding his then match, she would not intermeddle with matters of religion' probably came from Pym, who had marked the promise in his 1624 Parliamentary diary with the words 'worthy ye memorye'.[97]

[93] D'Ewes (N.), p. 448 (D'Ewes's capital). On 21 Nov. these alarms were given some unfortunate credibility when a recusant attempted to stab a Westminster JP who was collecting names of local recusants. This led Holles to express fears of a 'generall assassination', and such members as Capel, Hopton, and Digby joined in the general panic. D'Ewes (N.), pp. 55–7.

[94] BL Harl. MS 164, fo. 304ᵃ.

[95] D'Ewes (N.), pp. 89–91; CJ ii. 41–2; Northcote, pp. 19–21; BL Harl. MS 541, fos. 93–4.

[96] PRO SP 16/109/52. See also ibid. 16/464/15 and 16/478/69. I am grateful to Prof. Caroline Hibbard for helpful discussion of Pulford and his work.

[97] Northcote, p. 21; Russell, 1621–9, p. 154 and n. On the fears stirred up by the prospect of a popish royal marriage, see Thomas Cogswell, 'England and the Spanish Match', in Richard Cust and Ann Hughes (eds.), Conflict in Stuart England (1989), 107–33. Among future Parliamentarians, such feelings were very much alive in 1640.

Pym's point illustrated the fact that the Queen might well feel cause for alarm at the preferment of those who viewed her with such hostility. The House agreed to enquire into the Pope's nuncio and his authority, to investigate arms sold to recusants, to draw an Act against the growth of popery, to make a remonstrance to the King, and to impeach Secretary Windebank. Windebank decided to take flight, and remained for a long time on the other side of the Channel, waiting for the King to vindicate him and bring him back. He clearly did not know that the world had changed as totally as it had.

The next major issue which united the House was that of Ship Money. It had been referred to a committee chaired by Oliver St John, Hampden's counsel, which reported on 7 December.[98] St John's report relied heavily on the Petition of Right, and argued that Ship Money was condemned by the same arguments as the Forced Loan. They resolved, in the most restrictive terms, that the King could not, on any pretence of public danger or necessity of defence of the realm, raise any tax without consent in Parliament. Solicitor-General Herbert, for the King, desired that some other way be provided for financing the navy, but no notice was taken of this suggestion. Roe moved to take the resolutions to the Lords, and Wilde moved for a charge against the judges. Hyde agreed, claiming 'all our sufferings from the original of Ship Money'.[99] This apparently extreme declaration marked Hyde out as a moderate, since it was probably intended to distance him from what St John had just said, that the Forced Loan and the so-called excise commission of 1628 had been intended for the subversion of religion.[100] For Hyde, Ship Money was something evil in its own right, but not any part of a popish and Arminian conspiracy. Culpepper and Falkland supported the moves for the impeachment of Finch, whom one of them described as the Judas among the twelve judges.[101] The proposal to impeach Finch went ahead. Edmund Waller took the message to the Lords, and delivered it with more gusto than the occasion demanded. It should be stressed that the members who voted for the impeachment of Finch did not subsequently change their minds: Clarendon, in his *History*, remarked that 'if their rule were true, that an endeavour to alter the government by law, and to introduce an arbitrary power, were treason, was the most notoriously and unexcusably guilty of that crime of any man that could be nam'd'.[102] Having disposed of Ship Money, members then asked the King to send

---

[98] D'Ewes (N.), pp. 113–18; Palmer, fos. 86–9; Northcote, pp. 33–6.

[99] D'Ewes (N.), p. 116; Northcote, pp. 36–8.

[100] Palmer, fo. 89.

[101] Northcote, p. 39; DO, vol. i, fo. 16ᵛ. The sources disagree on whether Culpepper or Falkland used this phrase. The important point is that either could have done.

[102] Clarendon, *History*, i. 177. See also the reflections on Ship Money (ibid. 68–73) and on Finch (ibid. 131, 158).

out more ships against the Algiers pirates, the very task Ship Money had been supposed to finance.[103] The King may well have wondered where the Commons thought the money was coming from.

The House next moved on to a three-day set-piece debate on the canons of 1640, in which there was a rush to see who could condemn them most effectively. No member of the House seemed willing to defend the content of the canons in detail, and the discussion centred, not on whether these canons were unjustified, but on whether the clergy possessed power to bind the laity by canons under any circumstances. If we are looking for attempts to increase Parliamentary power, it is to this debate and the debate on Ship Money that we should be looking, rather than to more famous political confrontations. The claim to be ultimate interpreters of both religion and law was one which, if established, would give the Parliament a very considerable importance, and it was a power for which they had to fight against established and well-qualified rivals in the persons of the bishops and the judges. The claim for the church to be governed entirely by Parliamentary statute was one which Robert Beale and his fellows had pressed hard under Elizabeth, but though it had been pressed many times, it had never been established to the point where canons made by the clergy did not bind without Parliamentary assent. The central point which concerned many members of the Long Parliament was that they were not prepared to trust either law or religion to the judgement of those appointed by Charles I. In trying thus to reduce the significance of royal powers of patronage, they were attempting to bind the Crown in a way it had not been bound before.

On 9 December, when the canons first came up for debate, the discussion was opened by Francis Rous,[104] who condemned the canons in detail, and demanded that their makers be punished. He was answered by Dr Eden, a civil lawyer speaking in defence of his profession. He argued that the Henrician Act in Restraint of Appeals had left ecclesiastical jurisdiction in the Crown, and that under the Crown, the clergy might make canons if they had the King's licence, and that these canons could bind clergy and laity if not contrary to any existing law. He answered the objection that the laity were not parties to the making of canons, and therefore would be bound without their consent, by saying the laity were parties to the making of the statute, and so were parties to canons made in virtue of that statute, and bound by them. Edward Bagshaw, the next speaker, insisted on consent as the basis of

---

[103] D'Ewes (N.), p. 142; MP, 5 Mar. 1641. On pirates and the issues they raised, see D. D. Hebb, 'English Government and the Problem of Piracy 1616–1642', Ph.D. thesis (London, 1985). I am grateful to Dr Hebb for much useful advice on these questions.

[104] D'Ewes (N.), pp. 125–8; Palmer, fos. 91–103; Northcote, pp. 45–7. On all the debates on the canons, Palmer's are much the best reports.

obligation, and argued 'yt noe canons can binde the laity without consent'. He quoted the Act of Six Articles, and argued that the Act of Parliament was needed to make the articles binding. Similarly, he argued that the Thirty-Nine Articles made in Convocation did not bind until confirmed by an Act of Parliament. This meant, if correct, that only the articles of doctrine were binding, since the Act of 1571 had not confirmed the articles of discipline. So intense a stress on consent as the basis of political obligation was capable of having far-reaching implications during the next year. Alexander Rigby, the next speaker, was heir to a long Reformation and pre-Reformation tradition in objecting against the claim of the clergy to constitute 'the church': 'and altho the church bee the congregation of the faithfull yett they make it the churchmen'. Yet, though Rigby had a long tradition behind him, the wording of the preamble of the Act in Restraint of Appeals was against him. Richard King, who came next, hesitantly followed Eden in claiming that only those canons which were against existing laws were illegal. The last speaker of the day was Orlando Bridgman, son of the Bishop of Chester, who was so hesitant that D'Ewes was not sure on which side he was speaking. He seems to have been taking the same line as King, that the clergy could make canons, but not these canons.

The debate was then deferred to Monday 14 December,[105] when it was reopened by Whistler, who argued that the clergy had no power to make canons. He explained away the canons of 1604 by arguing that they had been received by consent, and therefore bound by custom. He claimed, in an argument which would have bewildered Henry VIII, that the King's confirmation aggravated the offence of those who made the canons, because they were laying responsibility for all their misdeeds on the King. Sir Thomas Widdrington attempted to answer Eden's argument that canons could bind if not contrary to law by subjecting it to a fork. He said that if they were agreeable to law, they bound by virtue of the law before they were settled and were redundant, and if they did not bind by virtue of existing law, they were new matter, and did not bind. Sir Francis Seymour proposed that the canons be burnt by the common hangman, but asked the House to be more charitable to those who made them. The debate was about to reach a conclusion when Robert Holborne, Hampden's counsel in the Ship Money trial, asked for one more day to prepare an argument for the canons. To the indignation of Perd, his request was allowed.

On 15 December came one of the paradigm confrontations of the Long Parliament.[106] Holborne and St John, Hampden's two lawyers in

---

[105] Palmer, fos. 106–9; Northcote, pp. 60–2; D'Ewes (N.), pp. 146–9.
[106] Palmer, fos. 110–19; D'Ewes (N.), pp. 152–7; Northcote, pp. 65–70.

the Ship Money cause, advanced major set-piece arguments against each other on the legality of the canons. Holborne argued the same case as Eden, that canons with the Royal Assent could bind if not contrary to law. He condemned the Etcetera Oath, while defending the clergy's power to impose an oath without Parliamentary action. Even he, one of the most committed defenders of the Laudian church in the whole House, expressed anxiety about the interpretation placed on the Thirty-Nine Articles by Santa Clara, and said that the clergy should not meddle with matters of property, for we 'must not measure our government by New Testament or Old'. Where he explicitly supported Charles and Laud, and was the only member of the House to do so, was in seeing church and state as two separate spheres of authority, to be governed by different people on different principles. 'Clergie and laitie in a state as soule and bodie in a man. They both under one governor that *quoad mores* to the king and his convocation, the other to the King and his Parliament'. As D'Ewes reported him, he said that 'surely the church ought to be governed by itself, and laymen not to intermeddle with it'. This came very near implying a descending theory of power, very different from Bagshaw's belief that all obligation rested on consent. It is a good example of how many meanings might be covered by the notion of 'popery' that Sir John Wray reacted to this speech by rudely demanding when and where he last received communion, to which Holborne mildly replied that he was a regular receiver at his parish church.

It was the notion of a separate sphere of authority with which Oliver St John joined issue. After a brief reminder that the laity paid the clergy their wages and tithes, designed to reinforce the seventeenth-century belief that the professions ought to be kept in their place, he argued that 'we are now all one body, and must be all bound by consent in Parliament'. He used the Act of Six Articles to prove the necessity of Parliamentary authority, arguing that 'princes do not usually in point of jurisdiction resort to their people if could do it without them'. He showed himself an adherent of Cokeian ancient constitution theory by arguing that in the Saxons' time constitutions and canons had been made in Parliament. He quoted Dr Standish to the effect that canons only bound those who consented, and concluded that no canons were to bind but by authority of Parliament. The general implications of this attempt to base obligation on the consent of the whole body politic were far-reaching. As always, attempts to tackle the vexed question of authority in matters of religion had stirred fundamental questions of political theory, which, once raised, were not likely to go away. After St John, Maynard held forth on the determination of clergy to enlarge their power. Sir John Wray 'spake in general against the innovations and usurpations of the bishops', and the House moved to the question. The canons were condemned *nem con*, and a request from Culpepper for a bill to confirm such canons as were thought necessary was ignored.

With the condemnation of the canons, the Commons were coming near the end of their agreed agenda. The punishment of delinquents, especially bishops and judges, was still ahead of them, and there was no end in sight to the hunt for delinquent minor clergy. These were not a full political agenda, and the House was in danger of coming to a halt while still halfway through the game. The failure to hold the unity of 1640 was not just because there were latent divisions of considerable significance separating members from each other. That was true, and clearly visible to many members. It was perhaps more important that, in their devotion to legality and low taxation, many members were pursuing something which could not be. With the attacks on Ship Money, monopolies, and forest fines (which were being slowly considered in committee), the House had made a considerable hole in the King's revenue. On 29 December, when the House took control of assignments on the customs, an even bigger hole was threatened.[107] The reassertion of the principle that customs revenue was under Parliamentary control would put the biggest part of the royal revenue at the mercy of a not very constructive House of Commons. Some very tentative attempts by Pym to reform the administration of the subsidy had produced no tangible result, and as yet, the only subsidies being voted were being paid to the two armies in the north. The King, while losing thousands a year, was not getting a penny. On 16 February the King fairly compared them to a watchmaker who had taken a watch to pieces, and expressed the hope that some time, they would put it back together again.[108] The point did not only apply to revenue. On 14 December the House discussed abuses of Deputy-Lieutenants, and resolved that they should draw a bill for the power of Deputy-Lieutenants, and for rating and assessing. The need was acute, since there was now no secure legal basis for the King to raise or finance armed force. That was a situation which could not continue: a kingdom not run by pacifists cannot long subsist in a situation where it is illegal for it to defend itself. Yet the proposal interested D'Ewes so little that he did not even record it. The House itself, having cleared its conscience by the resolution, diverted itself with the more entertaining business of attacking the 'horrible oppressions' of a Catholic Deputy-Lieutenant in Worcestershire.[109]

Having taken the King's government to pieces, the Parliament could not simply leave its work and go home. The first three months of the

[107] D'Ewes (N.), pp. 192–4.
[108] PRO SP 16/477/29.
[109] *CJ* ii. 50; D'Ewes (N.), p. 145; Northcote, p. 58. The Worcestershire debate is also noteworthy for the fact that Serjeant Wilde, one of the godliest members in the House, defended a Catholic neighbour to the point where D'Ewes reproved him for irrelevance.

Long Parliament had made it very difficult indeed for Charles to resume the task of governing without a new political settlement. In the process, members had given themselves a power they did not want. A member like Sir John Strangeways, for example, might be happy to defend the church against the Scots, but he and Edward Hyde had no urge to endow the King with an adequate revenue. In the militia debate of 14 December, Strangeways showed no desire to give the Crown secure authority over the militia, and was more interested in complaining that the militia had cost Dorset £2,000. The King's potential supporters in the House were potential supporters on the ecclesiastical issue, not on the financial. They were mostly in the tradition represented by Sir Francis Seymour, one in which the liberty of their countries was more important than restoring the power of the Crown. Among those who were to be the King's party a year later, only Sir John Culpepper had a serious constructive interest in making the Crown solvent.[110]

This fact gave the godly members a political importance in the winter of 1640–1 which they would not otherwise have enjoyed. Many, though far from all, of them wanted a further reformation of religion badly enough to be prepared to pay the very heavy price of making the King solvent in return for it. This desire was not confined to the group around Pym, who were engaged in the serious pursuit of office, and therefore was interested in the task of making the work of future office-holders possible. Willingness to give the Crown 'support', as a permanent addition to royal revenue had come to be called, extended to some not very important godly members such as Alexander Rigby.[111] Because these people had a vision of something they hoped to achieve, they would pay for it, when those who were beginning to think they already had most of what they wanted were perfectly prepared to leave things as they were.

The King, who needed a new settlement if his monarchy was to remain solvent, and possibly even if it was to survive, thus could not leave things as they were in January 1641. He had agreed to lay down those parts of his revenue which were grievous to his people, trusting, so he said, in their affection to restore his revenue.[112] In this, he had no doubt made a virtue of necessity, but having done so, he had made a necessity of virtue: he had to reach agreement with his Parliament. In January 1641 it was obvious even to Charles that he needed to negotiate a new settlement with his Parliament, but the fact was far from obvious to many of the Parliament. It was that awareness of his financial needs which had always distinguished Pym and his allies, as well as the need to

---

[110] See below, pp. 348–50, 357–60.
[111] *HMC Fourteenth Report*, IV. 60. See also above, p. 108.
[112] *LJ* iv. 143.

reunite the body politic, which forced Charles into serious negotiations with them. Those negotiations were, from the very beginning, conducted against the odds, and the presence of the Scots in London did nothing to make them easier.

6

The Projected Settlement of 1641

JANUARY—MARCH 1641

The idea that there should be a new settlement, broadening the base of government, was put up for discussion by the Privy Council in the week after the presentation of the Petition of the Twelve Peers. In Windebank's Privy Council notes of 1 September 1640 appears the question: 'whether some of the noblemen not counsellors shall not be called to counsell if it be but to engage them?'[1] The 3 September memorandum of the Privy Council to the King justifies the proposal on rather broader grounds. It says the ground of the Council's advice hath been the uniting of your Majesty and your subjects together, the want whereof the Lords conceive is the cause of all the present troubles'.[2] This memorandum was rapidly followed by the meeting, on 7 September, between the Privy Council and the Earls of Bedford and Hertford, as spokesmen for the Twelve Peers.

This very first appearance of the idea indicates what were to remain several of its central features. The first is a vital ambiguity between a scheme for winning men by places and a scheme to reunite the country by basing government on 'other counsels'. The hard-liners, of whom Windebank was undoubtedly one, were always interested in the first, and the more conciliatory members of the Privy Council in the second. It is also a key feature of the scheme that it is one floated by the Privy Council in the King's absence. It was neither a royal nor a Parliamentary scheme, but in its essence a court scheme. Its key advocates in public appear to have been Hamilton and Henry Jermyn, with warm support at a distance from Northumberland. Holland, Manchester, and Vane were almost certainly involved in helping it forward.[3] The Earl of Salisbury, who was given the keys of the King's privy garden on 14 January 1641, is

---

[1] PRO SP 16/466/5.
[2] *Clarendon SP* ii. 97–8. See above, pp. 153–5.
[3] On Holland, see Staffs. RO D 1778/1/i/14 and KAO De L'Isle and Dudley MSS C 114/9. It is a mark of how topsy-turvy court politics had become in Feb. 1641 that the latter document shows Holland trying to rely on the favour of Clotworthy to gain the Lord Deputyship of Ireland. Manchester's likely involvement is a deduction from his regular appearance in *LJ* as a reporter of key items in the negotiations, as well as from the fact that his son Mandeville was a likely beneficiary of them. In Vane's case also there was a father–son pipeline. See also Yale University, Beinecke Library, Osborn Shelves, Howard of Escrick MSS, Correspondence Folder 3.16, for an expression

not named as a supporter in any of the surviving correspondence, but his opinions and his circle of friends both make it an overwhelming probability that he was.[4] The other point illustrated by the first appearance of the scheme is that this was not in the first instance envisaged as a settlement with the Parliament: it was envisaged as a settlement with the Twelve Peers and their associates. On 3 September 1640 there was no Parliament in session, nor even yet one summoned. The Twelve Peers, however, represented a more powerful body of opinion than most of the Council could happily leave in a state of disaffection.

This is one reason why the key figure with whom Council supporters of a settlement set out to do business was Francis, Earl of Bedford, first signatory of the Petition of the Twelve Peers, and the man in whose house it had been drafted and approved. With Bedford came his two leading Parliamentary clients, Pym and St John, who are likely to have been responsible for a great deal of the hard work on the possible detailed terms of a settlement. Other likely beneficiaries in the redistribution of offices which was expected to follow the fall of the 'incendiaries' were Essex, Mandeville, and Saye in the Lords, and Denzil Holles in the Commons. The group planning for such a settlement were also able to draw on expert advice in matters of detail from a considerable number of people. Sir William Russell, Treasurer of the Navy, was a cousin and close friend of Bedford, as well as being an expert on the customs.[5] The younger Vane, the other Treasurer of the Navy, was a personal friend of Pym, and the two Vanes, father and son, are likely to have been one of the most effective channels of communication betwen Pym and the King.[6] On financial matters, the proposals relied on information from Sir Robert Pye, Auditor of the Exchequer, whose son had married Hampden's daughter, and from Sir Edward Wardour Clerk of the Pells, who was Pym's feoffee-to-uses.[7] On ecclesiastical matters, they could rely on information from Ralph Brownrigg, former Vice-Chancellor of Cambridge, who was married to Pym's niece, and from John Williams Bishop of Lincoln, a friend of

of gratitude by Hampden and the Parliamentary committee in Edinburgh for the regular supply of information they had received from Vane.

[4] PRO LC 5/134, p. 429.

[5] PRO A 4/18, fo. 357ᵃ; Huntingdon RO Manchester MS 19/3/1; Bedford Estate Office, Fourth Earl, draft wills of 1621, 1624, 1627, 1635, and other refs. I am grateful to Mrs M. P. G. Draper, Archivist of the Bedford Settled Estates, for information on the relationship between Bedford and Sir William Russell.

[6] Yale University, Beinecke Library, Osborn Shelves, Howard of Escrick MSS, Correspondence Folder 3.16. This tends to confirm the authority of Clarendon, History i. 180, 186–8.

[7] Keeler, p. 317; Somerset RO Pym MSS no. 146, and other refs. Wardour was also a friend of Bedford: Bedford Estate Office, Fourth Earl, draft will of 1634/5, and other refs.

Bedford's whose conversation is quoted in his commonplace book.[8] James Ussher Archbishop of Armagh was occupied, when the Long Parliament began, in a long series of lectures preached at Covent Garden, where Bedford controlled the vestry.[9] As Professor Aylmer has pointed out, this information does not mean these people should be construed as future Parliamentarians: they were advocates of negotiation and compromise, and not thereby committed to sides in a conflict which had not yet taken place.[10]

Bedford, the group's candidate for Lord Treasurer, was ideally chosen as the leading negotiating figure. Apart from Hertford, whose unity with the Twelve Peers was temporary and superficial, he and Essex seem to have been the only members of the group who were socially at all well known to the King. Unlike Pym and Saye, whose friends seem to have been almost entirely drawn from one narrow part of the political and religious spectrum, Bedford seems to have had friends in all parts of the spectrum. The friends whose private conversation is recorded in his commonplace book range from Saye at one end of the spectrum to Laud at the other, and his recorded house guests include George Goring and Lucy Carlisle. He was clearly a man able to talk to people of all sorts of opinion, and one of few such men in the group for which he acted as spokesman.[11]

The deduction of his opinions from the innumerable volumes of his commonplace books is a laborious process, since the majority of entries are in the form of unattributed quotations, with no clue to whether Bedford agreed with the opinion in question. It is only occasionally that one of his massive marginal notes of 'NO' indicates his own opinion.[12] The suggestions offered here are impressionistic conclusions from a much larger body of material than can be cited in a work of this sort. In religion, he emerges as a Calvinist episcopalian, whose favourite theological reading before 1640 seems to have been Bishop Hall, the only bishop ever mentioned without disapproval by Nehemiah Wallington.[13] He had read and understood Francis Rous's *Testis Veritatis*, his major anti-Arminian tract of 1626, but, in his annotations on Pym's 1625 Parliamentary diary, had shown no sympathy with pleas for those who

[8] On Pym and Brownrigg, see above, p. 109–10. For Williams, Bedford MSS vol. XI I p. 55.
[9] CUL MS Mm vi. 55; PRO Prob. 11/188/29; PRO SP 16/402/73.
[10] G. E. Aylmer, *King's Servants* (1961), 380–2, and other refs.
[11] See above, pp. 3–5.
[12] Bedford MSS vol. XI I pp. 67, 48; ibid., vol. 8, fo. 61. See also ibid., vol. XI i. p. 24 for quotation from Lancelot Andrewes, and ibid. 5 for remarks by Lord Brooke about French criticism of the Royal Supremacy. It underlines the point that Brooke and Digby were both his sons-in-law. His opinions can occasionally be deduced from index headings: e.g. ibid. 13: 'poopes see Antichrist'.
[13] Ibid., vol. 3, pp. 1–81; vol. XI I p. 4, and many other refs. Paul Seaver, *Wallington's World* (Stanford, 1985), 187.

did not conform in matters of ceremony.[14] There is every reason to suppose that the ideas advanced by Ussher, Holdsworth, and Brownrigg, the key advocates of modified episcopacy, commanded his instinctive sympathy. In matters of government, he was a believer in the collective authority of the Privy Council, rather than in royal prerogative or Parliamentary authority. He was awake to most of the main intellectual currents of his day, and his commonplace books are full of notes on such things as Harvey on the circulation of the blood and Reginald Scot's *Discovery of Witchcraft*, in addition to some very early texts of 'Dunse verses'.[15] His major disadvantage, of which historians cannot fail to be aware, is that he was left-handed, dyslexic, and suffered from writer's cramp.[16] His periodic attempts to restore order to his papers appear to have been a failure, and volume xi of his commonplace book, a laborious attempt to classify his notes by subject, is constantly punctuated by the heading 'Nots Escaped'.[17] However, a peer as prosperous as Bedford could rely on others to sort papers.

In 1640 he appears to have adopted a pro-Scottish position, and one of the King's anti-Scottish declarations is copied into his commonplace book with the most vigorous hostile annotations. One undated entry, probably during the summer of 1640, says that 'the Scots have delivered mi peticions', but he does not tell us what was in them. He was intriguingly aware of the possible parallels between the revolts of Scotland and Portugal, and seems to have been in favour of a concessionary approach to Scottish affairs. Yet he was also aware of the contrary case, and wrote down a quotation from 'Do. K' (probably Dr King, Jacobean Bishop of London) that 'it were better for K. to . . . [*illegible*] under the supremersy of the Pope then under the presbyterie of Scotland'. He absorbed the point of Bagshaw's Lent Reading of 1640, that a Parliament could be held without bishops, and noted that they had not been named in the enacting clause of the Statute of Provisors.[18]

Unfortunately, the commonplace book peters out after the first month of the Long Parliament, just when it would have been most interesting, and there are few clues there to his activities in trying to

[14] I am grateful to Dr Tyacke for the identification of quotations from Rous's *Testis Veritatis*. On Pym's 1625 diary, see Russell, *1621–9*, p. 231 n. He was, on the other hand, a patron of Cornelius Burges: Tyacke, pp. 78–9.

[15] Bedford MSS vol. XI I pp. 116, 119; vol. 3, pp. 223–38; vol. 26, fos. 50–4. The Donne texts are undated, but, judging from surrounding material, they probably date from about 1624. I am grateful to Prof. A. J. Smith for advice on these texts.

[16] The left-handedness is deduced from the extreme slant of the writing, the dyslexia from his constant inversions (e.g. 'King Charlse'), and the writer's cramp, more tentatively, from the extremely crabbed and jerky character of the writing.

[17] e.g. Bedford MSS, vol. 3, pp. 83–4. The notes are from Bishop Hall, and had escaped from the long section of notes on Hall which occupies pp. 1–81.

[18] Ibid., vol. 25, fos. 30, 51, and other refs. The bulk of this volume is unfoliated.

negotiate a settlement. A draft for a petition to the King, on an unidenti-fied subject, stops at the congratulatory phrases, and reveals nothing more unexpected than that he had read Machiavelli's *Prince*. Notes on Saye's attack on set forms of prayer are balanced without comment with notes on a sermon preaching the opposite case. Notes on one of Ussher's sermons show only that he was listening, and only the faintest whiff of irritation shows in his recording of a comment Gondomar had once made on the Earl of Bristol, that he would undo himself with reason.[19]

The first, and very faint, sign that Bedford may have been making political plans of substance comes in a letter from his son-in-law George Digby, written on 19 July 1640. This thanks Bedford for his good counsels, and says, in tones typical of Digby, 'in this I shew an obedience to you only in that wherein mine own reason hath a share in the commaund', and adds that he is not, as Bedford feared, swallowed up in contemplative studies.[20] There is no proof that the counsels referred to were political. This letter apart, the first mentions of the scheme as a matter of gossip are in two letters from Northumberland to Leicester and Lucy Carlisle to Lady Leicester on 3 December 1640. Northumberland said that 'the Treasurer is doubtlesse in the first place to be chosen, if Higgledy Piggledy [*deciphered by Leicester as Bedford*] get that tis not by the favour of the Parliament who is unsatisfied with him believing him to be gained by the King, but this discourse and some others of the like kinde are yet certainly without ground'. Lucy Carlisle was rather more explicit: 'what you hear conserning my Lord of Bed-ford is sartunly the news of the towne, and nothing of it aithere true or posible with out sutch a change as I dayr not thinke of. Theye have disposd and changd all the officers of this kingdome. The King makes himself merie at it, though I beleeve there is not much caus for that.'[21] This letter illustrates sharply both how much this was a court scheme, and how the court's addiction to playing musical chairs in Spain might build up to the point where it put the King under considerable pressure. Northumberland's remark that Bedford was incurring suspicion in Parliament is borne out by Edward Nicholas, in his later history of the Long Parliament, who says that in December Pym was reported in the town to be grown cold in the business of the commonwealth.[22]

In the Commons, Pym and St John were providing occasional hints of

[19] Ibid., vol. 25, unfol.
[20] Bedford MSS, Fourth Earl, Miscellaneous Papers. The dissenting phrases are heavily under-lined in Bedford's hand. There are very few people whose hand can be identified by underlinings, but Francis, Earl of Bedford is one of them.
[21] KAO De L'Isle and Dudley MSS C 85/22 (not in *HMC*) and 129/10 (*HMC De L'Isle and Dudley*, VI. 346).
[22] BL Add. MS 31,954, fo. 181ᵛ.

their willingness to back up the offers Pym and Rudyerd had made in their opening speeches, to supply the King with an adequate revenue in return for his agreement to adopt 'other counsels'. At the very beginning of the Parliament, Pym moved to adopt the principle of voting a lump sum instead of the traditional subsidy, thus protecting the yield from diminution by under-assessment. On 19 November he and Holles succeeded in carrying the principle. They were considerably helped in doing so by the fact that money was needed urgently to pay the Scots, while there was some feeling that a subsidy should not be voted at the beginning of a Parliament, or before redress of grievances. This made it much easier to argue that, when it was necessary to vote money to pay the Scots, it should be voted in some other form than the traditional subsidy. Nevertheless, the Commons were on their usual form in opposing accurate assessment of subsidies. On 19 November Pym faced considerable opposition, some of it from such close allies as Nathaniel Fiennes, to the attempt to abolish certificates, by which non-resident landowners (including Pym) had escaped subsidies in some places on the ground that they paid somewhere else.[23] On 10 December the Commons, in the face of Pym's vigorous opposition, overruled their former vote, and went back to the traditional subsidy.[24]

On 27 November Pym introduced the subject of Tonnage and Poundage, which was to be one of the key matters of negotiation most of the way through the Parliament. He 'declared that they would make the King the richest King in Christendome, and that they had noe other intention but that hee should continue their kinge to governe them, and pressed that hee might have Tonnage and Poundage graunted by Acte of Parliament which took well in the House'.[25] Following immediately on an attack on Ship Money, this speech was designed to meet one of the King's major anxieties, but the immediate motion of St John and Earle not to grant Tonnage and Poundage at the beginning of a Parliament suggests that the speech was designed as an earnest of future intention, rather than of present performance.[26] Pym was perhaps already hinting at what is now known in disarmament negotiations as the principle of 'linkage', in which concessions on one front are linked to equal and opposite concessions on another.

On 7 December, again in the context of the abolition of Ship Money, the subject of revenue came up again, and St John moved to provide otherwise for the navy.[27] On 14 December, again in the same context, St John was more explicit. He moved for a committee to consider the

[23] *CJ* ii. 29, 31; MP, 14 Nov. 1640; D'Ewes (N.), pp. 43–4.
[24] D'Ewes (N.), pp. 134–6.
[25] DO, vol. i, fos. 11–12; Northcote, p. 12 (dated the 28th).
[26] D'Ewes (N.), pp. 75–6.
[27] Northcote, p. 36; D'Ewes (N.), p. 116.

King's revenue, and to 'provide a high subsistence for Majesty'. Pym immediately seconded him, proposing to intimate their intention to the King, and asking for figures along the lines of Lord Cromwell's estimates of 1433.[28] Sir Robert Pye asked for the figures to include revenue by monopolies and the loss by them to the subject, and Whistler, whose personal connection with Bedford's group, if any, remains obscure, moved to revive the proposal of 1610, to give the King a constant revenue in return for wardship. Vane, for the King, welcomed the proposal, and asked for better assessment of the subsidy, and the only dissentient voice came from Hyde, maintaining that what had been issued in the past two years was enough to conquer Germany. On 17 December the King's leave was obtained,[29] and on 28 December Pye and Wardour brought in the 1635 revenue balance, offering to update it as soon as the bulk of work permitted. On 23 December Pym moved to raise the subsidies to the height of Queen Elizabeth's time, saying 'that the present necessity, not the satisfaction of the country, be looked to': a view not likely to be congenial to the House.[30] There was no performance here, but there was enough to offer a carrot of willingness to negotiate. Secretary Vane on 28 December told the House that 'King's revenue in such distraction that nothing but Parliament can repair it'.[31] It may be presumed that he and others told the King the same thing many times over, and the message may have done something to convince the King that he had less occasion to make merry at Bedford's proposals than he had believed at the beginning of December.

It would be possible to ascribe the timing of the beginning of serious negotiations to Bedford's health, since the minutes of the Scottish treaty list him as 'sick' from 9 December to 5 January, and he did not attend again until 7 January.[32] However, there is no evidence that Charles would have wished to negotiate with him in December if he had had the opportunity, nor that Charles had cleared his own mind about his negotiating terms. That process seems to have taken place during the first two weeks of January, and to have been hammered out in a long series of Privy Council meetings at which the King was present. He attended meetings of the Council on 18 and 23 December, and on 3, 6, 15, 17, 19, 24, 27, and 31 January.[33] On 14 January Lucy Carlisle said that 'I now beleeve wee shall have great change of officers, and contrary to what I thought . . . Bedford will be treasurer'. She now believed her

---

[28] Northcote, pp. 59–60.
[29] CJ ii. 52.
[30] Northcote, pp. 107–8.
[31] Ibid. 113–15.
[32] BL Harl. MS 457, fos. 25^r–50^r.
[33] PC Reg. XII. 66–81.

brother Northumberland would have a great power in these removes.[34] The next day, 15 January, the Privy Council considered two of the key areas of possible settlement, the military and the ecclesiastical.[35] The issue of military matters seems to have been raised by the Lords-Lieutenant present. Nicholas's notes record that 'the Lds. Lieutenants did make a ptestation what answer they yield to the pet. of Ps [Twelve Peers?] untill there were a lawe to doe the same thinges to ye publique safety of ye kingdome'. The Lords-Lieutenant were dissociating themselves from the view Charles had always held, that the prerogative was an adequate source of authority in military matters, and insisting that the King's military powers and the right to raise coat and conduct money be established by Parliamentary authority. It was a view which had commended itself to Pym since 1628, but in which Charles had never shown much interest. On this occasion it prevailed, and it was ordered 'the k. councell to drawe a bill for establishing ye powers of ye Lord Lieutenants and for providing of coat and conduct money'. These exchanges perhaps illustrate how much the case for a settlement arose from the need, after the Second Bishops' War, to re-establish the habit of obedience on a secure legal footing and a broader political base. The same points probably came up again in the meeting of 22 January, when Nicholas's brief note of '34 and 36 E 3 about pliaments' seems to indicate a discussion of the proposed Triennial Act. The 'heads from his Majesty', in the House of Lords Main Papers for 28 January, perhaps indicate, both the conclusion of this meeting, and the closeness with which the Privy Council was now working with the House of Lords. If so, Charles seems to have been persuaded that the stability of his authority depended on regular Parliaments. This is one issue on which Charles's change of heart appears to have lasted.[36]

It is less easy to say whether the same is true of the ecclesiastical issue, which came before the Council on 15 January, through the case of a group of separatists discovered in St Saviour's Southwark, which the Council decided to refer to the House of Lords. This issue produced 'debate whether y k. should make a declaracon that he will provide that all matters ecclall and ye ecclall government shalbe reduced to their former state as it was in ye times of Q. Eliz. which is esteemed ye best times'. This was, on paper, a full acceptance of the Lords' compromise

---

[34] KAO De L'Isle and Dudley MSS C 129/12; *HMC De L'Isle and Dudley*, vi. 361.

[35] PC Reg. XII. 78; PRO SP 16/476/19, 23, and 45. Of those attending, Manchester, Hamilton, Pembroke, Salisbury, Holland, Lanerick, Cork, Vane, and Littleton are likely to have been cautiously sympathetic to the proposals; Juxon, Lindsey, Berkshire, Roxburgh, Goring, Cottington, and Jermyn are likely to have felt reservations; and Arundel and Dorset, because their attitudes were least predictable, are likely to have been most influential.

[36] MP, 28 Jan. 1641; see above, p. 225. On the durability of Charles's change of heart, see PRO 31/3/73, p. 93 (Wat Montague to Mazarin, n.d. 1642–3).

formula of sticking to what was 'by law established', thereby ruling out Laudian and Scottish innovations with even-handed determination. With such a principle of settlement, everything would depend on the interpretation it was given. Charles had many times promised to eschew innovation, and the question would be whether he could absorb that many people believed that the bulk of the ecclesiastical policy of the 1630s constituted innovation.[37] Juxon, the only bishop present at these debates, was unlikely to interpret the principle in a way congenial to the House of Commons. At the meeting of 24 January Charles spelt out two of the implications he saw in this proposal: 'ye k. cannot in his conscience give way that episcopacy shalbe abolished either in the function or for their voyce in Pliament', and 'the k. would rather starve than have any of the church lands or livings'. The first, no doubt, was a good Elizabethan principle, but the second would have caused Elizabeth I, and even more her father, some surprise.

On 16 January, as agreed, the case of St Saviour's Southwark was presented to the Lords by Manchester at the King's command.[38] This congregation, which included Edmund Chillenden, possibly the later Fifth Monarchist, refused to go to their parish churches, held that there was no true church but where the faithful met, and that the King could make no law, because he was not perfectly regenerate. It was a provocative combination of opinions, and the Lords duly obliged. They ordered that divine service be performed as appointed by Act of Parliament, that all who disturbed it should be punished according to law, and that clergy should forbear to introduce any new ceremonies that might give offence, other than those established by the law of the land. It was a less complete victory for the King than it appeared to be: the invocation of Act of Parliament explicitly upheld a non-Caroline view of Parliamentary authority in the church, and the condemnation of new and offensive rites and ceremonies was not intended to offer any comfort to the Laudian clergy, or even to the Archbishop himself. To the bitter disappointment of Warner Bishop of Rochester, nothing was done to the offending sectaries; 'not so much as to reform their opinions or come to church'. When the tension between Bishop Hall and Mandeville got out of hand during debate, it was Hall who was made to ask pardon in his place. The Lords had duly supplied Charles with what Baillie called a 'procured ordinance', for which Manchester, Arundel, and Pembroke duly delivered the King's thanks.[39] However, they were not prepared to be used for merely partisan purposes. On 21 January, in discussing the case of Richard Powell vicar of Pattishull Northants, the Lords gave fair

---

[37] See above, pp. 49–50, 137.
[38] *LJ* iv. 133–4; BL Harl. MS 6424, fos. 6ʳ–7ʳ.
[39] Baillie, i. 293; *LJ* iv. 134.

warning of how they intended to interpret what they had agreed to. Powell appeared to Clarke and Sibthorp, the key local Laudians, to be orthodox and fully conformable, but the Lords found that 'Mr. Powell was no orthodox man, as informed, but popish and superstitious in divers practices, as crossing the bread and wine at the sacrament, and bowing to it afterwards, crossing himself a mornings before he drank etc.' They underlined their increased involvement in executive power by ordering that the two JPs who had been dismissed for their attacks on Powell, Sir Richard Samuel and John Crew, should be restored to the Commission of the Peace.[40]

The same week, there was a flurry of signals from court that the King was interested in proposals for settlement. On 19 January Littleton, who was probably sympathetic to the new trend, was appointed Lord Keeper in the place of Finch. On 20 January, when the Commons had just given the Triennial Bill an unopposed third reading, the younger Vane appealed for money for the support of the navy.[41] He had said this many times before, but the principle of reciprocity suggested that the withdrawal of royal resistance to the principle of the Triennial Bill demanded some return. On the 19th, it was given out at court that Strafford would have to secure his own acquittal, rather than relying on royal protection, the King again perhaps hoping that his own apparent concession would secure a reciprocal concession from the prosecutors.[42] By 21 January the new course had won the attention of the newsletters. The French Ambassador reported that Bedford, Pym, and Essex might get office, while adding that this was still 'fort incertain'.[43] The same day, Sir John Temple sent Leicester one of the fullest reports we have on the settlement negotiations.[44] He wrote:

I understand the King is brought into a dislike of those counsells that he hath formerly followed, and therefore resolves to steere another course. Hamilton and Jermyn have deeply contributed to this change. . . . My Lord of Bedford shall now presently be Lord Treasurer, my Lord Treasurer Archbishop of Yorke, Mr. Pimme shall certainly be Chancellour of the Exchequer and my Ld. Saye Master of the Wardes, my Ld. Cottington desireing to retire and glad if he may escape so. . . . This day my Lord Primate [Ussher] . . . Doctor Brumricke

---

[40] *LJ* iv. 136–7. One might suspect that this was a 'procured ordinance' for the other side, but such a suspicion would merely underline the basic point, that the Lords' objective was the partial satisfaction of all parties.

[41] D'Ewes (N.), p. 266.

[42] Staffs. RO D 1778/i/i/12.

[43] PRO 31/3/72, p. 406.

[44] *HMC De L'Isle and Dudley*, VI. 367–8: KAO De L'Isle and Dudley MSS C 114/7. Temple was acting for Leicester, who hoped to become Lord Deputy of Ireland, and was negotiating with Henry Jermyn, who was the source of his information. Morton, Ambassador to Savoy, believed that 'Heaven has blessed his Majesties conduct in this happy becalming of his domestique agitations'. He was getting his English news from Vane: PRO SP 92/23, fo. 382 (29 Jan./8 Feb. 1641).

[Brownrigg] and Dr. Oldsworth were sent for to waite upon the King about this business of episcopacy which is to receive a debate in the Lower House on Monday.

The willingness to listen to Ussher, Holdsworth, and Brownrigg indicated the possibility of a retreat much greater than had been spelt out in the Privy Council on the 15th, since Ussher's desire to have bishops reduced to the 'ancient primitive way' was sufficiently well known. This was no longer a scheme for winning men by places, but, in Temple's words, 'upon the bringing in of these new men to make up an entire union betweene the King and his people and so to moderate their demaundes as well as the height of that power wch hath been lately used in government'. It was, however, a plan for a purely *English* union: all that was to be done to the Scots was to pay them the Brotherly Assistance, which Temple expected to come to only £200,000, and 'so to cleare them away presently'. It was a programme the Scots might not welcome.

Two days later, when the King first enunciated his programme in public, he again chose the forum of the House of Lords, but committed himself to rather less than Temple's letter had suggested.[45] In his speech, he gave priority to the 'slow pace' of the Parliament, and the need to hasten the disbanding of the armies. He then repeated his need for help for caring for the navy and forts, and asked for help in ending 'present distractions', among which he included irreverent interruptions of divine service, tumultuous petitions, and the detaining or disputing of large parts of his revenue. In return, he repeated the offer of 15 and 16 January to 'reduce all matters of religion and government to what they were in the purest times of Queen Elizabeth's days'. He also made an offer he later had cause to regret,[46] that 'what parts of my revenue that shall be found illegal or grievous to the public, I shall willingly lay down, relying entirely upon the affections of my people'. He complained of petitions against bishops, and though he offered to restrain any excesses in their jurisdiction, he said he could not consent to taking away their voices in Parliament, or 'that bishops shall be no better than cyphers'. The last phrase suggests that Ussher and his colleagues had not yet succeeded in making a favourable impression on him. He claimed, in a striking statement of ancient constitution theory, that bishops had had voices in Parliament 'even before the conquest'. He and his supporters were perhaps beginning to discover that the notion of an ancient con-

---

[45] *LJ* iv. 142–3. The King was reported by Manchester.
[46] See *ECR* E 241(1), p. 520 (12 Aug. 1642) where Charles referred to the Houses' 'pretended care' to look into his revenue.

stitution was an even more effective defence for bishops than it was for
Parliaments.[47]

All this was well short of terms for an effective settlement, but it was
near enough for negotiations to begin. The chronology perhaps gives
some clues to what had converted Charles so far. The vote for the
abolition of Ship Money undoubtedly had some effect on him: as he had
said ever since the Short Parliament, if Ship Money was to go, he
needed some alternative means of support for the navy.[48] That, and the
more general need for some assistance for his revenue, undoubtedly
constituted one powerful motive for him to negotiate.[49] The desire to
save Strafford's life also constituted a motive which grew increasingly
urgent with the passage of time. How far he ever accepted or understood the Privy Council analysis, according to which he needed a new
settlement to restore his political authority, remains unclear. Probably
the Venetian Ambassador was right when he said, at the beginning of
January, that Charles's top priority was to separate the English and the
Scots. At all stages, the terms Charles offered Bedford and Pym were
ones which would have the effect of detaching them from their Scottish
allies. The Venetian Ambassador prophesied 'that every attempt to
separate them will prove vain, and that is the only stroke with which his
Majesty aspires to conquer the hydra of so many troublesome sedi-
tions'.[50] This was a correct prophecy, but by the end of February the
Scots felt it had been too close a call for comfort.

If this was the dominant issue, it is here that the chronology should be
scanned most closely. In the relations with the Scots, Charles's forced
concession on the incendiaries on 30 December is perhaps what first
made him think he needed new allies, and Bristol's success in avoiding a
breach at the conference of 12 January, on Scottish losses, what convinced Charles he had to negotiate seriously. Charles had, after all, been
brought low by an alliance of his English and Scottish opponents, and it
is possible to see his policy for the whole of the rest of his life as
dominated by the need to separate the English and the Scots by
whatever means came next to hand. Even at the height of the settlement
negotiations, Charles never put all his eggs in one basket, since he was
continuing throughout the period to negotiate through the Queen for a
papal loan sufficient to enable him to raise an army without Parliamentary assistance. This need not indicate that he was insincere in the
negotiations. It seems to be the same technique he had used with the

[47] See Dorset RO Bankes MSS vol. L, pp. 1, 13, 38 and other refs.
[48] *His Majesties Declaration* (1640), BL E. 203(1), pp. 13–14.
[49] PRO 31/3/72, pp. 359–60.
[50] *CSP Ven. 1640–2*, p. 111.

Covenanters in 1638–9, over the Irish army, or the plan to import Spanish veterans.[51] It was a negotiation by carrot and stick, in which the rewards for compliance and the threats for non-compliance might both be held out at the same time. There is no definite proof that Pym and Bedford knew of these papal negotiations, but if they did, the fact might provide an explanation of the strong line they took about papists during the negotiations.

Such tentative indications as we have suggest that at first, Bedford and at least some of his group would have been prepared to go along with the proposals for reformation of episcopacy with which Ussher and Williams Bishop of Lincoln became associated, but it must be admitted that the indications are extremely tentative, and that a number of members of the group, such as Hampden and Fiennes, are likely to have been exceptions. On 9 November 1640 the motion for Williams's release from the Tower was moved by Pym's step-brother Francis Rous, who by instinct was probably one of the most anti-episcopal members of the group.[52] On 23 January a petition for Lambert Osbaldeston, who had been sent to the Tower with Williams, was presented to the Lords by Bedford.[53] With these small indications should perhaps go the fact that Ussher had probably been brought to his existing position lecturing in Covent Garden by the influence of Bedford.

It is perhaps a better reason for this view that the surviving blueprints from the Ussher group were prepared to go very far indeed, and in particular that one of them, bearing the signatures of Ussher and Holdsworth, has a series of marginalia trying to indicate its compatibility with ecclesiastical arrangements in Scotland.[54] Ussher's proposals came from a clear line of descent which went back to Reynolds's proposals at the Hampton Court Conference, through Reynolds to his tutor Richard Hooker, and from him perhaps to Archbishop Grindal

[51] Hibbard, pp. 168, 179; *CSP Ven. 1640–2*, pp. 117–18. I am grateful to Prof. Caroline Hibbard for several helpful discussions of the papal loan, on which it is to be hoped she may publish further. For the parallels, see above, pp. 79–80.

[52] Holland, vol. i, fo. 13ʳ; D'Ewes (N.), p. 19. For Williams's addresses to the Parliamentary leaders, see Manchester MS 32/5/15 and Bodl. MS Tanner 88*, fo. 205. For Hampden's rejection of his advances in the spring, see PRO SP 16/453/24. The contrast between Hampden's reaction in Apr. and Rous's in Nov. is instructive.

[53] BL Harl. MS 6424, fo. 8ʳ.

[54] James Ussher, *Reduction of Episcopacie unto the Forme of Synodical Government received in the Ancient Church* (1656), Wing 216, repr. in *Whole Works of the Most Rev. James Ussher, D.D.* (Dublin, 1864), xii. 527–36. The text in the *Whole Works* omits the marginalia designed to prove conformity with Scotland. Nathaniel Bernard, in the Epistle to the copy in BL E. 897(1), confirms that these marginalia are authentic, but says Ussher wanted them omitted from any published version. On the provenance, see *Whole Works*, i. 209–12. See also *Original of Bishops and Metropolitans* (1641), in *Whole Works*, vii. 42–71.

and Lord Keeper Nicholas Bacon.[55] The central principle of this approach was to apply to bishops all the well-known principles about the need for counsel which conventional political theory applied to monarchs. The immediate result was to narrow the supposed gulf of principle between government by synods and government by bishops almost to vanishing-point. As Ussher summarized his proposals to the Prince of Orange's chaplain:

de droit divin les évesques et tous autres pasteurs sont d'un mesme ordre et ne doivent rien faire d'important que par conseil commun; que leur superiorité, que la coustume d'eglise leur a donné, n'a de difference avec les presidens de nos synodes, sinon que ceux-ci changent et les autres demeurent tousjours presidens; qu'il les faut regler aux synodes et astreindre a prendre conseil des autres pasteurs, leur oster la haute-commission, et les assubjetir aux censures.[56]

It was a brilliant attempt at squaring the circle, though it was perhaps to be expected that Charles should regard it as reducing bishops to ciphers, and that Henderson should regard the little matter of a permanent president as the crack in the door that let in the principle of popery. As Ussher and Holdsworth outlined the scheme, it allowed room for the participation of elders in the administration of discipline. The fourth Council of Carthage was invoked in support of the principle that bishops' judgements given without the counsel of their clergy were void. Parochial government in this conciliar form was compared to Scottish kirk sessions. Monthly synods, to be presided over by suffragan bishops and entrusted with the power of excommunication, were compared to Scottish Presbyteries. Diocesan synods, voting by majority, were to be created to parallel Scottish provincial synods, and a national synod was to be created to parallel the Scottish General Assembly. Only in the refusal to admit laymen does this proposal fall substantially short of Scottish practice.[57] The effort put into the attempt to prove that this was compatible with Scottish practice suggests strongly that this scheme was not ostensibly designed, as Charles wished, to 'clear them away presently', but rather to pay at least lip-service to Scottish desires for uniformity between the kingdoms. That would suggest that Ussher was at first working to meet the needs of Pym and Bedford, as much as to meet those of Charles.

We may gain some hint of how an Ussher-type settlement might have

[55] Ussher, *Judgement of Doctor Rainoldes touching the Originall of Episcopacy* (1641), in id., *Whole Works*, vii. 73–85; P. Collinson, 'Jacobean Religious Settlement', in Howard Tomlinson (ed.), *Before the English Civil War* (1983), 41–2; Richard Hooker, *Laws of Ecclesiastical Polity*, bk. VIII *passim*; P. Collinson, *Elizabethan Puritan Movement* (1966), 181–4. It is perhaps in this context, among others, that we should see Williams's proposal of July for the reviving of the *Reformatio Legum Ecclesiasticarum*: Gardiner, *Documents*, p. 179.
[56] Groen van Prinsterer, p. 440.
[57] Ussher, *Reduction of Episcopacie*, pp. 1–8.

been administered from a printed version of some of the conclusions of
Williams's committee on religion, set up by the Lords on 1 March.
These particular conclusions, which may be those reached at the meeting of 9 April, were published under the names of Ussher, Williams,
Prideaux, Ward, Brownrigg, Featly, and Hacket. The first section, on
matters of doctrine, disposes of some of Brownrigg's bugbears during
his Cambridge Vice-Chancellorship, such as confession and prayer for
the dead, upholds the authority of the Books of Homilies, and con-
centrates with overwhelming force on the condemnation of Arminianism: 'some have defended the whole grosse substance of Arminianisme,
that *electio est ex fide praevisa*, that the act of conversion depends on the
concurrence of man's free will, that the justified man may fall finally and
totally from grace'.[58] For Pym, something on these lines would have
been essential, and it left very little prospect that Charles could succeed,
as he had hoped on 21 January, in having Juxon as Archbishop of York
and Pym as Chancellor of the Exchequer, both at the same time.

The list of innovations in discipline was equally far-reaching: it condemned turning the table altarwise and calling it an altar, bowing to the
altar and to the east, candlesticks on the altar, compelling communi-
cants to come to the rails, crucifixes and images on the altar cloth '(so-
called)', and the suppressing of lectures by combination. For good
measure, the report maintained, in true Parliamentarian style, that
Elizabeth's Injunctions, which had no Parliamentary authority, had no
binding force, but were only a commentary. These and many similar
proposals covered most of the things Pym and his fellows might abolish
bishops to obtain, and if they were to gain secure possession of these
things within an episcopal system, many of them might well feel no need
to abolish episcopacy. Their problem, if they were to adopt this line,
would be one of security: could they trust true religion, defined in this
manner, to the power of bishops whom Charles would continue to
appoint?

Williams's bill for the better regulating of Archbishops and Bishops
was not made public until July, but it may be used to indicate the
criticisms of the past few months against which Williams thought episcopacy needed to be defended. The key point of that bill was to take
sole power of appointing bishops out of the King's hands. The bill
proposed, along lines following Ussher's *Reduction*, that the initial
power should revert, in true canonical style, to the Deans and Chapters.
They were to choose three names, out of whom the King was to select

---

[58] *Copie of the Proceedings of Some Worthy and Learned Divines, appointed by the Lords to meet
at the Bishop of Lincolns in Westminster* (1641), 1–4. The conclusion on Arminianism is item 13 in
the section on doctrine. This was almost certainly a pirate printing, possibly leaked in the hope of
reassuring the Scots. For the possible occasion of the meeting, see BL Harl. MS 6424, fo. 54ʳ.

one. In other words, Williams perceived it as the key objection to bishops that Charles appointed them. In England, as in Scotland, episcopacy was becoming a symbolic issue for testing the limits of royal control over the church.[59]

Two points were particularly stressed in the Commons in the early days of negotiations on the settlement. One was the need to secure the church from idolatry: on 22 January Sir Henry Mildmay, who may well have been privy to some of the negotiations, moved that the Commons should appoint commissioners to see that images and idols were 'utterly taken away'.[60] The other point they threatened to insist on was the removal of bishops from the House of Lords. On 2 January Sir Henry Anderson and Denzil Holles moved that the words 'Lords Spiritual and Temporal' be deleted from the enacting clause of the subsidy bill. Sir John Strangeways 'moved it might goe as it usuallie had done'. Pym, revealing an agenda, stilled the dispute by saying 'hee hoped that wee should have further time to dispute touching the spirituall lordes to better purpose'.[61] With these demands came demands for the abolition of the High Commission, and perhaps also of the Star Chamber, the latter apparently a late-comer to the list of demands.[62] The abolition of the High Commission Charles might be expected to resist as he had done in Scotland and was later to do in Ireland. The object of the reforms was so blatantly to prevent him from governing the church as he saw fit without Parliamentary sanction that he was almost bound to grow resistant as the proposals grew clearer. If Pym and his allies were only prepared to keep episcopacy at this sort of price, Charles might well conclude that the price was tantamount to abolition. The use of bishops to secure royal control over the church, which was in Charles's eyes their central function, was not intended to survive, whether the name did or not.

To win concessions of this magnitude, Bedford's group would have to offer a very substantial price, and the financial form was the obvious one in which to pay it. The centrepiece of the Pym–Bedford financial proposals was the scheme, mentioned by Whistler on 14 December, for reviving the Great Contract of 1610. Until August it was only the part of the Contract relating to wardship which was under consideration. The scheme is outlined in an undated memorandum in Bedford's papers,

[59] Gardiner, *Documents*, pp. 172–3; MP, 1 July 1641. There is a breviate of the bill in PRO SP 16/482/1. The provenance of the bill is suggested by the clause exempting the Dean of Westminster from the ban on secular jurisdiction.

[60] D'Ewes (N.), p. 270.

[61] Ibid. 209.

[62] Baillie, i. 280; *LJ* iv. 124; D'Ewes (N.), p. 244; Clarendon, *History*, i. 201.

entitled 'the proiect upon the wardes'.[63] The key to this was the proposal to transform tenures in knight service, liable to wardship, into tenures in fee farm, paying an annual rent and an entry fine to mark the beginning of the tenure. The combination of the rent and the entry fine allowed those handling the proposal to raise both income and capital, and to vary the proportions between the two to meet the needs of the moment at which the bargain was finally struck. The drafter assumed, building on foundations laid by Robert Cecil, that land was always worth ten times its old rent, but might in some cases be worth twenty times its old rent. One might imagine, if this scheme were implemented, that a flood of petitions to have land valued at the lower figure would provide opportunities to show favour to those to whom it was expedient to do so. The author of the document proposed to fix the proportions to raise an annual income of £48,000, and a capital sum of £239,000. The scheme would thus provide, as the settlement of 1661–2 did not, for paying the King's debts, and starting the new financial system with a clean slate.

This proposal was discussed, and did not remain a mere blueprint. We possess an undated draft for a reply to it, in Edward Nicholas's foul hand.[64] Nicholas was passionately opposed to this proposal, and his first objection is that the abolition of tenures by knight service would take the militia out of the King's hands. He had clearly not been convinced by the arguments he recorded during the Council meeting of 15 January, in favour of basing the militia on statute. He claimed, by implication, that the proposal was void as contrary to fundamental law: 'whereas the Lords and Commons in Parliament cannot assent to any thing that tends to ye disinherison of ye K. and his crowne, to wh. they are sworne.' It appears that the view that a Parliament had sovereign power to enact what it would was still far short of converting everyone in England. He played the anti-Puritan card, claiming that 'all persons will breed their relations, being wards, as they please, in heresies, schisms, etc', and, most unhistorically, that this proposal had been 'attempted first by a sort of phanaticks in ye beginning of K. James'.[65] Above all, Nicholas did not trust Parliaments enough to depend on them for regular income: 'being changed for a landtaxe, yt very taxe will be a grievance, and in another Parliament may be taken away, and so ye K. loose all'. Alternatively, he feared, the King might be induced to sell

[63] Bedford MSS, Fourth Earl, Miscellaneous Papers, 'The Proiect upon the Wardes'. The hand is not certainly identified, but is perhaps that of a clerk in Bedford's employment.
[64] PRO SP 16/487/35.
[65] See N. R. N. Tyacke, 'Sir Robert Wroth and the Parliament of 1604', *BIHR* 50 (1977), 120–5. Tyacke's argument apart, the man whose wife received the dedication of Ben Jonson's *The Alchemist* must be an unlikely candidate for the title of 'phanatick'. This passage seems to suggest that the partisan rewriting of English history was already under way before the Civil War broke out.

the whole Crown, and so they could make what kind of king they pleased, and dispose of the whole prerogative by Parliament. The Parliamentary record since 1610 did rather more to justify the first fear than to justify the second. Until the King and his allies were convinced that Parliaments had more financial literacy than they had yet shown, they were bound to feel anxiety about any proposal to depend on them for their daily bread.

There is one other clue to the terms of the proposed settlement in this document. Nicholas refers to possibilities 'if ye k. consents to exchange it for ye Excise'. That Bedford had a proposal for an excise has hitherto been known only through Clarendon, who claimed to know it of his own knowledge.[66] Clarendon's authority, by itself, is not sufficient, but Nicholas's use of the definite article suggests that, in this particular, he may have been right. If so, it was a very substantial addition to royal revenue, and filled what continental comparisons suggested was the major gap in the King's sources of income. On the other hand, as Pym was to find when he did introduce an excise in 1643, it was a matter of some political difficulty to get the Commons to agree to it. This may be why the proposal stayed under cover during what remained preliminary negotiations with the King.

The next major financial proposal on offer risked facing the opposite difficulty: it would have to rest on presumed support in the Commons to override the bitter hostility of the King. This was the proposal to take over the lands of Deans and Chapters as a permanent addition to the King's landed endowment. The proposal had obvious precedents, and D'Ewes, on one occasion, described the Deans and Chapters as the 'new abbies'.[67] The proposal is again outlined in a memorandum in Bedford's papers, 'the proiect upon the clergie and Colledges'.[68] This again rested on the assumption that the land was undervalued, and that the under-valuing was in all places such as to justify a tenfold increase, and in some to justify a twentyfold increase. The memorandum assumed a likely income of £120,000 per annum, and entry fines of £420,000. The profit was to be made at the expense of the tenant. The proposal encountered another vigorous rebuttal from Edward Nicholas, who viewed the pro-posal with considerable alarm, since he and his father were Dean and Chapter tenants.[69] He argued that it was unjust to punish the tenants for the default of their landlords, and also suggested that the market would

[66] Clarendon, *History*, i. 254.
[67] D'Ewes (C.), p. 313.
[68] Bedford MSS, Fourth Earl, Miscellaneous Papers, 'The Proiect upon the Clergie and Col-ledges'. For a later version of the scheme, see MP, 11 May 1641.
[69] PRO SP 16/470/112 (undated, after 12 May 1641). See ibid. 16/482/96 for Nicholas's complaint that he and his father would lose £1,500 in the value of their estates by the passage of what he there calls the Deans and Chapters Bill (29 July 1641).

be spoilt by the sense of many prospective purchasers that it was sacrilegious to buy lands given to sacred uses.

This proposal ran into a good deal more opposition than Pym and his colleagues foresaw. It remained on the table after the settlement negotiations were over, partly as a measure to help in paying the armies, and partly as an adjunct to the Root and Branch Bill. The longer it stayed before the House, the more opposition it seemed to draw. Cornelius Burges, the spiritual heir of Hugh Latimer, argued that it would be sacrilege to divert the money to civil uses.[70] A large part of the resistance seems to have been prompted by the Universities, whose influence in the Commons should not be underrated. A petition from Cambridge, read on 12 May, argued that they should spare cathedral Chapters, lest the loss of preferments should lead to the decay of learning. Vice-Chancellor Holdsworth, preaching at the summer commencement, preached 'the funeral sermon of learning'.[71] When the proposal was debated in the Commons on 26 March, the godly members were out in force, and D'Ewes, Reynolds, Sir Edmund Moundeford, Prideaux, and Fiennes spoke in favour of the proposal. D'Ewes names only Falkland and Culpepper on the other side, but says that 'most for them, that they might not be utterly abolished'.[72] Later, probably on 15 June, Rudyerd pointed out that the proposal was inconsistent with Ussher's proposals for limited episcopacy, and that those who thought bishops 'too absolute, too singular' needed Deans and Chapters as a check on them. He warned against financial optimism by telling a story to the effect that abbey lands under Henry VIII had been used to start a rumour that people would never pay subsidies again, and 'this was plausible both to court and country'. He joined in the expressions of anxiety about the decay of learning, saying that if there were no preferment outside Colleges, scholars would 'live and die as in cells'.[73] The proposal was last heard as a clause in the Grand Remonstrance, but 'in conclusion the episcopall partie were soe strong in the House as wee were faint to lay aside this clause also'.[74] As yet, most of this was in the future, but it suggests a potential for resistance too big to allow Pym and his allies to carry a proposal intolerable to the King.

There were numerous other minor proposals, including the usual ones for raising money from delinquents. It was hoped that it would be possible to recover the arrears of recusant forfeitures all the way back to 1617.[75] The draining of the fens, in which Bedford was deeply involved,

[70] BL Harl. MS 163, fos. 106ᵃ and 169ᵇ.
[71] Bodl. MS Nalson II fo. 2; DO, vol. ii, fo. 58ʳ.
[72] BL Harl. MS 164, fo. 145ᵇ.
[73] Yale University, Beinecke Library, Osborn Collection b. 297, fos. 60–1.
[74] D'Ewes (C.), p. 151.
[75] BL Sloane MS 3317, fo. 22ᵛ.

was recommended as a way of gaining the King a bigger landed endowment.[76] Apart from the excise, the biggest proposals were those concerning the customs, first hinted at by Pym on 27 November. It is in their treatment of the customs that Pym and his allies most clearly showed their determination to buy power, to grant the King large sums of public money while ruthlessly keeping control of it themselves. When the proposal first surfaced in public on 18 March, it was a proposal for a new bill for Tonnage and Poundage, to be granted for three years, and to be assessed on a new book of rates to be prepared by the House.[77] When the bill ultimately came, it reversed the judgement in Bate's Case, and thereby deprived the King of the right to raise any customs duties save the trivial Ancient Custom without Parliamentary consent.[78]

In the process, the bill made it necessary to prepare a new Book of Rates, since all recent Books of Rates, by which goods were valued for customs, had double-column entries for what they should be assessed at for custom, and what they should be assessed at for imposition.[79] A new Book of Rates would have to provide up-to-date valuations for customs, to prevent the King from suffering a serious net loss of revenue by the loss of impositions.[80] If the customs were to be used to increase royal revenues, valuations would have to be increased, as in the event they were, over and above the valuations of the Book of Rates of 1635. The price of this apparent generosity was the principle, offensive to both King and Queen, of the three-year grant.[81] Taken in conjunction with the Triennial Act, this means that the King's right to his customs would expire every time a new Parliament was due, and therefore it might be hoped that a failure to call another Parliament when it was due would be punished by the immediate loss of his biggest single item of revenue.

The difficulty in this scheme was that of ensuring that customs should cease to be collected when they were no longer legally due. Charles's relationship with his customs farmers had been generally good, and

---

[76] Huntingdon RO, Manchester MS 16/57/4.

[77] CJ ii. 107; DO, vol. i, fo. 63ʳ.

[78] Gardiner, Documents, pp. 159–62.

[79] See Rupert C. Jarvis, 'Books of Rates', Journal of the Society of Archivists, 5/8 (1977), 515–26; H. S. Cobb, 'Books of Rates and London Customs 1507–1550', Guildhall Miscellany, 4 (1971–3), 1–12. I am grateful to Dr Cobb for much helpful advice on Books of Rates. See Rates of Merchandizes (1610) (STC 7692–3); (1623) (STC 7694); (1635) (STC 7695); (1642) (Wing E 920). These books clearly demonstrate the impossibility of abolishing impositions without a new Book of Rates. They also show that the 1642 Book kept up all the increases of the 1635 Book, and added significantly to them. The final version was produced by Sir Robert Pye, John Harrison, Thomas Hoyle, Giles Green, Samuel Vassall, and John Rolle. The names are listed on the flyleaf of the Guildhall copy. I am grateful to Dr N. M. Fuidge for transcribing this list.

[80] On the success of the 1642 Book of Rates, see C. G. Chandaman, English Public Revenue 1660–1688 (Oxford, 1975), 11–14 and nn.

[81] BL Harl. MS 477, fo. 42ᵛ; DO, vol. i, fo. 63ʳ; BL Harl. MS 6424, fo. 74ᵛ; LJ iv. 554; Letters of Queen Henrietta Maria, pp. 53, 69.

after 1629, for example, the farmers had shown no inhibition about collecting customs the Parliament believed not to be legally due. The response of Pym's group to this danger was to form a plan to secure physical control of customs administration for themselves. This was to be ensured by granting Tonnage and Poundage, not to the King, but to commissioners for his use. This somewhat startling proposal was at first justified on the innocuous ground that the money had to be appropriated to the urgent task of paying off the armies, for which the commissioners were to be responsible, and to which their credit was to lend assistance. The leading figure among the proposed commissioners, Sir John Harrison, was an existing customs farmer, who tells us that he was acting in conjunction with his 'great and noble friend' the Earl of Bedford.[82] The justification of the principle was innocuous, but the duel fought over it during the summer, when Culpepper was its main opponent, suggests that more was at stake than met the eye.[83]

There is more evidence in favour of such an interpretation. Already on 29 December Pym had stopped all Charles's assignments of Tonnage and Poundage, and brought its administration under Parliamentary control. On this occasion, the House reversed its decision the next day, on the ground that it appeared to confer legal recognition on impositions, but the principle had been stated.[84] A succession of votes to investigate the customers on charges of delinquency were another method of ensuring their compliance. An anonymous memorandum in the Manchester manuscripts, probably dated between March and June 1641, discussed the customs in the context of proposals to confer places on 'persons well affected', and argued that it would be a good opportunity to dismiss persons 'ill affected' from the customs administration, especially in the Port of London. The memorandum argued that this would give them intelligence on preparations by foreign powers, and on the movement of suspected persons.[85] The suggestion that the group were concerned with gaining control of the collectorships as well as the farm is supported by a letter from Francis Rous to Pym, petitioning for the collectorship of Dartmouth.[86] The two plans together would give Pym and his friends a stranglehold on the customs administration, and therefore the power to bankrupt Charles whenever he failed to face his next Parliament. All these proposals were likely to be very difficult to

---

[82] D'Ewes (N.), p. 503; BL Harl. MS 162, fo. 377[a]; BL Harl. MS 477, fo. 42[v]; MP, 7 May 1641; BL Stowe MS 325, fo. 73[r].

[83] BL Harl. MS 163, fo. 716[b], and other refs.; see below, pp. 346–50.

[84] D'Ewes (N.), pp. 193–4, 197–9; CSP Ven. 1640–2, p. 112.

[85] Huntingdon RO, Manchester MSS 32/5/27. Sir John Nulls the customs farmer was Saye's son-in-law. I would like to thank Dr J. S. A. Adamson for this information.

[86] C. J. Sawyer and Co., Catalogue no. 155 (Jan. 1940), item 155. I am grateful to Messrs Sawyer's for permission to quote from their catalogue. I have not found the original of this letter, which comes from Pym's personal collection.

implement, as the House of Commons reminded them on 17 February, when a proposal to raise the rate of the subsidies was 'utterly disliked', but at least there was enough here to be worth talking about.[87]

The issue which first threatened to wreck the negotiations was not any of these but the issue of the persecution of recusants. The King, on the same day as his speech of 23 January, put this issue into the centre of the stage by granting a reprieve to a priest called John Goodman.[88] This was not merely a foolish aberration by Charles: it was the deliberate raising of a test case. Charles had no particular liking for popery, but he had that sort of concern that life should not be made impossible for them that many of his Council were prepared to show for Southwark separatists or New Englanders. He was prepared to disarm them, or to banish them from London, but he was not prepared to make England a place where a peaceable Catholic could not live in physical safety. The case of Goodman was a useful test case for this principle: he was not charged with winning converts, but simply with being a priest, and had been living quietly as chaplain to an exiled former French minister. Moreover, there was one particular Catholic whose safety was of special concern to the King. The Queen viewed the attitude of the Parliament to Catholics with some alarm, and Baillie said it 'puts no small discontent and feare to her stomach'.[89] She had no particular objection to the schemes for settlement, since, unlike her husband, she did not care about the difference between one sort of heretic and another. She was quite ready to further the schemes, but only provided she was assured of her own physical safety, and it was she who referred the case of Goodman to the King.

The Queen was entitled to her fears. There had been a considerable volume of protest about Charles's marriage, both before and since it had been made, and many of the godly had remained deeply alarmed about the presence of a Delilah so near the throne ever since. The Herefordshire draft for the Ministers' Remonstrance, among many others, began by proposing that the Queen be 'delivered' from all papists and that the King should be made to 'humble himself' for his presumptuous marriage. The text quoted for this view was Nehemiah 13: 25–6, which is an account of how 'outlandish women' caused Solomon to sin.[90] Here many of the images of popery came together, and the notion that its idolatrous tendencies were 'seductive' could be given a dangerously literal interpretation.[91] The Queen naturally felt some apprehension at the thought of power falling into the hands of people who thought in

---

[87] D'Ewes (N.), p. 368.
[88] Gardiner, *History*, ix. 264–5; Hibbard, pp. 182–3.
[89] Baillie, i. 295.
[90] BL Loan MS 29/172, fo. 363ʳ.
[91] Robin Clifton, 'Fear of Popery', in *Origins*, pp. 146–9.

this way. The prophet, in the text quoted in the Herefordshire remonstrance, had torn out the hair of the outlandish women who were married to Israelites, and Phinehas' treatment of the daughters of Moab, praised from the Long Parliament pulpit by Stephen Marshall, had been worse.[92] The Queen was entitled to want assurance that those who were admitted to power would treat her, not as an Israelite with a Moabite, but as gentlemen with a lady. When not sufficiently reassured on this point, the Queen started rumours that she was going to go to France. This was, no doubt, in part a negotiating tactic, designed, as the French Ambassador suggested, to raise some jealousy in the Parliament.[93] It was probably also designed to create the same effect in her husband, but it is probable that there was a genuine fear behind it as well.

If the Goodman case inspired these jealousies in the Queen, it inspired others in the Commons, and not only among the godly members. Those who joined in the outcry included Sir Francis Seymour. The only dissentient voice was Trelawny, who feared execution might 'exasperate' the Irish army. He was the only member of the Commons who pointed out that the treatment of Catholics might have implications for Charles's third kingdom, but there was an Irish Parliamentary committee in London, which was capable of making the point to Charles itself. The fears raised by the case of Goodman were the same raised by the King's continued refusal to disband the Irish army, by the reports of a Welsh popish army commanded by the Earl of Worcester, and by the continued presence of Rossetti the papal nuncio at court. The fears the case released included the fear of an armed attempt by the King to reverse the changes of the past few months, and for that reason, was always linked with demands for the disarming of papists. In addition, it drew on the providential theory of politics, documented all over the Old Testament, according to which toleration of sin was itself a sin, and liable to call down divine vengeance. It drew also on the fears, to which any proposed afforced council were liable, that the King might rely on advice from secret, rather than sworn councillors. For this reason, it was linked with demands for the banishment of Wat Montague, Kenelm Digby, Toby Mathew, and the Queen's secretary Sir John Winter from court.[94] It served to underline the basic point that Digby and Winter were both sons of Gunpowder Plotters. Just to underline the point that the basic godly objective was the eradication of sin, not liberty for error, D'Ewes picked this week to argue that 'the verie Inquisition of Spaine had a good couler in the first institution; being only intended against

---

[92] Stephen Marshall, *Reformation and Desolation* (1642), 40.
[93] PRO 31/3/72, pp. 416, 423, and other refs.
[94] D'Ewes (N.), pp. 286–92, 301; Rushworth, *Collections*, III. i. 158.

Moors and Jews'.[95] It had gone wrong only when it was used for the ruin of 'godly Protestants'. The Goodman case also produced vehement discontent among some in the City, expressed in Penington's threat to withhold loans to pay the armies, and fears about the possible content of a settlement may help to explain the timing of a flood of Root and Branch petitions, Kent on 13 January, Essex on the 14th, and Hertfordshire, Bedfordshire, and Cambridgeshire among others on the 25th. The presentation of the Ministers' Remonstrance, on the same day as the King's speech and the reprieve of Goodman, probably heightened the tension. If Pym and Bedford were to accept the proffered settlement, it was not only the Scots who would feel sold out by it. The King remained cool in the face of this agitation, and even selected this week for two significant conciliatory gestures. On 29 January he gave the post of Solicitor-General, vacant by the preferments following the flight of Finch, to Oliver St John. St John later gave the credit to Hamilton for his preferment.[96] Since Hamilton was negotiating to marry his son to Bedford's daughter, this appears credible.[97] It is not possible to be certain whether this was a unique offer, or whether, as is perhaps more probable, it was one of a round of offers of which only this one was accepted. If so, it would perhaps be significant that the man who accepted office was the most anti-Scottish member of the circle around Pym and Bedford.[98] The other conciliatory gesture, the next day, was towards Abbot's old chaplain Daniel Featly, who was invited to preach at court on 14 April in the place of Lawrence, who was sick, and to wait at court in May in the place of Gilbert Sheldon, who was excused. In the case of so extreme a hard-liner as Gilbert Sheldon, it is possible to wonder whether he had been manipulated out of the way.[99]

Meanwhile, backstairs negotiation was in progress. On 2 February Sir John Coke said he had heard from the 'popish party' that Bedford, Saye, and Pym had attended the Queen in private, and 'if these men come in by the Queen's side there is art enough somewhere'.[100] Some hint of what they had been discussing perhaps emerges from the King's speech to the House of Lords on 3 February. He said he had no wish for popery to increase, and in future he would execute the laws against priests and Jesuits. He said that Rossetti the papal nuncio had no commission but to the Queen, but he had 'persuaded' her that he should leave within a 'convenient time'. On the case of Goodman, he remitted the case to both the Houses, while warning them of the poss-

[95] D'Ewes (N.), p. 288.
[96] Hamilton MS 1657 (St John to Hamilton, 2 June 1642).
[97] Donald, p. 422; SRO GD 112/40/2/3/139.
[98] See above, p. 166.
[99] PRO LC 5/134, p. 435.
[100] HMC Twelfth Report III. 272.

ible consequences for Protestants abroad should he be executed.[101] The next day, he presented a petition he had received from Goodman, asking that, like Jonah, he should be cast overboard to still the tempest.[102] The next day, the Queen followed this up with a conciliatory message delivered by Sir Thomas Jermyn to the Commons. She said she would use her best endeavours for a good understanding between the King and the Parliament, and that she had helped the Twelve Peers who petitioned for a Parliament. She said that Rossetti would go, and that her attempt to raise a contribution from the Catholics for the Bishops' Wars (a matter of bitter complaint in the Commons) was the result of her ignorance of English law. She asked the Parliament to look forward and not back, and she would repay it with all her power.

It was a brave effort, even though it may have cost the Queen some equivocation, but the Commons did not know what to make of it, and when Jermyn finished reading his paper, there was a 'general silence'. At last Sir Hugh Cholemely moved that they should return thanks, 'but none saied well moved, or gave any great approbation to it'. D'Ewes was distressed at this neglect, but the resulting antiquarian discourse, to the effect that Queens were in law *femes soles*, and therefore they should receive this message as from a Queen in her widowhood, was hardly a courtly production. At last thanks were returned on the motion of the Speaker.[103]

By 6 February the leading men of the Parliament had had time to consult with each other, and decide that they were satisfied on the issue of Goodman. When Penington complained that he would not be satisfied unless Goodman were executed, the House directed the Speaker to write to the Lord Mayor to say that both Houses were fully satisfied. Goodman died in prison in 1645. Those satisfied appear to have included William Strode, one of the bitterest members of the group around Pym, and one of those least likely to agree to the King's suggested compromise. He was probably aiming at Penington in words, for which the House cleared him, about the sons of Zeruiah, who had been in trouble for insisting that David should execute Shimei.[104]

One issue had been smoothed over, but the issue disposed of was only that of Goodman himself, not the tensions his case symbolized. Demands for the disbandment of the Irish and Welsh popish armies, and for the banishment of the four papists about the Queen, and for the disarming of papists, continued unabated. When Hotham raised the four papists on 13 February, he added a proposal for the banishing of

[101] *LJ* iv. 151; Rushworth, *Collections*, III. i. 165–6; see Larkin, pp. 739–42.
[102] MP, 4 Feb. 1641.
[103] *Two Diaries*, p. 82; D'Ewes (N.), pp. 324–5; *CJ* ii. 78 is an excellent example of minutes which conceal more than they reveal.
[104] D'Ewes (N.), pp. 333–4; *CJ* ii. 80. For the sons of Zeruiah, see 2 Sam. 17: 9–12.

Scottish papists, which raises the suspicion that he may have been in communication with the Scottish commissioners.[105] Sir John Culpepper, in his speech in favour of the Irish army on 11 February, cleared his Protestant honour by adding a new demand, of which more was to be heard later, for the exclusion of popish Lords from the Upper House.[106]

The issue of money remained on the table, and on 9 and 10 February the Commons repeated their regular resolve to consider the King's revenue 'tomorrow'.[107] There was no sign of any compromise on the issue of Strafford, and when he asked for more time on 3 February, Saye, Mandeville, Brooke, Paget 'etc.' held the House in debate against it for two hours, and the proposal was only carried after a division.[108] On 16 February Pym for the Commons asked the Lords for haste on Strafford, adding ominously that 'when this trial is past, other counsels for the good of the king and kingdom may take place'.[109] In other words, there would be no progress on the settlement until the King gave way on Strafford. The Root and Branch debate on 8 and 9 February again suggested that settlement on that issue was still far off, and gave a stern reminder of the continuing power of the Scottish lobby in English politics.[110]

This depressing picture was suddenly changed by the King's assent to the Triennial Bill and the Subsidy Bill on 16 February. This, perhaps to the surprise of many of the participants, started a cycle of mutual exchange of favours which, for a few days, seemed likely to carry those who took part in it to a solution almost in spite of themselves. Immediately the Commons returned to their House, Holles moved for the second reading of the Queen's Jointure Bill, saying explicitly that this was 'to expresse some parte of our thankfulness'. The reading was interrupted by a message from the Lords asking the Commons to join in expressions of thanks, but was promptly resumed the next morning, and the bill was sent to committee. On the 16th, a committee on the Court of Wards was set up, possibly as a preliminary to a move to compound for wardship.[111] There was a sign of concession in the Lords on an even more significant issue, that of Strafford. A motion for him to

---

[105] Peyton, fo. 85 (D'Ewes (N.), p. 359 n). The man the Scots might have in mind could be Robert Maxwell, Earl of Nithsdale, who was talking of going to France and raising troops, with which he would return for the conquest of this country. The French Ambassador was probably right that he had vast designs lightly conceived, but in the light of the Queen's undoubted desire for French help, it was hard to be sure: PRO 31/3/72, pp. 434–5. See also PRO SO 3/12, fo. 127^v.

[106] D'Ewes (N.), p. 350.

[107] CJ ii. 81, 82.

[108] BL Harl. MS 6424, fo. 13^r; LJ iv. 150.

[109] BL Harl. MS 6424, fo. 21^v.

[110] See above, pp. 191–5.

[111] D'Ewes (N.), p. 365; CJ ii. 87. There is little suggestion that this committee concerned itself with any genuine feeling about abuses of wardship.

have more time was pushed to a division, but those who spoke for him included Bedford, Hertford, Saye, Savill, and Bristol, with Essex and Mandeville still against.[112] This was a significant staking of political credit by those who voted for the motion since, in the Commons, anger at proposals to give Strafford more time extended far enough across the spectrum to include Arthur Capel, whom the King was shortly to raise to the peerage as a potential ally.[113] On the 18th, the Lords sketched out a hint for a compromise by asking the Commons to join them in moving the King to sequester Strafford from his places. According to Diurnal Occurrences, this gave small satisfaction in the Commons, and it was there obscured in complaints about the time allowed to Strafford and about the proposal that he should be allowed counsel.[114] It was a discouraging response, but at least the Commons had not explicitly rejected it. A unilateral response by the King could have taken a lot of the wind out of the Commons' sails.

On the 19th, the King responded in a different way: he created seven new Privy Councillors, Bedford, Hertford, Essex, Saye, Mandeville, Savill, and Bristol. Bristol's preferment seems to be independent of the settlement negotiations, and should be seen rather as a reward for services rendered in the Scottish treaty. All the others were signatories of the Petition of the Twelve Peers, and their preferment should be seen as an earnest of good faith in the negotiations between that group and the King. The preferment did not signal that the negotiations were concluded: that would not happen until the group held the major offices, and therefore had their hands on the levers of power. It did indicate, however, that the mutual concessions since 16 February had breathed new life into the negotiations. Baillie and Temple agree in giving the prime responsibility to Hamilton, and Baillie is almost certainly right that the first motions for this preferment had been 'bittely rejected by the king, yet the Marqueis, by his wisdom, brought him unto it'. Temple was probably also right in ascribing a share of the responsibility to Jermyn.[115] It would be nice to know whether he was trying to do with Bedford, Saye, and Pym what he was trying to do with Leicester, and exact a bribe of £4,000 for his help in preferring them to major offices.[116] When the new Councillors arrived at the Board, they may

---

[112] Staffs. RO D 1778/1/i/14; *LJ* iv. 165; Baillie, i. 301–2. Baillie observed that 'those who were most for granting him bygone courtesies, will be his smallest friends when he comes to judgement'. This may be true, and doubtless represents what 'the good Lord Sey' was telling him, but this was a time in which politicians were manœuvring in symbols.

[113] D'Ewes (N.), p. 363.

[114] *LJ* iv. 168; DO, vol. i, fo. 46ʳ; D'Ewes (N.), p. 374. The Commons had no objection to sequestering Strafford: what gave them 'small satisfaction' was surely the hint of implied compromise.

[115] Baillie, i. 305; KAO De L'Isle and Dudley MSS C 114/12.

[116] KAO De L'Isle and Dudley MSS C 114/11.

have been a little deflated to find the King was not there. If so, they would have read the signals correctly. They succeeded in conciliating their followers by changing the Council day from Sunday to Monday, but the Council did not meet again till 1 March, and the frequency of its meetings dropped sharply thereafter. They had been given favour, but not yet power.[117]

In the continuing negotiations, there were three major unresolved issues, and a growing body of apprehension in the Commons and in the City. On 20 February the Commons were facing a renewed threat from the City to refuse to lend money. This threatened to deprive Pym of his freedom of manœuvre, by placing a veto, Fourth-Estate style, on any deal with the King that might be unacceptable to Penington and his allies. Pym, to Peyton's horror, proposed to deal with this threat by compelling the City to lend, a thoroughly arbitrary proposal which was opposed by Culpepper and Holles. Edward Baynton the younger proposed that he give satisfaction to the House for it. Strode, on the other hand, supported him, indicating that one of the most implacable men in Pym's group was still a party to the settlement negotiations.[118] Behind the refusal were the City godly, whose weight was likely to be thrown behind a series of godly bills, the bill abolishing superstition, the bill for clergy not to be JPs, the bill against pluralities, and a bill to prevent watermen from working on the sabbath.[119] There was also a considerable body of feeling in the Commons against any concession to Strafford, and on 18 February Arthur Goodwin and Henry Marten proposed that the Commons should adjourn in protest against the Lords' decision to grant extra time to Strafford.[120] It may here be important that Marten was a political pro-Scot, while the appearance of Arthur Goodwin might have alarmed Pym, since he was John Hampden's right-hand man. The risk that the settlement might divide the little group who were working for it was an acute one. There was also a risk, thanks to the level to which expectations had been raised, that they would be unable to carry their followers if they did make a settlement. The number involved would have been no more than a rump in the Commons, perhaps eighty members at the most, but it would have taken the gloss off a settlement designed to signal the full reuniting of the King and his people. This was

[117] PC Reg. xii. 100–1; Staffs RO D 1778/1/i/13. The Council met six times in the month from 19 Jan. to 19 Feb., and only three times in the next month. On 19 Mar. the new Councillors succeeded in winning the Scots exemption from the keeping of Lent: PC Reg. xii. 108. The order is signed by Hertford, Bedford, Essex, Bristol, Saye, and Vane. Only one old Councillor had attended the meeting.

[118] D'Ewes (N.), pp. 382–4; Peyton, fo. 85. Someone had induced Strode to reverse his position since 18 Feb.: D'Ewes (N.), p. 371 n. The appointment of the new Councillors might explain this reversal.

[119] CJ ii. 79, 94–5, 92, 93–4.

[120] D'Ewes (N.), p. 371.

not a difficulty which could be removed by further concessions from the
King. Even if that were an option, too much concession to Ussher and
Fealty and their allies could have had the effect of alienating people like
Hyde, Strangeways, and Digby. It was still possible to reunite the
country around a church led by John Williams, but the point of
equilibrium had become an extremely narrow one, and the unity it
could produce even more cosmetic than it had been under James.

Even if the negotiations had taken place in a vacuum, there remained
the issues of Strafford, of the Irish army and recusancy, and of Root and
Branch and the Scots. None of these were likely to be easily solved. On
the issue of Strafford, there was little progress. On 24 February, when
Strafford's answer to the charge was read, Mandeville moved that the
bishops might withdraw before it was debated. This was a long-standing
party demand, based on the doctrine that clergy should not give judgements of blood, and had first been mooted by St John in the Commons
back in November. On this occasion, it was supported by Arundel,
Manchester, Saye, Paget, Brooke, and others, a list which gave a
reminder that Strafford's enemies stretched beyond the limits of a
party.[121] The best hope for saving Strafford probably still rested on the
Lords' proposal of 18 February, for the King to sequester him from his
places, and this was a proposal to which both King and Commons had
still to react. The Scots' determination to see Strafford dead was likely to
be a further complication.

On the issue of the Irish army, the Lords came up with another
compromise on 19 February, after a debate in which Warner noticed
mainly the expressions of hostility to the Scots. The Lords proposed
that the new, and popish, Irish army be disbanded, and that 2,000 of
them be recruited to the old Irish army, in which they would be subject
to Protestant officers.[122] This satisfied all the King's legitimate interests
in keeping an Irish army, and also involved keeping quite as many
troops as he could afford. However, this proposal also was met by a
stony silence from both King and Commons. At least, though, even if
neither was happy with it, it was a proposal on which they might fall
back if they were to become determined to conclude a settlement for
other reasons.

On the issue of recusants, some progress was made. On 22 February
the new Councillors put their hands to a Proclamation embodying the
concessions the King had offered in his speech of 3 February. This
embodied the promise to banish all priests and Jesuits, and to execute

---

[121] BL Harl. MS 6424, fo. 39ʳ; Holland, vol. i, fo. 29ʳ, for St John's earlier offering of this
proposal in the Commons.
[122] BL Harl. MS 6424, fos. 23-4; *LJ* iv. 167. Anti-Scottish statements came from Berkshire,
Arundel, Dorset, and Bristol, and Warner records pro-Scottish sentiment only from Berkshire's son
Andover.

the laws against those who remained, but said nothing about Rossetti the papal nuncio.[123] It seems likely that that issue was waiting for the total conclusion of a settlement, and also for Charles's more complete success in 'persuading' his wife. The Proclamation embodied a protection for the Queen's priests, as guaranteed by the marriage treaty, but it does not seem to have satisfied the Queen, whose bitterest resistance to a settlement seems to be concentrated in this week. On 16 February a Scottish treaty paper, unconfirmed by D'Ewes or *Commons Journal*, reported that the Commons had resolved that no priest or papist should be admitted to the Queen, and no Mass was to be said in her court.[124] It was on 18 February, the day before the King appointed the new Privy Councillors, that the French Ambassador reported that she had sent Forster to France. Forster's message was a full-scale request for French assistance against the Parliament. This message received a dusty answer from Richelieu, who told her that whoever leaves the game loses it, and advised her to have a little patience, until the wheel of fortune changed again. This did not please the Queen, and her confessor reported that the Cardinal displeased her as much as the Parliament did.[125] It can only have heightened the tension about the Irish army that the Queen's reaction to Richelieu's refusal was to give out that she intended to go to Ireland.[126]

As always, the stick did not indicate absence of the carrot, and the Queen was still negotiating for terms on which she might fall in with the proposed settlement. Judging by the reaction of the Lords on 22 and 23 February, the crucial issue for the Queen seems to have been her ability to keep her own Catholic servants, for which her secretary Sir John Winter became a test case. Since the issue was one on which the King would not abandon the Queen, it became crucial to the whole settlement. The Lords joined with the Commons on the issues of disarming papists and banishing recusants from court, and on the Queen's servants, they tried the technique which had worked in the case of Goodman, of joining with the Commons while urging them not to exploit their victory. Holland and Dorset spoke to the Commons, both in favour of the Queen's rights by the marriage treaty, and to urge the case for having her served by Englishmen, answerable to English law, rather than by Frenchmen enjoying diplomatic immunity. The French Ambassador says they were joined by Bristol and by Bedford, and the *Lords' Journals* add the name of Hertford.[127]

If the French Ambassador is correct in including the name of Bed-

[123] Staffs. RO D 1778/1/i/14; Larkin, pp. 739–42.
[124] Hamilton MS M 9/119.
[125] PRO 31/3/72, pp. 456–60, 465.
[126] *CSP Ven. 1640–2*, p. 127.
[127] *LJ* iv. 167–70; PRO 31/3/72, pp. 467–8; D'Ewes (N.), pp. 392–3; *Two Diaries*, pp. 89–90.

ford, the issue had succeeded in splitting his group. This may be why it went underground for nearly a month, resurfacing in the Commons only on 15 March. When the issue emerged, the Queen's case was put by Digby and by her counsel Geoffrey Palmer. On the other side, Fiennes said there was no reason for the Queen to be incensed by their desire to have the laws put in execution, and Hampden argued simply that 'we sit here to see the laws observed, not broken'. St John, perhaps speaking *ex officio*, argued that by the Act of 1606, papists could be servants at court if they were licensed, and was surprisingly supported by Maynard. Gerrard, on the other side, argued that observing the law took priority over observing the marriage treaty.[128]

The issue of Winter came up again the next day on 16 March, when Strangeways pressed the case for concessions to the Queen in return for her help in persuading the King to call the Parliament and to pass the Triennial Bill. In reply, Pym, as reported by Moore, 'made a very excellent speech against it, and declared that we ought to obey God rather than man, and that if we doe not preferr God before man, he will refuse us, with many other good notions'. As reported by BL Harleian MS 1601, he said that 'the laws against papists founded on religion', presumably with the object of arguing that they were not dispensable, said that 'we ought not to forget our lawes though they may be forgotten in the treaty', and reminded the House that one of the statutes they were discussing was made after a great treason. This speech puts Pym firmly in the camp of those who opposed the final version of the settlement, and underlines the fact that he saw law, in the first instance, as a force for guaranteeing religion. He was supported by Rigby, and by Holles and Hampden, who produced the King's reply to the petition of religion in 1625, and the House resolved to insist on Winter's removal.[129] If the settlement had not already failed, this would have finally marked its end. It is true that Pym and Hampden had not come into the open with these feelings during February, but it is likely that they had held them in private, and in Pym's case, they are in line with all his previous Parliamentary career. It is religion which here impeded the settlement, and religion, not in the form of antipathy to bishops, but in the form of refusal to accept any sort of accommodation with popery. This resolute refusal was something a King with a popish wife could not come to terms with. If this is a fair guide to what had been going on in private for the previous month, it indicates enough division to explain why the issue remained under cover. It also shows the most pro-Scottish members of the group, and the strongest supporters of Root and Branch, as the Queen's sternest opponents.

[128] D'Ewes (N.), pp. 488–9; *Two Diaries*, pp. 20–1; BL Harl. MS 476, fo. 60^r, ibid. 1601, fo. 48^v.
[129] D'Ewes (N.), p. 493 nn.

The issue of Root and Branch sharply underlined the fact that one of the King's chief motives in preferring the new Privy Councillors was to induce them to break with the Scots. The King later said explicitly what was plain enough at the time, that one of his objects in preferring them was to induce them to abandon Root and Branch.[130] Baillie, for a little while, was afraid they would do so: 'incontinent, some of these new Councillors were found to plead for some delay to Strafford's processe, and to looke upon the Scottish affaires not altogether so pleasantly as they wont'. As a result, Baillie said, the Scottish commissioners were censured for advising Hamilton to prefer these men prematurely, though they denied having done so. It was perhaps to reassure the Scots that Pym brought forward the full articles against Laud. The trial of Laud had been persistently deferred, and, according to Baillie, they let him out 'as a pendicle at the Lieutenant's ear'.[131] This was because the King was conceding in Laud's case what he was refusing in Strafford's, and indicating that he would neither strive for his acquittal nor employ him further. Maurice Wynn on 9 March reported that Laud was ready to die, since the King did not now regard him.[132] As a result, the threat of proceedings in Laud's trial remained, right through to the Grand Remonstrance, a mere threat to be used as a whipping-boy to the King's conscience when his compliance was wanted on some other issue. It is possible, when Pym hurried the case forward on 22 February that he was concerned to exert leverage on the King, on Strafford, or on Root and Branch.[133] It is much more likely that he was engaged in a last-ditch attempt to head off the paper the Scots published on 24 February, demanding the death of Strafford and Root and Branch for England.[134]

This paper was designed to tell the Scots' English friends that they had to choose between the King and the Scots: it was designed to force 'our old friends, the new Councillors', to make a choice. It thus threatened the total collapse of the negotiations for settlement, which may help to explain the King's extreme rage against it. For a short while, Baillie feared that some, at least, of the new Councillors were going to go the wrong way, since they 'spake nothing for us'. Every Scottish comment indicates that the Scots' friends were at this point divided among themselves. Baillie says that some of their seeming friends turned countenance, and some of their true friends fainted for fear in the face of the reaction the King's clear lead had begun. Some of the most intelligent of their true friends, he said, indicated that the party for

---

[130] *ECR* E 241(1), pp. 517–18.
[131] Baillie, i. 305, 309.
[132] NLW Wynn of Gwydir MSS no. 1677.
[133] D'Ewes (N.), p. 388; *CJ* ii. 90, 91, 93.
[134] On the Scots' paper, see above, pp. 197–9.

bishops in the Lower House would soon be a majority.[135] This, perhaps, is better evidence on their own intentions than it is on Parliamentary psephology. The commissioners themselves reported that 'some of them are fallen in to have hand with the King'.[136] It is perhaps possible to extrapolate, very tentatively, from the line-up on the cases of Strafford and Winter to the likely line-up on the issue of Root and Branch and the Scots. There is no necessary reason why those negotiating for a settlement should have taken the same line on all the final list of disputed issues, but it is possible, both that some of them accepted or rejected the final settlement as a package, and that the same differences of belief and temperament that divided them on one issue might help to divide them on another.

Among those in favour, we should count St John, who had already accepted office, and who supported the Queen over Sir John Winter, and Saye, who accepted the Mastership of the Wards in the much less promising climate of May.[137] In Saye's case, the timing of his acceptance of office is easy to explain: it followed immediately on the death of Bedford on 9 May. The dangling of the Wards in front of Saye had probably always been designed to divide him from Bedford, whose financial proposals depended on the abolition of the Wards. He thus accepted the Wards at the first moment he was able to do so, but accepted it as a personal preferment, and not as any part of an overall settlement. The classification of him among those in favour in February also depends on his speech on Strafford on 17 February, and on the fact that, like St John, he did not emerge in later years as one of those who believed the Parliament's security depended on a continuing Scottish alliance. With these two should come Bedford, who was probably never a Root and Brancher, and Saville, whose limited sympathy with the Scots was rapidly detaching him from his former allies. Holland, who strongly supported the Queen over Winter, was an *éminence grise* of the settlement, and should also count among those in favour.[138]

On the other side, we should count Essex[139] and Mandeville, who spoke against Strafford on 17 February, and Hampden, Holles, Fiennes, and Gerrard, who spoke against Winter on 15 March. This involves the hypothesis that Fiennes disagreed with his father. This is possible, but it is also possible that he would have taken a more conciliatory line in February than he was to do in the changed circumstances of March. In the case of Hampden, we may possibly be dealing with one of the few committed Presbyterians in Pym's group. In the cases of Essex, Holles,

[135] Baillie, i. 306.
[136] NLS Adv. MS 33.4.6, fo. 133ʳ.
[137] Gardiner, *History*, ix. 374 and n.
[138] Staffs. RO D 1778/1/i/14.
[139] On the evidence that Essex had refused office, see PRO TS 23/1/12.

and Mandeville, we are dealing with three people who remained leading adherents of the view that the Scottish alliance was the only permanent security for a Parliamentary regime. Pym's speech of 16 March puts him among those refusing, but in his case, it need not be any guide to his views on other disputed issues.

The suspense did not last long. When Hyde raised the Scottish paper in the Commons on 27 February, he forced Pym's group to show their hand, and may, indeed, have forced them to make up their minds on the spur of the moment. When he asked Hampden for their intentions on episcopacy, Hampden may have been covering a division within his own group under the evasion 'that we are all of a mind in desiring what is best'.[140] It was perhaps inevitable, in a debate forced with the skill of a modern Question Time, that those who were in favour of the established line of loyalty to the Scots spoke out, while those who would have liked to change it were forced to remain silent and prefer a Scot in the hand to a King in the bush. Of the group which had been negotiating with Charles, Hampden, Gerrard, Earle, and Strode spoke in the Scots' favour, while Pym, Fiennes, Holles, St John, and many others remained silent. Short of having a public wrangle with their closest allies, no doubt to the great amusement of Hyde, Digby, and Strangeways, they had no other option.

This debate seems to have brought the settlement scheme to an end. Charles had preferred his new Privy Councillors in order to persuade them to abandon the Scots and Root and Branch, and, at the first opportunity they had in public, some of their key allies had refused to do so. In forcing Hampden and the others to make a declaration on the Scots' paper, Hyde had brought himself a degree nearer the King's favour, and civil war several degrees nearer. The King seems to have decided, probably within hours, on a change of policy. This was not just because his new Councillors had let him down: it was also because the new wave of anti-Scottish and anti-Puritan feeling for which Hyde, Culpepper, Strangeways, Hopton, and Digby spoke on 27 February offered him the possibility of raising a party against a group of people whose outlook had always been profoundly distasteful to him. It offered him a chance, not to reunite a country much of which he disliked, but to undertake what he always found the much more congenial task of leading a party.

On the same day, Sir Thomas Aston's Cheshire petition in favour of episcopacy was introduced in the House of Lords, indicating that the King too had a body of public opinion to appeal to.[141] By 3 March a charge was being contemplated against Hamilton, the architect of the

---

[140] D'Ewes (N.), pp. 417–18; *Two Diaries*, pp. 12–13.
[141] *LJ* iv. 174.

failed settlement.[142] D'Ewes said it was being put forward by 'the ill
partie of the House, . . . to have hinderd us from soe good an instrument
about the King'.[143] The advocates of conciliation in the King's counsels
were clearly now on the defensive. Temple, the next day, noted that
Hamilton was being defended by the efforts of Bedford.[144]

The centrepiece of the new policy, as of previous policies, was first
communicated to the House of Lords. When they considered the
Cheshire petition on 1 March, a new committee on innovations in
religion was set up to refer it to.[145] We possess the text of a speech,
apparently designed for delivery in the Lords in favour of the setting up
of this committee, in the fair hand of Edward Nicholas.[146] How a Lord's
speech comes to be in Nicholas's fair hand, which he did not use for
notes for his own benefit, is a question to which no clear answer
emerges. The speech was possibly delivered by Williams, who had
preached at court against the Geneva discipline on 24 January,[147] and
who became chairman of the new committee on 1 March.

The speech begins by arguing that the Commons should not be
allowed to settle the question of church government on their own, and
therefore that the Lords should set up a committee on the subject to
pre-empt their decision. Otherwise, it argues, there would be a risk of a
great rock of offence between the Houses. It proposes that the Lords
should set up a committee, and then demand a conference, so that the
business should be settled by consultation between the two Houses.
They should there argue that there was no precedent for church affairs
being decided entirely by laymen, and that there was a risk of a
'dangerous schism' if any new settlement was imposed without general
consent. It was necessary to give satisfaction to both parties, and to the
churches abroad. It concluded with a proposal for a national synod of
all three kingdoms: a proposal which could be relied on with the
greatest confidence to prevent a final decision within the next year. The
speaker asked for the Lords' leave to call assistants to this committee.
This was duly done, and when the committee first met on 12 March, it
agreed to call Ussher, Prideaux, Ward, Featly, Brownrigg, Holdsworth,
Hacket, Westfield, Sanderson, and Shute, and from the other side of the
fence, Twisse, Burges, Calamy, Marshall, Young, and Hill.[148] Before
then, the seal of royal approval had been set on the process by the

---

[142] On this charge, and those behind it, see Donald, pp. 422 n., 426 n.
[143] D'Ewes (N.), p. 430.
[144] KAO De L'Isle and Dudley MSS C 114/14; *HMC De L'Isle and Dudley*, VI. 389.
[145] *LJ* iv. 174; BL Harl. MS 6424, fo. 43ʳ.
[146] PRO SP 16/477/72.
[147] BL Harl. MS 6424, fo. 9ᵛ.
[148] BL Harl. MS 6424, fo. 49ʳ. Many of the godly clergy chosen had links with leading members
of the Twelve Peers.

preferment of Holdsworth and Brownrigg as royal chaplains.[149] At the very moment when Pym's group had rejected it, Charles committed himself, in public, to the Ussher scheme for reduced episcopacy. He took it up at precisely the moment when it no longer served to reunite the country, but had instead become a proposal for his partisan advantage. It seems unlikely that this timing was coincidental.

To reinforce this new line, the King by 3 March was negotiating, through Traquair, with the Covenanters' Scottish enemies.[150] This did not commit him to a breach with the Covenanters, but gave him a large extra lever to use in trying to get them out of England. It was no more than a couple of weeks since Richelieu had advised Henrietta Maria to wait for the wheel of fortune to turn, and it seemed she had not had long to wait. In bringing about the change of fortunes, as in bringing about the previous one, the influence of the Scots had been crucial. It was they who had pushed their Parliamentary allies into demanding terms for a settlement which went far enough to be themselves divisive, and therefore presented the King with the opportunity of raising a party against them. It was impatience with the Scots' continued stay in England, as repeatedly expressed by Bristol and Strangeways,[151] together with dislike of enforced godliness, which provided the driving force for the King's new party. The failure of the settlement was not necessarily final: the various blueprints continued to enjoy a half-life, ready to be revived if circumstances should again demand them. However, the likeliest resolution of the crisis, seen from the beginning of March 1641, was no longer either a settlement or civil war, but the same result Parliaments normally produced: a dissolution, leaving the King in sole possession of the stage, and therefore able to recover from many of the losses he had suffered during the Parliament. On 5 April John Barry reported back to Ireland that it would be necessary not to fly as high as other people,

for it is not safe to shew a will, where there is no poure, and though ye lyons clawes be pared close, yet in tyme they will growe out agen, and it is then better trusting to what his love and favor will oblidge him too, then to what his necessities may inforce him to promise nowe.[152]

This was good advice, to those whose religion allowed them to heed it. It was the misfortune of Pym and Baillie that they were not among that

[149] PRO LC 5/134, pp. 440, 442. Holdsworth became a Chaplain Extraordinary, and Brownrigg, who already held that status, became a Chaplain in Ordinary (5 Mar. 1641). See also Baillie, i. 308: he had some excuse for his view that this committee was a trick of the bishops.
[150] See below, pp. 312–13; Donald, pp. 424–8.
[151] See e.g. D'Ewes (N.), p. 398 for Strangeways's speech of 24 Feb.
[152] BL Add. MS 46, 925, fo. 1ᵛ. I would like to thank Dr J. S. A. Adamson for drawing my attention to this MS.

number. Nevertheless, though the long-term advantage was with the King, in the short term, Baillie was right that 'that which is the great remora to all matters is the head of Strafford'.[153] Unless the King could steer through that issue unharmed, the reaction in his favour might come to a halt.

[153] Baillie, i. 309.

7

The Trial of Strafford and the Army Plot

MARCH–MAY 1641

The failure of the settlement negotiations exposed the intellectual limitations of Pym's junto. By 1 March it was clear that the King would not
accept their settlement on any terms they found tolerable, yet they never
formed any workable alternative policy. Having learnt that the King
found their proposals unacceptable, they formed no new or alternative
proposals: they merely looked for ways of increasing the pressure on the
King. Having failed to persuade the King to take them into office, they
set out to force him to do so. The underlying assumption of this strategy
was that if they tried hard enough, they could threaten Charles with an
alternative worse than that of allowing them power on their own terms.
Not until 30 January 1649 were they finally persuaded this assumption
was false.

This group never formed any plans for regular 'Parliamentary government': they were later prepared to invoke Parliamentary power for
choosing the great officers, but it was in those great officers, under the
King, that they always saw power residing. As Saye explained at length,
probably in 1646, they could only see power as existing under the King,
and, while he lived, only under that King. They were happy to reduce
the King's power to a cipher, and to have it exercised, ministerially, by
others in his name, but that cipher was one without which they could
never see how to operate.[1] These assumptions remained in the Nineteen
Propositions, in the projected settlement of 1647, and even, for those
members of the group who were still alive, in their approaches to
Charles II in 1660.[2] It was therefore still true, as Pym had said in 1621,
that their principal labour consisted in winning the King, since without
his name, however reluctantly lent, all their plans remained dead letters.[3] Their strategy therefore had to depend on spelling out more and
more unpleasant alternatives to the King if he did not choose to co-
operate with them. As Lord Brooke put it in 1642, their objective was

---

[1] William Fiennes, Viscount Saye and Sele, *Vindiciae Veritatis* (1654), BL E. 811(2), pp. 6–8.
[2] J. S. A. Adamson, 'The English Nobility and the Projected Settlement of 1647', *HJ* 30/3
(1987), 567–602.
[3] *Commons' Debates in 1621*, ed. W. Notestein, F. H. Relf, and Hartley Simpson (New Haven,
Conn., 1935), iv. 448.

'to reduce the king to a necessity of granting'.[4] Whatever ascending element may have crept into their theories of authority during the next few years, it was never enough to allow them to envisage a legitimate title to power which did not emanate from royal grant.

This pursuit of power rested on more than simple desire for office, since it seems clear that if that had been all Pym and his fellows wanted, they could have had it. Indeed, Charles's last offer of the Exchequer to Pym seems to have been as late as January 1642.[5] They may have been driven by desire for security in power, a need of which their favourite precedents, 1258 and 1388, must have constantly reminded them. Yet for Pym, if not for all of his allies, the non-negotiable element in his demands always seems to have been first and foremost the religious. The purpose of power was to secure the eradication of 'popery', and since some elements in Pym's definition of popery probably comprehended Charles, as well as his wife, the chance of his gaining Charles's consent to eradicate them was always slender. It is one of the ironies of the relations between Pym and Charles that, though they had similarly inflexible religious consciences, each always approached negotiations on the assumption that the other would be willing to sell his religion for money, power, or position.[6] Neither of them ever seems to have been quite able to believe that the other actually held the beliefs he did.

In the short term, Pym and his allies kept up the pressure after 1 March on very much the same fronts as they had done before. The issues of the Irish army, the disarming of recusants, and the four papists at court continued throughout March and April. On 17 March the Commons belatedly rejected the Lords' proposed compromise on the Irish army, whereby 2,000 of the new Irish army would have been recruited to the old, and thereby put under the command of Protestant officers. The Commons' objection appears to have been that they thought no papists should be in the army in any form.[7] The Lords, with a slightly belated constitutional sensitivity, chose at this point to consult the Irish Parliamentary committee in London.[8] Finally, on 23 March they secured the agreement of the Irish Parliamentary committee to joining with the Commons.[9] The King, however, was no more ready to give way to a united approach from both Houses than he had been to one alone. On 14 April the King said he would consider a reply 'after

[4] *Two Speeches* (1642), BL E. 84(35), p. 6. I am grateful to Dr J. S. A. Adamson for this reference.

[5] Gardiner, *History*, x. 127 and n. It is not quite impossible that there might have been another offer after this.

[6] Russell, 'Pym', pp. 162–3.

[7] D'Ewes (N.), p. 498; *LJ* iv. 186; *CJ* ii. 104.

[8] *LJ* iv. 188.

[9] Ibid. 196.

these great businesses now in agitation are over'.[10] Since the King was that week spreading rumours that if the Scots used their army to secure the death of Strafford, he would use the Irish army against them, he could not complain if this reply provoked suspicion.[11]

This diplomacy by threat was being conducted on both sides. Nothing more was heard of the bill for the Queen's jointure, and on 22 March Charles complained, for the first of many times, that the Commons were holding up the bill to confirm the subsidy of the clergy.[12] On 17 March, a request by the two Vanes for the House to consider money for the navy was shunted aside in favour of the business of the Irish army.[13] Sir John Temple reported that the Houses were proceeding slowly in all matters to do with money,[14] and on Tonnage and Poundage, while the plans to grant and improve it were being put into place, it was becoming slowly clearer that their implementation would have to wait on much bigger royal concessions than had so far arrived.[15] Having at last succeeded, as a result of the work of the first three months of the Parliament, in making the power of the purse effective, some members were prepared to use it with great ruthlessness. This ruthlessness was unlikely to be restricted by the rank and file, whose enthusiasm for voting money was rarely great. D'Ewes, for example, reverted to attacking proposals to reform the subsidy by introducing the lump-sum system, saying that it was the point of a subsidy that its yield ought to be uncertain.[16] A clear lead from Pym and his allies could have carried members like D'Ewes and Hotham along, but in the absence of such a lead, their natural reluctance could be relied on to reassert itself. It was beginning to seem increasingly likely that Charles would have no money until he agreed to the death of Strafford, and possibly to Root and Branch as well. Charles's decision, announced on 23 January, to lay down whatever parts of his revenue might be grievous, and rely on the affections of his people, had made him desperately vulnerable to such a strategy. When the Commons decided on 26 March to grant Tonnage and Poundage for three months, they were ostensibly waiting only for the completion of the Book of Rates.[17] This, like all the best excuses, was true, but it remained an excuse. When, or whether, Charles got a long-term grant was likely to depend on what he did before the short-term grant expired.

[10] *LJ* iv. 216.
[11] PRO 31/3/72, p. 514 (8/18 Apr.).
[12] BL Harl. MS 164, fo. 952ª.
[13] D'Ewes (N.), pp. 498–9.
[14] KAO De L'Isle and Dudley MSS C 114/14.
[15] *CJ* ii. 107; DO, vol. i, fo. 63ʳ; MP, 7 May 1641.
[16] BL Harl. MS 163, fo. 118ª.
[17] Ibid. 164, fo. 145ᵇ.

The notion of linkage between matters of money and of religion was so much in the air that even so unsophisticated a politician as D'Ewes picked it up. On 2 April he reacted to a new subsidy bill, needed for paying the armies, by proposing that they send up with it the bill against pluralities and non-residence and the bill for abolishing superstition, and also the bill against the Star Chamber.[18] D'Ewes had got it wrong: the Commons could not afford to delay the bill, for fear of the response in the armies if they did, but the linking of such bills to Tonnage and Poundage, which would in the long term be for the King's own use, would be an entirely different matter. The two bills D'Ewes mentioned were among a succession of bills for religious reformation, many of them started by godly members alarmed by the settlement negotiations, and afraid their leaders might sell them short for the sake of a settlement with the King. It now entirely suited the plans of Pym and his allies to support such bills, in the hope of putting yet more severe pressure on the King. There was, of course, no prospect that any of them would be passed into law, since the Lords would pass such bills, if at all, only as a result of pressure from the King. They remained demonstrations, rather than a serious legislative programme, but as ways of persuading the King that the price of settlement would go up with time, they were well designed. In addition to the measures D'Ewes mentioned, there was a bill for the Free Passage of the Gospel, first read on 30 March, and sent to committee on 12 April. This bill would have enacted that every minister could preach in his own parish as often as he could, and created an obligation on the minister to procure two sermons every Sunday. It also enacted that no minister be troubled for not using the surplice or the Cross in baptism.[19] A clerical disabilities bill, designed to ensure that clergy should not be JPs, was replaced with a wider bill, excluding them from all secular employments, including membership of the House of Lords. Denzil Holles, who was one of those responsible for this change, doubtless welcomed the chance to repair his credit with Alderman Penington and his allies.[20] The issue of Bishops' Exclusion arose naturally from the Ministers' Remonstrance, which was still being debated clause by clause in committee. On 10 March the Commons debated the principle of Bishops' Exclusion. The reports of this debate give a good example of the extent of Baillie's dependence on his inform- ants, who doubtless wished to reassure him. He says the principle was carried 'unanimously, not ten contradicting', while Diurnal Occur- rences, reporting from the same political and religious bias, says there

---

[18] Ibid. 162, fo. 392ᵃ.
[19] *CJ* ii. 114, 119; Gawdy, vol. ii, fo. 34ʳ.
[20] *CJ* ii. 99, D'Ewes (N.), p. 452.

was 'great opposition'.[21] The reports of the debate do more to sustain Diurnal Occurrences' view than Baillie's, since the 'not ten contradicting' included Bridgman, Hopton, Hyde, Selden, Jermyn, Culpepper, and Waller. On the other side, however, the usual team enjoyed the support of Bagshaw and Falkland.[22] In Bagshaw's case, his position followed logically from his Lent Reading, while Falkland, according to Clarendon, had been won over by Hampden's assurance that if this passed, nothing further would be attempted against the church.[23] Strode claimed that the bishops 'live every one in popery or prerogative',[24] but it was becoming clear that such statements could lose support in the House, as well as winning it. Cromwell on 10 April moved that they add the enforcement of the sabbath to this list.[25] The longer the crisis went on, the more such proposals were likely to be added to the list. Time was also likely to add to the list of delinquents selected for prosecution. The priority at this time was going to John Cosin, who was in trouble primarily for his treatment of Peter Smart, whom Rous described as 'the protomartyr of the church of England in these days of persecution'.[26] The phrase is a very interesting example of how far Rous and his like remained loyal to 'the church of England' by identifying it as a body apart from, and even opposed to, its official hierarchy.

Other secular bills appeared, all designed to restrict the King's power to rule without co-operating with his Parliament. Bills to abolish the Star Chamber and the High Commission were before the Commons,[27] and Hyde followed them up at the end of April with a vigorous attack on the legality of the Council of the North.[28] In the Lords, Brooke, who seems to have had a knack for rushing in where Saye feared to tread, caused offence by referring to God, the Parliament, and the King, in that order.[29] In addition, Penington, almost certainly against the wishes of Pym and Saye, was still holding up money to pay the armies until he should have justice on Strafford. The King, if he should choose to make an issue of the attempt to save Strafford, would be facing very considerable pressure.

There were some conciliatory gestures being exchanged between the

[21] Baillie, i. 308; DO, vol. i, fo. 57ᵛ.
[22] D'Ewes (N.) pp. 464–70; Two Diaries, pp. 104–5.
[23] Clarendon, History, i. 234–6. The story of their division is repeated by Edward Nicholas in BL Add. MS 31,954, fo. 182ᵛ. Similar assurances from Saye appear to have won over Pembroke. See Two Speeches, BL E. 84(35), pp. 3–4. I am grateful to Dr J. S. A. Adamson for this reference.
[24] D'Ewes (N.), p. 467 n.
[25] BL Harl. MS 164, fo. 972ª.
[26] Ibid. 6424, fo. 50ʳ.
[27] CJ ii. 113, 114, 115, and 112 and 115.
[28] Ibid. 127; LJ iv. 227; BL Harl. MS 163, fos. 487ª–8ª; Clarendon, History, i. 238–42. Clarendon was distinctly disingenuous in claiming that he had not intended that this speech should inflame the Lords against Strafford.
[29] HMC Twelfth Report II. 273.

King and the Lords. An announcement by the Earl of Holland on 5 March that the King would consent to the forests being reduced to their ancient bounds, was matched by a vigorous effort from a Lords' committee led by Seymour to control printing, a measure particularly dear to the King's heart. Negotiations for a Dutch marriage for his daughter Mary were being shared with the House of Lords. Rumours were spread that the marriage might carry a covert condition of financial aid to Charles from the Prince of Orange,[30] but it must be said that if this is true, the Dutch Ambassadors knew nothing of it.[31] Perhaps the most unfortunate side-effect of the marriage negotiation was the unexpected and unwelcome arrival on 2 March of the King's nephew the Elector Palatine.[32] This created a fear that the King's opponents might acquire the one tool they conspicuously lacked: a potentially popular and eligible pretender. From this moment onwards, much of Charles's effort was devoted to keeping his nephew's sympathies, a fact which explains a number of otherwise unexpected foreign policy moves during the summer.

The central question facing the King was whether to play for time, and wait for a reaction in his favour to gather strength, or to attempt a violent retaliation either by dissolution or by a coup. In some ways, the signs looked set fair for the first. On 1 March the Commons had what was in effect their first party division. A clergyman called Dr Chafin was in trouble for saying in a sermon: 'from lay puritanes and lay Parliaments good Lord deliver us'. The House agreed, on Falkland's motion, to give him a 'sharp admonition', and then divided on whether to send him to the Tower as well. The motion was defeated by 190 to 189, in what remained the largest division in the Parliament.[33] Every time Pym and his allies tried to increase the pressure on the King, they were liable to find that the measures they proposed for the purpose lost them more support in the Commons. This was a promising line for the King, but it would take time, and time, it seemed, might be what Charles did not have.

The alternative prospects were not inviting. Baillie for a while feared dissolution, but the Dutch Ambassador was perhaps more realistic in saying that it was not practical with 'un peuple à demy eschappé'.[34] Apart from any blow to his authority in London, it was hard to see what

[30] NLS Wodrow MS Quarto 25, fo. 161ʳ; *CSP Ven. 1640–2*, p. 145. The Venetian Ambassador said the rumour originated 'at the palace'.

[31] Groen Van Prinsterer, p. 444. I am grateful to Prof. Jonathan Israel for a helpful discussion of this story.

[32] Groen Van Prinsterer, p. 393; *CSP Ven. 1640–2*, p. 130; PRO 31/3/72, p. 475; PRO SP 16/480/9; PRO SP 16/478/23.

[33] *CJ* ii. 94; D'Ewes (N.), pp. 419–20. The vote for Chafin was probably increased by the fact that he was a former chaplain to Pembroke: Clarendon, *History*, i. 58.

[34] Baillie, i. 310; Groen Van Prinsterer, p. 343.

Charles would then do with two unpaid armies. The question of time was probably in the minds of those members of the Commons who persistently pressed the Lords for haste on the trial of Strafford. From November to March, many of them probably had uncomfortable memories of the Lords' success in preventing any proceedings on the impeachment of Buckingham in 1626. The Lords were making preliminary moves, discussing procedure, and debating whether to allow Strafford counsel. They may perhaps have been hoping to repeat their achievement over Buckingham, but if so, they were defeated by Pym's success in winning a procedural point which had concerned him ever since 1621. In the 1620s the Commons had had no control over the conduct of the prosecution in trials before the Lords: the Lords themselves had been responsible for examining witnesses, weighing the evidence, and proceeding to judgement if they saw fit.[35] From 1621 onwards, Pym had been aiming at what has since become the classical pattern of an impeachment, with the Commons acting as prosecutors and the Lords as judges. It was in the trial of Strafford that he at last fully succeeded. The symbolic dispute in 1641 was over a deposition by Archbishop Ussher, taken by the Lords in the absence of the Commons. The Commons successfully insisted that this deposition was invalid, and that another must be taken by a committee including representatives of the Commons.[36] This completed a procedural victory already half won since November 1640, and it very much reduced the scope for delay available to the Lords. On 22 March, over four months after the charge, and three weeks after the failure of the settlement, the trial of Strafford at last opened.

The fact that Strafford, as an Englishman, was tried in the English Parliament has tended to obscure the fact that he was brought to trial at the suit of all three kingdoms, with the English, on the whole, remaining in third place. There were very few issues indeed on which such diverse people as Archibald Johnston of Wariston in Scotland, Sir John Culpepper in England, and Viscount Gormanston in Ireland could agree with each other. Indeed, the trial of Strafford seems to be a unique case, and the sheer fact of agreement between such diverse people would seem to suggest that he was the victim of something more than the partisan justice of an English Parliamentary clique. The trial of Strafford was one of the great issues of the Long Parliament, but it was not, at least initially, a party issue so much as one which tended to divide the King from the rest. The trial grew more divisive as it continued, partly because of the great skill of Strafford's defence, partly because of the

---

[35] Colin G. C. Tite, *Impeachment and Parliamentary Judicature in Early Stuart England* (1974), 218–19 and *passim*; Russell, 'Pym', p. 158.

[36] *CJ* ii. 113; *LJ* iv. 201; BL Harl. MS 162, fo. 373ᵃ.

increasingly visible vindictiveness of the prosecutors' demands for death, and partly because of the growing fear that the trial might bring the country to blows. Attempts to coerce the King to abandon a minister had led to bloodshed and civil war, and in the long term to deposition. The thought of such parallels was bound to make the more temperate supporters of the prosecution wonder whether the game was worth the candle.

The twenty-eight articles of the charge were held together by the attempt to portray Strafford as a man trying to set up 'arbitrary government', and to divide the King from his people. The underlying theme was the attempt to show him as an authoritarian ruler determined to have his own way regardless of any legal or political restraints. The man portrayed in the charge was one for whom the identification of dissent with disloyalty was instinctive. For example, the threat to hang some of the London Aldermen who refused to lend money for the Second Bishops' War appeared to Strafford an intelligible response to a near-treasonable sympathy with the enemy. It appeared to Christopher Wandesford, his best friend, as evidence that ill-health had unhinged his reason,[37] and it appeared to the prosecution as part of a systematic attempt to make authority independent of political or legal restraint. It was the quality Strafford recognized in himself under the admission that he was 'impatient'. The general charges, of subverting the law, and of making a division between the King and his people, were, for the prosecutors, very nearly synonymous. They saw Strafford as rejecting any need to operate by consent or to seek for consensus, and as prepared to use all the weight of authority, including armed force, to compel subjects to fall in behind the King's line of the moment.

Since Strafford had spent the bulk of his ministerial life in Ireland, it was his Irish record which supplied the bulk of the charge. On his Irish record, the Remonstrance of the Irish House of Commons supplied most of the charges, and the Irish Parliamentary committee in London co-operated with the prosecution. The Irish committee, as befitted a body which included the extremes of Catholic and Protestant, stuck firmly to secular issues in its charges. The key claim of the Remonstrance was that

loyal and dutiful people of this land of Ireland, being now for the most part, derived from British ancestors, should be governed according to the municipal and fundamental laws of England, that the statute of Magna Charta, or the great charter of the liberties of England, and other laudable laws and statutes, were in several Parliaments here declared and enacted.[38]

[37] See above, p. 141 and n.
[38] *CJ Ire.*, pp. 161–2. Irish, like colonial American, constitutional thinking, carried a certain built-in ambiguity about their relationship with England.

This wording cleverly combined a claim to English liberties and to the sovereignty of their own Parliament. Like most Irish constitutional thinking of 1641, this was securely in line with the Petition of Right, and well calculated for the task of making common cause with an English Parliament.

Articles 3–19 of the main charge dealt with Strafford's Irish record, and were in the main based on the Irish Remonstrance. Strafford rested much of his defence on the claim that Irish and English constitutional practice were very different, while Pym and his fellow-prosecutors argued that Ireland had been used as a pilot scheme for methods of government intended for introduction in England. Article 3, for example, accused Strafford of claiming that Ireland was a conquered nation. Strafford, pleading historical justification, said he would do a great injury to the memory of divers of their lordships' noble ancestors if he denied that Ireland was a conquered nation. Maynard, for the prosecutors, replied that 'though Ireland differ in some particular statutes from England, yet they enjoy the same common law, without any difference'.[39] The claim to title by conquest was certainly one to which much English common law thinking was deeply allergic. Article 4, alleging that Strafford had said an act of state should be as good as an Act of Parliament, pursued the same line of thinking. Articles 5–8 showed him exercising jurisdiction over lives, liberties, and estates simply by hearings in the Irish Council, rather than by judicial process, all actions to which the Wentworth of 1628 would have been profoundly hostile. Article 15, the most damaging of the Irish Articles, accused him of using soldiers to enforce such decisions, and therefore of levying war. Since the prosecutors, unchallenged by Strafford, assumed that any levying war against the kingdom was also against the King, they claimed that this was treason within the statute of 1352. Strafford's defence, mustered with the full force of his sarcasm, was that he had not levied war: 'these be wonderful wars, if we have no more wars, than such as three or four men are able to raise, by the grace of God we shall not sleep very unquietly'. Glyn, for the prosecution, fell back on a theory of war with something in common with Hobbes: ' 'tis as ill to be forced by 4 as by 4,000, and the force makes it levying war'. The claim is that the attempt to impose authority by force amounts to a state of war.[40] A case like this was bound to recall the debates on martial law in 1628. Strafford's actions were seen in 1641 as contradicting his Parliamentary record in a way they had not normally been in 1629. Strode, on article 19, recalled how active he had been in 1628 against

[39] Rushworth, *Trial*, p. 171.
[40] Russell, 'Strafford', pp. 43–4.

arbitrary imposition of oaths, and Bedford, who had remained amiable to him in 1629, copied into his commonplace book in 1640 a large extract from one of his major speeches in 1628, apparently with the innuendo that it helped to make a case against him in 1640. The distinction suggests that the sense that he had turned his coat was not based on his acceptance of office, but on what he did when he was in it.[41]

Article 19, the Ulster article, was the most British of all the articles. It concerned the arbitrary imprisonment of a number of Ulster Scots for refusing to take an oath which, though originally designed against the Scottish Covenant, was extended to make people swear they 'should not protest against any his Majesties royal commands'. In particular, it dealt with the case of one Henry Stewart, which had been taken up with some vigour by the Scots. This article combined the Covenanters' irredentist concern with the Ulster Scots and their hatred of the enforcement of Arminianism with the Irish concern with arbitrary government, and the conviction of the English Parliamentarians that the power to impose an oath was a legislative power, and demanded an Act of Parliament.

Article 20 was based on the Scottish commissioners' charge against Strafford, and accused him of being an 'incendiary' of the Bishops' Wars. It held him responsible for the breach of the Pacification of Berwick, and for urging an offensive war against the Scots. It further accused him of calling the Scottish nation rebels and traitors, and of threatening to root them out of Ulster 'root and branch'. His anti-Scottish sentiments were so widely known that it was difficult for him to defend himself against this charge. Articles 21–4 dealt with the Bishops' Wars, which were perhaps the one thing above all else for which Strafford was held politically responsible. Article 21 dealt with the Council meeting which decided to call the Short Parliament, and made one of the key points of the prosecution: that Strafford had reduced the need for consent to a rubber stamp by denying the right to withhold it. In the words of the article:

he counselled his Majesty to call a Parliament in England, yet the said Earl intended that if the said proceedings of that Parliament should not be such as would stand with the said Earl of Strafford's mischievous designs, he would then procure his Majesty to break the same, and by ways of force and power, to raise monies upon the subjects of this kingdom.

As Pym put it,

into what a miserable dilemma . . . did he bring the kingdom, that we must

---

[41] Bedford MSS, vol. 25, unfol. For the speech in question, see Gardiner, *History*, vi. 235–6. The famous description of Strafford as 'that grand apostate of the commonwealth' comes from George Digby, who had been only 17 in 1628: PRO SP 16/479/60.

either surrender the liberties of the kingdom in Parliament, or else be oppressed with force and violence out of Parliament.[42]

The charge was of exercising a sort of partisan leadership, which, because it rejected the need to look for consensus, was consequently compelled to rely on force. The weakness of the charge, as Pym and his allies were later to discover, was that it was one Strafford and his allies were quite capable of retorting on them. Article 21 dealt with the Short Parliament, and in effect reiterated the point that Strafford intended to rely on prerogative power if the Parliament did not do what he wanted. Article 23 dealt with his speech at the Council committee of 5 May,[43] in which he had told the King he was 'loose and absolved from all rules of government', and advised him to use the Irish army. Article 24 dealt with his attempts to raise illegal revenues during the Bishops' Wars, and the remainder with other Bishops' Wars' issues.

Much of the argument of the trial revolved round the question whether the articles should be taken severally, as Strafford thought, or jointly, as the prosecutors wished. The picture Strafford put before the Lords was of a piecemeal series of indiscretions, some of them no doubt unfortunate, but providing no systematic evidence of anything worse than an inability to guard his tongue. To the prosecutors, the individual incidents were important only as evidence of a systematic design to reject legal restrictions, and consequently to obviate the need to secure other people's co-operation for his actions. This was the picture they had in mind when they accused Strafford of subverting the fundamental laws: the chief purpose of legal restriction, in their eyes, was to preserve 'unity', to ensure that the King and his ministers were unable to escape from the need to bargain, compromise, and conciliate. To make such a charge politically effective, they had to make themselves appear as people Strafford could have conciliated if he had tried, and here, perhaps, lay their Achilles heel. Their greatest strength, perhaps, lay in the knowledge of many of the Lords that there was more to be said against Strafford than was being brought out in the trial. It may be this knowledge which explains the depth of hostility to Strafford inside the Privy Council: Vane, Pembroke, Arundel, and Manchester, for example, seem to have been as determined to see him condemned as most of the Commons.[44] The prosecution of Strafford was not merely an attack by an 'opposition' on a 'government': it was at least as much an attempt from within the government to ditch one of its members who had brought them all into grave political danger.

[42] Rushworth, *Trial*, p. 108. On the events referred to, see above, pp. 92–3.
[43] For this speech, see above, pp. 125–9.
[44] *Two Diaries*, p. 25; *HMC Twelfth Report*, II. 281; PRO TS 23/1/14; BL Add. MS 31,954, fo. 182[r].

The belief that there was more known against Strafford than came out in the trial does not rest on conjecture. We know, for example, that he had proposed to have the nucleus of a standing army in England. On 2 January 1640 Northumberland told Leicester that Strafford wanted some troops of horse 'constantly entertained after these troubles are ended'. Northumberland noted drily that he did not think this proposal would be approved by others.[45] Strafford's plan to call in Spanish help to fight the Second Bishops' War was not merely widely known about the court, and therefore to many of his judges: his letter to Olivares of 18 July 1640 was in the hands of Pym.[46] Pym never mentioned this letter in public, possibly out of desire to protect the King's 'honour', but it would be surprising if he were so abstemious in private. Strafford's speeches at the Great Council of Peers, demanding the renewal of war against the Scots, had been heard by the majority of his judges, but were never mentioned, possibly because they were regarded as being covered by Parliamentary privilege.[47] If we can discover so much now, it seems probable that, among the almost unrecorded debates of the Council, Strafford had committed other indiscretions. This may help to explain why hostility to Strafford was so obviously concentrated near the centre of power.

If all this had merely been designed to sustain the proposition that 'Strafford must go', it could have mustered very general support, including that of Strafford himself. His plea to resign, repeated at the beginning of the trial, was probably addressed to the King even more than to his prosecutors, for the central problem to which the trial was addressed was the King's refusal to let Strafford go.[48] This refusal was alarming. The offence charged against Strafford, of believing that government could be continued without co-operation and overriding legal restrictions, was so painfully similar to the alternative option the Parliament was trying to convince the King he did not possess that compromise could easily become impossible. It was, throughout the trial, an implied premiss of the prosecution that the King must settle with his Parliament on the best terms he could get, and that he could not use force to evade restrictions they had placed on him. It was perhaps the fact that the trial of Strafford came to symbolize this message which became the final reason why the prosecution was unable to retreat. It was thought that

[45] KAO De L'Isle and Dudley MSS C 85/5.

[46] Bodl. MS Nalson XII, fos. 1–4; J. H. Elliott, 'Year of the Three Ambassadors', in Hugh Lloyd-Jones, Valerie Pearl, and Blair Worden (eds.), *History and Imagination: Essays in Honours of H.R. Trevor-Roper* (1981), 177–9.

[47] See above, pp. 158–62.

[48] BL Harl. MS 476, fo. 107. For an example of the King's attitude, see PRO SP 63/258/57 (Charles to the Irish Privy Council, 15 Dec. 1640). He said there were 'some questions' depending concerning Strafford, 'whereof we doubt not but he will in due time acquit himself'.

nothing less than Strafford's execution could force a reluctant King to compromise.

This determination forced the prosecutors to engage with the heart of Strafford's defence, which was that the offences charged against him, though they might show political unwisdom, did not amount to treason. The prosecutors had a legal case for arguing that Strafford was guilty of treason: there were precedents for arguing that making a division between the King and the people could amount to treason, because it made force the arbiter of political decisions. This was a tenable view, though not an unchallengeable one.[49] Its two weaknesses were that it had normally been used, as in the charges against Empson and Dudley, in an extremely favourable political climate, and that it did not do quite what was required. Treason was of its essence an offence against the King's person, but the prosecutors wanted to condemn Strafford for what was, in effect, an offence against the state. This necessarily involved them in some legal legerdemain. Here they may have been influenced by Scottish treason law, and by the specific Scottish offence of leasing-making, which, like the charge against Strafford, was one of making division by giving ill counsel. This had been newly defined by the Scottish Covenanters, and must have been in the minds of at least some who advised on the trial. The Scots had also argued, in bringing a treason charge against the defenders of Edinburgh castle, that treason was an offence against the state as a whole.[50] These cases, though they may have been useful as sources of ideas, had no status in English law, and they left the prosecutors still open to Strafford's defence, which was, in effect, that he stood more for the rule of law than they did, because he stood for certain and known rules of law: 'and sure, it is a very hard thing, I should here be question'd for my life and honor, upon a law that is not extant, that cannot be shewed'. He derided the prosecution case that the articles should be taken together: 'that those should now be treason together, that are not treason in any one part, and accumulatively to come upon me in that kind; and where one will not do of it self, yet woven up with others, it shall do it; under favour, my Lords, I do not conceive that there is either statute-law or common law, that hath declared this endeavouring to subvert the fundamental laws to be high treason'. It is the same point encapsulated by Laud's counsel in the phrase that he never knew two hundred couple of black rabbits make one black horse. Strafford urged the Lords to 'cast from you into the fire, those bloody and mysterious volumes, of constructive and arbitrary treasons, and to betake yourselves to the plain letter of the

[49] On the legal issues, see Russell, 'Strafford', *passim*.
[50] *APS* 5. 286–7, 264, 282.

statute, that tells you where the crime is, that so you may avoid it'.[51] It was part of the strength of this defence that it carried the suggestion, not too subliminally, that the intransigence which was making a division between the King and the kingdom was not that of Strafford, but that of his prosecutors. The more stridently they insisted on his death, and the more they cut legal corners in doing so, the more they took the risk that their own arguments would rebound on them.

From 22 March to 10 April the trial was in progress more or less continuously, and the result remained in suspense. Anxious speculation did not produce any clear consensus on which way the Lords were likely to go. In particular, it was thought that much depended on whether the Lords were satisfied on the charge that Strafford had offered to bring the Irish army to subdue England. On this charge, the Commons had the double disadvantage, first that of all the people present, only Vane remembered the words, and second, that even if the words were admitted, it seemed more reasonable to suppose that they referred to Scotland than that they referred to England. Strafford was making the further claim that conviction for treason required two witnesses. On 10 April, after proceedings in the Lords had broken up in disorder about a claim by Strafford to call additional witnesses, the prosecutors tried to meet this objection. They produced the younger Sir Henry Vane, with a copy of his father's notes on the meeting of the Council committee of 5 May. The story ran that the younger Vane had been searching in his father's study for some family papers, found this paper, and began to transcribe it, and that while he was in the act of transcribing it, Pym 'casually' came in to visit him.[52] It was a story which took some believing, but at a time when the objection to hearsay in court was much less clear than it is now, it might technically meet the objection about a second witness. There was a public display of tension between the two Vanes, but granted the elder Vane's known hostility to Strafford, there is a distinct possibility that the whole performance was a collusive exercise between them and Pym.

The same day, some members of the House attempted to switch the method of proceeding, from impeachment to attainder. Impeachment, as a judicial process, involved the continuation of a trial before the Lords, whereas attainder, as a legislative procedure, could simply enact that Strafford's offences were to be treason. This changeover has been the subject of considerable conjecture. It could be taken as an admission of the inadequacy of the Commons' legal case, or it could be taken as an

---

[51] H. R. Trevor-Roper, *Archbishop Laud* (1940), 423; Rushworth, *Trial*, pp. 658–9.

[52] BL Harl. MS 164, fos. 162ᵇ, 167ᵇ. The performance was probably collusive between the two Vanes, as well as between the younger Vane and Pym. The elder Vane had probably just got wind of plans to bring the army south to interfere in the trial.

attempt to make the Commons equal judges with the Lords. These explanations, though highly plausible, are without adequate proof.

On 10 April the bill was moved by Sir Arthur Haselrig, who produced it out of his pocket.[53] On the 12th, the second reading was moved by Marten, while the committee for Strafford's impeachment were out of the House.[54] This fact, taken with the fact that Pym opposed the bill as soon as he was back in the House, suggests that Gardiner was right that the bill did not proceed from 'the party of Pym and Hampden'. On the other hand, Sir John Culpepper's support for the bill as 'the safest and the speediest way' suggests that it came from a group wider than 'the inflexible party' invoked by Gardiner. Among other members, Mr John Hotham and one of the Mr Tomkinses supported the move to go by bill, and Rudyerd opposed it.[55] It is a line-up from which it is hard to draw firm conclusions, but it provokes the faint suspicion that we are seeing a line-up of country members of all sorts against the would-be new court.

The best guide to the purpose of the bill is in the text of the bill itself. When it was introduced, Nathaniel Tomkins immediately remarked that it specified 'punishment by death (hanging drawing and quartering)'.[56] The final version of the bill no longer specified hanging, drawing, and quartering, but it did specify that Strafford 'shall suffer . . . pains of death'.[57] Since it was a well-established point that the King could not vary the words of legislation in giving his assent to it, the bill deprived the King of the power of commuting Strafford's sentence. In Baillie's words, it 'forces the King, either to be our agent, . . . or else doe the world knows not what'.[58] If a bill designed to prevent compromise was forced through against the resistance of Pym and Rudyerd, it suggests a suspicion in the Commons that settlement was once again in the air. It suggests further a desire, expected in Marten but rather less so in Culpepper, to prevent their leaders from negotiating any compromise involving Strafford's life.

There is evidence for this suspicion. On 26 April Nathaniel Tomkins reported that Pym 'hath been with the King twice of late'. There is evidence that this created an unfavourable reaction in the House. When George Digby was questioned about a paper the Strafford committee had lost, he 'said it must be some unworthie man who had his eye upon place and preferment, wherein he was supposed to allude to Mr Pym

[53] PRO SP 16/479/27; Gardiner, *History*, ix. 329–30.

[54] BL Harl. MS 164, fo. 164[b].

[55] Gawdy, vol. ii, fo. 35[r].

[56] PRO SP 16/479/27. This is a different Mr Tomkins from the one who spoke in favour of the bill.

[57] Gardiner, *Documents*, p. 157.

[58] Baillie, i. 350.

himselfe'.[59] Pym appears not to have been tempted beyond endurance, but Warwick on 28 April accepted membership of the Privy Council, and the negotiations which ended with Saye's appointment as Master of the Wards in early May were probably in hand at the same time. In Warwick's case, the King won nothing by the appointment, since he remained as firmly committed against Strafford as before, and took charge of the Attainder Bill in the Lords.[60]

The offices with which Pym and Saye were associated were vacated by the resignation on 27 April of Cottington, who claimed to be suffering from ill health.[61] His warrant for leave of absence from the Parliament is a royal holograph. He had very recently been alleged to enjoy more influence with the King than anyone else,[62] and he had been threatened by the remarks attributed to him in Vane's notes. It seems likely that his resignation was agreed with the King, as a device to tempt Parliamentary leaders with office. The temptation of Saye had the further advantage that an offer of the Wards, by interfering with Bedford's plan to abolish wardship, might create a division between Saye and Bedford.

In fact, it seems that these negotiations did not create any serious prospect of a settlement, though Sir John Temple was briefly optimistic that the King would offer an accommodation.[63] They were only part of a succession of cat and mouse manœuvres indulged in by both sides during the second half of April. Pym and his allies threatened to complete and produce what later became known as the Grand Remonstrance—a threat probably aimed, as later, as much at the Lords as at the King.[64] On the other side, Tomkins said 'I heare it whispered in ye court, yt the k. will not let ye earle goe, & yt the parliament is not likely to be long lived'.[65] Both of these were non-events, but the King's recruitment of Edward Hyde to his service had more lasting consequences. Since, according to Clarendon's account, they discussed the King's projected journey to Scotland, and the contact was made by Henry Percy, the interview is likely to have taken place between 21 April and 5 May. Curiously, the King does not seem to have succeeded in buying off his hostility to Strafford.[66]

While these manœuvres were in progress, the Attainder Bill went through the Commons. Once the bill was established as the chosen

---

[59] PRO SP 16/479/74.
[60] BL Harl. MS 6424, fo. 58ᵛ.
[61] *HMC Twelfth Report*, II. 279.
[62] PRO SP 16/479/74; Groen Van Prinsterer, p. 385; *HMC Twelfth Report*, II. 275.
[63] KAO De L'Isle and Dudley MSS C 114/20.
[64] *CJ* ii. 122, 130.
[65] PRO SP 16/479/74.
[66] Clarendon, *Life*, pp. 76–7. The King's journey to Scotland became public knowledge on 21 Apr., and Henry Percy fled abroad on 5 May. Hyde's attitude to Strafford is a subject on which the *History* should be viewed with particular suspicion: *CJ* ii. 127, 130 perhaps provides a safer guide.

method of proceeding, Pym on 15 April swung his weight behind it. Glyn, supporting him, tried to meet Strafford's argument that a mere endeavour to subvert the law was not treason by arguing that if the endeavour had succeeded, there would have been no law to try him.[67] Hampden on 17 April was still doubtful about going by bill,[68] but Fiennes on 19 April was unyielding: 'if it bee treason to endeavour to kill the governer, then sure 'tis treason to kill the government'.[69] This is a clear example of the idea of treason against the state. A considerable number of members, including Kirton, Waller, Holborne, Bridgman, and Selden, spoke against the bill, and it began to look as if Nathaniel Tomkins was right in calling Strafford's opponents 'the precise party'.[70] Yet the supporters of the bill included others besides the precise party, including Falkland, Culpepper, and probably Hyde, though he did not speak. When the bill came to the third reading on 21 April, the most damaging speech against it was made by one of those who had managed the impeachment, George Digby. He accepted Strafford's argument for settled rules of law: 'let the mark be set on the door where the plague is, and let him that will enter, dye'. Most damagingly, he revealed that Secretary Vane had failed to remember Strafford's words about the Irish army until the third time he was examined:

let not this, I beseech you, be driven to an aspersion upon Master Secretary, as if he should have sworn otherwise than he knew or beleeved, he is too worthy to do that; onely let this much be inferred from it, that he who twice upon oath with time of recollection, could not remember anything of such a businesse, might well a third time misremember somewhat.

He cast another shaft at Vane by complaining that his notes were an example of how not to keep minutes: 'such disjointed fragments of the venemous parts of discourses, no results, no conclusions of counsels, which are the only things that secretaries should register, there being no use at all of the other, but to accuse and to bring men into danger'. Having thus discredited both the accuracy and the motives of the chief prosecution witness, Digby immediately published his speech.[71] The most remarkable defaulter was Hampden, who went out at the beginning of the division, and stayed out till it was over.[72]

When the Commons came to a division, the bill was carried by 204 votes to 59, and the minority, whose names were taken down by John

---

[67] *Verney's Notes*, p. 48.
[68] Ibid. 50.
[69] Ibid. 54.
[70] PRO SP 16/479/27.
[71] Ibid. 16/479/60.
[72] BL Add. MS 31954, fo. 181ᵛ. Hampden was possibly still pursuing negotiations with the King. If so, it is interesting that, having been one of the most unyielding on the religious issue of Sir John Winter, he should have been one of the most flexible on the more secular issue of Strafford.

Moore the diarist and others, found their names posted up under the heading: 'These are the Straffordians, the betrayers of their country'. The majority, in turn, found themselves listed as 'the Anabaptists Jews and Brownists of the House of Commons'.[73] The list of the Straffordians includes such future stalwart Royalists as Sir Robert Hatton, Sir Frederick Cornwallis, Sir Edward Alford, Robert Holborne, and Edward Kirton, but it does not include Hyde, Falkland, Culpepper, Hopton, or Sir John Stawell. The vote against Strafford in the Commons was more than a party vote.

In the Lords, it seemed the same thing might happen. Arundel, who held the key office of Lord Steward for the duration of the trial, was as unsympathetic as his ancestor had been to Thomas Cromwell a hundred years earlier. The Commons continued, even while the bill was in progress, with the rituals of trial before the Lords. Strafford and Pym spoke their closing speeches on 13 April, Strafford's counsel was heard on 17 April, and St John, for the Commons, replied to Strafford's counsel on 29 April. The Earl of Bath, one of the moderate Lords whom both sides desperately needed to convince, told his wife that St John 'did excellently acquitte himself'. Not even to his wife did Bath reveal on paper whether this opinion was any guide to the way he intended to vote.[74]

From the very beginning of the trial, the central dilemma facing the King had been whether to remain quiet, and hope the resulting drop in the temperature would result in Strafford's acquittal, or to attempt to preempt the trial by a coup or a violent dissolution. It was a situation in which his usual policy of keeping both options open did not serve him well. If he intended Strafford to secure an acquittal, he could only do so by completely removing the fear that he would cling to him in the face of all opposition. Even more, he had to signal unambiguously that he was no longer attracted by the sort of violent counsels with which the prosecution were trying to associate Strafford. Conversely, if he was thinking of a coup, he needed, not to annoy people by indeterminate threats, but to move swiftly, secretly, and in overwhelming force. Neither for the first time nor for the last, Charles succeeded in getting the worst of both worlds.

When the Attainder Bill went to the Lords, Charles had in fact been preparing contingency plans for a violent response for over a month.[75] The idea of the Army Plot probably goes back to the Commons' debate of 6 March, when the Scots had demanded £25,000 extra for their army, and backed their demand by a threat to advance. The Commons

---

[73] For Moore's responsibility for listing the Straffordians, see BL Harl. MS 165, fo. 85ᵃ. For the 'Anabaptists, Jews and Brownists', see PRO SP 16/479/74. The latter list appears not to survive.
[74] KAO Sackville MSS C 267/12.
[75] For what follows, see Russell, 'First Army Plot of 1641', *TRHS* 38 (1988), 85–106.

promptly diverted to them £25,000 which had been intended for the English army. Willmott and Ashburnham, two of the English army officers in the Commons, were naturally incensed by this decision. When Strode found them in a state of great indignation in Westminster Hall,[76] the House realized it had made a bad mistake, but it was too late to rectify it. Henry Percy, another army officer in the Commons and a later leader of the Army Plot, had gone to see the King with a message about the Algiers pirates. It was probably at this encounter that the idea of the Army Plot was born. The plot drew on a considerable body of genuine discontent in the army, based on the perennial shortage of pay, on the feeling that the Commons were a collection of civilians who neither liked nor understood them, and on a deep anxiety about the issue of martial law. The army feared, probably rightly, that the civilian courts did not view them with favour, and that the absence of martial law meant that they would be exposed to a hostile jurisdiction. On 20 March the officers drew up a major petition to Lord General Northumberland, and this petition was brought to London by a junior officer called Captain Chudleigh.

When Chudleigh arrived in London, he was taken up by Jermyn, Davenant, and Suckling, three courtiers of standing, and asked to meet the Queen. From his arrival in London, serious plotting began. It seems that at first there were two plots. One was run by Henry Percy with the full support of the King, for the presentation of an army petition, asking, among other things, that the Irish army should not be disbanded, that episcopacy should be preserved, and that the King's revenue should be restored. These are three demands which have the royal hallmark. The other plot, run by Jermyn and Suckling, was a more far-reaching proposal to bring the army south (or at least southwards), to seize the Tower, and to procure Strafford's escape. When Chudleigh went back to the army, he tested support for this proposal at a meeting at Boroughbridge on 3 April. The proposal appears not to have found wide favour in the army, and was roundly opposed by the generals Conyers and Astley. When he heard the report of the Boroughbridge meeting, the King seems to have decreed that this part of the plot should be abandoned. However, it had become known, partly thanks to the vigilance of Sir John Conyers. On 6 April the Commons resolved that anyone moving the army, or the Yorkshire trained bands, 'without special order of his Majesty, with the advice and consent of both houses of Parliament . . . shall be accounted and taken for enemies to King and State'.[77] From then on, the plot continued in full view of the House of

---

[76] This is known only by Strode's later recollection: BL Harl. MS 164, fo. 837ᵃ.

[77] CJ ii. 116.

Commons. Apart from the news sent by Conyers to Lord General Northumberland, Sir George Goring, one of the conspirators, leaked the plot to Newport, Mandeville, Saye, and Bedford. Since he never appears to have suffered any royal disfavour for doing this, it is possible that he did so with full royal approval. If the Army Plot, like most of Charles's plots, was intended as a deterrent, it was essential that it should be known to the Parliamentary leaders.

The London end of the plot, which was managed by Sir John Suckling, continued after the Yorkshire part was abandoned. Suckling was recruiting mercenary forces, under a cover story that he intended to serve the new King of Portugal, a story the Portuguese Ambassador unfortunately denied. He succeeded in collecting a hundred men under the command of Captain Billingsley, an officer in Strafford's new Irish army. Charles intended these men to occupy the Tower, where they would have outnumbered the forty Yeomen Warders with some ease. Meanwhile, Strafford's brother had a ship waiting in the Thames, which was apparently designed for his escape. What Strafford, and even more Charles, were planning to do after that never appeared.

On 3 May, immediately before the Lords began to consider the Attainder Bill, Charles appears to have decided he could no longer go on trusting in Strafford's chances of acquittal, and sent Billingsley's men to the Tower. They were foiled, partly by the resistance of the Lieutenant of the Tower, and partly by the alertness of some of the citizens, who called in the House of Lords. The Lords instantly took charge, and sent the Earl of Newport, Master of the Ordnance, to take command of the Tower, undiplomatically telling him to let the King know 'what the House had ordered herein'. Essex, Hamilton, and Holland were sent to wait on the King. When the King was unimpressed by this deputation the Lords immediately sent it back, with the addition of Pembroke, Bath, Warwick, Bristol, and Saye. In the face of this pressure, the King gave in, and discharged Billingsley, directing that the Tower should be guarded by the usual guard from Tower Hamlets.[78] The Queen's plan to retire to Portsmouth, which she had been fortifying, continued for some days longer, and the Lords had to instruct her servants and the King's not to go. As soon as the Lords had finished with Billingsley, they went into committee of the whole to debate the Attainder Bill. The conjunction can have done Strafford no good.

At the same time, a large crowd of citizens was gathering outside the Houses to demand justice against Strafford. These were not sansculottes: Sir William Uvedale reported that they were 'citizens of very good

---

[78] P. Christianson, 'Obliterated Portions of the House of Lords' Journals', *EHR* 95/375 (1980), p. 347. The original appears to read 'Chamb' rather than 'Chanc'.

account, some worth 30 some 40 thousand pounds'.[79] The man who got himself noticed and questioned, as he was to do many times more, was a good deal less prosperous than this: he was John Lilburne.[80] The Lords' assessment of how these crowds were gathered is indicated by their decision to ask 'some of the ministers and best of the City of London' to try to get them dispersed.[81] Yet Pembroke, with his hat in his hand, treated the crowds with enough courtesy to encourage them, and led them to suppose that he would help them to obtain 'justice'.[82] This was quoted as a reason for the King's dismissal of Pembroke several months later.[83] Though the crowds undoubtedly heightened the tension in the Lords on 3 and 4 May, it seems likely that the Lords reacted to the Army Plot with no more hostility than they would have shown normally. When the Earl of Stamford called on some of the bishops to give thanks for their deliverance, which was greater than that from the Gunpowder Treason, he probably meant what he said. Immediately he sat down, Warwick brought in the Attainder Bill 'bound up in many Quires of Paper'.[84]

In the Commons, revelations of various parts of the Army Plot during 3 May produced a wave of anger such as had not been seen since the Parliament began. Bagshaw pointed at Strafford 'and saith that the Kingdom cannot be saff while he lives'. Culpepper called 'for the remonstrance, and petition of rights to be forthwith read, and then to goe to the lords, and by that we may try the affection of the kinge, and that if we should be dissolved, that we might be found doeinge the service we were hither sent for'. Strode complained that 'ill councell given to a kinge, doth make that the King understandeth not what treason is'. The key proposal, for an oath of association for the defence of 'king and church', was started by the pro-Scots Marten, Wray, Harley, and Perd.[85] The result of this proposal was the Protestation, which, in effect, was an oath of association to resist a potential coup. It bound those who took it to defend the King, the Protestant religion, laws, and liberties, and the privileges of Parliament, and authorized

---

[79] PRO SP 16/480/11.

[80] *LJ* iv. 233. Rous was raising Lilburne's case in the commons while the Lords were condemning him.

[81] BL Harl. MS 6424, fo. 59[r].

[82] DO, vol. i, fo. 123[v]. Pembroke 'with his hat in his hand prayed them to be quiet and what was in his power should be done'. It tells us a lot about Nehemiah Wallington that though he was an eyewitness on this occasion, his account of it is copied verbatim from D. O. Nehemiah Wallington, *Historical Notices*, ed. Rosamond Ann Webb (1869), i. 242.

[83] PRO SP 16/482/95; PRO TS 23/1/14. The Elector Palatine said he voted 'against the Lord Strafford contrary to the King's expectation'. See also *HMC Twelfth Report*, ii. 281.

[84] BL Harl. MS 6424, fo. 58[v].

[85] Ibid. 477, fo. 28[r].

what they did in defence of their oath.[86] Baillie said it was 'I hope in substance our Scottish Covenant'.[87] He grew less hopeful when he found that the bishops took it, but the parallel was exact in one respect: it identified loyalty with a cause, rather than with a person, and authorized those who took it to resist any threat to that cause. The next year, many Parliamentarians regarded it as supplying their title to be in arms. In the Lords, the House resolved that they should all take it, but showed no appetite for a Commons' bill that everyone in the country should be made to take it.[88] They evaded a motion by Essex, Mandeville, and Saye that those who refused the Protestation should have no votes on the attainder of Strafford. Showing their usual concern for the privileges of popish lords, they resolved that those who refused it only in point of religious doctrine might vote, but those who refused it on any other ground might not. In other words, they would protect the conscience of peaceable papists, but would not allow votes to those who dabbled in plans to use the army to destabilize the Parliament. The Army Plot had made the Lords very angry indeed, but not so angry that they lost their concern to avoid unnecessary divisions.

The Lords' anger, and their fear that Charles had still not relinquished plans for a coup, showed to more telling effect in their treatment of the bill providing that the Parliament should not be dissolved without its own consent. This bill was rushed through the Commons in two days, and reached the Lords on 7 May.[89] It could be justified by the need of those who were lending money to pay the armies for future Parliamentary subsidies as security,[90] but it is hardly likely to have been a coincidence that a bill rushed through at this speed came during a dissolution scare.[91] If the King should decide to veto the Attainder Bill, he would probably feel the need to dissolve the Parliament at the same time. The Lords immediately gave this bill two readings, and sent it to Committee of the Whole House on the day they received it. The Lords, while sympathetic to the principle of the bill,

[86] For the text of the Protestation, see Gardiner, *Documents*, pp. 155–6. The key phrase is the last sentence of the preamble: 'and lastly, finding the great cause of jealousy, that endeavours have been, and are, used, to bring the English army into a misunderstanding of this Parliament, thereby to incline that army by force to bring to pass those wicked counsels, have therefore thought good to join ourselves in a Declaration'. The document then passes straight to the engagement to defend the Protestant religion, the King, the law, and the privileges of Parliament 'with my life'. The threat to fight is more than implicit.

[87] Baillie, i. 351.

[88] BL Harl. MS 6424, fo. 60ʳ; Gawdy, vol. ii, fo. 39ᵛ. The compromise by which recusant Lords were allowed to take it in civil matters only was not taken advantage of by the recusant peers during the trial of Strafford: BL Harl. MS 6424, fo. 63ᵛ.

[89] *CJ* ii. 136–7.

[90] This was the reason given in public when the bill was before the Lords: BL Harl. MS 6424, fo. 65ʳ.

[91] See ibid. 163, fo. 512ᵃ, and above, p. 289.

were worried by its indefinite duration, and proposed that its operation be limited to two years. They amended the bill the day they received it, and asked for an immediate conference.[92] At the conference, Culpepper for the Commons was inflexible: he reported that the Lords 'made some scruple yet at length they were satisfied relieing upon the judgement of this house and that it would passe this afternoon.'[93] The opponents of the bill forced a division in the Lords, but it was carried by the 'major part',[94] and the Lords had agreed to deprive the King of one of the key parts of his prerogative. It was a measure they would have been unlikely even to consider six weeks earlier.

This bill reached the Lords on the day they were to reach their final decision on the Attainder Bill. The Lords began their consideration of the bill on 4 May, when it was uncomfortably sandwiched between debates on the Army Plot and the tumults, and the Commons' delivery of the Protestation.[95] Since the Attainder Bill was a legislative, rather than a judicial, process, the bishops might perhaps have claimed to vote, but they appear to have thought that they would face too much hostility by doing so. On Williams's motion, they withdrew on the ground that they had not heard the proceedings on which the bill was to be based. The next day, when consideration of the bill was resumed, the Earl of Southampton tried to refuse the Protestation, on the ground that its preamble was close enough to the charge against Strafford to prejudge the issue. The fact that the only response he got was from the Earl of Bath, who said 'he gives no reason but a woman's', tends rather to confirm than to deny his charge that the Protestation helped to create a heavy bias against Strafford. The Lords then settled one of the crucial issues against Strafford by deciding that they would weigh his actions by statute law, by common law, and by the legislative power of Parliament. They thereby rejected the argument of Strafford's counsel that there were no treasons except those specified in the 1352 statute, accepted the argument of some of the Commons that there were treasons at the common law, and affirmed their right to create new treasons by legislative action. These three decisions, together with Manchester's proposal that 'upon bill we go not to the legality, but upon our belief and conscience', overruled the heart of Strafford's defence.[96]

At this point, one after another, Lords began to slip away from the final vote. The recusant lords were already absent, and so were the bishops. Bristol, Berkshire, Holland, and Conway asked not to be judges because they had been witnesses. Savill, who ultimately stuck it

[92] LJ iv. 238.
[93] CJ ii. 139; BL Harl. MS 477, fos. 43ʳ, 45ᵛ, 47ᵛ; also D'Ewes (C.), p. 244.
[94] LJ iv. 241.
[95] BL Harl. MS 6424, fos. 58ᵛ–9ᵛ.
[96] Ibid. 6424, fos. 61ᵛ, 63ʳ; Christianson, 'Obliterated Portions', p. 349.

out and voted for Strafford, desired a night's time 'wherein to recollect his notes', which was refused. Feilding asked leave of absence because he had not been present at most of the evidence. Cumberland was refused leave on the ground of partiality. The next day, after the Lords had voted on some of the clauses of the bill, Hertford, Seymour, Dunsmore, Hamilton, Mowbray (Arundel's son), Coventry, and Strafford's brother-in-law the Earl of Clare asked leave of absence. Later that day, Exeter and Hamilton reported sick. All these Lords had left before the House came to consider the crucial charge on the Irish army. These absences are sometimes ascribed to the tumults. This may be correct, but by 6 May the worst of the tumults were over. Moreover, this argument is weakened by the fact that it is by no means clear that all these Lords would have voted for Strafford if they had been present. The common factor uniting them is not their allegiance to either side in the trial up to that point, but the fact that they were a group who had no wish to lose the favour of the King. Their absence looks more like the proverbial jury turning away from the prisoner than a forced absence due to fear. Coming in the middle of further revelations about the Army Plot, many of these withdrawals may be of Lords who were expected to vote for Strafford, but could no longer bring themselves to do so.[97]

With these Lords absent, the House voted Strafford guilty on the crucial Irish army charge. On 7 May, having voted the matters of fact proved, they asked the judges whether these offences were legally treason, and the judges replied that they were. Southampton, Bath, and Savill asked the judges to say by which laws, whether common or statute, but Paget, Brooke, 'etc' 'denied this request for that it would take too much time'.[98] Thus fortified, the Lords passed the bill on third reading. According to Vane, the bill was passed by 51 votes to 9.[99] Since there had been a division on almost every individual clause, it is hard to be certain to which division Vane is referring. If it was the vote on the third reading, it remains possible that some of the votes on individual clauses were much closer. However, if 51 Lords were prepared to vote for condemnation, it is difficult to explain the vote simply in terms of the absence of Strafford's potential supporters. Fifty-one votes might constitute a majority in a full House, and the number suggests that in

[97] BL Harl. MS 6424, fos. 63^r–4^r; *LJ* iv. 236; Christianson, 'Obliterated Portions', pp. 349–50. For a parallel case, see Warwicks. RO, Feilding of Newnham Paddox MSS C 1/17, Su Denbigh to her son Feilding, advising him to absent himself rather than giving offence by voting for Bishops' Exclusion.

[98] BL Harl. MS 6424, fo. 64^v; Christianson, 'Obliterated Portions', pp. 351–2, where it is recorded that the offences were charged as treason 'by the common lawe'. The Lords' votes, and the judges' resolution, are in House of Lords Braye MS 2, fos. 142–3.

[99] PRO SP 16/480/20; Baillie (i. 352) says that 19 of Strafford's friends and allies went out before the vote. It is not clear whether he refers to those who already had leave of absence, or to a second exodus.

the Lords, as in the Commons, the readiness to condemn Strafford stretched far beyond the confines of a party.

On the same day the Lords passed the Attainder Bill, the King at last decided to disband the Irish army. This, remarkably, was not a concession designed to win political support, but simply the result of shortage of money. The Council committee which considered the issue agreed with what the Irish Privy Council had said on 10 April, and simply told Charles that since he could not maintain the army, he had no option but to disband it.[100] Charles had thus lost a large amount of political credit by showing a public determination to do what he turned out to be unable to do. He was thus left to consider whether to pass the Attainder Bill with no prospect of being able to use the Irish army, and with the two Houses rapidly taking control of English armed force out of his hands.

The measures the two Houses took in response to the threat of armed force are among the most striking events of the Parliament, and go a long way towards anticipating the Militia Ordinance of the next year. The Commons on 5 May declared that anyone who brought foreign forces into the kingdom without the consent of both Houses was a 'publick enemy to the King and kingdom'. They also directed their members to take a survey of ammunition in their counties, and to report whether Deputy-Lieutenants and Lords-Lieutenant were 'persons well affected to the religion, and to the publick peace'.[101] The Lords were less hesitant: when some of those suspected of being Army Plotters fled, the Lords stopped the ports and issued a Proclamation to apprehend them entirely on their own authority. The Proclamation says euphemistically that it was issued on the 'advice' of the Lords, but the *Journals* contain not so much as an order to tell the King after the event.[102] They 'recommended' to the King that Salisbury should be joined with Cottington as Lord-Lieutenant of Dorset, and Southampton with March and Portland as Lord-Lieutenant of Hampshire.[103] The next day, they sent Mandeville and others to gather forces to defend Portsmouth, where the Queen was still expected to take refuge, and directed the Lord Admiral to put ships into the hands of 'persons of trust'. They agreed with the Commons' request for the trained bands of Yorkshire to be 'put into a safe hand', and sent Pembroke, Hertford, Warwick, Hamilton (rapidly recovered from his illness), Holland, and Saye to

---

[100] *LJ* iv. 239; PRO SP 63/274/21 and 63/274/22.

[101] *CJ* ii. 135. For one of the required surveys, presented by Earle to Salisbury as the new Lord-Lieutenant of Dorset, see *HMC Salis.* XXII. 353–4.

[102] *LJ* iv. 236, 238; Larkin, pp. 742–4. The use of the Sign Manual seems to establish the King's formal consent.

[103] *LJ* iv. 238.

move the King to appoint Essex.[104] On 11 May they took to themselves authority to open all foreign letters.[105] The Lords, with the assistance of many of the great officers, were acting as the ultimate repository of supreme authority. This was not in order to justify a coup of their own, but in order to prevent a threatened coup of the King's. In an ironical, but thoroughly English fashion, they were defending established authority against its lawful king. Perhaps the most important long-term consequence of the Army Plot was the training it gave law-abiding people in believing they could take control of armed force out of the King's hands for essentially defensive and law-abiding purposes.

Over the weekend of 8–9 May the King was left to decide whether to assent to the Attainder Bill, and the bill against dissolution. The Lords sent Pembroke, Bath, Hertford, and March to move him to give his assent to the bill against dissolution, and sent Lindsey, Bath, Hertford, Salisbury, Hamilton, March, and Bristol to ask, in a significantly different form of words, 'what tyme he will appoint to give his royall assent to the bill of attainder of the Earl of Strafforde'.[106] On the Sunday, the King consulted the Privy Council. The meeting does not appear in the Council register, so we have no attendance list, but if the attendance were the same as on the previous full meeting of 27 April, it would probably have shown a clear majority in favour of signing the bill. In addition, he consulted bishops Ussher, Morton, Williams, and Potter, who were reported to be in favour of signing the bill, and Juxon, who presumably was not. Perhaps most alarmingly, the Elector Palatine was in favour of the bill.[107] The country seemed to be in such a mood that, if the King should refuse to give his assent, civil war might result. This was not just a matter of the crowds again gathering, this time outside Whitehall Palace: it was a matter of the mood of people with some authority. Ussher on 2 May went to the Dutch embassy to ensure a refuge in exile in case of the worst, and Lord Brooke on 15 May took delivery of six

---

[104] Ibid. 241.

[105] Ibid. 245.

[106] Christianson, 'Obliterated Portions', p. 353.

[107] PRO 31/3/72, fo. 555; NLW Wynn of Gwydir MS 1685; PRO TS 23/1/10. The Elector Palatine's precise words were that Charles 'hath shewed himself a good master and a good Christian, and at last a good king'. The Elector also says the King was in tears at the Council table. For the Privy Council attendance of 27 Apr., see PC Reg. xii. 126. Those present were Juxon, Manchester, Hamilton, Arundel, Lindsey, Pembroke, Hertford, Bedford, Essex, Berkshire, Holland, Cork, Saye, Savill, Mandeville, Vane, Jermyn, Roe, and Bankes. Of these Bedford and Roe cannot have attended, Bedford because he died on 9 May, and Roe because he was abroad. Of the others, only Juxon and Savill can be confidently classified as in favour of Strafford, while Manchester, Hamilton, Arundel, Pembroke, Essex, Holland, Cork, Saye, Mandeville, and Vane can be classified with some confidence as against him. The group it is hard to classify, Lindsey, Hertford, Berkshire, Jermyn, and Bankes probably showed a majority in Strafford's favour, but even if they had all been in his favour, there would still have been a Council majority against him.

carbines which must have been ordered some time earlier.[108] The King, with his regular capacity to fear for the lives of his wife and children, must have had an uncomfortable night. On the engrossed Original Act for the attainder, there are several large blobs of candle grease, and it is tempting to speculate on the circumstances in which they may have come to be there.[109] For whatever reason, the King's courage failed him, and on Monday morning 10 May he gave his Royal Assent by commission.

Having given his Royal Assent, the King then tried, much too late in the day, to repeat his successful move in the Goodman case, and sent the prince to the Lords, with a letter asking whether, now he had satisfied the justice of the kingdom, the House would allow mercy 'if it may be done without a discontentment to my people'. Essex, Saye, and, significantly, Bristol, seized on the King's 'if' to argue that it could not be done, and the Lords sent a deputation to the King to tell him bluntly that what he wanted could not be without danger to himself. Holland, as if he were dealing with a child, moved to send a deputation to the King to 'comfort' him. Strafford was executed on Tower Hill on the morning of 12 May.[110]

In this long-drawn-out crisis, none of the parties had achieved their real objectives. The King had not saved Strafford, and instead had sacrificed the Irish army and the prerogative of dissolution. In addition, he had entirely thrown away the political reaction which had been gathering in his favour at the beginning of March. Once again, as much and more than in November, he was facing the solid opposition of men like Culpepper, Hertford, and Bristol, without whose support no viable party for the King could be gathered. Above all, he had suffered a vital blow to his political credit, not only from the deep discredit which came from his known willingness to use armed force against a duly constituted Parliament, but also from having precipitated a showdown, and lost. Sir Thomas Roe, the Stuarts' Greek chorus, expressed both feelings. He told Vane that if the situation did not change 'I shall envy those that perish with honour than they yt outlive the honour and peace of their countrye'. He said that 'the tydes return with every season, but obedience will be long lame, if ye Parlament every way restore it not'.[111]

Yet if the King had not achieved his objectives, Strafford's enemies

---

[108] Groen Van Prinsterer, p. 439; Warwicks. RO Warwick Castle MSS, Halford's accounts, vol. i, Gifts.

[109] House of Lords RO, Original Acts, 16 *Car.* 1, *cap.* 38, classified as no. 23 in Original Acts. The text is otherwise clean.

[110] *LJ* iv. 245; House of Lords RO, Original Journals, vol. 16, p. 24; BL Harl. MS 6424, fos. 66^r–7^r.

[111] PRO SP 16/480/26.

had not achieved theirs either. Their real aim was not so much to have Strafford dead, as to convince the King that he could not use that sort of policy. They hoped, in Secretary Vane's words, that 'his Matie is resolved to reconsile himselfe with his people, and to relie upon their counsels, there beinge now noe other left'.[112] What happened seems to have been precisely the opposite. Once the dust of the Army Plot had settled, the feeling that there was something discreditable about the condemnation of Strafford remained, and the poem recorded by John Rous, that he had been 'hurried hence betwixt treason and con-venience'[113] struck an uncomfortably persuasive note. The shedding of blood raised the stakes, and increased the fear of revenge. Verney, on the page in his diary which recorded the execution, marked it with a large red stain.[114] Instead of convincing Charles that he must co-operate with his people, the execution, by pressing him beyond his conscience, convinced him that he must not do so. He ascribed his subsequent misfortunes to his sin in agreeing to the execution, and the question which came to concern him was whether his punishment would be confined to this world, or whether it would extend to the next. He wrote to Hamilton in December 1642 that

I have sett up my rest upon the justice of my cause, being resolved that no extreamitie or misfortune shall make me yeald, for I will eather be a glorious King or a patient martir. . . . the failing to one frend has indeed gone very neere mee; wherfor I am resolved that no consideration whatsoever shall ever make mee doe the lyke; upon this ground I am certaine that God has eather so totally forgiven me, that he will blesse this good cause in my hands, or that all my punishment shall bee in this world, wch without performing what I have resolved, I cannot flatter my selfe will end heere.[115]

There was one other person the King might be pressed to abandon as part of the price of unity with his people. That person was well aware of the risk, and therefore had a special desire to hear Charles repeat remarks like the one quoted above. The attempts to reassure that person were one of the most important reasons why Charles could never cease to stress his sense of guilt for the death of Strafford. That person was his wife. From May 1641 onwards, Charles's need to reassure her that she would not go the way of Strafford took priority over any attempts to restore the political unity of his kingdom. Kings, like subjects, cannot be coerced beyond endurance without harmful consequences. With a King

[112] Ibid. 16/480/20.
[113] *Diary of John Rous* (Camden Society 66, 1856), 117–18.
[114] Yale University, Beinecke Library, Uncat. MS 226, fo. 81ʳ. I am grateful to Dr Maija Jansson for drawing my attention to this folio.
[115] Hamilton MS 167.

so bent on non-political objectives, it is hard to see how collapse could have been avoided. The fact that civil war did not come for another fifteen months is a deep tribute, both to the stability of English society, and to the skill of English politicians.

8

The King and the Scots

MAY–NOVEMBER 1641

In England, the summer of 1641 was the slow movement of the political crisis. Compared with the period from January to April, or from November 1641 to January 1642, it was one in which very little happened. This was because the King, who throughout set the agenda for the periods of acute instability, had his attention fixed elsewhere. This is not to say that the King had no English policies during the summer: there was no time when he confined himself to one objective. He continued, to his opponents' alarm, to hanker after the possibility of support from the English army, and he continued with the possibly incompatible aim of winning a party in the English House of Commons. He may have hoped to use the growing hostility to Root and Branch to bring this aim about. Nicholas in June may have been reflecting the King's thinking when he said: 'it is conceived it will never passe to be made a law'.[1] Whether this hope related to the Commons or to the Lords, or to both, Nicholas did not say. It is during the period when he did least that the King's support grew fastest.

The King's prime objective throughout these months was that of getting the Scots out of England, and, if possible, of doing so through a settlement which would put an end to the risk of future combination between his Scottish and English critics. Gardiner and Stevenson have both suggested that he hoped to go further, and actually obtain Scottish assistance *against* his English Parliament.[2] This is possible, but it is a view for which it is surprisingly hard to find any direct evidence. By contrast, there is a good deal of direct evidence to suggest that he was simply concerned with getting the Scots to leave England alone. Nicholas, who was growing increasingly close to the King during the summer, was certainly convinced that the mere absence of the Scots was enough to turn the tide in the King's favour. He told Vane in August that 'if the King shall settle and establish a perfect quietness with the Scots, it will make open a way to a happy and good conclusion of all differences here'.[3] Writing to the King on 18 August, he was more frank than he ever dared to be with Vane:

---

[1] PRO SP 16/481/21.
[2] Gardiner, *History*, ix. 418; Stevenson, p. 223.
[3] PRO SP 16/483/41.

your majesties partie here begins (as I am credibly told) to have more power
than heretofore, and thus if your Majesty shall settle there such a peace and
quyetnes as may conteyne at home the Scotts, in good obedience, they shalbe
no sooner returned hence . . . but . . . those that have depended upon them will
. . . fall flat.[4]

This is a view of the English situation which, until the outbreak of the
Irish Rebellion, was probably correct.

It cannot be proved that Charles held this view, but he behaved in the
manner which would have logically followed if he had held it. He
consistently pursued the objective of getting the Scots out, and it should
cause no surprise to anyone used to Charles's political methods that he
pursued it by two widely different methods at the same time. He could
aim at his objective either with the Covenanters or against them: he
could, relying for leverage on the Scottish army's desperate shortage of
money, try to induce them to go home and they accept a devolutionary
settlement, by which they would give up their influence in England in
return for power in Scotland. The alternative method was to link up
with the growing body of dissatisfaction with the Covenanters in Scotland, and use such power as the Scottish monarchy possessed to
manœuvre the Covenanters' opponents into power. From March to
October Charles pursued both methods at the same time. In the context
of continuing negotiations, the combination was not as illogical as it at
first sight appears. In negotiating with the Covenanters, he could use the
threat implied by his negotiations with their opponents as a way of
preventing them from being too intransigent about terms and conditions. In negotiating with the Covenanters' opponents, he could aim at
overcoming their natural reluctance to come into the open while their
enemies were in control by threatening to conclude a settlement with
the Covenanters unless proved they had the strength to provide him
with a viable alternative. It is a technique which won him considerable
concessions, but it was one to which there was a limit: there was a risk
that, sooner or later, he would try to twist men's arms into doing what
one side would not, and the other could not. If he reached that point,
his negotiating strategy would collapse, and that point he appears to
have reached by the middle of October.

Saye, writing many years later, probably in 1646, alleged that after the
Army Plot, the King was no longer in a hurry to conclude the treaty,
because he knew that if the Scots' army were disbanded, his own must

---

[4] Guildford MS 52/2/19(8). I am grateful to Dr J. S. A. Adamson for bringing this important
collection of MSS to my attention. They are Nicholas's rough drafts for letters whose originals
the King burnt on his insistence. This particular passage is a rough draft unusually heavily
corrected, and it is hard to be certain which parts of it Nicholas intended to remain in the final
version.

be also, and he would then not be able to use it to master the Parliament and the City.[5] There is not very much evidence that the motives here imputed to the King are correct: where Saye is perhaps more accurate is that he and his fellows behaved in the manner of men imputing such motives to the King: they no longer seriously attempted to delay the treaty. The Army Plot had served as a sufficient warning that it was not necessarily in their interest to keep two armies permanently on foot on English soil. If so, perhaps it had achieved at least some part of its original purpose. On 26 May, when Rothes called for the speedy conclusion of the treaty, it was Essex, not Bristol, who backed him up, saying that 'the Parliament hath reason to dispatch this, for it cannot be for the good of the kingdome to keepe two armies on foot'.[6]

By far the most important reason for the delay of the treaty from May to August was the perpetual hunt for enough money to pay off the two armies. This became something like the mathematicians' curve of pursuit: the Parliament perpetually chased a target, and as they got near it, a new month began, a new month's money became due, and the target receded in front of them. Their methods of tackling this problem are more significant in English than in Scottish history, and need not be discussed here.[7]

Many other issues in the treaty seem to have temporarily faded away. Issues which made up the biggest and most constructive parts of article 8 were remitted for further negotiation between commissioners of the two Parliaments. No agreement was reached on the claim that neither nation should make war without the consent of the other, nor on the Scots' claim to trade with the English colonies. The Scots' claim for religious uniformity between the kingdoms, which had been a serious demand, also temporarily faded into the background. In this case, however, the Scots' retreat was the result of facing the fact that the demand was, for the moment, unobtainable. The aspiration did not go away, and returned in the General Assembly of 1642, and later in the negotiation of the Solemn League and Covenant, and in the Westminster Assembly. It was not until 1707, in a different intellectual universe, that the Scots and the English finally abandoned hope of pushing each other into religious conformity, and it was not until they did so that a stable union between the kingdoms became possible. Other issues were successfully papered over. The King replied to the demand that he should reside regularly in Scotland with the face-saving formula that he would come as often as he could. On the issue of removal of papists from about the King's person, the Scots in the end proved more accom-

---

[5] William Fiennes, Viscount Saye and Sele, *Vindiciae Veritatis* (1654), BL E. 811(2), p. 30.
[6] BL Harl. MS 457, fo. 89ʳ.
[7] See below, ch. 9 *passim*.

modating than the English: the King replied that he believed they wanted to express zeal, not to deprive him of the choice of advisers, and he would do what would give satisfaction to the kingdom.[8] Whether the Scots would have proved so accommodating if they had expected the King to reside regularly in Edinburgh is a matter for speculation.

One of the remaining issues, which occupied the commissioners for much of June, was that of the incendiaries. This had already been settled once in the Scots' favour, but the increasing weakness of the Scots' army, and perhaps also his sense of guilt over the death of Strafford, encouraged the King to reopen it through the wording of the Act of Oblivion, which was to conclude the treaty. Since the Scots had always insisted that no agreement on any article should be taken as final until they were all agreed, they were hoist with their own petard. On 3 June, when the wording of the Act of Oblivion was discussed, Loudoun protested that 'to have it generall without exception is destructive to their instructions'.[9] On 7 June the issue came up again. Loudoun protested that they had instructions to have the Act of Oblivion with provisos, and, thinking of a possible compromise, offered a letter from Edinburgh 'wherein they have assurance that all rigid courses shall be avoided, when parties cited shall appear before the Parliament there'. There followed 'great arguments': Bristol asked 'how can it be honourable to the King to leave threeskore men that have adhered to him to prosecution, when an Act of Oblivion is passed for all others that have borne arms?' Rothes replied that they were not cited for adhering to the King, but for heinous crimes against the law, to which Bristol replied that it was the King who pardoned crimes against him and his laws. Rothes's reply has been crossed out. Loudoun repeated the argument that they could not dispense with the Acts of their Parliament, and Bristol concluded the discussion with the words: 'we must leave you to the King'.[10]

The King was reacting to this intransigence by saying it was 'small encouragement' to his plan to visit Edinburgh,[11] yet as June progressed, the Covenanters' intransigence on this issue increased, rather than diminished. Traquair, who remained the chief 'incendiary', was still at court: he signed an English Privy Council letter on 5 May and attended a meeting on 31 May.[12] He also became increasingly involved, perhaps for motives of self-preservation, in the King's negotiations with anti-Covenanter Scots. On 14 June the Covenanters complained of

[8] BL Stowe MS 187, fos. 67[r]–8[r].

[9] BL Harl. MS 457, fo. 93[r]; *HMC Salis.* XXII. 354–6. The Covenanters blamed the incendiaries for this proposal.

[10] BL Harl. MS 457, fo. 95[r–v]; *HMC Salis.* XXII. 356.

[11] EUL MS Dc 4.16, fo. 107[v].

[12] PC Reg. xii. 129, 134.

incendiaries 'incensing the King in England'. The next day they rehearsed Traquair's recent efforts in this direction, and demanded that he be sequestered from the King and sent to answer in Scotland.[13] On 27 July they also complained specifically of Sir John Hay's presence at court.[14] Sir Robert Spottiswoode and Walter Balcanquall, the other named incendiaries, were not specifically charged with such negotiations, but it is likely that they were suspected of them. The King's two policies were not necessarily incompatible, but they were certainly hard to follow together. On 30 July the Scots announced a decision to appeal to the Parliament.[15] They succeeded in getting the incendiaries exempted from the Act of Oblivion, but there was no reason for believing that the King's second concession on this issue would be any more final than the first. The issue remained to be argued out in Scotland.

The other major live issue was the disposition of Scottish offices. The King had agreed in principle back in April to Parliamentary involvement in the choice of great officers, but between the concession of the principle and its application in detail, a great gulf remained. One party would have to nominate, and the other to approve, but each seems to have retained the hope of being the nominating party. There was also disagreement about whether all existing officers should resign and go through the process of renomination, or whether the process should be confined to future appointments. There was also continuing disagreement about how offices should be filled if they became vacant during intervals between Parliaments. This issue was less prominent in the public negotiations of the treaty, perhaps partly because Charles's anti-Covenanter contacts were urging him to keep offices vacant until he arrived in Edinburgh. On 4 August the Scots were still objecting to the King's answer,[16] and the issue was clearly to await resolution in Edinburgh.

The disposal of offices was an issue of personal concern to some of the Scottish commissioners. Rothes on 25 June reported to Johnston that he had been offered a place. The Covenanters, in this a true party, had agreed that none of their members should accept office without general consent, for which Rothes asked. He asked Johnston to tell Argyll and Balmerino that 'I deser to accept the place', and said that Hamilton, Roxburgh, and Will Murray had assured him that it was for the good of the kingdom that he should take it. He said that 'we have had hard worke with the King', but appeared to believe their efforts had

---

[13] BL Harl. MS 457, fos. 100ʳ, 101ʳ.

[14] Ibid., fo. 109ʳ.

[15] Ibid., fo. 110ʳ.

[16] Ibid., fo. 111ᵛ. See Tollemache MS 4314, for a draft letter from Charles asking his Scottish officers whether they would accept reappointment on such terms.

been successful.[17] Baillie on 2 June expected that he would take a place in the Bedchamber, and be 'little more a Scottish man'.[18] The phrase is one in which condemnation has been read, yet it is worth noticing that it was part of a message intended for Rothes's daughter, and therefore unlikely to be sent with overt hostile intent. It perhaps represents the ambivalence inherent in the status of the Anglo-Scot. Patrick Hepburn of Wauchton had also been offered a reward on the conclusion of the treaty, and was much dismayed in November that it had not yet appeared.[19] These issues were still open when the treaty was concluded on 9 August, and, by general consent, were remitted for solution in Edinburgh.

These policies represented the King's carrot. Meanwhile, his stick was being used concurrently. At the same time as the King was discussing giving Rothes a post in his Bedchamber, his allies were also discussing the possibility of charging him with treason.[20] It would have been hard to make the combined pressure of hope and fear much more intense. At the same time, charges against Hamilton had been being discussed since the failure of the settlement negotiations at the beginning of March. Hamilton had been more closely associated than anyone else with the policy of concession, and if that policy should be held to have failed, Hamilton's own career might fail with it. Charges against Argyll, with whom Hamilton now had a marriage alliance, were also under discussion.[21] In any possible charge against Argyll, Charles would enjoy the help of potential allies eager to offer him a body of evidence.

Among these, the symbolic figure was James Graham, Earl of Montrose, previously distinguished as Leslie's only rival for the title of the Covenanters' best general. He had originally been prominent in the opposition to the Scottish service book, and a willing participant in the abolition of Scottish episcopacy. He was a full and willing participant in the Acts of the Scottish Parliament of 1639–40, and his approaches to Charles, which had been under way since 1639, seem to have been always on the understanding that they were aimed at a settlement involving Charles's acceptance of these Acts.[22] Montrose was not a champion of an episcopal church of Scotland, nor of government by Proclamation.

Among the forces which led Montrose to a breach with his former

---

[17] NLS Wodrow MS Fol. 66, fo. 183; PRO SP 16/481/42.
[18] Baillie, i. 354 (but see also p. 356). Only Rothes's death in August appears to have frustrated these expectations. When he died, it was said that the King had expected much service from him: PRO SP 16/483/96.
[19] Hamilton MS 1461.
[20] Donald, p. 428 and n.; Baillie, i. 356.
[21] Donald, pp. 426, 428.
[22] Above, p. 272.

allies, a personal rivalry with Argyll seems to have been one. There is an amusing emblematic expression of this tension between them in a letter of the Scottish Privy Council of 7 June 1641, which the two of them signed above the others, and in a much bigger hand than the others.[23] This determination to be top dog could have perhaps pulled them apart without any ideological reinforcement.

The evidence is slender, but it is possible that there was more dividing Argyll and Montrose than a personal, or even a clan, rivalry. Montrose, during the summer of 1641, said that while he had been at Newcastle (mainly the winter of 1640–1) he had not wished to mar the treaty for anything beyond their Acts of Parliament.[24] It is perhaps straining the evidence to draw from these words the conclusion drawn by Gardiner, that 'beyond Scottish territory and Scottish men Montrose's thoughts did not travel', yet it would fit the chronology of Montrose's career to assume that he was, as his words imply, reluctant to jeopardize the Covenanters' Scottish achievements for the sake of the unionist ambitions of Henderson or Johnston of Wariston.[25] The first chink between Montrose and his Covenanting allies came during 1639, when Scottish propaganda first began to take up the theme of liberating England. His doubts do not seem to have hindered his loyalty to the Covenanting cause in the Second Bishops' War, when he was the first to cross the Tweed.[26] In that war, he was fighting for the preservation of the Covenanters' Scottish achievements. His breach with the Covenanters became total sometime between September 1640 and June 1641, that is, during the period when the Covenanters risked sacrificing the achievements of Newburn for the sake of their English allies. The other theme which occurs constantly in the writings of Montrose and his key ally Lord Napier is a belief in preserving the power of the Scottish monarchy. Lord Napier, in justifying his negotiations with Charles during June 1641, argued that the King must settle religion and liberties, by which he seems to have meant, in effect, that the King should recognize the changes of 1639. In return, he argued, they must settle the King's authority, which was much shaken by the troubles. The effects of weak sovereign power, he said, were anarchy and confusion, the oppression of the weak by his stronger neighbour, and 'the tyranny of subjects, the most insatiable and insupportable tyranny of the world'.[27] This, perhaps, is the theoretical conviction behind Montrose's reluctance to risk the treaty for the sake of Parliamentary election of the great offi-

[23] Hamilton MS 1354.
[24] Napier, i. 357.
[25] Gardiner, *History*, ix. 151; see also Stevenson, pp. 206–7.
[26] Gardiner, *History*, ix. 189.
[27] Napier, i. 286.

cers.[28] Napier and Montrose seem to have believed that Scottish peace could only be preserved by the power of the monarchy to act as umpire and supreme patron in the disputes of the great nobles.

Montrose's widening breach with the Covenanters may also have been helped by the rising status of Argyll in Covenanter counsels, since the personal breach between Montrose and Argyll goes back to the summer of 1640. Their hostility goes back to an incident at the Ford of Lyon in June 1640. According to the story told to Montrose by Sir Thomas Stewart and John Stewart of Ladywell,

the Erle of Agyle being in his awin tentt at the fured of Lyone, declares that he being in Edinburgh at the Parliament that it wes agitatt ther whether or not ane Parliamentt might be holdane without the King or his commissioner: at last it wes resolvitt, be the best divyns and laweouris in the kingdome, that ane Parliament might be holdane without ather the King or his commissioner; and that a king might be deposit, being found giltie of anie of thir three: the first *venditio, 2 desertio, invasio.*[29]

This story, of course, offered grounds for a treason charge against Argyll. It may perhaps have been of as much interest to Charles that if Argyll were shown to be contemplating an alternative king, almost the only alternative available to him was Hamilton, with whom he then proceeded to contract a marriage alliance. No evidence ever connected Hamilton with the Ford of Lyon story, but he was so much its likely beneficiary that widespread belief in the story could easily have discredited him beyond the point of recovery. It is, at the very least, possible that the telling of this story did something to undermine Charles's trust in him, since Charles was already alert to the fact that Hamilton enjoyed a claim by blood to the Scottish throne.[30] Montrose, curiously, seems not to have seen this particular danger, and was more preoccupied with the danger that Argyll might set himself up, Roman style, as a dictator.[31] In the summer of 1640, when this issue was fresh, Montrose's suspicion seems to have been rather that Argyll might take the opportunity of the Covenanting army's absence in England to reach agreement with Charles behind their backs.[32]

Argyll, of course, hotly denied the whole story of the Ford of Lyon, but it is not necessary to take his denial as the last word. In June 1641 he brought a charge of leasing-making against Stewart of Ladywell for spreading this story. Stewart of Ladywell, faced with an investigation by

---

[28] Napier, i. 357.
[29] NLS Wodrow MS Fol. 65, fo. 85, no. 30, printed in Napier, i. 266–7. At the beginning of the Second Bishops' War, the reference to invasion was alarmingly topical.
[30] Rothes, p. 138.
[31] NLS Wodrow MS Fol. 65, fo. 60, no. 18.
[32] Napier, i. 284.

the Committee of Estates, and under the threat of execution, panicked, and tried to save his life by submission. Yet even when his fears were at their height, the furthest he retreated was to say that 'the Erle of Argyle, having spoken of kings in generall, and cases quherin it is thought kings mycht be deposed, the deponer did tak the words as spoken of our king'.[33] Ladywell's conclusion is one in which a historian might well follow him. Argyll's own charge against Ladywell is preserved, and the profusion of adjectives with which it is littered shows at least that Argyll had been deeply frightened by the charge. He described it as 'wicked and odious calumnies and lies', and said it was 'notorious and monstrous false lies and calumnies against me intending no less tharby nor ye utter ruine and overthrow of me and my estate', and that the story had been repeated to Montrose 'out of ane deep hatefull and precogitat malice against me my honor creditt and estaite'. Argyll was quite entitled to be frightened, since the story had been told, not only to Montrose, but to Traquair, who was perfectly capable of repeating it to the King. Yet, even after making full allowance for this, there is at least one historian who feels that Argyll protests too much, and that the best reason for believing him guilty is the unconvincing quality of his own denial.[34]

Whether we believe Argyll guilty or not, Montrose appears to have done so. His immediate response appears in the Cumbernauld Band of August 1640. It is hard not to sympathize with Stevenson's comment on the Cumbernauld Band, that 'the wording of the Band is so vague that it is impossible to know quite what it was meant to achieve'.[35] It bound its signatories to loyalty to their religion, king, and country, and to resist 'the particular and indirect practicking of a few'. It was signed by eighteen Lords, including Montrose, Home, Marischall, Kinghorn, Seaforth, and Almond, the Covenanter Lieutenant-General.[36] It was at the time secret, but became public knowledge by the deathbed confession of Lord Boyd at the end of 1640.[37] This caused some embarrassment to the Scottish Committee of Estates, which produced a joint declaration 'that none . . . joined in Covenant . . . may harbour . . . uncharitable thoughts of another'.[38] The actual declaration subscribed by Montrose and his associates on 28 January 1641 is unlikely to have achieved that effect. It argued that the Cumbernauld Band was not incompatible with

[33] Ibid. 297–9.
[34] Scottish RO, PA 7/2/63. It must be admitted that this is an individual reading of the document, but the impression, however hard it may be to justify formally, does not go away.
[35] Stevenson, p. 207.
[36] For the text of the Band, see Napier, i. 254–5. For Montrose's justification of the band on the ground that some had considered deposing the King, ibid. 304.
[37] Donald, p. 425.
[38] NLS Adv. MS 33.4.6, fos. 115–16.

the Covenant because it was aimed at 'some indirect practising against the publick', an explanation which can only have increased the personal tension between Montrose and Argyll.[39]

The news of this visible crack in Covenanter ranks must have reached London a few days before the first debate on the Root and Branch Petition, at a time when Charles's irritation with Scottish intervention in English affairs was at its height. It presented him with an opportunity too good to be missed. Serious negotiations between Charles and the Montrose group began on 3 March, in the same week in which hopes of an English settlement were abandoned, and in which rumours of a charge against Hamilton were first circulated.[40] The three things were clearly logically interdependent. Our record of the first contact is in the form of a paper, apparently prepared by the Montrose group, and altered for grammar by Traquair, who was their main court contact. The paper begins with three Scottish demands, first, for the confirmation of the Acts of the last General Assembly; second, for an Act of Oblivion (without any request for exceptions); and third, that the subjects should be governed by the laws in time to come. Traquair, who seems to have shown this paper to the King, reported his agreement to these propositions. In return, Montrose and his allies offered to maintain the King's 'honor, personne and royall authoritie against all men'. They asked him to attend the next Scottish Parliament, and to keep all Scottish offices vacant until then, and then to bestow them on those who should best deserve them.[41] Charles agreed to this also. Walter Stewart, Montrose's messenger, was later more explicit, and claimed that this meant that offices should not be bestowed by the advice of Hamilton, 'lest he crush the king'. Lennox, as well as Traquair, seems to have been a party to these negotiations. As yet, the King seems to have been using them only as a contingency plan, though it is worth noting that he did not in the event bestow any Scottish offices until after his arrival at Edinburgh. Whether Charles finally committed himself to these plans would perhaps depend on the Covenanters' willingness to make concessions on withdrawal from England, the King's share in disposing of offices, and the future of Traquair and the other incendiaries. The terms Montrose and Napier were offering him were much more inviting than those offered by the Covenanters, but their chances of delivering an agreement were correspondingly less.

From March until June these discussions remained under cover, though many Covenanters had their suspicions. These were, on occa-

---

[39] Hamilton MS 10774/9. I am grateful to Dr Peter Donald for explaining the context of this document to me.

[40] NLS Wodrow MS Fol. 65, fo. 56, no. 17 (Walter Stewart's deposition); see above, p. 272.

[41] NLS Wodrow MS Fol. 65, fo. 72^{r-v}, no. 24.

sion, comically misplaced, and on 27 May Drummond of Riccarton, one
of the Scottish commissioners in London, warned Keir against a plot in
which Keir was himself a participant.[42] The plot officially became public
knowledge at the beginning of June, when Montrose's emissary Walter
Stewart was intercepted, and the letters found in his saddlebag were
placed before the Committee of Estates. They included a letter to
Montrose, in which Charles repeated his intention to attend the Scottish
Parliament, and to confirm their religion and *just* liberties: an adjectival
addition from which Montrose might have taken more warning if he had
been more familiar with Charles's record in England.[43] There was also a
document of instructions for Montrose, Napier, Kier, and Blackhall,
which repeated the substance of Walter Stewart's paper of 3 March,
while half-concealing the characters under the names of animals. The
key proposition was that offices were not to be granted by the advice of
'the elephant', 'for fear he crush the King'. According to Walter
Stewart, the elephant was Hamilton. They were also to try the information against 'the dromedary', who, we are told, was Argyll.[44] From then
on, Charles's alternative policy was not merely known by whispers, but
open to public scrutiny.

This made it possible for the Covenanters and their allies to conduct
convincing counter-propaganda. It was almost certainly Traquair's role
in these negotiations which produced the Scottish commissioners'
attack on 14 June on Scottish incendiaries incensing the King in England. The Scottish commissioners also took the chance to interest their
English friends, and Loudoun and some of the other commissioners
showed the intercepted instructions to some of the English commissioners. The result was a debate, initiated by Haselrig, which led directly to
the passing of the Ten Propositions.[45] The unsuccessful threat to
Covenanter control of Scotland thus weakened Charles's English, as
well as his Scottish, position, and once again Charles had been shown
that his technique of following two policies at once carried a big risk of
spoiling them both. Charles on 12 June wrote a skilled and disingenuous
letter to Argyll, in which he gave every appearance of disowning
Montrose. In fact, the only specific assurance Charles gave Argyll was
that he had made no particular promises for disposing of any specific
office.[46] This assurance did not disown Montrose, who had asked him

[42] Ibid., Fol. 66, fo. 177, no. 91. I am grateful to Dr Peter Donald for this reference. See Donald,
pp. 438–9.
[43] BL Harl. MS 292, fo. 142 (copy).
[44] Yale University, Beinecke Library, Osborn Shelves fb 158, fo. 78 (copy in the hand of John
Browne Clerk of the Parliaments, with marginal decipherings in his hand). Another text is NLS
Wodrow MS Fol. 65, fo. 41, no. 12.
[45] BL Harl. MS 163, fo. 725[b]; Holland, vol. ii, fo. 83[r].
[46] Napier, i. 282.

not to make any such promises. For the time being, the combination of hope and fear led Argyll to go to great lengths to give the appearance of making himself agreeable. It remained to discover whether this appearance would be deceptive.

During the next two months Montrose, Napier, Keir, and Blackhall remained imprisoned in Edinburgh Castle while investigation into their 'plot' continued. Strictly speaking, what they had done was not a plot, but an alternative policy, and it deserved the title of 'plot', if at all, only for breaching the Covenanter rule against private negotiation with the King. Meanwhile, preparations for the King's visit to Edinburgh continued. The main cause of delay was in London, since it was generally agreed that the King could not come and hold a Scottish Parliament until the treaty was concluded, the armies disbanded, and the Covenanters no longer formally his enemies. The delays in London seem to be more part of English than of Scottish history, and to have been caused first and foremost by the difficulty in raising money to pay off the armies. In particular, the Parliament's new poll tax proved much less successful than its advocates had hoped.[47] For Charles, the English Parliament's deep anxiety at the prospect of his journey to Scotland was probably more an incentive than a disincentive, since it was difficult to see what his Parliament could do to stop him.

Negotiations on the issue of the incendiaries continued in Scotland, as well as among the commissioners in London. At the end of June Loudoun and Dunfermline returned to Scotland for consultations. They reported to the King on 12 July that the preservation of Traquair 'and passing from him upon his submission is most difficult of all your majesty's desires'. This, they said, was the truer because all men were convinced of his 'having hand in these lait unhappy plottis with the Earl of Montrose'. On the same day the Scottish Privy Council told Charles that it intended to continue proceedings against the incendiaries.[48] Montrose and Traquair were now coming to occupy the position in Scottish politics that Strafford had occupied in England: their lives were in potential danger because of their participation in the King's plans, and therefore all the King's guilt at his consenting to the death of Strafford was likely to be on the surface in negotiations about their future.

The day after his letter to the King, Loudoun explained his thinking more frankly in a private letter to Hamilton's brother Lanerick, Secretary of State for Scotland. He said a treason charge against Montrose was to be put before the Parliament, 'and although the Erll of Argyll bee verie much injured by these malicious calumnies I beleeve he will

---

[47] Below, pp. 336, 402.
[48] Hamilton MSS 1380, 1381.

endevore the cleiring of his own loyalty and integritye more nor revenge against those who have wrongit him'.[49] Read between the lines, this perhaps says that Loudoun would try to induce Argyll to compromise, but doubted his power to do so. For the incendiaries, he said, echoing the attempts at compromise which had been made over Strafford, that if they would be sensible of their error as penitent delinquents, their punishment would be more mild than their fault deserved, but if they added contumacy to their guiltiness, the Parliament might have a deeper resentment of the wrongs they had committed.[50] Read carefully, this carried the subliminal message that Montrose and Traquair, like Strafford, could only be further endangered by the King's attempts to save them. Any suggestion of 'cover-up' would only increase the fear that the King had not abandoned the policies with which these men were associated. It was a message Charles had not heeded over Strafford, and he was unlikely to heed it now.

The physical preparations for Charles's visit were also encountering some difficulty. Charles proposed, on the route from Berwick to Edinburgh, to spend one night at the Earl of Winton's house, but Winton said, in most un-courtier-like tones, that he would rather leave house, fortune, life, and all, before he would undergo any such charge.[51] At Edinburgh, the poverty of the Scottish Crown was causing even more acute difficulties. Argyll, who was increasingly taking the lead in the preparations, told Lanerick on 14 June that he had been meeting with the Greencloth every day, and had prepared things 'as far as they can without money, but I feare the want of that will doe much hurt'.[52] On 17 June, before charges against the plotters had been preferred, there was a meeting of a Council committee with the uncomfortable membership of Argyll, Napier, Hope, Blackhall, and Winton, which reported 'extreme defects' in the state of Holyrood, which needed timber, slates, windows, glass, and matting, for none of which was there any money.[53] On 2 July Carmichael of the Exchequer acknowledged the receipt of £1,600 from England, which had been distributed to caterers and butchers, but was little more than an earnest to them. He said he could not disburse the money needed for Holyrood, since Argyll had failed to borrow it.[54] A week later, it seems Argyll had succeeded, since it was reported that the repairs at Holyrood would be finished in two or three days, and Argyll

---

[49] Ibid. 1382.
[50] Ibid.
[51] Ibid. 1360. For Charles's announcement that he had 'changed his resolution' see Tollemache MS 3750, fo. 2ʳ.
[52] Hamilton MS 1363.
[53] Ibid. 1361.
[54] Ibid. 1374.

had taken great pains in the service.[55] Finally, Lanerick, in spite of
Scottish sense that it was a dishonour to entertain their King at the
charge of England, had to say that the King would bring plate, linen,
and £6,000 with him from England. The Scottish Council were still
saying that it was difficult to pay the bills for entertaining the King
before those for 1633 and for King James, and it seems to have been
only when Hamilton and the Committee of Estates agreed to become
bound for the King's expenses that the visit was able to go ahead.[56] In
spite of all attempts to keep the King's party small, it was swelled by the
inclusion of the Elector Palatine, whom, according to the Venetian
Ambassador, the King took with him for fear.[57] Otherwise, the only
prominent Englishman in the King's party was Secretary Vane.

The King eventually arrived in Edinburgh on 14 August. His first full
day in Edinburgh, he had to be reproved by Alexander Henderson for
missing the afternoon sermon. He did not make the same mistake again,
and Baillie said he 'hears all duelie, and we hear none of his complaints
for want of a liturgie, or any ceremonies'.[58] Vane, in some surprise, told
Nicholas that 'we had prayers and preaching the Scottishe way', 'so as
you see now one may heare tow sermons the Sunday att court; and I will
assure, prayers also twice a day dulie, wheare wee have *ex tempore*
prayers and singeing of pshalmes, his Majestie present, and Mr.
Henderson, when he sayes not prayers allwayes at the kings chayre in
the same manner I have seene the Bishop of Canterbury attend'.[59] This
is one of the few occasions in the whole story when we can feel reasonable confidence that Charles did not merely qualify his conscience, but
acted directly against it. His willingness to do so is perhaps a mark of the
importance he placed on the success of the visit. Vane, writing to Roe on
the 22nd, gave a measure of what the importance was: 'and thus your
Lop. may see, that by the blessing of Almighty God, these troublesome
stormes and tempests are ending in a peacable calme, wch doubtlesse
cannot but produce that happy union, soe much now desired by both
nations'.[60] In the view of Charles's entourage, the English troubles had
come in with the Scots, and they would go out with the Scots. Plans to
prorogue the English Parliament were already in hand, and waited only
on the King's return from Edinburgh. For a victory of this size, a few
Scottish sermons would have been a small price to pay.

As the time dragged on, it became a steadily increasing fear among
the King's friends and supporters that he might throw away all these

[55] Hamilton MS, 10774/2, 1377.
[56] Ibid. 1391, 10774/2; Tollemache MS 3750, fo. 3ʳ.
[57] *CSP Ven. 1640–2*, p. 228.
[58] Baillie, i. 385–6.
[59] *NP* i. 24; also PRO SP 16/483/68 and 104.
[60] PRO SP 16/483/81.

benefits by overreaching himself. The King's visit to Edinburgh lasted just over three months, and with the end of his troubles apparently waiting for him as soon as he returned to London, it is something of a problem what he was waiting for. His own servants do not appear to have known the answer.[61]

The disbanding, which appeared to be the key to the whole process, began smoothly by reciprocal stages. A brief scare about Holland's delay in disbanding the English horse was passed over, and the Scots left Newcastle on 21 August, and began disbanding on the 22nd.[62] By the 27th, all but three regiments had been disbanded, leaving the Scots with 5,000 foot and 500 horse. Delay after this point was apparently a reaction to the King's deliberate decision to delay disbanding the garrison of Berwick.[63] This left the Scots with three regiments, of which one, commanded by Colonel Cochrane, remained in the neighbourhood of Edinburgh. Cochrane, it so happened, was and remained a client of Montrose.[64] He may also have been identical with the Colonel Cochrane who was serving as the Covenanters' agent in Denmark in 1640, and gave regular information to the King, or with the Cochrane who was employed by the King in Edinburgh Castle in 1639, and was instrumental in betraying it to the Covenanters.[65] It thus came about, whether by chance or by someone's planning is not clear, that military force in Edinburgh passed into hands favourable to Montrose. This fact, which was certainly known to the King, may have encouraged him to hold out for more concessions than he might otherwise have hoped for.

Some potentially explosive issues were passed over smoothly. When the King came to the Scottish Parliament on 17 August, the Covenanters restrained him from touching the Acts with his sceptre, and thus avoided any claim that the Acts had been invalid till the King ratified them.[66] It was a move with considerable implications for Parliamentary autonomy. The King also failed to resist a move that those Scots in his entourage who had been out of Scotland during the crisis should take the Covenant before they were allowed to sit in Parliament. Richmond and Lennox jibbed briefly at this requirement, but Hamilton, Morton, and Roxburgh appear not to have done so.[67] It cannot have eased the hurt for the King that Lennox and Hamilton justified their decision by

[61] Evelyn, iv. 85, 86, 94, 105–6, and other refs; PRO SP 16/484/63.

[62] Yale University, Beinecke Library, Osborn Shelves, Howard of Escrick MSS, Correspondence Folder 1.1.

[63] Ibid., Correspondence Folder 2.1; PRO SP 16/485/22; CJ ii. 289, 190–1; Yale University, Beinecke Library, Osborn Shelves, Howard of Escrick MSS, Correspondence Folder 2.14.

[64] Napier, i. 302–4; NLS Wodrow MS Fol. 65, fo. 56, no. 17, fo. 92, no. 34. HMC Second Report, 176.

[65] PRO SP 75/15, fo. 475; Hamilton MS 864.

[66] Baillie, i. 388–9.

[67] NP i. pp. 12–13; Guildford MS 52/2/19(4).

saying it was no more than the Protestation, which they had already taken in England.[68] A manifesto drafted for Charles, declaring his determination to restore the Elector to the Palatinate, was placed before the Parliaments of all three kingdoms, and was probably put forward to convince the Elector that loyalty to Charles was worth while. It caused no great worries to the Scots, whose pan-Protestant inclinations made them agreeable to it.[69]

This left three issues, which appear to have taken most of the time from 14 August to early October, and none of which appear to have been entirely resolved in that time. The issue of the incendiaries created much less documentary record than that of the granting of offices, but was not necessarily therefore less important. On 20 August Nicholas wrote to the King that if Montrose were not released and Traquair cleared 'we shall account as feigned counterfeit all y Scots expressions and affeccions to y mats person'.[70] In this Nicholas may have been playing the courtier's part of providing a mirror to his master's opinion. On 3 September it was rumoured that the King would not wait until the end of the process against Traquair, but would go home before it was over, a course which at least one English adviser recommended as likely to be for the incendiaries' benefit.[71] On 28 September Nicholas explained the silence about incendiaries by saying the business had been not so much as entered upon yet.[72] It is possible that their trials were being delayed, as Strafford's had been, pending a settlement which might make judicial proceedings unnecessary. Much later, Baillie reported that by the middle of October Argyll had 'brought all things verie near to that poynt the king desyred'.[73] Baillie's judgement appears to be confirmed by a series of notes in the Tollemache manuscripts,[74] concerning negotiations on this subject, and apostiled in the King's holograph. They are undated, but a summary of them was minuted as a record of negotiations taking place on 8 October, and they may well have taken place on that day. The substance of the agreement was that the Parliament would insist on bringing Traquair and Montrose to trial, thereby acquiring the opportunity to wash their dirty linen and discredit

[68] PRO SP 16/483/91.

[69] Ibid. 16/483/82 and 94.

[70] Guildford MS 52/2/19(10).

[71] Yale University, Beinecke Library, Osborn Shelves, Howard of Escrick MSS, Correspondence Folder 2.10; PRO SP 16/484/63.

[72] PRO SP 16/484/44.

[73] Baillie, i. 393.

[74] Tollemache MS 4105, apparently minuted in MS 4109. I am very grateful to Dr J. S. A. Adamson for these references. The bulk of this collection is the papers of Will Murray, but it includes also the papers of Lord Maitland, second Earl of Lauderdale. It seems possible that these documents, which were clearly once in the possession of Lord Chancellor Loudoun, came from him via Lauderdale. I am grateful to Dr Adamson for advice on these points. Quotations are from MS 4105.

their accomplices. However, 'taking into consideration his Maties gracious goodnes towards his native kingdom', and 'that his Matie. may joyfullie return . . . to the settling of his royall affaires in his other dominiones', they would refrain from passing 'finall sentence'. Charles's suspicion shows raw in his annotation on this point: 'this to be understud, no sentence at all, except in so far as to fynde the relevance of the ditto'.[75] In return, Charles, in his own hand, undertook that

I taking in good part the respect & thankefulness of this Parliament in remitting to me those that they call incendiaries, & others, according to there declaration; I doe declare that I will not imploy anie of those persons in anie office of state Councell or Session without consent of Par. nor grant them access to my Person wherby they may interrup or disturbe that firme peace that is so happilie concluded.

Ruthven, the defender of Edinburgh Castle, was to be restored to favour, and summonses to minor figures were to be withdrawn. This is the agreement which came into effect on the final settlement a month later, and if it had been reached on 8 October, it seems that the issue of the incendiaries was not the one which led to the breakdown of negotiations which resulted in the Incident. Agreement on the issue had been reached with great difficulty, but it was reached.

   The issue of appointment of officers is easier to follow, because more of the negotiation took place in public. The King viewed the Scottish proposal for Parliamentary choice of the great officers, Councillors, and Lords of Session with some misgiving, since he took it to be 'a speciall part of his prerogative, a great sinew of his government, the long possession of kings in Scotland, the unquestionable right of kings in England'.[76] He was also deeply anxious, with reason, as the event proved, about the danger that if he made such a concession in Scotland, the English would want to copy it. Nicholas repeatedly warned Charles that if he made this concession, the English would press to imitate it.[77] Even Webb, the Duke of Richmond and Lennox's secretary, was ready to press for equal treatment: 'I am cleere of opinion with you, what is done here will be a rule to us; and I thinck it most just that a nation from whom a king injoyes all those benefitts which ours affords him should receive from him at least as much as an other place which yealds him nothing but trouble'.[78] There was also tension because the Scots wanted the concession to extend to all officers, while the King insisted, as he was later to do in England, that he would not displace existing officers

[75] The 'ditto', or 'dittay', was the formal paper of accusations against Traquair.
[76] Baillie, i. 389.
[77] Guildford MS 52/2/19(30); Evelyn, iv. 89, 105, and other refs. See also *HMC Salis.* XXII. 365.
[78] *NP* i. 52.

against whom no crime had been alleged.[79] There was also tension about how the procedure would work. The Scots clearly envisaged a procedure in which the Parliament nominated a list, among whom the King chose, whereas the procedure the King attempted to use was one whereby he nominated, and the Parliament had to give or refuse its approval.[80] There was further dispute about whether the Council should have power to fill offices during the intervals between Parliaments.[81] It was not only the King who began to be in favour of resistance on some of these issues. On 21 September Webb reported the existence of a faction which wished 'his Majesty would propose it like a man, and stand upon it'. 'These swearers say that ye king might carry everything, if he did not undoe himself by yealding'. Morton is the only one of these hard-liners named.[82] These rumblings signal the beginning of hard-line, in addition to soft-line, pressure on Charles, which was to increase steadily until 1642.

By comparison, the identities of the officers was a simple problem, and yet that caused trouble enough. On 20 September Charles proposed Loudoun as Treasurer and Morton as Chancellor. The nomination of Loudoun was acceptable, but that of Morton was not.[83] Morton encountered passionate opposition from Argyll, and, as Baillie commented, 'factions began here evidentlie to appear'.[84] On 25 September Wemyss named 'Argyll and his faction' as the source of opposition to Charles on officers, and also reported hot words on a proposal of the barons, that none who had been out of the kingdom and adhered to the King during the Bishops' Wars should hold office. This would have had the effect of excluding Roxburgh, as well as Morton, and Roxburgh was unwise enough to protest in public, saying 'Argyll told him comparisons were odious', to which Argyll chose to take exception. The King, Wemyss said, was 'glad . . . when he sees any man he thinks loves him yit'.[85] On 30 September the King tried again, offering Loudoun this time for Chancellor, and Almond for Treasurer. Almond had been a signatory of the Cumbernauld Band, and Argyll appears to have chosen to draw attention to the fact in public: 'Argyle had been before allwayes to that man a most speciall friend; bot he said, he behooved to preferr the publick good to private friendship, and so did avowedlie oppose that motion; as indeede it was thought Almond in that place, might have

---

[79] Guildford MS 52/2/19(13b).

[80] NLS Wodrow MS Fol. 64, fo. 115; PRO SP 16/483/96; *HMC Salis.* XXII. 369.

[81] *HMC Salis.* XXII. 363.

[82] *NP* i. 49–51.

[83] Yale University, Beinecke Library, Osborn Shelves, Howard of Escrick MSS, Correspondence Folder 3.17.

[84] Baillie, i. 390.

[85] Bodl. MS Carte 1, fos. 457–60.

been also a head and leader to his old friends, the banders and malcontents, as any other of our nation'.[86] Almond might well have said that with friends like that, he did not need enemies, and this intervention of Argyll's may do something to explain his actions in the next two weeks.

The nomination of Loudoun was agreed, but according to Vane, there was no further progress achieved in the next three weeks.[87] The tension was growing dangerous, and grew more so on 29 September, when Lord Ker, Roxburgh's son, accused Hamilton of being a 'juglar' with the King, and challenged him to a duel. The challenge was sent by his 'furious and drunken second', the Earl of Crawford, one of the officers who had been cashiered from the King's English army for his Catholicism. Hamilton, with a show of courtesy which can only have increased Crawford's fury, said he would give an answer if he would return the next day, clearly giving those present the message that he would answer Crawford when he was sober. Meanwhile, as Baillie put it, 'the wise man did make use of the injury', and obtained a declaration clearing him from both the King and the Parliament.[88] The issue of offices appeared to have a considerable capacity to inflame faction, and went a long way to illustrate the truth of Napier's view that Scotland needed an effective monarchy.

Yet though the issue of offices did most to inflame Scottish passion, the third remaining issue may well have been the most important to the King. That is the issue of Scottish involvement in English affairs. It was essential to Charles to ensure that the withdrawal of the Scottish army was not just a tactical retreat, but an abandonment of the claim to be interested parties in English politics. It was equally essential to Pym and his allies to ensure that the Scottish withdrawal should not mark this sort of withdrawal into isolationism, but that the Scots should remain ready to treat any revival of Laudianism in England as a threat to Anglo-Scottish peace. Shortly after the King went to Edinburgh, he was joined by a committee from the English Parliament, consisting of Howard of Escrick, Hampden, Fiennes, Sir Philip Stapleton, and Sir William Armyn. Charles made it slightly plainer than courtesy permitted that this committee was unwelcome, but it did not go away. It was officially charged with overseeing the disbanding and the conclusion of the treaty, but it is hard to imagine that, in two months, this is all it did. It must have enjoyed social contacts with some of the Covenanter leadership, especially with those on its interventionist wing. If we knew more of this committee's activities, it is possible that the events of October might be rather clearer than they are. Sir Philip Stapleton on 17 September

---

[86] Baillie, i. 390–1.
[87] NP i. 57.
[88] Baillie, i. 391.

told Lord Wharton that they had received many courtesies, especially from Hamilton and Argyll.[89] Charles and his friends appear to have drawn the obvious conclusion, and on 28 September the committee reported to Mandeville, one of the clearest pro-Scots in London, that 'very great jealousyes are raised upon us, as if wee were here onely to support a party and faction against his Majesty'. The committee appear to have thought the King's anger was bringing them into danger, and persistently petitioned for recall, saying they could not see they could do any service to countervail the hazard.[90] In Hamilton's case, the survival of his papers makes it possible to trace his English contacts, and he was keeping up a friendly correspondence with Essex, Mandeville, and Saye. Essex commended Howard of Escrick, and Mandeville advised him to trust Hampden. Saye recommended 'the union of both kingdoms without faction in either', advice which was not friendly to Montrose or Traquair.[91] Hamilton, as a member of the English Council, could not cease to involve himself in English affairs, but the King was likely to take a dim view of any attempt to involve Argyll or other resident Scots in these contacts. Sometime before he left Scotland, the King obtained promises of non-intervention in English affairs from Loudoun and Argyll, but since these are known only from Charles's later reminders, we do not know when they were given.[92] It was clearly one of Charles's major objectives to obtain them, and it is the balance of probability that, by the middle of October, he had not yet done so.

The conspiracy which became known as the Incident had existed as a contingency plan as far back as July, but the decision to put it into effect appears to have been taken very suddenly between 1 and 9 October. Endymion Porter, who was more in the King's confidence than most people, had not seen it coming. He told Nicholas he had left Edinburgh to see some famous towns of the kingdom, expecting to leave for England the day after his return. Instead, he found watching and warding, and deadly feuds.[93] This letter suggests that Charles's decision to commit himself to the Incident may have been a sudden one, taken between 1 and 9 October, and probably towards the end of that period. By great good fortune, we happen to possess a set of notes by Lord Chancellor Loudoun on the negotiations of 6 and 7 October. What is

[89] Bodl. MS Carte 103, fo. 84. This is the pencil, not the ink, foliation.

[90] Yale University, Beinecke Library, Osborn Shelves, Howard of Escrick MSS, Correspondence Folder 3.23. See also Donald, p. 433 and n. The committee's insistence that there was nothing for them to do suggests, either that their letters were written in more than usual fear of interception, or that Charles's suspicions were, for once, unjustified.

[91] Hamilton MSS 1410, 1412, 1505, and other refs.

[92] Ibid. 1585, 1586. Charles reminded Loudoun and Argyll of these promises in Jan. 1642.

[93] Christ Church, Evelyn MSS, Nicholas Box, no. 78 (my numeration), Endymion Porter to Nicholas, 19 Oct. 1641. I am grateful to Dr J. S. A. Adamson for drawing my attention to this collection.

more, we possess Charles's comments on these negotiations, in the form of holograph instructions to Loudoun, endorsed: 'Notes for my L. Chancelors memorie, that he may the better apply himself to my mynde in the intendit way of accommodation'.[94] We have, in fact, a vignette of the negotiations within forty-eight hours of their breakdown.

On some issues, these negotiations show progress. On 6 October they reached agreement to put the Treasury into commission, and Charles proposed for the commissioners Loudoun, the Earls of Mar and Southesk, Lord Lindsay, and Sir James Carmichael the Treasurer Depute. Of these names, only Loudoun and Carmichael were ultimately approved, but agreement on this issue does not appear to have been out of reach. On the issue of whether the existing officers should stay in place or whether their places should be filled by Parliamentary advice, they reached the face-saving compromise that the Parliament should approve the existing officers. There were still arguments in progress about which of the Acts considered in the current Parliament should be approved. There is a consistent thread underlying the detailed disagreements, which is about how much power the King personally should have in the new Scotland. This was a dangerous issue, but it was not impossible that the disagreements could be smoothed over.

The same issue appeared in a much more difficult form in a deep disagreement about the meaning of Parliamentary participation in the choice of great officers, Councillors, and Judges of the Court of Session.[95] The Covenanters had been hoping for Parliamentary nomination, and at the least, for a considerable influence on the list of names. Charles's understanding merges most clearly in his comments on the appointment of Councillors and judges of the Court of Session: 'I expect that those that I have or shall nominate shall be approved except sufficient cause (whether privatlie or publiclie I doe not care) be showen me, of which nature I nether esteeme the gen. citation, nor having been a Bander, to be anie'.[96] It was the same position he was to take up in England in the summer of 1642: if any specific fault could be shown in any of his choices, he would listen, but otherwise, he would not allow

---

[94] What follows is based on Tollemache MSS 4109 and 4110. I am deeply grateful to Dr J. S. A. Adamson for drawing my attention to these MSS. MS 4109 is a record of Scottish negotiating proposals, partly in the hand of a secretary, and partly in a hand which may be Loudoun's. It covers discussions taking place on 6, 7, and 8 Oct. MS 4110, addressed by Charles to Loudoun, is his holograph comments on the proposals made on 6 and 7 Oct. This MS gives the impression of having been written continuously, rather than day by day, but it is hard to see how such an impression could be proved.

[95] This tends to justify and strengthen the comments of Gardiner, *History*, x. 19, 21.

[96] The Banders, signatories of the Cumbernauld Band, might be suspected of being allies of Montrose. For a list of signatories, see Donald, p. 425. The signatory under discussion was probably Almond, Charles's candidate for Lord Treasurer. On delay caused by the problem of choice of officers, see Yale University, Beinecke Library, Osborn Shelves, Howard of Escrick MSS, Correspondence Folder 3.21 (Howard of Escrick to the Lord Keeper, 28 Sept. 1641).

his freedom of choice to be interfered with. This same insistence on his personal authority emerges in an aside on a reference to the committee for the relief of public burthens: 'I thinke that the Kings ar part of the publike'. It was the same cause for which he took his stand in England. He would not allow the creation of an impersonal state, but intended to remain personally the ultimate source of authority. This determination seems to have been incompatible with Covenanter plans for Scotland.

This disagreement about the ultimate seat of authority perhaps became irreconcilable on the morning of 7 October with the raising of the old issue of 1639, the control of the Scottish royal castles.[97] Loudoun forwarded to Charles a proposal 'that the castles may not be occasion of terror to the kingdome, it is thoght fitt, that the fortificationes of the castles of Edinburgh, Dumbartaine & Stirling may be demolished'.[98] Charles wrote: 'I see not how my castelles in the keeping of honnest men, can be a terror [to] the kingdome'. Reading over what he had written, he altered it to 'my castelles or other men's in the keeping of honnest men'. Anyone familiar with Dr Cust's work on 'Charles I and a Draft Declaration' will recognize the mental processes which went into this addition, and will see the tapping of deep-seated fears of his subjects' loyalty, which the Covenanters had already done enough to provoke.[99] Once these suspicions had been roused, they can only have been inflamed further by a proposal, made later the same morning, for yearly musters and preserving a stock of arms and ammunition within the country, but on this Charles confined himself to saying that 'I must see the particulars of this before I answer to it'. It is, in fact, the strongest reason for thinking that it was the proposal about the royal castles which made Charles lose faith in the negotiations that there is a clear change in the quality of his annotations from then on. Up to that point, he had been making numerous criticisms, like a man who, if not satisfied, still hoped to improve the terms. From then on, his comments grow more and more cursory and uninformative. They give the impression of a man avoiding commitment, rather than of a man trying to change terms.

This is particularly clear in the business of the afternoon of 7 October, when the Scots introduced a proposal for commissions to end the remaining business of the treaty, which Charles probably hoped they had allowed to lapse. They raised first the proposal for Scots of 'qualitie and respect' to attend the King, the Queen, and the Prince, in effect a proposal to revive the Anglo-Scottish Bedchamber of James VI

---

[97] On this issue, see above, ch. 2, pp. 63, 67–8.

[98] The inclusion of Dumbarton suggests Scottish fears that Charles might bring over some of the newly disbanded Irish army.

[99] R. P. Cust, 'Charles I and a Draft Declaration', *Historical Research*, 63/151 (1990), pp. 143–61.

and I.[100] This was a request which Charles had heard with sympathy, and it was not his fault that Rothes, whom he had planned to appoint, had instead died. Now, however, he seemed unwilling to hear more of the issue, and wrote: 'in this I suppose that the Par. hes more reason to thanke then to importune me'. The Scots then revived several of the proposals from their old widow's cruse, article 8 of their treaty demands. They wanted to raise the issues of leagues and confederations, of mutual supply in the case of foreign invasion, and of trade, commerce, naturalization, and mercantile privileges. These were all reasonable subjects of discussion. What was likely to be more offensive to Charles, because it contained a proposal to change the domestic constitution of England, was a proposal for 'not making or denouncing of wars with forraners without consent of both Parliaments'. Charles confined himself to the comment that 'I have nothing to say to this, but that great care must be had in the drawing up of the severall commissions & in the choice of the comissioners'. These proposals, with their implications of renewal of the Anglo-Scottish partnership, would have been anathema to Charles, and, if he had still been negotiating seriously, might have by themselves turned his mind back to plotting. However, the blankness of his reply to this proposal raises the suspicion that serious negotiation was already over. If it was not then, it very soon was. By 9 October the plot which became known as the Incident was well under way.

The plot which took shape between 9 and 12 October is best followed through the subsequent depositions of the conspirators.[101] The chief organizer appears to have been Will Murray, Groom of the Bedchamber, and a man closely in the confidence of the King and Queen. On the day after the King's arrival in Edinburgh, Murray had opened confidential discussions with Colonel Cochrane. Some time afterwards, he admitted 'casuallie being in the castell with the Earl of Montrose, and discoursing on the publict bussines'. Montrose asked to be admitted to the King's presence to deliver business 'of very hich nature'. After three letters, the King suddenly granted this request on 11 October. Cochrane admitted to his conversations with Will Murray, and said that 'religion and liberties being established', he had proferred his services against any who would hinder the peace of the kingdom, specially naming Hamilton and Argyll. Murray's reply was to ask whether he was certain of the loyalty of his regiment, to which he gave an encouraging answer. Cochrane's Lieutenant-Colonel testified that Cochrane came to

[100] On this, see Neil Cuddy, 'Revival of the Entourage: The Bedchamber of James I 1603–1625', in David Starkey (ed.), *The English Court* (1987), 173–225.
[101] *HMC Fourth Report*, i. 163–70.

his regiment on 9 October, 'drank liberallie' with them, and said that if they were of his mind, he hoped to make them a fortune.

The Earl of Crawford testified that the next day, 10 October, Will Murray supped at the Earl of Airth's house with Lord Ogilvie, Lord Gray, Colonel Cochrane, and Crawford, and told them that Montrose had written to the King offering to accuse Argyll and Hamilton of high treason. Contact was then established with Almond, the Earl of Home, and Lord Kirkudbright. Crawford then gave dinner to Lieutenant-Colonel Hurry (a soldier formerly in Spanish service),[102] and Lieutenant-Colonel Alexander Stewart, who were to be the key front men in the plot.

On the morning of 11 October the final stages of the plot took shape. Lieutenant-Colonel Alexander Stewart, who was in charge of the final recruitment of soldiers, explained that the whole country was governed by two, Hamilton and Argyll, but there was now a faction strong enough to suppress them. Porter, who described Hamilton and Argyll as 'the two great guiders of the affaires of this state', seems to have been told a similar story. The final plot, as Stewart recounted it, was that Will Murray should fetch Hamilton and Argyll to the King's withdrawing room, and that Almond and Crawford, with four hundred men to help them, should arrest them. Crawford then proposed to murder them, and Almond to imprison them pending a legal trial. In order to avoid possible tumults caused by their followers, they were to be imprisoned on a King's ship. In case of any disorder, the plotters were assured that the Earls of Home and Roxburgh would bring in their 'friends'. Roxburgh's optimistic claim to Nicholas that the story was 'not worthe the blackinge of so mutche paper' does not altogether free him from suspicion. Alexander Stewart claimed further armed support in Lothian, Linlithgowshire, and Stirlingshire. Since Hamilton later discovered that Almond's tenants in Linlithgowshire had been alerted for a muster with muskets, powder, and ball, this report may well be true.[103]

It was a well-planned plot, which might easily have succeeded. The last-minute character of much of the organization meant there was the less time in which the plot might leak. This might suggest that, unlike many of Charles's other plots, it was meant, not to terrify, but to succeed. Had it done so, there were enough banders ready to move in behind it to provide Charles with the basis of an alternative government.[104] This alternative government would have been one which would have had no truck with any future plans for English intervention, and,

[102] Hamilton MS 9572 (undated). See *HMC Second Report*, 176 for Cochrane's and Hurry's later presence as knights in Montrose's service.

[103] Hamilton MSS 1544, 1554; Christ Church, Evelyn MSS, Nicholas Box nos. 78, 36.

[104] The depositions also name Mar and Kirkudbright among those whose names were taken by the conspirators, whether genuinely or in vain.

with its opponents leaderless, might well have had enough physical power to remain in control. The King's involvement, though not finally proved by the depositions, is so overwhelmingly probable that only the most hardened of defence lawyers would think it open to reasonable doubt. Will Murray, both because of his nearness to the King and because of his menial status, was not the man to start a plot independently. When Hamilton selected Will Murray as the intermediary charged with making his subsequent peace with the King, he signalled plainly enough that he did not believe Will Murray to be the seat of the animus against him.[105] When Hamilton reported the plot to his brother-in-law Feilding, he said it had become 'a poynt of respect to his Majestie not to wrytt to anie of particulares which I have observed'. He enclosed instead a copy of some of the official depositions.[106] Moreover, although Nicholas repeatedly complained that the King's service suffered 'infinite prejudice' by his silence, the King never sent any official account of what happened to London.[107] The report from the Parliamentary commissioners was for a long time the only official report received in London.[108] Secretary Vane, when reproved by Nicholas for not reporting the true story to London, said that the King had forbidden him to do so: 'I must doe in businesse of this nature as his Majestie commands mee, but Secretarys have hard games to play att this time'.[109]

The Mounteagle of the plot was Lieutenant-Colonel Hurry, who, apparently having cold feet at what he was asked to do, told the story to General Leslie, who in turn took him to repeat it to Hamilton and Argyll. They at first were uncertain whether to believe it, and went into hiding overnight. It was only the next morning, on hearing that the King was going to Parliament escorted by an armed force made up of those named as plotting against them, that they decided on flight.[110] They went, accompanied by Hamilton's brother Lanerick, to Hamilton's house at Kenneill, a few miles outside Edinburgh. Lord Chancellor Loudoun then took charge of the slow and painful process of patching up an accommodation which would at least make a show of saving everyone's face. The difficulty was to make a submission which avoided a direct slur on the King's honour. Hamilton's first version proved unacceptable, but, after revisions according to the advice of Will Murray, a second version was happier. The King pressed for a public investigation, perhaps in the hope that this would inhibit witnesses, but the

---

[105] Hamilton MSS 1493, 1567, 1568.
[106] Warwicks. RO Feilding of Newnham Paddox MSS C 1/104; ibid. R 6 is probably the enclosure referred to in this letter. It duplicates what is available in *HMC Fourth Report*.
[107] Guildford MSS 85/3/2(19, 20, 23) and 52/2/19(25, 28).
[108] Hamilton MS 1446; PRO SP 16/485/22.
[109] *NP* i. 57, 58, 59; PRO SP 16/485/36.
[110] Hamilton MSS 1440, 1441.

Parliament was successful in achieving investigation by a private committee. On 1 November this committee reported a face-saving compromise asking for the fugitives' return. According to the report Lauderdale sent to Hamilton, Mar spoke 'I know not what', Yester was inaudible, and Spynie opposed it, while Morton criticized its grammar, and Lennox neither approved nor disallowed it.[111] With these reservations, it went through, and Hamilton and the others returned to Edinburgh. Hamilton, who seems to have believed the King guilty, showed himself a true professional courtier by his willingness to return to duty as if nothing had happened.

After this, both sides seem to have lost stomach for the fight, and they rapidly reached agreements which could have been had, with enough good will, many weeks earlier. The Treasury, the office which had caused most dispute, was put into a commission consisting of Loudoun, Argyll, Glencairn, and Carmichael, a committee of one figure acceptable to each side, one conciliator, and one financial professional. Ruthven and Nithsdale, two men highly unpopular with the Covenanters but not officially listed as incendiaries, were allowed to come home. On the incendiaries, both parties again agreed to a formula close to the one for which Loudoun had been working since June and which had been minuted on 8 October, whereby they were to be tried, but their sentence remitted to the King. In return for the remission of the sentence, the King promised not to employ them in future without the consent of the Parliament.[112] The King agreed to let a trial go forward without trying to intervene, but Argyll agreed not to insist on the punishment of those involved. The new Privy Council, named by the King with the 'advice and consent' of the Parliament, was designed, as far as possible, to satisfy all parties. Argyll, Hamilton, and Lanerick were included, together with the committed Covenanters Balmerino and Burghley. So, on the other side, were Almond, Morton, Roxburgh, and Mar.[113] Negotiations ended where the whole story had begun in 1637, with the issue of the Royal Supremacy. In a formula so qualified that it can have been designed for no purpose but to save the King's honour, they agreed to an oath of allegiance repudiating any foreign prince, and recognizing the King as 'onelie supreme governor of this kingdome' according to the Covenant.[114] Since the King recognized that his ordinary residence would be in England, he committed the 'administration and government' of the kingdom to the Privy Council, and, with a final request to the Scots not to forget his birthday, the King retired to London.[115]

[111] Hamilton MS 1562.
[112] APS 5. 388, 375, 409.
[113] RPCS vii. 142–3.
[114] Ibid. 147.
[115] Ibid. 482–3.

Endymion Porter was probably right in his fear that the plot would leave all worse than they found it.[116]

If he hoped to return to a concentration on English affairs, the King had left it too late, for on 22–3 October rebellion had broken out in Ireland. Charles's immediate reaction to the news was to go and play golf, leaving Vane to grapple with the rebellion and a purge together.[117] By the time he reached Berwick on 18 November, the King had been forced to recognize that he was going to need Scottish help in suppressing the rebellion, and sent back a letter written by Lennox to ask for it. So far from retreating into comfortable English isolation, Charles was now facing a wider phase of the British crisis. Ireland was an English dominion, not a British one, and therefore any attempt to recruit Scottish help was going to involve co-operation between the Scots and the English Parliament, and therefore another instalment of Scottish commissioners in London. What was more, he was going to have to face the potentially disruptive effects of Scottish intervention in Ireland. There was now no prospect of the kingdoms of Britain going their separate ways in peace. The English Parliament saw its opportunity, and its request for Scottish help arrived at Edinburgh together with the King's.[118]

[116] Christ Church, Evelyn MSS, Nicholas Box, no. 78.
[117] Hamilton MS 1447.
[118] *RPCS* vii. 150.

9

The Slow Movement

MAY–SEPTEMBER 1641

On 12 May 1641, a few hours after the death of Strafford, the Lords asked the Commons for a conference about settling the King's revenue.[1] It was, at least superficially, a reasonable request. It was one without which no long-term stability could be achieved, and it appealed to the generally accepted code of values, by which, if the King had done something for them, they should do something for the King. However, after the Army Plot, there was no prospect that this suggestion would be accepted. Instead, the Commons asked the Lords for haste in dealing with the bill to exclude bishops from the House of Lords.[2] There was no possibility that this request would be acceded to either. Much happened during the summer which was important to the long-term movement of opinion, but in terms of any movement towards resolution of the crisis, the period was one of deadlock. When Vane told Roe on 18 June that 'neither our Parliament doth as yet affoorde any matter worthie your knowledge', he did not mean there had been no interesting debates: he meant that there had been no movement towards a solution: 'wee are heare still in the labirinth, and cannot gett out'.[3]

After the Army Plot and the death of Strafford, Pym and Charles had both probably been coerced beyond endurance, and if they had been entirely free agents, they might have been ready for civil war then and there. Their difficulty was that there was no parallel perception of crisis in the country at large, nor even in a large proportion of the two Houses of Parliament. In particular, the two of them were almost handcuffed together by the resolute dedication of the House of Lords to the search for consensus. Individual members of the Lords were growing more frankly partisan, and heated exchanges between them began to find their way into the newsletters with increasing frequency. However, the House as a whole managed to keep up an appearance of consensus politics, largely through the efforts of Manchester, Bristol, and Williams, who, together, seem to have managed to hold the middle ground for most of the summer. The Lords had been deeply shocked by the

---

[1] *LJ* iv. 246.
[2] *CJ* ii. 145.
[3] PRO SP 16/481/44.

Army Plot, and throughout the summer, they were prepared to co-operate with the Commons in measures aimed at depriving the King of the power to conduct any future coup. They were also prepared to co-operate in measures designed to subject the King more firmly to Parliamentary statute, and therefore to deprive him of the power to follow policies which did not enjoy general consent. On the other hand, they remained adamantly opposed to a 'further Reformation' in religion, which, to the majority of the Commons, was becoming increasingly indispensable. All through the summer, bills for the reformation of religion were going up to the Lords, followed by requests for haste, and the bills were not being concluded.[4] A faction among the Lords was prepared to support such bills, but there was no likelihood that they would enjoy a majority in the House. The Lords were not prepared to pass any bill which had the effect of forcing people out of the political nation. They defended the rights of their own order, including the bishops and the popish Lords, with a stern determination. For example, when the Lords rejected the Commons' bill for compulsory taking of the Protestation, the Commons protested that it was 'a shibboleth to discover a true Israelite'.[5] In these words, they explained, however unwittingly, precisely why the Lords felt the need to reject it. The Lords' underlying message, both to the King and to the Commons, was that there was no alternative to co-operation.

The King was willing, at least superficially, to go along with this attitude, and the Venetian Ambassador said that he was relying on the division between the Houses to recover his fortunes.[6] The King was also relying on an increasingly articulate team of supporters in the Commons, among whom Sir John Culpepper was becoming more prominent. This group, though it won the occasional division, remained tantalizingly short of a majority, but its existence was a considerable check on Pym's freedom of action, since any provocative measures could shift votes and lose Pym his majority. The King, though he doubtless hoped for a majority in the Commons, could afford to wait in patience, since it seemed the overwhelming balance of probability that, on his return from Scotland, he would be able to end the session. Even if he did not get members' consent to dissolution, he could expect consent to an extended prorogation, and after a cooling-off period of some six months, Pym would find it difficult to start where he had left off.

By May 1641 the Parliament had already become a Long Parliament

---

[4] *LJ* iv. 247, 280, 308, and other refs. See below, pp. 337–44.
[5] *LJ* iv. 338.
[6] *CSP Ven. 1640–2*, p. 161. On the King's later reliance on divisions between the Houses, see M. J. Mendle, 'Politics and Political Thought 1640–1642', in Russell (ed.), *Origins*, pp. 239–45.

by previous standards, and members' impatience grew increasingly articulate during the summer. On 22 May Sir Percy Herbert wrote to his wife: 'sweetheart, the Parliament lasts but until Whitsun, and then it is done'.[7] Roger Hill was one of the more committed godly and his wife, who was a Gurdon, even more so, yet they were newly married, and even their devotion to the cause began to wear thin. On 15 June Hill complained that divers members 'will not let me goe'. On 10 August he wrote: 'I wish I were with thee under the plumb and payre trees'. On 29 August he said: 'I resolve to break through all boundes', and said he was coming to join her on Monday.[8] This sort of emotion was one of the King's major political resources.

For the group around Pym, the summer was a difficult time, since the Commons could not do anything without the Lords. It was necessary to maintain the atmosphere of political crisis, and to avoid any circumstances in which the King might be able to contemplate a dissolution. Ths meant, first and foremost, restraining the King's power to carry through a forcible dissolution. In this, Pym's group could rely on the co-operation of the Lords, but only so long as they did not alienate them by excessive obstinacy or enthusiasm. It was also necessary to prevent the King from being able to carry through a peaceable dissolution or prorogation. It was not safe to assume that the consent of the Houses would be withheld, since Roger Hill, for example, would have found it very hard to vote against such a proposal. The only likely way of achieving this objective was to reassert the King's dependence on Parliamentary authority for taxation, without getting round to providing him with a new revenue settlement.

In setting themselves this objective, Pym's group were able to work with the grain of traditional House of Commons' prejudices. Attacks on the vintners' monopoly, or bills against forest laws and knighthood fines, were popular with many members, such as Selden, who had absolutely no sympathy with the programme of religious reformation. The permanent settlement of Tonnage and Poundage, without which the King would find it difficult to dissolve, required a positive effort from Pym and St John, which they could easily refrain from making. Similarly, after the success of Pym's attack on military charges in the Short Parliament, the King knew he needed a measure providing for a legal settlement of the militia. This was the sort of constructive measure which went against all the ingrained country reflexes, and it was unlikely to go through unless or until Pym and his friends exerted themselves to

---

[7] PRO 30/53/7, no. 26.
[8] BL Add. MS 46500, fos. 11^r, 12^r, 15^r. I am grateful to Dr J. S. A. Adamson for drawing my attention to this MS.

ensure that it should. The junto did not have many cards in the summer of 1641, but in taking refuge in the area where inaction, rather than action, could achieve their objectives, they were playing the few cards they had with considerable skill. The ultimate objective still seems to have been the great offices of state, but the terms seem to have subtly changed. After the Army Plot, it was clear enough that they would never enjoy power on acceptable terms by Charles's consent. It therefore became more essential to aim at achieving office by coercion. If they did so, it would be essential to ensure that Charles should never recover the full power to govern: if he did, their execution could be expected to follow. Offices gained by coercion had to be kept by the same method. The aim therefore seems to have been to Merovingianize Charles, leaving him as a figurehead while real power remained with the Council and the great officers. It was not an easy strategy. It had last been used in 1388, and had led to loss of life among those who used it.

At first, the Army Plot did not have the same impact on all members that it did on Pym and his friends: on 19 May Pym complained that 'it is conceived by some that this design is of no importance'.[9] On the other hand, an incident the same day showed that many other members were in a considerable state of alarm. A board in the gallery cracked, and at the noise 'Sir Walter Earles sonne cried out Treason, Treason, many of the burgesses ran away, some wth their swords drawn, but they all returned well laughed at by the rest which stayed in the House.' Sir Arthur Haselrig, in his alarm, clutched hold of an image, 'but was much jeered for flying to the hornes of the altar'.[10] Meanwhile, the Army Plot was being investigated by a committee consisting of Pym, Hampden, Holles, Fiennes, Stapleton, Clotworthy, and Strode, and, with the benefit of being able to impose an oath, by a select committee of the Lords. During the month after the plot, the Lords' committee assembled the body of depositions which is the basis of our knowledge of the plot today, and Fiennes, for the committee of seven, reported the findings to the Commons. This report, made in a series of instalments from 8 June onwards, established to the satisfaction of most members that the plot needed to be taken seriously. Moreover, the public reading of the depositions provided rich material for members' newsletters to wives and friends. Sir Norton Knatchbull, for example, sent his wife almost the whole of Goring's deposition, with its damning implication of the King, asking her if she knew what the word 'cabal' meant. He asked her 'to be sparing to communicate it for a while', but it is doubtful whether

[9] BL Harl. MS 163, fo. 591ᵃ.
[10] West Devon RO, Drake of Colyton MS 1700 A/CP 19, BL Harl. MS 163, fo. 588ᵇ, Peyton, fo. 121.

all those to whom this advice was given took it.[11] Until the attempt on the Five Members, it is doubtful whether anything did as much to blacken Charles's reputation as the circulation of the Army Plot depositions. These depositions also established, for the benefit of any reasonable reader, that military preparations undertaken against Charles might be purely defensive in their intention. Resisting a coup, even one headed by the King, need not be classified as rebellion, but once that lesson had been learnt, it would become possible to apply it in many places where it did not honestly belong.

Meanwhile, since the treaty with the Scots required Parliamentary ratification, the two Houses were periodically occupied in discussing the conclusions of the treaty commissioners. These conclusions were taken clause by clause. In the Lords, they caused little trouble, since the House agreed with Bristol's determination to reach a quick conclusion and free the kingdom from the burden (and the threat) of the two armies. In the Commons, occasional clauses caused trouble, usually as a result of the objections of the anti-Scots. On 17 May the Commons discussed the Scots' request for conformity in religion between the kingdoms, and Hyde moved to agree with the Lords Commissioners' rather brusque answer of 15 March. D'Ewes 'marvelled at Mr. Hyde's motion, which would not only slight the Scots and their affection, but also utterly lay aside the work of reforming religion'. D'Ewes succeeded in adding the words 'that this House doth approve of the affection of their brethren of Scotland, in their desire of a conformity in church government, between the two nations; and doth give them thanks for it'.[12] This not very substantial addition drew protests from Digby and Falkland, and was probably the occasion of a speech by Waller, which 'gave some notes out of Buchanan about their tumultuous government, with the cruelties of its first beginning'.[13] Perhaps the most interesting point was the indignation caused by D'Ewes's description of the Scots as a 'potent nation': he had to defuse criticism by saying the word had only been in the positive, and he was prepared to use the comparative or the superlative for the English. On the 19th, Waller objected to the clause providing that the kingdoms should not make war on each other without the consent of their Parliaments, saying it was manifestly against the King's prerogative, but though 'divers' supported him, he did not carry his point. The Scots seemed to have lost none of their ability to

---

[11] KAO Knatchbull MSS U 951/C261/37. I am grateful to Dr J. S. A. Adamson for this reference. The Army Plot depositions were not printed until the summer of 1642, but they appear to have been widely circulated in manuscript newsletters.

[12] BL Harl. MS 163, fo. 580[a–b], CJ ii. 148; Gawdy, vol. ii, fo. 50[r]. There was a disputed election to the Chair, in which the pro-Scots tried to get Culpepper (not Hyde) called to the Chair in order to stop him speaking.

[13] BL Sloane MS 3317, fo. 22[r].

polarize English opinion.[14] The only other issue which caused serious dispute was that of the incendiaries, in which the King's case was powerfully put, not in the Lords, but in the Commons. Selden fired a warning shot on the incendiaries' behalf on 22 May, arguing, characteristically, that in handing them over for trial in Scotland, 'we would come to be judged by a law we knew not'.[15] The issue was argued out on 19 June, when the Scots' proposal for the incendiaries to be excepted from the Act of Oblivion came before the Commons. Pym 'spake verie effectuallie' for the Scots' clause, and was supported by Holles. St John, who opposed them, may possibly have been speaking *ex officio* as Solicitor-General. Glyn and Perd supported Pym and Holles. The anti-Scots then moved a brilliantly conceived amendment, which would have made the Parliament of England the judge of the Scots' claims in each individual case. According to D'Ewes, many 'mistaking the great danger of this addition', were prepared to vote for it. Nathaniel Fiennes, as well as young Mr Strangeways, acted as teller for it, with the pro-Scots Holles and Marten telling on the other side, and it was defeated only by 138 to 131. Culpepper, in an ill-tempered speech, suggested that the division had been settled because the ayes had to go out. The main clause was then carried by 166 to 123, which was a normal majority.[16]

Further delay in the treaty was caused mainly by the endless search for money. Sir John Hotham on 17 June set out a startling series of figures: there was £462,050 due to the King's army, of which they had had £150,000, and £220,750 due to the Scots, of which they had had £105,000. In addition, £80,000 of the Brotherly Assistance was due to the Scots on disbanding, so they needed to have £507,800 in Yorkshire within the next fifteen days. As Hotham pointed out, if the money were not there, they would need even more, since another month's money would become due. At the time, his figures came out £242,800 short, and that sum could be expected to increase.[17]

There were, as always, two different problems in raising the money. One was that of voting enough taxes to cover the sum needed, and the other was of finding the credit to borrow the money in order to pay the troops before subsidies could be collected. It was a familiar problem, but the scale of it had become startling. The bulk of the money was to be raised by the bill of £400,000, a subsidy to be raised on the new lump-sum principle. Attempts were made, as had been suggested by the

[14] BL Harl. MS 163, fo. 590ᵃ-1ᵃ; ibid. 5047, fo. 3ᵛ.

[15] Ibid. 163, fo. 611ᵇ.

[16] Ibid., fos. 719ᵇ-720ᵇ; *CJ* ii. 180-1. I have followed *CJ* on the tellers and D'Ewes on the voting figures. See Gawdy, vol. ii, fo. 81ᵛ. For an occasion when St John spoke by the King's command as Solicitor-General, and was collusively opposed by Pym and Holles, see *PJ* i. 175-7.

[17] *CJ* ii. 177-8; MP, 17 June 1641.

Privy Council in 1628[18] to combat under-assessment by making each
county pay the sum it had paid in 1593. Like other attempts to get
realistic taxes out of the House of Commons, this ran into difficulties,
and the bill suffered considerable delays.[19] In the end, this sum not
proving enough, the Commons settled on a graduated poll tax, an idea
which appears to have come from Alderman Penington and Secretary
Vane.[20] Thomas Smith, Northumberland's secretary, believed the tax
would yield 'a million at least', but by the end of August only £54,064
had come in.[21] The graduated assessment, based on men's assessment of
their own status, was designed to tax snobbery, but the desire to avoid
taxation appeared to be even stronger than the desire for social climb-
ing: 'reputed Esquires' valued themselves as mere gentlemen, and the
graduated assessment encountered such difficulties as whether barris-
ters were necessarily Esquires, and that no one in the City knew how to
define a yeoman.[22] The fate of the tax suggests an England in which the
marks of status were more fluid and more diverse than they had been a
hundred years earlier.

The need to borrow these sums caused even more difficulties. The
customs farmers, to the apparent annoyance of Denzil Holles, escaped
punishment as delinquents by offering to lend £150,000. As usual, fiscal
rather than economic considerations governed Parliamentary attitudes
to the Merchant Adventurers. Matthews, of Dartmouth, made the usual
objections to the Adventurers, and enjoyed the support of Nathaniel
Fiennes, but Pym came down firmly in favour of their offer to lend
money to pay off the armies.[23] After deciding to raise the poll tax, the
House decided it did not need a loan from the Merchant Adventurers,[24]
but it was so likely that the need would recur that any action against
them remained obviously unwise.

One of the intriguing reactions to the Army Plot was a tendency to
blame the bishops.[25] This reaction for a while turned such unexpected
people as Sir John Conyers and Baynham Throckmorton into supporters of Root and Branch.[26] In fact, there seems to have been no reason at
all for believing that the bishops were involved in the Army Plot. Some

[18] *APC 1627–8*, pp. 516–17.
[19] MP, 27 May 1641, and other refs.
[20] BL Harl. MS 163, fo. 715[b]; Holland, vol. ii, fo. 76[r].
[21] PRO SP 16/481/72; *CJ* ii. 269.
[22] PRO SP 16/482/110, BL Harl. MS 163, fo. 782[b]; Holland, vol. ii, fo. 130[v].
[23] BL Harl. MS 163, fos. 629–30, 715[b]. See also Robert Ashton, *The City and the Court 1603–
1643* (Cambridge, 1979), 154–5.
[24] *CJ* ii. 179.
[25] e.g. see BL Add. MS 6521, fos. 167[v]–8[r]; BL Harl. MS 163, fo. 694[a]; KAO Knatchbull MSS U
951/C261/37.
[26] PRO SP 16/480/73; Bristol RO Smyth of Long Ashton MSS 136(e); Bedfordshire RO St John
MS J 1384.

of this was a familiar searching for scapegoats. Yet there was also a certain logic in this reaction. One of the reasons why Charles had refused the projected settlement was undoubtedly his desire to continue to run the church along lines acceptable to himself, but not to many others. The bishops represented the main constitutional means by which he was able to do this. It was thus possible to see depriving Charles of bishops as a means to deprive him of the power to mould the church in his own image, and therefore of a possible incentive for future plotting. This reading of the reaction of the early summer against the bishops is perhaps sustained by the fact that the hostile reaction seems to have been confined to the government of the church: there was no corresponding reaction against its liturgy and worship. If Root and Branch were seen first and foremost as a means of restricting Charles's power, this might help to explain the paradox of a House which, throughout the summer and autumn, remained against bishops, but in favour of the Book of Common Prayer.[27]

On at least one occasion, this paradox led Hampden to misread the mood of the House. On 21 May he moved that ministers, on institution to livings, should be required to subscribe only to what was warranted by Scripture. Instead, the House left him with a requirement that ministers should be required to subscribe to what was required by statute, or, according to Gawdy's report, by the laws *and canons*. If Gawdy is correct, godly ministers had been left worse off, if anything, than they had been before.[28]

The heart of the godly cause during the summer of 1641 did not rest in Root and Branch, but in a series of bills designed to ensure reformed worship and a preaching ministry. Many of these languished in the House, and it would be possible to deduce from this that the godly enthusiasm of the Commons was less than total. In some cases, this deduction would be correct, but in a higher proportion of cases, the subsequent history of the measures during 1642 suggests that the delay was not due to lack of enthusiasm, but simply to the obvious impossibility of securing the Lords' assent until a thorough purge had taken place.

Probably the most enthusiastically supported of the godly bills was Penington's bill for abolishing idolatry and superstition, which provided for removing communion tables that stood altarwise, removal of pictures and images, and taking down of rails. It provided, like many of the godly bills, for the appointment of lay commissioners to see the task

---

[27] See below, pp. 368–9, 426.
[28] BL Harl. MS 163, fo. 599ᵃ; BL Add. MS 6521, fo. 164ᵛ; *CJ* ii. 152; Gawdy, vol. ii, fo. 52ʳ. *CJ* is perhaps more likely to be correct than Gawdy.

done.[29] This bill was being actively considered in committee all through the summer, but had to wait for execution until the Commons decided on reformation without tarrying for the Lords.[30] The bill for the free passage of the Gospel was another which did not reach the Lords, in this case perhaps because it was a fall-back bill to be used in case of failure to secure a real reformation. It provided that no minister should be troubled for the cross and surplice, in effect repeating the Millenary Petition's provision for tender consciences. It permitted parishioners to go to sermons in other parishes if there were none at home, provided that every minister might preach in his parish as often as he would, and created an obligation on the minister to ensure the preaching of two sermons every sabbath.[31]

The Pluralities Bill enjoyed wide support and was a major part of a programme of reformation. It was an amalgamation of two bills, and, in addition to providing that no man should hold more than one benefice, provided that a minister should lose his living for forty days' absence, and that no University man should have a living more than ten miles from the University unless he resided. All ministers scandalous in their lives or erroneous in their doctrine were to be put out, the latter almost certainly intended as an anti-Arminian clause.[32] It was originally supported by Rigby, and was reported from committee on 29 May by Wheeler, later a lay member of the Westminster Assembly.[33] On 19 June it was taken to the Lords by Hampden, 'with a recommendation of the said bill'. The Lords did not give great weight to the recommendation. On 2 July the bill was sent to Committee of the Whole alongside Williams's bill for the reformation of episcopacy. On 12 July Hampden from the Commons again asked for dispatch. On 31 December 1641 the Lords added two bishops to the committee dealing with the bill, and on 14 February 1642 Harley brought it back from the Lords heavily amended. The Commons agreed to *some* of the amendments, and again asked for haste on 1 and 12 April 1642. Finally, in a much changed House of Lords, Saye reported on 3 May 1642 that the Lords would not insist on the amendments the Commons had not assented to. The bill was sent to the King on 20 June 1642, and nothing more was heard of it. This was clearly not a bill with which the Commons showed any reluctance to persist.[34]

The bill for scandalous ministers was designed to appoint lay commis-

[29] DO, vol. i, fo. 42[r–v].
[30] CJ ii. 183, 191, 199, 246; BL Harl. MS 164, fos. 816[b], 818[a]; see below, pp. 367–72.
[31] CJ ii. 114, 119; Gawdy, vol. ii, fo. 34[v].
[32] *Two Diaries*, p. 142; DO, vol. i, fo. 57[r–v]; D'Ewes(N.), p. 464; CJ ii. 92, 100.
[33] CJ ii. 161, 181.
[34] LJ iv. 280, 297, 298, 308, 330, 404, 410, 437, 447, 451, 457, 469, 500, 577, 582; CJ ii. 431, 438; LJ iv. 609, 660, 665, 687, 713, v. 40, 43, 151.

sioners, to be named by the knights and burgesses for their counties, to
purge the church of unsuitable ministers. This gave effect to a proposal
which had been under discussion in the Commons for some time.[35] It
was first read on 23 June 1641, and given a second reading the next day.
On 12 July knights and burgesses were asked to name commissioners
for their counties. In this case, the godly in the Commons seem to have
decided it was necessary to wait for the purging of the Lords, since
nothing more was heard of the bill till it was reported by Corbett,
chairman of the scandalous ministers' committee, on 22 March 1642. It
was given a third reading on 7 April 1642, after the elimination of
signatories of the Kentish petition from the list of commissioners, and
the addition of John Pyne for Somerset. Stapleton took it to the Lords
on 12 April 1642, and the Commons asked for expedition on 4 May.
The Lords considered the bill in Committee of the Whole on 20 June
1642, and referred it to a select committee to draw amendments on 23
June. The bill did not emerge. Even after the exclusion of the bishops
and the departure of most of the Royalist Lords, this remained a bill the
Lords were reluctant to pass.[36]

The bill to prevent bargemen and watermen from working on the
sabbath might have been one of the most effective godly bills, since it
could have had a devastating effect on the economic life of London on
the sabbath. Perhaps for this reason, it seems to have been one of the
less enthusiastically supported bills. It was first read on 24 May, and was
reported from committee by Whitelocke on 14 July. It completed its
passage on 29 July, but was not sent to the Lords until 24 December. A
pause of this length at this stage of the proceedings surely tells its own
story. Even after the departure of the bishops, the Lords did not give it
so much as the courtesy of a first reading.[37] Apart from a request to the
assize judges not to travel on the sabbath,[38] very little more seems to
have been done about the sabbath until September. It is possible to
suspect that it was not one of the most popular items of godly
reformation.

It is not possible to say the same about measures for the restriction of
recusants. Recusants seem to have suffered even more severely than the
bishops from being used as scapegoats for the Army Plot, and proposals
for their disarming seem to have been regarded as an essential security
measure against a future coup. On the day of Strafford's execution, the
Commons proposed that 'the prime persons of the Romish religion may
be seized, and delivered, as publick hostages, into the custody of the

[35] Above, pp. 185, 222–3.
[36] *CJ* ii. 183, 184, 208, 491, 493, 516; *LJ* iv. 713, v. 35, 42, 151, 156.
[37] *CJ* ii. 155, 165, 211, 229; *LJ* iv. 488.
[38] *CJ* ii. 197.

power of the county'.[39] This was the sort of proposal the Queen regarded with fear, and the Lords with distaste, and nothing more was heard of it for the time being. A proposal that recusants should not be able to be guardians of wards is likely to have found favour with Saye and Sele, the new Master of the Wards, but the survival of Wards records from this period is too fragmentary for proof to be possible.[40] In August the Commons revived an old Elizabethan proposal, that no recusants should have the educating of their children after they were seven years old.[41] The real eradication of popery would, no doubt, have required measures of this sort, but once again, there was no point in putting any such measure before the Lords. In August Pym delivered one of numerous complaints against the Lords' 'pretence of privilege of Parliament' for recusant peers, but the issue was one on which the Lords remained unyielding.[42]

The *reductio ad absurdum*, and therefore in some ways the most revealing expression, of anti-popish feeling came on 19 July, in a proposal from Sir John Clotworthy the Ulsterman, backed by Sir John Hotham, to geld priests and Jesuits, to which Pym replied with a laborious Aristotelian disquisition, condemning the proposal on the ground that it was against nature.[43] This proposal, together with Pym's sense that it needed a serious reply, cannot be dismissed as mere political scare-mongering. Even if that had been its intention, it would only have been effective for the task in a House in which fear of popery was a deep and urgent emotion. The same arguments apply to some highly impolitic speeches on 20 August. The House was discussing a proposal to list the Queen's priests, to prevent accused priests from making spurious pleas that they were in the Queen's service. 'Divers' opposed this suggestion, 'and shewed that by allowing of this list wee should bee guiltie of countenancing the idolatrie it selfe wh. the preists committed in celebrating masse'.[44] No exposition of anti-Catholic feeling can make sense without allowing for the sense many Protestants felt, that the Mass was not merely evil, but an obscene and disgusting form of evil as well.

The bulk of the Commons' effort was concentrated on a bill 'to prevent the dangers which may happen by popish recusants', which was, in effect, a bill for disarming recusants. This bill had been read twice in March, and was reported from committee by Alexander Rigby

[39] *CJ* ii. 144.
[40] Ibid. 182; Holland, vol. ii, fo. 82[r].
[41] *CJ* i. 245.
[42] Ibid. 261.
[43] BL Harl. MS 163, fo. 791[a]; BL Add. MS 31,954, fo. 185[r-v]. I am grateful to Prof. Anthony Fletcher for drawing my attention to this incident.
[44] BL Harl. MS 164, fo. 880[a].

on 2 June.[45] It was taken to the Lords by Hampden on 9 June. On the 19th, Hampden from the Commons asked for dispatch. He asked again on 12 July, and on the 24th the bill came back from the Lords heavily amended, and disappeared back into the Commons' committee. There it rested until the King's departure for Scotland, when the decision was taken to try to pass the measure by ordinance, and commissioners were named to enforce it in the counties.[46] There is no way of explaining the effort the Commons put into this bill except on the assumption that they believed they were dealing with a country whose conversion to Protestantism was still far from complete. This assumption, true or false, is one they share with a good deal of recent research. On this issue, only Henry Marten, who presented a petition on behalf of lay Catholics on 7 August, was conspicuously out of line.[47]

All these measures illustrated the difficulty the majority in the Commons faced in dealing with the Lords. They were not content to let their cause spread in the country by unofficial methods: they would take advantage of that method if nothing better was available, as repeated orders in favour of parish lecturers showed. It was not what they wanted, since it was a route which did not lead to power. Most of the Parliamentary leaders were as much in favour of order and discipline as any Laudian, provided only that what was enforced should be true and not false. They were deeply committed to a national visible church, and to the punishment of sin and error. Many of them sympathized with the King's repeated expressions of horror at the growth of unlicensed and seditious printing. On 5 June Denzil Holles, acting on a complaint from John White 'grand minister' of Dorchester, complained of 'mechanical men that preached up and down the town, some publicly, some privately, which did very much redound to the scandal and dishonour of this House, as if instead of suppressing Popery we intended to bring in atheism and confusion'. Not all the Parliamentary leaders were of one mind on this question: the list of unlicensed preachers Holles complained of included Lord Brooke's former coachman, who may have enjoyed at least his master's tacit connivance. It is probably this fact, rather than any theological conviction, which accounts for Pym's caution on this subject. Otherwise, 'all disliked the practice of these men'.[48] The House was later further horrified by a group of Brownists, who declared that a church was no holier than a house of office.[49] Such

[45] ii. 106, 113, 165.

[46] Ibid. 171; *LJ* iv. 270, 272, 278, 280, 299, 305, 306, 308, 312, 316, 319; *CJ* ii. 223, 261.

[47] BL Harl. MS 5047, fo. 57ʳ.

[48] Ibid. 163, fo. 662ᵃ; *Two Diaries*, p. 48; Gawdy, vol. ii, fo. 65ʳ. See Lord Brooke, *A Discourse opening the Nature of that Episcopacie which is exercised in England* (1642), p. 106, for his praise of lay preachers, who 'thinke the wayes of Gods spirit are free, and not tied to a University man'.

[49] BL Add. MS 6521, fo. 200ʳ⁻ᵛ. A house of office was a lavatory.

stories reminded them that the unofficial propagation of their cause was no substitute for real power, and power could not come without control of the Lords.

The immediate battleground on this issue was the bill for the exclusion of bishops. This, in its original form, was a clerical disabilities bill, preventing clergy from serving in the Star Chamber, in the Privy Council, or as JPs, as well as preventing them from sitting in the House of Lords. The bill refrained from taking a fundamentalist position, since it allowed exemptions for Doctors of Divinity in the Universities, for noblemen in Holy Orders, and for the Dean of Westminster, and for Ely, Durham, and Hexham. The bill was taken up to the Lords on 1 May by Arthur Goodwin, Hampden's key ally in Buckinghamshire. On 13 May the Commons sent Arthur Goodwin back to the Lords to ask them to consider it soon.[50] The Lords' response to this pressure was to ask for a conference about tumults, and the resort of people to the House from London and other places. This was in part an objection to the growth of public petitioning.[51] It was also a fear of resumption of tumults, and Bishop Warner noted a libel set up at the entrance to the Parliament, saying that the voice of God was the cry of the people, and that bishops were limbs of Antichrist and plagues of the people: their destruction, it said, meant the taking away of Antichrist.[52] It seems the tumults of May, as well as the Army Plot, had left long-term fears behind them. These continued to surface, and in June the Lords showed signs of splitting over the question of 1642, whether royal or popular violence was the greater danger. Saye, in speaking on the Army Plot, said he would never sit in Parliament in fear of an army, but would venture his life and his fortunes rather than be in such subjection. Savill replied that he hoped they would not again be frightened 'here' with a rabble of the base multitude, and was again answered by Essex.[53] In May these divisions remained latent, and the Lords confined themselves to protecting their freedom by resolving that if the people assembled in a tumultuous manner during the hearing of the bishops' cause or at any other time, the House would take order to suppress them, or else adjourn till it was done. This resolution was a potentially effective protection against future threats, since the adjournment of the House would prevent the passage of any bill.[54]

Having thus protected themselves, the Lords considered the bill at

[50] *CJ* ii. 131; *LJ* iv. 231, 247.

[51] *LJ* iv. 252. On the growth of public petitioning, see Fletcher, pp. 92–102.

[52] BL Harl. MS 6424, fos. 69ᵛ–70ʳ.

[53] Bedfordshire RO St John MS J 1384.

[54] *LJ* iv. 253; BL Harl. MS 6424, fo. 70ʳ. It was presumably this resolution that the Duke of Richmond and Lennox was attempting to apply in his motion of 26 Jan. 1642, for the Lords to adjourn for 6 months: Fletcher, p. 256.

great length in Committee of the Whole.[55] The bill enjoyed some vocal supporters in the Lords, of whom Saye and Essex were probably the most articulate, but it is doubtful whether more than some twelve or fifteen peers supported the measure in principle. Those who did, however, enjoyed the tactical support of some of the conciliators in the House. Feilding's support for it[56] may shed some light on the views of his brother-in-law Hamilton. On 25 May, the third day in Committee of the Whole, the Lords decided to consider the bill in sections. They then voted that bishops should continue to sit in the Lords. According to Warner, twenty-five lay Lords voted in the minority, while the majority was made up of thirty or forty lay Lords and sixteen bishops. Having voted against the Commons on the major point, the Lords then voted for them on all the minor ones, and agreed to exclude clergy from the Star Chamber, the Privy Council, temporal courts, and from sitting as JPs. They then asked for a conference with the Commons, to see whether a compromise bill could be put together. They pointed out to the Commons that the exemptions in the Commons' bill debarred them from arguing that it was absolutely unlawful for clergymen to exercise secular jurisdiction, and that therefore their bill was understood as referring only to convenience, not to lawfulness. They therefore argued that they found that by common and statute law and by long practice, it was an unquestionable right for bishops to sit in Parliament.[57]

Faced by this reply, the Commons considered whether to restore logic to their own proposals by removing the exemption, which D'Ewes said had 'destroyed the bill itself'. This produced a division, with Sir Thomas Barrington and Mr Goodwin telling on one side, and Mr Strangeways and Lord Wenman on the other. The attempt by the godly to remove the exemption was defeated by 148 to 139. This vote was an important reminder to the godly of the risk of losing their majority if they were too rigorous in their logic, and perhaps also a reminder of the voting strength of 'our mothers the Universities'. The bill was thus sent back to the Lords unaltered, and the Lords were presented with an opportunity to consider it for a second time.[58] When the bill came back, Bishop Williams read a long speech against the Commons' reasons for the bill. He was reproved for this speech by Saye and Essex, and it perhaps gave the occasion for the Lords' resolution that reading speeches 'is no Parliamentary way'.[59] When the bill ultimately came to

[55] *LJ* iv. 255–7.

[56] That Feilding had voted in favour of the first Bishops' Exclusion Bill seems to be implied by his mother's warning not to vote in favour of the second, 'that you make not the last eror wors than the furst': Warwicks. RO Feilding of Newnham Paddox MSS C 1/17.

[57] BL Harl. MS 6424, fos. 70ʳ–1ʳ.

[58] Ibid. 163, fo. 658ᵃ⁻ᵇ; *CJ* ii. 165–7; *LJ* iv. 265.

[59] Bedfordshire RO St John MS J 1383; *LJ* iv. 267.

the vote, Bishop Warner said that there was a majority of at least 16 against it among the lay peers, though one newsletter said the lay peers showed a majority of 4 in favour of the bill. However, there appear to have been no more than one or two lay votes against the exclusion of bishops from the Privy Council and the Star Chamber.[60]

Thus thwarted, the Commons turned to the bill to abolish bishops root and branch. This was introduced on 27 May after the Lords' first rejection of Bishops' Exclusion. It was heralded by an anti-episcopal petition from Lincolnshire, preferred by Sir John Wray, and was moved, somewhat unexpectedly, by Sir Edward Dering, who said 'mere necessity' had driven them to it.[61] The bill at once encountered heated opposition. Culpepper argued that episcopacy was not yet past all hope of reformation, and Sir Charles Williams said he would divide against the bill if there were but six noes. Strode forced him to acknowledge that he had spoken 'rashly'. In a clash of two rival ecclesiologies, Hyde said that this government had continued many hundred years, and D'Ewes replied that it was not yet a hundred years old. Behind this exchange was all the difference between the belief that the church of England was a reformed heir of the Roman church, and the belief that it was a new church. D'Ewes also recommended the government of the continental reformed churches, and said that if popery were to return, 'many of us here must look for very little better safety than the fire'. A division was forced, although some of the noes confessed that the ayes were the greater number, and the bill was carried by 139 to 108.[62]

Nothing more happened until 11 June. On that day D'Ewes had gone out for a walk, when he was stopped by Stephen Marshall, who told him to go back to the House because the Root and Branch Bill was about to be discussed. Marshall said this decision had been taken the night before by himself, Pym, Hampden, Harley, and 'others'.[63] The debate on the preamble which followed lasted from seven in the morning till four in the afternoon, and only fragments of it survive.[64] Culpepper moved an amendment which speaks volumes about members' attitudes to the 1630s, in which he proposed that the statement in the preamble that the government of bishops had been found by 'long experience' to be harmful to the church should be amended to read 'late experience'.[65]

---

[60] BL Harl. MS 6424, fo. 71ʳ; Bedfordshire RO St John MS J 1383. It is possible that there was more than one division.

[61] BL Harl. MS 163, fo. 625ª; Gawdy, vol. ii, fo. 57ᵛ; Peyton, fo. 124ᵛ.

[62] BL Harl. MS 163, fos. 626–7.

[63] Ibid. 164, fo. 1031ᵇ. It should be noted that, on internal evidence, this passage must have been written long after the event. What is perhaps perturbing is that, had D'Ewes not chosen to allude to Hyde's preferment to the peerage, nothing in the physical appearance of the passage would have given any clue to its late date.

[64] BL Add. MS 6521, fos. 183ᵛ–4ʳ.

[65] BL Harl. MS 164, fo. 1019ª.

Rudyerd, with the frustration which increasingly afflicted those who had been happy with Archbishop Abbot, said that 'he turned round till his reason was a virtigo that ther could not be found a way off reformation', and claimed that there was no 'original sin' in episcopacy. St John, taking a fundamentalist line, argued that bishops had disrupted the church ever since Augustine of Canterbury quarrelled with the Britons, and that the bishops had opposed all attempts at reformation since 1559. Holles claimed that bishops were 'antimonarchical', to which Hopton replied that a presbytery would be worse, for bishops could at least offer a legal title to their independency. Crew, in a rare touch of political caution, argued that if they passed the preamble, any further bill for reformation would be 'shot downe by the Lords'.[66]

In fact, the Root and Branch Bill was never presented to the Lords. It ran on in committee all summer, taking a steadily more Erastian form. The commissioners who were to govern the church were changed from six lay and six clerical to nine lay and three clerical, and bishops' lands were voted to the King as a sweetener for the pill.[67] This last vote perhaps gives the clue to the strategy behind Root and Branch. It was not, whatever the leaders gave out at the time, a mere tactical manœuvre to secure the passage of Bishops' Exclusion. On the contrary, it was probably now part of their minimum terms for participation in any final settlement.[68] For many of them, this was probably not the result of a principled conversion to Presbyterianism, but of an equally principled determination that Charles should never again control the church. Since the Lords could not be induced to pass it, the strategic objective was to put enough pressure on the King to force him to agree to it, in the hope that the withdrawal of the King's opposition would lead the Lords to follow his example. Since the Commons had more means of bullying the King than of bullying the Lords, the strategy was worth attempting.

The key point of the strategy was first hinted on the afternoon after the second reading of Root and Branch, when the Commons gave two readings to a bill for Tonnage and Poundage. The implicit linkage is, at this stage, merely hinted at by the timing. Such linkage between reform of the royal revenue and reform of religion and disposition of the great offices grew steadily more explicit as the Civil War approached, and it seems to have been a settled strategy from 27 May onwards.[69] This

[66] Holland, vol. ii, fos. 54^v–7^v.

[67] BL Harl. MS 163, fos. 722^b; Holland, vol. ii, fo. 80^v; BL Harl. MS 163, fo. 772^{a-b}; DO, vol. ii, fo. 39^v; BL Harl. MS 163, fo. 773^{a-b}; DO, vol. i, fo. 40^v–40A^r; DO, vol. i, fo. 47^v; BL Harl. MS 163, fo. 790^a; DO, vol. i, fo. 63^{r-v}. For the text of the bill at the beginning of the committee stage, see PRO SP 16/539/59. For a fuller account, see A. J. Fletcher, 'Concern for Renewal in the Root and Branch Debates of 1641', in Studies in Church History, 14 (1977), ed. Derek Baker, pp. 279–86.

[68] For the evidence for this statement, see index entries s.v. 'linkage'.

[69] Hamilton MS 1397; BL Harl. MS 5047, fo. 57^r; Evelyn, iv. 115–16; D'Ewes (C.), pp. 44–7; Gardiner, Documents, pp. 231–2; Rushworth, Collections, iii. i. 697; LJ v. 98, 160.

linkage of reformation and revenue came to cover many issues, but the identification of the issues of Root and Branch and Tonnage and Poundage is where it appears to have begun. The King could have his bishops or his revenue, but not both. It was because Pym, St John, and Holles had the weapon of Tonnage and Poundage ready to hand that they believed they had more chance of persuading the King to agree to Root and Branch than they had of persuading the Lords.

Tonnage and Poundage was by far the most effective issue on which to exert this leverage, because the sums involved were exceptionally large. Once the Commons had resolved on 25 May that 'all collections of any sums of money under pretence or couler of subsidie imposts or aids upon anye merchandize whatsoever not granted by consent in Parliament, are against the law, the libertye and proprietye of the subject', the King's legal title to the whole of his customs revenue had come to depend on a new bill of Tonnage and Poundage.[70] Sir Robert Pye on 16 August reported the sum involved as £482,305 out of a total ordinary revenue of £899,402. He estimated that the King was losing another £139,403 raised by other 'waies and meanes held illegall', and therefore that only £277,774 of ordinary revenue remained. According to these figures, the King's need for Tonnage and Poundage was truly desperate.[71]

The Commons resolved on 26 May, immediately before the Root and Branch Bill, to bring in a bill for Tonnage and Poundage. Holles proposed the bill should be drawn, and St John was charged with drawing it. St John, showing a haste unusual in revenue matters, brought it in the next afternoon, immediately after Root and Branch. The House gave it two readings, and resolved to draw a new preamble.[72] The new preamble settled the question of right by declaring that 'no subsidy, custom, impost or other charge whatsoever ought or may be laid or imposed upon any merchandise exported or imported by subjects, denizens or aliens without common consent in Parliament'.[73] The care taken in this phrase to deny the King's right to tax aliens without Parliamentary consent marks it as a reversal of the judgement in Bate's Case of 1607. By passing this bill, the King would legally sign away his right to any customs duties other than those a Parliament might vote to him.

In return for this, the King was getting only a temporary bill, legalizing the duties from 25 May to 15 July. This, as was explained in the

[70] BL Harl. MS 163, fo. 616[b]; *CJ* ii. 156.
[71] Bodl. MS Clarendon, vol. 20, no. 1539: another copy in PRO 30/24/7, pt. 1.
[72] BL Harl. MS 163, fos. 620[b], 627[b], 628[a]. St John's ready agreement that the bill needed a new preamble, although he had brought the old one in ready drawn, raises the suspicion that he may have introduced the bill by royal command, as Solicitor-General.
[73] Gardiner, *Documents*, p. 160.

body of the Act, was because a permanent grant of Tonnage and
Poundage required a new Book of Rates. This was not an equivocation:
all Books of Rates since 1607, including the Book of 1635, which was
current, laid out a double-column liability on the goods they valued, one
column for customs, and one for impositions.[74] If impositions were to
be declared illegal, the Book of Rates had to be replaced, and if the King
were to avoid a large loss of revenue, the two columns had to be
consolidated in one single valuation for legal customs. If there was to be
a permanent improvement in royal revenue, some valuations would
have to be enhanced even above the raised values of 1635. In the event,
the Book of Rates which was published in 1642 did this, and would have
been the basis for a significant improvement in royal revenue. In the
mean time, however, no Book of Rates was in evidence. By the time it
appeared, the Long Parliament had passed no less than eight temporary
Acts, each granting the King Tonnage and Poundage for a few weeks.[75]
Behind these temporary Acts lies an extended game of cat and mouse.

The preparation of a Book of Rates was undoubtedly a time-consum-
ing task, especially if carried out in so public a forum as a Parliament.
Young Sir John Coke, who proudly reported that 'we have prevailed at
the committee to have the 48s. impost upon a fother of lead reduced to
20s. which is of great moment to the miners of the Peak, and I have not
been wanting to them herein'[76] was doubtless not the only member who
saw the preparing of a Book of Rates as a chance to do service to his
country. Yet it seems doubtful whether all this delay was involuntary:
the revenue settlement, which was expected alongside a grant of Tonnage and Poundage, suffered parallel delays. The number of occasions
when the revenue was ordered to be considered 'tomorrow' is long
enough to imagine Charles feeling like Macbeth.[77] If we add references
like 'next week' and 'Saturday-peremptorily', the list becomes far
longer.[78] It is hardly surprising that by September the King was commenting that 'I pray God it be to good purpose, and that there be no
knavery in it'.[79] By May 1642 Charles was asking:

And are all the specious promises, and loud professions, of making us a great

[74] The point becomes clear from reading any Book of Rates. See *Rates of Merchandizes* (1635)
(STC 7695) and ibid. (1642) (Wing E 920). The 1642 Book consolidates the valuations for custom
and for imposition under a common heading for custom, and increases some values above the
combined figure for the two. See also Russell, *1621–9*, pp. 283, 387, and other refs.

[75] *16 Car.* I, *caps.* 8, 12, 22, 25, 29, 31, 36. There is no Act in either *Statutes of the Realm* or
Original Acts to cover the period 1 Feb.–25 Mar. 1642. Such an Act existed, since it is rehearsed in
cap. 31, and the Royal Assent is recorded in *LJ* iv. 554. There is no obvious explanation of its
absence from Original Acts.

[76] *HMC Twelfth Report*, II. 289.

[77] *CJ* ii. 81, 87, 88, 89, 218, 219, 220, and other refs.

[78] Ibid. 212, 220, 288, 289, and other refs.

[79] Fletcher, p. 159; Evelyn, iv. 91.

and glorious king, of settling a greater revenue upon us, than any of our ancestors have enjoyed, of making us to be honoured at home, and feared abroad, resolved into this; that they will be ready to settle our revenue in an honourable proportion, when we shall put our self in such a posture of government, that our subjects may be secure to enjoy our just protection for their religion, lawes and liberties. What posture of government they intend, we know not.[80]

All but the last sentence of this statement is entirely credible.

On 31 May the Commons referred the task of preparing a Book of Rates 'in convenient time' to the committee for the customers, chaired by Giles Greene and added six members, including Sir Robert Pye, to help with the task. The resolution, on Sir Hugh Cholmeley's motion, that all that would come should have voices at the committee to prepare the Book of Rates illustrated how easily Pym could rely on country sentiment to provide any delay that might be needed.[81]

On 1 June Sir John Culpepper took over the issue. He explained that the King needed a settled revenue, and only the customs were left to raise it from. Otherwise, he said, it would have to be raised on land. Having raised the spectre of a land-tax, with all the fears of accurate valuation it invoked, he then diverted the House to the motion that they should lower the rates on home commodities, and lay them on imports and superfluities. This traditional appeal to restrain excessive imports was a carefully calculated attempt to gather votes. 'Some' followed this with a proposal to sit morning and afternoon till the Book of Rates was settled. This otherwise unpopular proposal was designed to benefit from members' desire to go home. The surprise of Denzil Holles shows in his remark that morning sittings would be a disservice to the House, and would not settle the business as quickly as they thought. On the proposal to tax imports more heavily, he warned that it might prejudice trade abroad. Accurate though this warning might be, it also betrayed the pique of a man who has had his business snatched away by someone else. The House's resolution directly followed the wording of Culpepper's speech, and he had won the first round.[82]

Culpepper was clearly entering on an attempt to finish Tonnage and Poundage before Root and Branch could be concluded. This attempt very nearly succeeded, and came so near succeeding that on 26 July Culpepper wrote a long letter to Hamilton which was, in effect, a report of success. He told Hamilton that the Book of Rates was ready, and that it was important to approve it before it could be used 'to draw on his

[80] *ECR* E 241(1), pp. 252–3.
[81] *CJ* ii. 164; BL Harl. MS 163, fos. 636ª, 638ª.
[82] BL Harl. MS 5047, fo. 9ʳ, MS 163, fo. 638ª; BL Add. MS 6521, fo. 176ᵛ; *CJ* ii. 163.

[the King's] consent to such other bills as may be lesse acceptable'.[83] If Culpepper had in fact succeeded in this attempt, the whole course of the Long Parliament might have been different. Culpepper at this stage seems to have been contemplating a grant for three years, which would have been less than the King wanted, but enough to allow him to dissolve the Parliament, and enough to stay within the limits of Pym's original proposals. Holles's acceptance of this time-limit, in his argument for commissioners on 3 June, suggested that it was a proposal his group could not see their way to fight.[84]

At this stage, according to Lisle, who chaired the Tonnage and Poundage committee, the greatest difference was about whether the temporary bill should grant Tonnage and Poundage to the King, or to commissioners for his use.[85] The proposal for the commissioners was officially intended to pay off the armies, since the proposal was that the commissioners should lend the money to disband the armies, and recoup themselves through the farm of Tonnage and Poundage.[86] The issue also appears to have been a power struggle, in which the question how far the King could be trusted with control of his own revenues was never far below the surface. On 1 June the committee voted for commissioners.[87] On 28 May Holles and Strode had been 'vehemently' for commissioners,[88] and on 3 June it was Holles who outlined the proposal for commissioners. On 10 June Secretary Vane, alleging difficulty in agreeing with the prospective commissioners, proposed that it be granted to the King instead of commissioners, and after 'a little debate', it was carried.[89] In the absence of a proper report of the debate, it is hard to know how to read this reversal. Vane could have been giving the real reason, or the King might have conveyed that he would veto a bill for commissioners, or Culpepper might have won a victory, or Holles and his friends could have retreated because they intended to debate Root and Branch the next day. The effect, however, was clear enough: Culpepper had won the second round.

From this point onwards, the bill progressed rapidly. The Lords were in full sympathy with the principle that taxation required Parliamentary consent, and passed the bill with great haste. It received the Royal Assent on 22 June, when it was the subject of a somewhat barbed exchange between Charles and Speaker Lenthall, which was subsequently printed. Lenthall reminded Charles that 'compulsory

[83] Hamilton MS 1397.
[84] *HMC Montagu of Beaulieu*, p. 130; Holland, vol. ii, fo. 36[r].
[85] BL Harl. MS 163, fo. 638[b].
[86] MP, 2 June 1641.
[87] BL Harl. MS 163, fo. 640[a].
[88] Ibid., fo. 631[b]; Gawdy, vol. ii, fo. 63[v].
[89] BL Harl. MS 163, fo. 690[a], ibid. 5047, fo. 15[v].

obedience, advanced by the transcendant power of prerogative, is too weake to support the right of government; it is the affections and estates of your people, tyed with the threads of obedience, by the rules of law, that fastens safety and prosperity to the Crowne'. Charles, in reply, admitted he had given over his claims of right: 'therefore you will understand this but as a marke of my confidence to put my selfe wholly upon the love and affection of my people for my subsistence'. His confidence appears to have been uncertain: he said he was showing 'that affection to my people that I desire my people would shew to mee', and said that 'I no way doubt, but that you will performe that which you have intimated unto me, and that in due time, you will performe the rest, when you have leisure'.[90]

At the third reading of the Tonnage and Poundage Bill in the Commons on 17 June, there were 'many noes'. The only speakers' names mentioned by D'Ewes are Pym and Culpepper, who were for the bill, and Holles and Robert Goodwin, who were against it.[91] The suspicion remains that this, like some other contests between members of Pym's junto, may have been a collusive opposition, in which they played the prearranged parts of hard man and soft man. This suspicion is strengthened by Pym's first action after the Royal Assent to the temporary bill, which was to propose what became the Ten Propositions, the most far-reaching restrictions proposed for an adult King since the Protectorate of Richard, Duke of York. Propositions so far-reaching need a context, and the events of June provide several.

One, undoubtedly, is Charles's tentative resumption of army plotting: he had sent Daniel O'Neill to the army with an initialled draft, proposing, among other things, that the army should petition that, since 'some turbulent spiritts backt by rude and tumultuous mechanick persons, seemed not to be satisfied, but would have the totall subversion of the government of the state', the army 'might be called up to attend the person of the Kg. and the Parlamt. for their security'.[92] The suggestion that O'Neill meant to back this proposal with negotiations aimed at Scottish neutrality must have been made more credible by the news of the Napier, Keir, and Blackhall 'plot', rehearsed to the House immedi-

---

[90] *His Majesties Speech* (Wing C 2797: BL 190 g. 12(104)), noted in Holland, vol. ii, fo. 87^{r-v}. For a draft of this speech, see Hamilton MS M 9/93/6. I am grateful to Dr Peter Donald for this reference. The two texts are not identical, and the printed version shows a hardening of the line which seems to bear Charles's hallmark: e.g. thanks for Commons' dutiful affections are changed into thanks for the beginning of their dutiful affections.

[91] BL Harl. MS 163, fo. 716^b.

[92] House of Lords, Braye MSS vol. 2, fo. 209^{r-v}. The depositions of Astley, Conyers, Hunkes, and Legge, which are almost the only good evidence on the second Army Plot, occupy ibid., fos. 201–11. These depositions give the impression that it was a faint carbon copy of the first Army Plot, and the most precise date they give is 'about midsummer'. Hunkes had been Will Murray's partner in a suit for a monopoly, and was a likely agent for a court-based plot: Tollemache MS 3747.

ately before the debate on the Ten Propositions began.[93] In the context
of the King's impending journay to Scotland, which would take him
through both armies, these fears seemed real enough. They were barely
concealed by Pym in the opening phrases of his speech: 'that the King
might bee petitioned to assigne his journey into Scotland as might bee
safe for this kingdome, after such time as the armyes should bee disbanded'.[94] His further proposal 'that this kingdome may bee put into a
posture to defend it selfe in the kings absence' looked perilously like a
proposition that it be put into a position to defend itself *against* the
King, if he should return from the north at the head of a hostile army.
This appearance is strengthened by one of the propositions which, in
the event, proved too plain-spoken to be adopted. Pym proposed

that the forces off every county may bee put into a posture off defence, and ther
may bee provisions of armes and ammunition made in every county; and lord
lieutenants and deputy lieutenants men off trust and such as shall bee nominated in the Parliament for the ordinary commanding off the forces off the
severall counties as occasion shall require.

This proposal was toned down by Pym's own colleagues of the committee of seven, but it shows that the ideas of the Militia Ordinance of 1642
were already fully formed in Pym's mind.[95] Together with the proposal
to make all Lords-Lieutenant, Deputy-Lieutenants, and officers of the
trained bands take an oath, this amounted to a proposal to confer a
monopoly of military force on Pym's allies. It is a proposal which
indicates a determination that Charles should never reign again: he
would remain on the throne, but authority was to be exercised in his
name by others.

  This determination, together with the timing of the introduction of
the Ten Propositions, suggests that, among other things, they were
intended as a statement of the minimum terms on which Pym would
agree to a permanent grant of Tonnage and Poundage. The existing
reference to the revenue settlement in the propositions is not explicit,
but it is a good deal plainer than the formula in which the threat to the
militia was ultimately concealed, and it is likely that the relationship
between statement and intention is very similar in the two cases. The
precise formula of the Propositions runs:

That some of the bills now depending in Parliament, whereof divers are sent up
already to the Lords, and some proceeding in this House, may receive the Royal
Assent before he go to Scotland; and that we may have time to pass the bill of

---

[93] Above, pp. 312–14.

[94] Holland, vol. ii, fo. 86ʳ; BL Harl. MS 163, fo. 730ᵃ.

[95] The final version of the proposal was simply that there should be 'good' Lords-Lieutenant and
Deputy-Lieutenants: Gardiner, *Documents*, p. 165. See Holland, vol. ii, fo. 90ᵛ for evidence that
the revised wording came from the committee of seven.

Tonnage to his Majesty for supporting of the royal estate, and to settle his Majesty's revenues for the best advantage of his service; and for these reasons, to allow some time before he go into the North.

The reference to bills not yet sent up to the Lords must be intended to refer to the bill for abolishing superstition or to Root and Branch or to both of them, and their conjunction in one sentence with Tonnage and Poundage is at least suggestive.

Culpepper's reaction to these proposals is interesting. He decided not to fight the Ten Propositions, and it was on Culpepper's motion, as well as Earle's, that they were referred to the Committee of Seven, dominated by Pym's allies, for final drafting.[96] His passionate hostility to the Army Plot in May suggests that he may have been in agreement with so many of the Propositions as were intended to deprive Charles of the power to plot. Beyond that, he seems to have hoped to complete the Book of Rates before Root and Branch could emerge from committee. This reading is suggested by his report to Hamilton on 26 July that 'the bill of episcopacy hath been retarded in the subcommittee all that possibly it could be'. He hoped that Williams's bill for the reformation of episcopacy might 'much advance the work'.[97] If he should succeed in getting the Book of Rates completed before Root and Branch, his key test would then come in the attempt to win a majority, in the face of Pym's covert opposition, for passing the Book of Rates before Root and Branch was completed.

It would be nice to know how much of the remainder of the Ten Propositions commanded the agreement of Culpepper and his allies.[98] The first two, asking for the disbandment of the armies and the delay of the King's journey to Scotland, surely commanded his full agreement, including the aim of 'suppressing of the hopes of persons ill-affected, that may have designs upon the army to disturb the peace of the kingdom'. The third, calling for the removal of Councillors who had stirred up division, and the appointment of 'such officers and Councillors as his people and Parliament may have just cause to confide in' is a form of words to which Pym and Culpepper probably gave very different interpretations.[99] The fourth proposition, concerning the Queen, is the one which probably annoyed Charles most. Read literally, it appears to deprive the Queen of the attendance of any priests whatsoever, and it demands that some of the nobility be set about the Queen 'by the advice of his Parliament'. During the King's absence, it proposes

[96] BL Harl. MS 163, fo. 730[a–b].
[97] Hamilton MS 1397.
[98] For the text of the Propositions, see Gardiner, Documents, pp. 163–6.
[99] A similar proposal for Scotland was already known to be the subject of varying interpretations. See above, pp. 319–21, 323–4.

that these nobles, 'with competent guards, may be appointed to attend the Queen's person, against all designs of papists, and of ill-affected persons'. There was some room for doubt about who was being protected from whom, but Culpepper, whose anti-popery was deep so long as the targets were popish *recusants*, might well not have opposed this clause. The concern that the Prince be brought up in 'religion and liberty', and that the Pope's nuncio should be sent away, would have commanded bipartisan support in the Commons. The seventh, on the militia, would have needed careful interpretation to make it generally acceptable, but it was designed to meet fears which were not confined to Pym's group. The proposal for a General Pardon was vital to those who had corresponded with the Scots, and innocuous to others. The ninth, which proposed a standing committee of the two Houses, carefully refrained from specifying whether it was to last only during the Parliament, or whether, like the Scottish Committee of Estates, it was to outlive the Parliament.[100] If the second, it could have been a vital constitutional innovation, but in the climate of June 1641 it could command support from many who felt Charles could not be trusted to reign as he pleased between Parliaments. The tenth, proposing that papists be removed from court, and that some of the most 'active' papists be 'restrained', was uncontroversial in the Commons. The Propositions seem to have come close enough to meeting the general mood to go through committee and the House in two days, and were taken up to the Lords by Pym on 24 June. His speech presenting them includes one passage suggesting that he had understood the doctrine of the double covenant of the *Vindiciae Contra Tyrannos*, but, like many of Pym's most radical suggestions, this remained subliminal.[101]

The Lords' reaction to the Ten Propositions is a remarkable example of how far they were prepared to go in taking power out of the King's hands. Some of them may have had a hand in the framing of them, but it is the agreement of the others which is interesting. They agreed to the vital third proposition about the appointment of Councillors. They agreed to the proposition on the militia, a fact which perhaps does more

[100] The proposal was for 'a select committee of the Lords to join with a proportionable number of the House of Commons, from time to time'. There was nothing in the text to say whether this committee should, like the Scottish Committee of Estates, outlive the Parliament: *LJ* iv. 287. The Venetian Ambassador took them for commissioners 'to take part in the government of the country when Parliament is not sitting, and that body will no longer be dissolved, but be permanent': *CSP Ven. 1640–1*, p. 174.

[101] Pym's words were: 'they are so united and weaved duties, which we owe to God, our King and our commonwealth, that we cannot duly and truly serve God, but thereby we serve our King: nor serve God and our King as we ought, without our service to the commonwealth.' (*LJ* iv. 285.) I am grateful to Mrs Alexandra Boscawen for a discussion of this text. Pym's comment on the proposal for a guard on the Queen also deserves quotation: 'it was a blessed thing to be kept from temptation'. (Ibid. 286.)

than anything else to suggest that the second Army Plot should be taken seriously: nothing less than fear of a coup ever made the Lords agree to taking military power out of the King's hands. They agreed on the upbringing of the prince, on banishing papists from court, and on the papal nuncio. As always, the Lords showed their deepest reservations on questions affecting the rights of papists, especially the Queen. They resolved to lay aside the proposition on the Queen until they had seen the marriage treaty. On popish ladies at court, they made the character-istic reply that 'there is but one English lady about the Queen who is a papist, and to acquaint them [the Commons] with the quiet condition of that lady'. On the proposal to restrain 'active' papists, the Lords desired 'to know of the House of Commons who they mean by active papists, and how far the extent is to be'.[102] They also dissociated them-selves firmly from the King's current policies by voting to remit the incendiaries for trial in the Parliament of Scotland.[103]

The Lords were ready to pass other bills which restricted the King's power to raise revenue or to follow policies which did not command Parliamentary assent. They passed the bills for abolition of Ship Money, forest laws, and knighthood fines without any difficulty, thereby de-priving Charles of a large part of his extraordinary income.[104] Since these items were never classified as part of the King's ordinary income, they do not appear in any of the balance sheets designed to show the King's loss of income by Parliamentary action, and their absence means that these balance sheets considerably understate the extent of the King's financial losses at the hands of the Parliament. They passed the bill for the abolition of the High Commission, and ultimately, after 'long and serious debate', passed the bill for the abolition of the Star Chamber.

This bill seems to have infuriated the Earl of Manchester, who had been a high prerogative lawyer ever since James's reign. On this occa-sion, it was said that he spoke such high prerogative language that he was likely to have been called to the bar. He 'affirmed the kings preroga-tive to be soe rivitted and inhaerent in him that it could not be limited by any lawe, that he might take any cause out of any court of justice and judge it himselfe'. He claimed that it was 'by the fundamentall law that the King shall be judge of his people', and that the power of judging was 'inseparable' to the Crown. It is easy to hear the voice of the man who had embodied the reaction against Coke, and it is essential, if the Civil War is to be understood, to remember that this is the voice of a man who was to be a Parliamentarian in 1642. He was answered by Essex,

[102] *LJ* iv. 289–91.
[103] BL Harl. MS 6424, fo. 77ᵛ; *LJ* iv. 281. On the King and the incendiaries, see above, pp. 178–9, 183–4, 306–7, 314–15, 318–19.
[104] *LJ* iv. 284.

who said they had laboured all the Parliament to make themselves freemen and not slaves, and to have an 'arbitrary court' as a continual scourge over them suited not with their liberties and freedom. Manchester was 'sharply reproved' by Saye, and taxed by Seymour with 'sordid bribery' in his own Court of Requests. Seymour, the only future Royalist whose speech is recorded, clearly wished to be associated with the legalism of Essex rather than with Manchester's cult of prerogative.[105] In the end, the Lords carried the bill by the 'major part',[106] but before they did so, they cut out of it a clause designed to give statutory effect to the clause of the Petition of Right prohibiting imprisonment by the Council table. This threatened to cause a quarrel between the Houses, but, after an uncomfortable conference, the Commons agreed to deal with imprisonment by the Council table in a new bill.[107] The Commons finally dealt with this problem by tacking a clause to the bill abolishing Ship Money, providing that 'all and every the particulars prayed or desired in the said Petition of Right shall from henceforth be put in execution'.[108] The Lords decided not to make an issue of this clause, and it duly reached the statute book. The Lords' underlying message was clear enough: they were telling both King and Commons that they could not get on without each other. Their detailed strategy seems to be dominated by a search for the points of least resistance, at which progress towards compromise might be made. Of all political groups, it was the Lords, who were the most tightly knit social body, who were the most resistant to the emergence of adversary politics.

Among the more heated spirits in the Commons, there was no such willingness to compromise, and William Strode spelt out the attempt to dictate terms by offering a bill to enable members of Parliament to discharge their consciences. This was a place bill, which would have debarred members of the Commons from being capable of any honour unless it came by descent, or with leave of both Houses of Parliament. This bill was given two readings, and remained a threat only, but it perhaps indicated a desire to imitate the Scottish Covenanters, and bind themselves not to accept office without general agreement.[109] Strode's anxiety indicates the possibility of more talk of a new distribution of offices. There was clearly such talk about the court, and Edward Nicholas on 29 July recorded a rumour that Saye was to be Lord

---

[105] Bedfordshire RO St John MS J 1386; BL Harl. MS 6424, fos. 73ʳ–4ʳ.

[106] *LJ* iv. 298.

[107] Ibid. 296.

[108] Gardiner, *Documents*, p. 191.

[109] BL Harl. MS 5047, fo. 7ʳ; Gawdy, vol. ii, fo. 63ʳ; BL Harl. MS 163, fo. 643ᵃ *bis*; Holland, vol. ii, fo. 112ʳ. The bill would also have had the effect of inhibiting the royal prerogative of creating peers. This would have contributed directly to Strode's immediate concerns, and was a cause for which he was later to show great enthusiasm. I am grateful to Dr J. S. A. Adamson for this point.

Treasurer, Hampden Chancellor of the Duchy, Pym Chancellor of the Exchequer, Holles Secretary, and Brooke a Privy Councillor, among other preferments. These rumours, even more than those earlier in the year, seem to have been a case of musical chairs in Spain.[110] The fact that the vacant offices were not yet disposed of, and the fact that many people expected the government of England to be settled before the King went to Scotland, were sufficient basis for a rumour that the offices were to be filled. That in turn would be sufficient basis for interested parties to begin discussing likely candidates. In July, in contrast to February, there is no evidence that the King was a party to any such negotiations. There were a few changes in offices during the summer. The Lords, during their investigations of the Army Plot, became perturbed by the suggestions of Newcastle's involvement, and began discreetly suggesting that someone else might make a more suitable governor for the Prince. The name of the Earl of Berkshire was mentioned, on the ground that he was 'un homme fort modéré'.[111] The King responded to this by a typical token concession: he dismissed Newcastle from his Governorship, while signalling that he had not lost favour by making him steward and Keeper of Sherwood Forest, and continued his personal attendance on the Prince by giving the office of the Prince's Gentleman of the Robes to Newcastle's second son, and directing that Newcastle was to discharge the office until his son was old enough.[112] There was no concession here to the Lords' view that an Army Plotter was a dangerous person to be attendant on the Prince: the gesture said plainly that, though Charles conceded the request, he was not convinced of the reasons for it. Pembroke also provided the King with an opportunity to dismiss him, in this case by fighting with Lord Mowbray in the House of Lords in full session.[113] The new appointments, in place of Newcastle and Pembroke, who doubtless encouraged each other to accept, were the brothers-in-law Hertford and Essex. The choice of Hertford as Governor to the Prince was a brilliant appointment: not only was he one of the figures in the centre whose political confidence was crucial to Charles: he was also a potential pretender. For that reason, the offer constituted a mark of trust which Hertford could not dare reject, and another potential candidate for the throne had been neutralized.

Beyond this, the evidence does not suggest that the King was contemplating any major reshuffle of offices. On 9 July the Lords sent a deputation to the King on the head of the Ten Propositions which dealt

[110] PRO SP 16/482/96 and also 94 and 104.
[111] PRO 31/3/72, p. 584.
[112] PRO SO 3/12, fos. 156^r, 159^r.
[113] BL Harl. MS 6424, fo. 82^v.

with evil counsellors, and the King replied that 'his Majesty knows of no ill counsellors':[114] he was prepared to dismiss those against whom specific offences had been proved, but he did not recognize any general obligation to choose such counsellors as the kingdom could feel confidence in. On the same day, the Lords did not dissent from Parliamentary demands for control of the militia: in a guarded formula, they reported: 'concerning the Lords Lieutenant and Deputy Lieutenants, considering the state this kingdom now stands in, the House of Commons desires they may be such persons as both Houses approve of'.[115] There is no formal expression of agreement, but there is a readiness to entertain the idea which the King should have found disturbing. There was also considerable suspicion in both Houses about the Queen's plans to go to take the waters at Spa.[116] It was widely feared that her departure was with hostile intent, and the Venetian Ambassador recorded a rumour that she might never come back.[117] The fears were mutual.

This was not a promising atmosphere for settlement, and if Culpepper were to succeed in producing his Book of Rates, and securing Parliamentary approval for Tonnage and Poundage, there would be no need for Charles to settle with critics whom his wife regarded with profound apprehension. All through July Giles Greene's committee worked on the Book of Rates. On 26 July Culpepper told Hamilton it was ready. On 30 July the Commons resolved that 'Mr. Greene shall make report of the Book of Rates'.[118] On 31 July Greene told the House the Book was ready. The House resolved that the Book of Rates should be considered on 'Tuesday next', 3 August.[119] On that day Greene began a report by dealing with the vexed business of customs on tobacco. He was interrupted by a report from Serjeant Wilde on the plans to impeach thirteen bishops for making the canons.[120] The House resolved that Greene should resume his report on Thursday at eight. On Thursday 5 August Greene began to report on one of the other issues before his committee, the delinquency of the customers, and was again diverted by a bill for naming Parliamentary commissioners to take charge of the militia.[121]

This looks, at first sight, as if those who wanted to make the Book of Rates wait on a settlement of Root and Branch had won the day: the sidetracking of revenue issues by introducing other exciting issues, like

[114] *LJ* iv. 306, 310–11.
[115] Ibid. 309.
[116] *CJ* ii. 210, 215; *LJ* iv. 316–7; Fletcher, p. 63.
[117] *CSP Ven. 1640–2*, p. 183.
[118] Hamilton MS 1397; *CJ* ii. 231.
[119] BL Harl. MS 5047, fo. 52^v.
[120] *CJ* ii. 233; BL Harl. MS 163, fo. 802^a; Holland, vol. ii, fo. 175^{r-v}; DO, vol. i, fo. 76^v.
[121] BL Harl. MS 163, fo. 805^{a-b}; BL Add. MS 6521, fo. 260^r.

impeachment of the bishops or Parliamentary control of the militia, was a technique in which the godly members were skilled. There is certainly evidence in this week that some members wanted to make a settlement wait on more stringent conditions. On 30 July, when Greene and Culpepper reported that the Book was ready, Rudyerd tried to add to the momentum by a speech to settle a revenue for the King, and was answered by Fiennes, whose speech is reported only in the words 'no till ill officers reparacons'.[122] This could be a speech in support of the clause about Councillors in the Ten Propositions, or it could be against delinquent customers. What is not in doubt is that the speech was meant to obstruct a settlement of Tonnage and Poundage. On 8 August Strode was much more explicit: 'Mr. Stroud was said lately we had donn nothing for k. that nothing wilbe till ill councellors and bps. be removed'. Here, for the first time, the linkage of Tonnage and Poundage with Root and Branch is explicit. The next day, other members supported him.[123] Mr John Hotham, the son, complained that a great part of the revenues went into the hands of incendiaries and traitors. Glyn obliquely supported him. Haselrig expressed a lack of confidence in the three new appointments to the Privy Council (Bath, Seymour, and Dunsmore), and Cromwell moved for Bedford and Saye to be 'added' to the Prince. There was clearly an organized group of godly members ready to obstruct Tonnage and Poundage until they had achieved both the abolition of bishops and the appointment of suitable great officers: in effect, till they had taken power out of Charles's hands.

Is the disappearance of Greene's report to be seen as a victory for the godly group, and a political defeat for Culpepper and his allies? This is the impression given by the surviving Parliamentary sources, but it does not explain why Greene did not make further attempts to report, and instead, the business appears to have disappeared until winter. If Culpepper had simply been procedurally outmanœuvred, he could have continued to try to seize a favourable moment to reintroduce the issue. If there had been a formal resolution to defer the issue, it would probably have left a less ambiguous record than it appears to have done.[124] In fact, the explanation seems to be recorded in an undated document in the papers of Lionel Cranfield. This is a report, addressed to 'this honourable committee', on a draft Book of Rates. The report says it is from 'certain merchants', to whom the Book had been referred by the committee, of whom we may presume Lionel Cranfield to have been one. The report records, among much else, that Coke had been

---

[122] BL Harl. MS 5047, fo. 52ᵛ.

[123] Ibid., fos. 57ʳ, 61ʳ.

[124] Ibid., fo. 55ʳ shows that a proposal to grant Tonnage and Poundage for three years was not read a second time at that time. See also DO, vol. i, fo. 65ʳ. For undated notes of proceedings in the Committee for the Book of Rates, see Holland, vol. ii, fos. 186ᵛ–8ᵛ.

successful in easing the imposition on Derbyshire lead, that the pretermitted custom was to be abolished, and that the commodities on which the rates had been raised were mostly ones which were very little traded. The report said that the new Book would result in a revenue loss of £140,000 a year, and that the rates on strangers had been raised to a level 'which is in effect to command the stranger not to trade with us at all'.[125] In short, Greene's committee had taken too literally the instruction the House had given them on 1 June, to lower rates on natives and raise them on aliens. Culpepper's proposals of 1 June had been designed to win votes for the new Book of Rates. In this objective, they would doubtless have succeeded, but in the process, they had defeated the other objective of raising revenue. The dilemma encapsulates the problem of dealing with a seventeenth-century House of Commons on revenue matters: what was politically acceptable was financially unviable, and what was financially viable was politically unacceptable. Culpepper, concentrating on the struggle to win votes, had made his proposals financially unworkable. The report is undated, but it would fit the Parliamentary chronology if it had reached Greene between 30 July and 3 August.

Being addressed to the committee, it did not need to be laid before the full House, and it is possible to understand Greene's readiness to save himself embarrassment by not confessing publicly that his Book of Rates was a failure. He may have seized on the efforts of Fiennes, Strode, and their allies to defer the business with considerable relief. By the time Greene brought the Book back, early in the next year, it had been thoroughly revised, and turned into a Book which provided the basis for adequate customs administration well into the Restoration.[126] Meanwhile, Pym and his allies had had a very narrow escape. Narrow though it may have been, it was complete. The King had to leave for Scotland on 10 August with no adequate settlement of Tonnage and Poundage behind him, and therefore he was no longer in a position in which he could easily contemplate the prorogation or dissolution of the Parliament. Once he understood that the revisions Greene had been sentenced to undertake were not a matter of last minute corrections, but of major and fundamental rethinking, he would have to digest the lesson that his plans to free himself of the Parliament had failed. This lesson

---

[125] KAO Sackville MSS U 269 O 294. The document is undated and in a secretary hand. The reference in the future tense to the abolition of the pretermitted custom supplies a *terminus ante quem*, since it was abolished by the temporary bill of Tonnage and Poundage which became law on 10 Aug. The *terminus post quem* is supplied by the existence of a completed Book of Rates for comment, which cannot have been significantly before Culpepper's letter to Hamilton of 26 July. Withing this period, the report is likely to have taken several days to prepare. It is then a serious possibility that the report reached Greene between 30 July and 3 Aug, when the Parliamentary timetable hit an otherwise unexplained snag.

[126] C. G. Chandaman, *English Public Revenue 1660–1688* (Oxford, 1975), 11.

seems to have taken Charles some time to learn, and he was still hoping for the end of the Parliament for some time after this. In the end, though, he would have to accept that he and his Parliament were still tied together in a deadlock from which neither could escape. After the King had been encouraged to hope for so much from this attempt to settle Tonnage and Poundage, it is not surprising that he viewed subsequent proposals to settle his revenue with a deepening suspicion. That suspicion, in the end, became one of the forces which drove him towards war as the only remaining method of resolving the deadlock.

The delay in completing the Book of Rates had made the business run on until the last week before the King's much-postponed journey to Scotland. The days immediately before the King's departure were among the tensest in the whole history of the Parliament. The fear that the King might seek to resolve the tension by force was heightened by the fact that he was moving towards the armies, which were not yet disbanded. The fear that the King might make use of the English army for an attempt to recover power by force was one which was never far from the surface during August. On 23 July Saye, Mandeville, Brooke, Wharton, and Paget made what was clearly a prearranged demand that the whole of the English horse, the part of the army which seems to have been most distrusted, should be disbanded before the Scots.[127] The Lords, though persistently willing to support the Commons in demands for the disbanding of the horse, were not willing to insist on their disbandment before the Scots.

A desperate attempt to persuade the King to defer his journey till the armies were disbanded procured only a delay of one day, until 10 August. The growth of a reaction in the King's favour is suggested by the fact that the Lords only agreed to this request by a majority of 3, 28 voting in favour, and 25, including 9 bishops, against.[128] After the King's departure, with the armies still undisbanded, these fears grew more explicit, and a letter from Lord General Holland, with 'darke words', increased the apprehension.[129] On the 16th, Pym reacted to this letter by saying they had cause to provide for their defence. Earle immediately supported him, and Wilde claimed that the Lord Keeper could use the Great Seal without royal warrant.[130] Culpepper's protest that this proposition was doubtful was ignored, and the Commons resolved to ask the Constable to reside in the Tower, and to write to the Mayor of Hull not to deliver the arms and ammunition in the town until he had further order from both Houses of Parliament. Strode was sent to take these

---

[127] BL Harl. MS 6424, fo. 84[v].
[128] Ibid., fo. 88[v].
[129] BL Add. MS 6521, fo. 276[r–v].
[130] BL Harl. MS 5047, fos. 73[r]–6[r].

two resolutions to the Lords, who agreed to both propositions.[131] The Lords' agreement is surely evidence that the fears of a coup on which Pym and Strode were playing were genuine and deep. Some Lords wished to save the King's face by saying that the Mayor should keep the arms for the King's service, 'but the L. Say, Wharton, Mandeville would by no means admit this last clause'.[132]

The fears in the end proved not to be justified. It is now hard to tell whether the King had planned to use the army, and was dissuaded by the Lords, or whether the fears had never been justified in the first place. The evidence of royal plotting with the army which later surfaced in the depositions of Conyers and Astley relates to June and July, and there is no direct evidence to suggest that in August the King had any other plans than disbandment. His previous record, combined with the guilty consciences of those who had coerced a King beyond endurance, make the fears natural enough, but it is probable (though not certain) that in this instance they were wrong. The balance of the evidence suggests that the King still hoped, in spite of the failure of the Tonnage and Poundage settlement, that he could prorogue, or at least adjourn, the Parliament as soon as he returned from Scotland, and that the absence of the Scots would be a sufficient condition to enable him to do so. This seems to have remained his hope until the outbreak of the Irish Rebellion.

Some of Charles's servants believed this was a misplaced confidence. Edward Nicholas on 11 October wrote to Webb, the Duke of Richmond and Lennox's secretary, to say that 'for ye houses to adjourne to another time wilbe very prejudiciall to his Matie. unless they first passe ye Act of Tonage and Poundage for ye king; this would be well considered of you there; for here is noe man yt I can see, yt takes care of anything'. This letter suggests that Nicholas felt that others in the King's circle did not share his sense of urgency about Tonnage and Poundage. The next day, he made the same points, rather less bluntly, to the King. He said that an adjournment to another time without passing Tonnage and Poundage, 'would put your Matie to a great straight for want of monny to uphold your house and for divers other occasions'. He asked what the King wanted his servants to insist upon before an adjournment, but received only the reply that 'I would have the adjurnment furthered by anie meanes'.[133] The King made no reply to any of Nicholas's remarks about Tonnage and Poundage. His silence suggests that he may have been hoping to repeat his coup of 1629 when, in the

---

[131] *CJ* ii. 259; *LJ* iv. 366, 369.
[132] BL Harl. MS 6424, fo. 93[r].
[133] Guildford MS 52/2/19(21); Evelyn, iv. 104. The context shows that Nicholas was envisaging another temporary bill.

face of a Commons' ban on the collection of Tonnage and Poundage, he had nevertheless succeeded in collecting it. It remained the case, as it had been then, that merchants could not refuse payment except by giving over trading.[134] It is possible that Charles might have succeeded in such an attempt, but without the support of the peerage, he would have found the task harder than it had been in 1629. Since the attempt was not made, we cannot say whether it would have succeeded: we can only say that Charles appears to have contemplated it. His willingness to do so is a measure of his total repugnance to the conditions the majority of the Commons were trying to force on him.

The best evidence that the King was contemplating the end of the session at or near the time of his return is the General Pardon. The King left a text for a General Pardon on his departure for Scotland, and it is now in the House of Lords Main Papers.[135] A General Pardon, by long and well-established tradition, was the last Act of a Parliament, and its appearance therefore signalled the conclusion of a session.[136] The passage of a General Pardon in the two Houses could legitimately have been taken to signal the Houses' consent to dissolution or prorogation, according to the terms of the Act against Dissolution. The Privy Council, according to Nicholas, resolved not to tender it until they found by friends in both Houses that it would be accepted. On 6 August the Lords asked for a General Pardon, and thereby signalled their willingness to end the session, presumably with a further temporary bill of Tonnage and Poundage to avert a crisis before the revisions of the Book of Rates were completed.[137] Soon it was being reported that the Commons were not willing to pass the General Pardon. The reason given was that it pardoned all treasons, thereby offering an amnesty to the Army Plotters, but however genuine this reason may have been, it is probably more important that the Commons would not agree to the end of the session.[138]

The King's response to this news was to ask whether the pardon

---

[134] On the fate of the campaign of refusal in 1629, see B. E. Supple, *Commercial Crisis and Change in England 1600–1642* (Cambridge, 1959), 104–25, and also the comments of Bishop Williams, in *CSPD 1628–9*, vol. cxlii, no. 19: 'he ever told the Lord Treasurer they would be weary of this new habit of statesmen, and turn merchants again when they heard from their factors that their storehouses grew empty. God send those men more wit who living in a monarchy rely upon the democracy'. It would have been very interesting to discover whether these words could have been repeated after a dissolution in 1641. See also Ashton, *The City and the Court*, pp. 130–3. I am grateful to Prof. G. E. Aylmer for a helpful discussion of this question.

[135] *NP*, pp. 6–7; House of Lords RO, Parchment Box 178; *CJ* ii. 247.

[136] *LJ* iii. 69 (I am grateful to Dr Bill Bidwell for this reference); Rushworth *Collections*, vol. i, app., p. 2. There had been no General Pardon in 1614, 1621, 1625, 1626, or in 1628. In all other Parliaments, well back into the reign of Elizabeth, it had always been the last Act passed. In 1628 the General Pardon would have been the last Act if the Commons had not rejected it.

[137] *LJ* iv. 316, 345.

[138] BL Sloane MS 3317, fo. 33ᵛ; Evelyn, iv. 76.

could be passed without the Commons, under the Great Seal. It seems that plans continued for a while to pass it without Parliamentary authority, since there are notes on the General Pardon in the Clarendon manuscripts which include the reflection that there is 'more need to be wary in a patent than in an Act', and therefore that more care was needed than in the drawing of the General Pardon of 1624.[139] This can only indicate that Charles was prepared to adjourn the Houses in the face of the Commons' resistance, hoping either that when the adjournment was put to the vote in the Commons, it would be carried, or that the consent of the Lords might serve for the consent of the Parliament as a whole.

It may have been in hope of preparing public opinion for an adjournment or a prorogation that the Privy Council on 13 August decided to write letters to the justices of assize, directing them in their Michaelmas circuits to publish a list of bills the King had passed, and to declare the King's grace and favour in doing so 'for ye ease and benefitt of ye subiect'. The sequel suggests that the matter was the occasion of some division in the Council, for when Bristol attended Dorchester assizes at the end of August, he found Mr Justice Foster had received no such letter, and asked Nicholas to 'informe yr. selfe of ye cause of this omission'. It is not beyond the realms of conjecture that some members of the Council may not have wanted to encourage the belief that the public could be adequately prepared for the end of the Parliament.[140]

Against a measure so deeply popular as an adjournment was likely to be, there was not much a Commons majority could do. If there was any doubt about the popularity of an adjournment, it was dispelled when on 16 August plague was discovered near the Parliament house.[141] The Commons could hope to achieve another turn of the revenue screw: they were already delaying the bill for the Queen's jointure and the bill for the Subsidy of the Clergy.[142] These were not measures of profound importance, but there was rather more potential leverage in a bill against purveyance, which was introduced on 7 August. The sources

---

[139] Bodl. MS Clarendon, vol. 21, no. 1602. For another memorandum submitted to Charles assuming the end of the Parliament, see Hamilton MS M 9/93/3. I am grateful to Dr Peter Donald for this reference.

[140] PC Reg. xii. 178; Christ Church, Evelyn MSS, Nicholas Box, nos. 65, 70.

[141] LJ iv. 365; Paul Slack, *Impact of Plague in Tudor and Stuart England* (1985), 146, 221, and other refs. The similarity of the Parliament's plague orders to the Book of Orders, to which Dr Slack draws attention, would seem to follow from the fact that both were largely the work of the Earl of Manchester. This fact is a useful symbol to show that King and Parliament did not stand for rival social policies: LJ iv. 391.

[142] On the Queen's jointure, see above, pp. 224, 262, 276. On the Subsidy of the Clergy, CJ ii. 213, 247; Holland, vol. ii, fo. 160ᵛ; CJ ii. 294; D'Ewes (C), 36 n, 202, 313; Bodl. MS Clarendon, vol. 21, no. 1634, fo. 125ᵛ.

conflict about whether this was a bill to abolish all purveyance, or simply to end the arrangements for composition, but those in the King's circle were used to reading the Commons' language by this time, and in the Bodleian revenue balance, completed on 16 August, purveyance is listed among revenues 'held illegal'. The sum at stake was assessed as £36,237.[143] The third temporary Tonnage and Poundage Act, which was completed on 10 August, just in time to be sent post-haste after the King on his journey, abolished the pretermitted custom, valued by Pye at £17,863 8s. 5d.[144] Yet these measures, in a contest on this scale, were only capable of annoying: they had limited coercive power.

Pym seems to have placed more faith in a renewed threat to revive the Grand Remonstrance, which might be used to call on public support in ways some of which might be dangerous.[145] This was accompanied by another threat to revive the impeachment of Laud.[146] Again, however, it was highly unlikely that Charles would abolish bishops in order to save Laud's life, or even that Laud would have welcomed such an exchange. The King was likely to take a different line about any threat to his family, and it seems that Pym's circle may have been threatening the King by leaking rumours of plots against his family. The style was very much Charles's own, and, as with the plots Charles leaked, it should be assumed that the initial objective was not to carry out the plot, but to use the threat to secure compliance. On 18 August a story was being spread that Sir John Clotworthy had told Lord Lanerick, and Lanerick had told the Queen, that Newport, Mandeville, and others at Mandeville's table had been discussing plans to take and keep the Queen and the Prince. This appears to be the same story Charles chose to make public in December, when he wanted to justify his charge against the Five Members. It was then alleged that those present were Essex, Newport, Saye, Mandeville, Wharton, Cork's son Lord Dungarvan, Nathaniel Fiennes, Clotworthy, and Pym, and that the precise words spoken by Newport were a comment on rumours that Charles had a plot to the effect that 'if there be such a plot, yet here are his wife and children'.[147] These words fall short of the interpretation placed on them, yet they were ideally designed to inspire fear in Charles while falling short of the guilt of genuine plotting. These threats were

[143] Hamilton MSS 1397, 1411; CJ ii. 243; BL Harl. MS 164, fo. 811ᵇ; Holland, vol. ii f. 183v; Bodl. MS Clarendon, vol. 20, no. 1539.

[144] 16 Car. 1, cap. 22. On the pretermitted custom, see Russell, 1621–9, pp. 52, 60 and n., 199 and n., and other refs.

[145] CJ ii. 232, 234, 253, 257; BL Harl. MS 164, fo. 815ᵃ⁻ᵇ.

[146] CJ ii. 233.

[147] BL Harl. MS 6424, fo. 94ʳ; LJ ii. 490, 497–8. It could be argued that the story contains little more than the suggestion of the Ten Propositions for a guard about the Queen.

backed by a rumour, of uncertain origin, that the Crown would be offered to the Prince or to the Elector Palatine.[148]

The Commons' energies were then concentrated on the proposal for a *Custos Regni*, to whom the royal authority should be committed in the King's absence. For the first time since 1453, the union of multiple kingdoms was forcing the English to give serious thought to the problems, familiar to Ireland and Scotland, of authority under an absentee king. The proposal looks like a revival of the medieval Justiciar, but others may have thought rather of the Protectorate of Richard, Duke of York. The *Custos Regni* was to have power of military command, and power to pass Parliamentary bills in the King's absence. This proposal was put by the Commons to the Lords on 30 July, and again on 4 August.[149] The response of the Lords was to agree that the *Custos Regni* should have power to raise forces, but to agree only that he should have the power to pass a limited list of bills to be specified in advance. They delivered an implicit rebuke to the King by including military powers, and one to the Commons by including the subsidy of the clergy among the named bills the *Custos Regni* was to be empowered to pass.[150]

The proposal to limit the powers of the *Custos Regni* caused some irritation in the Commons. Orlando Bridgman supported the Lords, but those who opposed them included Culpepper and Falkland, and Culpepper argued that specifying what bills a commissioner might pass could lead to the King directing the Parliament what bills it might pass 'as now in Ireland'. St John offered the far-reaching argument that a *Custos* might do all things a King might do, as well in Parliament as out of it.[151] When the Commons on 9 August spelt out some of the bills they wished the *Custos* to have power to pass, there were enough alarming inclusions to make the Lords' caution appear justified. They included the bill for scandalous ministers, the bill for abolishing superstition, Strode's place bill, any bill or bills against delinquents, the disarming of recusants, the bill for pluralities, a bill for 'removing of officers and placing others in the king's absence', and a bill for raising forces by sea and land. Even the omission of Root and Branch was not enough to sweeten this list: it was a proposal for a full-scale regency.[152] The proposal looked the more sinister beside a proposal from Holles for a new Lord Steward. Arundel, the previous Lord Steward, was going abroad to take the Queen Mother out of the country, and therefore could not be a candidate. The office was one with which viceregal and almost

---

[148] *CSP Ven. 1640–2*, p. 200. There is no reason to believe there was any actual plan for deposition, since none of the possible alternative candidates seem to have been available.
[149] *LJ* iv. 335; *CJ* ii. 235.
[150] *LJ* iv. 342.
[151] BL Harl. MS 5047, fo. 55ᵛ; Holland, vol. ii, fo. 180ᵛ; *CJ* 240, 242.
[152] BL Harl. MS 5047, fos. 60ᵛ–1ʳ.

viceregal claims had been associated, and Pembroke, Holles's candidate, was not the man to miss the chance to magnify an office which he held. Together with this proposal, the younger Hotham advanced a proposal for Salisbury to be Lord Treasurer. Salisbury anxiously assured Hamilton that this proposal had been made 'much against my will'. His assertion may well be true, but does not compel belief.[153] Taken together, these proposals amount to a proposal to Merovingianize Charles, with Pembroke as a highly convincing candidate for Mayor of the Palace. These proposals illustrate how far the Parliamentary leaders' hostility was not to the powers of monarchy, but to the policies Charles I used those powers to pursue. This proposal was not one to diminish the powers of monarchy: it was one to transfer them to a different holder, without incurring the guilt of deposition. In the Lords, the proposal for Pembroke to be Lord Steward secured the expected support of Mandeville, and the rather less expected support of Andover, but did not find favour with the House.[154]

It was only after their failure to get the powers of regency vested in a single person that members turned instead to the attempt to vest them in a Parliament. On the morning of 10 August, as the King was departing, Mr Grimston, one of the more moderate members, claimed that 'the power of Custos Regni is in the Parliament', and Strode advanced the claim to make ordinances: 'by the Act for continuance of Parliament we have power to make ordinances of Parliament which as binding as an Act of Parliament'.[155] In 1641, as at any time between 1640 and 1660, most members regarded moves towards Parliamentary government as a *pis aller*, to be adopted only if they were unable to find a single person to exercise the powers in the right spirit. What the debates on the *Custos Regni* show is that the attachment to the single person no longer extended to the person of Charles Stuart.

The commission which the King eventually left on 9 August was along the lines recommended by the Lords. It was not given to one person, but to a commission, consisting of Littleton (recently recovered from illness), Manchester, Lindsey, Hertford, Arundel, Essex, Northumberland, Dorset, Salisbury, Bath, Warwick, Bristol, Danby, Berkshire, Bridgwater, Newcastle, Saye, Mandeville, Saville, Goring, Bankes, and Sir Peter Wych, a commission so balanced that it was unlikely to do

---

[153] BL Harl. MS 5047, fo. 61[r]; Hamilton MS 1495. On 29 Nov. Pembroke sent a disconsolate message to the King via Nicholas, saying he hoped that nothing said in the Commons suggested he claimed any title to the King's service any way but by the King's grace and nomination. It would be nice to know whether this was the first time Pembroke had sent such a message: Christ Church, Evelyn MSS, Nicholas Box, no. 27.

[154] BL Harl. MS 6424, fos. 89[v]–90[r].

[155] Ibid. 5047, fo. 62[r–v].

very much.[156] Military power was entrusted to Essex, but, as Essex complained, without any clarification of his legal powers.[157] Before his departure, the King gave the Royal Assent to the bill to confirm the treaty, and the bills for Ship Money, forests, the Public Faith for the Brotherly Assistance, for free buying of gunpowder, for knighthood, and for the Clerk of the Market. When the Commons accepted that the King's departure could no longer be postponed, and that no stable settlement could be reached before his departure, 'ther was much saddnes amongst us'.[158] The future was deeply uncertain, but it was likely that, with the departure of the Scottish army, the House of Commons would find that their glory was departed. Northumberland, writing to Nicholas on 13 August, agreed with this estimate, saying that:

the manner of the kings goeing away and the actes he did immediately before his departure doth very much amase me, surely there is a strange alteration and change in the present affaires els the king would never have given such a farewell to the Parlament, if they swallow this pill quietly there is no question but the king will easily overcome all difficulties that can arise in that place.

It seemed that the wheel of fortune had spun, and once again, in a contest between a King and a Parliament, time had proved the King's ultimate weapon. At the time when he reached it, Northumberland's assessment was surely correct. It was to take a further turn of the wheel of fortune to falsify this judgement, and that turn did not happen in Parliament.[159]

The Houses sat through August, to ensure that the disbanding of the armies was safely completed, and resolved to adjourn early in September. Before they went, they tried to leave their mark as firmly as possible on the world to which the King would return. On 30 August the Lords unexpectedly agreed to the ordinance for the disarming of recusants, which rehearsed that many papists who outwardly conformed nevertheless harboured most dangerous designs against the State, and therefore arms were to be taken away from all those who had not taken communion in the past year. A formidable list of commissioners were named to carry this out, though, in the ironic way such things worked, at least one of the commissioners for the East Riding (Sir Marmaduke Langdale) became a papist himself.[160]

It remained to give effect to the bill for abolishing superstition. Pym was already under pressure on this subject. On 8 August, when the

[156] PRO SP 17, Case F, no. 2.
[157] *LJ* iv. 367.
[158] BL Harl. MS 164, fo. 815ª.
[159] Christ Church, Evelyn MSS, Nicholas Box, no. 23.
[160] *LJ* v. 384–5. It is a great pity that Bishop Warner appears not to have been present on this day. On Langdale, see J. T. Cliffe, *Yorkshire Gentry* (1969) 346.

Houses acted against their own consciences by sitting on a Sunday in order to complete business before the King's departure, they were particularly in need of measures to quiet their consciences. Penington pressed for a Declaration by the House to abolish superstition in churches, as in setting communion tables altarwise and enclosing them with rails. That the proposal was likely to be controversial was illustrated by Mr Grimston's immediate response, which was to demand an order against disobedience to laws settled, as had been done by the House of Lords. D'Ewes added to Penington's request by calling for an end to the profaning of the sabbath by the Book of Sports. Pym's reply to this was that 'hee did hope that wee should in due time suppresse it'.[161]

The due time Pym selected was immediately before the recess, when members could go home and ensure the immediate enforcement of any order which might be concluded, and while the King was out of the country and could not quickly issue any contrary commands. On 30 August the House resolved to consider the issue of rails 'tomorrow'. This 'tomorrow', unlike the many over the King's revenue, was intended seriously. On 31 August a committee was set up, consisting of Pym, Holles, St John, Harley, Selden, Wilde, Falkland, Culpepper, D'Ewes, Crew, Barrington, Marten, and Mildmay.[162] The membership of this committee gave the godly and their allies a majority of ten to three, and they were empowered to consider communion tables, the Book of Sports, and all other matters of innovation that had been debated that day. The text reported by Pym on 1 September is almost the form now known as the Commons' order of 8 September. This ordered church-wardens to remove communion tables from the east end, to remove rails, to take away crucifixes, scandalous pictures, and pictures of the Virgin Mary, to abolish bowing (the original wording said 'adoration'), and to call on Vice-Chancellors, Mayors, and JPs to execute this order, and report by 30 October next. This could make a large amount of destruction a *fait accompli* before the King returned to stop it. D'Ewes added a requirement to level the chancels, and a condemnation of the Book of Sports.[163]

Culpepper's reaction to this order was to move that they should add a clause against those who vilified and condemned the Book of Common Prayer 'established by Act of Parliament'.[164] D'Ewes immediately opposed this with one of the stock nonconforming arguments, that the existing Prayer Book 'altered by Dr. Cousins' was not the same as the

---

[161] BL Harl. MS 5047, fo. 58^r, ibid. 164, fo. 818^a.
[162] *CJ* ii. 277–8.
[163] Ibid. 279; BL Harl. MS 164, fo. 888^b.
[164] BL Harl. MS 164, fos. 887^{a-b}, 888^b–9^a, 890.

Book established by law. He was much surprised when Sir Thomas Barrington and Oliver Cromwell 'spake against the Common Prayer Book it selfe that was established by Act of Parliament'. D'Ewes, as his vote showed, agreed with them, but was not used to such plain speaking. Nevertheless, when the issue was forced to a division, it was the supporters of the Prayer Book who won. The vote was 55 to 37, with Sir Robert Pye and Sir Thomas Bowyer telling for the Book, and Sir Henry Mildmay and Sir William Masham telling against it.[165] There was then another partisan dispute about whether to refer the drawing of an order in favour of the Book of Common Prayer to a new committee, or to the committee which had drawn the main order. Those who had been for the addition wanted a new committee, and those who had been against it wanted it referred to the existing committee 'without anie addition of others'. This time, on the procedural question, the godly won, and the task of drawing an addition in favour of the Prayer Book was referred to a committee with a clear godly majority. The result was a form of words to which Culpepper was the first to object, and after a confused series of divisions, the House agreed not to put the main question on whether the addition should be included in the order.[166]

At this point, proceedings stopped for the day of thanksgiving for the completion of the treaty with the Scots. The Houses there listened to sermons from Stephen Marshall and Jeremiah Burroughes, which were probably designed to increase their courage in pushing through this order. Marshall's first doctrine, that 'God, and God alone, is on his people's side to deliver them in all their most deadly and desperate dangers' was designed to reinforce the providentialist theory of politics, according to which compromise, where a divine imperative was involved, was an imprudence and not a prudence. In this context, his assertion that 'persecuting kings and princes have become nursing fathers and nursing mothers' was an exhortation to persist with the cause of reformation even in the face of the bitterest royal disapproval.[167]

With this exhortation fresh in their ears, the Commons resolved that their order should be printed and published. They followed it up, on Cromwell's motion, with another order to the effect that the parishioners of any parish where there was no lecture might set up an 'orthodox' lecturer at their own charge.[168] This order was repeatedly taken advantage of by parishes practising their own measures of reform

---

[165] *CJ* ii. 279.

[166] BL Harl. MS 164, fo. 895[a–b]; *CJ* ii. 280–1.

[167] Stephen Marshall, *Peace-Offering to God* (1641), 4–5, 8. See also Jeremiah Burroughes, *Sions Joy* (1641), 26, 45, 19, 34, 27, and other refs. It is hard to dispute the topicality of these two sermons.

[168] *CJ* ii. 283; BL Harl. MS 164, fo. 905[a].

by a kind of non-separating congregationalism. The developments it encouraged were perhaps more congenial to Cromwell than they were to Holles.

The order of 8 September was a calculated snub to the Lords, who decided to reply in kind, by publishing and printing their order of 16 January, demanding that divine service be performed according to law. The division in the Lords was on whether they should publish and print their order before demanding any conference with the Commons, and this proposal for tit for tat was carried by 11 votes to 9. Bedford, Warwick, Clare, Newport, Wharton, and Kimbolton (Mandeville) protested against the decision. The other Lords in the minority were Lord Keeper Littleton, Manchester, and Hunsdon. The Lords voting with the majority were Denbigh, Cleveland, Portland, Dover, Bishop Williams, Mowbray, Wentworth, Kingston, Dunsmore, Coventry, and Capel. The division should not, perhaps, be taken as a straight party division. Not all the Lords voting in the minority were necessarily committed to supporting the Commons' order by their vote to confer with the Commons about it. Nevertheless, it seems a reasonable deduction that those who voted to confer with the Commons were less offended by their order than the Lords who voted in the majority, so, in a very imprecise sense, the vote is some guide to party sentiment in the Lords.

The Earl of Dover, who began his Lords' diary from this incident, noted: 'whether ye Howse of Commons have power of them selves, to enjoyne ye whole kingdome any thinge wch is not settled by ye lawes'.[169] The best answer D'Ewes could make, when faced with this objection, was that the order was not against law, because the statute of 1559 had abolished all popery and superstition.[170] In the Commons, Pym, reverting to his 1621 persona, could think of nothing to suggest but to send to the King to ask him to suspend the Lords' order by Proclamation.[171] The remark is a good illustration, both of how desperate the Commons' majority had become, and of how far their real quarrel in the summer of 1641 was with the Lords as much as with the King. They could exert leverage on the King far more easily than they could on the Lords, and therefore, as Stephen Marshall's reference to the conversion of 'persecuting kings' had suggested, their strategy was aimed at securing, by whatever coercive means came to hand, the conversion of Charles I. This, in the literal sense of the word, was hoping for a miracle.

---

[169] *LJ* iv. 394–6; Bodl. MS Clarendon, vol. 21, no. 1603; BL E. 669, p. 3(18). The printed report appears to emanate from the protestors. If it has an independent provenance, its confirmation of Dover's division list is the more impressive. For the growth of the hostility between the Houses which came into the open on 8 and 9 Sept., see Bedfordshire RO St John MS J 1383; *CJ* ii. 261; Holland, vol. ii, fo. 100ᵛ.

[170] D'Ewes (C.), p. 20.

[171] BL Harl. MS 5047, fo. 85ʳ.

Meanwhile, the country was faced for the first time with what became a normal problem over the next year: the imposition of contrary commands from two different authorities. The list of seditious words reported to the Commons over the next few months suggests that resistance to the order of 8 September may have become a rallying point for those who were opposed to the Commons majority and their call for further reformation. On 20 October, immediately after the recess, a churchwarden from Lancelot Andrewes's old parish of St Giles Cripplegate was before the Commons accused of saying 'hee wondered why the howse of Commons was so invious against the railes, that they were all asses'.[172] On 6 November Mr Carter minister of Highgate was accused of saying 'they were mad that would read the order of the House of Commons concerning innovations'.[173] In April 1642 Nathaniel Fiennes reported the case of a man in an inn at Bromsgrove who had linked the religious and constitutional issues in this order: he claimed that

the church windows had been pulled down, had it not been for him: but now that his Majesty had proclaimed that no ordinance of Parliament did bind without his Majesty's assent unto it; he cared not a fart for the Parliament's orders: and that a company of asses had sat about a twelvemonth together for nothing but to set divisions between his Majesty and his people.[174]

By attempting to enforce their order without the consent of King or Lords, the Commons, for the first time, were making it possible to turn the rule of law into an effective Royalist slogan. They also turned the law into an instrument to protect those opposed to further reformation, and an instrument for the defence of rails and stained glass windows.[175]

It is difficult to draw clear evidence from churchwardens' accounts on how widely or how swiftly this order was enforced, since the presence of builders in church seems to have been so pervasive that the absence of a specific record of enforcement cannot often be taken as negative evidence: it may be concealed under the heading of 'work done in the church'. One parish which enforced the order rapidly was Great Staughton (Hunts.), which recorded: 'paid to Raphe Warner for helping to take down the railes in the chancell, 8d.'. In Great Staughton, this swift compliance is more likely to be evidence of efficiency than of godliness, since the same parish had acquired a copy of the Book of Canons before 31 May 1640. They ceased to pay for washing their surplice in 1642, yet wrote an indignant note in the margin of their

---

[172] D'Ewes (C.) pp. 17, 19. I am grateful to Dr Kenneth Fincham for information on Andrewes.

[173] CJ ii. 307; D'Ewes (C.) pp. 98, 104.

[174] PJ ii. 178; CJ ii. 530. Though the words were not questioned until much later, their reference to the Parliament having sat 'a twelvemonth' would suggest that they were spoken around Nov.

[175] On the legal issues raised by the ordinance for disarming of recusants see Fletcher, pp. 76–7, 147–8, 195, and other refs, and below, p. 421.

inventory when it was taken away by soldiers in 1645.[176] Great
Staughton was probably not alone in regarding the order as yet another
example of irritating central interference, and that attitude, as well as
Laudian devotion, was capable of breeding Royalists in suitable
conditions.

Some indication of quite how disruptive the enforcement of the
Commons' order might be can be gathered from Sir Robert Harley's
attempts to enforce it in the unfavourable surroundings of Herefordshire: at Wigmore, he pulled down the Cross,

he caused it to be beaten in pieces, event to dust, with a sledge [hammer]; and
then laid it in the footpath, to be trodden on in the churchyard . . . upon the
30th day [of September], being Thursday, he pulled down the cross at Leint-
wardine, and broke the windows in the church and chancell and beat the glass
small with a hammer and threw it into [the] Teme, in imitation of King Asa 2
Chronicles 15–16, who threw the images into the brook Kidron, and because he
could not come at Kidron, he threw it into the Teme, as Mr. Yates one of his
chaplains said. He was also at Aymestry, to have done the like, but the parish
and Mr. Lake the minister withstood him, and so he departed for that time.[177]

This report is surely not only a measure of how near the country was
being brought to civil war, but also a remarkable tribute to the spiritual
power credited to the symbols of popery in a country which had supposedly been Protestant for eighty years.

[176] Huntingdon RO 2735/5/1 (Great Staughton Churchwardens' Accounts), fos. 30[r], 4[r], 32–6,
4[r].

[177] Jacqueline Levy, 'Perceptions and Beliefs: The Harleys of Brampton Bryan and the Origins
and Outbreak of the First Civil War', Ph.D. thesis (London, 1983), 215–7; Jacqueline Eales,
*Puritans and Roundheads: The Harleys of Brampton Bryan and the Outbreak of the English Civil
War* (Cambridge, 1990), 115–16.

10

The Origins of the Irish Rebellion
NOVEMBER 1640–DECEMBER 1641

On 1 September 1641 Edward Nicholas said he had just heard from the Lords Justices, in charge of the Irish government in Dublin, 'who write that all is in that kingdom very quiet and in good order'.[1] Within less than two months after this, Ireland had been engulfed in one of the biggest rebellions in its history. Since that rebellion had been in gestation since February 1641, this letter reveals the extent to which what went on in the Irish community was a closed book to such pillars of the 'English empire' as Lord Justice Parsons. Even as late as 2 October, less than three weeks before the outbreak of the rebellion, Sir John Temple told Nicholas 'this kingdome gives nothing worth your knowledge'.[2]

Yet, on a deeper level, such a comment was not quite as absurd as later events have made it look. Much recent comment on the Irish Rebellion has stressed that it did not arise from the sort of settled national hatred perceived by post-Cromwellian hindsight, but, in Aidan Clarke's phrase, was a 'startling interruption of a mood of peaceful cooperation'.[3] It is possible that, in expressing such a view, we are, to an extent, the prisoners of our documents. It would be an exaggeration to say that the surviving records are not the records of the Irish, but the records of the English in Ireland, but it would be an exaggeration containing some measure of truth. Those individuals our records allow us to identify include some Irishmen, as well as Englishmen, but these are almost invariably the most Anglicized Irishmen, as perceived through English records, and, above all, as perceived in the English language. The destruction of the rebel archive at Kilkenny has left a gap in Irish sources which nothing else has satisfactorily filled, and the picture of 'peaceful cooperation' may in part result from the built-in bias of documentary survival.

Nevertheless, the surviving documents must represent at least some part of the truth, and it is one of which we must take account. There is, for example, evidence of intermarriage which has been described as

---

[1] PRO SP 16/484/2.
[2] The phrase is Parsons's own: *NHI* iii. 235; Christ Church, Evelyn MSS, Nicholas Box, nos. 39 and 40.
[3] Aidan Clarke, 'Ireland and the General Crisis', *Past and Present*, 48 (1970), 86.

amounting in some places to 'fusion'.[4] Much of this applies to the native Irish and the Old English, pre-Reformation settlers who often retained sympathy for Catholicism in varying degrees of explicitness. It is more striking to find evidence of improving relations in the life of such a dedicated Protestant and New English figure as the Earl of Cork. Between 1603 and 1641 Cork seems to have grown increasingly secure of the English future in Ireland. He employed Irish servants, and continued to do so even after the rebellion, and his son Roger, possibly as a result of having an Irish wet-nurse, was said at the age of four to have enough Irish to act as his father's interpreter.[5] This more relaxed mood had extended to some of Cork's neighbours, and after the rebellion had broken out, John Fitzgerald wrote to him from Kerry, complaining in alarm that his house had been built for peace, having more windows than walls. He asked to take refuge from the rebels in one of Cork's castles.[6]

Paradoxically, some of the best evidence for increased harmony between the races comes from the study of the rebel leaders themselves. To one used to the view of the Irish Rebellion as seen from Westminster, one of the major surprises of work on Irish history has been the discovery of the deep Englishness of many of the rebel leaders. Figures like Viscount Gormanston were concerned with securing for themselves the rights of Englishmen, and, like Benjamin Franklin or Mahatma Gandhi, were led into challenging the English because this came to appear the most effective way of securing for themselves the rights of Englishmen. This does not only apply to Old English figures like Gormanston, but to some of the Irish leaders. Lord Macguire, for example, was an Oxford man, and even Sir Phelim O'Neill, who became the key man in the rebellion, was able to capture Lord Caulfield's castle at Charlemont by the simple expedient of dropping in for dinner. As Aidan Clarke has remarked, the real lesson of this episode is that the two men were on casual visiting terms.[7] Caulfield was not the only settler with whom O'Neill was on such terms: Rawdon, Conway's Irish informant, wrote in some alarm when the rebellion was two weeks old that he feared the commander was 'my friend Sir Phill. O'Neille'.[8]

Such evidence of the Anglicization of many of the rebel leaders, and of the English ideals which dominated much of their propaganda, must call for thought about the original aims of the rebellion. Nationalist

---

[4] *NHI* iii. 148.
[5] Nicholas Canny, *Upstart Earl* (Cambridge, 1982), 126–7, and other refs.
[6] BL Egerton MS 80, fo. 6^r.
[7] Aidan Clarke, 'Genesis of the Ulster Rising of 1641', in Peter Roebuck and J. L. McCracken (eds.), *Plantation to Partition* (Belfast, 1981), 35.
[8] PRO SP 63/260/35.

hindsight (on both sides of the water) tends to see the rebellion as, from the outset, a direct challenge to English rule. This is an assumption which should not be accepted uncritically. It may have been true from the beginning for some rebels, but it is clearly not true of all, and is certainly not true of the early Irish confederate propaganda.

On 29 December 1641 the confederate peers, in an appeal to the gentlemen of Galway, wrote that they had seen

how much the majesty of our prince in what concerns the kingdom has suffered in the essential rights of it by the management of the affairs of the state by the Parliament of England, as if, not content with the blessing of the presence of our common father his sacred Majestie, they would force upon us a further subordination at the same distance.

They said their aim was 'to preserve the freedom of this kingdom under the *sole* obedience of his sacred majesty'.[9] This, if it had come from fellow-Protestants, is a vision of the relations between the three kingdoms the Scots would have been able to understand: a view of three autonomous kingdoms, subjected to a common monarchy but not in any way subject to each other. Bishop Warner, in the English House of Lords, saw the similarity: he noted that the Irish 'as the Scots did, require liberty, religion, laws, etc'.[10] In December 1641 the Lords, knights, and gentlemen of the Pale, writing to the King and Queen, asked for 'a construction no worse than your Majesty hath made of others of your subjects, who upon less or the same occasions have done the like'.[11] One of the captured rebel leaders said they took arms 'to imitate Scotland, who got a privilege by that course'.[12] The example of Scotland, in a three-kingdom context, was likely to be profoundly attractive to the Irish, since it suggested the possibility of a relationship of equality with England, without breaking the links which bound them together. The visible existence of such an example just across the Irish Sea is likely to have been one of the strongest incentives to rebellion.

If this is correct, it would support Aidan Clarke's stress on the limited objectives with which the rebellion began.[13] This, of course, was not the view of the Irish Privy Council. They were saying, from the very begin-

---

[9] Gilbert, i. 244–5. Italics mine.
[10] BL Harl. MS 6424, fo. 99r.
[11] Gilbert, i. 236.
[12] *LJ* iv. 415. See also J. Nalson, *Impartial Collection of the Great Affairs of State* (1683), ii. 551 for the rebel leaders' efforts to recruit him, 'it being for religion, and to procure more liberty for their country, as did (they say) of late Scotland.'
[13] Clarke, 'Genesis of the Ulster Rising', *passim*. The use of the word 'rebellion' here is without prejudice to the arguments advanced by Clarke. In English parlance, the word is normal for any armed resistance, which, however limited its aims may have been, the movement of Oct. 1641 undoubtedly was.

ning, that they feared for the lives of all the British in Ireland and for the loss of the King's sovereignty.[14] When the rebellion was six weeks old, the Irish Privy Council was taking an entirely fundamentalist view of its purposes:

they profess they will never give over until they leave not any seed of an Englishman in Ireland. Nor is their malice towards the English expressed only so, but further, even to the beasts of the fields and improvments of their lands, for they destroy all cattle of English breed, and declare openly that their reason is because they are English'.[15]

The Irish Council was dominated by such figures as Lord Justice Parsons, one of the key advocates of Protestant supremacy. Such people could see a long-term interest in presenting the rebellion in this light, as a justification of their long-held fears. Above all, though, the early testimony of the English and Scots on the rebellion is, like English reports from India during the Mutiny, such a vivid measure of sheer physical fear that it is hard to use it as an accurate indicator of much else.[16] Such reports may well have amounted to a self-fulfilling prophecy, since they served to determine the nature of the English response, but they should not be accepted uncritically.

Perhaps the most balanced of the original reports on the rebellion are those from the Earl of Ormond, who was, somewhat unusually, both Old English and Protestant, and was writing to the King on being appointed Lieutenant-General against the rebels. On 12 December he reported the decision of many of the Old English Lords of the Pale to join with the rebels, and said he was *told* that their accession would moderate the rebels' demands—a phrase which hints strongly at some sort of private contact. He said they would stand for the repeal of all statutes laying penalties on the Roman religion, and for taking away the incapacity of 'natives' to bear office either in respect of birth or religion. Others, he said, went higher, and said the question was whether there should be no Protestant or no papist. On 1 December he had told the King that among the rebels there were many of good heart, who did not aim at shaking the King's government, but had only been seduced into 'a rebellious way of remonstrating'. He was almost certainly right in seeing a division between moderates and fundamentalists among the rebels, and in identifying the Old English, whose decision to join in an

[14] *HMC Ormond*, NS II. 6–8. 'British', in an Irish context, normally denotes English and Scots together.
[15] Ibid. 35. Attacks on English tillage were probably no more random than English reasons for imposing it: it was part of the colonial ideal of 'civility': see *NHI* iii. 176.
[16] See, among other refs., PRO SP 63/260/23.1, 23.2, 23.3, 26, 29, 30, 32, 33, 37 (letter of Payne to the Earl of Kildare).

Irish rebellion was one of the most startling events of 1641, as the source of many of the counsels of moderation.[17]

Aidan Clarke's picture of the rebellion as 'a startling interruption of a mood of peaceful cooperation', like Falkland's description of the 1630s in England as 'the most serene, quiet and halcyon days that could possibly be imagined',[18] creates a considerable historiographical problem. Both in England and in Ireland, the amount of discontent visible before 1640, though significant, does not appear to be on a scale cosmic enough to justify the upheavals which came afterwards, and both English and Irish historiography have had considerable difficulties in coming to terms with this fact. In both cases, it is possible that appearances are deceptive, and that the impression that discontent was not enough to explain what came afterwards is an accident of archival survival. This case is stronger for Ireland than it is for England, because the Irish government was so rarely able to pick up what was not spoken in the English language. There is one story of a priest exhorting disbanded soldiers to disloyal courses, in the presence of an English officer, and blissfully unaware that that officer spoke Irish, which gives a tantalizing glimpse of how much may have gone on under the noses of the English without their knowledge.[19]

It is perhaps an easier case to argue that the scale of the upheaval in Ireland was influenced, not only by merely Irish considerations, but by Ireland's involvement in the problems of the other two kingdoms of Britain. It is not necessary, to argue this case, to prove detailed Irish knowledge of events in England and Scotland, since royal policy towards Ireland was liable to change suddenly and unpredictably as a result of events in other kingdoms. In Ireland, as in England, the crisis began with the assembly of Parliament in 1640. In both kingdoms, a Parliament was called in 1640 for the very specific purpose of obtaining aid against the Scots. It is hard to imagine Irish politics in the winter of 1640 taking the course they did without the removal of Strafford, in which the co-operation of his English, his Scottish, and his Irish critics was an essential part of the process.

In fact, confederate propaganda in the early months suggests very considerable awareness of what was going on on the other side of the Irish Sea. There is no reason why this should not have been so. The disputes about passports during the early months of the rebellion reveal that considerable numbers of the Old English community were in

---

[17] Ibid. 63/260/49 and 44. On the counsels to which Ormond was probably referring, see below, pp. 396–9. His phrases have a close resemblance to the letter taken to the King by Lord Dillon of Costello; PRO SP 63/260/37.

[18] Rushworth, *Collections*, III. i. 86.

[19] PRO SP 63/259/44.1 and 44.2.

London during the months before the rebellion broke out,[20] and it is not to be imagined that they refrained from doing as other gentlemen in London did, and sending home some examples of the startling news which was being made. From December 1640 to August 1641 there was also an Irish Parliamentary committee in London negotiating with the King, and it is hard to see how they could have done their duty without being aware of the contrary pressures Charles was under, both from his English Parliament, and from the Scottish commissioners in London. The correspondence of the Irish committee has not been found, and we have to rely, for a sample of news coming back from London, on the correspondence of a junior officer in the English army called John Barry. Barry was himself a future rebel, and his correspondence shows, both an intense alarm at the growing wave of anti-popery in London, and a profound suspicion of the Scots of the type characteristic of anti-Puritans on the other side of the Irish Sea.[21] In addition, there was a steady stream of Irish witnesses in London to testify at the trial of Strafford, and it is likely that most of them made some additions to the stock of English and Scottish news available in Ireland.

In places, confederate propaganda shows quite detailed knowledge of what had happened in England. One confederate pamphlet of 1642 answers atrocity stories by saying they were 'no truer than that Colonel Lunsford did eat children about Kingston'. This shows knowledge of a rather obscure rumour, which, moreover, was not current until over three months after the rebellion had broken out.[22] The knowledge of it tends to confirm Aidan Clarke's judgement that 'those who planned the rebellion were not beyond the Pale'.[23] Some of the rebels or potential rebels who tried to approach the King through Lord Dillon at the beginning of November said that 'the papists are severely punished (though they be loyall subjects to his Mty.) in the neighbouring countries which serve them as beacons to look to their own countrey'.[24] That popery and political loyalty were compatible was a central item of the Old English creed, and the growing reluctance of those in power in

[20] LJ iv. 437, 518, 542, 657; CJ ii. 304, 308, 358, and other refs.
[21] HMC Egmont, I. 122, quoted above, p. 177. For his suspicions of the Scots, see HMC Egmont, I. 131, 132. For an attitude to the King and his prospects which may be typical in Anglo-Irish circles, see BL Add. MS 46,925, fo. 1ᵛ: 'Though ye lyons clawes be pared close, yet in tyme they will growe out agen, and it is better trusting to what his love and favor will oblidge him too, then to what his necessities may inforce him to promise nowe'. This sentence, written on 5 Apr. 1641, carries an implicit criticism of Pym which is hardly likely to be accidental.
[22] Discourse between Two Councillors of State, the one of England, and the Other of Ireland, ed. Aidan Clarke (Analecta Hibernica, 26, 1970), 172. I concur with Dr Clarke's verdict that this is a pamphlet 'comparing more than favourably in style, cogency and restraint with its English equivalents'. (ibid. 161.)
[23] Clarke, 'Ireland and the General Crisis', p. 89.
[24] PRO SP 63/260/37.

England and Scotland to believe any such thing was an outside threat
capable of having a severely disruptive effect in Irish politics.

Perhaps the most lucid invocation of the outside threat as a justification of rebellion comes from Viscount Gormanston, in an unsuccessful
appeal for support addressed to his fellow Old Englishman the Earl of
Clanricarde in January 1642:

It was not unknown to your lordship how the Puritan faction of England, since
by the countenance of the Scottish army they invaded the regall power, have
both in their doctrine and practice laid the foundation of the slavery of this
country. They teach that the laws of England, if they mention Ireland, are
without doubt binding here, and the Parliament has wholly assumed the
management of the affairs of this kingdom, as a right of preheminence due to it.
And what may be expected from such zealous and fiery professors of an
adverse religion but the ruine and extirpation of ours.

As an analysis of events in London, this could not easily be improved,
and Gormanston took it the more seriously because he feared the
growth of an axis between the Lords Justices in Dublin and 'their
patrons the Parliament of England'.[25] It was certainly true that Lord
Justice Parsons wished to influence policy in an anti-Catholic direction,
and that the support of Pym in London could become a powerful asset
to any attempt to do so. It thus seems reasonable to consider the
hypothesis that the Irish Rebellion, as well as the English Civil War,
owed some part of its origin to the force of outside intervention, and
that both events are in part expressions of the problem of multiple
kingdoms. For how many of the Irish rebels such a hypothesis might
hold true is a question which might call for future work. It seems likely
that it held more truth for Old English rebels than for Irish, and that
among the Old English, it held more truth for peers than it did for
commoners. It is also a plausible hypothesis that it held more truth for
Gormanston than for others. Yet, even with all these notes of caution,
there is a case here to be investigated. Since it was the Irish Rebellion
which made the peaceful dissolution of the English Parliament impossible, and thereby made civil war likely, the importance to English
history of establishing the causes of the Irish Rebellion is considerable.
The case argued here is that the rebellion was not a *diabolus ex machina*,
not a random intervention of an outside force, but in part a logical
consequence of an Anglo-Scottish *rapprochement* whose key term was
an increased hostility to popery. Gormanston was not the only resident
of Ireland who viewed such a *rapprochement* with alarm. One of the

[25] Gilbert, i. 255. Gormanston had been in London both as a witness against Strafford and as a
member of the committee of the Irish House of Lords. For the passage about the laws of England
binding if they mention Ireland (because Ireland was a conquered country), see Palmer, fo. 185ᵛ,
quoting Coke, *Seventh Report*, i. 17. Gormanston quoted it correctly.

general statements of grievances shows what could be made of Gormanston's insights when they were placed in unsophisticated hand: it claims that:

the English and Scotts combined and joined in a petition to his Majestie to bee licenced for to come into Irland, with the Bible in one hand and the sword in the other, for to plant their Puritan, anarchical religion amongst us, otherwise utterly to destroy us.[26]

Some of the Irish themes which run through the Irish crisis of 1640–1 go back to the beginning of the reign of Charles I. When Charles was having difficulty financing the wars at the beginning of his reign, some of his advisers looked to the example of the Union of Arms in Spain for the proposition that all three kingdoms ought to contribute to their joint defence.[27] These efforts led to the raising of one Scottish and one Irish regiment in 1627.[28] It was not a great contribution, but the political disturbances it gave rise to were much more long-lasting than the Union of Arms itself. It was essential to the financing of an Irish army to induce the Irish to vote money for it, and as part of the negotiations to that end, Charles in 1628 granted a series of concessions known as the Graces.[29] These offered a series of detailed concessions, mostly designed to make life easier for Catholic Old English landholders. For example, those whose land had been in wardship were to be entitled to receive livery on taking the oath of allegiance, which most Old English Catholics could take, rather than having to swear to the Supremacy, which many of them could not. The key concession of the Graces was the application to Ireland of the English Concealment Act of 1624, which said that sixty years' possession of an estate was to confer a good title.

In England, this Act had merely stopped an abuse. In Ireland, its effects would be likely to be much more far-reaching. As in other English colonies, there was considerable trouble when the English freehold doctrine of property came into conflict with more collective indigenous notions of property.[30] Property in Ireland had often been regarded as belonging to lineage groups rather than to individuals, while English lawyers could find no valid title to land until they discovered an individual or corporate owner. Moreover, the lawyers needed to find an owner with a valid feudal tenure, derived immediately or mediately

[26] Gilbert, ii. 4, from Bodl. MS Carte 2, fo. 217ʳ. The passage was written after the English Parliament had called for Scottish help in suppressing the rebellion.

[27] PRO SP 16/527/44.

[28] G. E. Aylmer, 'St. Patrick's Day in Witham, Essex', *Past and Present*, 61 (1973), 139–48. For the Scottish regiment, see above, p. 27.

[29] Aidan Clarke, *Old English in Ireland* (1966), pp. 28–60 and *passim*.

[30] *NHI*, iii. 169. I would like to thank Dr T. Venables, of Yale, for helpful discussions of this question. It seems to have arisen almost every time the English common law was put in a colonial context, from the Welsh Act of Union onwards.

from the Crown. For lawyers such as Sir John Davies, Solicitor-General to King James, these attempts to introduce English land law were a vital part of their efforts to make the Irish 'become English'.[31] It was even more important to Protestants in Ireland that these investigations into land titles were an essential part of the policy of plantation. Before land could be planted with Protestant settlers, it was essential to find the King's title to it. Since very few Irishmen could prove the requisite feudal tenure, it was usually possible to find the King's title to land destined for plantation, and so to dispossess the occupants. If sixty years' possession were to confer a valid title, such efforts would become very much more difficult, and the policy of plantation would, in effect, be at a halt. For Catholic Irish landholders, therefore, the Graces represented a concession of quite exceptional importance.

For New English and Protestant interests, the Graces created the ugly fear of an alliance between Charles and the Old English against settler and Protestant interests. That fear was the uglier because the army for which the Graces were a concession was to be collected by the arming of papists. The Irish Privy Council in 1626 protested indignantly at any such notion: 'thereby we should have put arms into their hands of whose hearts we rest not well assured'.[32] The alarm was increased by the fear that such a deal would involve *de facto* toleration of popery: Archbishop Ussher called it a proposal to sell Christ for thirty pieces of silver.[33]

No sooner had Charles been forced to realize that the Graces were running him into a storm, than the making of peace in 1629–30 put an end to the need for an army the Graces had been designed to meet. The recall of Lord Deputy Falkland therefore led to the elevation of Loftus and Boyle as Lords Justices, and the restoring of Irish policy to impeccably Protestant hands, and the Graces disappeared into limbo. Sir Thomas Barrington, in England, noted this development with relief, and hoped for much better times because the Lords Justices were suppressing priests and friars.[34] For the Old English, on the other hand, their alliance with the King against the Protestant interest had been snatched from their hands almost at the moment of its conclusion, and they spent most of the next thirteen years striving to recover it.

Strafford, during his Lord Deputyship, showed no patience with requests for confirmation of the Graces, and told the Parliament of 1634 that the Graces were 'more . . . than their six little subsidies were

---

[31] Ibid. 187.
[32] Clarke, *Old English in Ireland*, p. 35.
[33] Ibid. 39.
[34] *Barrington Family Letters 1628–1632*, ed. Arthur Searle (Camden Society[4], 28, 1983), 138.

worth'.[35] Perhaps the key to Strafford's Irish administration was the determination that Ireland should not be a drain on the English Exchequer, as it had been for most of the reign of James, but that it should raise enough revenue to be self-sufficient. This is an example of Irish policy being determined for non-Irish reasons, and appears to have been a decision of the English Privy Council, given to Wentworth as an instruction.[36] He dealt with the problem of 'little subsidies' by introducing the system of lump-sum assessment, later brought in by Pym in England, but, with a typical indifference to legal forms, did so by administrative action rather than by an Act of Parliament. He also decided that the need to increase revenue and the abandonment of the policy of plantation were incompatible objectives. He told Lord Treasurer Portland in January 1634 that he hoped to raise £5,000 per annum by the plantation of Connacht, and a further £3,000 per annum by discovering concealed Crown lands, and that the Graces would have to wait until he had done this.[37] The proposed plantation of Connacht was the first one in which the Old English on any significant scale faced confiscation as papists, and therefore were liable to find they had a common interest with the native Irish.[38] Yet, though the revival of the policy of plantation brought Strafford into conflict with the Old English, he did not rely on any alliance with the New English, and his determination to recover church property, among other things, led him into equally bitter conflict with the Earl of Cork. His attempts, in conjunction with Laud and Bramhall Bishop of Derry, to bring the Protestant church of Ireland into conformity with the Laudian church of England brought him into conflict with much of the Protestant church of Ireland, and his fear of hidden Covenanter sympathizers led him into even deeper hostility to the Ulster Scots.[39] When these things are put together with such personal insensitivities as lying on the Earl of Clanricarde's best beds in his riding boots,[40] it is easy to understand why Strafford made enemies. There is justice in Aidan Clarke's comment that 'one of the features of his administration had been the impartiality with which it had trespassed upon the interests of all and sundry'.[41]

For a short while in the winter of 1640–1, Strafford appears to have achieved the distinction of being perhaps the only Englishman to have

[35] Clarke, *Old English*, p. 88. According to *Two Councillors* (p. 166), he also described the Concealment Act as their 'Delilah'.

[36] Knowler, i. 160.

[37] Ibid. 190.

[38] Clarke, *Old English*, p. 110.

[39] David Stevenson, *Scottish Covenanters and Irish Confederates* (Belfast, 1981), 17 n. In this case, the impetus seems to have come from the King, but Wentworth responded with alacrity.

[40] *Two Councillors*, p. 170.

[41] Aidan Clarke, 'Policies of the Old English in Parliament', in J. L. McCracken (ed.), *Historical Studies*, 5 (1965), 88.

obliterated the religious divide in Irish politics. The Irish Remonstrance, passed without debate in order to prevent an attempt to adjourn the House, was carried unanimously on 7 November 1640. The Remonstrance was one long attack on the arbitrariness of Strafford's government, and it was carried by Catholics and Protestants acting side by side. In the attack on Strafford, Gormanston, a Catholic with a nephew in the service of the King of Spain, worked side by side with Sir John Clotworthy the Ulster Presbyterian.

The Remonstrance shows immediately the debt of the Irish Parliament of 1640–1 to the Petition of Right. It recounts that the 'loyall and dutiful people of this land of Ireland, being now for the most part derived from British ancestors, should be governed according to the municipal and fundamental laws of England'. It claims that Magna Carta is in force in Ireland, and condemns illegal impositions and increases in the Book of Rates, arbitrary decisions on civil causes at the Council table, the denial of the Graces, the abuse of monopolies, the creation of the Court of High Commission, the Proclamation against leaving the kingdom without the Lord Deputy's licence, Quo Warranto proceedings against boroughs' rights to return members, and the interference of ministers with the 'natural freedom' of the Parliament. It is an enunciation of the ideal of the rule of law in terms Sir Edward Coke could have been proud of.[42] There is no better refutation of the view that there is some inherent link between Catholicism and support for prerogative than a reading of the Irish *Commons' Journals* for the winter of 1640–1.

They immediately appointed a committee to go into England to secure a hearing for their Remonstrance. The committee spans the full spectrum of Irish politics, from Sir Donagh McCarthy, an Irishman an a future rebel, on one hand, to Sir Hardress Waller, a New Englishman and a future regicide and New Model colonel, on the other. Taking a leaf out of the Scots' book, they empowered the committee to remain in being in the name of 'the commonalty of Ireland' if the Parliament should be dissolved, and raised the sum of £5,086 for the support of the committee in England.

The Lords were slightly less precipitate, but no less determined. Gormanston and Kilmallock on 12 November raised a list of grievances which added to the Commons' list the use of the proxies of Lords with no lands in Ireland to secure a majority in the House. The Lords did not complete the appointment of a committee before they were prorogued, but prorogation did not stop them. Thirteen or fourteen Lords, 'the most then in town', unofficially appointed Gormanston, Dillon of Costello, Muskerry, and Kilmallock to go to England to represent their

---

[42] PRO SP 63/258/65; *CJ Ire.* i. 162–5; PRO SP 63/258/48.

grievances, and when the House reassembled after the prorogation, it gave retrospective legitimation to their actions.[43]

Since they were not supposed to appeal to the King without the permission of Dublin Castle, and Christopher Wandesford, Deputy in Strafford's absence, was unlikely to give any such permission, the Irish Commons, without any sense that they were creating a Frankenstein Monster, appealed to the English House of Commons to get the King to hear their Remonstrance, 'calling to mynd the neere linkes and great tyes of blood and affinitie betwixt ye people of this kingdome, and the famous people of England, from whose loynes they are descended, and being therefore flesh of there flesh and bone of there bone, subjects to one gracious sovereigne and governed by the same lawes'.[44] By a smooth exercise in which it is tempting to see the hand of Clotworthy, the Remonstrance was then delivered to the committee on Irish affairs by Pym.[45] It looks like a co-ordinated effort, and it is unlikely to be a coincidence that the Irish Remonstrance was read on the same day on which Clotworthy began the attack on Strafford's government of Ireland in the Westminster Parliament.[46]

This co-operation could continue only granted two provisos. One was that the Parliament of England should refrain from claiming any authority to legislate for Ireland, for if it should do so, the moves aimed at autonomous status for Ireland inside Britain would backfire very badly indeed, and subjection to the King would be transformed into subjection to the much more anti-Catholic English Parliament. Any move to alter the comparative status of King and Parliament in England would carry such risks for Ireland, since subjection to the King was perfectly compatible with independence from the municipal authority of England, whereas subjection to a Parliament in which they were not represented would carry for the Irish the risk of unambiguously colonial status. The other proviso was that the issues in dispute should remain civil and not religious. The excessive rate of the subsidies of the nobility, for example, was an issue on which Protestants and Catholics could easily unite. The issue of plantation, on the other hand, was not.

The issue of the status of the English Parliament in Ireland was one on which the Scots committed error so consistently as to create the suspicion that it was not accidental.[47] The Anglo-Scottish axis proposed by the Petition of the Twelve Peers was an anti-popish one, being

---

[43] *LJ Ire.* i. 142, 148, 149, 150, 151; PRO SP 63/258/70.1.

[44] BL Egerton MS 1048, fo. 13ʳ. This document appears to be a genuine original, with some hundred signatures. The MS originally belonged to Henry Elsynge Clerk of the Commons. I am grateful to Dr J. S. A. Adamson for this information.

[45] Holland, vol. i, fo. 138ᵛ.

[46] D'Ewes (N.), p. 13; Peyton, fo. 6.

[47] BL Stowe MS 187, fo. 54ᵛ; Scottish RO, PA 7/2, no. 78B; above, pp. 103, 128.

designed for 'uniting of both your realms against the common enemies of the reformed religion'. The colonialist implications of that 'both' were noticed in Ireland, and subsequently picked up in confederate propaganda.[48] In their paper of 10 March, which was printed, the Scots called for a time when 'papists and recusants shall despair to have their religion set up againe, and shall either conforme themselves or get them hence'.[49] When Pym, on the outbreak of the rebellion, said there should be no peace with the rebels unless the laws against recusants were executed, he was saying no more than the Irish expected of him.[50] The Commons' instinctive assumptions about the Irish were betrayed by their resolution, on the news of the rebellion, that 'there is just cause to suspect, that divers of his majesties subjects in Ireland have had some hand in the conspiracy and rebellions of the Irish'.[51] The temptation to regard Catholic Irish as lesser breeds without the law was acute, and the Irish committee was in London quite long enough to observe this attitude.

This sort of religious pressure was not the only force making for an assumption of English Parliamentary authority over Ireland. It was difficult to impeach Strafford without claiming authority in Irish affairs, and in addition, the admission of petitions against Strafford opened the door for disappointed Irish litigants to take their cases to Westminster, and many did so. Pym's claim on 6 November 1640 that 'all the subjects of Ireland have power to come here' almost invited such a flood of Irish appeals.[52] Speaker Lenthall's letter of 13 November, ordering the arrest of Strafford's ally Sir George Ratcliffe in Ireland and claiming that 'this shall be your sufficient warrant', risked overstepping the jurisdictional bounds. The King saved him from himself by issuing the identical order two days later.[53] In February 1641 the Irish Council protested at a rumour that the Lord Chancellor and the Lord Chief Justice of the Common Pleas were to be summoned to England.[54] The English Parliament did not as yet explicitly reach the position taken by Henry Parker in 1642, that 'England and Ireland are one and the same dominion, there is as true and intimate a union betwixt them, as betwixt England and Wales',[55] but by February acute observers could see that there was danger. The Irish House of Lords appears to have seen the dangers before the Irish House of Commons, and on 23 February 1641 they

[48] PRO SP 16/465/16, noticed in *Two Councillors*, p. 171.
[49] BL E. 157(2), p. 4.
[50] PRO SP 16/485/66. Pym was also ensuring the failure of Lord Dillon's peace mission, but it is not clear whether he was yet aware of the fact. See below, pp. 396–9.
[51] MP, 10 Nov. 1641.
[52] D'Ewes (N.), p. 3.
[53] PRO SP 63/258/51 and 53.
[54] Ibid. 63/258/68.
[55] Henry Parker, *Observations on His Majesties Late Answers and Expresses* (1642), 36.

rebuked the judges for delaying an answer because matters were depending in the Parliament of England, saying they had spoken 'as if this Parliament were subordinate to the Parliament in England'.[56]

The Irish Commons continued for a little longer to argue claims to be governed by English law, without, apparently, seeing the danger that such claims might make them appear subject to the Parliament of England as makers of that law. The Queries, passed by the Irish Commons on 16 February 1641, represent the fullest flowering of this Anglo-Irish constitutionalism, and again show how deeply Irish thinking had been influenced by the Parliament of 1628. The Queries began with the claim that the subjects of Ireland were to be governed

by the common laws of England and statutes in force in this kingdom, in the same manner and form as his Majesty's subjects of the kingdom of England are, and ought to be, governed by the same common laws and statutes in force in that kingdom, which of right the subjects of this kingdom do challenge, and make their protestation to be their birthright and best inheritance.

The individual queries asked, among much else, whether monopolies were according to law, in what cases the Lord-Lieutenant might fine and imprison, whether they were subject to martial law in time of peace, and whether an Act of State might bind liberty or goods, or alter the common law.[57] They then proposed to transmit the queries to the Parliament of England for comment, claiming that they were 'totally British and English, and having received their laws from England, and being governed by the common laws thereof, to their great comfort, for five hundred years'.[58] This insistence on claiming that English law applied in Ireland may have originated, in part, from their determination, in the face of bitter royal resistance, to impeach their Lord Chancellor and Lord Chief Justice of the Common Pleas, since the Irish Parliament could only claim a right of impeachment by claiming that English precedents were binding in Ireland. This appears to have led to growing anxiety in the Irish House of Lords: when the impeachment proceedings were reported, there was a 'long silence' before Lord Lambert moved that they follow English precedents such as the case of Strafford.[59] Four days later on 3 March, the Lords were brought face to face with the growing claims of the Parliament of England by a request from the Bishop of Ardagh, one of their members, to appear before the English Parliament to answer a private complaint from one Teige O'Roddy. They refused him leave, and, on the motion of the future rebel leader Lord Macguire, went into Committee of the Whole to

[56] *LJ Ire.* i. 161.
[57] *CJ Ire.* i. 174–6.
[58] Ibid. 189, 191.
[59] Ibid. 185; *LJ Ire.* i. 165–6.

consider the cases of other people summoned by the Parliament of England.[60]

Meanwhile, the committee in London was approaching the most important part of its work. It is not clear how far Charles appreciated that the Irish committee on the one hand, and the Scottish commissioners and the English Parliament on the other, were asking him for incompatible things. The Scots and their English allies were asking for an unremittingly Protestant alignment, in which the world would be made as unsafe for Catholics as possible, while the Irish committee, in their request for the Graces, were asking for a world in which the rights of Catholic landholders would be fully secured. For the Irish committee, the possibility of offering to pay for the upkeep of their army represented, as it had done ever since 1625, the only possible concession of sufficient weight they could offer in return for any such favour, while for Pym or Loudoun, the disbanding of the Irish army was the first step towards the security of any possible settlement they might reach with the King. It was hard to see how Charles could possibly satisfy both parties. It seems likely that the Irish committee understood the symbolic importance of the Queen's household in the struggle for the safety of Catholics, since in later confederate propaganda, the breach of the Queen's marriage treaty was invoked as evidence of the untrustworthiness of the English Parliament.[61] It is likely that this rests on some careful Irish observation of what was going on in London in February and March 1641.

The absence of the correspondence of the Irish committee is one of our most serious archival losses. There are frequent allusions to the existence of such correspondence,[62] but the reconstruction of what it may have contained is a difficult exercise in conjecture. At first, to their intense indignation, the King referred their business to Strafford through Sir Philip Manwaring Secretary for Ireland.[63] They did, however, succeed in preventing the appointment of two figures closely associated with Strafford to fill the vacuum left by his departure. First, they appear to have succeeded, in alliance with Arundel, in preventing the appointment of Ormond as Lord Deputy. They then succeeded in forcing Charles to rescind the appointment of Strafford's ally Lord Dillon of Kilkenny West as Lord Justice alongside Sir William Parsons. It is typical of Charles that he rescinded Dillon's appointment while insisting that he remained in his good opinion.[64]

[60] *LJ Ire.* i. 174, 176.
[61] Gilbert, ii. 5, from Bodl. MS Carte 2, fo. 217ᵛ. On the material being cited, see above, pp. 266–7, 352–4.
[62] *CJ Ire.* i. 168, 172, 179, 180–1.
[63] KAO De L'Isle and Dudley MSS C 114/5.
[64] PRO SP 63/258/57 and 58.

Having cleared some of the obstacles out of their way, the committee were able, during the first quarter of 1641, to approach the central item of their business, the petition for the Grace confirming the Concealment Act, and therefore the stopping of the policy of plantation. At first, they were forced to argue on paper with Strafford's imprisoned henchman Sir George Ratcliffe, who put up a standard defence of plantations in terms of the King's revenue, claiming that the Concealment Act would cost £20,000 a year in terms of lost revenue.[65] On 9 March, significantly the week after the failure of the English settlement negotiations, Charles began to consider the Irish demands more seriously, and set up a Council committee, consisting of Littleton, Manchester, Arundel, Hertford, Bedford, Bristol, Cottington, Vane, and Bankes, to consider the Graces and the Remonstrance of the Irish House of Commons.[66] On this committee, in mirror image of English alignment, Arundel and Cottington were probably the conciliators, and Manchester and Vane the hard-liners. It was probably this committee which received a set of papers from Ratcliffe and from the Irish committee, which they appear to have considered on 13 March. Ratcliffe, in addition to raising his points about revenue, asked how Charles could keep up the army if he lost the revenue from plantations, and feared the loss of 'the securing and civilizing these parts by planting etc'. He dismissed the complaints of the inhabitants of Connacht by saying they were 'all in a manner natives and Catholics'. In reply, the gentlemen of Connacht, led by Patrick Darcey, seem to have made an offer of composition to keep up the army in return for the stopping of the plans for plantation.[67] There are numerous allusions to such an offer, but though the original was in the hands of the Clerk of the Council on 3 June 1641, it does not now appear to survive.[68] Like the original offer from which the Graces had first resulted, this provoked deep suspicion among the Protestant interest in Dublin, and Sir Adam Loftus the Vice-Treasurer told Vane that 'this doubtless is a fearfull plott to woorke the Kinge to certaine present ends and then leave him in more distress'. He said that, having dispersed the army, they would then 'fall upon all the new English societies'.[69] It seems that the divisive potential of the issue of plantations may have been splitting the committee itself. John Barry on 8 March reported that the committee suspected Bourke and Plunkett, two of its Catholic members, of having gained private access to the King through Cottington 'and some others well wishers (as they conceave) of the Catholique party', and favourably disposed him to the stopping of

[65] PRO SP 63/258/74.
[66] PC Reg. xii. 107.
[67] PRO SP 63/258/74.
[68] PRO 31/3/72, pp. 356–7; PRO SP 63/258/96 and 83; PRO SP 63/259/38.
[69] PRO SP 63/258/96.

plantations and the granting of all the Graces. Other members of the
committee were defending plantations, both for the revenue, and for 'ye
chiefest and mayne reason of all, ye propagation of ye Protestant religion'. He said it was possible to hear them abuse one another.[70] Most of
this struggle seems to be for ever lost to sight, but the upshot of it was
that on 3 April the King confirmed the Graces.[71]

It is important to note the stage in the English and Scottish story at
which the King did this. He had given up his efforts to reach a settlement with Pym, and instead was planning the Army Plot, and about to
reveal his plan to go to Edinburgh. A hard line towards Protestants was
being matched by a soft one towards Catholics, and the conciliation of
the Old English worked very sensibly as part of a common policy with
his approaches to Montrose and his allies. He had also not given up his
hope of keeping the Irish army, and seems to have been as determined
as ever to keep it until the Scottish army was disbanded. The inclusion
of the keeping up of the Irish army in the petition Henry Percy was to
circulate during the Army Plot makes a logical whole with the decision
to grant the Graces.

It is important to remember, as the Irish committee undoubtedly did,
that Charles was now granting the Graces for the second time. Their
desire for security was deep, and turned out to be well justified, since for
the second time, the Irish did not enjoy the benefit of them. During the
month after he granted the Graces, Charles learnt that he would not,
after all, be able to keep up the Irish army. Until the Treaty of Ripon, it
had been a charge on the English Exchequer, but there was no way the
English Exchequer could continue this payment while paying the costs
of keeping the English and Scottish armies as well. Charles hoped that
he could obtain regular support for it from Ireland, but on 10 April the
Irish Council firmly explained to him that any such hope was vain. The
rule of law, as always, had turned out to be in part a device for reducing
royal revenue. They explained that 'this subject standing now upon the
lawes of the land, whereby, they alledge, their goods ought not to be
taken from them by soldiers, or any other, but in a legall way' they could
not raise money for them, billet them, or discipline them by martial
law.[72] In the absence of evidence, it is impossible to tell why the Connacht men's offer to raise money for the army came to nothing. It is
possible that the offer turned out, on investigation, to be insufficient, or
it is possible that Charles got cold feet about the English political
consequences of accepting any such offer. As a result, the English
Council committee which met on 7 May to consider the Irish Privy

---

[70] BL Add. MS 46924, fo. 209^{r-v}; ibid. 46925, fo. 1^{r-v}.
[71] PRO SO 3/12, fo. 142^{r}; PRO SP 63/258/82; *CJ Ire.* i. 211–12.
[72] PRO SP 63/258/85.

Council's letter of 10 April reported simply that since Charles could not afford to continue the army, he must disband it.[73] He thus appears to have lost what may have been the foremost political benefit for which he had accepted the Graces.

The fate of the Graces appears to have remained in doubt most of the way through the summer. Because the previous granting of the Graces had come to nothing, the Irish committee wanted statutory confirmation.[74] This meant, under Poynings's Law, that bills would have to be prepared for transmission to the English Privy Council before they could be presented to the Irish Parliament.

One of the immediate questions of dispute was who should be responsible for drawing such bills. Under the interpretation of Poynings's Act which had prevailed under Strafford, only the Irish Privy Council had the power to draw and transmit bills for approval by the English Privy Council, a procedure which, in effect, deprived the Irish Parliament of any independent right to initiate legislation. The Irish Parliament wanted an 'explanation' of Poynings's Act, according to which they themselves would have been empowered to prepare and transmit bills for English approval. This was a modification to which the King was adamantly opposed, and which, in the end, he refused.[75] This meant that the task of preparing bills to implement the Graces fell on the Irish Privy Council, which remained opposed to the concession, not least because Charles had made it 'without consulting his ministers here'. On 24 April they offered another lengthy defence of plantations. They stressed the increased revenue from wardships which could result (Lord Justice Parsons was Master of the Irish Court of Wards), and carefully explained that the purpose of plantations was to ensure that the lands 'cannot in point of interest come into the hands of the Irish'. They said that 'there was noe way to reduce this kingdome to the English lawes and obedience of the Crowne, and to free England from the perpetual charge thereof, but only a full conquest, or a politique reformation, by plantations'.[76]

The Irish Privy Council continued this rearguard action against the Graces all summer, and the issue on which they fixed was the loss of revenue involved. They rightly stressed, as in duty bound, the losses of revenue which resulted from the reassertion of the rule of law after the departure of Strafford, and argued that if plantation were stopped as well, the kingdom could not continue without a subsidy from England. In the financial circumstances of the summer of 1641, this was some-

---

[73] PRO SP 63/274/21 and 2.
[74] Ibid. 63/259/4 and 20.
[75] CJ Ire. i. 167, 183; PRO SP 63/259/9 and 11; PC Reg. xii. 167.
[76] PRO SP 63/258/93.

thing Charles could not contemplate. On 7 June they rehearsed a catalogue of the fall in revenues: the customs, they said, needed 'strict and
watchfull supervision', and in the then political climate, they could not
interpose the King's authority, as others had done, lest they diminish it.
The profits of the Court of Wards were much lessened, because the
plantations were not settled, the Castle Chamber was yielding no profit
because it had not sat, the tobacco monopoly was yielding very little
because they could not punish offenders by proclamation until the
Queries were cleared. The commission for defective titles was at a stand,
and the debt had reached £140,000. At the end of this catalogue of woe,
they formally requested a subsidy from England.[77] The figures backed
up these complaints. The customs in the full year of 1639 had yielded
£51,874, and in the first half year of 1640 had yielded only £18,519.[78]
The yield of a subsidy in County Cavan had fallen from £1,250 to £204,
and in Westmeath from £1,350 to £180. Sir Adam Loftus the Vice-
Treasurer said that these were such contemptible sums as were not
worth the King's acceptance.[79] Revenue from the Wards fell from
£8,251 in 1639 to £5,897 in 1640, and revenue from respite of homage
from £622 in 1639 to £242 in 1640.[80] Loftus explained that the negotiations on the Book of Rates proceeding in London would lead to further
revenue losses, and that the Irish Council could not repair these losses:
'in truth the tymes will not now admitt of the former harsh and strickt
way'. Loftus proposed that the rectifying of this problem be linked to
the passage of the bills to confirm the Graces, for, he said, if these bills
received the Royal Assent before the King's business, 'that which concerns his Majesty will have but slow motion'.[81]

By 15 July these constant reiterations, combined with the financial
disasters daily happening in England, had convinced the English Privy
Council. The King was now demanding legislation to improve the Irish
Book of Rates and the customs on wine and tobacco, and two further
subsidies, raised to a height sufficient to pay his debts. Some, at least, of
the concessions the Irish committee wanted were to be held back until
the necessary legislation was completed.[82] These delays seem to have
run on too long to permit the necessary bills to confirm the Graces to be
sent over before the Irish Parliament began its summer recess on 7
August. At the last moment, however, the English House of Lords
supplied Charles with an excuse to blame someone else for the non-
appearance of the Graces. At the end of July the Irish Privy Council and

[77] Ibid. 63/259/26.1.
[78] Ibid. 63/258/89.
[79] Ibid. 63/273/8 and 9, probably the enclosures mentioned in PRO SP 63/259/63.
[80] Bodl. MS Carte 1, fos. 319, 321.
[81] PRO SP 63/259/46 and 63.
[82] Ibid. 63/259/61; ibid. 63/274/26; NP i. 4–5, 20–1.

the Irish House of Lords protested at a series of summonses, in one of which the whole of the Irish Privy Council were summoned to appear before the English House of Lords as delinquents. This remarkable summons was in response to Scottish pressure, being concerned with the case of Henry Stewart, an Ulster Scot who had been imprisoned for refusing in 1639 to take an oath renouncing the Scottish National Covenant. It was a case in which the Scots felt their honour to be concerned, and the English Lords could not safely leave it alone.[83] The Lords, in order not to offend the Scots, had to take offence at the Irish protests at this summons, and they chose to ask the King to stay the Graces, and to declare the subjection of the Parliament of Ireland to the Parliament of England.[84] In fact, it was already too late for the Graces to be sent over for that Parliamentary session, so the Lords were asking the King to do what he had already, in effect, done. However, they presented him with an ideal opportunity to blame someone else for it, and also explicitly asserted the dependency of the Irish on the English Parliament. It was these events which provided the Irish rebels with the excuse for asserting that the Parliament of England, by drawing the King's prerogative out of his hands, had disabled him to grant the Graces 'which always we found him inclinable and ready to grant'. The incident also provided the clear justification for the rebels' assertion that the Parliament of England were 'of opinion that the statutes of England shall binde the natives of this kingdome contrary to laws and the liberties and freedoms of this kingdom'.[85] For once, Charles had succeeded in passing the buck with distinction: he had bitterly disappointed the Old English, while allowing them to blame the Parliament, and to continue to rely on him for support against the English Parliament and the Lords Justices in Dublin.

In fact, the planning of the rebellion had been under way, at least on a contingency basis, since February, and these events were crucial more to the raising of extra support than to the decision to make plans for rebellion. Our knowledge of the original planning comes mainly from a confession by Lord Maguire, one of the leaders who was captured in Dublin on the day the rebellion broke out.[86] In the absence of any means of checking it, it is hard to know how trustworthy this confession is, but it seems in the main credible. Roger Moore, who first approached Maguire, dwelt on the fact that they were put out of their ancestors'

---

[83] MP, 9 Sept., 30 Jul., 4 Aug. 1641.

[84] *LJ* iv. 339; KAO De L'Isle and Dudley MSS C 114/23; BL Harl. MS 6424, fo. 87ᵛ.

[85] Gilbert, ii. 5–6 from Bodl. MS Carte 2, fos. 217–18; *Two Councillors*, p. 171, blames 'the puritan faction' for the disappearance of the Graces.

[86] Nalson, *Impartial Collection of the Great Affairs of State*, ii. 543–54. I have not found a manuscript original of this text.

estates by plantation, and applied this to 'both the natives, to wit, the old and the new Irish' — a significant reclassification of the Old English. He argued that the Scottish troubles provided a good opportunity to recover their estates, and added that the Parliament in England intended 'the utter subversion of our religion', a charge Pym would have found hard to deny. According to Maguire, these fears were much increased by the English anti-Catholic Proclamation of March 1641.[87] He also said it was 'very confidently reported that the Scottish army did threaten never to lay down arms, until an uniformity of religion were in the three kingdoms, and the Catholic religion suppressed'. This, in fact, seems to be a reasonably accurate report of the Scots' paper of 10 March.[88] The rebellion, he said, was timed for 'towards winter', in the hope that England would not be able to send help until the next spring. The timing was also nicely designed to wait until the Scottish army was disbanded, and could not be used to suppress them. They planned not to meddle with the Scots at the beginning of the rebellion (as was in fact done for the first few weeks) in order not to provoke Scottish opposition.[89] For Roger Moore, support from the Old English was the crucial part of the plan. He claimed that the native Irish 'would be ready at any time', but 'that all the doubt was in the gentry of the Pale'. If they had refused to support the rebellion, it seems possible that Moore might have wished to call it off, and it was their support which remained in suspense right through the summer. An unambiguous and complete concession of the Graces would have been likely to deprive the rebels of most of their Old English support. The non-appearance of the Graces at the beginning of August did not create the plans for rebellion, but it was probably the occasion for those plans to be taken out of the status of contingency plans, and put into top gear.

During the summer, interest centred on what happened to the army, whose disbandment was decided on 7 May, since it provided by far the likeliest source of able men on which a potential rebellion might draw. So far as our sources go, they suggest that the disbandment proceeded smoothly. Charles wrote to Ormond on 8 May, the day after the decision was taken, to instruct him to disband the army, and saying the King was giving leave to transport the soldiers from the disbanded army for the service of foreign princes, to avoid disorders they might commit after disbanding. Vane's covering note, telling Ormond to disband 4,000 out of 8,000 'presently' is perfectly in line with this instruction.

---

[87] Larkin, ii. 739–42. See above, pp. 265–6.
[88] Above, p. 199.
[89] On this brief initial period during which the rebels spared the Scots, see Michael Perceval Maxwell, 'Ulster Rising of 1641 and the Depositions', *Irish Historical Studies*, 21 (1978–9), 159–61. The period may have been designed to ensure the conclusion of the residue of Scottish disbanding.

Disbanding by instalments, as the English and Scottish examples show, was a perfectly normal procedure, designed both to avoid bottlenecks in the supply of money, and to avoid the disorders resulting from turning a large number of men loose at the same time.[90] On 26 May Vane reiterated the need to complete the disbanding, saying 'itt is a service yt both kinge and Parlemt. will not bee well satisfied until they shalbe advertised yt itt bee done'. Ormond replied on 10 June that the army was disbanded.[91] On 1 June the Lords Justices and Council reported to the same effect, saying that 'wee have now by orderlie degrees disbanded the new armie' and saying the work 'is now fully don'.[92] On 17 June Lord Justice Borlase reported that the army were gone to their own homes, save those to be transported by Colonel Belling, who was to embark them 'this day'.[93]

It is necessary to stress this evidence because of a story told by the Earl of Antrim to the victorious Cromwellians in 1650, according to which Charles was said to have been responsible for keeping a large part of the army together, in the hope of using them for his own political purposes. According to Antrim, it was Charles's own plan, in which he claims to have been an agent, which got out of control and turned into the Irish Rebellion. The biggest obstacle to believing this story is that it does not seem to have been in Charles's interest: the months of June and July, when it was supposed to have taken place, were the ones when he believed that Culpepper, in England, would secure him a legal and adequate grant of Tonnage and Poundage, and therefore that he could look forward to the legal end of the English Parliamentary session. It was one of the times when Charles had no need to plan to use force. Even after July he seems to have been setting his hopes on an English adjournment, and the soothing effects of a quiet period in which no Parliament was sitting. If he had any use for military force in August and September, it would have been in Scotland, in support of the plans which grew into the Incident.[94] For any such plans, Antrim was an unlikely and unsuitable instrument, since he was a long-standing friend and client of Hamilton. The second obstacle to believing this story is that there is no direct evidence in its favour from any earlier date than 1650. The third obstacle is that, so far from being deep in conspiracy with the King, Antrim during the summer of 1641 was unable to get the King to answer his letters, and appears to have believed the troops were

[90] Bodl. MS Carte 1, fos. 381–3.
[91] Ibid., fos. 411, 426.
[92] PRO SP 63/259/24.
[93] Ibid. 63/259/39 and 44. The Irish Council reported labouring by 'priests, friars and Jesuits' to stop the soldiers leaving the kingdom. See also ibid. 63/259/44.2.
[94] Above, pp. 322–9.

about to depart for the service of the King of Spain. Charles I was guilty of many plots, but this appears not to have been one of them.[95]

The story of why the troops did not in the end go to the service of the King of Spain is a complex one, but it does not appear to involve bad faith on the King's part. At first, the proposal seems to have enjoyed the tacit support of the English Parliament. This situation changed rapidly after the publication of the King's Palatine manifesto on 5 July, since the prospect of war for the Palatinate created the fear that Irish levies might be used against England. The first objections to the sending of Irish troops, from Pym and Rudyerd, followed rapidly after the publication of the Palatine manifesto on 8 July.[96] The key speech in the Commons against sending these troops to Spain, on 28 August, came from Sir Richard Cave, Elizabeth of Bohemia's agent in England.[97] Sir John Clotworthy, who seems to have suspected trouble in Ireland, was a lonely dissentient from growing Commons' opposition to sending these troops to Spain.[98] The King appears to have reacted with considerable anger to this resistance to sending the men abroad.[99] The Irish Parliament was also initially in favour of sending the men abroad, but also swung against it during the summer. In their case, the tell-tale presence of the rebel general Sir Phelim O'Neill on the committee which made the objections suggests that the future rebels had seen the advantage of keeping the men at home. This is the same story told in Lord Maguire's confession, though there too, no contact between the rebels and the colonels is admitted before August. The resolution of the Irish Commons also stresses the Palatine issue, and seems likely to have been supported by Protestants on that ground, as well as by some Catholics on rebellious grounds.[100] When the Spanish Ambassador went to see Charles about these delays on 6/16 August, Charles convinced him entirely of his good faith, engaging himself 'on the honour of a gentleman', and offering a secret licence for transport of men. He said he was moved by gratitude for Spanish assistance in getting the Queen Mother out of England. Since the Spanish Ambassador was deeply suspicious of all delays in his levies, this testimony needs to be taken seriously.[101] It

[95] Hamilton MSS 1355, 1356, 1389. For a fuller discussion of this issue, see my article, 'British Background to the Irish Rebellion', *Historical Research*, 61/145 (1988), 166–82.

[96] Holland, vol. ii, fos. 124^v–5^r.

[97] BL Harl. MS 164, fo. 878^b.

[98] Ibid. 5047, fo. 78^r.

[99] He told the English committee in Edinburgh that he 'holds himself ingaged in his reputation', and that if they were not sent, it would 'tend highly to his dishonor with other princes': Yale University, Beinecke Library, Osborn Shelves, Howard of Escrick MSS, Correspondence Folder 2.12 (3 Sept. 1641).

[100] *CJ Ire.* i. 273–7. The list of reasons given provide a fascinating study of the terms of Protestant–Catholic co-operation in the Irish Parliament.

[101] B. Jennings, *Wild Geese in Spanish Flanders* (Irish Manuscripts Commission, Dublin, 1964), 352–3.

seems that the plan was finally stopped by the English Parliament in September, but the main reason why the men were still in Ireland to be stopped was the familiar difficulty in getting money out of Madrid. Whoever was to blame for the failure of these men to leave Ireland, it seems clear that it was not Charles. The officers themselves appear to have still expected to go, and on 8 September John Barry bound himself to the Spanish Ambassador in a substantial sum to take his men for Spanish service.[102] The fact that Barry was still in Ireland to join the rebellion appears to be nothing more than an accident.

It does seem, however, that some of the Old English may have made one last approach to Charles, in the hope of averting the necessity for rebellion, which did not come naturally to many of them. The intermediary they were employing during the first two weeks of the rebellion was Lord Dillon of Costello, a Protestant Old Englishman who had been a member of the Lords' Parliamentary committee in London. The fact that Lord Dillon was with Charles in Edinburgh during the weeks before the rebellion broke out raises the possibility that he may have been engaged before the rebellion on the sort of negotiation which was occupying him when it broke out. On 25 September Ormond's Scottish correspondent Lord Wemyss reported that he was a great traitor, if he could make use of it.[103] In an undated letter during October, Wemyss said that the King had authorized Dillon to spread a report that the King was going to come to Ireland the next spring or summer.[104]

If this report was designed to help to avert the rebellion, it came too late, and when the rebellion broke out, Dillon had to go to see the King in London, bringing with him, according to the Irish Privy Council, 'a writing signed by many papists of the nobility and gentry of this kingdom, which writing, as we are informed, imports a profession of loyalty to his Majesty and offer of themselves by their power to repress this rebellion without aid of men forth of England'. The Irish Council said that Dillon, though a member of the board, had not told it of this negotiation, and that the plan was as dangerous as a surprisal of Dublin Castle. Force, they said, was necessary to 'reducing this kingdom to civility and religion'.[105] The 'writing' is probably one which later came to the hands of the Council, which asked for an Act of Oblivion, a repeal of all statutes against papists, and 'a charter of free denizen in ample manner for ye meere Irish'.[106] By 8 December this letter was in

[102] BL Add. MS 46925, fos. 137–9.

[103] Bodl. MS Carte 1, fo. 457ʳ.

[104] Ibid., fo. 467ᵛ. On Scottish internal evidence, this letter must have been written between 1 and 12 Oct.

[105] *HMC Ormond*, NS II. 25–6. They said Dillon was acting on instructions from the Irish House of Lords.

[106] PRO SP 63/260/37.

the hands of Pym, who reported it accurately to the English House of Commons. They resolved 'that this House doth declare, that they will never give consent to any toleration of the popish religion in Ireland, or in any other of his Majesty's dominions.'[107] Dillon, on his arrival in England, was arrested on the orders of the House of Commons, and Sir John Clotworthy, the man who had proposed to geld priests and Jesuits, reported that he was 'suspected to have been employed by the rebels to negotiate with his majestie for a toleration of the popish religion to be granted them'.[108] Pym, who reported from the committee which examined him, extracted one further vital piece of information: there had been a plan to remove the Lords Justices and replace them by Ormond. Ormond's letter to the King on 12 December, drawing attention to the weakness of 'our counsels', and saying that 'unlesse other managers of them be sent, all succours will be lesse, if at all, useful', creates a strong suspicion that he may have been privy to this plan.[109]

Dillon's scheme, like Bedford's, is a fascinating example of the historical might-have-been. For Charles himself, there was probably no insuperable reason why he should not govern Ireland on terms which involved toleration of Catholicism, civil rights for the native Irish, and the independence of the Irish Parliament from England. Indeed, Charles might have been happier as such a King of Ireland than he ever was as King of England. He did not like Catholics, but never felt for them the sort of deep allergic dislike he felt for Puritans. He was well aware, as he was not in the case of Puritans, that they could combine their religion with political loyalty. Dillon's scheme would no doubt have caused mortal offence to the New English interest, but that disadvantage was not necessarily insuperable. The New English interest depended so heavily on the political backing of England, with military support if needed, that it had very little scope for resisting any settlement with the full weight of English authority behind it.

The obstacles to Dillon's scheme, as the reactions of Pym and Clotworthy illustrate, were not Irish: they were English. Where Dillon saw an attempt at a new consensus, Pym and his allies saw treason. For him and his allies, any attempt at suppression of the Irish Rebellion which involved toleration of Catholicism was a cure worse than the disease. If Charles had in fact accepted the Dillon scheme, as his Irish interest arguably dictated, he would not have lost Ireland, but he probably would have lost England, and possibly Scotland as well. In England, any

---

[107] D'Ewes (C.), pp. 250–4; CJ ii. 335. See Edward Nicholas's note on the dorse of PRO SP 63/260/46.
[108] Gardiner, History, x. 112–13; D'Ewes (C.), p. 349.
[109] D'Ewes (C.), p. 351; PRO SP 63/260/49; CJ ii. 358.

scheme involving acceptance of papists as subjects enjoying a share of power and privilege on equal terms was simply not practical politics. The Old English of the Pale who waited to join the rebellion till December were probably waiting to see the fate of Dillon's mission. If so, it must have convinced them that they were entirely correct in the analysis which saw the rising power of the English Parliament, and the deep hostility to Catholics which came with it, as the fundamental obstacle to peace in Ireland. Just as the settlement advocated by Pym and Bedford would have made Ireland ungovernable, so the settlement advocated by Dillon would have made England ungovernable. In the event, English plans for the reconquest of Ireland, based on plans for wholesale confiscation through the scheme for the Irish Adventurers, turned the Irish Rebellion into a fundamental challenge to English rule in a way it had not been when it broke out. Cromwell's ultimate suppression of the rebellion seven years later, left behind it a bitterness to which there are few historical parallels. However, granted that the point of equilibrium in Ireland was incompatible with peace in England, and that the point of equilibrium in England was incompatible with peace in Ireland, it is hard to see what else Charles should have done. In the event, he agreed to Pym's plans to draw on Scottish help for the reconquest of Ulster, and so contributed to the importation of yet another kingdom's interests into Irish politics. In the process, the decision to call on Scottish help for the reconquest of Ireland meant more Scottish commissioners in London, and therefore held out the hope of the renewal of the axis between the Parliament and the Scots which had been Pym's standby at the beginning of the Parliament.

The outbreak of the Irish Rebellion did not, by itself, make civil war inevitable, but it closed off one of the alternative exits from the crisis. As the Army Plot and the execution of Strafford had closed off the exit marked 'settlement', so the outbreak of the Irish Rebellion, by calling for a new military effort from England, closed off the exit marked 'dissolution'. The Irish Rebellion meant that King and Parliament were left as it were handcuffed together, and unable to escape from each other. For two parties which could not settle with each other, this was an uninviting prospect. Nevertheless, there still remained two alternative solutions other than civil war. One was the possibility of a coup, leaving one side, by a bold stroke, in possession of the field. The other was the possibility that when the crisis came, a movement of opinion would leave one side or the other without sufficient support to start a war, and therefore force it to accept the other's terms. These, no doubt, were remote possibilities in November 1641, but they were possibilities, and until they had been eliminated, no party wished to take the ultimate risk of civil war. It seems likely that the leaders on both sides, like party leaders in an election campaign, tended to overestimate their support, and therefore showed an undue optimism about the prospect that the other might prove unable to fight. Remote though these possibilities were, the two parties spent the next ten months exploring them.

11

The Grand Remonstrance and the Five Members

SEPTEMBER 1641–JANUARY 1642

I

From the King's departure for Scotland on 10 August 1641, to the raising of the standard on 22 August 1642, was a period of a little over a year. In that year the King and his Parliament only succeeded in remaining in the same place for some six weeks, from 25 November 1641 to 10 January 1642. Those six weeks were alarmingly eventful. Unless or until they could learn to live in the same place, their long-term prospects of avoiding war would not be high. Some part of this fear is undoubtedly due to misunderstanding. Neither the King nor his leading opponents could ever understand how the world looked from the opposing perspective, and they were therefore often unable to read the likely reactions to their actions. There is a lack of political sure-footedness such as deep misunderstanding tends to provoke.

Yet misunderstanding is not a sufficient explanation. From the publication of the 8 September order onwards, Charles knew that the majority of those attending the Commons intended a further reformation of religion, while the leaders in the Commons were in no doubt that Charles intended no such thing. No doubt both sides failed to understand that the other was (or hoped it was) sincerely defending the church of England as it understood it, but whether understanding would have produced any fundamental changes in policy is doubtful. The chief reason why the King and the Commons' majority did not succeed in dispelling each other's fears is that they never seriously tried. Indeed, they did not wish to dispel each other's fears. From the day of Newburn and the Petition of the Twelve Peers onwards, the strategy of Charles's opponents had been to use threat to secure the King's compliance with measures to which he would not otherwise consent. From the Army Plot onwards, if not earlier, the King had replied to this strategy in kind. If they were to learn to live in safety together, the King and the Parliamentary leaders would have had to eschew diplomacy by threat. There is no sign that this happened: from May 1641 onwards, the evidence of serious negotiation between Charles and the Parliamentary leaders is negligible. Negative evidence is not necessarily conclusive, but the discrediting of the conciliators in the King's counsels, of whom Hamilton and Vane had been the chief, does not suggest that the King and his allies any longer felt in need of the sort of services they had provided.[1] The lesson learnt on both sides seems to have been, not that diplomacy by threat had been a failure, but that it was necessary to increase the threat till it became effective. That there could be such a point remained an article of faith.

The area in which compromise had proved impossible was the one area in which it was widely held by conventional wisdom not to be a virtue: that of religion.[2] Charles had accepted the principle that he could not raise taxes with Parliamentary assent, and was sticking to it in the face of near-bankruptcy. He had accepted the principle of Triennial Parliaments. He had accepted the Act against dissolving the Parliament without its own consent. He had accepted, with intense reluctance, that his ministers were subject to Parliamentary impeachment. He had retreated to the point where members predominantly concerned with issues of legality, like Culpepper, Hyde, Strangeways, Kirton, and Seymour, were willing to work with him. The members who continued to oppose Charles were those, like Pym, St John, Harley, Wilde, Barrington, and Cromwell, to whom a further reformation of religion was an essential pre-condition of any settlement. These men were not irreconcilable: they were the men Charles did not choose to reconcile. It was in order to force on him a policy to which he could never consent that they were so determined to deprive him, first of his bishops, and then of the right to appoint his secular ministers. The policy was to be enforced over his head, and he was to be deprived of the power to fight back. So long as what Charles called 'decency' was the same as what Pym called 'idolatry', it was hard to see how it could be otherwise.

The period from the beginning of the recess to the King's final departure from London breaks into four phases. The first is the period of the recess from 9 September to 20 October, during which committees of the two Houses carried on something which the Venetian Ambassador said approached the Dutch form of government.[3] The second period, though short, is worth taking in isolation, since it helps to isolate one causal influence from another.[4] It is the period from the reassembling of Parliament on 20 October, to the arrival of the news of the Irish

[1] For Bristol's warning to Nicholas on 28 Aug. 1641 to address his dispatches to the King and not to Vane, see Christ Church, Evelyn MSS, Nicholas Box, no. 65 (my numeration). I am grateful to Dr J. S. A. Adamson for this reference.

[2] Richard Hooker, *Laws of Ecclesiastical Polity*, V, Dedication 5. This is perhaps the passage referred to at the beginning of Hamilton MS M 9/93/3, a memorandum to Charles of about this date on how to bring about the dissolution of the Parliament. I would like to thank Dr Peter Donald for this reference.

[3] *CSP Ven. 1640–2*, p. 220.

[4] I am grateful to Prof. Anthony Fletcher for this point.

Rebellion on 1 November. The third, the period when the two Houses came nearest to being an effective government, stretches from the news of the Irish Rebellion on 1 November, to the King's return from Scotland on 25 November. The fourth stretches from the King's return to his departure, and from that point, the long descent into civil war begins.

It is a revealing paradox that the biggest swing of public feeling towards the King comes in the first of these periods, when he was doing nothing in particular. His opponents, on the other hand, were experiencing the miscellaneous unpopularities that come with power, however transient. The Venetian Ambassador said there was considerable resistance to taxes, and that the Parliament was losing credit because of their size.[5] He is not, perhaps, the ideal witness on this point, yet there were manifold complaints about the poll tax, and the sheer weight of taxes imposed to disband the army must make it inherently probable that he was right. Sir Thomas Barrington is perhaps a better witness, and when he went home to Essex, he found

a great and strong iusle against divers of our proceedings, by a commixture of malcontents severally disaffected; in so much as I find a straunge tepiditye, full of needles scruples, in ye execution of yt brave ordinance of both houses, for disarming of papists, and an indisposition in many commissioners to make a review of ye service of poll-money, and indeed such an undervalew of ye orders of Parlt. as if it bee not sharply vindicated at our next access, ill wishing minds will extremely prejudice the priveleges of Parliamt.[6]

He said that the body of the county was nevertheless as firm to the Parliament as Caesar's troops, but, coming from what was perhaps the most firmly Parliamentarian county in England, this report should have caused some alarm.

Barrington said nothing about the 8 September order, which others regarded as the most important cause of resistance to the Commons. The Venetian Ambassador said that some parishes obeyed the Lower House, and some the Upper, and some vigorously resisted innovation.[7] It makes a major point about 1641 that by this last phrase, he meant exactly the opposite of what Pym would have meant by it. Pym himself admitted that there were many parishes where 'they were at blows and likely to come to blows' over the order, though he claimed that 'all honest and godly ministers did readilie receive and publish the same', and only 'scandalous ministers' had disobeyed it.[8] For Pym, this statement was probably tautological. Cottington, writing to Nicholas from

---

[5] *CSP Ven. 1640–2*, p. 215.
[6] Yale University, Beinecke Library, Osborn Shelves, Howard of Escrick MSS, Correspondence Folder 1.1.
[7] *CSP Ven. 1640–2*, p. 222.
[8] *CJ* ii. 289; D'Ewes (C.), p. 12.

Wiltshire on 16 September, gave a description which, *mutatis mutandis*, is very much the same as Pym's:

I am very much afraid that these printed contradictory orders will do much harme amongst us here in the countrey, and breed no little distraction, at least very much disorder, for every man makes use of them according to their severall pallets and humors. But God Almighty his will must be done, and these things are not without his divine providence, the issue whereof we must expect with patience.[9]

The Parliamentary committee had already dealt with a disturbance in St George's Southwark, where the churchwardens put up the rails again after they were pulled down, and they became equally perturbed by a churchwarden in St Mary Woolchurch, London, who had proceeded 'as if wee meant to deface all antiquities'.[10] One of Sir John Coke's correspondents gave a picture of how this activity appeared from the other side:

as for the affairs here, they are in a distempered way by those that would have themselves thought to be most holy, and judge themselves fitter to regulate the church affairs, than the law and the judges. In the Old Jewry, a good number of them in the time of divine service came into the church and did tear the Book of Common Prayer, and some misdemeanours against the minister; and upon Sunday last I hear an assembly of them would have come into the church in Paul's to have overthrown the organs and defaced divers other ornaments in the church. What difference is concerning the votes set out by both houses is here inclosed.[11]

For the first time since his reign began, dislike of disruption of the established order was becoming a force which worked for the King and not against him.

This reaction against the order seems to have been strongest in London, perhaps because attempts to enforce it were strongest there also. Thomas Wiseman Remembrancer of the City said that 'the Brownists and other sectaries make such havock in oure churches, by pulling downe of ancient monuments glasse windows and railes that theire madness is intollerable. I thinke it will be thought blasphemye shortly to name Jesus Christ, for it is allready forbidden to bow at his name'.[12] Another, writing anonymously, probably to Vane, said that 'England is much converted without any other preacher but that of error and schisme, for ye confidence of ye late prevailing party unmask't them soe fast that their deformity appeared, and their lovers fell off. If London

---

[9] Christ Church, Evelyn MSS, Nicholas Box, no. 61.

[10] D'Ewes (C.), pp. 3, 6.

[11] *HMC Twelfth Report*, II. 291. The enclosure, which does not appear to survive, was probably the printed text of the orders of the two Houses which survives in PRO SP 16/484/16.

[12] PRO SP 16/484/68.

turne proselyte ye need not doubt ye generall conversion'. For him, the best evidence of this conversion was the election of Sir Richard Gurney, the candidate opposed by the 'Puritans', as the new Lord Mayor. The same letter is one of the first two to imply the new derogatory title, 'King Pym',[13] a title which carried an immediate suggestion of usurpation.

The same author expressed a swing of opinion against conciliation which was becoming characteristic of these weeks, calling for 'courage — and I will never be wizard more if that word and not accommodacon be not the plaster for this ages sore'. There is here a deliberate move away from consensus politics towards a franker party spirit, carried on 'in hope old England shall not be new'.[14] In the rude remarks about New England, Scotland, and sectaries, the junto's opponents were building up a demonology to rival anti-popery. The way two sides were building up rival demonologies, each reading events in line with their previous religious convictions, shows very clearly in a pair of weekly newsletters, both addressed to Sir John Penington in command of the fleet. It is a useful corrective to modern myths that of the two, it is Thomas Smith, secretary to the Lord Admiral and a government servant, who was the Parliamentarian, and Thomas Wiseman Remembrancer of the City who was a Royalist. Where Wiseman thought peace should be secured by repressing Brownists and sectaries, Smith was in favour of securing the kingdom by disarming papists.[15] Since each interpreted every event in the light of previous convictions, their pictures of what was happening diverged rapidly, and by November they hardly seemed to be reporting the same events. By contrast with either of these, Vane's clerk Henry Cogan, who thought the Commons' order was 'for placing the communion tables as they were in Queene Elizabeth's time', was already beginning to sound rather old-fashioned.[16]

With the denigration of conciliation came a denigration of the conciliators. Nicholas, perhaps encouraged by the Queen, allowed his dislike of Hamilton to show freely, describing him as 'a person that ever perfectly hated our nation'.[17] Nicholas even allowed himself to complain

[13] PRO SP 16/484/63. The author, who signs himself 'P. W.' is commonly taken for Sir Peter Wroth. This identification rests on the probable, but uncertain, belief that the author was a member of the Commons' recess committee. If this assumption is discarded, then, on grounds of opinion, Philip Warwick and the new Comptroller of the Household Sir Peter Wych would become more probable candidates. The two letters from 'P. W.' do not appear to be in the same hand. On the election of the Lord Mayor see Pearl, pp. 124–5 ff. Edward Nicholas used the phrase 'King Pym' on the same day: Guildford MS 52/2/19(16).

[14] PRO SP 16/484/72.

[15] Ibid. 16/485/28.

[16] Ibid. 16/484/20.

[17] Guildford MS 52/2/19(25); Evelyn, iv. 94.

that many found the King 'faynt in his owne cause'.[18] From September onwards, if not earlier, it was an important limit on Charles's freedom of manœuvre that there was a considerable head of party feeling behind him. With it came desire for revenge. Nicholas, writing to Vane on 9 October, said that 'I wish that those who have been the cause of these miserable distraccons in his Mats dominions may feele ye weight of punishment wch they deserve. I doubt not but they will doe in due time'.[19]

For Pym's junto, fear that such wishes might come true was a strong force making for intransigence. They knew enough about the fate of their predecessors in coercing the King to know that a settlement with the King was no guarantee against subsequent royal revenge, and showed a steadily increasing determination to make any change they achieved irreversible. Charles's record, and especially the Army Plot, did nothing to discourage this sort of fear. Yet it must also be said that their fear of Charles rested, not only on what he had done to them, but also on what they had done to him. The coercing of a King, especially by the death of his servants, creates its own fear of retaliation. Thomas Webb, the Duke of Richmond and Lennox's secretary, thought these fears could never be stilled: 'there is no buckler safe enough to feare, nor for ye ill deserver. Therefore they will never be secure'.[20] It was an unfriendly view, but not necessarily incorrect, and it may help to explain why fears of royal retaliation were liable to create horrors worse than what actually came. The soldiers who came to arrest the Five Members, for example, did not actually shoot the Commons in their places, but it is possible that members' consciences, as well as Charles's record and the propaganda needs of the moment, contributed to the fear that they might do so. The Incident was not part of a plot to be extended to England, but it made a good deal of sense to Edward Nicholas that his English opponents feared it would prove otherwise.[21] Such fears also had the vital consequence of blocking off the junto's retreat: they could only pursue security, not by retreating, but by demanding more and more cast-iron concessions. It was not in Pym's temperament to be a Hamilton, who could go back to court believing the King guilty of an attempt to kill him, so the search for security was liable to become 'a perpetual and restless desire of power after power, that ceaseth only in death'.

The junto's immediate objective during the recess seems to have been

[18] Guildford MS 52/2/19(21) (Nicholas to Webb, 12 Oct.).
[19] Ibid. 52/2/19(18). It is possible that this passage was aimed at Vane himself, whom Nicholas correctly suspected of leaking information to the Parliamentary leaders.
[20] *NP* i. 39. Webb was formally referring to the Covenanters, but there is surely an English message between the lines.
[21] Guildford MS 52/2/19(24) (Nicholas to Richmond, 21 Oct.).

to insist on Parliamentary choice of the great officers, using Charles's Scottish concession as a precedent to wring the concession out of him. Their only likely lever, which Nicholas warned Charles they would use, was to insist on the concession as the price of a life grant of Tonnage and Poundage.[22] Beyond that, they could only hope to recover 'ye people's good opinion, wch is their anchor-hold and only interest'. Nicholas thought it likely that they would attempt this by doing something against papists, but could not foresee how good an opportunity the Irish Rebellion would provide for such a policy.[23] It is possible that they again provoked Charles's fear for the Queen's safety, by spreading the rumour of a meeting to secure her which they had begun in August. This is possibly the subject of the 'enclosed paper' which Nicholas sent to the King on 27 September, saying he had been given it by Lady Carlisle, who had been given it by Mandeville.[24] The threat to the Queen seems to be for the Parliamentary leaders what the Irish army was for Charles: there is no sign that they meant to carry the threat out, but they were certainly guilty of inflaming fears that they meant to do so, and could not complain if they were believed.

The King, according to his own subsequent account, left for Scotland believing he had done all that could legitimately be asked of him:

We undertook that journey, not doubting, but that when we should have dispatched the affairs of that kingdome, which we hoped speedily to do, and both our Houses of Parliament should have refreshed themselves in the visitation of those, for whom they had so well provided by our favour, we should meet again with mutuall confidence one in another, and that it would be our turn to receive such testimonies of that confidence and affection we had deserved.[25]

In other words, Charles expected a revenue settlement. This, no doubt, he expected to follow up with a few good bills, a General Pardon, and a dissolution. The order of 8 September appears to have awoken Charles's fears that this vision might not come to pass.[26] He took comfort for a while from the fact that the order had been made in a very thin House, but he remained convinced that it was an illegal order and 'for suspension of those laws in force which concerned the government of the

[22] Evelyn, iv. 91. See also *NP* i. 52.
[23] Evelyn, iv. 93.
[24] Ibid. 92. The King promised to conceal the 'enclosed paper', which has not yet reappeared. See above, pp. 345–6 and below, pp. 412–13.
[25] *ECR* E 241(1), pp. 525–6, Charles's Declaration of 12 Aug. This Declaration contains a history of the Long Parliament as seen by Charles after the event. It must be used with caution.
[26] Hamilton MS M 9/93/3 is an anonymous memorandum to Charles on steps that needed to be taken to bring about a dissolution, apparently with consent. For the last mention of an adjournment or dissolution, see Evelyn, iv. 120, by Charles, a week *after* the news of the Irish Rebellion reached Edinburgh.

church'. More seriously, he retained his conviction that the House of Commons 'in truth hath no authoritie to make any orders in business of that nature'. The use of the words 'of that nature' suggests that this is not merely the conviction that the Commons could not make law without the Lords, but his old conviction that church matters were not properly under the control of Parliamentary legislation. This would have become a future bar to co-operation with Culpepper as much as with Pym, since, for the overwhelming majority of both Houses, the control of the church by Parliamentary statute was a minimum condition of consent. Charles recognized the constitutional threat behind the Commons' order, saying it was 'an apparent evidence that they meant the whole managery of the kingdome, and the legislative power should be undertaken by the House of Commons, without the consent, either of us, or of our nobilitie'. Charles was equally offended with the order in favour of parish lecturers, later complaining that they used it 'to commend such lecturers as best suited with their designes, men of no learning, no conscience, but furious promoters of the most dangerous innovations which were ever introduced into any state'.[27] In most cases, this was as much a travesty as godly pictures of popish, Arminian, and immoral clergy on the other side: beyond a certain point of religious passion, accurate observation of facts seems to have become impossible.

In the short term, Charles seems to have hoped to meet this situation by relying on the disagreement between the Houses. When their initial disagreement about the order was reported to him, he replied 'I am not much sorie for it',[28] and when the Houses reassembled, he relied heavily on the efforts of Nicholas and the Queen to exercise a whip to secure the attendance of sympathetic lay Lords and of *well-affected* bishops'.[29] He did not intend to allow any further reform in the church, and relied on the desire for finality to bring in support behind this position. He was reluctant to allow further measures against papists, and rejected a suggestion from Edward Nicholas that he should send away the Queen's Capuchins.[30] Beyond that, Charles hoped for an adjournment, either to another time or to another place. For a while, the gathering threat of a plague epidemic looked likely to be a useful ally in bringing this end about. Edward Nicholas told the King on 12 October that Holles was in favour of an adjournment to Salisbury, 'but Mr. Pym and others will not yeild that it shalbee by any meanes adjourned to any other place, but wished rather that they should sit heere at Westminster and dye here

---

[27] *ECR* E 241(1), p. 526.
[28] Evelyn, iv. 85.
[29] Ibid. 100; Guildford MSS 85/5/2(11), my italics, and other refs. See Christ Church, Evelyn MSS, Nicholas Box, no. 72 (my numeration) for Bath's reply to the whip in a style any modern whip would find painfully familiar. I am grateful to Dr J. S. A. Adamson for this reference.
[30] Evelyn, iv. 90.

together, but I beleeve Mr. Pym will find few (besides those of his Juncto) of that opinion'.[31] If, as seemed likely for a few weeks, the plague epidemic of 1641 had grown into a major epidemic on the scale of 1625, the Civil War might never have happened. The petering out of the plague perhaps deserves to be ranked alongside the Irish Rebellion as one of Charles's major strokes of ill fortune.

When the Parliament reassembled on 20 October, the King had little new to offer it, since he did not accept that anything new was needed. He sent a Declaration to Edward Nicholas, apparently timed for the reassembly of the Houses, saying that 'I am constant for the doctrine and discipline of the church of England, as it was established by Queene Elizabeth and my father, and resolve by the grace of God to live and dye in the mayntenance of it'.[32] Most members would have accepted these words as they themselves understood them, but not so many would accept them as Charles understood them.

II

When the Commons reassembled on 20 October, they began with a long report by Pym from the recess committee.[33] He dealt at length with the disbanding and with the 8 September order, drew attention to the King's obstruction of the disbanding of the garrison of Berwick, and explained that they had not been able to do more towards settling the King's revenue than obtaining a new balance sheet. He reported the continuing investigations of the second Army Plot, but found no time to mention Samuel Vassall's pet project for creating a West India Company.[34] The big new item on the agenda was the Incident. The Houses thanked their committee in Scotland for sending them a full report, stressing that they had had no other public intelligence of it. The Earl of Essex, acting by his authority as Captain-General in the King's absence, decided, to the patent surprise of some of the Lords, to place a guard, to 'secure the houses against other designs, which they have reason to

•

---

[31] Guildford MS 52/2/19(22). See also Christ Church, Evelyn MSS, Nicholas Box, no. 78, Endymion Porter to Nicholas, Edinburgh, 19 Oct., where he says he thinks the English Parliament will not let Nicholas remove from the plague.

[32] PRO SP 16/485/2.

[33] CJ ii. 289–90.

[34] BL Harl. MS 164, fo. 880[b]; BL Add. MS 6521, fo. 294[v]–5[r]; BL Harl. MS 5047, fo. 79[r–v]. Vassall's original proposal was for a company to take advantage of the growing weakness of the Spaniards, and possess ourselves of the rights of Africa and America, and for 'no peace with Spaine beyond tropick line of cancer'. It was supported with equal enthusiasm by Culpepper and Pym, and narrowed to a proposal for a West India Company by the Palatine agent Sir Richard Cave the next day: BL Harl. MS 164, fo. 888[a].

suspect'.[35] Many in the two Houses assumed that this was another army plot, and that it probably had an English branch also. As soon as Pym concluded his report, Rudyerd called for a conference with the Lords.[36] D'Ewes supported him in a speech which is an interesting example of members' tendency to fall back on basic reflexes when faced with events they did not understand: 'let us but looke to the ultimate end of all those conspiracies and wee shall finde them to bee to subvert the truth which I am confident the papists would never have hope offe were they not assured of a party they have in our church which being once taken away by our proceeding in the matter of religion as wee have begun they will have no further hope'. This is also a very good example of the thesis that the way to security was by carrying through an irreversible change. Falkland and Hyde, though much handicapped by the lack of any official account of the Incident, moved that they should leave it to the Parliament of Scotland, 'and not to take upp feares and suspicions without very certaine and undoubted grounds'.[37] The House overruled them, and 'Mr. Pym and others' were sent to prepare heads for a conference. At the conference the next day, Pym asserted three points, first that the Incident was likely to be part of a design for both kingdoms, second that this fact justified a guard, and third that the peace of the kingdoms was indivisible. He threatened 'to employ the power of Parliament, and of the kingdom, for suppressing such as shall, by any practice or other malicious attempts, endeavour to disquiet and oppose the peace of Scotland, and to infringe the late treaty and pacification made betwixt the two kingdoms'. The Lords 'agreed with the House of Commons in all their desires'.[38] In Pym's mind, the Anglo-Scottish alliance of 1640 was still alive, and he was quite ready to offer to return the favour the Covenanters had done him the year before. The speech also served notice that Pym would not abandon the attempt to interest the Scots in any threat to the reformation of religion in England. In October 1641, immediately after the disbandment, Pym could not play a Scottish card, but he continued to look to the time when he could play it again. Whether this may have continued to influence his religious strategy is a suitable matter for conjecture.

On 21 October the Commons took up the case of the contentious churchwarden of St Giles Cripplegate, who had disobeyed both the order of 8 September and the order in favour of lecturers, abusing a member's servant with the words 'the House of Commons were nothing but a company of asses, and sent such as Chambers was up and down

---

[35] LJ iv. 396.
[36] D'Ewes (C.), pp. 14–15.
[37] See Evelyn, iv. 107–8, 112, and other refs. for the dismay of the King's servants at the absence of any official account of the Incident.
[38] LJ iv. 398–9.

with their fables and bables'.[39] Captain Venn, who raised this case, was no doubt hoping for an exemplary punishment, but instead he provoked a careful attack by Dering, Bridgman, and Thomas Coke on the validity of the order itself. Dering said that the country sent them to make and unmake laws: 'they know they did not send us hither to rule and govern them by arbitrary, revocable and disputable orders; especially in religion. No time is fit for that, and this time as unfit as any: I desire to be instructed herein'. The House does not seem to have succeeded in doing so, and the debate was adjourned to 4 November, by which time the Irish Rebellion had overtaken it.[40]

The same day, Sir Gilbert Gerrard, one of the long list of capable first lieutenants who made the godly such a powerful Parliamentary team, reintroduced the bill for Bishops' Exclusion.[41] Since the Parliament had had an adjournment and not a prorogation, this was not a new session, and therefore the bill should not have been reintroduced in the same session in which it had failed. However, orders are not proof against the desire of a majority to break them, and the bill went ahead. It was given two readings at once, and went to Committee of the Whole on 22 and 23 October, where the debate began. There was an attempt to remove the Pauline phrase in the preamble that the office of the ministry was of such great importance that it would take up the whole man. The issue concealed the disagreement which had helped to wreck the first bill, between those who thought the exercising of secular jurisdiction by the clergy was absolutely wrong, and those who thought it merely inconvenient. It concealed a disagreement, both about the nature of the ministry, and about the relations between church and state. The clause was carried on a division, but by the narrow majority of 70 to 59. The next day, Dering revived Williams's proposal of March for a national synod, and Hyde tried to defer the business because of the thinness of the House. Having lost their division on the preamble, the opponents of the bill decided not to press it to a division, and it was sent up to the Lords with a request for expedition.[42]

The Commons were returning immediately to the strategy of the late summer, of continual pressure on the Lords, to get them to create a majority for further reformation. If they could not do this by Bishops' Exclusion, they would do it by means of the impeachment against the thirteen bishops for making the canons, on which Holles asked the Lords for dispatch on 22 October. The Lords guardedly replied that

---

[39] D'Ewes (C.), p. 19; BL Add. MS 34485, fo. 81r.
[40] Rushworth, *Collections*, III. i. 392; *HMC Twelfth Report*, II. 293; D'Ewes (C.), pp. 19, 79. D'Ewes confirms that Dering spoke, but our only knowledge of what he said is from the text he subsequently printed.
[41] D'Ewes (C.), p. 21.
[42] Ibid. 25, 28–9, 30–2; BL Add. MS 34485, fos. 86r–7v; *LJ* iv. 402.

they would answer 'in convenient time'.[43] In pressing the Lords for haste, the Commons were visibly acting in alliance with the minority within the Lords themselves: when Bishops' Exclusion came up from the Commons, Essex, Mandeville, and Brooke pressed for it to be debated 'presently', which the Lords refused. Instead, some of the Lords trumped one of the Commons' main arguments against the thirteen bishops: the Commons argued that since the canons had been condemned, the bishops were *ipso facto* condemned for making them, but Bath, Bristol, and Brudenell insisted that when the Lords had refused to hear the bishops before condemning the canons, they had resolved that the vote would not prejudice them personally. Browne the Clerk said they were right.[44] The presence of Brudenell was significant, since he was a recusant Lord, and his presence doubtless lent colour to Pym's attempts to lump together 'the lords and bishops that were papists'.[45] On 27 October the Lords were treated to major speeches for Bishops' Exclusion from Pym and St John, but instead of responding, the Lords deferred the issue till 10 November. The King directed Nicholas to thank the Earl of Southampton for this result.[46] The godly peers also tried to revive the bill against pluralities, urging the committee to hear the cases of those deprived for opposing the Book of Sports, but instead they got bogged down in questions of the King's chaplains, the privilege of noblemen, and that favourite standby of those who desired to obstruct the anticlerical lobby, the rights of Oxford and Cambridge Heads of Houses.

It appeared that the majority in the Commons were no nearer getting the Lords to agree to a further reformation than they had been before the recess. If a majority in either House were to shift, it was more likely to be in the Commons than in the Lords. Meanwhile, so long as the Houses disagreed, the King could go on claiming that he had refused nothing his Parliament had asked except the last request to defer his journey to Scotland. The King, after lengthy consultation with Nicholas and Juxon, decided to follow up his advantage by filling five vacant bishoprics, whose new holders he intended to attend and vote in the Lords.[47] Those chosen were, in the phrase of Nicholas, 'persons, of whome there is not the least suspicion of favouring the popish partie', in Charles's phrase, evidence that 'I have altered somewhat frome my

[43] *LJ* iv. 400.

[44] BL Harl. MS 6424, fo. 97[r–v].

[45] Yale University, Beinecke Library, Osborn Tracts 1, 2, Box 2, no. 45h. This is a variant DO, quoting Pym's report of 20 Oct. If it is a misreport, it is perhaps an example of Pym's knack of communicating a point subliminally.

[46] *LJ* iv. 408–9; BL Harl. MS 6424, fo. 98[v]; Evelyn, iv. 114.

[47] Evelyn, iv. 88–9, 116, and other refs.

former thoughts, to satisfye the tymes', and in D'Ewes words, men 'who if this Parliament had not happened should assoone have been sent to the gallies as have been preferred to bishopricks'.[48] The list was Dr Prideaux, Regius Professor of Divinity in Oxford, and long-standing opponent of the Arminians; Henry King; Ralph Brownrigg, husband of Pym's niece; Dr Winniffe, Dean of St Paul's; and Richard Holdsworth, Vice-Chancellor of Cambridge and D'Ewes's former tutor. In May this would have been a popular list: in October it provoked an outcry from Earle, D'Ewes, Cromwell, and others, and on a division, the objection to making any new bishops was carried by 71 to 53.[49] All the candidates except, somewhat surprisingly, Holdsworth accepted appointment.[50] For Pym, the decision of Ralph Brownrigg, who had been close to him, was probably a bitter disappointment. Brownrigg had gone along, at least on paper, with the 8 September order.[51] His decision brought schism into Pym's inner family circle, and indicated Pym's failure to communicate his distrust of the King to someone who must have been very familiar with his reasons for it.

The day before this, 21 October, the Commons had considered a proposal which showed more plainly than most how far the objective had become to deprive Charles of the power to govern. This was a proposal for Parliamentary choice of the great officers, in the mildest of the forms discussed in Scotland, whereby the King was to nominate, and the new Parliament to advise and consent. The sting in the proposal, unnoticed by D'Ewes, was that 'untill such things as these shalbe granted, they cannot with a good conscience supply your Maties necessities'. Nicholas remarked that 'your maties long absence encourages some to talk in Parliamt. of high matters', while D'Ewes, for once deriving perception from his precedents, commented that most of the precedents for such a proposal came from royal minorities. The observation illustrated the key thrust of most Parliamentary constitutional thinking between the recess and the Civil War. It was in favour of government by Council or great officers, rather than by Parliament, and it owed more to Simon de Montfort, the Lords Ordainers, and the Lords Appellant, and perhaps to the *Modus Tenendi Parliamentum*,[52] than it did to any notion of Parliamentary sovereignty. The idea was to take as much power as possible out of Charles's hands, while leaving unchanged as much of the shell of the existing form of government as

[48] Evelyn, iv. 89, 99; D'Ewes (C.), p. 46.

[49] D'Ewes (C.), pp. 51–4.

[50] Holdsworth, in the teeth of the Bishops' Exclusion Bill, nevertheless accepted appointment as a JP: PRO C 231/5, p. 489.

[51] D'Ewes (C.), p. 49.

[52] Saye had possessed a copy of the *Modus* before 1640: Bodl. MS Tanner 88*, fo. 203ʳ.

possible. The aims remind us how deeply the Parliament was handicapped by the lack of a suitable Pretender.

The junto's big guns remained masked for this debate, and the proposal was put forward by Robert Goodwin and William Strode. Strode,
speaking with 'great violence', claimed that 'all wee had done this
Parliament was nothing unless wee had a negative voice in the placing of
the great officers of the King and of his councellors, by whome his
Majesty was led captive'. The extent to which ecclesiastical issues lay
behind the proposal emerged from an exchange between D'Ewes and
Hyde, who seem to have been developing a personal antipathy like that
between Pym and Waller. Hyde, showing the essentially secular sense of
priorities which had marked him from the beginning, claimed that with

the passing of the three bills against the Starre-Chamber the High-Commission
court and the shipp-monie wee had done verie much for the good of the
subject: and hee thought all particulars weere in a good condition if wee could
but preserve them as they weere.

D'Ewes replied:

For the church I cannot agree with the gentleman over the way (viz. Mr. Hyde)
who thinkes that all is well setled and constituted if wee cann but keepe them as
they are; trulie I rather thinke the church is yet full of wrinkles amonst us and
needes a great deal of reformation which I hope wee shall shortly see effected.

Edward Nicholas advised the King and send thanks to Falkland, Sir
John Strangeways, Waller, Hyde, and Holborne for their contributions
to this debate, of whom only Hyde succeeded in attracting the attention
of D'Ewes. The debate concluded with the appointment of a committee
to draw a petition to the King, a conclusion which illustrated the fact
that the issue of revenue gave the Commons a leverage on the King
which they did not possess with the House of Lords. The terms of
reference for the committee carefully stopped short of specifying the full
claim for Parliamentary approval of great officers.[53]

On 30 October Pym raised the temperature further by raising the
question of the safety of the Prince of Wales. He complained that the
Prince was 'often at Oatlands with the Queene', and 'that wee might
well doubt by reason of those persons about the Queene hee should
reseave noe good ther neither for soule nor bodie'.[54] This picture of the
Prince being kidnapped by his mother's entourage was perhaps only
likely to convince the converted, but in raising the fear of conversion by
the Queen's influence, he was raising what had been one of the standard
arguments against a popish match ever since the Reformation, and a

[53] D'Ewes (C.), pp. 44–7; Evelyn, iv. 115–16; DO vol. ii, fo. 115^{r-v}; CJ ii. 297. Nicholas's report
is alarming evidence of D'Ewes's capacity to miss the vital points in a debate.
[54] D'Ewes (C.), pp. 58–9; CJ ii. 299; LJ iv. 412.

point which, in relation to his younger children, worried even Charles I himself.[55] Pym's suggested remedy was that Hertford, the Prince's duly appointed governor, 'should take the Prince into his charge and looke to his saftie and suffer none to bee about him but such persons of whose fidelitie hee was well assured and for whome hee would answeare'. It says a lot about the genuineness of the fears on which Pym was playing that this proposal seems to have been accepted in the Commons without debate, and was immediately accepted by the Lords.[56] The Queen duly agreed to the proposal, allowing herself only one barbed comment, that 'she did make no doubt, but upon the King's return, the Parliament will express the like care, both of the King's honour and safety.'[57] On the eve of the Irish Rebellion, Pym and his allies had firmly committed themselves to the view that it was unsafe to trust the King with any significant amount of power. At a time when a major military force had to be raised, such a conviction was likely to cause difficulties.

III

The news of the Irish Rebellion reached London on 1 November, in the form of a letter from the Lords Justices in Dublin to the Earl of Leicester, the new Lord-Lieutenant. The treatment of this letter says a good deal about the power structure in London in the King's absence. Leicester laid the letter before the Privy Council. The Council felt the need to report to someone in authority, and, since the Lords were not sitting until the afternoon, they went to make their report to the Commons. This decision surely recognizes a considerable shift in the structure of power since 1640,[58] but whether such a shift was more than a temporary aberration was still in suspense.

If the Commons persistently misunderstood the Irish Rebellion, a great deal of the responsibility must rest on Lord Justice Parsons, since it was his letters which provided the official accounts available at Westminster. Parsons, as might be expected, consistently put the strongest anti-Catholic gloss on the events he was reporting. D'Ewes's report of Parsons' letter, 'that all the Protestants and English should be cut

---

[55] M. A. E. Green, *Lives of the Princesses of England* (1855), vi. 104–5.

[56] See *CSP Ven. 1640–2*, p. 241 for an unwilling testimony to the genuineness of these fears.

[57] *CJ* ii. 303. There are more ambiguities in the Queen's phrase than immediately appear.

[58] PRO SP 63/260/29; *CJ* ii. 300; *LJ* iv. 412. There is no record in PC. The rebellion was betrayed by Owen O'Connolly, servant to Sir John Clotworthy. It does not immediately appear how Clotworthy's servant had come to be in the inner counsels of the Irish rebels. For O'Connolly's equal success in being on the spot when Protestant riots had broken out in Antrim in the spring, see PRO SP 63/258/85.1 and BL Egerton MS 2541, fos. 235–6.

offe',[59] is admittedly a paraphrase, but it is probably nearer to Parsons's original wording than Parsons's wording was to the truth as it has since become apparent. The Lords Justices' decision to advise the English to read again their letter of 24 April, advising against abandoning the policy of plantation, was not only an exercise in saying 'I told you so': it was also an invitation to suppress the rebellion by the policy of confiscation which was afterwards followed.[60] The Commons admittedly needed little encouragement to turn an Irish war into a war of extermination against popery, but whatever encouragement was needed, Parsons was eager to provide.

The contribution of the Irish Rebellion to the polarization of opinion in England is probably far greater than the surviving evidence now allows us to discover. For the godly, it was a validation of all their worst fears, and a justification for the most stringent measures to root out the lingering popery in their midst. Thomas Smith's reaction gives no great ground for surprise: 'there is fallen out an horrible in Ireland' (*sic*). He said they intended to cut the throats of all the Protestants in Ireland:

thus much wee get by favouring of those popish hellhounds, this we may thank Strafford for in Ireland: here our lukewarme Protestants in England may do as much mischief by conniving at them. I pray God the busines ends thus. I feare plots here, but it shall go well with God's servants of which number God make me and thee two, yt you may not raile on ye poor puritans as you use to do.[61]

Thomas Wiseman, writing a week later, was becoming increasingly allergic to this intense anti-popery:

but oftentimes wee have much more printed then is true, especially when any thing concerns the papists, who, though they are bad enough, our preciser sort strive yet to make them worse, and betweene them both are the causes that in no discoveryes wee can hardly meete wth the face of truth.

For Wiseman, anti-popery was not the remedy:

problems will not yet cease untill the buissenes of religion bee better settled; and that the sectaryes and separatists, whereof in London and the parts contiguous are more then many may bee supprest and punisht.[62]

What these two ways of thought have in common is perhaps as important as what divides them. Perhaps the best illustration of how far anti-

---

[59] D'Ewes (C.), p. 61; BL Harl. MS 162, fos. 60–2. The agitated and disjointed appearance of these folios is a good example of how the most perfect of editions cannot convey all the evidence visible in the original, though the editor did his best.

[60] PRO SP 63/258/93: see above, p. 390.

[61] PRO SP 16/485/57.

[62] Ibid. 16/485/72. Wiseman said there would be no peace till those who carried the greatest sway in the Commons ceased to attempt to make the church government of England conform to that of Scotland.

popery was part of the instinctive intellectual equipment of ordinary Englishmen is the reaction of Edward Nicholas: 'there is advertisement come out of Ireland of a great rebellion there made by the papists, whoe have been imprudenty connived att or rather tollerated there a long time, and especially by the Earl of Strafford'.[63]

So long as the King was securely absent, and the two Houses could control their own war effort, they showed considerable eagerness to suppress the rebellion. Leicester the Lord-Lieutenant, Newport the Master of the Ordnance, and Northumberland the Lord Admiral, all commanded the confidence of the Houses, and any measure which could be channelled through them, without being referred to the King, was likely to command the support of both Houses. The Houses' reliance on these three during the King's absence is a very good illustration of the actual working of the ideal of monarchy without the King which had been adumbrated in the proposals for Parliamentary choice of the great officers. The Commons immediately sent over £20,000, which was all the money in their custody, gave orders for raising volunteers, ordered that the munitions at Carlisle should be sent to Carrickfergus, that the Lord Admiral should set out ships for guarding the Irish coasts, and many other such orders.[64] The Lords could understand the reasons for such actions, but were aware that they were technically irregular. They justified them because 'in this time of his Majesty's absence, his royal commission cannot be so soon obtained as the necessity of that kingdom doth require'. They authorized Leicester to levy men, and Newport to issue arms to Leicester, 'and for his so doing, this shall be a sufficient warrant'.[65]

However excusable it might be in the immediate circumstances, the issuing of arms from the King's stores without his authority was a precedent which caused the King some anxiety. His immediate response was to issue his own warrant confirming the warrant of the Lords, 'and for so doing, *this* shall be your warrant', but the power to issue arms remained a continuing source of anxiety to the King, and a continuing source of potential conflict.[66] The Lords' decision of 6 November, though taken for the most loyal of motives, was another step down the slope towards the point where civil war would become possible.

The Irish Rebellion also forced into the open the underlying disagreement about legal authority to levy troops. This disagreement had been on the agenda ever since Pym's opening speech to the Short Parliament:

[63] PRO SP 16/485/56.
[64] *CJ* ii. 304–5.
[65] *LJ* iv. 424–5.
[66] MP, 15 Nov. 1641: my italics. For the continuing tension on the issue, see PRO SP 29/6, fo. 158ʳ, which is the story told by the surviving Ordnance Officers to Charles II. I owe my knowledge of this document to Dr Howard Tomlinson.

Charles believed that he was entitled to raise forces by his prerogative, while Pym and his allies believed that there was no valid legal authority for raising troops until the Parliament passed a Statute to provide one. From the outbreak of the Irish Rebellion onwards, this was an issue on which the parties could no longer afford to agree to differ. The Commons' response was to prepare a bill to legitimize conscription for this particular service only, but since the preamble of such a bill would necessarily rehearse the reasons why it was thought to be needed, it was hard to see how the King could see his way to consent to it.[67] Equally, it was hard to see how the Commons' majority would see their way to allowing Charles to raise troops, as they saw it, illegally. The Irish Rebellion therefore made it impossible to avoid the debate which ultimately led to the Militia Ordinance. In the Commons, however, the only overt opposition to the Impressment Bill seems to have come from Marten and Sir John Hotham, who argued that the bill was against the liberty of the subject. This appears to be a libertarian opposition to all conscription, rather than any defence of the King's prerogative. This is further suggested by the fact that the man who defended the bill against Marten was Waller, arguing 'that what is done by Act of Parliament is done by consent of the subject'. Waller's support for the bill again illustrates how much the sort of legalism which lay behind it was a creed Royalist and Parliamentarian had in common.[68]

For the majority, the easiest way round these dilemmas appeared to be to accept the eager offers of help which had already been made by the Scottish Parliament, and not discouraged by the King. Others felt some misgivings about this idea. Nicholas feared it 'will make ye rebells there the more desperate by reason of ye great hatred ye Irish beare to ye Scottish nacon'.[69] The Lords also felt considerable misgivings about relying on large numbers of Scots. The anti-Scots in the Commons, led by Sir John Culpepper, rallied against this proposal with a vigour which suggests that they feared the return of the Anglo-Scottish axis of the previous winter.[70] On 6 November the Scottish Parliament appointed commissioners to go to London to negotiate terms for Scottish help in Ireland. They were the Earls of Lothian and Lindsay, Balmerino, Sir Thomas Myretoun, Sir Thomas Hope, Johnston of Wariston, Sir John Smith, Patrick Bell, and Robert Barclay of Irvine.[71] The King went to

---

[67] *CJ* ii. 305; *LJ* iv. 422, and other refs.

[68] D'Ewes (C.), p. 83; Holland, vol. iii., fo. 3[r].

[69] PRO SP 16/485/90; also Evelyn, iv. 138–9.

[70] D'Ewes (C.), pp. 91, 93, 130, 293, and other refs. In the polarization of pro- and anti-Scots, only Sir John Hotham took a different line from the one he had taken the previous winter.

[71] Scottish RO, PA 13/2, unfol. Their instructions of 22 Nov. enjoined them to keep a right understanding between the King and his people, and 'to confirme that brotherlie affection begunn betwixt them'. They also made clear that the Scots expected plantation land to be the reward of their efforts. Robert Barclay had been in London during the Short Parliament: see above, p. 122.

great lengths to conciliate them, even to the length of giving Lothian and Lindsay the keys of his privy garden,[72] but the possibility that they could provide a new line of communication between Parliament and Covenanters could not be removed. The eagerness of the inner ring of members to conciliate them appears from the tragi-comedy of the efforts to provide them with a house. The Lord Mayor, perhaps express-ing his political sympathies, tried to lodge them in a house where the plague had recently been,[73] and from then on, a small group of members were involved in constant efforts to find them something more satisfac-tory.[74] In the short term, the issue of Scottish help produced numerous rapid changes of front, but in the end, Scottish help materialized, and made a major contribution to holding Ulster for the Protestants.[75]

The raising of money, almost equally, thrust the Commons upon politically sensitive issues, since it gave considerable extra leverage to those in the City who dreamed of using the power of the purse in order to act as a Fourth Estate. When a Commons' committee went to the City, the City were unanimous in stressing the need for the Parliament to do something about the abuse of protections, by which members and their servants could run up large debts under the protection of Parliamentary privilege. They argued reasonably that unless they could recover the money which was owed to them, they would not have enough to lend. There was a bill already on the stocks to deal with this abuse, but it ran into heavy resistance in both Houses, and was perpetu-ally being sent back to committee. Rather more controversially, the City tried 'not by way of contract', to persuade the Houses to arrest the popish Lords and expel the bishops from the House of Lords.[76] By increasing the political power of an already divided City, the Irish Rebellion encouraged the spread of the political conflict into another major theatre, and in the next two months, the struggle for control of the City was arguably as important as the struggle for a majority in the Lords or the Commons.

It had long been traditional for the Commons, faced with the need to organize an anti-popish war-effort, to devote a large part of their energies to hunting for a fifth column. This sort of displacement aggres-sion was a well-established political reflex, and in November 1641 it also served some very immediate political purposes. To Pym, popery was

---

[72] PRO LC 5/135, unfol. (surveyor, 6 Dec. 1641).

[73] PRO SP 16/486/14.

[74] D'Ewes (C.), p. 220; CJ ii. 328, 330, 352; D'Ewes (C.), pp. 311, 331, 337, and other refs. The members involved were Pym, Hampden, Stapleton, Penington, Spurstow, Sir John Evelyn of Surrey, Marten, Venn, Vassall, and Richard Moore.

[75] On the subsequent story, see David Stevenson, *Scottish Covenanters and Irish Confederates* (Belfast, 1981), *passim*.

[76] CJ ii. 314; D'Ewes (C.), p. 133.

always an indivisible evil, and for the next few months, he busily tried to identify his Irish and his domestic enemies with each other. Speaking to the Lords on 9 November, he again rehearsed his complaints of 'those who have been admitted into very near places of counsel and authority about him [the King], who have been favourers of popery, superstition and innovation', and claimed that 'we have just cause of belief, that those conspiracies and commotions in Ireland are but the effects of the same counsels', and that he feared 'some such like attempt by the papists and ill-affected subjects in England'.[77] Pym always presented the Irish Rebellion as part of a popish conspiracy active in all three kingdoms, and continually insinuated the suspicion that the root of this conspiracy was within the court. He never directly charged the King with responsibility for this conspiracy, though his incidental remark that 'diseases which proceed from the inward parts, as the liver, the heart or the brains, the more noble parts, it is a hard thing to apply cure to such diseases' at least risked giving that impression to his audience. It is very difficult now to judge Pym's sincerity in this suspicion. By 9 November he knew about the Dillon mission, which established the King's willingness to tolerate popery as a condition of peace.[78] For Pym, this may have been tantamount to partnership in guilt with the rebels. It is also possible, though, that he was convinced by the case for regarding the King as an active partner in inciting the rebellion. An anti-popish case which convinced S. R. Gardiner and Aidan Clarke may well have convinced Pym also. If he was convinced of the King's complicity, he had a large extra reason for distrust. If not, he had been given a formidable political weapon, which he was perfectly capable of cynically exploiting.[79] Perhaps, though, this is another case where we should be thinking, not about cynical exploitation, but about guilty conscience. Pym suspected the King of planning to coerce a recalcitrant Parliament with the armed aid of Irish papists. It is relevant to remember that he had himself coerced a recalcitrant King with the armed aid of Scottish Presbyterians. Having used the tactic successfully, Pym was bound to fear that the King would use the same tactic to retaliate against him: he knew it could work.

Within hours of hearing the news of the rebellion, Pym was using it to justify a proposal that the Earl of Portland, whom he believed to be a papist, should be deprived of the strategic position of Governor of the

---

[77] *LJ* iv. 431.

[78] Above, pp. 396–9.

[79] On the King and the Irish Rebellion, see Russell, 'British Background to the Irish Rebellion', *Historical Research*, 61/145 (1988), 166–82. The conclusion of that article is that the King was not guilty of any complicity in the Irish Rebellion, but the contrary case has been strong enough to convince many better scholars than Pym. It should never be forgotten that we probably know much more about Charles I's intentions than Pym ever could.

Isle of Wight. This proposal was immediately opposed by Falkland, who said he went to church, and by Waller, who said he had a true English heart. For Pym, going to church was never a sufficient refutation of a charge of popery, and he pressed ahead. This proposal ran into considerable resistance in the Lords, who were as usual ready to defend one of their own order. Their first reply on 8 November was that they would consider the proposal when the Commons showed reasons for it. On 16 November the Commons asked for haste, and the Lords repeated their previous reply.[80] On 18 November the Commons supplied their reasons, saying that Portland's father, mother, and wife were recusants, and that his sister married one. Portland, who was a regular attender at the House of Lords, replied that his father was a Protestant, and he could make it appear by witnesses who were with him when he died, and that if his wife was a recusant, it was against his will. For himself, he said his father bred him a Protestant, and he would live and die one. The issue, which had been in dispute since Elizabethan times, was whether attendance at church was a sufficient refutation of a charge of 'popery': to those, like Pym, who saw papists as an outwardly conforming fifth column, it was not.[81] The Lords, after 'long debate', were unconvinced, and the issue rumbled on until it became merged in the dispute over the Militia Ordinance. At first sight, it is not obvious why the Irish Rebellion should logically have led to a demand for the dismissal of the Governor of the Isle of Wight. The political capital Pym dissipated on this issue is only explicable on the assumption that he regarded Portland and his like as a genuine threat, but whether he regarded them as potential allies in a popish conspiracy, in a Royalist coup, or in some combination of the two, our sources do not tell us.

This wave of anti-popish proposals of course included another attack on the Queen's attendants. The Commons, within hours of the news of the rebellion, again demanded that the Queen's Capuchins be sent away, to which the Lords agreed.[82] They also agreed to a demand for the listing of the Queen's priests.[83] Pym added to this the much more damaging proposal that the oaths of allegiance and supremacy should be tendered to all servants of the King, Queen, and Prince. Since nothing was said about any exemption for priests, this should have had the effect of preventing the Queen from enjoying the services of any priest at all. This proposal appears to have gone through the Commons on the nod. The Lords, perhaps unexpectedly, eventually agreed to this

---

[80] D'Ewes (C.), pp. 63–4; *LJ* iv. 427, 442.
[81] *LJ* iv. 446. On the issues involved, see Lake, *Puritans*, pp. 171–80.
[82] *CJ* ii. 300–1; *LJ* iv. 427.
[83] *LJ* iv. 427, 438.

proposal also.[84] The Commons also insisted on the questioning of Father Philip the Queen's confessor, who was still under investigation for his part in the Army Plot. Father Philip ran into worse trouble by refusing to take the oath on the Protestant Bible, because it was not a true Bible. After some resistance by the Commons, the Queen eventually recovered his services.[85]

The rebellion also provoked another drive for the disarming and arresting of prominent recusants, including recusant peers. The issue was raised on 2 November by Whitehead, Whitaker, and Strode.[86] The Lords agreed in principle to the demand on 9 November, but showed no great signs of haste in furthering it.[87] On 16 November the Commons supported their demand with a list of prominent recusants they wanted secured. On 18 November the Lords insisted their concession only applied to convicted recusants, and the Commons, in a phrase Charles would not have dared to offer to the 1628 Parliament, demanded immediate proceedings because 'it would ask too much time to stay for putting the laws into execution at this time'.[88] On 22 November the Lords again bowed before the storm: it was debated 'whether the kingdom was in such danger at this time as requires the securing of the persons of recusants and it was agreed it is'. At least one Lord then cocked a snook at this vote by naming to the resultant committee Goodman Bishop of Gloucester, the only genuine papist on the bench of bishops. Perhaps not surprisingly, the issue became bogged down, and no action resulted.[89]

It is amusing, and a necessary exercise in understanding anti-popery, to look at the occasions on which the godly themselves asked for exceptions from their own rules. The first to do so was, of all unlikely people, William Strode, who moved that a Latin psalter might be restored to a popish gentlewoman. He was solemnly reproved by D'Ewes, who 'wondred at the gentlemans motion and hoped wee would not restore it to her and soe be guiltie of her idolatrie and superstition'. Strode's request was turned down. Ironically, the next request for exemption came from D'Ewes himself, on behalf of his fellow-Fleming the Count of Egmont, who was 'come into England to crave the assistance of his Majestie against the King of Spaine'. 'Tis true that he is a papist, but a

[84] D'Ewes. (C.), p. 115; *CJ* ii. 315; *LJ* iv. 501. The Lords' agreement immediately followed the King's message for the impeachment of the Five Members.

[85] *LJ* iv. 419, 449, and other refs. The Lords soon recommended the release of Father Philip, but the Commons took some time to agree.

[86] D'Ewes (C.), pp. 68–9. Lawrence Whitaker Clerk of the Council is more likely to have been the speaker than William Whitaker, Pym's lawyer.

[87] *LJ* iv. 429.

[88] Ibid. 441, 446.

[89] Ibid. 449, 450. It is impossible to know who was responsible for committee nominations. The business of this committee seems to have been managed by Manchester.

presbiteriall one, and one that hates the Jesuits'. There were many good anti-papists who were able to say, like Sir William Pelham, that some of their best friends were papists.[90]

With these general anti-popish measures came a series of measures more directly concerned with members' own security. A deep anxiety about the use to which troops raised for Ireland might be put surfaced in the proposal from Sir Robert Cooke and Perd that any officers serving in Ireland should be made to take the Protestation. This proposal, together with the demand for a census of Irish living in London, appear not to have been controversial.[91] Demands for a guard were also in principle acceptable, but Oliver Cromwell, in asking for the Earl of Essex to have power to assemble the trained bands 'at all times', was perhaps asking for rather more than the occasion warranted. The Lords accepted the demand in principle, but after drafting an ordinance whereby the Lords and Commons 'do hereby appoint and ordaine', they retreated to the more legal position of asking Essex and Holland to have the trained bands in readiness by virtue of their authority, by the King's commission, as Captains-General on either side of Trent.[92] The Lords were more agreeable to the proposal that the ammunition at Hull should be immediately shipped to London, since it was needed for Ireland.[93]

The atmosphere of course bred more stories of popish plots. The most famous of these is the Beale Plot, perhaps the most hare-brained of all the plot stories spread during these years. Beale, a London tailor, said he had been lying behind a hedge when he heard a group of Catholics on the other side of it discussing a plan for 108 of their fellows to kill one member of the Lords or Commons each, and each one to have the goods of the man he killed. These papists ultimately detected Beale's presence and 'ranne him through his cloke and clothes', and left him, as they thought, dead. Beale, miraculously uninjured, hastily made his way to the Parliament and told his tale.[94] The Lords' response to this story was typical of them: they ordered all recusant peers to attend the House on the day when this plot was to be acted.[95] The anti-popish Lords, remembering the case of Lord Mounteagle in 1605, could hardly com-

[90] D'Ewes (C.), pp. 141, 173–4. I am grateful to Prof. M. J. Mendle for drawing my attention to the 'presbiteriall papist': PRO SP 14/159/28. Pelham's words were: 'I love many of their persons and hate none'.

[91] D'Ewes (C.), pp. 107–8; BL Add. MS 34485, fo. 94ʳ. Cooke had only just secured his seat after an unusually complex election dispute. He was a valuable recruit to the godly cause: LJ iv. 428; MP 13, 17 Nov. 1641. We possess fragmentary returns for the census of Irish in London, but, unfortunately for historians, little progress seems to have been made on it.

[92] D'Ewes (C.), pp. 97–8; LJ iv. 441, 445; MP, 16, 17, 29 Nov. 1641.

[93] LJ iv. 421, 444–5.

[94] PRO SP 16/485/93; MP, 15 Nov. 1641.

[95] LJ iv. 439–40.

plain of this decision, but nevertheless, the Lords had succeeded in using an anti-popish scare to reassert the right of recusant peers to attend the House. Pym and Hampden, on the other hand, repeatedly interrupted debates on the Grand Remonstrance with new revelations about this plot. If there is any point at which the charge of cynical exploitation of plot scares can be made to hold good, it is surely here.

The point where all this anti-popish fear merged with Pym's immediate political objectives was the Additional Instruction of 5 November. The instructions were being sent to the Parliamentary committee in Scotland, which, since the King was still in Scotland, was charged with the task of communicating with the King about the suppression of the Irish Rebellion. Pym proposed to add to the instructions for what the committee were to tell the King 'that if such counsells continued the aydes off his subiects will be employed towards their destruction. Therefore humbly to desire a remove of such counsellors and take to him the councell of Parliament'. If the King did not agree to this, he said, they should not hold themselves responsible for suppressing the Irish Rebellion.[96]

It was, to put it no higher, a startling proposal, and was opposed by Hyde and Waller. Waller perceptively compared it to Strafford's advice that the King was 'loose and absolved from all rules of government' if the Parliament did not do what he wished. Pym in reply demanded that either the House should give him the same punishment as Strafford, or they should make Waller withdraw, which they duly did. When the House returned to the proposal the next day, it 'occasioned a great deale of debate'. Perd compared the proposal to a refusal to lend more money to a spendthrift, but Culpepper argued that Ireland was a part of England, and they ought to defend it. D'Ewes, while opposed to the proposal in this form, suggested they should put it in the next bill of Tonnage and Poundage.[97] St John argued that they were only asking for the approbation of Councillors, not the naming of them, and optimistically argued that it was no breach of the King's prerogative, being petitionary.[98] On 8 November Pym brought in a revised wording, in which the direct threat not to relieve Ireland was replaced by the ambiguous phrase that 'wee should take such a course for the securing of Ireland as might likewise secure our selves'. Waller and Culpepper again spoke against the proposal, and were supported by Bridgman. Pym, in reply, claimed that 'it will discourage the rebels who have

[96] D'Ewes (C.), pp. 94–5; Holland, vol. iii, fo. 12ᵛ. The words quoted are those reported by Holland on 6 Nov. It appears that Pym made, in effect, the same speech on both days, and that Holland's is the pithier report.

[97] D'Ewes (C.), pp. 99–101.

[98] Holland, vol. iii, fos. 12ᵛ–13ᵛ. He also argued, in terms which would have worried Gormanston, that Ireland was part of the demesne of the Crown of England.

bragged that they have in and about the king friends'. In its revised form, this article was carried by 151 to 110.[99] On 9 November Pym took this proposal to the Lords, with an eloquent plea 'to beseech his Majesty to change those counsels, from which such ill courses have proceeded, and which have caused so many miseries and dangers to all his dominions; and that he will be graciously pleased to employ such Councillors and ministers as shall be approved by his Parliament'. The Lords, after some hesitation, resolved that this proposal would take great debate, and that it should be left to further time.[100] The Lords' anxieties about 'great debate' were well founded: when Charles heard of the Additional Instruction, he told Nicholas to 'cross this in the Lords House if it be possible'.[101] In addition, the Lords were still delaying Bishops' Exclusion, and Northumberland said that 'whether we shall get it passed or not is very doubtfull, unless some assurance be given that the voting out of the function is not afterwards intended'.[102]

When the Commons' leaders finally unveiled the Grand Remonstrance on 8 November, it seems they intended it as a reproach as much to the Lords as to the King. There had been consultation with their allies in the Lords, and when Northumberland said it stopped in the Lords, it had not been presented to them. The decision to go ahead without the assent of the Lords, like many other decisions, was probably taken with the approval of the minority faction in the House of Lords, and was probably designed by them, as much as by the Commons, to put pressure on their recalcitrant colleagues. Charles, looking back on the Remonstrance from August 1642, described it as 'an attempt to incense the people against us and the House of Lords',[103] and he seems to have been quite right. In the same paragraph, he repeated his claim that he had not refused to consent to anything asked in the name of the two Houses of Parliament, and so long as the Lords would turn down all the Commons' extremer proposals for him, he had no need to do so. So long as the conflict was between Lords and Commons, Charles could sit serenely above the battle, and the Commons could not even effectively confront him. As the Remonstrance itself said, 'what can we the Commons, without the conjunction of the House of Lords?'[104]

The Remonstrance was many things. It was, as Northumberland put it, a plea to the King that 'he would be pleased to change his counsels'.

[99] D'Ewes (C.), pp. 104–5; Holland, vol. iii, fos. 15ʳ–16ᵛ.

[100] *LJ* iv. 431, 435. For the Commons' threat on 13 Nov. to send the Additional Instruction without the Lords' consent, see *CJ* ii. 315.

[101] Evelyn, iv. 129.

[102] PRO SP 16/485/76. The use of 'we' is worth remark.

[103] Bodl. MS Clarendon, vol. 21, no. 1634, fo. 125ᵛ.

[104] Clause 181: Gardiner, *Documents*, p. 228. See also M. J. Mendle, 'Politics and Political Thought 1640–1642', in Russell (ed.), *Origins*, pp. 237–41. These four pages are the source of a large number of the ideas developed in this chapter.

It was an attempt to justify the Commons to the public, and to end the 'disvalewing' of the orders of the Commons of which Barrington had complained in September. It was also a minimum statement of terms on which the majority were prepared to grant supply: as Strode put it on 11 November, 'that wee might not debate of the giving of monie till the Remonstrance were past this howse and gone into the cuntrie to satisfie them'.[105] Strode's wording suggests that there was never any plan to invite the Lords to consider the Remonstrance: it was to go direct from the Commons to the country. To spell out the linking of the Remonstrance with supply, St John, four days after the introduction of the Remonstrance, proposed the revival of the committee to prepare a new Book of Rates.[106] He and Charles were both well aware that the existing Act of Tonnage and Poundage expired on 1 December. On 23 November, the day after the passage of the Remonstrance, St John moved that the Book of Rates be brought in speedily. The Book of Rates of course was not ready, so on 25 November St John, having dangled his carrot in front of the King, brought in a new temporary bill to keep the issue in suspense for a few more months.[107]

The body of the Remonstrance was designed to set out 'a malignant and pernicious design of subverting the fundamental laws and principles of government, upon which the religion and justice of this kingdom are firmly established'. A complete catalogue of what had gone wrong since 1625 was thus held together by the binding force of belief in a conspiracy to subvert the religion of England. It was a case Pym, St John, and Rous had been arguing for a long time,[108] but here, for the first time, they had space to develop it. On 9 November, members were given the opportunity to add any extra grievances they wished to have included. Cromwell added the abuse of the Commission of Sewers, Wilde the felling of timber by recusants in the Forest of Dean, and Smyth the Court of Wards, which it is interesting to discover had been unmentioned in the original document.[109] Since most members agreed that the individual things mentioned were grievances, debate on the Grand Remonstrance tended not to concentrate on the justice of the individual grievances mentioned. It concentrated either on the use of anti-popery to turn a scattered set of abuses into a conspiracy, or on the expediency of telling the full story in that way at that time.

[105] D'Ewes (C.), pp. 120–1. Strode, as usual, had jumped the gun, but see also clauses 197 and 204.
[106] D'Ewes (C.), pp. 125–6; CJ ii. 312.
[107] D'Ewes (C.), pp. 189, 196–7.
[108] See above, pp. 14, 105–6.
[109] CJ ii. 309. There are five possible candidates for the identity of 'Smyth'. The clauses on wardship concern such matters as excessive fines and undue proceedings for finding offices. They contain no suggestion whatsoever that wardship itself was regarded as a grievance.

The 'prophetical' part of the Remonstrance, as Rudyerd called it, outlined what the leaders still wished to see happen. It called for the removal of bishops and popish Lords from the House of Lords, for the imposition of 'discipline' in religion, in words which would have been more pleasing to Holles than to Cromwell, for a British synod, no doubt to pursue the aim of uniformity with Scotland, for a purge of the Universities, for attempts to discover 'the counterfeit and false conformity of papists to the church', and for a standing commission, named in Parliament, to enforce the laws against recusants.[110] It was for the execution of this sort of programme that the King was to be asked to employ such Councillors 'as the Parliament may have cause to confide in'. As Professor Fletcher has pointed out, this clause fell far short of its framers' real intentions, and thereby put those opposing it in the difficult position of arguing against what was not formally in the document.[111]

On 15 and 16 November the House considered the Remonstrance clause by clause.[112] The opponents of the Remonstrance began by attacking a clause, whose text we do not now possess, which criticized the Book of Common Prayer. According to D'Ewes, 'wee saw that the partie for episcopacie was soe strong as wee weere willing to lay the clause aside without further trouble'. It was sent back to committee, with instructions to draw a clause which did not condemn the Book of Common Prayer, and did uphold a set form of prayer. Pym at this point broke into the debate with a request that Lord Petre's house be searched for priests and Jesuits, but this did not save him from an assault by Harbottle Grimston on the 8 September order. This issue was laid aside as out of order, but the trouble was not over. They went on to a clause on the disposal of bishops' and deans' lands, but 'the episcopall partie were soe strong in the howse as wee were faint to lay aside this clause also'. The two sides then engaged over a clause saying that the bishops had ushered in idolatry. Dering immediately opposed it. D'Ewes does not give us the arguments, but we have some report of them when this clause was again discussed in the final debate on the Remonstrance on 22 November. Pym claimed that 'altar-worship is idolatry, and that was enjoined by the bishopps in all there cathedrals'.[113] Dering conceded that some bishops had introduced

---

[110] Clauses 170, 182, 185, 187, 193, 194. For another call for a national synod, and for a call to avoid 'anarchy and confusion (under a false guise of Christian liberty)', see the Epistle to Cornelius Burges's sermon for 5 Nov. Clauses 182 and 184 may have originated from the success of the 'episcopal partie' on 16 Nov. in calling for a clause defending a set form of worship, but the drafting bears the stamp of Denzil Holles and what was later to be the Presbyterian interest.

[111] Clause 197; Fletcher, pp. 146–7.

[112] D'Ewes (C.), pp. 149–52.

[113] *Verney's Notes*, p. 123.

superstition, but denied that they had ushered in idolatry. He defended Morton and Hall, and said that though this was 'a very accusative age', he had heard no charge of idolatry, or even superstition, against the bishops of London, Winchester, Chester, Carlisle, or Chichester. By his inclusion of London and Chichester, he committed himself to the view that an Arminian might be a true Protestant.[114] The clause was carried by 124 to 99, but, when again challenged on 22 November, was left out of the final Remonstrance.

On 22 November the House considered the Remonstrance as a whole. D'Ewes withdrew with a cold some hours into the debate, at about four in the afternoon, and it seems to have continued until about two in the morning.[115] Holland, Peyton, and Verney, none of them among the fullest of diarists, stayed on to report the debate. Between them, they give us reports of fifteen speeches in a debate which may have been as much as twelve hours long. It is hard to believe that this represents more than a small fraction of the speeches delivered, and the bulk of the debate on the Remonstrance must be regarded as wholly lost. This said, the extent to which the three diarists report the same speeches suggests, either that these were the first speeches, or else an impressive degree of consensus about what were the most important speeches. If numbers of speeches reported are any guide, the diarists suggest that the Royalists won the debate, since they report nine speeches against the Remonstrance, from Hyde, Falkland, Dering, Bagshaw, Culpepper, Bridgman, Waller, Coventry, and Palmer, five for it, from Pym, Hampden, Holles, Glyn, and Maynard, and one doubtful, from Rudyerd.

The argument against the Remonstrance concentrated heavily on the impropriety of a Remonstrance from the Commons alone, and of addressing the people. Culpepper, in perhaps the most impressive speech against the Remonstrance, said that 'the declaration going but from this House goes but on one legg. We never desierd the Lords to join. All remonstrances should be addresssed to the King, and not to the people, because hee only can redresse our greevances. . . . We are not sent to please the people'.[116] Dering made the same points, complaining that 'I did not dream that we should remonstrate downward, tell tales to the people, and talk of the King as a third person'. He said that 'the use and end of such a remonstrance I understand not: at least I hope I do not'. Dering rather spoiled the effect by printing his speech, but his

---

[114] Rushworth, *Collections*, III. i. 426. This is again the text subsequently printed by Dering. It appears that he delivered much of it, since Hampden's phrases about the moon and stars are incomprehensible unless as an answer to Dering: *Verney's Notes*, p. 124.

[115] D'Ewes (C.), p. 185.

[116] *Verney's Notes*, p. 122; Holland, vol. iii, fos. 48ʳ–9ʳ.

question was, and remains, difficult to answer.[117] Culpepper, who had drafted much of the Remonstrance, but was none the less opposed to passing it in this way, said that the malignant party would take advantage of it to 'exasperate' the King, and so to put out a contraremonstrance in the King's name. The point underlines the difference between those, like Culpepper, who were still working for the King's good opinion, and those, like Pym, who were simply aiming to coerce him. Hyde objected to the narrative part, saying it looked too far back, and Falkland said that much of the matter mentioned was fitter for an Act of Oblivion. Falkland argued against the religious part of the Remonstrance, and said, in a phrase which, if accurately reported, shows why he was always a lone wolf: 'Arminians agree no more with papists than with Protestants'.[118]

On the other side, Glyn and Denzil Holles concentrated on the need to satisfy the people. Glyn argued that 'the people trust us, ergo no dishonour to strive to satisfie them'. Holles reminded them that they had made remonstrances without the consent of the Lords in 1626 and 1629, but omitted to mention that on both occasions, impending dissolution left them unable to offer them to the Lords.[119] The most powerful, and the most alarming, speech in favour of the Remonstrance came from Pym, showing that Cromwellian certainty that marks out the true providentialist politician with his mind made up. He defended the decision not to go to the Lords, saying that 'the matter of this declaration is not fit for the Lords, for the matters were only agitated in this House, and againe, many of them are accused by it'. Nothing says more plainly how much the Remonstrance was directed against the House of Lords. In an exhortation which summed up a life's creed, he once again linked the King's revenue with the extirpation of popery:

It was time to deale plainely with the King and posterity; and come nearer home yett; since all projects have been rooted in popery. Shall we forget that a Lord Treasurer died a papist? That a Secretary was a papist? If this king will ioyne with us wee shall set him upon as great grounds of honour and greatness in that all the world shall not be able to move him.[120]

He did not say what should be done with the King if he did not join them, but in the context of an appeal to the people, Sir Edward Dering thought he could guess. It is likely that the King thought the same.

At the end of the debate, the Remonstrance was carried by 159 votes

---

[117] Rushworth, *Collections*, III. i. 425.

[118] *Verney's Notes*, pp. 121–2; Holland, vol. iii, fos. 45ᵛ–6ʳ.

[119] *Verney's Notes*, pp. 124–5.

[120] Peyton, fo. 149; Holland, vol. iii, fo. 49ʳ; *Verney's Notes*, pp. 122–3. Pym's plain statement that 'let a law bee made against sectaries' may be a clue to his likely factional sympathies if he had lived beyond 1643.

to 148, a very small majority, and, for a division in the small hours, evidence of a remarkably conscientious attendance on both sides. The House then divided again on a motion, possibly from Dering,[121] that the Remonstrance should not be printed or published. The supporters of the Remonstrance moved to delete the word 'published' and, in a suddenly thinned House, carried their proposal by 124 to 101. It was thus not permitted to print the Remonstrance, but it was permitted to give out manuscript copies. The London scriveners were probably delighted. It was apparently during this debate, and in reply to a proposal by Perd to print the Remonstrance, that Palmer nearly precipitated a fight by demanding the right, like dissident members of the Lords, to enter a Protestation against the decision. After prolonged debate and numerous divisions, the House later decided to send Palmer to the Tower, but not to expel him from membership.[122] It was at this point, with the Remonstrance just completed, and the talk of the town, that the King came back to London. It is hard to believe that the timing of the Remonstrance was accidental.

IV

The King did not visit the Parliament when he returned to London, telling the House of Lords on 26 November he was 'hoarse with a cold'.[123] This cold did not prevent him from undertaking a triumphal entry into the City on 25 November. He came, with a large escort, including all four possible pretenders (Hamilton, Richmond and Lennox, Hertford, and the Elector Palatine), and was treated to a banquet and a speech of welcome by the Recorder. The Recorder, speaking in the name of the Mayor and Aldermen, 'the representative bodie of your citie', congratulated the King on 'the defence of our established religion', and asked him in return to uphold 'that ancient forme and frame of government, which hath been long establisht in the Citie'.[124] The Mayor and Aldermen were offering Charles a chance to make common cause against their enemies in the City and in the Parliament. The King, in reply, said that disorders had only arisen from the baser sort of people, and that the 'better and mayne part' of the City had always been loyal to him. He regranted Londonderry to the City, to be held whenever they could recover it, and repeated his pledge to uphold the

---

[121] See D'Ewes (C.), p. 117. Dering was a teller in the division: CJ ii. 322.
[122] D'Ewes (C.), pp. 192–9.
[123] LJ iv. 452.
[124] Ovatio Carolina, BL E. 238(4), pp. 9–10.

Protestant religion as it had been under Elizabeth and James.[125] He somewhat spoilt the effect by withdrawing to Hampton Court, to the great detriment of the City's trade. On 3 December a company of Aldermen, led by the Recorder, went to see Charles to ask him to come back to London. They dissociated themselves from disorders, and tried to further an old suit by claiming that they could not repress disorders in the suburbs unless the King gave them jurisdiction over them.[126] The King agreed to come back to Whitehall, and knighted all the Aldermen present except those who were already knights, whereof, Wiseman told Sir John Penington, 'your cozin the Alderman was none, whose wayes, as you partly knowe are rather to please him selfe then to strive to do any acceptable service for the King if it stand not with the sense of the precizer sort of the House of Commons'. Wiseman, who was an officer of the City, was well aware that a struggle had been joined for control of the City. He said that 'insolent and seditious meetings of sectaries' at the House of Commons were not the representative body of the City, which was the Lord Mayor, Alderman, and Common Council, who entertained the King.[127]

The story of the struggle for control of the City has been well told by Professor Pearl, to whose account this can add very little. One side relied on the Mayor and Aldermen, the other on the City members, on the organization, with the members' co-operation, of public petitioning, and almost certainly, as Charles I believed, on the organization commanded by the City godly ministers. Referring to the week after his return from Scotland, Charles later claimed that the clergy were the Commons' 'chief agents to derive their seditious directions to the people, and were all the week attending the doores of both Houses to be employed in their errands'.[128] Charles's reading was confirmed in February 1642 when the Commons decided, minutes after the Lords had passed the Bishops' Exclusion Bill, that they had had enough of tumults. They sent notice to 'the several ministers in and about London', which was immediately effective.[129] The intense royalism of the Lord Mayor and the majority of the Aldermen led the struggle for the City to assume a constitutional form, in which the King's opponents aimed to enlarge the powers of the wider assemblies of Common

---

[125] PRO SP 16/485/109 and 110; *Ovatio Carolina*, BL E. 238(4), pp. 11–12; Pearl, pp. 126–30. It would be nice to know the author of the suggestions for the King's speech in PRO SP 16/485/109. The handwriting may possibly be Juxon's.

[126] *Ovatio Carolina*, BL E. 238(4), pp. 23–8.

[127] PRO SP 16/486/29. See also the rather more dubious comments of the French Ambassador, PRO 31/3/72, p. 644.

[128] *ECR* E 241(1), p. 528.

[129] *PJ* i. 288.

Council and Common Hall, and to diminish those of the Mayor and Aldermen.[130]

This constitutional form of the struggle for the City has perhaps distracted attention from the fact that the City was very far from unanimous: there was a good deal of City opinion ready to stand to the Lord Mayor and the Cross—the City equivalent of church and king.[131] Professor Woolrych, describing the riot which attacked Praise-God Barebone's conventicle in December 1641, has rightly described it as 'a time when hostile mobs could be drummed up against sectaries almost as readily as against bishops'.[132] Some City parishes in January 1641 even presented petitions in favour of bishops.[133] In June 1641 there were petitions in favour of rails round the communion table from St Olave's and St Saviour's Southwark, and from St Magnus.[134] In St Olave's Southwark in July 1642 a Commission of Array was stuck on a maypole. In the winter of 1642, according to Saye, the decision to engage Rupert at Turnham Green was taken for fear of the amount of Royalist support he might tap inside the City.[135] It is hard to know how big an iceberg this is the tip of. It probably remains true that the godly were stronger in the City than their opponents, and they were certainly much better organized, and could be turned out in very much less time. What remains clear is that Recorder Gardiner was right that 'the citizens are not all . . . of one mind':[136] determined leadership from the Mayor and Aldermen might tap a well of support, and no one was sure how large that well might be.

The first City trial of strength came over a petition organized by Alderman Fowke and the minority faction among the Aldermen, which was against the votes of bishops and popish Lords, who had obstructed 'many good bills', and for the kingdom to be put into a posture of defence and for the removal of evil counsellors. It also repudiated the rumour that the City had turned against the Parliament.[137] The petitioners also complained of attempts by the Lord Mayor and Recorder

---

[130] See *Letter from Mercurius Civicus to Mercurius Rusticus, Somers Tracts*, ed. Sir Walter Scott, iv. (1810), 588–9.

[131] *LJ* v. 247, 256–7; *HMC Twelfth Report*, ii. 304. The Cross in question was Cheapside Cross, whose standing had been in dispute for a very long time. I am grateful to Dr Kenneth Fincham for information on earlier disputes about the Cross. See also Russell, *1621–9*, p. 277.

[132] A. H. Woolrych, *From Commonwealth to Protectorate* (Oxford, 1982), 224.

[133] PRO 31/3/72, p. 419.

[134] MP, 10 June 1641; *CJ* ii. 695. Southwark, though not part of the City, was well within crowd-gathering range.

[135] William Fiennes, Viscount Saye and Sele, *Vindiciae Veritatis* (1654), BL E. 811(2), p. 68.

[136] For Recorder Gardiner's use of the phrase in the spring, see above, p. 196. For D'Ewes's approving citation of it, while opposing a suggestion of adjourning to the Guildhall on 30 Dec., D'Ewes (C.), p. 366.

[137] D'Ewes (C.), pp. 271–2; Peyton, fo. 162; Holland, vol. iii, fo. 71A^{r–v}, Pearl, pp. 222–3, 233–4.

to obstruct the gathering of signatures to this petition, eliciting the ominous reply from Pym that 'we would give them justification in what concerned my Lord Mayor whensoever they should ask it'.[138] This was little less than a threat to impeach the Lord Mayor. Both the Lord Mayor and the Commons seem to have investigated the gathering of support for this petition. The Commons found that Recorder Gardiner had said that those that set their hands to it deserved to be disfranchised, that it tended to tumult and the cutting of throats, and that they did not know the danger they incurred by it.[139] The Lord Mayor found that Christopher Nicholson, one of Penington's allies on the Common Council, had helped to collect signatures. In Ludgate Street, a mercer backed by a constable had told people who refused to sign the petition that they were 'neither good Christians nor honest men, nor well affected to the commonwealth'.[140] All this must have generated a considerable debate around the election of the new Common Council, which was due on 21 December 1641. This election, it seems, was a major victory for Penington and his allies, and it seems to have been the new Common Council, at the crucial moment in January 1642, which delivered control of the City Trained Bands into the hands of supporters of the Parliament.[141] The City Trained Bands were a far more powerful force than unorganized crowds, and it was they, in the end, which delivered control of the streets into the hands of the Parliament. During December, however, the Trained Bands remained under the control of the Lord Mayor, and therefore potentially at Charles's disposal. As late as 28 December Charles ordered the Lord Mayor to be ready to clear the streets by ordering the Trained Bands to shoot to kill 'with bullets or otherwise'.[142] So long as the Trained Bands took the King's orders, he was, however tenuously, in control of his capital. Since the whole of the politics of December revolved round the control of armed force, this power was vital.

Without control of the Trained Bands, crowds could not conduct a coup, but they could make life extremely uncomfortable for those they did not like. On 29 November, a week after the passage of the Grand Remonstrance, the Lords were told that there was a great company of men in the Court of Requests, armed with swords and clubs, and crying 'downe with the popish lords and the bishops'. The Lords asked the

---

[138] KAO Sackville MSS F 1/3, Parliamentary diary of Richard Sackville, Lord Buckhurst, fos. 2ᵛ–3ʳ. I am deeply grateful to Dr J. S. A. Adamson, who discovered this diary, for lending me a photocopy of it.
[139] D'Ewes (C.), p. 319; *Verney's Notes*, pp. 133–4.
[140] PRO SP 16/486/30, 32, 45. On Nicholson, see Pearl, p. 148.
[141] Pearl, pp. 132–40, 344–5. The dating of this 'crucial moment' is uncertain. Pym believed that it had come by 30 Dec., Charles that it had not come by 3 Jan. 5 Jan. is the *terminus ante quem*.
[142] PRO SP 16/486/99.

Commons for assistance in dispersing these crowds, but received little satisfaction.[143] On 30 November the King's friends in the Commons took up the issue. Hyde complained of the citizens coming with swords and staves, and Sir John Strangeways, who had been recognized by the crowd (luckily in the moment of making his escape) as 'one of the greatest enimyes we have', complained that the inciting of the crowds was little less than high treason. He and Edward Kirton offered detailed information on how the crowds had been gathered. Kirton's, which is the fuller, seems to fasten responsibility on Captain Venn, one of the members for the City, but the chain of proof ran no higher up.[144] Kirton and Strangeways persistently demanded an investigation of these charges, but though the charges persistently appeared in the Commons' agenda, they only joined the King's revenue on the list of things to be debated 'tomorrow' or 'Wednesday next'.[145] For a little while, other members tried to force discussion of the issue: Waller on 2 December complained of the Londoners crying 'no bishop! no bishop!', only to meet a reply from D'Ewes that 'though some of them came armed with swords, yet that might well be excused alsoe because they came in the evening'.[146] On 3 December Strode claimed that there had been no tumults, which was indignantly denied by Sir John Culpepper.[147] It is impossible now to be certain how severe these tumults were: there seems to have been no significant injury caused, and though they caused very acute fear to some people, the gravity of any contemporary assessment of the tumults measures the prejudice of the assessor too exactly to tell us very much else. The fact remains that, both at the beginning and at the end of December, the fear caused by crowds, whether justified or not, was undoubtedly real. It is also a fact that Pym and his junto, whether directly responsible for these tumults or not, made no effort to stop them, and, by passing the Grand Remonstrance, had given a clear signal to encourage them.

Argument about the crowds merged with an increasingly heated debate about whether the Houses needed a guard, and if so, by whom and against whom. On 26 November Essex reported to the Lords that his commission as Captain-General was ended by the King's return, and that therefore he could not provide a guard for the Houses. The Lord Keeper then reported that the King had dismissed the guard because he hoped his presence would be a guard to the Parliament. The Commons

---

[143] MM, 29 Nov. The information is not in *LJ*. *CJ* ii. 327–8.

[144] D'Ewes (C.), pp. 213–6; Holland, vol. iii, fos. 56ʳ–7ᵛ; *Verney's Notes*, p. 129. Kirton's information is in Bodl. MS Clarendon, vol. 20, no. 1542. For the involvement of Venn in the crowds in May, see MP, 3 May 1641.

[145] *CJ* ii. 332, and other refs. See also D'Ewes (C.), p. 309; *CJ* ii. 348.

[146] D'Ewes (C.), pp. 225–6.

[147] Ibid. 230–1.

petitioned to have the guard back, and the 'major part' of the Lords agreed to join them. The King said that 'to secure them, not only from real, but even imaginary dangers', he would supply a guard under the command of the Earl of Dorset, and at the same time would take care for his own safety.[148] On 29 November Dorset's guard thrust the people crying 'down with the papist lords and the bishops' out of the Court of Requests.[149] This was not why the Commons wanted a guard, and they dismissed it on their own authority. Instead, Pym asked Glyn and Wheeler, as Westminster JPs, to set a strong watch.[150] Meanwhile, the King's claim that his presence was a sufficient guard was causing sarcastic comment: some were saying that if the King could not protect Hamilton in his own bedchamber, he could scarcely protect them in the Parliament chamber. In fact, it was becoming painfully clear that some members wanted to be guarded, not by the King, but against him. Some were already talking of adjourning to the Guildhall, but there was not, as yet, a majority for any such drastic step.[151]

The issue rested there until 10 December, the day Alderman Fowke's petition was expected. That day, the House found a guard of Trained Bands, sent by Middlesex JPs by warrant from the Lord Keeper. They indignantly resolved that to set a guard about the House without its own consent was a breach of privilege, and sent George Long, the unfortunate JP involved, to the Tower.[152] What the Commons wanted was a guard against the King, which would not impede tumultuous petitioners. What the King wanted was a guard against tumultuous petitioners, and the thought of any guard not under his own control filled him with fears for his own safety. What the Lords wanted was a guard against disturbance by all and sundry. There was no way this circle could be squared, since the Commons would not accept any guard that was under the King's control, and the King would not accept any that was not. The issue rested there until 23 December.

Meanwhile, other measures for control of armed force were being debated. The Impressment Bill was before the Lords, and the King on 2 December delivered a distinct but oblique threat to veto it.[153] He was not prepared to accept any doctrine by which his power to raise armed force would be made to rest on statutory consent. Littleton and Manchester argued that the King had an undoubted prerogative, which

[148] *LJ* iv. 452–3, 455.
[149] Holland, vol. iii, fo. 56ʳ. Bodl. MS Clarendon, vol. 20, 1544 provides a useful chronology of the debate on the guard.
[150] *CJ* ii. 328; D'Ewes (C.), p. 219.
[151] *HMC Buccleuch*, I. 286–7.
[152] *CJ* ii. 338–40; Bodl. MS Clarendon, vol. 20, no. 1544. It is surely disingenuous of D'Ewes to ascribe Fowke's deferring of his petition to the next day to 'a strange providence of God': D'Ewes (C.), p. 271.
[153] PRO SP 16/486/55.

had continued for three hundred years, to which Saye replied that the abolition of Ship Money was to little purpose if the King kept the power to press. The Lords agreed to hear the Attorney-General, who developed an argument based on Calvin's Case, to the effect that the power to command military service was personally inherent in the King.[154] The Lords failed to square the circle, and the bill remained in limbo. The country was paying a very heavy price for the failure of earlier Parliaments to clarify the law on military service before the crisis began. Meanwhile, if the bill was not passed, there was little which could be done to suppress the Irish Rebellion.

The Impressment Bill asserted a constitutional principle the King found alarming, but at least the power it was to confer by act of Parliament was to be conferred on duly constituted authority: it posed no *immediate* threat to the King. The same could not be said of Haselrig's militia bill, introduced on 7 December. This was to appoint three generals, two this side of Trent, and one beyond, 'suppose Essex, Holland and Northumberland'. On these people (whose names were left blank in the bill) it conferred 'martial law, power of life and death, power to pardon, and whatever may erect an absolute tyranny'.[155] Strode seconded this bill, but Culpepper and Waller moved to have it cast out on the first reading. Culpepper 'wondered that the gentleman in the gallerie . . . should bring in such a bill, having soe often complained of the exorbitant power of the Deputie Leiftenants in his cuntrie'. Barrington suggested that this bill was too unlimited and arbitrary and that a better bill could be brought in, but St John, suggesting some division in the junto, supported the bill, saying 'there ought to be a plenitude of power in some person'. He said this bill did not settle the militia, since the person to be appointed had no successor. Mallory moved that the bill be burnt in Palace Yard, but on the division, the attempt to throw it out was defeated by 158 to 125.[156] Nothing more seems to have been heard of Haselrig's bill, and on 21 December, after advance warning from Hampden, a new bill was brought in and read a first time.[157] Such measures might well make Charles fear insurrection. In fact, however rational such fears may have been, they seem not to have been correct. The Houses' firm determination to ship as many munitions as possible off to Ireland seems to indicate a determination to

[154] Bodl. MS Clarendon, vol. 21, no. 1603, fos. 56–7 (Earl of Dover's diary).

[155] *HMC* Twelfth Report, II. 296. The words are those of Secretary Coke's son. Thomas Coke got into trouble for quoting the case of Haxey's Bill in 1397. 1397 was not, perhaps, the most tactful precedent to throw at a set of latter-day Lords Appellant.

[156] D'Ewes (C.), pp. 244–8; Holland, vol. iii, fos. 62Aᵛ–3ʳ; *CJ* ii. 334. Mallory was either the veteran who had been sent to the Tower in 1621 or his son. The family were suspected of popery, and William Mallory's career illustrates the discontinuity between the 1620s and 1642.

[157] D'Ewes (C.), pp. 326–7; *CJ* ii. 351.

keep force out of Charles's hands, rather than to get it into their own. They could not complain, however, if this distinction was not as clear to Charles as it may be to us.

Charles, on his return to London, gave many signals of a hardening political line. His disposal of offices indicates a desire to surround himself with political friends. Secretary Vane was dismissed from both his posts, the Secretaryship going to Nicholas, and the Treasurership of the Household to Lord Savill. Windebank's former Secretaryship remained vacant. The younger Vane was dismissed from his post as Treasurer of the Navy. Some in the Commons thought of trying to preserve him by putting his name into the bill of Tonnage and Poundage, but thought better of it,[158] possibly for fear Charles might veto the bill and collect Tonnage and Poundage illegally. The Lord Stewardship, vacated by Arundel, who wanted to go abroad to protect his Catholic wife,[159] went to Richmond and Lennox, who was becoming increasingly prominent as one of Charles's partisans. Rumours circulated that Holland, Hamilton, and Newport might lose their places, and Bankes was tipped for the still vacant Lord Treasurership. Smith, Northumberland's secretary, feared his master might lose his place also 'if the feminine gender might have their will'. Smith feared the King 'might lose all the best frends and servants he hath'. Wiseman, on the other hand, was happily spreading rumours of the possible preferment of Bristol, Digby, Viscount Scudamore, and Sir Arthur Hopton.[160]

With this harder line came an increasing impatience with the Commons' bargaining over Tonnage and Poundage. On 29 November, when the temporary bill was given its third reading in the Commons, the House linked it with a petition to make Salisbury Lord Treasurer and Pembroke Lord Steward.[161] The Lords on 30 November gave the temporary bill three readings in one day, and sent a message to the King to 'let him know' that the old bill expired the next day. Charles duly gave his Royal Assent on 2 December, only one day late.[162] By 11 December the King's patience with the delay of Tonnage and Poundage

---

[158] PRO SP 16/486/36 and 29; Holland, vol. iii, fos. 81^{r-v}; CJ ii. 349. The restoration of Strafford's son to his father's Earldom was also seen as a hard-line signal: PRO C 231/5, p. 491. William Montagu commented on this news that 'certainly the good party is tottering': HMC Buccleuch, i. 288.

[159] CSP Ven. 1640–2, p. 230; Hibbard, pp. 34–5. See also LJ iv. 581.

[160] PRO SP 16/486/36 and 29.

[161] D'Ewes (C.), pp. 207–8, 216; CJ ii. 326. Robert Goodwin moved to link both the appointment of Salisbury and the securing of recusants to the bill, and Morley added the name of Pembroke for the Lord Stewardship.

[162] LJ iv. 457, 459. Wiseman (PRO SP 16/486/15) said the Lords agreed to the request for Pembroke and Salisbury. If so, they recorded the fact neither in their Journal nor in their Manuscript Minutes.

was at snapping-point: he told the assembled Privy Council to enter into a 'serious consideration' of his expenses, so that he should no longer live from hand to mouth because the bill of Tonnage and Poundage was not passed for continuance. He said it was 'dishonourable' to take any more that way, or to be 'starved or bought out of any more flowers of his crown', and asked them to make such a retrenchment that he could subsist, though 'far below his kingly dignity', on his own revenues.[163] This was of course impossible, as Charles was eventually told at the end of December, but the frustration in this document is palpable.[164] It perhaps sheds some light on why the Lords had felt the need to 'remind' him to pass the temporary bill eleven days earlier.

The day before he put these questions to the Council, Charles had issued a Proclamation on the church which in effect repeated the Lords' order of 16 January 1641.[165] He would prevent innovations against law, but he would not change the law. This seems to have remained his consistent position from January 1641 onwards: it cost him a considerable effort, but it was within the limits of his conscience, and his preferment policy seems to indicate that he meant to stick to it. If peace had come, a revitalized Caroline church, under the influence of James's old Lord Keeper Williams, recently preferred to York, would have been, at least for a while, as close to James's church as to the church of the 1630s. This policy, and especially the defence of the Book of Common Prayer, seems to have appealed to a large body of opinion. When the Proclamation was read at Archcliff Fort, Dover, it 'caused much reioycing, the people crying out God bless his Majestie we shall have our old religion setled againe'.[166] Behind this policy, a series of county petitions for episcopacy and the Book of Common Prayer were being organized. The Commons usually succeeded in keeping such petitions at bay, though Sutton succeeded in presenting one for Nottinghamshire.[167] The Lords, on the other hand, accepted pro-episcopal petitions from Somerset, Cheshire, and Huntingdonshire.[168] The King was beginning to have a party behind him. He could also draw on the impatience, for which Wiseman was an articulate spokesman, with the growth of separatists and sectaries. On 17 December, when the Lords were debating yet another attempt by the Commons to procure a declaration that

---

[163] PC Reg. xii. 200; PRO SP 16/486/37. There is a misplaced copy in PRO SP 16/138/63. I am grateful to Dr R. P. Cust for this reference.

[164] For further proceedings on Charles's request, see Russell, 'Charles I's Financial Estimates for 1642', BIHR 58 (1985), 109–20.

[165] Larkin, pp. 752–4. The text is very nearly a direct copy of the Lords' order of 16 Jan., on which see above, pp. 244–6. Among the Councillors, Warwick, Saye, and Mandeville refused their assent to this Proclamation: HMC Buccleuch, I. 289.

[166] PRO SP 16/486/72.

[167] D'Ewes (C.), p. 290. Sutton's petition was laid aside and not read.

[168] LJ iv. 469, 482, 467. These petitions were careful to disown Laudian innovations.

neither in Ireland nor anywhere else would they ever tolerate popery, Bristol offered to amend the proposal, to draw a declaration that no religion should be tolerated 'but what is, or shall be, established by the laws of this kingdom'.[169] The feeling that religion was not open to change, even by Act of Parliament, seems to have been very deep-rooted. On 20 December Robert Holborne, in a phrase closer to Thomas More than to Thomas Cromwell, said: 'a Parliament may doe a thing unlawfull, as to change our religion etc, and then wee are bound to ask leave to protest against it'.[170]

Meanwhile, the Commons' majority were still trying to find ways of putting pressure on the Lords. On 3 December Pym, in a move which must surely have been made in concert with his allies among the Lords' minority, proposed to draw up a list of good bills which had stopped with the Lords, and to join with the minority Lords, who 'have a liberty to protest', to represent their case to the King. He also proposed to 'make a declaration to the people, to let them see where the obstructions lie'. Sidney Godolphin, making the obvious riposte, suggested that the minority of the Commons should go to the King together with the majority of the Lords, and found himself forced to withdraw.[171] On 6 December Cromwell hit on a new method of harassing the House of Lords. When the House was debating a disputed election for the borough of Arundel, he moved to invalidate it because the Earl of Arundel had written a letter on behalf of one of the candidates.[172] A committee was named of 'Mr. Pym, Mr. Cromwell and others', from which Cromwell reported four days later, to the effect that all letters from Lords in favour of particular candidates for election violated the privileges of Parliament. On Sir Gilbert Gerrard's motion, all members were ordered to send copies of this order to their constituencies.[173] Coming from a man such as Gerrard, or indeed from Pym, who had only once secured election to the Commons without support from a peer, this cannot be taken to represent principled hostility to the peerage. It can only be taken to represent a ruthless pursuit of immediate partisan advantage. The majority persisted, in the face of division, in treating dissent as if they were the representatives of a united nation, and on 11 December Cromwell complained that many of the House spoke in favour of delinquents. His target on this occasion was his favourite target, Sir Cornelius Vermuyden the fen drainer, but it is likely

---

[169] *LJ* iv. 480; MM, 17 Dec.
[170] *Verney's Notes*, p. 136. The debate was on an attempt by the King's partisans to sustain Palmer's claim of 22 Nov. that they, like the Lords, had the right of protestation.
[171] D'Ewes (C.), p. 228 and n; *Verney's Notes*, p. 131; *CJ* ii. 330.
[172] D'Ewes (C.), p. 236.
[173] Ibid. 260; *CJ* ii. 337.

that he meant his remarks to be of wider application.[174] There did, however, remain some places where the godly recognized the limits of the possible. On 17 December Edward Partridge moved for a committee to consider suppressing whoring, swearing, and drinking. The House instead appointed a committee to put the laws in execution against swearers, drunkards, and sabbath-breakers.[175]

Such a deadlock invited desperate measures to break it: the only problem was what measures were open to a desperate man to take. The patience of all parties seems to have snapped just before Christmas, on 23 December. The Commons decided to publish the Grand Remonstrance, producing a comment from Smith that it was 'full of modesty and truth, yet the popish adherents traduce it'.[176] The King immediately published his reply, which had been ready since the beginning of December. On their notion of the 'malignant party', he said that 'we cannot at all understand them', and he said he was not aware of having any evil counsellors. On the church, he said:

we are persuaded in our consciences that no church can be found upon the earth that professeth the true religion with more purity of doctrine than the church of England doth, nor where the government and discipline are jointly more beautified and free from superstition, than as they are here established by law.[177]

With the decision to go public came the attempt to raise force. Having unsuccessfully tried to induce the Lieutenant of the Tower to resign by offering him £3,000,[178] Charles dismissed him, and appointed Thomas Lunsford. Apart from the rare distinction of having fought with credit at Newburn, Lunsford enjoyed an unsavoury reputation. He had never recovered from a particularly unpleasant case which many people regarded as attempted murder.[179] Lunsford, as the sequel proved, could be relied upon to clear away tumultuous protesters without too much concern to avoid shedding of blood.

The question was whether the appointment presaged an assault on the House of Commons as well as on demonstrators. Pym, on Christmas Eve, said it proved that the design of the papists was growing to a

[174] KAO Sackville MSS F 1/3, fo. 1ᵛ. The attempt to repress dissent was proving painful, and Wiseman complained that there were 'few dayes, but one or other is sent to the Tower': PRO SP 16/486/62.

[175] D'Ewes (C.), p. 308; CJ ii. 348; D'Ewes (C.), pp. 343–4.

[176] PRO SP 16/486/89. For Wiseman see ibid. 16/486/90.

[177] Gardiner, Documents, pp. 233–6; PRO SP 16/486/3.

[178] D'Ewes (C.), p. 330. The money was to be channelled through Sir Richard Wynn the Queen's Receiver, suggesting that, as with the Army Plot, Charles was financing spending he did not wish to avow out of his wife's private money.

[179] Anthony Fletcher, County Community in Peace and War: Sussex 1600–1660 (1976), 54–5, 279.

maturity, and on Stapleton's motion, the House asked Newport, as Constable, and therefore as Lunsford's superior, to take up residence in the Tower.[180] Charles's response was to dismiss Newport.[181] A petition from Randall Manwaring and some of Penington's allies on the Common Council spurred the Commons to action against Lunsford.[182] Everything depended on the attitude of the Lords, to whom the Commons applied immediately, and on the afternoon of 23 December the Lords resolved 'after a long debate', not to join with the Commons in asking for Lunsford's removal. It was an unexpected decision, and perhaps a measure of how angry the Lords had become at the continuing threat from the crowds. Pym was back the next day, reminding them of the Irish army and the Army Plot, and complaining of the advantages received by the 'malignant party', by delays caused by the great number of bishops and papists in the Lords. He ended by appealing, in a clear hint, that 'if *any* of your lordships have the same apprehensions that we have, we hope they likewise will take some course to make the same known to his Majesty'. The Lords, on a division, resolved to defer the issue until Monday. Twenty-two peers out of sixty present then took advantage of Pym's hint and entered their protests, thus initiating a period of public side-taking in which the allegiances of individual Lords became apparent as never before.[183] Fourteen of the protesting peers represented the group associated with the Twelve Peers, and the hard core of the faction in the Lords. They were Essex, Bedford, Warwick, Bolingbroke, Saye, Stamford, Wharton, St John, North, Kimbolton (Mandeville), Brooke, Grey of Wark, Robartes, and Howard of Escrick. A godly peer was often a good deal less godly than a godly commoner, but with this rider, these represented a group whose votes would be cast against the King with reasonable consistency. With them, now and later, came three old Privy Councillors, Northumberland, Pembroke, and Holland, who, though not personally very godly, had clearly decided that government could no longer be safely left to Charles. The junto had not got very far with picking up the votes of Lords in the middle of the spectrum. Newport, whose honour was perhaps touched, had joined them, and so had Suffolk, Carlisle, Clare, and Spencer. On the other side was Salisbury, who might have been expected to join the protesters, eight bishops, and the serried ranks of what was to become the Royalist

---

[180] D'Ewes (C.), pp. 346–8.

[181] PRO SO 3/12, fo. 179ᵃ (undated, but by surrounding material, probably either 26 or 27 Dec.). In spite of the Kensington story, this does not indicate a personal distrust of Newport, since Charles gave him the keys of Whitehall on 30 Dec.: PRO LC 5/135, unfol. (surveyor, 30 Dec.).

[182] MP, 23 Dec. 1641; Pearl, pp. 223–4.

[183] LJ iv. 489–90; MM, 23 and 24 Dec. We cannot be certain that those who were listed as present and did not protest refused to do so, since they may have left before the vote. On an issue of this importance, absence might amount to a calculated abstention. The possibility that some voted against Lunsford but did not protest at the result cannot be eliminated.

peerage, Northampton, Berkshire, Bristol, Portland, Hertford, Saville, Dunsmore, and many more. It becomes possible to guess how far the Lords' official posture in favour of consensus had been masking a bitter division within their own House. At this point, the Houses adjourned for Christmas or for Christ-tide, as the case might be. Since 26 December was a Sunday, they did not reassemble till 27 December.

On Sunday the 26th, the King was persuaded to dismiss Lunsford from the Tower. This, it seems, was the achievement of the Lord Mayor, who told the King that the 'well affected partie' was as discontented with Lunsford's appointment as the other.[184] The Lord Mayor had to be taken seriously, since loss of the well-affected in the City would carry loss of control over the City Trained Bands, which were still the major force in the capital, and on whom Charles was still relying. Charles instead appointed Sir John Byron, whose loyalty to him was undoubted, but who enjoyed none of Lunsford's unsavoury personal reputation. Charles, however, chose to exhibit his continued confidence in Lunsford by knighting him and giving him a pension of £500 a year. The Commons were not free of Lunsford, since the only result of his dismissal from the Tower was to shift the sphere of his operations from the City to Westminster. On 27 December his men, armed, were on duty outside the Houses. Charles followed this up on 28 December with an order for building a Court of Guard outside Whitehall, and on 31 December Edward Nicholas prepared a warrant to issue £200 for payment of the guard of Trained Bands 'daily attending upon his Majesty'.[185] There appears to have been an attempt to rally other force to Whitehall, including a number of disbanded former officers, and a group from the Inns of Court. The purpose of these men appears, as yet, to have been primarily defensive: their activities seem to have been confined to protecting the immediate environs of Whitehall Palace, the House of Lords, and Westminster Abbey. They are a reminder that it was not only the Commons who were capable of fearing for their safety.

The citizens' persistence in the face of this threat made the five days after the Christmas holiday the most uncomfortable time of the whole two years: Slingsby on 30 December said 'I can not say we have had a merry Christmas, but the maddest one that ever I saw'.[186] On 27 December the Lords found a crowd around the door, and sent the gentleman usher to command them to be gone 'in the King's name'. The crowd said they dared not go, because Colonel Lunsford and other soldiers were lying in wait for them with drawn swords in Westminster Hall. The

---

[184] Pearl, p. 131; West Devon RO Drake of Colyton MSS 1700M/CP 20.
[185] PRO SO 3/12, fo. 181ᵛ; PRO LC 5/135, unfol. (surveyor, 28 Dec.); PRO SP 16/486/120.
[186] PRO SP 16/486/110.

Lords appointed a committee to investigate.[187] In their ultimate retreat through Westminster Hall, the crowd encountered Lunsford, and 'divers were lightly hurt, but without further danger'.[188] It is hard to be certain of the extent of serious injury, since it is possible that some may have concealed wounds for fear of having prosecution added to injury. The only person known to have been seriously hurt is Sir Richard Wiseman, described by Bere as one of their leaders. Sir Richard Wiseman was not a figure to lend great credit to the crowds. He had lost a major case in the Star Chamber, and spent much of the 1630s in prison for accusing the Lord Keeper of taking a bribe in that case. The House of Lords had released him pending an investigation. When he found, like all other petitioners, that his case was delayed by the press of business, he accused the assistant clerk of the Lords of taking another bribe to suppress the justice of his cause.[189] Sir Richard Wiseman's motives for attacking the Lords are likely to have been in part personal. Smith, who is likely to have wished to magnify the incident, said some of the apprentices had been wounded, but his need to add that they had lost their hats and cloaks suggests that he was reporting a small, rather than a large, disturbance. Nehemiah Wallington said the citizens drove back the soldiers by tearing bricks and tiles off the walls and throwing them at them.[190] The man who came nearest to being a major casualty was Archbishop Williams, who unwisely took hold of one of the crowd to bring him before the House of Lords, and the rest 'came upon him'. Williams appears to have escaped with no more than a bad fright.[191] This fact alone is perhaps enough to show that the crowd were something less than a revolutionary mob. Williams seems to have spent the rest of the week occupied in his other capacity as Dean of Westminster, defending the Abbey against apprentices trying to pull down the organs and altar.[192]

On 28 December only two bishops took the risk of attending the Lords.[193] The Commons spent two hours debating a request from the Lords to join in a declaration against the crowds, but 'the greater part of the howse thought it unseasonable to make any such declaration at this time to discontent the cittizens of London our surest friends when soe many designes and plotts were daily consulted of against our safetie'. Instead, they repeated their request to the Lords to join in asking for a

---

[187] *LJ* iv. 491.
[188] PRO SP 16/486/108. The report comes from Vane's clerk Sidney Bere, who is perhaps the least partial of the reporters.
[189] LJ iv. 124; MP, 10 Jan., 4 Aug., 5 Aug. 1641.
[190] PRO SP 16/486/109; Nehemiah Wallington, *Historical Notices*, ed. Rosamund Ann Webb (1870), i. 277.
[191] Drake of Colyton MSS 1700 M/CP 20.
[192] PRO SP 16/486/110.
[193] MM, 28 Dec.

guard commanded by the Earl of Essex.[194] Once again, there was no agreement on a guard because there was no agreement on whom it should be guarding from what. The Lords seem to have reacted by starting a debate on whether it was still a free Parliament, in which George Digby appears to have argued that it was not.[195] He did not carry the House, but he seems to have done enough to bring to a head plans in the Commons to impeach him and his father Bristol. Sir John Hotham, no doubt working with an ally in the Lords, produced a copy of Charles's letter of 1626 out of the Lords' Journal, accusing Bristol of having advised Charles to turn papist while he was in Madrid. It is possible that some of the suspicion of popery which clung to Charles went back to the suspicions which had surrounded and followed his trip to Madrid as Prince.[196] The Commons spent most of the rest of the day issuing orders for sending munitions to Ireland. On the 29th, no bishops attended the House of Lords.[197] The Lords refused to join the Commons in asking for a guard commanded by Essex, and at the end of the day, the Commons carried Pym's motion to ask the JPs of West-minster to ensure the keeping of a strong watch that night. It was a small step, but a real one, towards the disposal of military force on the authority of the Commons alone.[198]

On 30 December there were no bishops present at the Lords in the morning, though the Bishop of Winchester took the risk of attending in the afternoon.[199] Early on the 30th, the Lords were faced with a petition from twelve bishops, led by Archbishop Williams, which the King forwarded to the Lords. The bishops alleged that 'they dare not sit or vote in the House of Peers till your Majesty shall further secure them from all affronts, indignities and dangers', and protested against all votes passed in their 'forced and violent absence' since 27 December. This protest, directly contradicting the Lords' vote that they were free on the 28th, appears to have irritated the Lords enough to give the godly peers a temporary majority, and they informed the Commons that this protest was a breach of privilege and of high and dangerous consequence.

This swing of opinion in the Lords seems to have been due to a change of heart, rather than to differential absence among the lay peers. Of the twenty-seven lay Lords who had not protested against the vote

[194] D'Ewes (C.), p. 356.
[195] MM, 29 Dec.; *LJ* iv. 494, 495.
[196] D'Ewes (C.), pp. 352–3, 357, 361; *CJ* ii. 361; PRO SP 16/491/78; *HMC Salis.* XXII. 179–85. Mandeville, who had attended the Prince in Spain, and may have derived his view of Bristol from Buckingham, is among the candidates for the ally in the Lords. See *LJ* iii. 544.
[197] MM, 29 Dec.
[198] D'Ewes (C.), p. 364; *CJ* ii. 362.
[199] MM, 30 Dec.

on Lunsford on the 24th, eleven were absent, and of the twenty-two who had protested, eight were absent. The fall in attendance seems to have affected both sides in equal proportion. There is no sign that Royalist lay Lords had been frightened away by the crowds, and even the elderly and Catholic Marquess of Winchester was present. The Commons reacted by impeaching the twelve bishops for treason, and they were duly sent to the Tower, thus eliminating twelve votes.[200]

The reaction of Pym and his junto to the bishops' protest could be described by their admirers as dramatic, and by their detractors as melodramatic. Pym moved that the doors be locked, and others added that the outward room should be cleared, and none should go into the committee chamber. When D'Ewes protested, the Speaker modified the proposal to an insistence that no one should speak to anybody out of the windows, or throw any writing out of them. After this preparation, Pym

moved that there being a design to be executed upon the howse of Commons this day wee might send instantly to the Cittie of London that there was a plott for the destroying of the howse of Commons this day, and therefore to desire them to come downe with the Traine Bands for our assistance.

'Some few' seconded this motion, but others opposed it, and some moved instead for an adjournment to the Guildhall.[201]

Pym, it seems, had taken the protest of the bishops that the Parliament was not free for a harbinger of an angry and forcible dissolution, or, in other words, for the Army Plot come again. The charge of duress, by depriving the Parliament of the power to give a free consent, might have been held to override the statute against dissolving it without its own consent. The proposal to adjourn to the Guildhall, whose source we do not know, only makes sense if it is supposed that some members believed they were on the point of facing an armed attack. Pym's proposal, on the other hand, crossed a line Charles was watching very carefully indeed: it proposed the calling out of military force without royal authority. To Charles, this was, it seems, the point which marked the line between politics and rebellion.[202] As Pym believed that Charles and Lunsford intended to attack the House of Commons, so Charles seems to have believed that Pym and his City allies intended to attack Whitehall Palace. Both of them, it seems, were wrong. The evidence stops well short of sustaining the view that either intended an armed

---

[200] *CJ* ii. 362–3.

[201] D'Ewes (C.), pp. 365–7; *CJ* ii. 363 is a skilled example of the use of minutes to cover up what had happened. Pym appears to have believed that his allies in the new Common Council were now able to respond to such a message.

[202] See e.g. MP, 15 Nov. 1641; PRO SP 16/488/7 (King to Lord Mayor, 3 Jan.) and PRO SP 29/6, fo. 158ᵛ (King to Ordnance Officers, 7 Jan.). Charles was also persistently opposing Parliamentary pressure for Newport to have a general warrant to issue arms for Ireland without referring to the King each time, something for which Pym had asked on 29 Dec.: *CJ* ii. 361.

assault on the other, yet such was the danger of allowing the other a pre-emptive strike that neither could afford to wait to be proved right or wrong.

The proposal seemed to illustrate, not only that Pym was planning rebellion, but also that, by overreaching himself, he was losing control of the House. D'Ewes, a man liable enough to panic, bluntly pronounced the grounds of suspicion 'not sufficient', and proposed to limit precautions to adjourning for dinner so that they should not all be taken together. Others were not quite so sanguine as D'Ewes, but the House confined itself to impeaching the twelve bishops for high treason on the ground that they were claiming a legislative veto (something their petition had specifically disclaimed). They once again asked the Lords to join in asking for a guard commanded by Essex, to which the Lords replied that they were willing to agree to a guard, but would not name any person to command it.[203] The naming of a particular person to command armed force was coming to sound dangerously near rebellion, and was therefore beyond the limit of what the Lords would countenance. Having failed to secure a guard, the Commons asked the Westminster JPs present to supply twenty halberts, and asked all their servants to come with pistols.[204] It was a force useful for defence, but not for offence. It was enough to provoke the King, but not enough to threaten him. Pym ended the day of 30 December in the unfortunate position of having made a military threat which he was not yet in a position to carry out. It was a position which invited a pre-emptive strike.

On New Year's Eve the focus of interest shifted to Whitehall. Some two hundred citizens, carrying swords and staves, came up to the gate at Whitehall, and one of them 'clapt his staffe to the ground, crying out stand!', whereat they shouted 'no bishops! No popish lords', and turned to beat a retreat. One of the gentlemen standing within the rails drew his sword, whereat one of the citizens threw a clod of 'dry durt' at him. The gentlemen then came over the rails with their swords drawn, and some of the citizens were hurt.[205] This was an ugly scene, but it does not seem enough to justify Charles's later claim that he was facing a threat to his life and to those of his wife and children.[206] The House of Commons also sent a committee to the King to ask for a guard commanded by Essex, and asked the committee 'if his Majesty shall not vouchsafe to send any, to consider what then shall be done for the safety of the king, the kingdom and this House'. It was a threat to call out force

[203] This is clear in MM but suppressed by the careful wording of *LJ* iv 498.

[204] *CJ* ii. 364; D'Ewes (C.), p. 369. D'Ewes failed to carry a proposal to limit the number of men with pistols to 50. See also Gardiner, *History*, x. 123-5.

[205] PRO SP 16/486/103, 104, 105, 113, 114.

[206] Bodl. MS Clarendon, vol. 21, no. 1634, fo. 126ᵛ.

without authorization if the King should not comply. Like so many other threats during this period, it was intended to secure compliance, rather than to be carried out. Yet, again like so many others, it succeeded in creating belief without securing compliance. There is no more evidence from this week that the Commons intended an armed insurrection than there is that the King intended a massacre of the Commons, yet both sides, partly because they knew they themselves were willing to fight rather than give in, ended the week believing in the imminence of an armed assault from the other. It seems probable that both beliefs were natural but wrong.

Such beliefs, even if mistaken when formed, might constitute a self-fulfilling prophecy. Lord Brooke spent much of the Christmas season seeing to the ordering and delivery of great guns from 'Wopping'. He is not likely to have intended to wheel a minion and two falcons about London. Until they were sent to Warwick, the guns are more likely to have been used to guard Brooke House than for any offensive purpose. Being a prudent man, Lord Brooke also tipped the King's guards, and, for good measure, his trumpeters, but this year, unlike the year before, he refrained from giving the King a New Year's Gift.[207] Sir Thomas Barrington on 4 January bought four muskets, but again, the number does not seem sufficient to organize a successful revolution.[208]

On 1 January a Commons' committee for the safety of the House and the kingdom, and the committee of both Houses for Irish affairs, both met at the Guildhall. It may have been on this occasion that the Commons decided, no doubt with the assistance of the new Common Council, to call out the Trained Bands on their own authority. Such a decision was certainly taken by the full House when it reassembled on the morning of Monday 3 January. At some time on 3 January Charles wrote to the Lord Mayor to ensure 'that none of our trained bands be raised without speciall warrant from us'.[209] In this document, Charles made the crucial claim that: 'wee understand that the House of Commons hath sent to have a guard of the trained bands of that City'. In other words, he was claiming, a few hours after committing himself to the impeachment of the Five Members (which is mentioned in the same letter), that the other side had turned to force first. It is a crucial claim, and it would be nice to know to what Charles referred. Such a decision to call out the Trained Bands without Charles's authority might have

---

[207] Warwicks. RO Warwick Castle MSS, Halford's Accounts: vol. ii *sub* Necessaries, Foreign Payments, Gifts; vol. i *sub* Taxes. It is interesting to note that 'taxes' was the heading under which Brooke accounted for his New Year's gift to the King. It makes a point about English unpreparedness for war that Brooke accompanied his purchase of the guns with the purchase of 'the booke called Smithes Arte of Gunnerye'.

[208] Essex RO DD/BA A 14, fo. 23ᵛ.

[209] *CJ* ii. 366; PRO SP 16/488/7.

been made by the almost unrecorded committee which met at the Guildhall on 1 January. If that committee made no such proposal, then Charles may have been referring to Pym's unsuccessful motion of 30 December. Though Pym had then proposed such a course, the Commons had not approved it. If this was what Charles referred to, he was straining the evidence.

The committee for Irish affairs on 1 January certainly gave orders for issuing a large amount of munitions for Ireland, which provoked Charles on 7 January to send another instruction to the Ordnance Office that no arms should be issued without his warrant.[210] The committee for the safety of the kingdom decided 'in regard they received as yet no answer from his Majesty concerning a guard', to prepare a new remonstrance, which, among much else, demanded a repudiation of the Dillon mission.[211] It was also rumoured that the committee at the Guildhall discussed a plan to impeach the Queen. There is no proof of this rumour, but when it became public a few weeks later, Pym did not go out of his way to stop it.[212] This rumour may explain the warrant at the beginning of January to issue £600 to the Countess of Denbigh, the Queen's Mistress of the Robes, for 'secret service'. If the Queen were to have to fly, at least she should do so properly equipped.[213] The decision to swear Southampton of the Bedchamber on 30 December 'at 7 o'clock at night' is another sign of hardening resolution.[214] After having apparently made one last effort to get Pym to take the Exchequer without strings, the King bestowed it upon Culpepper, and the vacant Secretaryship on Falkland.[215]

If this story of the offer of the Exchequer to Pym is correct, the decision to impeach the Five Members cannot have been final until sometime on 1 January. Nevertheless, some such plan had existed as a contingency plan ever since the King in September 1640 had told the Council that his subjects' treasonable correspondence with the Scots 'shall not be forgotten'. It is so well established in English folk memory that the charge against the Five Members was a political disaster, and

---

[210] BL Loan MS 29/46/25; PRO SP 29/6, fo. 158ᵛ.

[211] DO, vol. ii, fos. 170ᵛ–1ʳ.

[212] *CSP Ven. 1640–2*, p. 272; *HMC Montagu of Beaulieu*, i. 141; Gardiner, *History*, x. 127. For the failure to dispel the suspicions, see *PJ* i. 63, 70, 74. If the Declaration contained any phrase like the one ultimately included, to the effect that 'Her Majesty hath been admitted to intermeddle with the great affairs of state' (*PJ* i. 544), this would make the rumour intelligible without making it necessary to believe it. If so, it is hard to believe Pym was unaware it was likely to be so interpreted. The suspicion again arises that Pym may have been tempting the King to overreach himself.

[213] PRO SO 3/12, fo. 183ʳ. It is rather more difficult to explain a warrant of 28 Dec., to issue £1200 to Saye, 'to disburse in his Mats. special and private service according to his Mats. directions already given him therein'. £40 was paid on this warrant on 5 May 1642: PRO SO 3/12, fo. 179ʳ; PRO E 403/2814, fo. 23ᵛ. On possible plans for the Queen's flight, see also PRO SP 16/488/51.

[214] PRO LC 5/135, p. 5, 30 Dec.

[215] Gardiner, *History*, x. 127. Culpepper was sworn on 1 Jan.: PC Reg. xii. 207.

the belief contains so much truth, that it is hard to remember that Charles's legal case against them might have been very strong. Since the case was never tried, we cannot know how much Charles knew, but it seems likely that, following Waller's hint on 6 November, he could have made a better case against them than they had made against Strafford. The first article of the charge, of subverting the fundamental laws, and placing an arbitrary and tyrannical power in subjects, could have been sustained by expounding the attempt to legislate by ordinance of the two Houses, and even more, by expounding the Commons' attempt to legislate alone by the order of 8 September. The charge that they had endeavoured to alienate the people's affections from the King could easily have been sustained by reference to the printing of the Grand Remonstrance, and it was they themselves, in the case of Strafford, who had argued that this constituted treason. The charge that they had encouraged a foreign power to invade England was true, and Montrose, as a member of the Scottish Committee of Estates, would have been in a position to supply the King with all the necessary evidence. The charge that they had raised and countenanced tumults against King and Parliament had been advanced, and called treason, by such good Parliament men as Strangeways and Kirton. Pym's speech of 30 December could have sustained the charge that he had actually levied war against the King. To make this charge lie against the named individuals, it would have been necessary to persuade one of the middle rank organizers, such as Captain Venn, to turn King's evidence. Whether the King was able to do this, we cannot know, but it was at least plainly on record that Pym and his allies had made no attempt to discourage the assembly of crowds outside the Lords. Finally, in spite of all Parliamentary argument to the contrary, the charge was not a breach of privilege, since treason was universally agreed not to be protected by Parliamentary privilege. Under these circumstances, the agreed fact that the charge was a political disaster is itself evidence that Charles had already lost a large part of his authority to govern.

The persons accused were Pym, Hampden, Haselrig, Holles, and Strode, with Lord Mandeville as a last-minute addition.[216] The King instructed the Attorney-General, who delivered the articles to the Lords, to object against Essex, Warwick, Holland, Saye, Wharton, and Brooke if they were named to a committee to investigate the charge, because he wished to call them as witnesses. Mandeville, who was in the House, promptly submitted for trial, but the Lords would have none of it. Instead of appointing a committee to examine witnesses, as the King envisaged, they appointed a committee to consider whether the charge

---

[216] BL Egerton MS 2546, fo. 20 is the King's holograph instructions to the Attorney-General, in which the last-minute insertion of Mandeville is plainly visible.

'be a regular proceeding according to law'. This committee included Warwick, Saye, Wharton, and Brooke, all peers to whom the King had specifically objected. Later that day, the Lords agreed to join the Commons in their requests for a guard, though they still did not agree to the naming of Essex. Their request to the King was for 'such a guard as himself and both Houses of Parliament should approve of'.[217] This was, no doubt, an impossible request, since no such guard could exist, but it did indicate a significant shift away from the King and towards the Commons. In the Commons, the charge first came to their attention because the studies of Pym and Holles had been sealed up. The House directed the Serjeant to break open the doors and break the seals off their trunks. They issued a further order that if anyone tried to arrest a member or to seal his papers, the members should call on the aid of the constable to put the offending officer into safe custody. The order further stated that, according to the Protestation, it was lawful for such a member to defend himself. This order surely came close enough to rebellion to suggest that the charge was justified.

On the morning of 4 January, on Pym's motion, the Commons sent Penington, Soames, and Venn to ask for help from the Lord Mayor, Aldermen, and Common Council.[218] It seems to have been on the receipt of this message that the new Common Council elected a Committee of Safety, which was clearly dominated by Penington's allies in the City. On 5 January this committee condemned the charge against the Five Members, and it appears to have been they, in the very nick of time, who delivered military control of the City into the hands of Pym's allies.[219] Meanwhile, the Commons remained in session, while Nathaniel Fiennes anxiously watched the officers gathering at Whitehall.

According to the King's later account, it was the Commons order of 3 January, authorizing members to defend themselves, which encouraged him to come to the House himself, in the hope that his presence would make it possible to arrest the members without bloodshed. He clearly expected that, faced with his own royal presence, the House would peacefully give up its members.[220] After dinner on 4 January the members took their seats in the House, possibly in the hope of tempting the King to overreach himself as he did. The King, accompanied by the Elector Palatine and the Earl of Roxburgh, and followed by a large body of armed men, promptly set out for Westminster. The Commons were ready, having received a warning by the French Ambassador, who

[217] *LJ* iv. 501–2.
[218] *CJ* ii. 366–8; D'Ewes (C.), pp. 379–80. For a similar order by the Lords, see *LJ* iv. 502.
[219] Pearl, pp. 139–44; PRO SP 16/488/13. The possibility remains that the events of 5 Jan. rubber-stamped a change already several days old.
[220] *ECR* E 241(1), p. 535.

described four of the six accused as his 'friends', and also by Essex.[221] The members withdrew, though 'it was a pretty while before Mr. Strode could be perswaded to it'. The King came into the House, still bringing the Elector Palatine with him, found the members absent, and 'went out of the howse in a more discontented and angry passion than he came in'. The indignation this day provoked was not merely the result of the King's presence: it was also a reaction to the eighty or so armed 'ruffians', or, as Roger Hill had it, Frenchmen, panders, and rogues, who crowded the lobby behind him, allegedly ready to begin a 'massacre' if the House should refuse to give up its members. The House, having had enough for the day, immediately adjourned.[222]

The next day Hopton and Culpepper bravely attempted to defend the King, on the ground that he usually came with a guard.[223] Instead, the House voted that the King had broken their privileges, and that they could not sit there in safety until they had vindicated them. Being unable to adjourn as a House to any other place, they resolved to adjourn as a committee to the Guildhall. This decision was forced to a division, and was carried by 170 to 86, the biggest majority Pym and his allies had enjoyed for a very long time. It was the same proposal which had been rejected on 30 December. The King's action, which had been designed to reassert his authority, had simply alienated the Lords, and tipped the Commons' majority over the edge into what was very near a state of legal rebellion. Moreover, it was a state from which, in the face of the King's charge, it was hard to see how they could return with safety. At no time did the Commons, or the Lords, ever consider the charge against the Five Members as a charge which required a legal answer. On 5 January Charles went to look for the members in the City. He was given an uncomfortable reception, and Wiseman reported that he was moved, 'and I beleive was glad when he was at home'. Even Wiseman, a congenital optimist about the religious temper of the City, now said that 'the puritan faction with the sectaryes and schismatikes are to prevalent both in cittie and country, soe that no man can tell, if the king and parlament should not agree, which partie would be strongest'.[224] The King was reduced to issuing a Proclamation for the apprehension of the Five Members. It was the crowning mark of how

---

[221] PRO 31/3/73, fo. 10r–v; D'Ewes (C.), pp. 383–4; PRO SP 18/94/71 and 71/1. I am grateful to Dr Richard Stewart for this last reference.

[222] PJ i. 9–13; Verney's Notes, pp. 138–9. Strode, being 'a young man and unmarried', had to be pulled out by his cloak by Sir Walter Earle.

[223] PJ i. 15; KAO Sackville MSS F 1/3, fo. 7v. Culpepper, newly appointed as Chancellor of the Exchequer, may have been speaking ex officio.

[224] PRO SP 16/488/27. The French Ambassador, who was in the City that day, said there were 20,000 men under arms. It is not clear whose orders these men were taking: PRO 31/3/73, fo. 7v.

comprehensively Charles had lost the middle ground that Lord Keeper Littleton refused to put the Seal to it.[225]

In the City, the Commons' committee passed a long series of resolutions about the control of armed force. They resolved that the Lord Mayor's commission was a commission of Lieutenantcy, and illegal. In the absence of any settled law for the militia, they resolved that the power to name guards and officers rested with the Lord Mayor, Alderman, and Common Council, 'or the greater number of them'. In practice, this bare invocation of the majority principle meant the majority of the most numerous body, which was the Common Council. The change in the City government was now under the direct protection of the House of Commons. To underline the point, the committee resolved that they had power to treat with the Common Council. They further resolved that the sheriffs were entitled to raise the *posse comitatus* for the safety of 'the king, kingdome and Parliament', and that if they failed in this duty, members of the public were bound to defend 'every member' of the Parliament by their Protestation.[226] On 10 January Clotworthy reported from a subcommittee appointed to advise with 'some' of the Common Council. They resolved that Serjeant-Major Skippon should take command of the City forces until the City should order it otherwise. He was to accompany the Commons back to Westminster with a guard of eight companies, all of whom were to take the Protestation, with eight pieces of ordnance, and ammunition out of the chamber of London. With the aid of armed watermen, some of the trained bands of Southwark, and 'divers thousands' out of Buckinghamshire who had come to defend their member, this made a formidable escort.[227]

On receipt of this news, Charles took fright, and decided, in great haste, to leave London for Hampton Court. He took with him only the Queen, his children, Secretary Nicholas, and the perennial Elector Palatine. Essex and Holland, who had been ordered to attend as Lord Chamberlain and Groom of the Stool, refused and remained at Westminster.[228] Almost the first thing Charles did when he was safely out of London was to write to the Scottish commissioners to remind them not to involve themselves in the differences between him and his English Parliament without acquainting him first.[229] It was a useless request: the peace of the kingdoms was, as the Covenanters had always said, indivis-

---

[225] Larkin, pp. 757–8. The Proclamation includes no command for the apprehension of Mandeville, who had offered to stand trial. For the refusal of the Seal, see *HMC Twelfth Report*, II. 303, and PRO SP 16/488/54. Bere said that Littleton offered his resignation, which was refused.

[226] PRO SP 16/488/39; *Verney's Notes*, pp. 140–1.

[227] *PJ* i. 30–1; *Verney's Notes*, pp. 141–3. In Sidney Bere's phrase, they were accompanied by such multitudes 'as had as much of the triumph, as gard': PRO SP 16/488/54.

[228] Fletcher, p. 184; *ECR* E 241(1), pp. 537–8.

[229] Scottish Record Office, PA 13/2, unfol. (14 Jan. 1642).

ible. On 17 January the Scottish commissioners submitted a petition, which was immediately carried to the Commons by Walter Long, and presented by Sir Philip Stapleton. In it, they claimed that Scotland and England must stand together, and what disturbed the peace of one must disturb the peace of the other, 'so that they are bound to maintain the peace and liberties of one another, being highly concerned therein'. They blamed the troubles on 'papists, prelates and their adherents', advised the King to take the sound and faithful advice of his Houses of Parliament, and offered their services as mediators. The Commons thanked them warmly, and resolved, on Hampden's motion, to pay the costs of the house they had hired.[230] In taking this line, the Scots were acting in their own interest: if Charles should succeed in suppressing trouble in England, it was not to be expected that he would leave the Covenanters in control in Scotland. Lord Chancellor Loudoun reminded Charles that he had already involved the Scots. The charge against the Five Members that they had incited the Scots to invade England infringed the Act of Oblivion, and any threat to the Act of Oblivion crated widespread anxiety in Scotland.[231] The Covenanters thus had a vested interest in ensuring the safety of the Five Members. Any investigation into Anglo-Scottish correspondence during the Bishops' Wars was likely to threaten them at least as much as it did the Five Members.

Meanwhile, the House of Commons marched back to Westminster, escorted by 2,400 men in arms, many of them carrying copies of the Protestation 'like a little square banner' on top of their pikes.[232] When safely back in their own house, they reacted, like any burgled house-holder, by ordering a new lock for their door.[233] They had secured their safety for the time being, but both they and the King had taken up a position from which it was very difficult to retreat. Once King and Commons had publicly taken up the position that they could not be safe together in the same place, it was hard to see any possible compromise. After the attempt on the Five Members, following after the Army Plot and the Incident, the majority in the Commons were unlikely to accept any situation in which they did not enjoy a guard which was not under the King's control. Equally, after having fled from something very near an insurrection, it was hard to see how the King could feel safe in the near neighbourhood of a military force not under his control. Compromise was now finally impossible. Peace could now only come by the

---

[230] *To the King's Most Excellent Majesty*, 17 Jan. 1641, St Ang. (BL D 1 3/4); *PJ* i. 91. The decision to compose this 'courteous letter' was taken on 15 Jan.: Scot. RO PA 13/2, unfol. (15, 17, 18), Jan. 1642.

[231] Hamilton MS 1723.

[232] *PJ* i. 39.

[233] *CJ* ii. 371.

surrender of one party, which would only happen if that party was unable to raise military force to defend itself. Since both sides were firmly equipped with a mythology to aid in the task of thinking about the unthinkable, this was unlikely. For Smith, on 29 December the country was on the edge of a war between the Protestants and the papists, and when he wrote about the 'Protestant Lords', he meant the minority in the House of Lords. For Wiseman, the next day, what was taking place was a move to rebellion by 'separatists and sectaryes whoe rage that they cannot have their wills in putting downe the bishops and abolish the booke of commen prayer'.[234] Both myths contained enough truth to make it unlikely that their holders would be compelled to abandon them by pressure of events. So long as division was interpreted according to these two rival myths, it was a self-sustaining process: every disagreement, by strengthening the rival interpretations of what was wrong, in turn gave rise to further disagreement. In December 1641 the fears of Smith and Wiseman had not yet spread far outside London: it was to the task of propagating them in the country that efforts now turned. Perhaps the most sensible comments on the whole episode were those made at a safe distance by Argyll: 'the power of princes is best maintained when most feared bot least used'. He condemned those who allowed the King to be engaged but never looked to his retreat, and said that 'it can never be for his Majesty's honor nor advantage to mak himself head of ane pairtie'. His condemnation was impartial: 'subiects will ever finde it best to yeeld in sumthings to their king'.[235] If they did not, they forced the King to become head of a party, and a party, in Scottish parlance, was normally a group organized for war.

[234] PRO SP 16/486/102 and 111.
[235] Hamilton MSS 1735, 1749, 1748.

12

The Road to York

JANUARY–MARCH 1642

After the King's departure from London on 10 January, the historian's major task is not to explain why there was a civil war: it is to explain why there was not a civil war for another eight months. What had taken place since Christmas was a partially successful *coup d'état*: the King had lost military control of his capital, which was now dominated by forces which did not take his orders. The failure to arrest the Five Members showed that, in the most literal sense, the King's writ no longer ran in London. That kings who lose military control of their capitals should wish to recover it, by any effective means to hand, does not require explanation. If Charles wanted civil war from January 1642 onwards, he was only doing the obvious thing for a king in his position to do. Equally, those who are publicly charged with treason do not usually wish to trust their futures to those who have preferred the charges. Clarendon's later claim that after the attempt on the Five Members Pym had no thought of moderation, is not contradicted by anything in the day-to-day record.[1]

If the King on the one hand, and the Parliamentary junto on the other, were willing to fight by January 1642, the problem becomes one of explaining why they did not do so. This is partly a matter of their tactical needs of the moment, but much more a commentary on the state of England in 1642. If the country had been ready to fight in January 1642, it is hard to see what forces at the centre might have held it back. In fact, the history of 1642 suggests that Strafford had been right in May 1640 when he said that 'the quiet of England will hold out long'. The French Ambassador on New Year's Eve said that 'si c'estoit une autre nation que celle cy, je croirois que la ville seroit à feu et à sang dans 24 heures: il sera pourtant malaisé que l'affaire se passe sans scandale'.[2] The country was in fact deeply divided, but what seems to have lasted is the depth of social tolerance which held local communities together, combined with the devotion to consensus politics which led both the Lords and a large part of the country to go on believing in a political solution long after such a thing had ceased to be a practical possibility.

---

[1] Clarendon, *History*, iii. 464.
[2] PRO 31/3/73, fo. 5ᵛ.

In a way, the devotion to consensus politics may have made civil war in the long term more likely, since it made it harder for people to appreciate that there were such things as non-negotiable demands. The bulk of the petitions which came in from the counties in support of the Parliamentary junto during the first quarter of 1642 were in fact asking for things Charles could never concede, but there is very little reason to believe that their framers often understood this fact. Professor Fletcher, who has undertaken a thorough study of these petitions, concluded: 'At Westminster there was a sense of outright confrontation with the Crown from which there could be no drawing back. We find this entirely absent in the petitions'.[3] Lists of seditious words, on which Cromwell and other members were keeping an increasingly close eye, indicate the presence of a number of people willing to take part in belligerent talk, often taking the form of threats to kill Pym because he was a traitor.[4] What is surely significant is that these incidents were continuing to stop at words: not once between January and March was the Parliament told of any incident involving violence between the partisans of the two sides.[5] Even the anti-Catholic scares which grew commoner from the Irish Rebellion onwards normally continued to exempt friends and neighbours from the strictures aimed at 'papists'.[6] This continuing local peace may well have reinforced the tendency to look for scapegoats for the breakdown of order at the centre: the less natural a crisis appears, the more a scapegoat is needed to explain it.

The delay in the outbreak of civil war is not only a political phenomenon: it is also a measure of how extraordinarily demilitarized a country England had become. That England had reached January 1642 with no unquestionably legal method of raising troops is a symptom of this demilitarized condition. It is both a large part of the explanation of why the monarchy was allowed to reach the point of collapse, and an important reason why that collapse was not immediately followed by civil war. On 13 January the French Ambassador said that in another eight days two-thirds of the population would have taken arms.[7] This remark betrays the fact that he had not been in England long, and barely knew the country outside London. There were occasional gatherings to meet immediate crises, but large assemblies of men under arms were not a regular feature of the situation until July, and even then, it is doubtful

---

[3] Fletcher, pp. 223, 191–228. The absence of a full discussion of these petitions is because I have very little to add to Prof. Fletcher's account.

[4] See e.g. CJ ii. 409; PJ i. 101, 114, 257, 348–9; PJ ii. 8–9, 39.

[5] See also J. S. Morrill and J. D. Walter, 'Order and Disorder in the English Revolution', in Anthony Fletcher and John Stevenson (eds.), Order and Disorder in Early Modern England (1985), 137–65, esp. p. 157.

[6] Fletcher, pp. 203–8; Robin Clifton, 'Fear of Popery', in Russell (ed.), Origins, pp. 163–7; Anthony Fletcher, A County Community in Peace and War: Sussex 1600–1660 (1975), 94–104.

[7] PRO 31/3/73, fo. 13ᵛ.

whether his proportion of two-thirds of the population under arms was ever reached. To those more familiar with the inertia which had always attended English musters, this probably came as much less of a surprise. The county militias, because they were so deeply rooted in county society, were not likely to have much stomach for a fight until they felt a deep threat to their own local communities, and that time had not yet come. Neither King nor Parliament possessed the money for hiring large numbers of mercenaries, and the professional soldiers who had gathered round the King at Whitehall were numbered in hundreds and not in thousands.[8] There were probably not many countries in Europe where a major panic could be created by a military force costing only £200. Above all, the Lords, though they still kept a sense of their own importance which dated from the days when they had been a military power in the land, no longer had large numbers of armed men at their disposal. Major political figures like Saye or Bristol may have added a great deal to the political strength of any side they might join, but in terms of armed men, their contribution might be numbered in single figures. Some of the Lords who still had a territorial base, such as Pembroke, Hertford, or Warwick, may have been able to do rather better, but even they were not able to make any significant military contribution. If 1642 is compared with, for example, 1399, one of the most striking differences must be the lack of any force of soldiers instantly available. England in 1642 was, in a very real sense, a society in which power could only be exercised by consent, and therefore, for a considerable period of time, the absence of consent meant there was an absence of power. This absence of power was an important part of the reason why the King and his enemies were not yet able to start a civil war.

There were also more immediate tactical reasons why a war did not start in January 1642. If what had taken place is seen as a successful *coup d'état* by the junto and their City allies, it should emerge that the person who had an immediate incentive to fight was the King. On 8 January he said that the order of the Commons' committee in defence of the Five Members on 6 January was such a thing 'as noe sovereigne can or ought to suffer from subiects'.[9] He seems to have contemplated the idea of using force to back up this view, and Smith said on 7 January that some had tried to persuade him to use force to fetch the Five Members out of the City. The King seems to have been brought face to face with the fact that in a society still dedicated to ideals of compromise, attempts to reassert his authority only succeeded in weakening it further. Smith, who was Northumberland's secretary, said that 'some well affected

---

[8] PRO SP 16/486/120.
[9] Ibid. 16/488/38.

nobles to both sides do labour to pacifie the K.'.[10] These nobles are likely to have spelt out to the King that any such attempt on his part would simply drive them into the arms of his opponents.

When he left London, the King seems to have again briefly contemplated an immediate resort to force. Much of our information on the attempt by Lunsford and Digby to rally force to Kingston comes through the medium of the House of Commons, which is not necessarily the best source. However, when the House of Commons paid 20s. to the watermen who had been hired to take saddles to Kingston, so that they should not lose their fare for their public spirit in revealing the business, this has the ring of truth.[11] Slingsby, whose account, though entirely hearsay, is at least informed by an attempt at balance, said that Lunsford was reported to have made a proclamation for all the King's party to come to him, but felt the need to add that 'if any such thing were I beleeve it was but some drunken flourish'.[12] There was rather more purposefulness about the immediate decision to send Newcastle and Legge to take control of the armoury at Hull, and in the instruction to Nicholas not to enter their warrant in the Signet Office. Nicholas, typically, kept a record of his authorization not to make a record.[13] Nicholas has also left us a marginal allusion to 'the purveyors that attend the soldiers'.[14]

If the King had such ideas during the period 10–13 January, he must have soon learnt that in terms of practical politics, he had no such option. The attempt on the Five Members, like the Army Plot, caused a temporary but severe blow to his political credit, and he had suffered a loss of support so great that he did not have the option of fighting. On 13 January, feeling himself unsafe at Hampton Court, he withdrew further to Windsor. At Windsor, he heard a report that 1,000 citizens were coming with a petition, and called out the *posse comitatus*, 'the whole power and arms of the country, but there was not any came to him'.[15] The rot had extended into his own circles: he was not accompanied by any great number of Lords or 'old courtiers'.[16] Orlando Bridgman, who did attend the King at Windsor, said 'he never saw so

---

[10] Ibid. 16/488/37. On the fear caused in the City by this report, see Pearl, pp. 142–3.

[11] *CJ* ii. 375.

[12] PRO SP 16/488/56. On the 'hurly-burly' at Kingston, see also *LJ* iv. 509, 516; MP, 15 Jan. 1642; *CJ* ii. 372, 373, 395. For Digby's view on 21 Jan. that it was too late for accommodation, see *LJ* iv. 582–3, and BL E. 138(10).

[13] PRO SP 16/488/50.

[14] Ibid. 16/489/36.1. This document, which is undated, is about the ships to take the Queen to Holland, and probably dates from the first week of Feb. I have found no further information in PRO LS.

[15] PRO SP 16/489/3.

[16] Ibid. 16/488/56.

small a court'.[17] Those few who did attend included the vultures of seventeenth-century politics—unpaid creditors. These were present at Hampton Court and Windsor in considerable numbers, including some whose debts went back to the expeditions to Rhé and Cadiz.[18]

These, doubtless, were signs to which the many people calling for accommodation were able to point with telling effect. The French Ambassador told the King and Queen that if they went on, 'ils sont ruinez sans ressource'.[19] From the King's point of view, the most alarming of the voices calling for a reconciliation with his Parliament was probably that of the Elector Palatine, who could have become a William of Orange at very short notice.[20] The Venetian Ambassador at the end of January said Charles's hopes of using force were dwindling.[21] He appears to have briefly contemplated the idea of looking for support in Ireland, which the French Ambassador believed to be the only recourse left to him.[22] If so, he is likely to have been considering an initiative along the lines of the Dillon mission, offering toleration to Catholics in return for laying down their arms. Slingsby on 6 January said that 'the ill affected partye, (wch are those yt follow the court) do now speak very favourably of the Irish, as those whose grievances were greate, there demands moderate, and may stand the king in much stead'.[23] Months later in June, Clanricarde, apparently on his own initiative, tried out terms resembling those of the Dillon mission, at the surrender of Galway. The results showed that the Irish results were all that could be hoped, and the English all that might be feared.[24] Whether for fear of further loss of English support or for some other reason, Charles put the Dillon plan into cold storage, though he does not appear to have abandoned it. Instead, with his message to the Parliament of 20 January, he adopted a conciliatory position, no doubt in the hope of waiting until Pym could provide him with a party. If he was to adopt a waiting strategy, as his English interest seemed to dictate, he had to ensure the safety of the Queen. Both the French Ambassador and the Elector Palatine reported that it was the Queen, rather than the King, who was

---

[17] *PJ* i. 71.
[18] PRO 30/5/6 (Book of Petitions), pp. 455–6, 460, 461. I am grateful to Dr J. S. A. Adamson for drawing my attention to this volume. PRO LS 8/1 shows no diets for any person of distinction.
[19] PRO 31/3/73, fos. 14ᵛ, 25ᵛ.
[20] PRO SP 16/489/9 (Elizabeth of Bohemia to Sir Thomas Roe, 7/17 Feb. 1642).
[21] *CSP Ven.* 1640–2, p. 283.
[22] PRO 31/3/73, fos. 11ʳ, 14ʳ.
[23] PRO SP 16/488/29.
[24] On the surrender of Galway, see *HMC Ormond*, NS II. 148–51, in which the Irish Council cast oblique doubt on Clanricarde's loyalty. MP, 23 June 1642; *LJ* v. 166, 167; BL Harl. MS 164, fos. 207ᵇ, 214ᵇ, 224ᵇ; Hill, p. 106. The story tends to support the view that Ireland was only governable on terms which rendered England ungovernable.

the centre of resistance to their efforts at mediation. The Queen had had no reason to trust her safety to the Parliament, and if, as the French Ambassador said, she found herself 'ne pouvent souffrir les puissances du Parlement',[25] it was hardly a matter for surprise. When she was safely out of England, she wrote to her old governess Mme St Georges, to explain why she had no longer felt safe in England:

their design was to separate me from the King my lord, and they have publicly declared that it was necessary to do this; and also, that a Queen was only a subject, and was amenable to the laws of the country like other persons. Moreover than that [sic], they have publicly accused me, and by name, as having wished to overthrow the laws and religion of the kingdom, and that it was I who had roused the Irish to revolt; they have even got witnesses to swear that this was the case, and upon that, affirmed that as long as ever I remained with the king, the state would be in danger, and many other things too long to write, such as coming to my house, whilst I was at chapel, bursting open my doors, and threatening to kill everybody; but this I confess did not greatly frighten me; but it is true that to be under the tyranny of such persons is inexpressible misery.[26]

Much of this appears to be the Queen's deductions, rather than direct and public statements by the Parliament, but as deductions, they are entirely plausible. The Parliament had said it was unsafe for her son to remain in her company, and it required no great imagination to suppose that they might extend the same principle to her husband.[27] Sometime late in January the King and Queen decided that she should go abroad. Once that decision had been taken, the King's policy was dominated for several weeks by the desire to ensure that the Parliament was not provoked to stop her departure.[28] War would have to wait until his wife and son were in safety, and his wife in a position to buy arms abroad.

At Westminster, as much as at Windsor, a desire to postpone action coexisted with a desire to avoid any genuine accommodation. The leading members of the Parliamentary junto were well aware of the extent to which moves towards war might risk alienating the support on which they would depend to win that war, and any time they might forget it, such people as D'Ewes could volubly remind them of it. When civil war was referred to in such euphemisms as that 'the worst of all should befall, in the superlative degree',[29] there was no political capital to be won out of appearing to be guilty of such a thing: it seemed a safe political prediction that whoever was blamed for the outbreak of civil

[25] PRO 31/3/73, fo. 25ᵛ.
[26] Letters of Queen Henrietta Maria, pp. 71–2.
[27] See the Queen's comment in CJ ii. 303.
[28] Fletcher, pp. 228–30.
[29] PRO SP 16/488/76. The words are those of Sir William Boswell, Ambassador to the Hague.

war would lose it. In this situation, there was no advantage in a pre-emptive strike. In January 1642 it appeared possible that Charles, like James II, would find himself too friendless to fight. This was a possibility not lightly to be thrown away, and if it did not turn out to be a justified hope, there was every advantage in ensuring that, in any civil war that might result, Charles should appear to be the aggressor. Having pulled off this feat on 4 January, the junto had every incentive to try to repeat it.

The need to avoid any appearance of resistance was not just a matter of political tactics, since most of the House of Commons had been bred on the belief that rebellion was a sin. The doctrine preached in almost every godly pulpit was firmly based on Romans 13: 1 and the 'Homily on Obedience'. For a century, and even more since 1588 and 1605, the godly claim to a place in the sun had rested on the belief that they were the loyal ones, and that it was papists who indulged in rebellion, treason, and conspiracy. To reject so thorough a process of indoctrination (in the literal sense of the word) was not easy. Moreover, even if some members did reject their upbringing in the doctrine of non-resistance, they could not afford to say so, since in a debate which was designed to win public support, even a whiff of rebellion could be enough to drive all the waverers to the other side. So taboo was the notion of resistance that even ascribing it to others was liable to get a speaker into trouble. On 13 January Sir John Northcote opposed a proposal for Hertford to take control of the Prince, 'it being already reported by some that there was an intention to crown the prince and make him king', but he provoked such interruptions that he was unable to finish his speech.[30] The doctrine of resistance was literally unmentionable.

This does not make it easy to understand how far members of the leading group in the Commons had been converted to a belief in resistance, since any who were would have had more wit than to say so. There is evidence that some members knew many of the major writings of resistance theory. John Crew, chairman of the committee on religion, possessed the *Vindiciae Contra Tyrannos*, and works by Buchanan, Pareus, and Knox. At some time, probably during the summer of 1642, he noted that Venice, Genoa, and Lucca were free states, and credited Machiavelli with the office of Recorder of Florence.[31] Pym on 26 January 1642 referred to the Commons as 'united in the public trust, which is derived from the commonwealth, in the common duty and obligation

---

[30] *PJ* i. 63.
[31] Cheshire RO DAR 1/29, fos. 6ᵛ, 14ʳ. I am grateful to Dr J. S. A. Adamson for this reference. The source does not reveal which works by these authors Crew possessed.

whereby God doth bind us to the discharge of that trust'.[32] This looks remarkably like a doctrine of the double covenant which could have been derived from the *Vindiciae*. Edmund Calamy, preaching to the Houses on 22 December 1641, made the impeccable point that God warns us by the death of his servants. Three of his examples, Augustine, Luther, and Ambrose, would have been acceptable to any Protestant, but his fourth was Pareus, whose views every Jacobean graduate at Oxford had to swear to renounce as a wicked example of resistance.[33] It would be a matter for considerable surprise if William Strode, Sir Henry Ludlow, or Henry Marten could be shown to be principled believers in non-resistance.[34] Yet, though such hints are undoubtedly the tip of an iceberg, it is impossible to have any idea of the size of the iceberg underneath them.

Moreover, even if we were to take all the junto as closet resistance theorists, they still needed to justify their actions to a sceptical public, and for that purpose, they consistently fell back on the one justification widely acceptable to conventional opinion, that of self-defence. This was the more necessary for the fact that the cause in which they were opposing the King was that of the further reformation of religion, and that was a cause which could only be contradicted, not served, by rebellion. The godly had for years been telling impatient semi-separatists that it was necessary to tarry for the magistrate, since reformation could only be virtuously done by due and lawful authority.[35] Saye, writing against a Scottish opponent whose culture put him under no such inhibitions, later spelt out these points with some firmness:

I never heard of any sober divine that would justifie the carrying on of reformation in that manner, by private men against the laws and government established in a kingdom; the removing of idolatry out of a kingdom, and introducing the truth of the Gospel, is a blessing to be desired and preferred before all earthly things, but we must wait upon God for it; that we may have what he promiseth in his way, and in his time, and not think to help him by our

---

[32] *LJ* iv. 537. See also above, p. 353 and n.

[33] Edmund Calamy, *Englands Looking Glasse* (1642), 15. On Pareus, see Gardiner, *History*, iv. 297–9. He concentrated on the two themes of self-defence and the rights of the inferior magistrate, both likely to be helpful to the Parliament.

[34] *PJ* i. 248, 249, 313. Marten's speech of 8 Feb., denying the King's negative voice, on the ground that 'the king's vote was included in the lords' votes as the whole commons of England were included in ours because he elected the peers as the commons did us', sounds like political theory made up on the spur of the moment, and is certainly something he might not have said a week earlier. By contrast, Ludlow's speech of 1 Feb., arguing that 'the king is derivative from the parliament, and not the parliament from the king, and if he govern not by parliament, then he govern by force and abuseth the law', sounds like a rare example of a genuine alternative political theory.

[35] P. Collinson, *Religion of Protestants* (Oxford, 1982), 153–5, 161–70, 173–82, and many other refs. See ibid. 177 for the description of Samuel Ward's preaching as 'within its own perspectives, as factious and subversive as the homily of Obedience'.

government of this state in regard of her interest with the king, is the cause of the evils and distempers'.[45] The approving of this clause on this day must be read as a deliberate refusal to remove the fears raised by Cholmeley. It was the classic counsel of Achitophel, designed to make the division irreconcilable.

On the 15th, Pym, Hampden, and Strode rubbed salt in another of the King's wounds by proposing to impeach the Attorney-General for obeying the King's command to impeach the Five Members, Strode claiming that the Attorney-General was in the head of the conspiracy 'to kill such as would maintain the privilege of Parliament'.[46] After the case of Strafford, Charles's allergy to having his servants punished for obeying him must surely have been well known. On the 17th, Pym proposed to imitate the Scots by a proposal to 'evacuate' all the existing Privy Council, and elect such as should be allowed by Parliament, as had been done in Scotland.[47] On the 18th, following Cromwell's motion of the 14th to put the kingdom into a posture of defence, a committee resolved that the power of the militia should be in Lords-Lieutenant and Deputy-Lieutenants to be named by ordinance of Parliament.[48] On the 19th the House discussed a proposal that peers created in future should have no vote without the consent of both Houses. Strode added a proposal that the six new Lords created since the beginning of the Parliament should be deprived of their votes in the Lords. This was too much even for Sir Robert Cooke, but Hampden declared that 'the commonwealth is now sick and this will be one remedy'.[49] On the same day, Hampden reported a letter, drawn up at Grocers' Hall, instructing sheriffs and JPs to organize the tendering of the Protestation to all within their areas, and to note the names of refusers. This action was taken in spite of the Lords' persistent refusal to consent. The letter described the attempt on the Five Members as an assault on 'the very being of Parliament'.[50] The use of the singular, without the article, represents a considerable conceptual change, and it is a usage which was rapidly becoming commoner.

The Commons' majority had made their position clear before the arrival of the King's message of 20 January, which was his first effort at negotiation. He had, by this stage, presumably discovered that he was unable to fight, and thus had nothing to lose from negotiation. If it proved, as he doubtless suspected, that no settlement on any plausible terms was available, at least that discovery could be counted upon to

[45] *PJ* i. 63, 75.
[46] Ibid. 82.
[47] Ibid. 99.
[48] Ibid. 67, 105.
[49] Ibid. 108–9.
[50] Ibid. 109; *CJ* ii. 389.

make him less friendless than he had been. The message so much resembles the technique Bristol had used for handling the Scots in the previous March that the resemblance may provide a clue to authorship: in effect, the message called on the Houses to state their uttermost demands. It asked for proposals for the settling of the King's revenue, the establishment of their privileges, the security of their property and persons, the security of 'the true religion now professed in the church of England', and the settling of ceremonies in such a manner as might take away 'just' offence. The central theme of the message was the question of what the King had to do to secure a revenue settlement.[51] It was a proposal which, it seemed, could at least be relied on to start a negotiation.

The message appeared to be widely welcomed. The Lord Keeper, reporting it to the Commons, called it a 'joyful message', and the Lords composed a form of words for the answer which offered thanks, and said they would take it into speedy consideration. The Commons approved the Lords' answer.[52] At this point, with the tide running strongly in favour of negotiation, Hampden moved 'most unseasonably, and as the issue proved, very unluckily', to add a clause onto the answer to ask that the Tower, the forts, and the 'whole militia' of the kingdom should be put into hands the Parliament could confide in, 'that so we may sit in safety'. This motion was carried, and it plainly told Charles that he was now himself the issue: his opponents intended to ensure that they should not live under his power, before they would discuss any other issues. For the King, the failure to respond to his message of 20 January became a sore point, and remained one right up to the outbreak of the war. It is hard to share D'Ewes's belief that Hampden was 'unlucky' in achieving the effect he did.[53]

On the same day, the House received a petition from Colchester, which expressed hostility to the Book of Common Prayer. King and Bridgman moved that the petitioners should not be given thanks for this clause, but were overruled. The next day, debating more clauses of their pending Declaration, the House voted that the want of a due reformation of church government and of the liturgy now used was a cause of the evils of the kingdom.[54] For the first time, the House had voted against the Book of Common Prayer, which had been upheld in every previous vote. This vote marks a change in the character of the Commons which appears to have lasted. The extremer godly members, such as Wilde, Cromwell, and Sir Robert Cooke, were becoming increasingly

---

[51] *LJ* iv. 523; *PJ* i. 125 and n. Moore omits the words 'now professed in the church of England'.
[52] *PJ* i. 124; *CJ* ii. 388.
[53] *PJ* i. 118–19, 126; *CJ* ii. 389. D'Ewes says that 'the lords, it seems disliking our addition, gave us no answer this night'.
[54] *PJ* i. 123–4, 131.

before the Lords, and had the effect of asking the Lords to rule on the issue of the militia. It is not surprising that the Lords rejected Parliamentary control of the militia. What is surprising is the strength of the Parliamentarian protest, which rose to thirty-two, or, according to Moore, to thirty-four.[65] These people insisted that Parliamentary control of the militia was 'absolutely necessary to the settling of the present distempers'. In other words, they would no longer trust Charles with power. The protesters included Peterborough, an ex-papist and ex-Ship Money refuser about whom it would be nice to know more; Thanet, who had left his proxy with Bath in August, and must therefore be regarded as a swing vote; and Clare and Conway, two Lords as near the centre of the spectrum as it was possible to be. This vote seems, in terms of numbers, to represent about the high-water mark of the Parliamentarian cause in the Lords. From this point on, its increasing success seems to represent changes in attendance, rather than any further conversion. Nevertheless, the protest represented about a third of the lay peerage. For a third of the lay peerage to insist that the King was unfit to be trusted with armed force was a very considerable vote of no confidence.

The response of the Commons' leaders to the rebuff was predictable: they turned to support outside the walls, and on 25 January Pym came to the Lords with four massive petitions, from London, Middlesex, Essex, and Hertfordshire.[66] All these petitions asked for the removal of bishops and popish Lords, the further punishment of delinquents, and the more effective prosecution of the war in Ireland. Middlesex complained of the 'evil counsels, crafty devices, desperate plots' employed by the malignant party 'lest perfect reformation should follow'. Essex complained of 'a great stop of reformation in matters of religion' and feared that papists in England were 'ready to act the parts of those savage bloodsuckers in Ireland, if they be not speedily prevented'. They called for the kingdom to be put in 'a warlike posture of defence'. Hertfordshire recalled how before 1640 the kingdom had been brought to an almost desperate condition by the prelates and their allies the popish party, and that the Parliament was the only means under God to effect reformation. They too recounted how the malignant party had 'endeavoured to hinder all through reformation in church and commonwealth'. Just in case any Lord should miss the point, Lord Brooke, at about this time, said in open House that any Lord who did not join with the Commons was of the malignant party.[67]

[65] *LJ* iv. 532–3; *PJ* i. 168 n. Hill (*PJ* i. 173) says 32 'good lords' protested. Moore's extra 2, Northumberland and Suffolk, perhaps associated themselves with the protest after the event. The incident shows how carefully some members of the Commons were scanning the Lords' Journals.

[66] *CJ* ii. 394, 395; *LJ* iv. 537–40.

[67] Bodl. MS Clarendon, vol. 21, no. 1603, *sub* 31 Jan.

In presenting these petitions to the Lords himself, Pym was throwing the full weight of the House of Commons behind them. He complained of the power of bishops and popish Lords, and pointedly warned the Lords of the dangers of tumults. Beyond that, he attempted, in his most polished subliminal technique, to fasten suspicion on the King. He complained that 'diseases of the brain are most dangerous, because from thence sense and motion are derived to the whole body'. After two sentences, to prevent the innuendo from being too blatant, he continued: 'this evil influence hath been the cause of the preparation of the war with Scotland, of the procuring a rebellion in Ireland; of corrupting religion, suppressing the liberty of this kingdom, and of many fearful and horrid attempts to the subverting the very being of Parliament,[68] which is the only hopeful means of opposing and preventing all the rest'. In another part of the speech, he complained that many now at the head of the Irish rebels had been suffered to pass the ports 'by his Majesty's immediate warrant'. He was careful to say that this was 'without his Majesty's knowledge and intention', but Charles, for one, always remained convinced that he had been personally accused by this passage. It is unlikely that he was alone in the belief. The innuendo that the King was the head of a popish and malignant faction was, from Pym's perspective, perfectly true, and the fear Pym expressed elsewhere in the speech that the King would later attempt to restore ceremonies which were removed was entirely reasonable. The charge of complicity in the Irish Rebellion is another matter. Unless Pym referred only to Charles's dealings with the Dillon mission, the charge was false. Whether it was made in sincerity, however, is a different question, to which present evidence does not permit an answer.[69]

When the Lords began to debate these petitions, they were well aware that they were again under threat. Having co-operated in handing over military control to the City Committee of Safety, they could no longer hope to raise any guards to protect them against the crowds. When the Parliamentarian peers reintroduced the subject of the militia, the Duke of Richmond replied by moving for the House to adjourn for six months. In doing this, Richmond was attempting to activate the resolution the Lords had taken after the tumults of May.[70] Moreover, as D'Ewes pointed out the next day, he 'moved that which might have been effected'. The adjournment of the Parliament was covered by the Act against Dissolution, but there was no legal restriction on the voluntary adjournment of one House, 'and thereby the Parliament would

[68] The singular without the article again deserves remark.
[69] *LJ* iv. 540–3.
[70] See above, p. 342.

not measures to force a new cause on the country. For many Lords who went along with the Militia Ordinance, such as Littleton, Leicester, and Bankes, the object seems to have been, not to enable the Commons to start a war against the King, but to disable the King from starting a war against the Commons. Such people, by accepting office under the Militia Ordinance, seem to have hoped they could ensure that no belligerent use was made of the militia in the counties under their control.[83] The allegiance of men like Manchester, Northumberland, Pembroke, Salisbury, and Holland does not seem to have been to anything resembling Parliamentary sovereignty, but to a sort of aristocratic conciliarism which would enable the peers and the great officers to continue government in the King's name unless or until he came to his senses and tried to reach an agreement with his opponents.

These people showed no eagerness to further the measures of godly reformation for which the Commons and most of the country petitions were still calling. The call of the Kentish petition on 8 February 'to suppresse Masse, both in publick and private',[84] was greeted with stony silence. The reiterated demands to exclude the popish Lords were met with an equally deaf ear. Even in the Nineteen Propositions, the one time when the Lords entertained such a proposal, they wanted to apply the proposition, not to 'popish' Lords, but to 'recusant' Lords, a very different proposition indeed.[85] The Lords, in the teeth of Pym's deepest convictions, adhered to the view that attendance at Protestant worship was to be deemed sufficient proof of Protestantism. They still showed no eagerness to pass the bill of pluralities, with its innuendoes of a parochial calling to the ministry, and Harley continued to manage unsuccessful conferences about Lords' amendments on which it was never possible to reach agreement. Nor did the Parliamentarian Lords show much more enthusiasm than the full House had done for the 8 September order. The Commons gave a first reading to a bill embodying the order on 16 February. It was reported by Wilde on 12 March, and recommitted to meet objections from D'Ewes.[86] Wilde took it to the Lords on 24 March, and it was given a second reading on 29 March. The Commons asked for expedition on 1 and 12 April. On 15 July the bill was considered in Committee of the Whole, and accepted subject to amendments. The amendments were all accepted by the Commons save

[83] For a blunt expression of this sort of thinking, see KAO Sackville MSS U 269/O294, a memorandum, possibly of July 1642, partly in the hand of Lionel Cranfield. It proposes that each shire should have two Lords Lieutenant, one named by the King, the other by the two Houses, and that no troops should move without the command of both. Bankes was not a lord, but appears to have given his opinion as an assistant: *LJ* v. 115–16.

[84] PRO SP 16/489/15.

[85] *LJ* v. 91; *CJ* ii. 600.

[86] *CJ* ii. 436, 437–8, 476; *PJ* i. 407, ii. 32.

one for the privilege of peers, which would, in effect, have exempted the Lords from the operation of the bill. There the bill rested, to be remembered only as a part of one of the Nineteen Propositions.[87] It does not show the Lords as zealots for further reformation. The Root and Branch Bill was still not offered to the Lords, presumably because it was taken for granted that they would reject it.

It seems the strength of true godliness in the Lords was very small. Brooke, and perhaps Warwick, fully qualify, and so does Saye within the limits permitted by his intense Erastian anticlericalism. There are other possible candidates, such as Lincoln, or Spencer, whose father-in-law Leicester described him as having an inclination to the 'brotherhood'.[88] Mandeville counted as one of the political godly, but Ralph Josselin refused his family living on the ground that it was a 'loose' household.[89] Salisbury, Essex, and Northumberland, whose religion may have been typical of the Parliamentarian peers, were good Calvinists, but nothing obviously more radical, and in Northumberland's case, an Erastian almost as firm as Saye.[90] A number of peers, such as Conway (Brilliana Harley's brother) had a devout Calvinist upbringing, but seem to have never given much more than formal assent to its principles.

Whatever drove a third of the lay peerage to the edge of rebellion seems to have been something much more secular than impelled most of the majority in the Commons. On 25 February, when deeply irritated by an attempt by the King to influence attendance by incompetent whipping, the Lords debated what ill counsels had been given to the King. One of the peers, possibly Essex, offered three questions: 'who have gone about to extend the king's prerogative beyond the ancient bounds? Who were the authors and procurers of monopolies? Who gave counsel for the breach of the pacification with the Scots, which hath cost the kingdom five millions, besides many other mischiefs and inconveniences that happened thereupon. But, not being resolved at this time, the House was resumed.'[91] The third question, which was the most damaging, recalls the Deposition Articles of Edward II, and expresses a similar conviction that they were living under a King who simply could not cope. It is probably this sense which accounts for the prominence of old Privy Councillors in the Lords' opposition to Charles: they, of all people, knew quite how difficult the task of hand-

---

[87] *LJ* iv. 669, 679, 687, 713, v. 212, 214; *CJ* ii. 677, 691, 600.

[88] *HMC Eighth Report*, II. 55.

[89] *Diary of Ralph Josselin*, ed. Alan Macfarlane (Oxford, 1976), 8. I am grateful to Dr J. S. A. Adamson for this reference. Josselin's remarks tend to confirm the claim of Clarendon that Mandeville was of a 'licentious life': Clarendon, *History*, i. 145.

[90] On the religion of the Lords, see J. S. A. Adamson, 'The Peerage in Politics 1645–1649', Ph.D. thesis (Cambridge, 1986), 59–115, esp. on Northumberland.

[91] *LJ* iv. 612–13. For similar sentiments from Essex, see Bedfordshire RO St John MS J 1386.

his attempts to deceive, Charles told the Lords that he would answer on the militia when the Queen was on board.[101] On the 24th, against his better judgement, Charles accepted the Parliamentary scheme for private enterprise finance of the Irish war, by granting confiscated Irish land in return for investment in the war. The Commons had recommended the scheme because it was voluntary, and it was in effect, like Digges's proposal for a West India Company in 1626, a proposal for the privatization of war.[102] In fact, Cromwell's congratulations to Sir John Clotworthy for his care in the scheme showed what interests were behind the proposal: it in effect delivered control of the royal prerogative of mercy, and therefore of an important part of policy, into the hands of what was to become a new plantation interest in Ireland.[103] Charles, again showing the residual honesty which often prevented his concessions from being persuasive, said he was granting it without taking time to examine whether it might retard the reducing of Ireland by exasperating the rebels, and making them desperate of being received into grace if they returned to obedience.[104] It seems plausible to suppose that an Irish policy devised by Clotworthy was designed to have exactly that effect. The next day, 23 February, the wind was at last fair, and the Queen set sail, with Charles galloping along the cliffs to keep her in sight as long as possible. She took with her a considerable part of Charles's jewels,[105] to be sold or pawned to raise a war-chest.

With his wife safely out of harm's way, Charles turned his attention to his son. On the 26th, he was back at Greenwich, and commanded Hertford Governor of the Prince to bring the Prince to meet him there. This order was reported to the Lords on 24 February by Hertford's brother-in-law Essex. Hertford's full brother Seymour said that Hertford intended to go with the Prince himself, and the Lords agreed to let the Prince go provided that Hertford went with him.[106] Hertford appears to have fallen ill, and told his wife that he was unable to go with the Prince. The King insisted that the Prince should come none the less, telling Hertford that 'we cannot imagine that it can be disagreeable to any that our children meet us, especially so near London'.[107] Charles was soon forced to imagine such a thing: on 26 February Gerrard, from the Commons, asked the Lords for a joint deputation to go to Greenwich to ensure that the Prince was sent back to Whitehall 'forthwith'. To this the Lords, remarkably, agreed, and sent Newport and

---

[101] *LJ* iv. 600.
[102] Ibid. 593–5, 607–8. On the 1626 proposal, see Russell, *1621–9*, pp. 293–4, 299–300.
[103] *PJ* i. 395.
[104] *LJ* iv. 608.
[105] Gardiner, *History*, x. 168; PRO SP 16/489/59.
[106] *LJ* iv. 608, 610.
[107] *HMC Bath (Seymour)*, IV. 217.

Seymour to accompany Hyde to Greenwich to bring the Prince back
'this night'.[108] This deputation encountered an extremely angry King,
and Hyde was able to assist in drafting a reply to the Parliament on the
militia: he does not tell us whether he assisted in drafting the answer to
himself about the Prince. The King told Hyde that 'now I have gotten
Charles, I care not what answer I send to them'.[109] His conciliatory
phase was at an end.

In his message on the Prince, Charles professed himself bewildered
by references to 'fears and jealousies' about the Prince's visit to
Greenwich, and said that 'he hopes that these fears and jealousies will
be hereafter continued only with reference to his Majesty's rights and
honour'. On the militia, he replied bluntly that 'he can by no means do
it'. He repeated his offer to accept the people named by the Parliament,
except in the vital case of the City of London whose powers he believed
to be governed by its charter. He did insist that, since 'more shall be
thought fit to be granted to these persons named than by the law is in
the Crown itself', the power should first be granted to him by Act of
Parliament before he delegated it to the men appointed by his Parliament. He insisted that the power could not continue indefinitely, but
must be subject to a time-limit, since 'he cannot consent to divest
himself of the just power which God and the laws of this kingdom have
placed in him, for the defence of his people, and to put it into the hands
of others, for any indefinite time'. He again asked the Parliament to
consider his message of 20 January, vigorously disclaimed any hostile
intent against the whole House on 4 January, and asked for any people
who meddled with the militia without authority to be proceeded against
according to law.[110] This last request was perhaps aimed at a petition
received three days earlier from Cambridgeshire, asking to arm and
execute the militia, to which one of the signatories happened to be
Thomas Symons, Pym's son-in-law.[111] With these words, the King and
Prince set out for York, taking the Elector Palatine with them.

The effect on the Commons was not soothing. Herbert Morley and
Pym moved that the answer be taken for a denial, a motion it is interesting to find they felt the need to make. Another member, illustrating the
sort of pattern of thought which came naturally to Parliamentarians in a
crisis, compared the problem raised by the King's behaviour to that
which would arise 'if the King should be desperate and would lay
violent hands upon himself'. The innuendo, presumably, was that it
would not be resistance to stop the King committing suicide. He also

---

[108] *LJ* iv. 614; *CJ* ii. 459.
[109] Fletcher, p. 230; Clarendon, *Life*, i. 101.
[110] *CJ* ii. 459–60.
[111] *LJ* iv. 612.

Plot, and Digby and Lunsford's attempts to gather force at Kingston. They pointed out the resemblance of one of the Irish rebel manifestos to Henry Percy's petition during the Army Plot,[120] and claimed to have 'manifold advertisements' from foreign parts, 'that still expect that your Majesty has some great design in hand, for the altering of religion, the breaking the neck of your Parliament'. The first three words of this quotation make it stop short of a direct assertion that the King had such a design, but Sir Ralph Hopton certainly saw the innuendo, and vehemently objected to the Declaration on the ground that it charged the King with apostacy. He had read between the lines and 'acknowledged his error proceeding from his mistake'. The acknowledgement was not enough to save Hopton from the Tower,[121] and Pym, once again, had shown how effectively his subliminal technique had enabled him to have his cake and eat it. He had spread the slur that the King was a papist, without being forced to admit to having done so. This Declaration passed the Lords, with fourteen Royalist Lords protesting,[122] and on 9 March was presented to the King at Newmarket.

The King, while deferring a full answer to this 'strange and unexpected Declaration', allowed himself a few brief verbal comments. He again expressed dismay at the neglect of his message of 20 January, expressed surprise that 'any more general rumours and discourses should get credit with you', and expressed his own fears for the 'true' Protestant profession. He asked rhetorically 'Have I violated your laws?', and added 'I do not ask you, what you have done for me'.[123] An additional Declaration from the Commons, which claimed that the 'rebels' in this kingdom would be encouraged by his departure from London, he passed over without comment.[124] The King's formal answer to this Declaration, sent from Huntingdon on 15 March, seems to have been composed by Hyde, whose covering letter to the King is much in the style Hamilton had used to him in 1638. It warns him that there was talk 'of your Majesty's designs of immediate force, of a retreat into Scotland, of the divisions there', and instructs him 'to none of which your servants give the least credit'. His servants, Hyde said, were 'assuring themselves that, however your affairs and conveniences may have invited you to York, you intend to sit as quietly there as if you were at Whitehall'. He

[120] For the resemblance, which is genuine, see Gilbert, ii. 3. For the significance, Charles could with equal justice have replied that the document in question was a parody of the Parliament's Protestation.

[121] *PJ* i. 502–3; *CJ* ii. 467. Hopton, like most other members sent to the Tower, was released after a few days.

[122] *LJ* iv. 631. The list of protesting Lords is closely similar to the list for the Militia Ordinance. It adds Northampton, and omits Bath, Monmouth, and Portland. All these are likely to be changes in attendance.

[123] *CJ* ii. 475.

[124] Ibid. 470. For Fiennes's responsibility for this draft, see *PJ* ii. 5.

warned Charles that 'neither can there be so cunning a way found out to
assist those who wish not well to your Majesty (if any such there be), as
by giving the least hint to your people that you rely upon any thing but
the strength of your laws and their obedience'.[125] Such counsel as this
goes a long way to explain the delay in the outbreak of war, and it was
good counsel in that it was true that the least hint that Charles intended
force would increase the strength of his opponents. Whether Hyde
really had the confidence in the possibility of peace which this dispatch
suggests, or merely intended to prevent Charles from alienating too
much support before the war began, perhaps Hyde himself was not
sure: the dispatch certainly does not tell us.

Hyde's Declaration, which was sensibly short, concentrated on the
assertion 'that his subjects cannot be obliged to obey any Act, order or
injunction, to which his Majesty hath not given his consent'. It called for
obedience to established laws, and enjoined subjects not to obey 'orders
or ordinances, to which his Majesty is no party, concerning the
militia'.[126] In its sensible concentration on the present, rather than
entering into recrimination about the past, the message was very different in tone from Charles's message of 2 March, and provoked the
suspicion in the Lords that it had been written nearer at hand than
Huntingdon. The next day, it was followed by the Proclamation the
King had promised for enforcing the laws against recusants, this time
issued from Stamford.[127]

The suspicion that Hyde's reply had been written at Westminster
arose in part from the directness with which it contradicted the Commons' votes of 15 March, to the effect that in 'an urgent and inevitable
necessity' the Militia Ordinance 'doth oblige the people, and ought to
be obeyed by the fundamental laws of this kingdom'.[128] This, especially
the appeal to 'necessity', was very close to the reasoning with which the
King had justified the Forced Loan. Some opposed this, but 'others'
said that it was warranted by 'the law of God, the law of nature, and of
necessity'. D'Ewes argued that it was legal because it was done 'by the
assent of the whole kingdom in their representative body of the House
of Commons', 'whereas if particular men did this of themselves, they
might be guilty of raising war and tumults within the realm'.[129] The idea
that the whole community could be in rebellion against itself seemed to
many members a strange one, and yet the theory of Parliamentary power
implied in these remarks is one which D'Ewes himself had not held even
a few weeks earlier. There is a strong suspicion here that members were

[125] *Clarendon SP* ii. 138–9.
[126] *CJ* ii. 481.
[127] Larkin, p. 763.
[128] *CJ* ii. 479.
[129] *PJ* ii. 41.

the Militia Ordinance, saying that those who made it 'would make law without us, and impose it upon our people'. He denied, to his knowledge, having any evil counsellors, and, taking responsibility in his old style, said that 'we could wish that our own immediate actions (which we avow) and our own honour might not be so roughly censured under that common stile of evil counsellors'. He reiterated his attachment to the 'true' Protestant profession, reassured the Scots by pleading the Act of Oblivion as an excuse for not answering the charges about the Scottish war, and roundly condemned the Irish Rebellion, 'so odious to all Christians'. He entered into a long denial of the Army Plot, and angrily listed his concessions since the Parliament had assembled, reiterated his fear for himself and his wife and children during the tumults at the end of December, and repeated his calls for the suppression of seditious pamphlets and sermons. He demanded that 'the government of the City of London may recover some life, for our security', and somewhat menacingly appealed to the law, 'which we always intend to be the measure of our own power, and expect it shall be the rule of our subjects' obedience'.[136]

Five days later he was ready with an answer to the Parliament's further Declaration of 19 March. It begins with a reproach to the Houses for not having the patience to wait for his answer to their previous Declaration. On the militia, he complained that if 'we must neither deny the thing you ask, nor give a reason of refusing it, without being taxed of breaking your privileges . . . you will reduce all our answers hereafter into a very little room'. He complained again that the militia was being asked for 'a time utterly unlimited'. He answered the request to name seditious pamphlets by listing three, and saying that listing more 'would be too much excuse for the rest: if you think them not worthy the enquiry, we have done'. On the issue of a Parliamentary guard, he reasserted his right to deny anything 'which, in our understanding (of which God hath surely given us some use) is not fit to be granted'. He admitted the charge that some of his ministers' actions before the Parliament had been against the laws, but added that he had abandoned them 'upon observation of the mischief which then grew by arbitrary power, though made plausible to us by the suggestions of necessity and imminent danger; and take heed you fall not into the same error upon the same suggestions'. It seems Pym's arguments from necessity and imminent danger had reminded him too of his arguments in favour of the Forced Loan. On the Army Plot, he offered what sounded like a categorical denial: 'we defy the Devil to prove that there was any design (with our knowledge or privity), in or about the time of passing those bills, that, had it taken effect, could have deprived our

[136] LJ iv. 667–8.

subject of the fruit of them'. This, though it sounds like a complete denial, was in fact an equivocation: the object of the Army Plot had not been to subvert, for example, the Triennial Bill, but to allow him sufficient power to exercise his undoubtedly legal prerogative of mercy. Sweeping though the statement sounds, what it denies is something different from what he had done. On the Parliament's rejection of his offer of a General Pardon, on the ground that they had done nothing requiring pardon, he said: 'it is a strange world, when princes proffered favours are counted reproaches: yet, if you like not this our offer, we have done'.[137]

This reiterated refrain recalls Wyatt's poem:

> Now cesse, my lute, this is the last
> Labour that thou and I shall wast,
>   And ended is that we begon:
> Now is this song boeth sung and past,
> My lute be still, for I have done.[138]

If this was the poem on which Charles was drawing, the image is accurate: he now felt a sense of rejection too deep to think it worth trying any longer, and was soon attempting to gain control of the arsenal at Hull. He was well aware that 'we have and do patiently suffer those extreme personal wants, as our predecessors have seldom been put to'. All his attempts to discover the terms on which a revenue settlement might be available to him had failed, and the time he could endure without one was rapidly coming to an end.

The House of Lords, when this Declaration was presented to it on 1 April, appears to have reacted to the anger rather than to the hurt. Their immediate reflex was to take out of mothballs an old Declaration the Commons had sent them on 19 February. They had taken no action on it all this time, presumably because they thought it either too extreme or too provocative, but the King seems to have made them angry enough to be ready to pass it. This Declaration's gestation went back to the meeting of the Commons' committee at the Guildhall on New Year's Day, and its resurrection at this stage could only add to the general mood of retrospective recrimination.[139] In it, the Commons recounted the 'efforts made against the very being of Parliaments', but congratulated themselves that 'yet have we so kept ourselves within the bounds of modesty and duty, that we have given no just occasion of your Majesty's absence at this time, nor of any offence or displeasure to the Queen's Majesty'. This was on a level with Charles's denial of the Army Plot.

---

[137] Ibid. 686–7.
[138] *Collected Poems of Sir Thomas Wyatt*, ed. Kenneth Muir (1949), 49–51.
[139] LJ iv. 689–91.

13

The Road to Nottingham

APRIL–AUGUST 1642

When Charles chose York for his refuge, he issued a reminder that he still was, however tenuously, king of three kingdoms. At York, he was better placed than he would have been in London either to withdraw into one of the others, and wait for the new government in London to make enemies, or to attempt to draw directly on the resources of one or both of his other kingdoms to restore his control of England. As he had tried in 1639 to rely on the resources of England and Ireland to recover Scotland, so he might try to rely on the resources of Ireland or Scotland to recover England.

The first such plan to emerge in public was a plan to go to Ireland, of which Charles officially notified Ormond and the Lords Justices at the beginning of April.[1] His objective, so he told the House of Lords, was 'to chastise those wicked and detestable rebels (odious to God and to all good men) thereby to settle the peace of that kingdom and the security of this, that the very name of fears and jealousies may be no more heard of amongst us'. Such a thing was easier said than done. Charles assured the Lords that he 'will never consent (upon whatsoever pretence) to a toleration of the popish recusants in that kingdom',[2] yet in fact the plan made very little sense unless Charles intended to revive the Dillon mission and hoped to make peace with the rebels by offering to tolerate Catholicism. Apart from the rebels, the only considerable force under arms in Ireland was the Scottish army in Ulster, whose loyalties, in case of dispute, were more likely to be to the Parliament than to the King. Henrietta Maria on 5 May believed Charles had been planning 'to join the army of the Catholics'.[3] What Charles might do at the head of a Catholic army was something Pym was well able to guess.

What Henrietta Maria could believe, others could believe also. The Lords Justices and Irish Privy Council on 23 April wrote to 'cast our-selves at your Majesty's feet', and to explain with great care how wicked the rebels really were. They said the rebels intended 'which we tremble to write, and cannot think without horror and astonishment at their

---

[1] PRO SO 3/12, fo. 193ʳ.
[2] *LJ* iv. 709.
[3] *Letters of Queen Henrietta Maria*, p. 66.

impiety) ... to deprive you of your royal crown and dignity, and to put over them some of themselves or some foreign prince, and so altogether to shake off the English government'.[4] This was not an impartial assessment of the rebellion, but it did say plainly that the Irish Council would oppose any negotiations along the lines proposed by Dillon. Lord Grandison, an Irish friend of Hyde's, wrote to him saying Hyde might 'easily imagine' how dissatisfied he was with this proposal 'till I understand from you, how it agrees with the sense you have of what is fitt for him to doe at this time'.[5] Discontent at this plan extended deep into English Royalist circles: the Countess of Lindsey, wife of one of the few truly committed Royalists in the Privy Council, told Lord Montagu the King's plan troubled 'all the good people of the kingdom'.[6]

If the proposal produced this sort of reaction among English Royalists, it may be imagined what sort of reaction it produced in Pym. We are fortunate in possessing Pym's rough draft for a reply to this proposal, which is considerably more extreme than the version ultimately approved by the House.[7] He was clearly unconvinced by Charles's promise not to tolerate popery in Ireland. He said the journey would risk the King's life 'especially *if* your mat. continues your profession to maintayn the Protestant religion in that kingdome'. He said the journey would 'make way to the proseqqution of that crewell and bloody design of the papists every where to root out and destroy the reformed religion', and added that the design would be attempted elsewhere 'if the confederation of the strength and union of the two nations of England and Scotland did not much hinder the discovery and proseqqution of any such design'. He announced that if the King went to Ireland they would not be bound to submit to any governors the King might choose for his absence, but 'according to the right devolved to us', would choose 'guardians' to govern the kingdom 'by the counsell and advice of Parliament'.[8] Most of this was not allowed by the Commons, but what they allowed was fierce enough. For Pym himself, this may be the moment at which the last vestiges of his allegiance to Charles disappeared.

It is hard to know how seriously Charles ever contemplated going to Ireland. Henrietta Maria certainly imagined he might go, but she seems to have taken more seriously an alternative plan that he should go to

---

[4] *HMC Ormond*, NS II. 116–17.

[5] Bodl. MS Clarendon, vol. 21, no. 1588.

[6] *HMC Buccleuch*, I. 297. The Earl of Newcastle was another.

[7] Bodl. MS Nalson XII, fos. 80–2. This text is a much-corrected Pym holograph. For the final text, from which most of the material here quoted has been omitted, see *CJ* ii. 527–8: italics mine. Pym has crossed out the 'if'.

[8] The use of the word 'devolved' prompts the question whether Pym knew the work of Christopher Goodman. For Pym's attempt to mollify his critics, see *PJ* ii. 169–71. This is one of the early examples of the use of 'Parliament' without an article.

expecting the English to adopt the Scottish form.[20] However, if the English wanted Scottish help, they would have to make at least a gesture of co-operation with these ambitions.

The English Parliament did not let its case go by default. They approved a small Declaration to go before the Scottish Council at its meeting in April, in which they said they would imitate the wisdom of the Parliament of Scotland, 'by giving a timely and right understanding of their proceedings unto the kingdom of England', and hoped that such testimonies of mutual affection 'may be reciprocal'.[21] So plain an attempt to cash political credit was unlikely to be sufficient by itself, and on 4 April Francis Rous moved 'that some divines might be appointed to prepare a way to settle the church in doctrine and discipline'.[22] This, in effect, was the Scottish proposal of the previous year for a General Assembly, and the germ of what was to become the Westminster Assembly. As in the previous year, the subject was fraught with difficulties for the Parliamentary leaders, for every concession they made to the Scots, while it might rally their friends, also served to increase the number and determination of their enemies. The proposal produced a not very specific declaration, reported from committee by Crew, saying they intended a due and necessary reformation of the government and liturgy of the church, but intended to take away nothing but what was 'justly offensive, or at least, unnecesary and burthensome'.[23] When Crew presented it to the Lords on 8 April, he combined it with a request for them to pass the bill confirming the 8 September order against innovations.[24] At the same time, the Commons completed the bill for scandalous ministers, and sent it up to the Lords.[25] On 12 April Sir Robert Cooke, another well-established pro-Scot, moved to name a day for naming divines for an assembly. The naming in fact started on 20 April. There is no proof that the timing of the revival of this proposal is connected with the competition for Scottish support, but the coincidence of dates is suggestive. The same suggestion occurred to Charles I himself, and on 12 April he wrote to Johnston of Wariston to warn him that good correspondency between the kingdoms would not be achieved by 'laying an aspersion on our actions, though clouded under the name of evill counsellors'. He was insisting that he remained the principle of unity between the kingdoms, and warning Johnston of

[20] Baillie, ii. 2.
[21] CJ ii. 520; Tollemache MS 3750, fos. 9–10 is a copy of this Declaration in Secretary Lanerick's letter-book.
[22] PJ ii. 126.
[23] CJ ii. 510–11, 515. The proposal included an early hint of what became the Westminster Assembly.
[24] LJ iv. 706.
[25] CJ ii. 516.

Wariston of possible retaliation if he continued to try to unite the two kingdoms against their king.[26]

On 21 April the Scottish Council had the opportunity to consider the cases put before them by King and Parliament, the English Parliament's Declaration having been offered to them by Johnston of Wariston, and referred to a committee consisting of Loudoun, Argyll, Morton, Lauderdale, and Southesk.[27] What the Council approved on the 21st seems to have been essentially their draft. It is the sort of antiphonal performance which results from the search for consensus in a deeply divided committee, on the one hand urging the Parliament to seek a right understanding with the King, and on the other, urging the King to return to his Parliament. Like other draws, it called for a replay.

This Declaration was read in the Commons on 9 May, and was immediately preceded by the first and second readings of the bill for the Westminster Assembly, moved by Sir Peter Wentworth.[28] On Pym's motion, the Commons decided to prepare an answer, which was completed on 18 May.[29] At the same time, Pym and Venn occupied themselves with finding £500 for the rent of the Scottish commissioners' house.[30] The Declaration, when finished, was, for Pym, a remarkably soothing document, proclaiming their determination 'to work in his Majesty a right understanding of their loyal intentions'. It was a phrase which must have stirred memories in old Covenanters. More significantly, it was accompanied by the bill for the Westminster Assembly, now described as a bill for calling an assembly 'to settle the doctrine of our church'.[31] The Lords, though still resisting the bill to confirm the 8 September order, had at last passed the bill against pluralities, so the Scots' English friends had something solid to offer them, however small.

Meanwhile, the King was equally busy. To the profound grief of Baillie, he was relying on Baillie's patron Lord Montgomery as one of his Scottish organizers, and appears to have had hopes of winning round General Leslie.[32] Baillie, in an almost Hildebrandine letter of rebuke to Montgomery, seems to have had no doubt that his purpose was to secure Scottish intervention on the King's side: 'to draw our counsell, and so our nation, upon the Parliament of England', and to 'make fire and sword to rage in all the isle'. Baillie also accused him of joining with

[26] *PJ* ii. 159; *CJ* iv. 535; Tollemache MS 3750, fos. 7–9.

[27] *RPCS* vii. 241–51. Argyll's account of the meeting is in Hamilton MSS 1757.

[28] *CJ* ii. 564–5; *PJ* ii. 296. Johnston of Wariston, who was one of the main agents of communication, appears to have chosen Samuel Vassall as his contact in the Commons: *PJ* ii. 294.

[29] *PJ* ii. 312; *CJ* ii. 578–9.

[30] *PJ* ii. 339.

[31] *LJ* v. 74, 72.

[32] NLS MS 81, fo. 24 (Roxburgh to Morton, York, 4 May). I am grateful to Dr Peter Donald for this reference.

Montrose and Morton.[33] On 25 May the Scottish Privy Council was asked to consider a long letter from the King, hoping that 'you may be the more able so to expresse your affection to our service as that you will not be willing to sie us suffer in our honour or auctoritie'. With this request, he asked their opinion on a series of events ranging from the tumults of December to Hotham's recent refusal to surrender Hull.[34] These were leading questions, and they were supported by a petition 'spontaneously' presented by Lord Montgomery and a group of Bander Lords. On the other side, Johnston of Wariston presented the Declaration of the English Parliament. He too was capable of producing 'spontaneous' support, which Lanerick found 'riding up the staires to the councell chamber' to present another petition. This was probably the pro-Parliamentary petition ultimately presented by Haddington and Elcho on 31 May.[35] Lanerick also warned his brother that there was a plan to combine these proceedings with pardoning the incendiaries. Between one courtier and another, his message to his brother that these were 'such things as I am most confident his matie never thought upon nor intendit' is both a plain condemnation, and a complaint of being kept in the dark. It is very like Vane's reaction to the Army Plot, or Hyde's to the attempt on the Five Members. On 2 June the Council, duly encouraged by Argyll, returned a polished answer answerless, and Charles's attempt to secure Scottish support collapsed.[36] The relief of the English Parliament was palpable. On 7 June Hampden wrote to Hotham at Hull: 'you cannot but heare how resolutely ye kingdome of Scotland hath carried themselves at Edenburgh'.[37] D'Ewes, less discreetly, said in the House that 'the Scots have so declared themselves in their last petition to the Privy Council there as we may rest assured of them'. He therefore claimed confidently that 'the greatest strength is held by us'.[38] From this point on, it was the King, not the Parliament, who had to hope for Scots neutrality.

Charles had learnt by the beginning of June that he would have to rely on English force to reduce the English Parliament. He had, in effect, already lost two of his three kingdoms, and the fact must have made him the more determined to hang onto what authority he had left in the third. When Charles arrived at York, Henrietta Maria and Hyde had two contradictory ideas of what he intended to do there. For Henrietta

[33] Baillie, ii. 35–6. For a recent dispute between Baillie and Montgomery which may have contributed to Montgomery's impatience with godliness, see ibid. 6–7.

[34] RPCS vii. 256–7; Gardiner, History, x. 203; Stevenson, pp. 248–9.

[35] Hamilton MS 1653; RPCS vii. 260–3. Lanerick on 28 May told Hamilton he hoped to be able to defer the presenting of this petition for a few days.

[36] RPCS vii. 264–5.

[37] Hull University Library, Hotham MSS DD/HO/1/4.

[38] BL Harl. MS 163, fo. 153b.

Maria, it was too late to talk of accommodation, and she told Charles that if he returned to London, she would retire into a convent, for 'I can never trust myself to those persons who would be your directors, nor to you, since you would have broken your promise to me'.[39] She was perhaps remembering the fate of Strafford. She was waiting impatiently for news that Charles had seized the arsenal at Hull, and much annoyed to hear that 'everyone dissuades you concerning Hull from taking it by force, unless the Parliament begins—is it not beginning to put persons into it against your orders?'[40] As a strategic assessment, Henrietta Maria's was perhaps sounder than that of her Royalist rivals. There was no reason to believe that Charles's opponents at Westminster would consent to any settlement which allowed him any share in power, and, unless he wished to become a sort of Japanese emperor, Charles had no option but to fight or abdicate. It was Hyde, assuring Charles that 'your greatest strength is in the hearts and affections of those persons who have been the severest assertors of the public liberties', who was indulging in wishful thinking.[41] At least so far as Pym, Strode, and Holles were concerned, this was no longer the case. However, though Henrietta Maria's strategic assessment was correct, Hyde's tactical assessment was much more accurate than hers. Henrietta Maria wanted Charles to resort to arms almost immediately, while Hyde wanted him to go to York and 'sit as quietly there as if you were at Whitehall'.

To Henrietta Maria, who correctly saw rebellion, it was hard to understand that many level-headed Englishmen did not. She did not appreciate that many people, such as Bath and Seymour, without whose support Charles had little chance of so much as beginning a civil war, did not yet see a sufficient *casus belli*. It was not until such people came to share Charles's view of the Parliament as already committed to rebellion that he would be able to fight. Nor did Henrietta Maria understand the depth of English distaste for civil war or *coup d'état*, or the extent to which the crucial middle-ground support which would determine victory was likely to go to the side seen as less responsible for starting war.

It is also possible that Charles had not told Henrietta Maria quite how weak his position at York was during his early weeks there. At first, he was attended by only 39 gentlemen and 17 guards, and when he arrived, the Recorder's address of welcome urged him to 'hearken unto and condescend unto' his Parliament.[42] Even early in May, when he was rather better attended, the nobility at York advised him firmly against

[39] *Letters of Queen Henrietta Maria*, pp. 55–6.
[40] Ibid. 60.
[41] *Clarendon SP* ii. 138–9.
[42] Fletcher, p. 231.

war.[43] If Charles had started a civil war in May, he would probably have been captured without a battle.

The King's weakness in the early weeks at York was financial and administrative as well as political. His ordinary revenue had been reduced by Parliamentary action to £277,000, and since a large amount of this was tied up in standing commitments, he had barely enough money to run a household.[44] When the King arrived at York, he attempted to restore a normal atmosphere by summoning his musicians of the wind instruments, but they replied that their salaries were two years in arrears, and they could not afford to go.[45] His Ordnance Office was in London, and even if he could get material out of it by the device of issuing it to the navy, as he hoped,[46] there was very little there, because most of it had been issued to Ireland by the Parliament's command. Frequent requests to the Parliament to take care that the stock was replenished had been politely ignored.[47]

The records tell the story of a transfer of power already largely accomplished: the *Lords' Journals* and the *Commons' Journals* become bulky archives filled with routine business such as the granting of passports, which had previously gone to the Privy Council. On one occasion, D'Ewes was even given the chance to exercise his procedural ingenuity in working out the protocol for the Commons to receive an ambassador from Hamburg.[48] By contrast, the royal archives are those of a government in exile. The Acts of the Privy Council cease on the King's departure from London, and do not resume until after the beginning of the Civil War. The record of dockets for the Great Seal stops suddenly in the middle of a sentence.[49] The Signet Office docket book records the grant of a passport to a resident of the 'county of Esquire'. It is only because the recipient of this unusual passport took the precaution of getting another from the Commons that we know that the correct county was Essex.[50] Henry Wilmot the Army Plotter, looking back on this period from the rather brighter days of June, said the King 'very lately appeared almost abandoned by all his subjects'.[51] In this situation, there would be no civil war. The King did not start one

[43] PRO 31/3/73, fo. 54A[v].

[44] See Russell, 'Charles I's Financial Estimates for 1642', *BIHR* 58/137 (1985), 109–20.

[45] PRO SP 16/489/107.

[46] Ibid. 16/491/25. Charles clearly did not foresee Parliamentary success in gaining control of the navy. PRO E 403/2814, *passim* suggests that he spent considerable sums on munitions for the Navy, most of which must have fallen into Parliamentary hands.

[47] See PRO SP 16/489/44 (18 Feb. 1642) for an early inventory of munitions issued to Ireland and munitions remaining in store. The position had worsened substantially since that date. For the King's concern, see *LJ* iv. 518, and many other refs.

[48] BL Harl. MS 164, fo. 260[b].

[49] PRO C. 233/5 (IND 4225), unfol.

[50] PRO SO 3/12, fo. 207; *CJ* ii. 517.

[51] *LJ* v. 169.

because he could not, and the Parliament did not because it was still hoping for a walkover. On 18 May, as this hope was ceasing to be realistic, Pym wrote to Sir John Hotham at Hull, saying that 'we understand the proceedings in Yorkshire, and though there be some disaffected, yet there appears so great party of the county to be well disposed to the peace of the kingdom, that it is hoped they will so over-awe the other party as to keep them quiet'.[52] A month earlier, this would have been an entirely realistic hope. The Parliamentarians, because they were the more homogeneous group, and, in their godly capacity, had been in contact with each other for a very long time, were more quickly forged together into a party than the Royalists were. The King's first active supporters were a motley collection: friends of Ben Jonson such as Sir Francis Wortley, Arminians such as Richard Spencer, church papists such as Sir Thomas Danby, believers in the rule of law such as Sir Roger Twysden, churchmen such as Sir Ralph Hopton, Strafford clients such as Sir William Pennyman, and crusty country gentlemen such as Sir John Stawell were not easily welded together into a homogeneous group.

It is also possible that the King's sheer weakness discouraged supporters from rallying to him: a penniless King enjoys few of the advantages of majesty. Sir John Meldrum, a Scot who had been one of the monopolists complained of in 1621, rallied to hold Hull against the King, telling him that in thirty-six years' service to James and Charles, 'all your Majesty's favours have produced no other effects to me' than a debt of £2,000.[53] He was telling Charles, in effect, that he was not worth serving. Lord Feilding, son of the Duke of Buckingham's sister and one of Charles's most determined opponents in the House of Lords, felt equally strongly about the unpaid debts of his Venice embassy. For him, his visit to Geneva in 1631 and his concern about the money owed to him perhaps blended together into a single whole.[54] The Earl of Leicester, an absentee Lord-Lieutenant of Ireland when his presence was desperately needed, was attempting to claim the unpaid expenses from his Paris embassy before he went.[55] Wat Montague, shortly after the war had begun, told Mazarin that it had begun by the belief of the factious in Parliament in the King's weakness. He said they hoped to make the

---

[52] CJ ii. 577; LJ v. 72.

[53] Rushworth, Collections, iii. i. 628. It should not be suggested that this was Meldrum's sole concern. He expressed a deep hostility to the Bishops' Wars, which, as a Scot, he probably felt. On Meldrum's lighthouse patent, complained of in 1621, see Russell (ed.), Origins, pp. 15–16.

[54] LJ iv. 724; Warwicks. RO Feilding of Newnham Paddox MSS C 1/9. I am grateful to Dr Ann Hughes and Dr J. S. A. Adamson for several useful discussions of Feilding. The closeness of his relationship with his brother-in-law Hamilton probably helps to explain the depth of his distrust of the King after the Incident. See also J. Godwin, 'Steps of Descent', BIHR 60/141 (1987), 109–15. Mr Godwin and I have reached very similar conclusions by very different routes.

[55] LJ iv. 679.

King submit by necessity. Yet Montague did not think this a sufficient analysis: he said that the King had so lost the confidence of the people that all he refused the Parliament passed for crime.[56]

This loss of confidence goes too deep to be explained entirely by the King's weakness or by his recent actions. Its roots undoubtedly go back at least as far as the Bishops' Wars. The initial refusal of Bath, for example, to obey a summons to York in his capacity as a Privy Councillor cannot easily be explained in these terms. Bath in the end went to York, but left again in early June, telling his wife that he could do the King no service, and himself no good.[57] This letter seems to mark Bath as one of the large group of peers who went to York, not to help the King to start a civil war, but in the hope of persuading him to stop one. The Earl of Dorset, as late as August 1642, thought we lived under 'an arbitrary government even on both sides'.[58] Probably many of the King's natural supporters reacted to the fear invoked by the Commons of the King 'intending to return an absolute conqueror'.[59] This may account for the hope of Lord Savill, some months after the war had started, that neither side would win it.[60] It must also be suspected that the extreme reluctance of many of Charles's supporters to rally to him had something to do with their sense of his past errors. It is not to be imagined that Bristol, for example, had forgotten that he had warned Charles in 1640 that persistence in the Bishops' Wars would lead to precisely this sort of consequences. It may be in part the frustration of those who had warned Charles that he was heading in this direction while there was still time to draw back which explains the remarkable lack of support for the King among those who had been Privy Councillors in 1640: the King's new party, when it came, came from the country and not from the court.

One of the earliest signs of the sort of partisan Royalism the King would need to sustain a war was the Kentish Petition of March 1642. This petition was produced by the Grand Jury, though the Commons were later told that 9 out of 19 of the Grand Jury had opposed it. One of the moving spirits was Sir Edward Dering, now expelled from the Commons and free to devote himself to county affairs. He was working with Sir George Strode, Sir Roger Twysden, and Richard Spencer the Arminian. The most passionate passage in the Kentish Petition is its defence of the liturgy,

---

[56] PRO 31/3/73, fo. 91ʳ.

[57] *LJ* iv. 709; KAO Sackville MSS C 267/13.

[58] *HMC Salis.* xxii. 318. This letter is dated 1640 in the Calendar, but on internal evidence clearly dates from 1642. The last figure of the date on the original is totally obscured by a blot.

[59] *CJ* ii. 732.

[60] *CSPD 1641–3*, pp. 411–12, 445–6. See also Fletcher, p. 279.

celebrious by the piety of the holy bishops and martyrs who composed it, established by the supreme law of this land, attested and approved by the best of all foreign divines, confirmed with subscription of all the ministers of this land, a clergy as learned and able as any in the Christian world, enjoyed and with holy love embraced, by the most and best of all the laity, that this holy exercise of our religion may, by your authority, be enjoyed, quiet and free from interruptions, scorns, prophanations, threats and force of such men, who daily do deprave it, and neglect the use of it in divers churches, in despight of the laws established.

The framers agreed to leave out the phrase in their original draft that it was 'penned by the inspiration of the Holy Ghost', but their statement was strong enough without it. At the same time, they asked for the laws against papists to be put in execution, and for all children of papists to be brought up as Protestants. They wanted, as Dering had often argued, to refer religious differences to a synod, but specified that it should be of 'most grave, pious, learned and judicious divines, the proper agents'. In other words, it should be more like a Convocation than a Westminster Assembly. They asked to preserve episcopal government, 'as ancient in this island as Christianity itself, deduced and dispersed throughout the Christian world, even from the apostolical times', and wanted a severe law against laymen 'daring to arrogate to themselves and to exercise the holy function of the ministry'. They wanted a law for the militia which left as little to discretion as possible, and that no order of either or both Houses should be enforced if not grounded on the law of the land, and so that 'the precious liberties of the subject (the common birthright of every Englishman)' might be preserved. Finally, it was they, rather than Parliamentarian petitioners, who asked for legislation to help the cloth industry. In this combination of devotion to a 'traditional' church and to the rule of law, the Kentish Petition was the essence of what was to become the Royalist cause.[61]

The reading of this petition when nearly two thousand people were present[62] must have generated a good deal of debate. It is possible that the new freedom of debate led many people to learn that they had for a long time been more deeply in disagreement than they had ever discovered. Henry Oxinden of Deane said that 'I have heard foul languig and disperat quarrellings even between old and intire friends'.[63] The continual circulation of printed pamphlets, often in print runs of 9,000 at a time,[64] must have done much to increase such debate, and continual commands to sheriffs and clergy to read these Declarations, and not to

[61] *LJ* iv. 677–8; *CJ* ii. 502–3; *PJ* ii. 102, 106–7.
[62] *CJ* ii. 507.
[63] *Oxinden Letters 1607–1642*, ed. Dorothy Gardiner (1933), 272. This letter dates from Jan., and one imagines the point was even truer in Apr. or May.
[64] MP, 28 July 1642 (Parliamentary printing bill), and other refs.

read those of the other side, generated many more debates.[65] The forging of two parties out of these debates, and out of the contradictory Declarations and commands which gave rise to them, was a slow process, and the Civil War could not take place until it was well advanced.

The difficulty Charles and Pym experienced in fully involving the public in their quarrel was partly because the issue over which they had reached the point of no return was one too personal to be easily communicated: it was sheer physical fear. For Charles, the tumults at Whitehall were an essential part of his *casus belli*: he was not prepared to take the risk of returning to London until he received justice against those responsible, and recovered military control of his capital. One of the points for which Charles pressed most persistently through these months was the adjournment of the Parliament to a place outside London.[66] For Pym and his allies, that in its turn was an unsafe proposal: they did not dare sit in any place where Charles controlled military force, just as Charles did not dare sit in any place where he did not.[67] This issue was one on which compromise was impossible, and it was the price both sides had paid for two years of dedicated diplomacy by threat. To many in the country, who disagreed about similar issues, but had been living in peace together for years and were willing to continue to do so, the fears generated in the crucible of Westminster were very hard to understand. Yet, however strongly the country might deplore these fears, it could not make them go away. Until they went away, no stable government could be restored, and unless a stable government were restored, civil war and *coup d'état* were the only alternatives left. It is this agreed determination to communicate an atmosphere of panic which creates the rather eerie impression of alliance between Charles and Pym during the summer of 1642: the one cause in which they had a genuine common interest was that of convincing the public that they could not live with each other. However much the public might disagree with them, it could not make its disagreement effective: short of choosing another King and another Parliament, the public had nowhere else to go.

At the beginning of April Pym as well as Charles was having trouble with reluctant followers, and so long as Charles did nothing, this trouble seemed likely to increase: as always, inaction was serving Charles's cause better than any action he could undertake. Pym's attempts to answer the King's last Declaration hung fire all through April. Pym had a draft,

[65] See BL Harl. MS 163, fo. 152ᵃ for Harley's comparison of the pressure of the King's demands for the reading of his declarations to demands that the clergy read the Book of Sports during the 1630s.
[66] *LJ* v. 13–14, 162, and other refs.
[67] G. Bankes, *Corfe Castle* (1853), 138–9, and many other refs.

which D'Ewes described as 'full of asperity and fieriness etc',[68] but this draft was continually recommitted until it eventually secured approval as the Parliamentary Declaration of 19 May. On at least one occasion, Pym's closest allies decided his draft needed toning down: the House decided to delete a phrase accusing the King of laying a 'scandal' on the Parliament. The deletion was carried by 116 to 53, with Holles and Stapleton telling for the majority, and Marten and Glyn for the minority.[69] On two occasions, members got into trouble for remarks that went too far. Sir Peter Wentworth on 1 April said 'we could not confide in the King, nor trust him', to the indignation of Sir John Culpepper, still in his place in the House. The House called on Wentworth to 'explain himself', but, to D'Ewes's evident dismay, otherwise 'passed by his folly'. The next day 'Mr. Nathaniel Fiennes did most ignorantly and untruly affirm that the king had no negative voice in passing those acts of Parliament which both Houses had agreed unto but was to assent to them'.[70] For Charles, this would have been a propaganda gift, since it justified exactly what he had been saying since January. Unfortunately, D'Ewes reports his own indignation so fully that it is hard to discover the reaction of the rest of the House. Fiennes was one of the members with closest Scottish links, and may have been taking a leaf out of the Scottish book of 1639. The reaction in the House does not, in the first instance, seem to have been coming from Royalist members: with Dering expelled, Hopton and Palmer discouraged by their spells in the Tower, and Hyde, Holborne, and Sir John Strangeways rarely present, the Royalist members were thin on the ground. Falkland, Culpepper, and Waller still made contributions to debate, and Sir Edward Alford (son of a 1620s veteran) and Sir Thomas Bowyer were beginning to emerge as Royalist members of stature. Yet in the main, the Royalist members could manage only a rather unco-ordinated guerrilla rearguard action. The resistance was coming from peaceable Parliamentarians like Sir John Northcote, Harbottle Grimston, Sir Hugh Cholmeley, and Framlingham Gawdy. Unfortunately, D'Ewes was so committed to the emerging peace party that its activities are almost totally obscured in lengthy reports of his speeches.

Only the threat of armed action by the King could win back for Pym the firm support of the Parliamentary peace party. Pym desperately needed some dramatic action from the King, to prove that the threat he saw was not imaginary. He did not have to wait very long. Charles's initial moves were cautious, and did not create intense alarm. He tried

[68] *PJ* ii. 148. A large part of what is probably the draft complained of survives in Yale University, Beinecke Library, Osborn Collection, Pym File. It is in Pym's hand throughout, and closely resembles the text finally approved on 19 May.
[69] *CJ* ii. 508.
[70] *PJ* ii. 115, 119.

to put Sir John Penington in command of the fleet. The Lords took the lead in preventing this, backing the Earl of Warwick, who was appointed by Northumberland as Lord Admiral. However, the determination to keep armed force out of Charles's hands was not matched by any equivalent alarm at the person of Penington. Penington was capable of mocking his cousin the Alderman for his 'Puritanism', but found this no obstacle to sending his children to keep 'Christ-tide' with the Alderman.[71] He is a good example of the sort of social tolerance which had prevented the country away from Westminster from sharing in war fever, and this may be one reason why he never seems to have been regarded as a dangerous 'cavalier'.

At the same time, Warwick and Northumberland did not appear to most of the gentry as dangerous men committed to the subversion of church and state: the Lords' decision to send Warwick to sea provoked a protest from thirteen Lords,[72] but it does not seem to have done what Charles most needed, and convinced his wavering supporters that the men at Westminster were in rebellion. It is a measure which seems to have attracted the support of those who wished to keep armed force out of the King's hands simply in order to prevent a civil war. Charles had to devise measures which made his opponents appear in the guise of rebels. His first move was a shrewd one: he summoned four of his household officers to York. This was a move any gentleman could understand, and the stated purpose of the summons, for keeping St George's Feast, did not look like the beginning of a civil war. He summoned Essex Lord Chamberlain, Holland Groom of the Stool, Savill Treasurer of the Household, and Salisbury Captain of the Gentleman Pensioners. Essex and Holland had already refused a command to accompany the King when he left London in January, and the King therefore told them that if they refused again, he would request their resignations. He also summoned Seymour, Saye, and Bath as Privy Councillors. Of these seven only Seymour left for York, and he obeyed the order of the Lords to return when he had got as far as Northampton.[73] Essex and Holland accordingly resigned their places. The Lords resolved that in obeying the command of the House to stay at Westminster, they 'had done nothing but what they ought to have done', and that their staying at Westminster 'is no disobedience to the King's commands', an exercise in Parliamentary newspeak which made the Houses appear in what Charles believed to be their true colours.[74] They then invited the Commons to express their resentment 'that per-

---

[71] PRO SP 16/485/104 and 91.
[72] *LJ* iv. 697.
[73] Ibid. 697.
[74] Ibid. 713.

sons of their merit have suffered for their good affections to the public'.
The Earl of Dover, who thought the Lords' privileges were no concern
of the Commons, protested.[75] On the prompting of the Commons, they
further resolved that anyone who accepted the offices vacated by Essex
and Holland 'shall be accounted to do an ignoble act, and to offer an
affront to the Parliament, and thereby render himself incapable of any
place of honour or trust in the commonwealth'. In effect, they were
declaring the jobs black. The declaration was effective, and the offices
remained vacant.

The King's next move was hastened by the action of the Houses. The
Commons asked the Lords to agree to the removal of the magazine at
Hull, and the Lords, choosing to behave correctly, insisted on asking
the King's leave.[76] The King, of course, refused:

we rather expected (and have done so long) that you should have given us an
account why a garrison hath been placed in our town of Hull without our
consent, and soldiers billeted there against law, and express words of the
Petition of Right, than to be moved, (for the avoiding of a needless charge you
have put on yourselves) to give our consent for removal of our magazine and
munition (our own proper goods) upon such general reasons as indeed give no
satisfaction to our judgement.

He again reminded them of the need to replace the supply of munitions
carried out of the kingdom to Ireland, and finally reverted to the need
for a revenue settlement: 'will there never be a time to offer to, as well as
to ask of, us? We will propose no more particulars to you, having no
luck to please or be understood by you'.[77]

Thus prompted, the King took the advice Henrietta Maria had been
giving him for a long time, and decided to go to Hull in person: if he did
not do so at once, the arms would be gone when he got there. He
collected a party of 300 horse, and, accompanied by the Earl of Newport, Master of the Ordnance, and the inevitable Elector Palatine, rode
over to Hull. He sent Newport and the Elector as an advance party, and
sent a letter notifying Hotham that he was coming.[78] The King's tactical
objectives here need thought. If he had arrived unannounced, it is
highly likely that he would have succeeded in riding in before any
decision could be taken on whether to shut the gate in his face. Had he
wished to overpower the garrison, he would not have gone with a force
probably much smaller than Hotham's. The objective, it seems, was

[75] Ibid. 714, 719; Bodl. MS Clarendon, vol. 21, no. 1603.
[76] LJ iv. 708–9. For an inventory of the arms still in Hull, see PRO SP 16/490/77.
[77] LJ iv. 722–3.
[78] CUL Add. MS 7582 (Hotham to Lenthall, 29 Apr.), repeating an earlier letter which Hotham
believed to have been intercepted. I am grateful to Dr J. S. A. Adamson for this reference. For the
King's account, see LJ v. 16–17. For the unofficial eyewitness account given to the Commons, see
PJ ii. 223.

symbolic: to discover whether Hotham was actually in rebellion, and if so, whether the Parliament would support him in it. If Hotham let him in, this would be a very significant retreat from confrontation, and if he did not, Charles might hope that people would understand rebellion well enough to cease plaguing him with petitions for compromise. The King's visit to Hull, like his visit to the House of Commons on 4 January, was not an act of war, but a propaganda exercise.

Hotham's orders were to let no forces into Hull except by the authority of the King, signified by both Houses of Parliament. Sir Edward Alford and one of the Godolphin brothers tried to point out in the Commons that this was short of a specific authorization to shut out the King, but it was clearly the intention of the Houses that he should do so. Hotham had to make a snap decision while the King stood in the rain outside the wall, and decided to shut the King out. He told Speaker Lenthall that this decision ran some risk of being 'misconceived' by the King, and asked anxiously for a 'quick resolution' of whether he had performed his trust. The King asked Hotham whether he had a specific order to justify his claim that he could not let the King in without a breach of his trust to the Parliament, because otherwise 'his Majesty could not believe it'. The King invited the Houses to 'free themselves of this imputation' by assisting in bringing Hotham to justice. The Lords 'took this message of His Majesty's in a serious debate', and speedily resolved that Hotham had acted in obedience to the Houses' command, that the King's declaring him a traitor 'is a high breach of the privilege of Parliament', and that declaring him a traitor without due process of law was against the liberty of the subject and the law of the land.[79] The last vote confused charge and conviction, and in the second, breach of privilege seemed to be coming to have the sort of omnibus function prerogative had once had for the King. The Commons agreed to these votes, diverted only by Strode's attempt to add an explicit vote that Hotham should not admit the King in person, which Holles prudently 'modified'.

For the next month after the King's attempt to enter Hull, the paper war was at its peak. Two sequences of Declarations, one dealing with Hull and the other with the militia, were exchanged in a rapid succession. The second round of the paper war was very different from the first. During the first round, while the King was on his way to York, the parties were still, in a rudimentary way, addressing each other: they were still trying to communicate a sense of hurt they were amazed the other party could not understand. In the second round of the paper war, there are still occasional traces of this feeling, but in the main, the

<hr />

[79] *LJ* v. 17; *PJ* ii. 224–5. For Charles's message to Hotham the night before, warning him of his arrival, see *LJ* v. 16.

parties were openly appealing to the country for support. Both sides were appealing to sheriffs and clergy to publish their Declarations, and not to publish the other side's. It is hardly surprising that 'innovating clergy' published the King's Declarations, while godly clergy published the Parliament's.[80] The second round, unlike the first, was a frank call to arms, and a call to which people tended to react in the light of their previous religious convictions.

For the King, the case of Hull proved that 'actual war is leavied upon us'.[81] He hoped that at last it might be clear to his subjects that he was facing a rebellion, and needed help to suppress it. Unfortunately for him, however, this was not the only way the case of Hull could be read. To the Houses at Westminster, the only intelligible reason why the King might want to go to Hull was to secure arms to start a civil war, and the only way to keep the peace appeared to be to deprive the King of the power to break it. They asked the country to consider 'how desperate and ill-affected divers persons attending upon his Majesty have shewed themselves to the Parliament, and to his other good subjects'. If the King should raise forces, they called on the sherriff of Yorkshire to 'raise the power of the county, to suppress the same, and to keep his Majesty's peace, according to law'. The King was being accused of breach of the King's peace.[82]

The King and his propagandists of course attempted to laugh such doctrine out of court. The fact that, for a large part of middle opinion, they did not succeed in doing so tells us a large amount, both about the nature of authority in seventeenth-century England, and about the intellectual traditions on which the King's opponents were able to draw. The doctrine on which the King's opponents drew most heavily was the doctrine of the King's Two Bodies, a doctrine most economically expressed by the fact that it was treason against the King to kill one of his judges sitting on the Bench. The statement that allegiance was owed to the King did not only mean that it was owed to a natural person: it also meant that it was owed to a body of public authority established by law. When a judge in one of the King's courts gave a judgement, it was the King's judgement, and fortified with royal authority, even if the King in his private person happened to disagree violently with it. When a constable trying to apprehend a felon banged on a door and cried 'open, in the King's name', he was endowed, for his brief moment upon the

[80] Bodl. MS Nalson ii, fos. 72 (committee in Rutland to Lenthall, 14 July) and 79 (Sir William Brereton to Oliver Cromwell, 27 July). For the anger of the Commons at the sheriff of Northamptonshire, who said 'the King must be obeyed, for all the Parliament', see *CJ* ii. 480; *PJ* ii. 45–6, 47, 99. The fact that this case came from Northamptonshire is a reminder that there was no such thing as a 'safe' county for either side.

[81] Rushworth, *Collections*, iii. i. 574.

[82] *LJ* v. 70.

stage, with royal authority, even if the King in person had never heard of him or of the felon he was apprehending. As Shakespeare's Lord Chief Justice had it, 'I then did use the person of your father: the image of his power lay then in me'.[83] It was a familiar idea, and conceded by the King himself, that 'our authority may be where our person is not'. For great officers such as the Lord Keeper or the Lord Admiral, both of them still at Westminster, it was an idea by which they lived their daily lives. It was equally familiar to every gentleman in the habit of attending quarter sessions, and even to any local villager compelled to take his turn on the watch. For them, the King was often a face on their coins, and a name in which they apprehended malefactors: in fact, he was the symbol by which their power in their own communities was validated. The doctrine of the King's Two Bodies was ideally designed to appeal to the prejudices of a country in which authority had become quite exceptionally decentralized. As the King put it, 'these persons have gone about subtilly to distinguish betwixt our person and our authority, as if, because our authority may be where our person is not, that therefore our person may be where our authority is not'.[84]

Yet even that was a proposition the law was prepared, on occasion, to grant. Oliver St John, in the Ship Money trial, correctly argued that if the King commanded a traitor to be put to death without trial or indictment, an action would lie against the executioner.[85] The King could not say 'off with his head': he had to proceed through the proper channels, which were his courts. The precedents, which were valid ones, had been rehearsed by Wilde in March, in the impeachment of the Attorney-General.[86] It then remained for the Parliament to add to a standard defence of the privileges of the courts the claim, with plenty of precedent behind it, that Parliament was a court:

It is acknowledged that the King is the fountain of justice and protection, but the acts of justice and protection are not exercised in his own person, nor depend upon his pleasure, but by his courts and by his ministers, who must do their duty therein, though the King in his own person should forbid them: and

---

[83] *Henry IV Part II*, v. ii. 73–4. On the history of the doctrine, see E. H. Kantorowicz, *King's Two Bodies* (Princeton, NJ, 1957). There is a very fair summary of the sources in the King's Proclamation of 18 June, which was probably, from its resemblance to material in his commonplace book, written by Chief Justice Bankes: Larkin, pp. 770–5, Dorset RO Bankes of Kingston Lacey MSS, vol. M, p. 3. The most familiar recent precedent was Calvin's Case, in which the doctrine that allegiance was due to the law, rather than to the natural person of the King, had been the argument of the losing side. The doctrine was most fully developed (in a form later rejected) under Edward II. In 1308 the barons had argued that their allegiance to the Crown entitled them to disobey the King: Eleanor Lodge and Gladys A. Thornton, *English Constitutional Documents 1307–1485* (Cambridge, 1935), 11–12. I am grateful to Dr David D'Avray for this reference.

[84] Larkin, p. 773.

[85] Gardiner, *Documents*, p. 111.

[86] *LJ* iv. 635–6.

therefore if judgements should be given by them against the King's will and personal command, yet are they the King's judgements'.

If this had been justifying a judgement in a criminal trial, instead of the Militia Ordinance, it would have been an uncontroversial statement. The claim followed that they stood more for the King's authority than the King did:

what they do herein hath the stamp of royal authority, although his Majesty, seduced by wicked counsel do in his own person oppose or interrupt the same, for the King's supream and royal pleasure is exercised and declared in this high court of law and council after a more eminent and obligatory manner, than it can be by any personal act or resolution of his own.[87]

In short, the King's Two Bodies was a rudimentary doctrine of the State.

It was rather more difficult to use the doctrine of the King's Two Bodies to prove that Hotham had not levied war against the King, but in their Declaration of 26 May, the Houses made the attempt. They argued that:

the levying of war against his laws and authority, though not against his person, is levying war against the King; but the levying force against his personal commands, though accompanied with his presence, and not against his laws and authority, but in the maintenance thereof, is no levying war against the King, but for him.[88]

The King satirized this doctrine as a claim that 'we are the only person in England, against whom treason cannot be committed'.[89] He later accused the Parliament of a design 'to take up arms against our person, under a colour of being loving subjects to our office, and to destroy us, that they may preserve the King'.[90] It was a fair charge: the effect of extreme reliance on the doctrine of the King's Two Bodies was to drive the Parliament towards the situation to which that doctrine was most appropriate, that of a royal minority: the Parliamentary Declaration of 19 May claimed that 'the wisdom of this state hath intrusted the houses of Parliament with a power to supply what shall be wanting on the part of the prince, as is evident by the constant custom and practice thereof, in cases of nonage, natural disability and captivity'. They were trying to preserve Charles, like Henry VI during his insanity, as a name in which authority was exercised, without allowing him any personal say in the exercise of it, 'so we hope that his Majesty will not make his own understanding or reason the rule of his government, but will suffer

---

[87] Ibid. v. 112.
[88] Rushworth, *Collections*, III. i. 585.
[89] *LJ* v. 52.
[90] Rushworth, *Collections*, III. i. 749.

himself to be assisted by a wise and prudent counsel'.[91] The King protested that such precedents were inapplicable: 'we being no ideot, nor infant, uncapable of understanding to command'.[92]

From the Parliament's point of view, the doctrine of the King's Two Bodies had the great advantage of avoiding the need to justify rebellion altogether. It also avoided the need to argue any case for Parliamentary sovereignty: if the authority of the King could once be separated from the angry man in York, then members could claim to be truly loyal to it. They could claim that 'His Majesty's government must be carried on' in despite of his Majesty himself. Whether the doctrine was used as a cloak under which ideas of Parliamentary sovereignty might grow unseen is another question, and a much more difficult one to answer. The clearest common assumptions of the whole debate are that rebellion was wrong, that civil war was undesirable, and that authority was royal. Victory would therefore go to the side best able to appropriate these assumptions to itself. The cover was not merely a public one: on 17 June Roger Hill wrote to his wife that the King was coming with an army, but 'we shall not be wanting to defend his Majesty, our selves and kingdome, against that wicked brood that would destroy both prince and people, and make both a prey unto themselves'.[93] It is in the almost unconscious lapses of language, rather than in any deliberate claims, that ideas approaching Parliamentary sovereignty most easily emerge. On 5 May the Houses complained of the danger of the King's withdrawing himself from his Parliament, 'so as the disaffected and malignant party, under colour of his service, go about to raise a faction and a party against the Parliament, which at last may break out into open rebellion'.[94] If it was rebellion in the King to resist the Parliament, this came very near a claim that the Parliament was the legitimate seat of authority. Serjeant Wilde, at the end of his exposition of the King's Two Bodies to justify the impeachment of the Attorney-General for obeying the King's orders, allowed himself a very similar slip of the tongue. He claimed that, in trying to arrest the Five Members in the House, Charles had tried to take them 'even from the horns of the altar'.[95] The symbol clearly referred to the ultimate seat of authority, and was familiar in that sense. It is possible, if difficult, to argue that this language covers a hidden determination to claim Parliamentary sovereignty. It seems, however, rather more reasonable to suppose that those concerned were hastily working out their justifications as they went along.

Other ideas are offered much less frequently: the doctrine of the

[91] Rushworth, *Collections*, III. i. 699, 702.
[92] Larkin, p. 773.
[93] BL Add. MS 46500, fo. 29^r.
[94] *LJ* v. 47.
[95] Ibid. iv. 636. On the previous meaning of the phrase, see Russell, *1621–9*, pp. 201–2.

King's Two Bodies takes up more space in the Parliamentary Declarations than all the other justifications put together. This is partly because most of the other claims advanced involved an even larger element of *petitio principii*: they assumed what was to be proved. There was, for example a stress on the good Aristotelian doctrine that power existed for specific ends, and was valid only for the ends for which it was ordained: 'the king by his sovereignty is not enabled to destroy his people, but to protect and defend them'.[96] It was pointed out that a general's commission, however largely worded, was not intended to empower him to turn his cannon against his soldiers.[97] This was a perfectly good idea, but its relevance to the situation in hand depended on the assumption that the trouble arose from the King's determination to attack his Parliament.

There was also a considerable difficulty in understanding that a Parliament, representing the assembled authority of a community, could be in rebellion against itself: 'how can that possibly be called a faction, which is done by both Houses of Parliament, the greatest court of England, and the most faithful Council his Majesty hath?'[98] Sir Edward Dering no doubt could have answered this argument. The Earl of Warwick, when accused of treason for detaining the fleet against the King's command, said 'obeying the Parliament is counted high treason; a doctrine I never heard of till this Parliament'.[99] The Houses claimed on 2 August that it was impossible that 600 in both Houses should agree in arbitrary acts,[100] a claim which was much weakened by the fact that only some 150 in the two Houses had agreed in the acts complained of. Some of their Declarations complained of 'so horrid and unnatural an act, as the overthrowing a Parliament by force, which is the support and preservation of them all'.[101] They complained there were 'never any such monsters before, that ever attempted to disaffect the people from a Parliament'.[102]

These ideas perhaps implied an ascending theory of power, but they stopped short of stating it. They came slightly nearer in their invocation of a doctrine of trust, pledging themselves, for example, to preserve the peace against the King's guard 'in duty towards God, and by the trust

[96] *LJ* v. 113.

[97] PRO SP 16/490/12 (*A Question Answered*, pamphlet complained of by the King). It is tempting to ascribe this pamphlet to Henry Parker: see M. J. Mendle, *Dangerous Positions* (University of Alabama, 1985), 187–8. The failure to discuss Henry Parker here is the result of a deliberate self-denying ordinance, involving a decision to concentrate on the official productions of the Houses. There will never be a shortage of Parker scholars.

[98] *LJ* v. 153; see also Rushworth, *Collections*, III. i. 772.

[99] *LJ* v. 216.

[100] Ibid. 258.

[101] Ibid. 121; *CJ* ii. 618.

[102] Rushworth, *Collections*, III. i. 578.

reposed in us by the people and fundamental laws and constitutions of this kingdom'.[103] There are a number of places from which they might have drawn in constructing a doctrine of trusteeship, but the most explicit statement of the case suggests that they were turning to the most familiar and least radical: English land law. In opposing the King's claim that in being shut out of Hull he had been deprived of his own property, they argued that kings

are only intrusted with their kingdoms, and with their towns, and with their people, and with the publick treasure of the commonwealth, and whatever is bought therewith: and by the known law of this kingdom, the very jewels of the Crown are not the king's proper goods, but are only intrusted unto him, for the use and ornament thereof . . . And as this trust is for the use of the kingdom, so ought it to be managed by the advice of both Houses of Parliament, whom the kingdom hath trusted for that purpose.[104]

The whole of this complex construction, in which King and Parliament are both trustees for the use of the kingdom, has a remarkably close resemblance to the double enfeoffment to use by which Pym had protected his estates in 1614.[105] Yet, before we pronounce confidently that this expresses an ascending theory of power, it is worth remembering that any gentleman brought up on Gouge and Perkins would also see his authority as a paterfamilias as a trust, and limited to certain ends for which he was trusted, but in that case the trust was a descending one, and came from God. He too could have used the words in which Roger Hill the lawyer summed up the case of Hull: 'he hath but the custody, which is trust and not *dominium utile*. He can open and shut for the public good of the people and state but not to make gain or for their hurt'.[106] It is worth remembering that, as in the double covenant of the *Vindiciae*, or in the divine right of husbands, or in the choosing of churchwardens, ascending and descending theories of power were very easily amalgamated.

By contrast, the King's case was simple and easy to explain. He complained that 'a subject, in defiance of us, shuts the gates against us'.[107] To argue that this was treason, the King only needed to assert two very simple points. One was that, when any new law was proposed, he had the right to say 'no'. The other was that, since he legally possessed

---

[103] *LJ* v. 77.

[104] Rushworth, *Collections*, III. i. 579. I am grateful to Dr R. P. Cust for pointing out the debt of the doctrine of trusteeship to the use, and to Prof. J. H. Burns for a helpful discussion of this and similar passages.

[105] Somerset RO Pym MSS 139–46.

[106] *PJ* ii. 346. It is not clear whether Hill is paraphrasing the declaration, giving his own opinion or reporting a speech by Nathaniel Fiennes. Any of these possibilities would make it a good guide to Parliamentary thinking.

[107] Rushworth, *Collections*, III. i. 573.

this right, any attempt to take it away from him was an attempt to subvert the law, and to introduce an arbitrary government. He did not accept any antithesis between the power of the King and the power of the Parliament, because 'we are still a part of the Parliament, and shall be, till this well-founded monarchy be turned to a democracy'.[108] He asserted that 'we called them, and without that call they could not have come together, to be our counsellors, not commanders'. Such trust as the Houses possessed, he thought, came from him: 'were they not trusted by us, when we first sent for them? And were they not trusted by us, when we passed them our promise, that we would not dissolve them? Can it be presumed, and presumptions go far with them, that we trusted them with a power to destroy us, and to dissolve our government and authority?'

He satirized their claim to declare the law, picking up the implications of their own comparison with the Pope's power to interpret Scripture, saying it implied that 'whatever they say or do should be lawful, because they declare it so'. In one of the cleverest passages in the whole of the paper war, he asked the Parliament to imagine their reactions if the papists had got a majority in the Parliament of Ireland, declared their religion and liberty to be in danger from a malignant party of Protestants and Puritans, and therefore resolved that the forts and militia of Ireland were to be put into such hands as they could confide in.[109] The justice of the parallel says as much as the obvious inability of the English Parliament to see it. He claimed that the only person trusted by God was himself, and that the trust was irrevocable. Having asserted his right to say no, he developed, in every piece he put out, the claim that the rule of law depended on that right being preserved. Echoing Phelips in 1628, he asked: 'if they declare, that by the fundamental law of the land, such a rash action, such an unadvised word ought to be punished by perpetual imprisonment, is not the liberty of the subject, *durante beneplacito*, remediless?'[110] It was an able case, well argued, and it seems, both in terms of intellectual coherence and in terms of immediate political benefit, that the King had the better of the paper war.

During the second half of May and the first half of June there was a steady flow of supporters to join the King at York. He seems, initially, to have given the signal for this flow to begin. On 18 May he gave leave of absence from the Parliament to twenty-eight Lords, and on 21 May he

---

[108] *LJ* v. 94.
[109] Rushworth, *Collections*, III. i. 591–2. The King was clearly involved in the writing of his own propaganda, but enjoyed assistance from Hyde, Falkland, Culpepper, Bankes, and probably Bristol. Bristol or Falkland, the son of a Lord Deputy of Ireland, are perhaps the likeliest authors of this passage.
[110] Rushworth, *Collections*, III. i. 711. For the speech echoed, see Russell, *1621–9*, p. 348.

summoned Hyde to join him at York.[111] Savill, having thought better of his earlier refusal, went to York, where he was in due course joined by Falkland, Culpepper, Bristol, Bankes, Dover, and a considerable group of the King's regular supporters. There were some surprises, both in the inclusions and the exclusions. The King decided on 21 May to take the seal from Lord Keeper Littleton, and sent an emissary to fetch the seal. He may have been somewhat surprised when Littleton voluntarily followed the Seal to York. Paget, who had been deep in the junto in the House of Lords, and who had recently executed the Militia Ordinance as a Lord-Lieutenant, caused general surprise by going to York in the middle of June, saying he would not fight against the King. His letter to this effect was described by the Commons as an 'objectionable publication'.[112] On the other hand, the Earl of Portland, heaping coals of fire on Pym's often expressed distrust of him, remained at Westminster well into August. So did the Earl of Peterborough, who may have been, as he claimed, medically unfit to go,[113] and Lord Spencer, who backed the Parliament to the last moment, and then broke away. Perhaps no one, not even those concerned, could be certain who would stick with the Parliament beyond the outbreak of civil war, and who would follow Paget in deciding they could not fight against the King.

On 20 May the King began summoning local forces for a guard. This provoked a Lords' committee led by Manchester and Mandeville to resolve that 'the King intends to make war against the Parliament'. It was the Commons, at Pym's instigation, who shrank from calling a spade a spade by adding the words 'seduced by wicked counsel'.[114] On 11 June the King went on to issue Commissions of Array, based on an unprinted statute of Henry IV, to levy men throughout the country. Since he had been told that commissions of lieutenantcy were illegal, he fell back on the Commissions of Array as a method of levying force according to a statute as yet unrepealed.[115] This did not save him from vigorous Parliamentary Declarations of the illegality of the commission. During June and July, attempts were made round the country to execute the Militia Ordinance and the Commission of Array, and in some counties, particularly Leicestershire, the two clashed head-on. As yet, such clashes were stopping at words, with very occasional exceptions. In the main, however, the delay in the start of the Civil War was now becom-

---

[111] Bodl. MS Clarendon, vol. 21, no. 1605.

[112] PRO SP 16/491/17; CJ ii. 633.

[113] Hamilton MS 1652.

[114] PJ ii. 348–9; CJ ii. 581; LJ v. 76–7. Herbert of Cherbury was committed to the Gentleman Usher for saying he would agree to the resolution if he were convinced the King would make war on the Parliament without cause.

[115] For Edward Alford's recommendation in 1628 of Commissions of Array as a legal way of levying troops, see Russell, 1621–9, p. 386.

ing a matter of the inertia and delay familiar in all English efforts to start wars for a long time: there was not much chance left of avoiding it altogether.

Attempts to bring about a settlement had not ceased. They have left little trace in the records, but the balance of probability is that there was much more communication between London and York than now survives, and, one may suspect, much more than was ever on paper. There were numerous cases in which the split between London and York was separating old friends, who were often divided only by the narrowest of margins. It is not, for example, to be supposed that Essex ceased to exchange ideas with his brother-in-law and closest friend the Earl of Hertford. Such exchanges must be assumed to have taken place, but no archival record of them appears to have survived. What need not be assumed is that any of these exchanges ever involved Charles and Pym, who appear to have been supremely uninterested in them.

One Councillor at York who did preserve some record of his correspondence with Westminster is Chief Justice Bankes, who had accepted office under the Militia Ordinance before going to York, and who allowed it to be known that he knew nothing of the King's attempt to rally the Yorkshire gentry to attend him. He took care to tell his former client Giles Greene, who was at Westminster, that the King was extremely offended with him for refusing to condemn the Militia Ordinance.[116] Having thus established his credentials as a man of peace, he made approaches to Northumberland, Saye, Holles, and Essex, with a fuller and franker exposition of his case to Greene.[117] The case he put to Greene was very much along the lines of the King's message of 20 January. He wanted the Houses to set down their 'desires', together with what they would do for the King's revenue. In return, the King should 'express what he desires to be done for him'. It is startling, and surely significant, that so limited a request for negotiating terms had been unmet from January to May. The mere discussion of terms implied a readiness to accept Charles's authority in some form, and it was that readiness Pym and Strode no longer had. To Northumberland and Saye, Bankes outlined more fully the points on which the King would expect satisfaction. He said the King feared the alteration of government, and attacks on the liturgy and discipline of the church, and attempts to bring in a Presbyterian government 'as an introduction to a commonwealth'. These things, he said, 'do very much perplex his Majesty, and make him look after guards to secure his person'. At the same time, he said that the differences were not too great to be reconciled, if there were a willingness on all parts. To Saye, he stressed that the King required

---

[116] PRO SP 16/490/50; *Corfe Castle*, pp. 134–6.
[117] *HMC Eighth Report*, I. 211; *Corfe Castle*, pp. 154–6.

satisfaction in point of honour about Hull, and asked again for a mutual exchange of propositions.

Northumberland, who was the first to reply, accepted the olive branch, and expressed his agreement with Bankes's desire to avoid civil war. He denied any intention to change the form of government, or to leave the King without a revenue settlement, but stressed that the fear of alteration of government existed on both sides: 'we believe that those persons who are most powerfull with the King do endeavour to bring Parlaments to such a condition that they shall only be made instruments to execute the commands of the King, who were established for his greatest and most supreame councel'.[118] This vision of Parliaments reduced to a rubber stamp surely rested on memories of the Short Parliament, rather than on any more recent events. Essex's letter, though apparently friendly, committed him to nothing, and Holles's offer of submission 'upon the first appearance of change in his Majesty' can hardly have been encouraging.[119]

Northumberland, however, was as good as his word. He wrote to Bankes on 19 May, and on 23 May he moved for an accommodation in the House of Lords.[120] On the 27th, Waller induced the Commons to make a similar request, though Strode insisted it was a proposal 'to no purpose'.[121] The result was that the Lords charged a twelve-man committee for the defence of the kingdom with the further task of considering 'how to prevent a Civil War'.[122] The next day Northumberland reported from this committee with the first draft of what became known as the Nineteen Propositions.[123] The Nineteen Propositions are so far-reaching that it is a shock to think of them as a proposal for accommodation, yet Feilding, who was a member of the committee, told

[118] *Corfe Castle*, pp. 122–3.

[119] Ibid. 124–7. The enclosure mentioned by Holles on 21 May may have been the Declaration of 19 May. Saye, to judge from Bankes's reproachful letter of 11 July (*HMC Eighth Report*, I. 211b) would appear not to have replied. Some indication of what Saye might have said may be gained from his letter to Hamilton of 3 June, in which he stressed that the Nineteen Propositions did not proceed from any fear of the King's cavaliers, and said that if they were met with scorn and reproach, he would be ready 'to maintaine the authority of Parliament against what power soever shall oppose it': Hamilton MS 1658.

[120] Bodl. MS Clarendon, vol. 21, no. 1608. This report says Northumberland followed up a speech by Bristol. It is tempting to identify this with the speech under Bristol's name in Rushworth, *Collections*, III. i. 714–17. Bristol's denial of this speech (*LJ* v. 87) carries weight, but it could only mean that it was a pirate printing, or even a deniable leak. Bristol's denial stops short of claiming that he did not deliver the speech.

[121] *PJ* ii. 376.

[122] *LJ* v. 85, 88. The committee consisted of Northumberland, Essex, Holland, Pembroke, Peterborough, Mandeville, North, Feilding, Wharton, Brooke, St John, and Hunsdon. Saye was not a member. The committee which produced the Nineteen Propositions thus included 3 members of the Privy Council of the 1630s, and 1 future Royalist. The Royalist (Hunsdon) was not one of the former Privy Councillors.

[123] *LJ* v. 89–91.

Hamilton that they 'have bene brought downe to the lowest degree of moderation and respect'. He insisted they were 'the only meanes which is left' to beget a better understanding between the King and the Parliament, and asked Hamilton, who had reluctantly gone to York, to further them.[124] Wharton supported the request in a hasty postscript to Feilding's letter, but Hamilton appears to have been unable to gain access to the King, and soon left York for Scotland.[125]

Northumberland's text includes the first fourteen of what are now the Nineteen Propositions. They asked for the Privy Council to be chosen in Parliament, and for the King not to take the advice of any 'unknown or unsworn counsellors'. The provision for vacancies in the Privy Council, significantly, is directly copied from the Scottish settlement of September 1641. The Propositions provide for the Parliamentary choice of the great officers, Lord High Steward, Constable, Lord Chancellor, Lord Treasurer, and others. They provide that those responsible for the education of the King's children should be chosen by the Parliament, or by the Council in between Parliaments, and that no marriage might be concluded for the King's children without Parliamentary consent. There were to be no more popish queens. The King was to be forbidden to dispense with the laws against Roman Catholics, and the votes of popish Lords on religious matters were to be taken away. The King was asked to agree to such a reformation of the church as the Houses and the assembly of divines should advise, and to pass such a bill to settle the militia as should be advised by the Houses. All members of either House displaced from office during the Parliament were to be restored,[126] and the judges were to take an oath to observe the Petition of Right. The King's comment, that 'it is not with the persons now chosen, but with our chusing, that you are displeased' appears to be a fair one. This is a proposal to exclude the King from the process of government, a proposal to which the only full parallels are during the captivity of Richard I, and the insanity of Henry VI. Charles said it 'were in effect at one to depose both our self and our posterity'.[127]

Nevertheless, Feilding's belief that these propositions represented the lowest possible level of moderation was confirmed by the fact that the Commons strengthened the Propositions.[128] It should come as no surprise to anyone who has followed the relations between the Houses so

[124] Hamilton MS 1655.

[125] Warwicks. RO Feilding of Newnham Paddox MSS C 1/106–8. The story of Hamilton's departure from York is far from perfectly understood: the story Hamilton told Feilding is the story he wanted to have believed at Westminster. See also Hamilton MSS 1668, 1667, 1671, 1679, 165, 168, and other refs. His underlying commitment seems to have been to Scottish neutrality.

[126] This was a carelessly drafted clause, since it would have had the effect of restoring the Earl of Newcastle to the Governorship of the Prince.

[127] Rushworth, *Collections*, III. i. 727, 728.

[128] *CJ* ii. 595–6; *PJ* ii. 396–7, 395.

far that it was the religious, and not the constitutional, aspect of the Propositions the Commons chose to strengthen. They removed the limitation to religious issues from the ban on popish Lords voting, transforming the proposition into an absolute ban on their participation in the Lords. They also changed the Lords' reference to 'popish recusants' into a plain reference to 'papists', continuing Pym's insistence that church attendance was not a sufficient proof of Protestantism. They added to the eighth proposition a demand that the King should confirm the bills for the 8 September order, against pluralities and against scandalous ministers. They also named a small committee, from which Pym inevitably reported, which added five further propositions.[129] These called for the commanders of forts and castles to be approved by Parliament, for the King's guards to be dismissed, for a more strict alliance with the United Provinces 'against all designs and attempts of the Pope', for an Act to clear the Five Members, and for another to restrain peers created in future from sitting in Parliament without Parliamentary consent. The additions show vividly how far fear of popery and fear of Charles had blended in Pym's mind into one whole. The preface, also supplied by Pym, ignored Mr Grimston's insistence that the petition should not be 'cloyed with any expostulation',[130] by blaming past troubles on 'the subtle insinuations, mischievous practices and evil counsels of men disaffected to God's true religion, your Majesty's honour and safety, and the public peace and prosperity of your people'. Pym did not do enough with the Propositions to entitle us to say that he wanted to wreck them, but he did not add a single syllable to make them more palatable to the King. The Commons' readiness to insist on the religious issues was further spelt out on 25 June, when the Book of Rates was at last completed, and the Commons asked for the bills for the Westminster Assembly, pluralities, innovations, and scandalous ministers to be sent to the King with it.[131]

The King's answer, though an extremely able work of propaganda, did not offer much in the way of concession.[132] It has since become famous for its retreat to the position of 1660, classifying the King as one of the three estates in Parliament. Yet, since the Propositions were the first attempt at genuine negotiation since the King left London, the Parliamentary peace party took the debate on the answer as a signal to

[129] For the final text, see Gardiner, *Documents*, pp. 249–54.
[130] *PJ* ii. 392.
[131] *LJ* v. 160. The Book of Rates was attached to yet another temporary bill, so the Commons had kept the power to make a longer grant depend on the King's assent to the proposed bills.
[132] For the *Answer*, see Rushworth, *Collections*, III. i. 725–35. On its significance in the history of English political thought, see Mendle, *Dangerous Positions*, pp. 5–20, 171–83, and *passim*. The present book tends to sustain Prof. Mendle's point that 'the pursuit of place was itself an aggressive act', and in the immediate context of the *Answer*, it supports the remarks on pp. 177–83 about the overwhelming importance of the attack on the King's negative voice.

rally. On 23 June, when the answer was debated, Gawdy estimated that some 260 members were present,[133] which was probably 100 more than had been present at most times in the past few months. Two hundred and sixty-four had voted on 16 June, when the answer was probably expected, and the rally of the peace party had probably begun. The last division before that in which over 240 had voted had been the division on the impeachment of the Duke of Richmond on 27 January.[134] The attempt to induce the Commons not to insist on the first proposition, for retirement of all the Privy Council, was opposed by Glyn, Fiennes, St John, and Pym. Pym, in an unusual historical exercise, claimed that Henry III was the first king to choose great officers without the consent of Parliament. More immediately, he said that 'he saw no alteration but from worse to worse till king incline to the Parliament. Ergo, Council chosen as they have been we shall soon return to the same mischiefs, and break through all laws made or to be made'. Nevertheless, in the face of all these big guns, the House resolved not to insist on the first proposition. Waller, Selden, Rudyerd, and Lenthall, free to speak because the House was in Committee of the Whole, seem to have been the leading speakers for the majority.[135]

This produced a few more days' break in the momentum, and was followed by a few other votes to retreat on individual propositions, but the King's continuing use of the Commissions of Array soon restored the advantage to the 'fiery spirits'. On 8 July Pym reported a Declaration justifying taking up arms, 'the war being thus by his Majesty begun'. This, after a long and familiar rehearsal of the history, insisted that the main issue was 'the alteration of religion, which is the main end of those who have been the authors and counsellors of his Majesty's undertaking this war'.[136] On 9 July the Commons voted, by a majority of 125 to 45, to raise an army of 10,000 volunteers. On the 11th, they resolved, on the motion of Holles, to raise an army, to appoint a general, and to petition for accommodation. This is a clear example of the belief in negotiating from strength. On the 12th, Essex was chosen General, and the petition for accommodation was brought in. The petition for accommodation had been entrusted to Pym, and the results were as might have been foreseen. His original draft contained a long historical catalogue of reproaches, which one or other House insisted on cutting out.[137] This reproached the King, among much else, with having besieged Hull, with

[133] Gawdy, vol. ii, fo. 142ᵛ.
[134] CJ ii. 626, 400.
[135] Hill, pp. 102–5; BL Harl. MS 163, fo. 207ᵇ; Verney's Notes, pp. 181–2; HMC Buccleuch, i. 306.
[136] CJ ii. 659; BL Harl. MS 163, fo. 267ᵇ; CJ ii. 668.
[137] MP, 12 July 1642, secretary's draft corrected by Pym. For the final version, LJ v. 207.

having put an 'illegal' garrison in Newcastle, with having executed an 'illegal' Commission of Array, and with having protected delinquents, including the Army Plotters and Lord Dillon. The formal proposal was for a laying down of arms on both sides, and the restoration of Hull to the King, but *without* the magazine. Pym, taking a leaf from Charles's linguistic book, offered to prevent any tumults which should give him 'just' cause of apprehension. The petition offered to settle the militia by a bill, granted guarantees that the strength of the kingdom should not be employed against itself, and also guarantees for the safety of those, both in England and Ireland, who '*still*' (my italics) desire to preserve the Protestant religion. Sir Philip Stapleton, one of those charged with presenting this petition to the King, believed it to be 'full of moderation', but it is easy to understand why the King thought otherwise.

It appears that there was no more real desire to make concessions at York than there was at Westminster. In July, probably for the first time, one of the vital conditions of a civil war had been achieved, in that both sides believed they were strong enough to be able to win. Stapleton, when he presented the petition for accommodation, reported that the King had 'noe foot', and thought the Yorkshire trained bands would only fight 'faintly' for him.[138] Feilding's mother, the Queen's Mistress of the Robes, was writing to tell him that 'I do beleeve the king will have the better of his enymies'. Feilding apparently felt equal confidence, since she wrote back to him: 'beleeve me, you are deceved, your party will have the worst'. She too hoped for an accommodation, but what she meant by accommodation was that 'they would humble themselves to the king, and acknowledg their erors': it was the very mirror image of Holles's readiness to submit on the first change in the King. She ordered her disobedient son to 'run to the King upon your knees'.[139] The King's reply to the petition for accommodation was in this spirit: as always, he was the one person Pym could trust to help his plans forward. The King's reply was in the form of an ultimatum. On 25 July Waller and Sir John Potts moved to accept the ultimatum, but 'Mr. Denzil Holles, Mr. Strode and other fiery sprits would not hear of it'. Pym opposed accommodation because 'the king is still ruled by the same counsels'. Marten said the conditions were worse than war, and that 'though the King be King of the people of England, yet he is not master of the people of England'. Long said he would as soon come with a halter about his neck as agree to the King's proposals. The most startling speech against accommodation was from that peaceable character Sir John Holland: 'that there is no security but in the actual going on with your prepara-

---

[138] Hamilton MS 1677.
[139] Warwicks. RO Feilding of Newnham Paddox MSS C 1/20, 22A, 26, 28.

tion'.[140] Pym, Marten, or Long can easily be dismissed as 'fiery spirits': if the King could not reach a settlement with them, the blame might as well be theirs as his: yet a King whom Sir John Holland would not trust with armed force was a King who had truly failed his people.

There was one more Declaration approved by the Lords on 2 August, to justify the resort to arms. It was reported from committee in the Commons by Holles, and revised in the Lords by Northumberland, Holland, Pembroke, and Saye, but the mind behind it is surely that of Pym. The vision which informed this Declaration had been Pym's since the introduction of Arminianism in the early years of the reign. It was of the alteration of government, in order to make way for the alteration of religion. It called for war against those who had 'possessed' the King against them, a word whose choice was surely not accidental. It complained of the resort to the King of all those who 'out of their desire of a dissolute liberty, apprehend and would keep off the reformation intended by the Parliament'. It looked back into the 1630s, when 'religion was made but form and outside', and 'the laws were no defence nor protection of any man's right; all was subject to will and power'. The great design for which all this had been done was 'the changing of religion into popery and superstition'. If these words were Pym's, they were probably not a mere smear, but a correct description of Pym's perception and definition of the vision of the church of England for which Charles stood. The key point in this Declaration was the attempt to make common cause with Scotland: the Scots were praised for the determination with which they resisted a 'popish service-book', 'for well they knew the same fate attended both kingdoms, and religion could not be altered in one without the other'.[141] In August 1642 these words surely meant more than the mere giving of credit where credit was due: they should be read as an immediate call for help.

If this hypothesis is tested against the actions of the Parliamentary junto from the beginning of June down to the King's raising of his standard on 22 August, it appears to be entirely correct. Throughout this period, the tactics of the Parliamentary junto, and of its most enthusiastic followers, were not aimed at exploring the possibility of accommodation with Charles I. They were aimed at securing the Scottish intervention which they eventually secured in the Solemn League

[140] BL Harl. MS 164, fo. 293[b]; Gawdy, vol. ii, fos. 170[r]–1[v]. Sir John Holland had been one of those who presented the petition for accommodation to the King at Beverley, and he had perhaps not liked what he found there. There is one more hint of negotiation for an accommodation. On 19 July when leaves for York were not readily granted, Sir John Hippisley was granted leave to go to York for a month: CJ ii. 680. Hippisley was an old client of the Duke, and therefore at home in court circles. He was now a loyal Parliamentarian, and Master of the Horse to the Earl of Northumberland. See J. S. A. Adamson, 'The Peerage in Politics 1645–1649', Ph.D. thesis (Cambridge, 1986), 32; BL Add. MS 18016, fo. 1[v]. I am grateful to Dr Adamson for this reference.
[141] CJ ii. 694; LJ v. 257–9.

and Covenant of 1643. The objectives were, of course, incompatible, since every measure designed to reassure the King would lose Scottish support, and every measure designed to appeal to Covenanter sense of solidarity would convince Charles further that he was right to fight. The object of the Scottish alliance was not to persuade Charles, but to prevent him forcibly from fighting. As the Scottish General Assembly wrote to the well-affected ministers of England at the beginning of August, if attempts were made to secure unity in religion between the kingdoms, opposition from Satan and worldly men would be vehement.[142] Charles was one of those 'worldly men', and every move for unity in religion between the kingdoms would assist him in making common cause with his fellow 'worldly men'. The people in Southwark who stuck a Proclamation for the Commission of Array on a maypole[143] were Charles's natural allies in resisting a Scottish reformation, but had never been allies to the regime of Archbishop Laud.

Charles, in writing to the General Assembly, tried to adopt a federal ideal for his three kingdoms which, if he had adopted it in 1635–7, might have saved him all the trouble he had since suffered. He attempted to convince the Assembly that the security of their reformation did not depend on the future of the English church settlement:

God, whose vicegerent we are, hath made us a king over diverse kingdomes, and wee have noe other desire, nor designe, but to governe them by there owne lawes, and ye kirkes in them by theire owne canons, and constitutions. Wheere anythinge is found to be amisse we will endeavour a reformation in a faire and orderly way, and where a reformacon is settled, we resolve wth that authority wherewith God hath vested us to mainteine and defend it.[144]

It was too late for this sort of reassurance: Charles's distaste for the sort of religion represented in the General Assembly had been shown too clearly and for too long for the Scots to have any great faith in his conversion. Moreover, the reassuring effect was spoilt by Charles's visibly continuing commitment to an ideal of the Royal Supremacy which was anathema to Covenanter theories of authority. The attachment to the Royal Supremacy, and the difficulty in admitting that it did not apply to Scotland, were something the King shared with his new English party. On 2 June Sir John Culpepper insisted on the setting up of a committee in the Commons because he found it a notion of 'dangerous consequence' that Scots in England were freed by the treaty from taking the Oath of Supremacy.[145] To the Covenanters, a Royal Supremacy in the hands of an uncovenanted king was necessarily a

---

[142] Hamilton MS 10774/17.
[143] CJ ii. 695.
[144] Hamilton MS 10774/14.
[145] BL Harl. MS 163, fo. 143ᵇ; CJ ii. 601.

permanent threat to their security. For them, even more than for the English godly, security against the religious proclivities of Charles I could be gained only by an irreversible change. As the General Assembly told the well-affected ministers of England, the kirk could not hope long to enjoy the purity and peace which had cost them so dear without unity in religion between the kingdoms. To this end, they suggested that, after preparatory meetings to clear the ground, the Westminster Assembly should include representatives of both kingdoms.[146]

These were the sorts of demands the 'fiery spirits' were setting out to satisfy from the beginning of June onwards. As always, the Scottish route to security risked deepening the divisions of England. This fact was quickly demonstrated when the final list of names for the Westminster Assembly came up for consideration. The Commons' list included some names the Scots might have preferred not to see there, such as those of Ussher and Prideaux, but at least the Calvinism of the Commons' nominees was almost entirely uniform. The Lords, on the other hand, chose to add a number of names, many of whom were holders of Lords' home livings.[147] Among these names was that of Dr Henry Hammond, holder of the Earl of Leicester's home living of Penshurst. Dr Hammond happened to be an extremely well-known Arminian. There is no need to assume that Leicester shared his views, but Hammond's nomination does identify Leicester as one of those, like Dering, who believed an Arminian could be a good Protestant. Such people were not likely to welcome a Scottish reformation in which Arminianism would have been even more effectively outlawed than Calvinism had been in the 1630s. To the Lords, with their instinctive tendency to search for consensus, such a move was alarming. When Sir Robert Cooke, for the Commons, objected to Hammond's nomination on the ground that 'they had nott satisfaction that hee was well enough affected to the Protestant religion', the Lords saw danger signals: 'the Earls of Pembroke, Holland, Bristol, Leicester and Northumberland, lord admiral, spake all very earnestly on the behalf of Dr. Hammond and to justify him to be learned and orthodox'.[148] These people, especially while the destiny of the fleet was not finally settled, were ones the Commons needed even more than they did the Scots, and they beat a hasty retreat.[149]

The retreat, however, was tactical and temporary. Scottish issues received rapid attention, and Hampden, for example, seems on occasion to have known of events in Edinburgh before the Scottish Commis-

---

[146] Hamilton MS 10774/17.

[147] The nominations are listed in *PJ* ii. 490–2.

[148] MP, 1 June 1642; *PJ* ii. 398. This must have been almost Bristol's last appearance at Westminster.

[149] *CJ* ii. 598.

sioners did.[150] Complaints that Scots in Northumberland were asked to pay the poll tax as aliens, and that some items in the Book of Rates bore harshly on the Scots, received rapid action.[151] The approach of the General Assembly produced a Declaration, reported by Fiennes from the Committee for the Defence of the Kingdom, designed to be put before the General Assembly. Francis Rous, a pro-Scot from the beginning, moved to strengthen it by adding the word 'dissoluteness' to a reference to the 'avarice and ambition' of the bishops. D'Ewes agreed, on the ground that the clergy who had brought in the 'wicked tenants' of Arminianism were mostly men of scandalous lives.[152] The final Declaration included the amendment. It claimed that the Houses were 'zealous of a due reformation both in church and state', and blamed a malignant party of papists and corrupt and dissolute clergy for their failure to achieve it to date. In a phrase which anticipates the famous wording of the Solemn League and Covenant of 1643, they offered such a reformation 'as shall be most agreeable to God's word', a phrase likely to have offered the same loophole to Fiennes as it later did to the younger Vane.[153] This Declaration made the right noises, but the Scots would want something more specific. Loudoun, a few days later, told Hamilton that this Declaration would move the General Assembly to renew their desire for unity of religion and uniformity of church government, which he heard was 'very offensive to the commissioner's grace'.[154] The Commons were surely aware of this Scottish concern on 11 August, when they accompanied their pledge to live and die with the Earl of Essex with a resolve to draw up a 'Covenant'.[155] This worried even so good a pro-Scot as D'Ewes, who feared it might be used for a device to interfere with freedom of speech.[156] Whether for this reason or because of disagreement among the committee charged with drawing it up, the Covenant never appeared. This committee was drawn from the inner ranks of the Parliamentary leadership, so if it is division within the committee which is responsible, the issue of uniformity with Scotland was already showing some of the divisive power within Parliamentary ranks which it was to show later in the war.

[150] *CJ* ii. 608; *PJ* ii. 296.
[151] *CJ* ii. 621; *LJ* v. 171.
[152] BL Harl. MS 164, fo. 284[b].
[153] *LJ* v. 229; Scottish RO, PA 13/1, pp. 59–60.
[154] Hamilton MS 1741. The commissioner was the Earl of Dunfermline, who had been from the beginning one of the Covenanters concerned to find common ground with the King. Hamilton was asked to act as his assistant: Hamilton MS 1679.
[155] *CJ* ii. 715, 718, 722.
[156] BL Harl. MS 164, fo. 261[b]. The committee named to draw up the Covenant consisted of Holles, Stapleton, Pym, Reynolds, Prideaux, St John, Sir John Holland, and Strode. The appointment of additional members on 15 Aug. is a pointer towards disagreement within the committee. If so, St John and Holland are perhaps most likely to have generated it.

Meanwhile, pressure was rising in Scotland for a meeting of the conservators, appointed under the treaty to avoid future division between the kingdoms. Loudoun warned Charles on 1 August that if there was a war, Scotland, having so near a relation to the King and to England, must be involved in the common calamity. He told the King that it was more for his honour that the conservators should convene by his command than without it. A meeting of the conservators was finally arranged for 23 September, and Will Murray warned Hamilton that Charles should expect to be pressed further for uniformity in church government, and if he did not respond to this pressure, 'the two kingdoms will shatt upon him in despight of what his best servants canne doe'.[157] The General Assembly, however, had learnt to be suspicious of Parliamentary promises in this area. In a Declaration offered to the Parliament of England just after the war had begun, they expressed their grief that 'the reformation of religion hath moved so slowly, and suffered so great interruption'. They warned the Parliament that the Lord's controversy with England would not be settled till the worship of his name and the government of his house were cleared. They then picked up where they had left off, by quoting the Scottish commissioners' paper of 10 March 1641, on the need for the kingdoms to share one Confession of Faith, one directory of worship, one public catechism, and one form of kirk government. This was the price of Scottish support.[158]

Pym, it seems, was already resolved to pay it, and on 10 September he brought to the Lords two Declarations, one for the Scottish Privy Council and one for the General Assembly. He told the Privy Council he agreed with the Scots on prelacy, and that the enemies of the English Parliament were the same people who had attacked Scotland. To the General Assembly, he offered hope for a full reformation, and the hope of agreement on the 'substantial parts' of their demands. He offered them the means of achieving this, in the form of an invitation to send divines to the Westminster Assembly.[159] In 1642, as in 1640, Pym was not prepared to challenge Charles without Scottish support. In 1642, as in 1640, the Scots asked Pym a price in the form of religious reformation designed to bring about unity between the kingdoms. To Pym, this was perhaps further than he would have gone left to himself, but it was a price to which he had no objection in principle. To others, to Cromwell and Milton as much as to Falkland and Culpepper, these Scottish demands for uniformity were to become just as offensive as Charles's

[157] Hamilton MS 1781. See Scottish RO, PA 13/3, unfol. (1 Mar.) for the Presbytery of Edinburgh's insistence that the English Parliament were mistaken in regarding Will Murray as an evil counsellor. They said Murray had acted as London agent of the kirk under James.

[158] *LJ* v. 324. On the paper of 10 Mar. 1641, see above, p. 199.

[159] Ibid. 348–50. On the Parliament's moves for Scottish help in Nov., see Stevenson, p. 256.

similar demands had been to many of the Scots in 1637. Moreover, as the delay in bringing about the Solemn League and Covenant may indicate, there was likely to be resistance to such demands north of the Border, as well as south of it. In fact, by committing himself to the Scots, Pym was buying himself opponents by the same transaction which bought him allies. The road on which Pym embarked when he made his second bid for Scottish support in September 1642 was not merely one which led away from any possibility of compromise with Charles and the English Royalists. It also led, not merely to Marston Moor, but to Preston, Dunbar, and Worcester. It illustrated what has been the central theme of this book, that measures designed to bring about unity in religion between England and Scotland, no matter in the name of which religion they were undertaken, could unite a faction across the Border, but only at the price of the internal division and disruption of both countries to which it was applied. In Britain, as in the Netherlands and Catalonia, the drive for uniformity within multiple kingdoms led only to disaster.

14

Conclusion

If this book has demonstrated anything, it is that the Civil War is not an enclosed English subject. It cannot be understood in any purely English context, which is perhaps why it has caused so much bewilderment to the English, both then and now. England before the beginning of the crisis was, no doubt, a country subject to considerable stresses and strains, but it was one which few of the participants remembered as a country deeply enough divided to justify the fate which fell on it. Andrew Marvell, looking back on the time before the war, wondered:

> What luckless apple did we taste,
> To make us mortal, and thee waste.[1]

This bewilderment perhaps measures the exceptionally insular character of the English within their British context. Men like Marvell or Twysden thought very little of British affairs, as distinct from English ones, and their successors who have written their history have not escaped from this fault. The result is that we have been trying to deduce the whole of the explanation from one part of the problem.

Between 1639 and 1642 Charles faced armed resistance from all three of his kingdoms. In two of them, and arguably in three, this resistance broadened out into an internal civil war. It seems improbable that we are dealing here with a random coincidence between three separate national crises: it is surely sense to look for some sort of common factor linking these troubles together. Such a common factor cannot be found in their economies or their social structures: the three were as different as could be found in most of Europe. Nor is it easy to find a common factor in their internal constitutions. If we look for common factors, we can find them in the two problems all three kingdoms shared: that of being part of a multiple kingdom, and that of being ruled by Charles I.

In committing himself to Arminianism, Charles destroyed the painstaking labour James had put into making a cosmetic unity between the kingdoms. He committed himself to that interpretation of the English religious settlement which had least in common with the kirk of Scotland. Under these circumstances, it is perhaps not surprising that, among Charles's three kingdoms, Scotland was the one where he enjoyed the least support, and England the one where he enjoyed the

---

[1] Andrew Marvell, *On Appleton House*, stanza 41.

most. In fact, if we look at England in the context of Charles's other kingdoms, the peculiarity which needs explaining is not its revolutionary character: it is the fact that it was the only one of the three kingdoms which created a Royalist party large enough to be an effective fighting force. It is the English Royalists, not the English Parliamentarians, who are the peculiarity we should be attempting to explain. It must contribute to the explanation that the wealth and prestige of the Crown of England, small as they were, were much greater than the wealth and prestige of the Crowns of Ireland and Scotland. Yet it is probably much more important that the cause in whose name Charles was trying to achieve uniformity between his kingdoms was that of one particular vision of the church of England. The church of England, like the Tory Party after it, was always much more popular in England than it could hope to become in Ireland or Scotland.[2]

The *primum mobile* of the British crisis, chronologically and probably logically as well, was the conflict between Charles and the Scottish Covenanters. This was a real clash of ideas as well as of interests. It enshrined visions of the church, and of authority, so far apart that no real compromise was ever likely to be possible between them. It was this conflict which was the vortex into which the other kingdoms were drawn. This is not to say that Charles was faced by a united Scotland: it has been one of the major findings of this book that that was not the case: all kingdoms, like all English counties, and even most English villages, were divided. Yet it was clearly in Scotland that the Calvinist-Presbyterian ideas to which Charles was most deeply allergic had taken the deepest root. It was the Scots who resorted to arms first, and who did so with the least compunction. It was Charles's determination to suppress them when he was physically unable to do so which caused his authority to collapse, and troubled the English waters enough to encourage the Scots to fish in them.

The intervention of the Scots goes a long way to explain the central paradox of the English Civil War: it divided the English along a line of division which had been visible for a very long time, but one which had never looked sufficiently bitter to constitute a *casus belli*. Those in England who fought against the King were, with very few exceptions, those to whom the slogan of 'further reformation' was and always had been congenial. This is true of the members who were most active in hastening the Civil War on: with the exception of Henry Marten, they were almost all people like Rigby, Strode, Cromwell, Pyne, Sir Robert Cooke, Harley, Penington, and Venn, to whom the cause of reformation was never one which had stopped in 1559. Many of them, such as

---

[2] It is not a coincidence that the word 'Whig' accuses those to whom it is being applied of being Scottish, while the word 'Tory' carries the accusation of being Irish.

Samuel Vassall and Sir John Clotworthy, were also men who had been prominent as the nucleus of a Scottish party in England as far back as 1638. Similarly, the Parliamentary volunteers, who played a crucial part in making it possible for the men at Westminster to start a civil war, came overwhelmingly from such places as Dorchester and Boston, where the cause of godly preaching had been established for a very long time.

If we say that it was mainly religion which divided the two sides in the Civil War, we do not have to follow Samuel Butler in seeing England as full of people who would

> Fight like mad or drunk,
> For Dame Religion, as for punk.[3]

We do not have to say that England was full of undisciplined religious enthusiasts. We do not even have to say that the men who made the war (with one possible exception) cared more about religion than anything else. In the opening debates of the Long Parliament, legal resentments left over from 1628 and the Ship Money trial affected quite as many people as religious passion. What divided those who put these issues first from those who put religious issues first was not that they felt less passion: it was Charles I himself. Charles, with whatever reluctance, decided to conciliate men like Sir Francis Seymour and Sir John Strangeways, who put legal issues first, when he chose not to conciliate men like Pym or Sir Robert Harley, who put religious issues first. It was religion which divided the parties because Charles decided it should be so. This was in large measure because Charles's own religious convictions were both deep and a long way off centre. Yet it was also, and perhaps equally, because of the intensity of Charles's concern, as Supreme Head, to conserve his 'authority'. So long as governments enforced religion, no complete separation between religious conviction and political authority could easily exist, and there was certainly none in Charles I's mind. In the end, what separated him from such men as Pym and Harley is that they would neither worship as he told them, nor desist from telling him to worship in a way he would not. It was enforcement which turned religion into a divisive issue.

This was not the only way in which religion divided parties. We are not the first people to have been bewildered by the complexity of the events which led to the English Civil War: we share that experience with those who lived through them. One of the great advantages of conspiracy theory is that, by providing an all-purpose explanatory tool, it can make it possible, without unacceptable effort, to impose order on an otherwise unintelligible mass of events. In trying to make sense of the

---

[3] Samuel Butler, *Hudibras*, lines 5–6.

confusion they were living through, Charles I and his subjects were by
no means immune from this temptation. Anti-popery provided one such
explanatory tool, and was put to good use by Northumberland's servant
Thomas Smith, to whom opponents of the Grand Remonstrance were
classifiable as 'papists'. Ever since Richard Bancroft's *Daungerous Positions*, anti-Puritanism, especially in its anti-Presbyterian form, had come
to be useful for a similar purpose. In the hands of Thomas Wiseman
Remembrancer of the City, this conspiracy theory was developing into a
form which placed the blame on Brownists and Separatists. This, as
much as anti-popery, was developing into an all-purpose explanatory
tool. When Charles spoke to his troops at Wellington, at the beginning
of the march to Edgehill, it was this explanatory tool he fell back on,
telling them they had few enemies to meet other than Brownists, Anabaptists, and atheists. This was as true as that Charles's army was made
up of papists and Jesuits, but it was equally useful as a device to make
sense of the unintelligible. For that reason, such beliefs helped to
determine what people believed to have happened. Such devices were
used by many whose personal religious convictions were well within the
bounds of moderation. Roger Hill, for example, was no doubt a devout
man, but in 1642 he was far more interested in the company of his newly
married wife. Yet, perhaps in part for that very reason, he relied as
much as others on such simple explanatory tools to explain what was
happening to him.

It is hard to sustain the Royalist–Anglican myth which sees such
people as a perpetual nursery of revolution, in training since 1559 if not
earlier. Pym under James I had been a peaceable subject, worshipping
and renting a pew in a church where they washed the surplice for the
Fifth of November.[4] It is hard to imagine him able to sustain such a
compromise in 1642. Similarly, Dorchester and Boston under James did
not appear as centres of revolution, though John Cotton had never been
a man whose first objective was to live at peace with his neighbours.
Cotton and White under James had been in a dominant position in their
parishes, and if the seeds of civil war and revolution are to be sought
under James, they should perhaps be sought in the undercurrent of
resistance in and around those towns to the enforcement of godliness.[5]
It is that undercurrent which Charles drew to the surface, and of which
he made himself the leader. This is a picture which shows Charles,

---

[4] City of Westminster Archives, St Clement Danes Churchwardens' Accounts, B10(1) and
B10(2) (1623–6). Where a church possessed a surplice, its ecclesiastical complexion is often
indicated by the date for which the surplice was regularly washed. 5 Nov. is the lowest possibility
compatible with the possession of a surplice.

[5] On Dorchester, see David Underdown, *Revel, Riot, and Rebellion* (Oxford, 1985), 51–2, 56–7,
89, 166–7, 205, and other refs. On Boston, see Clive Holmes, *Seventeenth-Century Lincolnshire*
(Lincoln, 1980), 49–50, 53, 92–3, 95–6, 107–8, 116, 118, 121, 148, and other refs.

Tyacke-style, as a leader of resistance *against* the Jacobean establishment. It is one which makes sense of the Parliamentary sympathies of pillars of that establishment such as Manchester or Sir John Coke.

To Pym, and to many like him, allegiance to the Jacobean church had always been a matter of compromise. The Town Council in Boston, who avoided idolatry by breaking the Cross off the town mace, can hardly have believed that they in all respects stood for the same cause as Bishop Williams of Lincoln. Yet such people were brought up on Calvin's doctrine of the marks of the true church: if they could find, anywhere where they could worship, the word of God duly preached, and the sacraments duly administered, then the overwhelming priority of the need to avoid the sin of schism had to keep them in line. For Pym, Arminianism destroyed the word of God duly preached: it deprived him of right doctrine, the consolation the godly back to Cartwright's days had always used to quiet their consciences when they worried about their continued membership of an imperfectly reformed church.[6] For Pym and Hampden, the introduction of altars, by ushering in idolatry, destroyed the other mark of a true church.[7] By 1637 Charles's turning to Arminianism and its attendant Laudianism had destroyed the basis of a compromise which had lasted most of a lifetime. The effect seems to have been very like that of taking the pin out of a grenade.

For such men, the Scots were manna from Heaven. There is no need to believe that the bulk of the Parliamentarians were that deeply alienated by 1637, though Pym is almost certainly far from alone. Yet others, even not particularly godly people like the Earls of Holland and Pembroke, seem to have realized that the country was ungovernable if men of Pym's stamp could not be induced to co-operate.[8] After their attempts to divert Charles from the pursuit of his own ruin in the Bishops' Wars, many such people realized that Charles would never voluntarily make the sort of concessions which allowed Calvinists a place in the sun. For them, the use of the Scots as guarantors of a settlement with Charles I had political, if not theological attractions. Henry Marten, to take one unexpected example, cannot have found anything other than that his gorge rose at the theological productions of Johnston of Wariston. Yet Marten, from his motion for the Brotherly Assistance onwards, functioned in the Commons as a political pro-Scot. It is hard to see what such an unholy alliance can indicate but the need to bind an untrustworthy king in chains.

For the Scots themselves, the man responsible for the publication of

[6] P. Collinson, *Elizabethan Puritan Movement* (1966), 261; Russell, 'Pym', pp. 159–61. I am grateful to Dr Peter Lake for many discussions on this question.

[7] For Hampden, see *LJ* iv. 112.

[8] See Clive Holmes, *Seventeenth-Century Lincolnshire*, p. 118 for Dorset's attempts to prevent the deprivation of John Cotton. I am grateful to Dr David Smith for helpful discussions of Dorset.

the *Large Declaration* was never going to be regarded as a trustworthy Covenanting sovereign. His distaste for all they stood for was too palpable by 1640 for them ever to trust their security to his goodwill. It is this knowledge which forced the Scots to adopt what Professor Levack calls the 'Scottish Imperial' vision of British unity, in which the export of a Scottish reformation would bring about an irreversible change, and turn defenders of the *status quo* in England into their natural allies. This was always as much of a pipe-dream as Charles's vision of a decent, ordered, liturgical church of Scotland, yet both dreams found people in the countries concerned willing to go along with them. It is not irrelevant that during Pym's early childhood his stepfather had been sheltering a refugee minister from the Black Acts in Scotland.[9] Yet the real problem in England is that of explaining the number of people, not previously committed to a Scottish vision of the church, and indeed in some cases never committed to it, who were willing to go along with the attempt to force a Scottish programme on Charles up to and beyond the point which led to war. Genuine pro-Scots like Rous and Sir Robert Cooke are easy to explain. It is not so easy to explain the readiness of Saye and Fiennes to go along with the Scottish programme, which is one they found deeply distasteful.

In explaining this, as indeed in explaining the triumph of the Covenanters in Scotland itself, it is necessary to place a very heavy responsibility on the King. He was not, in fact, nearly as duplicitous as he is sometimes taken to be, but he did feel a very profound incomprehension and distaste for the religious convictions of large numbers of his subjects. In England, and even more in Scotland, it was impossible to govern the country without its rudimentary consent, and anyone who had watched, for example, the determination with which Charles elbowed aside the Irish Articles of 1615 was going to find it very difficult to believe that he would for long voluntarily govern his kingdoms in a way to which the stricter Calvinists could consent. When this fact was seen beside his conspicuous material weakness, the temptation to coerce him became very big indeed. It was a temptation Saye and Fiennes failed to resist. Once the attempt at coercion had been embarked on, and inevitably failed, the cycle of threats was under way which ended with King and Parliament unwilling to live in the same place. It was this cycle of threats, rather than an unbridgeable difference of opinion, which made government at Westminster break down. It was the Parliamentary leaders, by going into alliance with the Scots in the Petition of the Twelve Peers, who began the process of politics by threat. It was that which began the use of the Scottish army to force Charles into making concessions he would never voluntarily make, and

---

[9] Collinson, *Elizabethan Puritan Movement*, p. 233.

that invited royal retaliation in the form of the Army Plot. That in turn invited further threats, in the form of attempts to gain control of the militia. The Twelve Peers, like Cromwell, found that 'the same arts which did gain a power, must it maintain'.

As the Arminian strategy for British uniformity most conspicuously failed in Scotland, so the Calvinist strategy for British uniformity most conspicuously failed in Ireland. If Scotland was ungovernable according to Charles I's premisses, Ireland was ungovernable according to Pym's. If Charles deserves the major share of the blame for forcing Scotland into rebellion, it is Pym and Argyll who deserve the major share of the blame for forcing Ireland into rebellion. It is a remarkable illustration of the extent to which religious bias affected political judgement that while in Scotland it is Charles who appears the ideologue unable to understand the effect of his measures, in Ireland it is Pym who bears this character, and Charles, by contrast, who appears an intelligent, if rather weak, politician. It is hard to be certain how far Charles's resistance to the Scottish imperial vision was based on the knowledge that it must lead to the loss or the reconquest of Ireland, but it seems likely that future rebel leaders like John Barry realized it fairly early in the crisis.

England, as always, was cast in the unhappy position of pig in the middle between Ireland and Scotland. Both had their attractions as a model for sections of the Englsh population which were not negligible. For Catholics and church papists, who were not an insignificant part of the gentry even in 1642, Ireland was a symbol of the fact that there was still room for Catholics in the British body politic. It was for precisely this reason that Pym, whose fear of Catholicism was like the fear of a modern Nazi-hunter, had to insist that Catholicism should not be tolerated even in Ireland. Yet the resistance to Scottish uniformity in England went far wider than the ranks of Catholics and church papists. England was a country where the success of the Reformation, though considerable, had been incomplete. It was, in very many senses, a country 'but halfly reformed'. For those who had first conformed to the church of England and then grown used to it, without ever going through a full-scale 'conversion' to the reformed faith, the pressure coming from Pym and the Scots may well have represented a threat that they had been beating off ever since 1559, when Bishop Horne and his fellows had begun their demands that they dispose of their 'trash' to pay for pulpits and homilies.[10] When Laud in 1635 demanded that London parishes restore organs, St Michael's Crooked Lane got out the organ it had carefully put away in storage in 1559.[11] This perhaps represents as

[10] Ralph Houlbrooke, *Church Courts and the People during the English Reformation* (Oxford, 1979), 169.
[11] *CSPD 1636–7*, vol. cccli, no. 102.

much of a continuity as the continual aspiration to complete and establish the Reformation of 1559. The intellectual and social antecedents of Royalism have not yet been studied with the care which has for many generations been lavished on the Parliamentarians, and the result is that we do not know nearly as well what continuities informed Royalism as we do what continuities informed its opponents. Yet it seems the continuities were there, and it would be very nice to know whether a man like Sir Frederick Cornwallis, who was in a real sense the heir of his family tradition, was a more common figure among the Royalists than Henry Jermyn, who had firmly turned his back on his.[12]

Above all, anyone who has tried to understand Falkland and Sir Henry Slingsby as well as Rous and Sir Robert Harley must be filled with a sense of the sheer impossibility of any attempt to impose religious uniformity on England in any cause whatsoever. Protestants, always trying to plead not guilty to the sin of schism, had spent a century denying that they had broken the unity of the church. The point had come when only by the most desperate attempts to reimpose it could they continue to exonerate themselves. It was not until the attempt to impose one religion on everyone had been slowly and painfully abandoned that peace, whether within England or between England and Scotland, finally became possible. As for Ulster, already in 1641 the crucible of the British problem, that is a place where the issue of this process is yet in the future.

[12] Diarmaid MacCulloch, *Suffolk and the Tudors* (Oxford, 1986), 97–100, 119, and many other refs.

Index